Based on

NIELIT 'A' Level Revised Syllabus of year 2020 for Module: A7–R5

'A' LEVEL *made simple*

DATABASES TECHNOLOGIES

by

Satish Jain

B.Sc., B.E.(IISc), M.E.(IISc), M.Tech.(IIT Kanpur),
Ex-Professor of Information Technology,
Institute of Information Technology & Management
GGS Indraprastha University, Delhi.

Shashi Singh

MCA, M.Phil

www.bpbonline.com

FIRST EDITION 2021

ISBN: 978-93-90684-11-3

Distributors:

BPB PUBLICATIONS
20, Ansari Road, Darya Ganj
New Delhi-110002
Ph: 23254990/23254991

DECCAN AGENCIES
4-3-329, Bank Street,
Hyderabad-500195
Ph: 24756967/24756400

MICRO MEDIA
Shop No. 5, Mahendra Chambers,
150 DN Rd. Next to Capital Cinema,
V.T. (C.S.T.) Station, MUMBAI-400 001
Ph: 22078296/22078297

BPB BOOK CENTRE
376 Old Lajpat Rai Market,
Delhi-110006
Ph: 23861747

Published by Manish Jain for BPB Publications, 20 Ansari Road, Darya Ganj, New Delhi-110002
Printed at Akash Press, Delhi

www.bpbonline.com

Dedicated to

Sri Raja Rajeshwari, Mata Sharda Devi and Sri Sai Baba

Whose blessings will overcome all the hurdles in life

PREFACE

This book is an up-to-date edition based on NIELIT '*A' Level* Module (A7–R5) syllabus for **Databases Technologies**. The objective of this book is to explain to '*A' Level* students the database management concepts in an easily understandable and simple language. It is observed that most of the books available in the market do not cover the entire syllabus for the course and fail to meet the entire need of the students. This subject matter requires a thorough study of Database Management Techniques and their Applications. Towards achieving this goal, we have pressed into service all our experience in computer science as well as in academic field in bringing out this book to meet the needs of all types of students from any stream.

When one goes to a temple to offer prayers, the priest asks you four things, namely your *Name*, your *Gotra*, your *Rashi* and your *Nakshatra*. These four things will be conveyed to the *Almighty* (similar to the concept of Database Administrator) by the priest (the online user). Almighty then, using the four search fields given by you, retrieves your past and present records from His massive database and blesses you accordingly. Thus, the ancient Hindu Astrological system can be considered as a pioneer in Database Management System. A similar method is followed in our modern Database System. Data are stored in an ordered manner which we call as the Database. Required information is retrieved from the database using the key(s) (search field(s)) and decisions are made accordingly. This book is designed with view to equip learner to acquire knowledge of current trend and technologies of Databases. We have discussed two types of databases - RDBMS and NoSQL databases. Separate chapters are included on introduction and manipulation of data using MariaDB database and to apply various SQL statements on it. The book also covers NoSQL database technologies - MongoDB and its features in detail.

We have made this book user friendly by adding very comprehensive glossary of technical terms. The glossary of technical terms will be specially helpful to a reader in answering objective type of questions asked in Part I of 'A7-R5' question paper of NIELIT 'A' Level examination. The book contains ample concise and practical example programs. Also many solved and unsolved examples are provided at the end of each chapter. An effort is made to explain all topics in layman's language with a large number of illustrations and examples. The book elucidates both basic and advanced topics in "Databases Technologies".

A special feature throughout this book is that the salient and crucial information has been encapsulated within parallel and horizontal lines with a (☞) mark to draw the attention of the reader.

We shall feel obliged if you could send us your critical opinion regarding the presentation, readability and coverage in this book and request you to mail your suggestions, if any, to improve the same.

2nd July, 2020

Authors

A7-R5 : Databases Technologies

Outline of Course

S.No.	TOPIC	Written Marks (Max.)
1.	An Overview of the Database Management System	4
2.	An Architecture of the Database system	6
3.	Relational Database Management System (RDBMS)	6
4.	Database Design	14
5.	MariaDB	20
6.	Manipulating Data with MariaDB	20
7.	NoSQL Database Technology	20
8.	Selecting the Right Database	10
	Total Marks	**100**

Detailed Syllabus

1. An Overview of the Database Management System 4

What is database? Why database? Database system, database management system (DBMS), advantages of DBMS.

2. An Architecture of the Database system 6

Three levels of architecture, Logical View, Physical View, Conceptual View, Logical data independence, Physical Data Independence

3. Relational Database Management System (RDBMS) 6

Introduction, RDBMS terminology, relational model, base tables, keys, primary key, foreign key, constraints, Codd Rules

4. Database Design 14

Normalization, Normal forms-1NF, 2NF, 3NF, BCNF 4NF and 5NF, E-R Diagram. Mapping ER-diagram to database tables.

5. MariaDB 20

Introduction to MariaDB, Data Types, SQL Commands, Create, insert, update, delete, drop, alter, SQL functions (String functions, date functions), indexing, key, primary key, foreign key

6. Manipulating Data with MariaDB 20

SQL Statements, Select, like clause, groupby, orderby, joins-leftjoin, naturaljoin, rightjoin, union. Correlated and nested queries. Backup and restore commands.

Module: A7–R5

7. NoSQL Database Technology 20

Introduction to NoSQL Databases, Difference between relational and NoSQL databases. NoSQL features, types, advantages, Architecture of MongoDB, Documents, Collections, Dynamic Schemas, Mongo Shell, MongoServer and Client, Data Types, Embedded Documents, Creating Configuration file for Mongo

JSON File format for storing documents, Inserting and Saving Documents, Batch Insert, Insert Validation, Removing Documents, Updating Documents, Document Replacement, Using Modifiers, Updating Multiple Documents, Returning updated Documents

Introduction to Indexing, Introduction to Compound Indexes, Using Compound Indexes, Indexing Objects and Arrays, Aggregation Framework, Pipeline Operations-$match, $project, $group, $unwind, $sort, $limit, $skip, Using Pipelines, MongoDB and MapReduce, Aggregation Commands, Introduction to Replication, configuring a Replica Set, Member Configuration Options

8. Selecting the Right Database 10

Selection of right databases, RDBMS or NoSQL, selection of database based on performance, data size, type of data, frequency of accessing data, business needs, type of application.

USEFUL TIPS FOR THE EXAMINEE

Dear Reader,

Every examination has its peculiarity and the best results are often obtained by identifying that particular feature and working with the help of right strategies, which in turn can be adopted by correctly analyzing the question paper.

The 'A' Level Examination being no exception to this rule, the authors present an effective aid to guide you to analyze the question paper and thus help to chalk out your own effective plan of action.

The instructions given on the first page of the question paper should always be read *very* carefully. As the answer sheets of Part ONE will be evaluated with the help of a computer, you have to be extra cautious.

The answer sheet contains separate boxes for writing answers to each question in this part. You should read the following paragraphs to avoid mistakes and clear the first part without any difficulty.

How to avoid mistakes?

If you are not sure about a particular answer - *do not fill* the box in the first try itself, but make an attempt later. After having given an initial reading to all the questions, first attempt only those questions about which you are very ***sure*** regarding the correct answer. It is while taking a second go at the questions, that you answer the remaining ones, always making sure that you spend only a *limited* amount of time on each one of them. Finally, go through all the answers once decided and fill the boxes with black ink as per the instructions given in the question paper.

How to answer the questions of Part TWO?

Once you have done well in Part ONE, rest assured, passing Part TWO will not pose much of a problem, if you have effectively followed the instructions given below. While answering Part TWO, the time limit should be strictly kept in mind and every effort must be made to complete all the questions, by keeping the answers brief and to the point. Remember you can also resort to making a sketch/diagram in your answer wherever possible, instead of describing it in words, because "a thousand words of description can be effectively expressed by a small diagram." As the number of questions are normally more for an average student, this precious time saved, enables you to have a wider coverage of the paper.

While attempting the descriptive type of questions, keep a check on the length of your answers and keep in mind the time frame available for answering the remaining questions.

The last stage, being the revision stage, you should save at least 5 to 10 minutes to revise all your answers. Try to find the gross errors, like units of measurement, or wrong question number you might have put for a specific answer, etc. This does happen because of the inherent tension of the examination.

This book has covered the complete syllabus in an easy to understand manner. It is advised, however, that in addition to this book, you should also refer to a few books on 'Databases Technologies'. This will enable you to broaden the horizon of your knowledge.

Make your own notes, by reading each topic from this book and other standard books. Once you are quite sure about the comprehension of the topic, try to answer the Exercises given at the end of each chapter of this book.

In the second reading, go through the sample papers given at the end of the book. Solve these papers without consulting any book. After you have answered them, compare your response with the relevant matter available in the text of this book. Where you find your answers differ, re-study that part again.

WISH YOU A GRAND SUCCESS in the 'A' Level Examination, and a very bright future in the field of computer science.

Authors

Contents

Databases Technologies

Chapter 3. Relational Database Management System (RDBMS) 37

Chapter 4. Database Design 47

Module: A7–R5

Chapter 5. MariaDB 76

Chapter 6. Manipulating Data with MariaDB 113

OTHER TITLES OF INTEREST

Agile Project Management
in Easy Steps
ISBN: 9789386551313

Agile, DevOps and **Cloud Computing** with **Microsoft Azure**
ISBN: 9789388511902

Machine Learning & **Deep Learning Algorithms**
ISBN: 9789388511131

Fundamentals of **Deep Learning** and **Computer Vision**
ISBN: 9789388511858

Deep Learning with C#, .Net and Kelp.Net
ISBN: 9789388511018

Pragmatic **Machine Learning** with **Python**
ISBN: 9789389845365

Machine Learning **Cookbook** with **Python**
ISBN: 9789389898002

Machine Learning for **Beginners**
ISBN: 9789389845426

Machine Learning for **Finance**
ISBN: 9789389328622

Data Science & **Machine Learning** Interview Questions Using **R**
ISBN: 9789389845846

Data Science & **Machine Learning** Interview Questions using **Python**
ISBN: 9789389845785

Data Science Fundamentals & **Practical Approaches**
ISBN: 9789389845662

Data Science for **Business Professionals**
ISBN: 9789389423280

R for Data Analysis in easy steps
ISBN: 9789387284227

Data Science with **Machine Learning - Python** Interview Questions
ISBN: 9789388176637

Data Science with **Jupyter**
ISBN: 9789388511377

CHAPTER 1

An Overview of the Database Management System

1.1 WHAT IS DATABASE?

A database is an organized collection of facts. In other words you can say that it is a collection of information arranged and presented to serve an assigned purpose.

☞ *A collection of data is referred as database.*

An example of a database is a dictionary, where words are arranged alphabetically. Another example is a telephone directory, where subscriber names are listed in an alphabetic order. Similarly, when you think of a box of cards with names and addresses written as a mailing list, then the box and its contents form a mailing database. Figure 1.1 contains cards with mailing addresses. All these cards are placed in alphabetic order of names and the collection of these cards would be called a database.

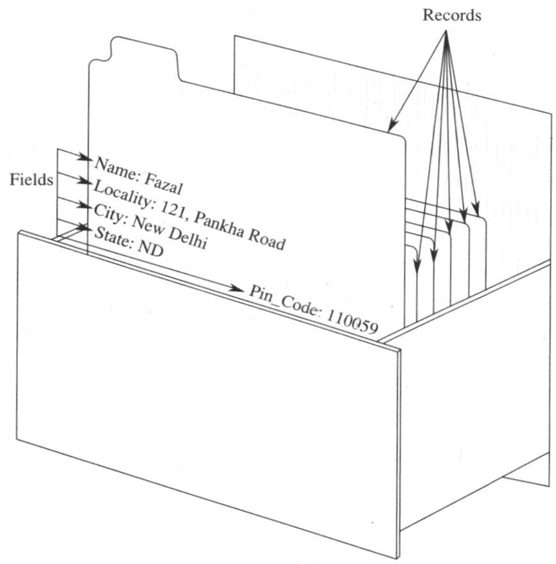

Figure 1.1 Each card represents a record in which information is organized into fields and records

☞ *Thus, information stored in a database is arranged in a particular order.*

In order to keep database updated, we may need to perform operations like adding information, removing information, editing existing information, etc. Take the case of a telephone diary, in which you note down the names, addresses and phone numbers of your friends. This is also a type of database. If you make a new friend, you note the information about him/her in the diary which is equivalent to *adding* data to a database. If address of your friend changes then you note the new address in your diary which means *editing* a database. If you want to send a letter to your friend then you look into the diary to locate the address. This is called *searching* a database.

In case your telephone diary contains a very large number of names, addresses, phone numbers. Moreover, the names are not arranged in any order. Thus, it would be very difficult to locate the names, addresses, and phone number of your friends. Thus, it is essential to arrange the names in some order, say alphabetically, to make the search easy. However, as the number of friends gets larger, managing the database manually becomes difficult. A database management software package is a helpful tool in such a situation.

1.2 WHY DATABASE?

Any organization, be it a Bank, Manufacturing Company, Hospital, University, Conglomerate or a Government Department, requires huge amount of data in some form or the other. All such organizations need to collect data, manipulate them and store them for future use. All such type of organizations require data for a number of purposes, say;

(a) Preparing sales reports
(b) Forecasting sales
(c) Preparing accounts reports
(d) Getting medical histories of patients

Thus, we can say that data are very vital corporate resources. The amount of data used these days in organizations can be measured in the range of some billions of bytes or characters. The financial investment involved is also very high. Many organizations have become critically dependent on the continued and successful operations of databases.

1.2.1 File Oriented Approach Vs Database Oriented Approach

The conventional approach for data processing is to store locally needed data and develop a program (or many programs) for each type of application. In the past, different users had programs that handled their own independent stored data. This resulted in more than one data files with same data for different applications. An example might be a payroll application used by the accounts department and employee record keeping system used by the personnel department. Both applications would have their master files containing many common data fields for example, employee names, addresses, and employee codes, etc. Therefore, although the same data may be required by two applications, the data will have to be stored in two different places in a computer because each application separately stores and maintains the data. Moreover, one application may require the file to be arranged on the basis of Emp_code and another application may require the file to be arranged on the basis of another field say Emp_name.

Thus, when separate departments in an organization maintain files that contain duplicate information, that would result in *data* duplication and hence the chances of errors. Figure 1.2(a) shows three files containing duplicate data fields, namely B, D, E etc.

Maintenance of information in separate file for each business application has the following disadvantages:

(a) Each file requires separate processing program.
(b) The practice of preparing two or more copies of each file for security purposes leads to the retention of at least six backup files which requires large disk storage space.
(c) Each department needs to keep its files updated separately.

In a database system, entire data is available without duplication. Instead of each program (or user) managing its own data, data for all applications are shared by authorized users using Database Management System (DBMS) package.

An example of a database approach for our three-file illustration in part (a) of Figure 1.2 is seen in part (b) of Figure 1.2. In this case, all three files have been combined into one, and data redundancy and duplication of fields available in the three files maintained separately, is eliminated. When all three applications utilize the same data file, operations are simplified and fewer backup files are needed for security purposes.

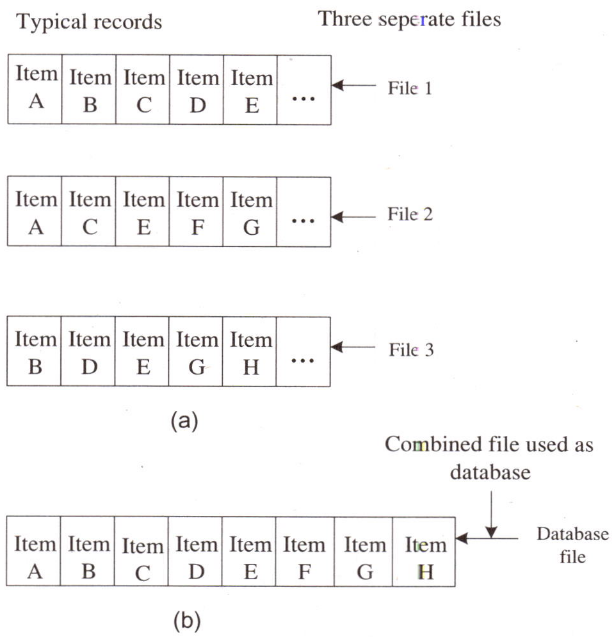

Figure 1.2 File based system versus a database approach

Disadvantages of File Processing Approach

The traditional approach of programming with file manipulation, has the following disadvantages:

(a) Redundancy in defining and storing data, results in wastage of disk storage space.
(b) Data definition is typically a part of the application programs themselves and hence file processing software can access only specified fields.
(c) The structure of data files is embedded in the application programs itself and so any change to the structure of a file may require changing all programs that manipulate this file.
(d) Does not support multiple views of same data file.
(e) Data for multiple applications may not be integrated and maintained in a single file.

1.2.2 Characteristics of Data in Database

Computer uses database by adopting a set of well defined rules. You should note that just as a mailing box, in Figure 1.1, is filled with *cards*, so is a computer database filled with *records*. And while each *card* in the box may contain several lines of written information, a *record* in a database contains several *fields* of data items. Thus, a mailing box contains cards, each of which has several lines of information on it. Similarly, a database contains records, each of which in turn has *fields* in it.

Assume that each card in the mailing box has five lines of data items, namely,

(a) Name;
(b) Locality;
(c) City;
(d) State; and
(e) Pin_code.

Then, all these fields combined to form a record. We shall now understand each part of a database one by one.

Field

The smallest piece of meaningful information in a file is called a *data item* or *field*. A data item is generally used for a group of alphanumeric characters. Figure 1.3 displays the data items (fields) in a record.

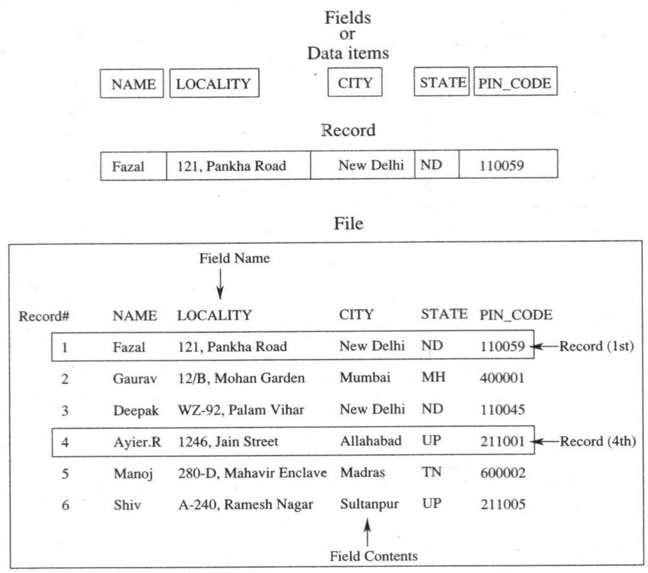

Figure 1.3 Concept of Fields, Records and File

NAME, LOCALITY, CITY, STATE, PIN_CODE are all known as data items or fields.

Record

The collection of related fields is called a *record.* For example, Figure 1.3 contains six records and each record has five related fields namely; **NAME, LOCALITY, CITY, STATE and PIN_CODE.**

File

File is the collection of all related records. In Figure 1.3, the file contains the list of addresses of six friends.

Database

Database is a collection of related files. Figure 1.2 shows Employees database having related files containing records of employees.

Key Field

In Figure 1.2 (a), File 1 contains employee records with fields **Emp_Code** and **Address**. File 2 contains employee records with fields **Emp_Code** and **Salary**. File 3 contains employee records with fields **Emp_Code** and **Name**. All the three files have one common field, namely Emp_Code. Such a field, called the *keyfield,* is used for identifying and relating records.

The combination of all the three related files, as shown in Figure 1.2 (b), is known as a database of Employees. It removes all data items in files 1, 2 and 3, containing common fields.

☞ *The keyfield in a record is a unique data item which is used to identify the record for the purpose of accessing and manipulating database.*

1.3 DATABASE SYSTEM

A Database system is a general term that refers to the combination of a database, a database management system and a data model. This system is responsible for data controlling, data retrieval, data maintenance and data definition. Basically, a database system is a software that sits between the end-user software and a database. A database is a container for information and a database system is a software that manages one or more databases.

The database system may be multi-user or single-user. The configuration of the hardware and the size of the organization will determine whether it is a multi-user system or a single user system. In single user system the database resides on one computer and is only accessed by one user at a time. This one user may design, maintain, and write database programs. Due to large amount of data management most systems are multi-user. In this situation the data are both integrated and shared. A database is integrated when the same information is not recorded in two places.

Database systems are basically developed for large amount of data. When dealing with huge amount of data, there are two things that require optimization i.e., Storage of data and retrieval of data.

Storage of data

According to the principles of database systems, the data is stored in such a way that it acquires lot less space as the redundant data (duplicate data) has been removed before storage.

Retrieval of data

Along with storing the data in an optimized and systematic manner, it is also important that we retrieve the data quickly when needed. Database systems ensure that the data is retrieved as quickly as possible.

1.4 DATABASE MANAGEMENT SYSTEM

DataBase Management System (DBMS) is a software package that allows data to be effectively stored, retrieved and manipulated. A DBMS system is basically a computer based record keeping system. The data contained in a DBMS package can be accessed by multiple application programs and users. Application packages such as SQL Server, Oracle, MS-Access are some commercially available DBMS packages.

A DBMS consists of the following three elements:

(a) **The physical database**: the collection of files that contain the data.

(b) **The database engine**: the software that makes it possible to access and modify the contents of the database.

(c) **The database scheme**: the specification of the logical structure of the data stored in the database.

1.4.1 Components of DBMS

A DBMS constitutes different components that help in the use and management of data in an organization. These are:

(a) **Database Engine:** Database Engine is the heart of DBMS. It is responsible for storing, retrieving and updating the data. This component is responsible for the speed (performance) and scalability of a database.

(b) **Data Dictionary:** A *data dictionary* is a database about databases. It holds all information about each data element in the databases, such as its name, data type, range of values, source, access authorization and indicates which application programs use this data item. Data dictionary is also known as metadata, i.e., data about data.

(c) **Query Processor:** Query processor is a functional component of database management system whose function is to break down query (SQL) statements (given by user) into instructions understood by the DBMS and which helps the database system to access and update data.

(d) **Security and Other Utilities:** DBMS must be responsible for establishing and maintaining security access controls. Security component of DBMS must identify the user and then provide or limit access to various parts of the database. Various administrative utilities such as backup and recovery, user management, data storage evaluation and performance monitoring tools are provided with most of the DBMSs.

(e) Other components include forms (data entry screens) generator, report (output screens) generator and data communication and networking utilities.

1.4.2 Applications of DBMS

Applications of Database Management Systems are:

(a) **Telecommunications**: In telecom database keeps track of the information such as calls made, network usage, customer details, monthly post paid bills etc. Without the database systems it is difficult to maintain huge amount of data that keeps updating every millisecond.

(b) **Library Management System**: There are thousands of books in the library so it is very difficult to keep record of all the books in a register. So, DBMS used to maintain all the information related to book issue dates, name of the book, author and availability of the book etc.

(c) **Industry**: In industry database keeps records of ins and outs data from different units such as manufacturing unit, warehouse or distribution centre. For example, distribution centre should keep a track of the product units that supplied into the centre as well as the products that got delivered out from the distribution centre on each day; this is where DBMS is used. Also in sales it stores customer information, production information and invoice details etc.

(d) **Banking System**: In banking system Database management systems is used for storing customer info, tracking day to day credit and debit transactions, generating bank statements etc. That is all possible just because of DBMS that manages all the bank transactions.

(e) **Airlines and Railways**: In airlines and railways it stores traveler details, reservation information along with flight or train schedule etc., in database. Also if flight or trains get late then people get to know delay status through database update.

(f) **Education**: Database systems are used in schools and colleges to store the data regarding student details, staff details, course details, exam details, payroll data, attendance details, fees details etc. The main purpose of database systems is to manage the data. Consider a university that keeps the data of students, teachers, courses, books etc. To manage this data we need to store this data somewhere where we can add new data, delete unused data, update outdated data, retrieve data, to perform these operations on data we need a Database Management System that allows us to store the data in such a way so that all these operations can be performed on the data efficiently.

(g) **Online shopping**: Online shopping has become a big trend of these days. The online shopping websites such as Amazon, Flipkart etc., store the product information, customers addresses, credit details, purchase information, invoice bills, payment, and provide you the relevant list of products based on your query.

(h) **Social Media Sites**: We all are on social media websites to share our views and connect with our friends. Daily millions of users signed up for these social media accounts like facebook, twitter, pinterest and Google plus. It is all possible because of DBMS.

1.4.3 Data Model

A data model is a description of the organization of a database. Data modeling is used for representing entities and their relationships in a database.

In a database, a group of similar information or data, which is of interest to an organization, is called an *Entity*.

Each entity can have a number of characteristics. The characteristics of an entity are called *Attributes*. For example, an entity, say client, can have characteristics like name, address, phone number, balance due, etc.

1.5 TYPES OF DBMS

Various types of Database Management Systems (DBMSs) are the following:

(a) Hierarchical DBMS (HDBMS)
(b) Network DBMS (NDBMS)
(c) Relational DBMS (RDBMS)
(d) Object Oriented DataBase (OODB)
(e) Distributed DBMS (DDBMS)

1.5.1 Hierarchical DBMS (HDBMS)

Database Management Systems based on the hierarchical *data model* are known as HDBMS. Hierarchical data model was developed by IBM in 1968 and introduced in IMS (Information Management System). This model is like a structure of a tree with the records forming the nodes and fields forming the branches of the tree.

In the hierarchical model, records are linked in the form of an organization chart. For example, in the organization chart shown in Figure 1.4, the boss or executive is placed at the topmost position of the chart. The managers are linked with the executive in the hierarchy. The junior managers are placed below these managers. Thus, personnel at the lowest post are linked with their immediate superior. These may or may not have further dependents. Also a dependent can have only a single superior. An assistant may not assist more than two managers.

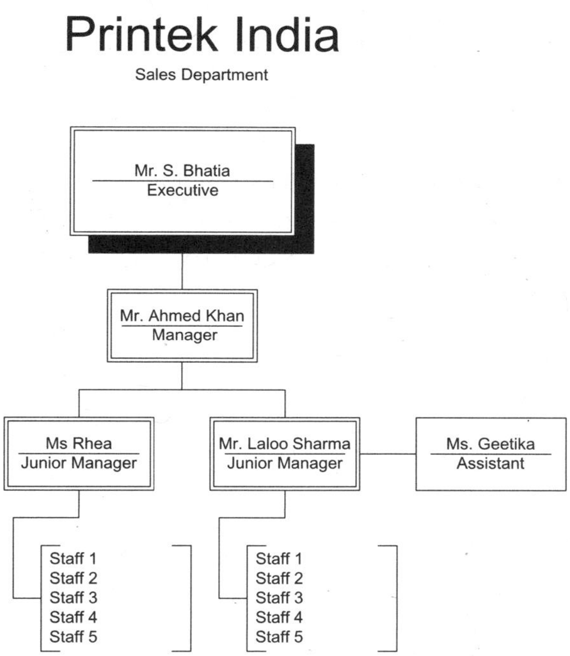

Figure 1.4 An organization chart

Similarly, in the hierarchical data model, records are linked with other superior records on which they are dependent and also on the records which are dependent on them. For example, in a customer-order database, order records are the *dependents* of the customer record (since customer places orders) and the hierarchical view for the same will be as seen in Figure 1.5. The customer record forms the *owner record*. Hierarchical database follows a tree structure where the root is at the highest level and leaves at the lowest level.

A tree structure may establish one-to-many relationship. Figure 1.6 illustrates the structure of a family. Great grandparent is the root of the structure. Parents may have many children exhibiting one-to-many relationship. The great grandparent record is known as the *root* of the tree. The grandparents, parents and children are the *nodes* or *dependents* of the *root*. In general, a root may have any number of *dependents*. Each of these *dependent* may have any number of lower level *dependents*, and so on, with no restriction of levels.

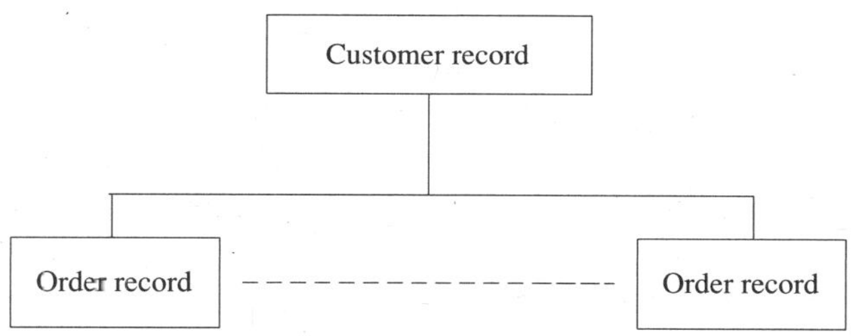

Figure 1.5 Hierarchical view

The different elements (e.g. records) present in the hierarchical tree structure have *Parent–Child* relationship. A Parent element can have many children elements but a Child element cannot have many Parent elements. That is, hierarchical model cannot represent many to many relationships among records.

IMS by IBM corporation of USA and SYSTEM 2000 are examples of hierarchical database management systems.

Advantages of Hierarchical Model

(a) It is a simple, straightforward and natural method of implementing record relationships.

(b) Hierarchical model is useful when there is some hierarchical character in the database.

Disadvantages of Hierarchical Model

The drawbacks of hierarchical model are as follows:

(a) The hierarchical model cannot represent all the relationships that occur in the real world.

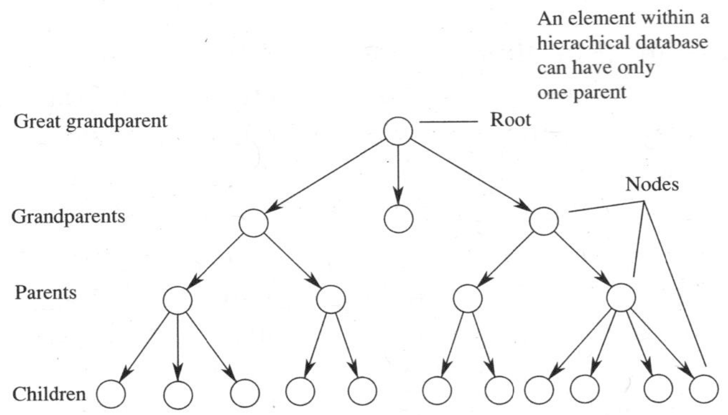

Figure 1.6 Basic structure of hierarchical data model

(b) It cannot demonstrate the over-all data model for the enterprise because of the non-availability of actual data at the time of designing the data model.

(c) The hierarchical model is used only when there is a hierarchical character in the concerned database. It cannot represent many to many relationship (a child can have only one parent).

(d) **Insert Anomaly**: It is not possible to insert data about a new dependent, if its superior record is not present. This is because a node cannot exist without a root.

(e) **Delete Anomaly**: Deletion operation in a hierarchical database leads to loss of many necessary information. For example, all shipment and payment related information about a product may be stored in a Customer record. Deletion of a customer would also lead to the deletion of corresponding shipment and payment details.

(f) **Update Anomaly**: Updation operation in a hierarchical database leads to several inconsistencies in the database. For example, suppose we wish to change the city of a customer from Mumbai to Goa, then we will face two problems. We need to search the entire database to find every occurrence of that particular customer and make changes everywhere wherever his/her details is appearing. If we miss out a single occurrence, we will face the inconsistency problem. The customer might be shown as being in Mumbai at one place and in Goa at other places.

Hierarchical structures were widely used in the Mainframe database management systems. However, due to their restrictions, they cannot be used to relate structures that exist in the real world.

1.5.2 Network DBMS (NDBMS)

In network database structures, a record type can have multiple owners. For example, in customer's order-processing system, orders are owned by both customers and also by products (See Figure 1.7), since that is the way they relate in the real world.

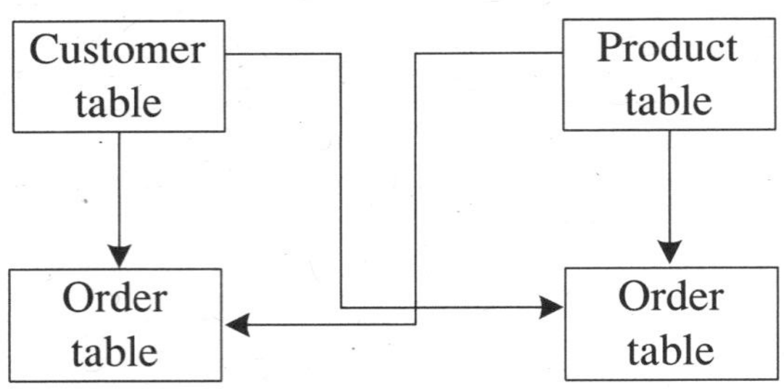

Figure 1.7 Orders owned by both customer and product

In Network model, data are represented by records using links among them. It is an improvement over the hierarchical model, since we can have many to many relationships among records.

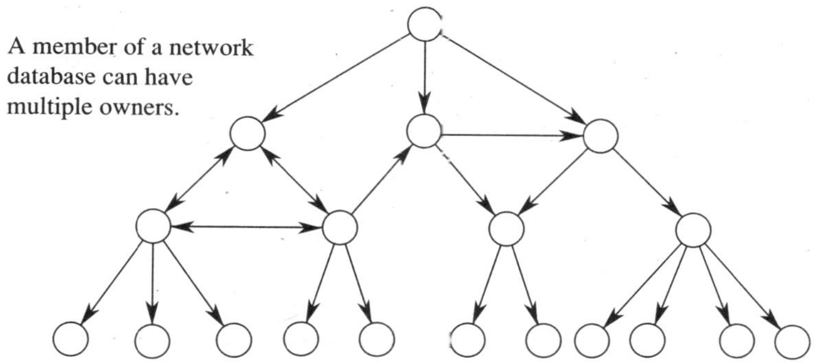

Figure 1.8 Network structuring

The network data model is similar to an hierarchical model, except that an entity can have more than one parent. As shown in Figure 1.8, data can belong to more than one parent. Note that there are lateral connections as well as top-down connections as seen in Figure 1.8. A network structure thus allows 1:1 (one:one), 1:M (one:many) or M:M (many:many) relationships among entities.

IDMS (Integrated Data Management System) and SYSTEM 2000 are examples of network database management system.

Advantages of Network Data Model

(a) Network model is useful for representing such records which have many-to-many relationships.
(b) Problem of inconsistency does not exist in a Network model because a data element is physically located at just one place.
(c) Searching a record is easy since there are multiple access paths to a data element.

Disadvantages of Network Data Model

The drawbacks of network model are given below:

(a) All the records are maintained using pointers and hence the whole database structure becomes very complex.
(b) Insertion, deletion and updation of any record would require pointer adjustments.

1.5.3 Relational DBMS (RDBMS)

In a *Relational Database Model*, data is organized in the form of rows and columns similar to a table. The tables are referred to as *relations* in a relational data model. Rows of the table are referred to as *tuples* and the columns of a table are referred to as *attributes*. A *domain* is a collection of all possible values from which actual values for a given column can be drawn. The number of records present in a relation is called *cardinality*. The number of attributes in a relation determines the *degree* of a relation.

☞ ***A relational model database is defined as a database that allows you to group its data items into one or more independent tables that can be related to one another by using fields common to each related table.***

Tables in a relational database is similar to the traditional file system with its records, fields and files. The table's rows, called *tuples*, contain records and columns, called *attributes*, contain fields. Each tuple or row, has values for the attributes. The attribute describes some feature or property of the objects. The full two dimensional table represents a file or 'relation'. For example, in Figure 1.9, there is an Employee-Service relation that describes the entity Employee by the attributes Emp_Code, Name, and Years of service (Year).

Attributes →	Emp _ Code	Name	Year
Tuples →	21130	Amar Jain	1
→	30143	Kuldeep	3
→	41894	Manoj	2
→	51207	Rita Bajaj	6

Figure 1.9 Employee-Service relation

☞ *Note that all the entries in each column are of the same kind. Each column has a unique name and no two rows in the table are identical.*

Concept of Keys in Relational Model

Each table in a relational database must have a unique identifier or field called *key*. A key consists of one or more fields. Without this unique identifier, there is no way to retrieve the unique record from a table.

Primary Key

The field or group of fields that is unique identifier for a table is called the table's *primary key*. The primary key uniquely identifies each record in the table and can never be the same for two records. It is always recommended to use the AutoNumber data type for primary keys, since this data type guarantees that no duplicated values are entered into the primary key field. For example, in an Employee relation, there can be more than one employee with the same name, say Ramesh Chadha. Therefore, if we say "Retrieve the joining_date of Ramesh Chadha", more than one records will be accessed. And the computer cannot distinguish among them. But if we have a unique field, say Emp_code, called *Primary Key*, defined in the Employee table, it would be easier to access the required record by saying "Retrieve the joining date of E105".

Composite Key

There are cases of various tables, in which a record cannot be uniquely identified by a single field. In such cases, a composite key may be used. A composite key is a group of fields that uniquely identify a record. A composite key can also be the primary key for that table. While duplicate values are allowed within any of the fields of a composite key, there cannot be duplicate values across all the fields that make up the composite key. For example, in the Employee table, the name of the Employee along with its address would form a composite key.

Oracle, Access, SQL Server, Sybase, MySQL, Ingress etc. are some examples of RDBMS packages.

Advantages of Relational Model

(a) The relational database structure can be efficiently used even with a PC that has limited main memory and processing capability.

(b) Relational database is very effective for small databases.

(c) Relational database is much easier to use because it enables a computer system to accommodate a variety of enquiries in an efficient manner.

(d) Relational database is only concerned with data and not with the structures, which improves the performance. Hence, the processing time and storage space is comparatively large in relational database but the user is not required to know the complexity of the structure design, thus making relational database easy to use and learn.

(e) Network and hierarchical databases use pointers to implement record relationship. But, in relational databases record relationship is implemented using primary key or composite key field(s). Hence it is very simple and represents the logical relationship among the data items rather than physical relationship (like hierarchical and network model).

(f) Relational model is very useful for representing most of the real world objects and the relationships among them.

1.5.4 Object Oriented DataBase (OODB)

Object Oriented databases (OODB) are dependent on the object oriented programming paradigm. It enables us to create classes, organize objects, structure an inheritance hierarchy and call methods of other classes. Besides these, it also provides the facilities associated with standard database systems. However, object oriented database systems have not yet replaced the RDBMS in commercial business applications.

Following are the two different approaches for designing an object oriented database:

(a) Designed to store, retrieve and manage objects created by programs written in some object oriented language (OOL) such as C++ or Java.
(b) Designed to provide object oriented facilities to users of non object-oriented programming languages (OOPLs) such as C or Pascal.

The user will create classes, objects, inheritance hierarchy, and so on and the database system will store and manage these objects and classes. This second approach, thus, turns non-OOPLs into OOPLs. A translation layer is required to map the objects created by user into objects of the database system.

☞ *Although a relational database can be used to store and manage objects, it does not understand objects as such. Therefore, a middle layer called object manager or object-oriented layer software is required to translate objects into tuples of a relation.*

Storing and Accessing Objects

The data part of all objects of a class are stored individually in a database. The program part of the class are stored as part of the database schema along with the type definitions of the classes. Objects can also be given names to allow their access. However, such an approach will not work when the number of objects in a database are large in numbers, say in the range of millions. Another method is to collect objects into a group. A group is given a name. The programs will then iterate over a group to find out the required object.

A special case of a collection is the *class-extent.* A class-extent is the collection of all the objects belonging to a class. Whenever a new object needs to inserted be inserted into a class, it is inserted into its class-extent automatically. Similarly, whenever a new object needs to be deleted, it is deleted from the respective class-extent.

A Sample Object Oriented Database

A sample object oriented database is shown in Figure 1.10. The solid lines (—) in the figure represents class-subclass link. The dash (---) represents attribute-domain link. The class *Vehicle* is the root of a class composition hierarchy that involves *VehicleSpecs* and *Company.* The class *Vehicle* is also the root of a class hierarchy that involves the subclasses *TwoWheeler* and *FourWheeler.* The class Company is in turn the root of a class hierarchy that involves the subclasses *DomesticCompany* and *ForeignCompany.* It is also the root of a class composition hierarchy that involve the class *Employee.*

Advantages of OODBMS over RDBMS

Following are the advantages of Object Oriented Database System over Relational Database System.

(a) RDBMS does not allow nested structure. Nested structure applications are found in CAD/CAE, aerospace science, etc. It is easier to navigate through these complex structures in the form of objects rather than in the form of tables and records.
(b) Relational databases have only a limited number of data types like integer, char, text, etc. Although we can create complex data types in relational database by combining fields, these are restricted by their base data types. But OODBMS allow arbitrary data types and subclassing with inheritance.
(c) Object oriented databases are favoured in those applications where the relationship among data elements are more important than data items themselves. However, relational databases are used in those applications where the values of data elements are more important. If a record makes sense only when used in context of other records, then an object oriented database would be more appropriate.

1.5.5 Distributed DBMS (DDBMS)

Some organizations use distributed database system rather than a centralized database system. In the centralized database system, data resides in one single location. But in a distributed database system, database is stored in several computers.

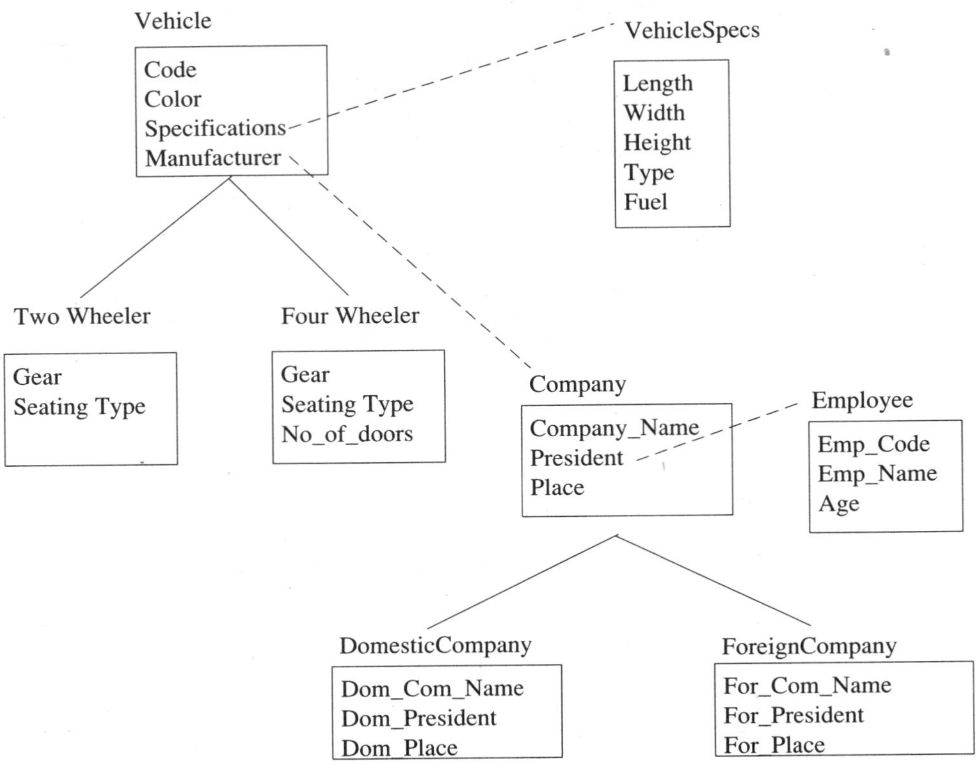

Figure 1.10 A sample Object Oriented Database

The computers in a distributed system communicate and exchange data among one other using leased lines, telephone lines or other means of communication. These computers do not share memory or clock. Each of the computers in a distributed system participates in the execution of transactions. These computers can also be known as *sites* or *nodes*.

Advantages of Distributed databases

(a) **Data Sharing:** Since data is distributed on multiple computers, user operating on one computer can work on data available on any another computer.

(b) **Distributed Control:** Unlike Centralized database system, where a single database administrator controls the database, in a distributed system responsibility of control is divided among local administrators for each computer. Thus, local administrators have a certain degree of control over the database stored locally.

(c) **Reliability and Availability:** Even if one site fails in the distributed system, the remaining sites can continue working. If data is replicated among multiple computers, failure of any one computer does not cause shutdown of the entire database system.

(d) **Faster Query Processing:** Queries involving data at several sites can be split into subqueries. These subqueries can then be executed in parallel by several sites. Such a parallel computation allows faster processing.

Disadvantages of Distributed databases

(a) **Increased cost:** It is more difficult to develop software packages to implement distributed database system. Also cost is involved in physically linking different sites.

(b) **More Error Prone:** Since the sites that comprise distributed database system operate in parallel, it is very difficult to ensure the correctness of data. The algorithms are more error prone and have greater potential for bugs.

(c) **Increased Overhead:** Maintaining physical links between the sites and exchanging messages among computers is an additional overhead associated with distributed systems, that are absent in the case of centralized systems.

1.6 ADVANTAGES OF DBMS

DBMS has got the following advantages:

(a) **Data independence**: In a database system the data is held independently of the application programs that use it. Changes to the data or the way it is stored will not necessarily affect the programs that use the data. In other words, the system data descriptions or data describing data (metadata) are separated from the application programs. This is possible because changes to the data structure are handled by the database management system and! are not embedded in the program itself.

(b) **Controls data redundancy**: Data redundancy means duplication of data i.e., information is repeated at various locations. In a database approach, any information usually appears at a single place. Hence, data duplication or redundancy is reduced.

(c) **Controls data inconsistency**: A database system is designed to reduce data redundancy. A database is in an inconsistent state if the same item of information is stored in at least two places in the database, but with different values. In database approach, items of data are ideally stored in one location only.! When updates are made to data, changes should only need to be made to this one location. This dramatically reduces that sort of repetition, making the risk of inconsistent data smaller.

(d) **Provides data management**: A DBMS provides a mechanism for easier management of the data held by an organization. It maintains data dictionary for the storage of information pertaining to data fields and data manipulation. It also represents complex relationships among different data items.

(e) **Data sharing**: The collection of data in a central data repository and managed by a DBMS ensures that data can be shared across all applications. A database can be used by many persons simultaneously or different times. And also has different interfaces through which users can manipulate data. It is not important for users to be aware of how and where the data they access is stored.

(f) **Enforces data access authorization**: In DBMS, the Database Administrator (DBA) has complete control over the database and ensures that the data is accessible only to authorized people. Not all users of a database system will have the same accessing privileges. For example, one user might have read-only access (i.e., the ability to read a file but not make changes), while another might have read and write privileges, which is the ability to both read and modify a file.

(g) **Transaction processing:** A database management system must include concurrency control subsystems. This feature ensures that data remains consistent and valid during transaction processing even if several users update the same information.

(h) **Backup and recovery facilities:** Backup and recovery are methods that allow you to protect your data from loss. DBMS provides an automatic intelligent backup and recovery procedure of data. If a hard drive fails and the database stored on the hard drive is not accessible, the only way to recover the database is from a backup. Also, if a computer system fails in the middle of a complex update process, the recovery subsystem is responsible for making sure that the database is restored to its original state.

(i) **Increased productivity:** File structures are already determined in the database structure. New application programs can then be developed that use these structures. This results in shorter development times.

(j) **Reduced maintenance:** A number of tools for maintaining the data are already built in to most DBMS. Tools may include report generators, query languages, form generators, code checkers, data dictionaries and maintenance logs.

1.6.1 Problems and Limitations

(a) Data Management approach bring up problems in data resource management.
(b) Developing a large database and installing a DBMS can be difficult and expensive.
(c) More hardware capability is required (storage and memory requirements are higher).
(d) Longer processing times may result from high-volume transaction processing applications.
(e) The security and integrity of an organization's databases are major concerns of an organization's data resource management effort.

1.6.2 DBMS Technologies

The database management system allows end-user software to connect to the databases and allow data to be extracted and saved. It also has many other purposes, like security management, performance improvement, etc. Popular types of DBMS technologies include:

- Relational Database Management System (RDBMS) is adaptable to most use cases, but RDBMS Tier-1 products can be quite expensive. In the case of a relational database, related data are stored in multiple tables. And each table has data stored in rows and columns. These tables are connected.
- NoSQL DBMS is well-suited for loosely defined data structures that may evolve over time. A NoSQL database is an approach to design such databases that can accommodate a wide variety of data models. NoSQL stands for "not only SQL." It is an alternative to traditional relational databases in which data is placed in tables, and data schema is perfectly designed before the database is built. NoSQL databases are useful for a large set of distributed data. Some examples of NoSQL database system are MongoDB, Coherence, and Big Table etc.
- In-Memory Database Management System (IMDBMS) provides faster response times and better performance.
- Columnar Database Management System (CDBMS) is well-suited for data warehouses that have a large number of similar data items.
- Cloud-based Database Management System is the cloud service provider and is responsible for providing and maintaining the DBMS. Cloud database facilitates you to store, manage, and retrieve their structured, unstructured data via a cloud platform i.e., it is a type of database where data is stored in a virtual environment and executes over the cloud computing platform. You can access your cloud-based database from any location, anytime. All you need is just an Internet connection. Cloud databases are also called a database as service (DBaaS) because they are offered as a managed service. Some best cloud options are AWS (Amazon Web Services), Oracle Database Cloud Services, Microsoft SQL server and Google cloud spanner.

Difference between DBMS and RDBMS

A DBMS is a software used to store and manage data. The DBMS was introduced during 1960's to store any data. It also offers manipulation of the data like insertion, deletion, and updating of the data.

Relational Database Management System (RDBMS) is an advanced version of a DBMS system. It came into existence during 1970's. RDBMS system also allows the organization to access data more efficiently then DBMS.

DBMS	RDBMS
DBMS stores data as a file.	Data is stored in the form of tables.
DBMS system, stores data in either a navigational or hierarchical form.	RDBMS uses a tabular structure where the headers are the column names, and the rows contain corresponding values.
DBMS supports single user only.	It supports multiple users.
Data fetching is slower for the complex and large amount of data.	Data fetching is rapid because of its relational approach.
Data elements need to access individually.	Multiple data elements can be accessed at the same time.
DBMS does not support client-server architecture.	RDBMS supports client-server architecture.
DBMS has low software and hardware requirements.	RDBMS has higher hardware and software requirements.

REVIEW QUESTIONS WITH ANSWERS

1. Multiple Choice Questions

1. Which one of the following is not a valid relational database?
   a. SYBASE b. IMS
   c. ORACLE d. UNIFY
2. Data about data is normally termed as
   a. Directory b. Data bank
   c. Meta data d. none of the above
3. In an object-oriented model, an object can access data of another object by passing
   a. Instance variable b. Message
   c. Variable d. None of these
4. Find the wrong statement:
   Database software
   a. provides facilities to create, use and maintain database
   b. supports report generation, statistical output, graphical output
   c. provides routine for backup and recovery
   d. all are correct
5. Which is not a DBMS packages?
   a. Unify b. Ingress
   c. IDMS d. All are DBMS packages
6. Data are
   a. Raw facts and figures
   b. Information
   c. Electronic representation of facts
   d. None of the above
7. Corporate information
   a. brings healthy relationship among employees and employers
   b. contains personal particulars
   c. means information derived from weekly meetings
   d. None of the above
8. DBA stands for
   a. Data Bank Access b. Database Access
   c. Data Bank Administration d. Database Administrator
9. Between the users and the database itself a DBMS will act as
   a. Barrier b. Interface
   c. Referee d. Obstacle
10. Which one of the following is not an object based logical model
    a. The binary model
    b. The entire relationship model
    c. The infological model
    d. None of the above

2. State True or False for the following:

1. A database is self describing.

2. IDMS is an example of network database system.
3. Database standards are provided by DBA.
4. All managers in a big organization use the same type of information.
5. Data items in records are also known as fields.
6. Classifying and sorting data are same.
7. Data and information are same.
8. Numerical data and character data are same.
9. Client/Server architecture is a special form of distributed processing.
10. Information is obtained by manipulating data.
11. DBMS is a collection of programs that enables user to create and maintain a database.
12. A table can also be called as relation.
13. Information stored in a database is arranged in a particular order.

3. Match the following:

1. Knowledge	a. Classifying
2. Data dictionary	b. Information at higher level of abstraction
3. Collection of logically related records	c. Database
4. Organizing similar items of data into groups	d. File organization
5. Manipulation of facts	e. Information about structure of a database
6. Information processing and retrieval	f. File
7. Decentralized processing	g. Data
8. Arrangement of records on files	h. Data item
9. Raw facts	i. Client/server
10. Smallest piece of meaningful information	j. Data processing
	k. Sorting

4. Fill in the blanks:

1. _________ contains the structure of the database.
2. ___________ is a hierarchical database system.
3. __________ is an example of network database system.
4. __________ model is preferred over hierarchical model by many organizations.
5. ____________ is a relational Database Management System (DBMS).
6. _________ is designed for heterogeneous database platforms.
7. ___________ is an organized collection of facts.
8. The smallest piece of meaningful information in a file is called ___________.
9. ___________ is responsible for physical design and maintenance of database.
10. Hierarchical, network and relational data models are __________ data models.
11. __________ provides support for logical data independence in the relational model.
12. In an oracle server the database writer is a ___________ process.
13. RDBMS does not allow _______ structure.
14. In a _________ model, data is organized in the form of rows and columns.

Answers

1. 1. b 2. c 3. b 4. d 5. d 6. a 7. d 8. d 9. b 10. c

2. 1. T 2. T 3. T 4. F 5. T 6. F 7. F 8. F 9. T 10. T 11. T 12. T 13. T

3. 1. b 2. e 3. f 4. a 5. j 6. c 7. i 8. d 9. g 10. h

4. 1. Data dictionary 2. IMS

3. IDMS	4. Relational
5. Security	6. DDBMS
7. Database	8. Field
9. DBA	10. Traditional
11. View	12. Background
13. Nested	14. Relational Database

Short Answers Questions

1. Write short note on the following:
(a) Object-Oriented Databases
(b) Hierarchical Databases
(c) DBMS

Ans a It is a type of database that uses the object-based data model approach for storing data in the database system. The data is represented and stored as objects which are similar to the objects used in the object-oriented programming language.

b. It is the type of database that stores data in the form of parent-children relationship nodes. Here, it organizes data in a tree-like structure. Data get stored in the form of records that are connected via links. Each child record in the tree will contain only one parent. On the other hand, each parent record can have multiple child records.

c. Database management system (DBMS) is a collection of interrelated data and a set of programs to access those data.

2. What is the use of Database Management Systems?

Ans Organizations use large amounts of data. A database management system DBMS) is a software tool that makes it possible to organize data in a database. The ultimate purpose of a database management system is to store and transform data into information to support making decisions.

3. Write advantage of centralized database.

Ans Advantage of centralized database are:

(a) Redundancy can be reduced.

(b) Inconsistency can be avoided

(c) The data can be shared

(d) Standards can be enforced

(e) Security restrictions can be applied

(f) Integrity can be maintained

4. How database, files, records, and fields are related?

Ans Database is a collection of related files while file is basically a collection of records and records are collection of fields. Fields give the individual information about an entity. The database system allows the user to access and manipulate the data contained in the database in a convenient and effective manner.

5. What is Data Base Management System? What are its characteristics?

Ans Database Management System is software which is used to store and retrieve data from the database i.e., it is software that supports management of large collections of data. Some popular DBMS tools are Oracle, MySQL, etc. Some of its characteristics are:

(a) DBMS provides the interface to perform the various operations like creation, deletion, modification, etc.

(b) DBMS allows the user to create their databases as per their requirement.

(c) DBMS accepts the request from the application and provides specific data through the operating system.

(d) DBMS contains the group of programs which acts according to the user instruction.

(e) It provides security to the database.

6. How DBMS controls data redundancy?

Ans DBMS stores all the data in a single database file, so it can control data redundancy.

7. Write disadvantage of DBMS.

Ans Disadvantage of DBMS are:

(a) Size: It occupies large disk space and large memory to run efficiently.

(b) Cost: DBMS requires a high-speed data processor and larger memory to run DBMS software, so it is costly.

(c) Complexity: DBMS creates additional complexity and requirements.

8. What is a data model?

Ans A data model is a collection of conceptual tools for describing data, data relationships, data semantics and consistency constraints. It thereby defines the infrastructure offered by a particular database system. The most popular example of a database model is the relational model.

9. Define Integrity.

Ans Integrity refers to the process of ensuring that a database remains an accurate reflection of the universe of discourse it is modeling or representing. In other words there is a close correspondence between the facts stored in the database and the real world it models.

10. List some of the disadvantages of using a DBMS. What are the circumstances under which file processing system is preferred over DBMS?

Ans Although a DBMS has got many advantages, it also incorporates certain overheads. These are as follows:

(a) High initial costs in hardware, software and training.

(b Overhead for providing security, concurrency control, recovery and integrity functions.

(c DBMS provides a generalized approach for defining and processing data. That is, it is not application specific.

File processing is preferable under the following circumstances:

(a) The database and applications are well defined and simple and are not expected to change.

(b) Some applications may have some real time processing requirements which may not be met because of DBMS overhead.

(c Multiple user access to data is not required.

(d) Database designers and DBA (Database Administrator) are ill trained or inexperienced.

11. What are the drawbacks of relational DBMS?

Ans Drawback of Relational DBMS are:

(a) RDBMS does not allow nested structure. Nested structure is required in such applications as CAD/CAE i.e. Computer Aided Design / Computer Aided Engineering.

(b) RDBMSs support only a limited number of data types like integer, char, text, etc.

(c) Applications developed nowadays are very different from the older data-processing style applications. However, the relational database model is fit for the latter type applications.

(d) In some cases it is impossible to represent every information in table (row and column) form.

12. Write advantages of DBMS.

Ans Advantages of DBMS are:

(a) Redundancy is controlled.

(b) Unauthorised access is restricted.

(c) Provides multiple user interfaces.

(d) Enforces integrity constraints.

(e) Provides backup and recovery.

13. Write disadvantages of File Processing System.

Ans Disadvantages of File Processing System are:

(a) Data redundancy and inconsistency.

(b) Difficulty in accessing data.

(c) Data isolation.

(f) Concurrent access is not possible.

(g) Security Problems.

14. Write short note on Network model.

Ans In Network model, data are represented by records using links among them. It is an improvement over the hierarchical model, since we can have many to many relationships among records.

15. What are the main differences between a file processing system and a database system?

Ans

File processing system	Database System
In a file processing system, the system stores permanent records in various files. Application programs are needed to extract records from, and add records to the appropriate files. As time passes new files and corresponding application programs are added to the system.	In the database system, there exists a collection of interrelated files and a set of application programs to access and modify these files. Details of data storage and maintenance are hidden from the users.
Supported by conventional operating systems such as MS DOS.	A database may be generated automatically or it may be computerized. The computerized database may be created and maintained by a database management system.
Since the files and application programs are created by different programmers over a long period of time, data in the files is likely to get repeated. Redundancy can lead to inconsistency that is, the various copies of the same data may contain different information.	A database system so designed does not involve the problem of data redundancy or inconsistency.
Not every user of the system should be able to access all the data. In a file processing system, since application programs are added in an adhoc manner, it is difficult to enforce such security constraints.	A database system so designed provides the security mechanisms to prevent unwanted users from accessing certain parts or whole of the database. For example, tellers in a bank see only that part of the database that has information on customer accounts. They cannot access information about salaries of employees.
Multiple user access to the information is difficult to provide through the conventional file processing system. This is due to the use of the application programs which have not been coordinated previously.	Almost all the database systems allow multiple users to update database at the same time.

16. Compare the three traditional data models. According to you, which is the best model and why?

Ans Following table brings out the comparison among three different data models.

Hierarchical Data Model	Network Data Model	Relational Data Model
Relationship between records is of the parent child form.	Relationship between records is expressed in the form of pointers or links.	Relationship between records is represented by a relation that contains a key for each record involved in the relationship.

Many to many relationship cannot be expressed in this data model.	Many to many relationship can be implemented in this model.	Many to many relationship can be implemented in this model.
It is a simple, straightforward and natural method of implementing record relationships.	Record relationship implementation is very complex due to the use of pointers.	Relationship implementation is very easy through the use of a common key or composite key field(s).
Hierarchical model is useful only when there is some hierarchical character in the database.	Network model is useful for representing such records which have many to many relationships.	Relational model is useful for representing most of the real world objects and relationships among them.
In order to represent links between records pointers are used. Thus relations between records are physical.	In Network model also the record relations are physical.	Relational model does not maintain physical connection between records. Data is organized logically in the form of rows and columns.
Searching for a record is very difficult since one can retrieve a child only after going through its parent.	Searching a record is easy since there are multiple access paths to a data element.	A Unique, Indexed key field is used to search for a data element.
During updation or deletion process, chances of data inconsistency is involved.	No problem of inconsistency exists in Network model because a data element is physically located at just one place.	Data Integrity maintaining methods like Normalization process, etc. are adopted to maintain consistency.

Out of these three, relational data model is considered to be the best model. This is so, because:

(a) Use of relational model for database design increases the productivity of application programmers by eliminating the need to change the application programs when a change is made to the database.

(b) Relational tables show only logical relationship.

(c) Users need not know the exact physical structure of a relation.

(d) Relational model can be used for representing most of the real world objects and relationships among them.

(e) Security and integrity are maintained easily by relational data model.

EXERCISE

1. Write short note on the following:
   (a) Object-Oriented Databases
   (b) Database system
   (c) Database
2. Discuss the main categories of Data models.
3. What is database system? What are the benefits of database?
4. What are the advantages of OODBMS over RDBMS?
5. What are the advantages of Distributed DBMS?
6. Define Field and Record.
7. How is a DBMS distinguished from a file-based system?
8. Differentiate between DBMS and RDBMS.
9. What is meant by database systems? What are the advantages and disadvantages of this system?

CHAPTER 2

Architecture of Database System

2.1 DATABASE ARCHITECTURE

The design of a DBMS depends on its architecture. It can be centralized or decentralized or hierarchical. The architecture of a DBMS can be seen as either single tier or multi-tier. An n-tier architecture divides the whole system into related but independent *n* modules, which can be independently modified, altered, changed, or replaced. DBMS architecture helps in design, development, implementation, and maintenance of a database. A database stores critical information for a business. Selecting the correct database Architecture helps in quick and secure access to this data.

2.1.1 1-tier Architecture

The 1-tier Architecture is simplest in all database architecture. In this type of architecture, the database is readily available on the client machine, i.e., any request made by client doesn't require a network connection to perform the action on the database. For example, lets say you want to fetch the records of employee from the database and the database is available on your computer system, so the request to fetch employee details will be done by your computer and the records will be fetched from the database by your computer as well. This type of system is generally referred as local database system. Database designers and programmers normally prefer to use single-tier architecture. But such architecture is rarely used in production.

2.1.2 2-tier Architecture

In 2-tier architecture, the database system is present at the server machine and the DBMS application (Presentation layer) is present at the client machine. These two machines are connected with each other through a reliable network. Whenever client machine makes a request to access the database present at server using a query language like SQL, the server perform the request on the database and returns the result back to the client. The application connection interface such as JDBC, ODBC are used for the interaction between server and client. 2-tier architecture also provides added security to the DBMS.

2.1.3 3-tier Architecture

The 3-tier architecture is an extension of the 2-tier architecture. In three-tier architecture, another layer is present between the client machine and server machine. In this architecture, the client application doesn't communicate directly with the database systems present at the server machine, rather the client application communicates with server application and the server application internally communicates with the database system present at the server. The 3-tier architecture has Presentation layer (client), Application layer (server), and Database (Data) server. This DBMS architecture contains an Application layer between the user and the DBMS, which is responsible for communicating the user's request to the DBMS system and send the response from the DBMS to the user. The Application layer also processes functional logic, constraint, and rules before passing data to the user or down to the DBMS. It is the most widely used architecture to design a DBMS.

☞ ***Presentation layer*** *is user interface which runs on end-user's computer (the client).* ***Application Server*** *is a business logic and data processing layer. This middle tier runs on a server which is called as Application Server.* ***Database Server*** *is a DBMS, which stores the data required by the middle tier.*

2.2 DATA ABSTRACTION

Abstraction is the process to hide the irrelevant things from the users and represent the relevant things to the user. Database systems are often used by non-computer professionals so that the complexity must be hidden from database system users. This is done by defining levels of abstraction at which the database may be viewed.

☞ *Data abstraction allow developers to keep complex data structures away from the users. The developers achieve this by hiding the complex data structures through levels of abstraction.*

DBMS is a collection of interrelated files and a set of programs that allow several users to access and modify these files. A major purpose of a database system is to provide users with an abstract view of the data. That is, the system hides certain details of how the data is stored and maintained. However, in order for the system to be usable, data must be retrieved efficiently.

The concern for efficiently leads to the design of complex data structure for the representation of data in the database. However since non-computer professionals often use database systems, this complexity must be hidden from database system users. This is done by defining levels of abstract as which the database may be viewed, there are logical view or external, conceptual view and internal view or physical view.

To understand it more clearly let us take an example, suppose you have to create a database of a college. So, entity sets involved are !Student, Lecturer, Department, Course and so on. Now, the entity sets Student, Lecturer, Department, Course will be stored in the storage as the consecutive blocks of the memory location. This is the physical or internal level and is hidden from the programmers but the database administrator is aware of it.

At the logical level, the programmers define the entity sets and relationship among these entity sets using a programming language like SQL. So, the programmers work at the logical level and even the database administrator also operates at this level.

At the view level, the users have the set of applications which they use to retrieve the data they are interested in.

2.3 LOGICAL VIEW

This the highest level of abstraction as seen by a user. It describes only the part of entire database, which is relevant to a particular user i.e., logical view is designed to suit the need of different users by representing data in a meaningful format. In a database there is only one physical view, but there can be multiple ways a user can view each item. The logical view is unique to any one user; each user can decide what they want to view and how they want to view items on a database.

☞ *The logical view/user's view, of a database program represents data in a format that is meaningful to a user and to the software programs that process those data.*

2.4 CONCEPTUAL VIEW

This is the next higher level of abstraction which is the sum total of Database Management System user's views. It describes what data is actually stored in the database. It contains information about entire database in terms of a small number of relatively simple structure.

2.5 PHYSICAL VIEW

This is the lowest level of abstraction. It describes how the data is physically stored. Physical view refers to the way data are physically stored and processed in a database. So while there can be numerous logical views of a database to suit the needs of the users, there can only be one physical view of a database because physical view deals with the physical storage of information on a storage device. Database specialists use the physical view to make efficient use of storage and processing resources. Users, however, may wish to see data differently from how they are stored, and they do not want to know all the technical details of physical storage.

☞ *The physical view deals with the actual, physical arrangement and location of data in the direct access storage devices.*

2.6 THREE LEVELS OF ARCHITECTURE

In the previous section we defined three levels of abstraction at which the database may be viewed. A database management system that provides these three levels of data is said to follow three-level architecture. These three levels are External level, Conceptual level, and the Internal level. The generalized architecture of a database system is called the ANSI/SPARC model. Many commercial systems and research database models fit within this framework. The architecture as per ANSI/SPARC is shown in Figure 2.1. The main objective of this architecture is to have an effective separation between the user interface and the physical database. So, the user never has to be concerned regarding the internal storage of the database and it has a simplified interaction with the database system.

Data is actually stored as bits, or numbers and strings in the database storage. It is very difficult to work with data at this level. So it is necessary to view data at different levels of abstraction. There are mainly three levels of data abstraction:

(a) External level or View level (Describes various user views)
(b) Conceptual level or Logical level (Structure and constraints for the entire database)
(c) Internal level or Physical level (Actual physical storage structure and access paths)

☞ *Database systems comprise of complex data structures. Thus, to make the system efficient for retrieval of data and reduce the complexity of the users, developers use the method of data abstraction.*

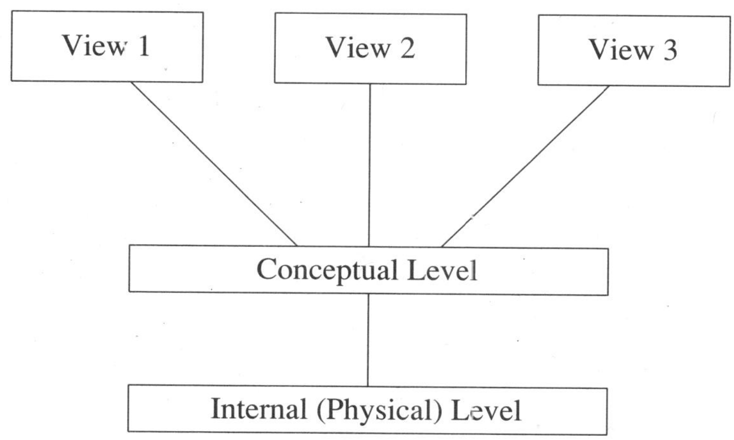

Figure 2.1 3-level architecture as per ANSI/SPARC

2.6.1 External Level (View Level)

The External or View Level of the architecture of a database system is the level closest to the users. This level is concerned with the way in which data are observed by individuals. Most of the users of database are not concerned with all the information contained in the database. Instead, they need only a part of the database relevant to them. For example, even though the bank database stores a lot more information, an *account holder* would be interested only in the account details such as the current balance and the transactions made. He/She may not need the rest of the information stored in the account holders database.

A DBMS may provide many different views for the same database. For example, FACULTY of a university is interested in looking course details of students, STUDENTS are interested in looking at all details related to academics, fees, courses and hostel details as well. So, different views can be generated for different users. The main focus of external level is data abstraction.

Figure 2.2 shows the interrelationship among the three levels of abstraction and presents the stored data at three different levels.

- An external level is the highest level of abstraction as seen by a user. It describes only the part of entire database, which is relevant to a particular user i.e., the data which is viewed by specific end users.
- This level includes some external schemas.
- The external schema describes the segment of the database which is needed for a certain user group and hides the remaining details from the database from the specific user group

☞ *The level of abstraction that describes only part of the entire database is called **view level**.*

2.6.2 Conceptual Level (Logical level)

Conceptual Level of DBMS abstraction describes the different types of data actually stored in a database i.e., data is represented in the form of various database tables. This level also indicates the relationships existing among data items. At this level, a database is described logically rather than physically in terms of data-structure. Users of this level are not concerned with how these logical data structures will be implemented at the physical level. Rather, they are only concerned about *what* information would be kept in a database. For example, UNIVERSITY database may contain STUDENT and COURSE tables which will be visible to users but users are unaware of their storage. (See Figure 2.2).

- Conceptual Level is the next higher level of abstraction. It describes what data is actually stored in the database. It contains information about entire database. Here it defines all database entities, their attributes, and their relationships.
- Security and integrity information.
- In the conceptual level, the data available to a user must be contained in or derivable from the physical level.

☞ *The conceptual level is also called as Logical level. It hides details of the physical level and gives logical view of whole database.*

2.6.3 Internal Level (Physical Level)

The lowest level of abstraction is the *internal level.* It is the one closest to physical storage device. This level is also termed as *physical level*, because it describes how data are actually stored on the storage medium such as hard disk, pendrives, etc. At this level, complex low-level data structures are described in detail. (See Figure 2.2)

- Internal Level is the lowest level of abstraction. It describes how the data is physically stored and it has complex data structures. Only the database administrator operates at this level.
- It helps you to keeps information about the actual representation of the entire database. Like the actual storage of the data on the disk in the form of records.
- The internal view tells us what data is stored in the database and how.
- It never deals with the physical devices. Instead, internal schema views a physical device as a collection of physical pages.

☞ *The level of data abstraction that describes how the data is actually stored on the storage device is called **physical view**.*

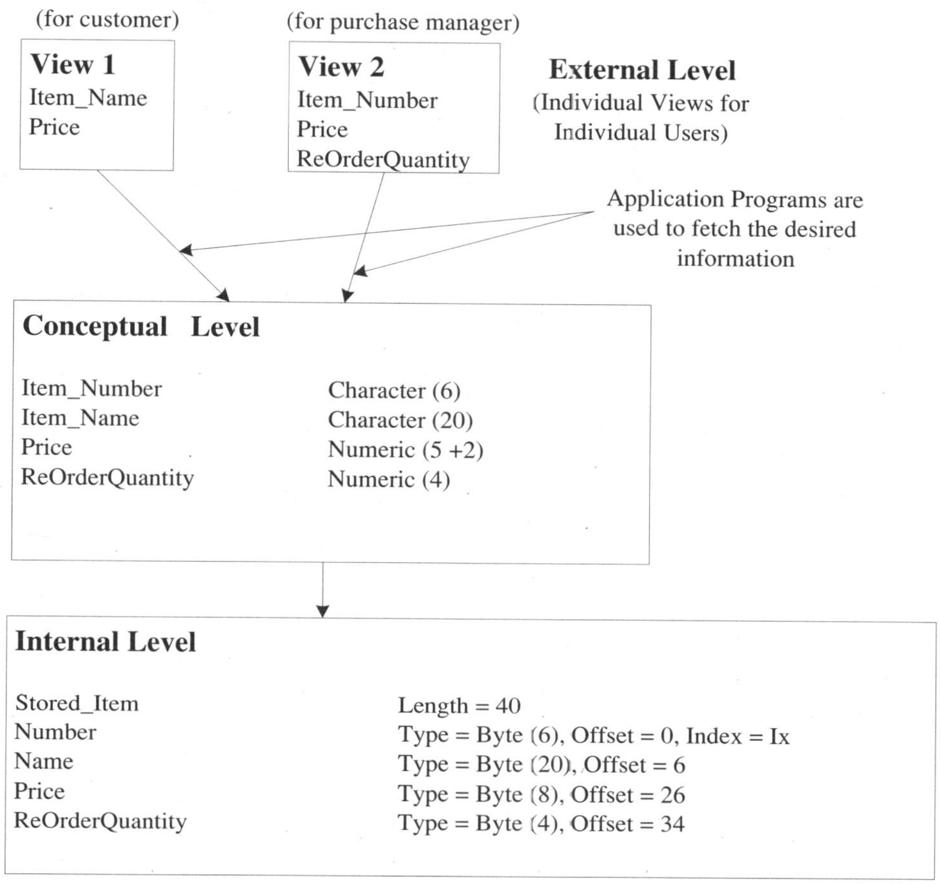

Figure 2.2 Inter-relationship between data at three levels of ANSI/SPARC model of DBMS architecture

2.7 MAPPING

We know that three view-levels are described by means of three schemas. These schemas are stored in the data dictionary. In DBMS, each user refers only to its own external schema. Hence, the DBMS must transform a request on a specified external schema into a request against conceptual schema, and then into a request against internal schema to store and retrieve data to and from the database.

The process to convert a request (from external level) and the result between view levels is called *mapping*. The mapping defines the correspondence between three view levels. The mapping description is also stored in data dictionary. The DBMS is responsible for mapping between these three types of schemas. There are two types of mapping.

(i) External-Conceptual Mapping
(ii) Conceptual-Internal Mapping

2.7.1 External-Conceptual Mapping

An extra-conceptual mapping defines the correspondence between a particular external view and the conceptual view. The external-conceptual mapping tells the DBMS which objects on the conceptual level correspond to the objects requested on a particular user's external view. If changes are made to either an external view or conceptual view, then mapping must be changed accordingly.

2.7.2 Conceptual-Internal Mapping

The conceptual-internal mapping defines the correspondence between the conceptual view and the internal view, i.e., database stored on the physical storage device. It describes how conceptual records are stored and retrieved to and from the storage device. This means that conceptual-internal mapping tells the DBMS that how the conceptual records are physically represented. If the structure of the stored database is changed, then the mapping must be changed accordingly. It is the responsibility of DBA to manage such changes.

Data Model Mapping is also called logical database design. During this phase the transformation of the conceptual schema into the actual implementation of the database, is done. This may be carried out as a DBMS package commercially available.

☞ *In terms of the three level DBMS architecture, the result of this phase is a conceptual schema in the chosen data model. In addition, the design of external schemas (views) for specific applications is often done during this phase.*

2.7.3 What is Schema?

The term schema shows an overall structure (organization) of all data-items including their record types stored in a database. A database schema is the skeleton structure that represents the logical view of the entire database. It defines how the data is organized and how the relations among them are associated. It formulates all the constraints that are to be applied on the data.

The first thing we must do to set up a database is to define its structure namely the *schema* definitions. This is done by identifying the characteristics of each field contained in a database.

☞ *Schema is the overall design of the entire database and is not changed frequently.*

☞ *A good way to begin defining the schema of a database is to list down on paper all the fields that need to be included in a database, and then determine the name, type and size of each of these fields.*

While defining the schema of a database, one should also consider possible future needs of all types of users. That is, all possible fields that may be needed in the near future should be included in the database structure at the time of defining it. Although it is possible to modify the database structure at any time, but making such a modification is time-consuming. Hence, it is always better to design a database very carefully in the beginning itself and minimize the need to modify it later.

A database schema can be divided broadly into two categories:

- **Physical Database Schema**: This schema pertains to the actual storage of data and its form of storage like files, indices, etc. It defines how the data will be stored in a secondary storage.
- **Logical Database Schema**: This schema defines all the logical constraints that need to be applied on the data stored. It defines tables, views, and integrity constraints.

2.7.4 What is Subschema?

The overall design of a database is known as the schema of a database. The term '*Subschema*' refers to an application programmer's view of the data-items and record types which the user would use. Many subschema can be derived from one schema. The subschema is also referred to as *logical view.*

☞ *External schemas are also called as subschemas.*

2.7.5 What is Instance?

An instance is the retrieval of information from the database at a certain point of time. An instance in a database keeps on changing with time. In short, at a particular moment; the data stored in database is called the instance, that changes over time when we add or delete data from the database. !Database schema defines the variable declarations in tables that belong to a particular database. For example, let's say we have a single table student in the database, today the table has 100 records, so today the instance of the database has 100 records. On another day we added 100 more records in this table now the instance of database becomes 200 records in table. So, the value of these variables at a moment of time is called the instance of that database.

☞ *The data stored in database at a particular moment of time is called instance of database.*

2.8 DATA INDEPENDENCE

Data independence means a change of data at one level should not affect another level. A database is viewed through different levels of abstraction. Any change at any level may affect other level's scheme (structure of database). As the databases keep growing, there may be changes made at some level. However, this should never lead to redesigning and re-implementation of a database. The concept of data independence proves beneficial in such a context.

☞ *The ability to modify a schema definition in one level without affecting a schema definition in the next higher level is called* ***data independence****.*

There are two levels of data independence. These are as follows:
(a) Physical Data Independence
(b) Logical Data Independence

2.8.1 Physical Data Independence

Physical Data Independence refers to the ability to modify the schema followed at the *physical* level without affecting the schema followed at a *conceptual* level i.e., any change in the physical location of tables and indexes should not affect the conceptual level or external view of data. That is, the application programs remain the same even though the schema at physical level gets modified.

☞ *Modification at the physical level are occasionally necessary in order to improve performance of the system.*

2.8.2 Logical Data Independence

Logical Data Independence refers to the ability to modify the *conceptual* schema without causing any changes in the schema followed at *view* level. The logical data independence ensures that the application programs remain the same. Modifications at the conceptual level are necessary whenever logical structures of the database get altered because of some unavoidable reasons. Such a case may be the introduction of maternity leave for female employees in the Employee table.

☞ *It is more difficult to achieve logical data independence than the physical data independence. The reason being that the application programs are heavily dependent on the logical structure of a database.*

The *abstract data types* in modern programming languages implement the concept of *data independence* to a larger extent. Both types hide implementation details from the users. This allows users to concentrate on the general structure rather than low-level implementation details.

2.9 DATABASE MODELS

A *Database model* is a collection of tools for describing data, data relationships, data semantic and consistency constraints. They can be broadly classified into the following categories:
(a) Conceptual database models
(b) Physical database models
(c) Logical database models

☞ *A collection of conceptual tools for describing data, data relationships data semantics and constraints is called data model.*

2.9.1 Conceptual Database Models

The conceptual database models are used in describing data at the conceptual level and also at the view level. They provide the flexible structuring capabilities. A number of conceptual models have been proposed, but Entity-Relationship (E-R) model is widely used. They are also known as object based database models. E-R data model is based on real world that consists of basic objects called entities and of relationship among these objects. Entities are described in a database by a set of attributes. Features of conceptual database model include:

- Includes the important entities and the relationships among them.
- No attribute is specified.
- No primary key is specified.

☞ *A conceptual data model identifies the highest-level relationships between the different entities.*

2.9.2 Physical Database Models

Physical database models are used to describe data at the lowest level. With the physical models it is possible to implement the database at the system level. Physical data model represents how the model will be built in the database. A physical database model shows all table structures, including column name, column data type, column constraints, primary key, foreign key, and relationships between tables. Two of the widely known models are *unifying model* and *frame memory model.*

Features of a physical data model include:

- Specification all tables and columns.
- Foreign keys are used to identify relationships between tables.
- Denormalization may occur based on user requirements.
- Physical considerations may cause the physical data model to be quite different from the logical data model.
- Physical data model will be different for different RDBMS.

2.9.3 Logical Database Models

Logical database models are also used in describing data at the conceptual and view levels. However, in contrast to conceptual database models, these models are used to specify both the overall logical structure of the database and a higher level description of the implementation. They are also known as record-based database models. Features of a logical data model include:

- Includes all entities and relationships among them.
- All attributes for each entity are specified.
- The primary key for each entity is specified.
- Foreign keys (keys identifying the relationship between different entities) are specified.
- Normalization occurs at this level.

☞ *The three widely accepted logical data models are **Relational model**, **Network model** and **Hierarchical model**.*

In the record-based logical models, the database is structured in fixed format records of different types. Each record type defines a fixed number of fields, or attributes and each field is of a fixed length. There are three types of record-based data models. These are the following:

(a) **Hierarchical data model**: It was developed to model the many types of hierarchical organizations that exist in the real world. It uses tree structures to represent relationship among records. In hierarchical model, no dependent record can occur without its parent record occurrence and no dependent record occurrence may be connected to more than one parent record occurrence.

(b) **Network data model**: It was formalized in the late 1960s by the Database Task Group of the Conference on Data System Language (DBTG/CODASYL). It uses two different data structures to represent the database entities and relationships between the entities, namely record type and set type. In the network model, the relationships as well as the navigation through the database are predefined at database creation time.

(c) **Relational data model**: The relational model was first introduced by E.F. Codd of the IBM Research in 1970. The model uses the concept of a mathematical relation (like a table of values) as its basic building block, and has its theoretical basis in set theory and first-order predicate logic. The relational model represents the database as a collection of relations.

The three logical models are described in Sections 1.5.1, 1.5.2 and 1.5.3, of Chapter 1, respectively. In the subsequent sections, a comparative study of the three models are given, in order to select the suitable data model.

2.9.4 Comparison of the three Models

Table 2.1 gives a comparative study of the three traditional database models.

Table 2.1 Comparison of the three data models

S. No.	Hierarchical Data Model	Network Data Model	Relational Data Model
1.	Relationship between records is of the parent child type.	Relationship between records is expressed in the form of pointers or links.	Relationship between records is represented by a relation that contains a key for each record involved in the relationship.
2.	Many to many relationship cannot be expressed in this model.	Many to many relationship can also be implemented.	Many to many relationship can be easily implemented.
3.	It is a simple, straightforward and natural method of implementing record relationships	Record relationship implementation is quite complex due to the use of pointers.	Relationship implementation is very easy through the use of a key or composite key field(s).
4.	This type of model is useful only when there is some hierarchical character in the database.	Network model is useful for representing such records which have many-to-many relationships.	Relational model is useful for representing most of the real world objects and relationships among them.
5.	In order to represent links among records, pointers are used. Thus relations among records are physical.	In Network model also the record relations are physical.	Relational model does not maintain physical connection among records. Data is organized logically in the form of rows and columns and stored in table.
6.	Searching for a record is very difficult since one can retrieve a child only after going through its parent record.	Searching a record is easy since there are multiple access paths to a data element.	A unique, indexed key field is used to search for a data element.
7.	During updation or deletion process, chances of data inconsistency is involved.	No problem of inconsistency exists in Network model because a data element is physically located at just one place.	Data integrity maintaining methods like Normalization process, etc. are adopted for consistency.

2.9.5 Which Data Model to Use?

The data model that best suits an organization depends on the following factors:

(a) The organization's primary goals and requirements.

(b) The volume of daily transactions that will be done.

(c) The estimated number of enquiries that will be made by the organization.

For example, in the hierarchical view of customer-order table a dependent, cannot have more than one superior and hence an order cannot be placed by multiple customers. This is against business rules. Therefore when an organization wishes to create a database for order processing it must *not choose* hierarchical model.

Among the traditional data models, the widely preferred one is the *relational* model. This is because, relational model can be used for representing most of the real world objects and the relationships among them. Security and integrity are maintained easily by relational model. Also, use of relational model for database design increases the productivity of application programmers, since it eliminates the need to change the application program when a change is made to the database. Moreover, relational tables show only the logical relationship. End users need not know the exact physical structure of a table or relation.

2.10 ROLE OF DBA (Database Administrator)

Database Administration is implemented by a person or group of persons under the supervision of a knowledgeable person called administrator. This person, known as the DataBase Administrator (DBA), is responsible for supervising the creation, modification and maintenance of the database.

☞ *The DBA controls the database structure and sets up the definition for physical as well as logical implementation of the database.*

The overall function of the database administrator include:

i) **Schema definition:** The original database schema is created by writing a set of definitions which are translated by the DDL compiler to a set of tables that are permanently stored in the data dictionary.

ii) **Storage structure and access method definition:** Appropriate storage structures and access methods are created by writing a set of definitions which are translated by the data storage and definition language compiler.

iii) **Schema and physical-organization modification:** The DBA carries out changes to the schema and physical organization to reflect the changing needs of the organization, or to alter the physical organization to improve performance.

iv) **Granting of authorization for data access:** DBA also maintains that the database is not accessible to unauthorized users. The DBA is responsible for granting permission to use the database and stores the profile of each user of a database. This profile describes the permissible activities of a user on that portion of the database which is authorized to him. The user profile can be used by the DBA to verify that a particular user is only allowed to perform a given operation on the database, within the limited time frame.

v) **Routine maintenance:** The DBA is responsible for defining procedures to recover data from failures due to human, natural or hardware malfunctioning with minimal loss. This recovery procedure would thus enable an organization to continue working with the available intact portion of the database.

He also ensures that enough free disk space is available for normal operations and upgrading disk space as required.

vi) **Maintaining integrity:** DBA ensures that appropriate measures are taken to maintain the integrity of a database. Integrity constraints are kept in a special system structure that is consulted by the database manager whenever an update takes place in the system.

REVIEW QUESTIONS WITH ANSWERS

1. Multiple Choice Questions

1. The relational model is concerned with:
   a. Data structure and Data integrity
   b. Data manipulation
   c. Both a and b
   d. None of these

2. A view of a database that appears to an application program is known as:
   a. Schema b. Subschema
   c. Virtual table d. None of these

3. Model based on user's requirements is:
   a. Logical model b. Physical model
   c. Conceptual model d. None of these

4. The Data model which describes how the data is actually stored is:
   a. Internal model b. External model
   c. Logical model d. None of the above
5. The scheme for hierarchical database is:
   a. A tree b. A graph
   c. A B– tree d. None of these
6. A relational model which allows non-atomic domains is:
   a. Nested relational model
   b. Non-atomic data model
   c. Hierarchical data model
   d. Such a model cannot exist
7. Which of the following is an example for network database?
   a. IDMS b. Ingress
   c. Oracle d. DBMS
8. Which of the following is an example for hierarchical database?
   a. Oracle b. DBII
   c. Ingress d. SYSTEM2000
9. In most of the implementations of hierarchical databases, parent-to-child links are stored with the help of:
   a. Pointers b. Virtual records
   c. Reference variables d. Preorder threads
10. A hierarchical data model is:
    a. Partially ordered b. Not ordered
    c. Totally ordered d. Concept of ordering does not appear
11. Which of the following design is both software and hardware independent?
    a. Logical b. Physical
    c. Conceptual d. None of the above
12. The level of data abstraction which describes how the data is actually stored is:
    a. Conceptual level b. Physical level
    c. File level d. None of the above

2. State True or False for the following:

1. IMS (Information management system) is a hierarchical database system.
2. The design of a DBMS depends on its architecture.
3. An hierarchical data model is partially ordered.
4. Hierarchical model is preferred over relational model by many organizations.
5. In an hierarchical database, modelling of many-to-many relations is achieved by record duplication.
6. The DBA controls the database structure and sets up the definition for physical as well as logical implementation of the database.
7. The internal level describes the physical storage structure of the database.
8. The conceptual level is a level of indirection.
9. The conceptual view is a view of the total database content.
10. System tables are catalog in relational system.
11. The database schema and an instance of the database are the same thing.
12. Hierarchical data model uses the concept of SET.
13. Relational data model provides better data independence than network model.
14. In the ANSI term internal schema, it is also called 'stored record'.
15. The internal schema defines the physical storage structure of the database.
16. The conceptual schema describes the Database structure of the whole database for the community of users.
17. An external schema describe the part of the database which specific user is interested in.
18. In a single-tier system the database is centralized, which means the DBMS Software and the data reside in one location and the dumb terminals were used to access the DBMS.
19. Program data independence is the same as data Independence.
20. Data consistency and Integrity are the responsibility of DBA.
21. The subschema must contain all the descriptions of certain data, that are in the scheme.
22. Network model cannot handle many to many relationship in natural way.

23. The 3-tier architecture is an extension of the 2-tier architecture.
24. In data independence the schema at higher level remains unchanged.

3. Match the following:

1.	Hierarchical model	a.	Hierarchical database system
2.	IMS	b.	View level
3.	Subschema	c.	Sets
4.	Physical model	d.	An object in the real world that is distinguishable from all other objects
5.	View	e.	Data are represented by collection of records and relationships among them is in parent child form
6.	Network model	f.	External model
7.	External Level	g.	Logical view
8.	Schema	h.	Highest level of abstraction
9.	2-tier architecture	i.	Overall structure
10.	An external level	j.	Provides added security to the DBMS.

4. Fill in the blanks:

1. The process to convert a request (from external level) and the result between view levels is called _______.
2. ANSI/SPARC report proposed ________ level architecture for a database system.
3. Data on a last level of a database tree is called _________.
4. _________ is a collection of entries where each entry corresponds to a data record.
5. In the relational data model, the columns of a table are called ___________.
6. The ___________ model is based on the mathematical concept of a relation.
7. Relational model of data management is based on ___________.
8. An internal schema describes __________ structure of the database.
9. The level of abstraction describes only part of the entire database is called ___________ .
10. The level of data abstraction that describes how the data is actually stored is called __________.
11. The _______ Architecture is simplest in all Database Architecture.
12. _________ layer is user interface which runs on end-user's computer (the client).
13. ________ Server is a business logic and data processing layer.
14. The _______ architecture appears as improvement over two-tier architecture.
15. ________ Server is a DBMS, which stores the data required by the middle tier.
16. ________ is the process to hide the irrelevant things from the users and represent the relevant things to the user.

Answers

1.	1. c	2. b	3. a	4. a	5. a	6. a
	7. a	8. d	9. d	10. c	11. c	12. b
2.	1. T	2. T	3. F	4. F	5. T	6. T
	7. T	8. F	9. F	10. T	11. F	12. F
	13. T	14. T	15. T	16. T	17. T	18. T
	19. T	20. T	21. T	22. F	23. T	24. T
3.	1. e	2. a	3. g	4. d	5. f	6. c
	7. b	8. i	9. j	10. h		

4.

1. Mapping	2. Three
3. Leaf	4. Index
5. Attributes	6. Object
7. Set theory	8. Physical storage
9. View level	10. Physical level
11. 1-tier	12. Presentation
13. Application	14. Three-tier
15. Database	16. Abstraction

Short Answers Questions

1. What are the objectives of using Three schema Architecture?

Ans Objectives of using Three schema Architecture are:

(a) Every user should be able to access the same data but able to see a customized view of the data.

(b) The user need not to deal directly with physical database storage detail.

(c) The DBA should be able to change the database storage structure without disturbing the user's views.

(d) The internal structure of the database should remain unaffected when changes made to the physical aspects of storage.

2. Explain the difference between two and three-tier architectures.

Ans A three-tier architecture includes a client and two server layers. The application code is stored on the application server and the database is stored on the database server. A two-tier architecture includes a client and one server layer. The database is stored on the database server.

3. Differentiate between Database Schema and Database Instance.

Ans Database schema is the skeleton of database. It is designed when the database doesn't exist at all. Once the database is operational, it is very difficult to make any changes to it. A database schema does not contain any data or information.

A database instance is a state of operational database with data at any given time. Database instances tend to change with time.

4. What is Data Independence?

Ans Data independence means that "the application is independent of the storage structure and access strategy of data". In other words data independence defines the extent to which the data schema can be changed at one level without modifying the data schema at the next level.

5. What is the use of Logical View?

Ans The logical view is a simple term, which helps the user only view the items they need for their specific task. The logical view is a view that is logical to the database user. The database only has one physical view, but can have many logical views. Each user can have their own logical view that is unique to the user and unique to a specific task.

6. Differentiate between Logical view and Physical views of the data.

Ans The DBMS relieves the programmer or end user from the task of understanding where and how the data are actually stored by separating the logical and physical views of the data. The logical view presents data as they would be perceived by end users or business specialists, whereas the physical view shows how data are actually organized and structured on physical storage media.

7. Differentiate between Conceptual schema and Physical (internal) schema.

Ans The logical description of the entire database showing all the data elements and relationships among them is called the conceptual schema, whereas the specifications of how data from the conceptual schema are stored on physical media is termed the physical schema or internal schema.

8. What is subschema?

Ans The specific set of data from the database, or view, that is required by each user or application program is termed the subschema. For example, for the human resources database an employee retirement benefits program might use a subschema consisting of the employee's name, address, adhar card number, pension plan, and retirement benefits data.

9. How Logical Data Independence is different from Physical Data Independence?

Ans Logical data independence describes the degree up to which the logical or conceptual schema can be changed without modifying the external schema. The changes to data schema at the logical level are made either to enlarge or reduce the database by adding or deleting more entities, entity sets, or changing the constraints on data.

Physical data independence defines the extent up to which the data schema can be changed at the physical or internal level without modifying the data schema at logical and view level. The physical schema is changed if we add additional storage to the system or we reorganize some files to enhance the retrieval speed of the records.

10. Explain two types of Data Independence.

Ans The ability to modify the schema definition in one level should not affect the schema definition in the next higher level. Two types of Data Independence are:

Physical Data Independence: Modification in physical level should not affect the logical level.

Logical Data Independence: Modification in logical level should affect the view level.

11. What is a view? How it is related to data independence?

Ans A view may be thought of as a virtual table, that is, a table that does not really exist in its own right but is instead derived from one or more underlying base table. In other words, there is no stored file that direct represents the view instead a definition of view is stored in data dictionary.

12. What is an instance?

Ans We can define an instance as the information stored in the database at a particular point of time. For example, the database comprises of several entity sets and the relationship between them. Now, the data in the database keeps on changing with time. As we keep inserting or deleting the data to and from the database. Now, at a particular time if we retrieve any information from the database then that corresponds to an instance.

13. What is schema?

Ans Schema is the overall design of the entire database. Schema of the database is not changed frequently.

14. What is three-level abstraction of data? Explain.

Ans View of data in DBMS describes the abstraction of data at three-level i.e. physical level, logical level, view level.

The physical level of abstraction defines how data is stored in the storage and also reveals its access path.

Abstraction at the logical level describes what data would be stored in the database, the relation between the data and the constraints applied to the data.

The view level or external level of abstraction describes the application which the users use to retrieve the information from the database.

15. Discuss all the three record-based data models in detail.

Ans Classification of Record-based Data Models:

(a) Hierarchical data models
(b) Network data models
(c) Relational data models.

Hierarchical data model

In the hierarchical data model, data is organized in a ordered tree manner. Moreover, in this model, database is a collection of disjoint trees. The nodes of the tree represent record type. In a hierarchical model, no dependent record can occur without its parent record occurrence. And no dependent record occurrences may be connected to more than one parent record occurrence. Thus, the hierarchical data model can represent one to many relationship but not *many to many* relationship.

Network data model

In the network data model, the data is represented by records using links among them. It is an improvement over the hierarchical model, since we can have *many to many* relationships among records, which was not possible in the hierarchical model. The network data model is similar to a hierarchical model, except that an entity can have more than one parent. The relationships as well as the navigation through the database is pre-defined while creating a database.

Relational data model
In relational data model, the relation or table is the only construct required to represent an association among the attributes of an entity as well as relationships among different entities. In this model users need not know the exact physical structure of a database, yet manipulation of database using some query language is possible.

16. Describe the three-schema architecture. Why do we need mappings between schema levels? How do different schema definition languages support this architecture?

Ans The three-schema architecture separates the user applications and the physical database as seen in Figure 1. Schemas can be defined at the following three levels:

(a) The internal level has an *internal schema*, which describes the physical storage structure of the database.

(b) The conceptual level has a *conceptual schema*, which describes the structure of the whole database for a community of users. The conceptual schema describes entities, data types, relationships, user operations and constraints. It hides the details of physical storage structures.

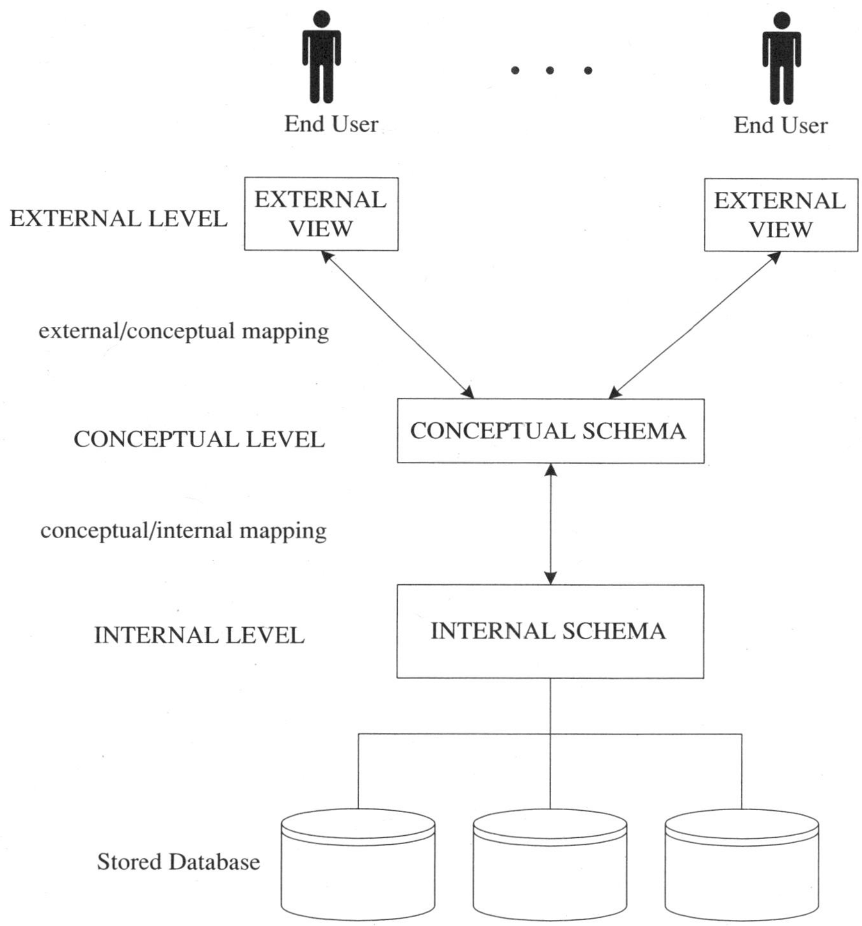

Figure 1 Three schema architecture

(c) The external level has a number of *external schemas* or *user views*. Each external schema describes the part of the database that a particular user group is interested in and hides the rest of the database from that user group.

Data actually exists at the physical level. Users interact with the DBMS through the external schema. Hence, the DBMS must transform a request by the user on an external schema into a request against the conceptual schema and then into a request on the internal schema for processing over the stored database. The data extracted from the stored database must be reformatted to match the user's external view. This process of transforming requests and formats among the different levels is known as *mapping*.

In those DBMS packages where no strict separation of levels is present, *data definition language (DDL)* is used by DBA and database designers to define conceptual and internal schemas.

However, in such DBMSs where a clear separation is present between the conceptual and internal levels, DDL is used to specify the conceptual schema only. And another language, called the *storage definition language (SDL)* is used to specify the internal schema.

Although most DBMSs use DDL to define both conceptual and external schemas, for a true three-schema architecture, we would need a *view definition language (VDL)* to define the external schemas.

EXERCISE

1. Write short note on the following:
   (a) External level or View level
   (b) Conceptual level
   (c) Internal level or Physical level
   (d) Subschema
   (e) Data Independence
2. What is difference between Physical and Logical data independence?
3. Explain 2-tier Architecture.
4. Compare and Contrast Physical and Logical data independence.
5. Discuss all the three record-based data models in detail.
6. Describe the three-schema architecture. Why do we need mappings between schema levels? How do different schema definition languages support this architecture?
7. Compare the three record-based database models. According to you, which is the best model and why?
8. How 3-tier Architecture is different from 2-tier Architecture?
9. Explain Three levels of Architecture.
10. What is Data abstraction?
11. Discuss role of Database Administrator.
12. Compare Relational, Network and Hierarchical data models. According to you, which is the best model and why?
13. Explain the distinction between the representation of association and relationship in the network and hierarchical models.
14. What are the advantages and disadvantages of Relational database model as compared to other traditional models?
15. Describe Conceptual, Logical and Physical database models.
16. What are the five major functions of a database administrator?

CHAPTER 3

Relational Database Management System (RDBMS)

3.1 INTRODUCTION

Relational Database Management System (RDBMS) is a software package used to store and retrieve data that is organized in the form of tables. In other words Relational Database Management System stores information in rows and columns and conducts searches by using data in specified columns and rows of one table as well as to find additional data in another related table.

Two dimensional table is a natural way to represent data to a user. A table must be set up in a way that no information about the relations among data elements is lost.

A table should contain the following properties:

(a) Each entry in a table should only represent one data item and no two column headings with the same name.
(b) In each column, the data items are of the same data type.
(c) Each column is assigned with a distinct heading.
(d) All rows are distinct; duplicate rows are not allowed.
(e) Both the rows and the columns can be viewed in any sequence at any time without affecting the information.

A relational database model uses a collection of tables to represent both data and the relationships among those data items. Each table has multiple columns, and each column has a unique name.

A Relational Database Management System (RDBMS) has the following properties:

(a) Stores data in the form of tables.
(b) Does not require the user to understand its physical implementation.
(c) Provides information about its content and structure in the system table.
(d) Supports the concepts of NULL values.

3.2 RDBMS TERMINOLOGIES

3.2.1 Relation

All data items and relationships among them are represented in a two dimensional table called a *relation*. For example, the table shown in Figure 3.1 is referred to as a relation. A database constructed using relations is referred to as a *relational database*. Relational database is constructed from flat arrangement of data items. In Figure 3.1, there is an Employee Service relation that describes the entity[1] *Employee* by Emp_code, Name and Year of Service (Year).

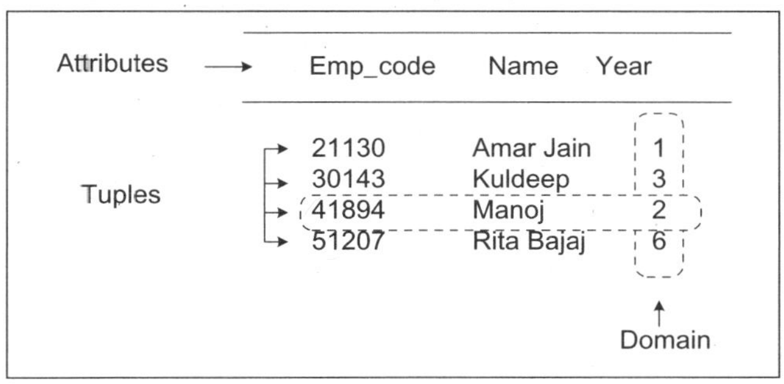

Figure 3.1 Employee Service relation in table form

All relations have three components:

(a) Name
(b) Degree
(c) Cardinality

Name

Name is represented by the *title* or the *entity–identifier*. For example Employee Name and years of Service relation as seen in Figure 3.1.

1 An entity is person, place, event or concept about which we need to capture and store data.

Degree

The number of columns associated with a table or relation among them is called the *Degree*. In the table Employee Service relation, degree is 3, i.e. there are 3 attributes or fields associated with the table.

Cardinality

The number of rows in a table is called as *Cardinality*. In the table (Employee Service relation), cardinality is 4, i.e. there are 4 rows or records (tuples) associated with the table.

3.2.2 Attributes and Tuples

Two dimensional tables in a relational database are much like the traditional file system with its records, fields and files. Rows of a relation are referred to as *Tuples* of the relation and columns are referred to as *Attributes*.

☞ *A relation consists of number of records or row-wise information **(tuples)** and column-wise information **(attributes)**.*

An entity usually has an attribute whose values are distinct for each individual entity in the collection. Such an attribute is called a *key attribute* and its values can be used to identify each entity uniquely. For example, *Emp_code* attribute is a key of the *Employee* entity in Figure 3.1, because no two employees will have the same Emp_code.

☞ *Each attribute of a relation has a distinct name.*

Each tuple or row has a set of permitted values for the attribute called the *Domain*. For example, the domain of attribute *Name* is the set of all alphabetic strings of finite length. The domain of attribute Year is the set of all whole numbers, as shown in Figure 3.1.

☞ *A **domain** is a collection of all possible values from which the values for a given column or attribute is drawn. There are domains defined for every attribute in each table.*

3.2.3 Entity, Entity Set and Instance

An *entity* is an object that exists and is distinguishable from any other object. In other words, an entity is a real-world person, place or thing, or a conceptual (logical) person, place or thing, of significant interest to the organization and about which the organization must collect and maintain data. Each entity has particular properties called attributes that describe it. For example, an *Employee* entity may be described by employee's Name, Address and Age. Figure 3.2 shows an entity and the values of its attributes.

For example, Employee entity has three attributes Name, Address, and Age with the values "Ramakrishna", "D-428, Vivek Vihar" and "27" respectively.

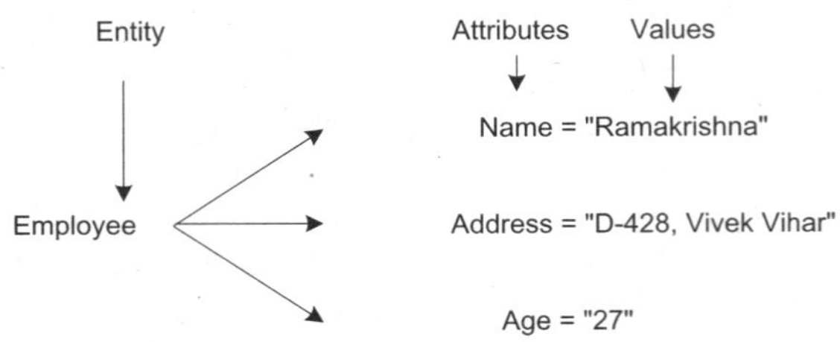

Figure 3.2 Entity and the values of its Attributes

☞ *An entity set is represented by a set of attributes.*

The collection of information stored in a database at a particular moment is called *instance* or *occurrence*, of the entity.

3.3 RELATIONAL DATA INTEGRITY

When many users enter data items into a database, it becomes important that all data items and association among such data items are not destroyed. Hence, data insertions, updations, etc. have to be carried out in such a way that database integrity is maintained.

Integrity check is to be performed at the data entry level itself. By checking the data 'values' conforming to certain specified rules, the names, value lying within a specified range. For example, the age of the employee should be in the range of 18 years to 70 years.

The relational model includes two general integrity rules. These integrity rules define the set of consistent database states and changes of state or both.

3.3.1 Integrity Rule 1 (Entity Integrity)

"If an attribute of a table is of prime attribute (unique identifier), it can not accept null values, or in other words *no component of a primary key*[2] *values may be null*".

Entity Integrity ensures that instances of the entities are distinguishable and thus no prime attribute (component of a primary key) value may be null. By definition, all entities must be distinguishable i.e. they must have a unique identification of some kind. Primary keys perform that unique identification function in a relational database. Hence, an identifier (Primary key value) that was completely null would be a contradiction.

☞ *If two entities are not distinguishable from each other, then by definition such entities are not two entities.*

3.3.2 Integrity Rule 2 (Referential Integrity)

"To ensure that a value that appears in one relation for a given set of attributes also appears for a certain set of attributes in another relation. Such a condition is called the referential integrity."

Integrity Rule 2 is concerned with the concept of foreign key i.e. with the attributes of a relation having domains. The domain of foreign keys[3] are those of the primary key of another relation. For example, if a base relation[4] includes a foreign key, then it must have a primary key to match in some other relation, or contain a null value completely. (See Figure 3.3).

☞ *The value of a primary key which appears in the base table (entity set) whenever their is a cardinality (entity relation) then the value of a primary key, which becomes a foreign key in the entity relation, the value of foreign key and primary key should be the same.*

The designation code 'X01' in master file is not allowed, as it does not have a primary key match in other table, namely the control file.

Employee with Emp_code 104 joins the organization, and his designation is not clearly specified at the time of data entry. Hence, the designation can be a null, so that the same can be updated later.

Master File

Emp_Code	Dept_Code	Name
100	A01	Raj
102	C01	Lalit
104	X01	Govind

Control File

Dept_Code	Designation
A01	Director
B01	Manager
C01	Officer

Figure 3.3 Referential Integrity

☞ *Referential integrity constraints are created in order to ensure that data entered into one table is matchable or compatable with corresponding data in the other related tables. Values from one column are dependent on the values of columns in other tables.*

3.4 DOMAIN CONSTRAINTS

Domain constraints include entity integrity and referential integrity. The domain is a set of values that may be assigned to an attribute. The entity integrity rule states that no part of a primary key may be null. Referential integrity states that each foreign key value must match a primary key value or be null.

3.5 RELATIONAL MODEL

This portion is already covered in Chapter 1.

3.6 BASE TABLES

The base tables are those tables that are created prior to their use. It is a set of rows. A row is an ordered list of values. The row is the smallest unit of data that can be inserted in or deleted

2 The field or group of fields which forms the unique identifier for a table is called its *primary key*.

3 In a relation, column whose data values correspond to the values of a key column in another relation is called a *Foreign key*.

4 The *base relations* are those relation which are created prior to use.

from a table. Each row in a table has the same number of columns and contains a value for each column.

☞ *Base table is a table that is physically stored in the database.*

3.7 RELATIONAL DATA MANIPULATION

RDBMS is a database management system where data are organized in the form of tables and all database manipulation are carried out on these tables. Users of RDBMS can create a new relation from two or more existing tables thus permitting them to manipulate data in creative ways. For example, suppose a relational DBMS maintains two relations: the Employee Service relation (Figure 3.1) and Employee Education relation (Figure 3.4).

A query about employees with more than two years of service in the organization and an MCA degree can be obtained by using the following procedures:

(a) A relationship is implied between the Employee Service relation (Figure 3.1) and Employee Education relation (Figure 3.4).

Emp_Code	Degree
21130	High School
30143	MCA
41894	M.Sc
51207	MCA

Figure 3.4 Employee Education relation

(b) A temporary table of employees who have been in the organization for more than two years is obtained from the Employee Service relation and placed in a temporary table.

(c) The information in the temporary table is taken along with the Employee Education relation to determine which employee has been in the firm for more than two years and also qualified as MCA. This results in a second temporary relation. From this second temporary relation is inferred that *Kuldeep* and *Rita Bajaj* are the only employees who qualify for the two conditions put together. Thus this method is very useful to manipulate several tables together to bring out informations. This is the method used in RDBMS for manipulating and extracting informations.

3.8 KEYS

A *key* is that data item that exclusively identifies a record. For example, *Account_number*, *Product_code*, *Employee_number* and *Customer_number* are used as key fields because they specifically identify a record stored in a database.

3.8.1 Super Key

A *Super Key* for an entity is a set of one or more attributes whose combined value uniquely identifies the entity in the entity set. For example, for an entity set Employees, the set of attributes (emp_name, address) can be considered to be a super key, if we assume that there are no two employees with the same emp_name as well as the same address.

3.8.2 Primary Key

The primary key uniquely identifies each record in a table and must never be the same for two records. For example, emp_code can be primary key for the entity set Employees.

The primary key should be chosen such that its attributes are never or very rarely changed. For instance, the address field of a person should not be part of the primary key, since it is likely to change. Emp_code, on the other hand, is not changed, till he is working in the organization.

☞ *The primary key of a relation can be said to be a minimal super key.*

3.8.3 Candidate Key

A *Candidate Key* is an attribute or set of attributes that uniquely identifies a record. These attributes or combinations of attributes are called candidate keys. In such a case, one of the candidate key is chosen to be a primary key. The remaining candidate keys are called *Alternate keys.*

☞ *There is only one primary key in a table. But there can be multiple candidate keys.*

3.8.4 Composite Key

In many cases, as we design a database, we will have tables that will use more than one column as part of the primary key. These are called *Composite Keys* or (concatenated keys). In other words, when a record cannot be uniquely identified by a single field, in such cases a composite key is used. A composite key is a group of fields that are combined together to uniquely identify a record.

3.8.5 Secondary Key

A *Secondary Key* is an attribute or combination of attributes that may not be a candidate key but classifies the entity set on a particular characteristic. For example, the entity set EMPLOYEE having the attribute *Department*, which identifies by its value which means all instances of EMPLOYEE who belong to a given department.

More than one employee may belong to a department, so the *Department* attribute is not a candidate key for the entity set EMPLOYEE, since it cannot uniquely identify an individual employee. However, the *Department* attribute does identify all employees belonging to a given *department*. Hence, it can be considered as a secondary key.

3.8.6 Foreign Key

In a relation, the column whose data values correspond to the values of a key column in another relation is called a *Foreign Key*. The supp_code key is a Foreign Key as seen in Figure 3.5.

☞ *In a relational database, the foreign key of a relation may be the primary key of another relation.*

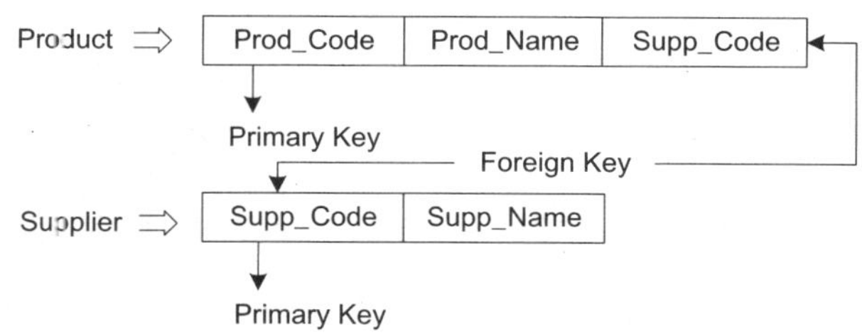

Figure 3.5 Concepts of foreign key

3.9 CODD'S RULES

There are twelve rules formulated by E.F. Codd for RDBMS in 1970. If an RDBMS satisfies all these twelve rules, then full benefits of the relational database results can be obtained.

The twelve rules are having the following main points:

(a) Information Representation
(b) Guaranteed Access
(c) Systematic Treatment of Null Values
(d) Database Description Rule
(e) Comprehensive Data Sub-Language
(f) View Updating
(g) High-Level Update, Insert, Delete
(h) Physical Data Independence
(i) Logical Data Independence
(j) The Distribution Rule
(k) Non-Subversion
(l) Integrity Rule

3.9.1 Information Representation

In a relational database model, all information should be explicitly and logically represented by entering the data values in the form of tables. The information such as view and column names should be in the table form. Data stored in data dictionary[5] should also be in the tabular form.

3.9.2 Guaranteed Access

This rule refers to the fact that a table can be taken as a storage structure and at the intersection of each column and row, there will necessarily be only one specific value of data item (or null).

5 A data dictionary is a database about databases. It holds information about each data element in the database.

Every value of data item must be logically addressable by using a combination of table-name, primary-key-value and the column-name.

3.9.3 Systematic Treatment of Null Values

In relational database management system null values should be supported for the representation of missing and inapplicable information only. The database management system must have a consistent method for representing null values. For example, null values for numeric data must be distinct from zero or any other none numeric values and for character data, it must be different from a string of blanks.

3.9.4 Database Description Rule

The description of a database is stored and maintained in the form of tables. This allows the users with appropriate authority to query information using similar ways and using the same language. This implies that a data dictionary should be present within the RDBMS that is constructed out of tables and/or views that can be examined using the Structured Query Language (SQL).

3.9.5 Comprehensive Data Sub-Language

The RDBMS must be completely manageable through its own extension of SQL. The SQL should support Data Definition, Views, Data Manipulation, Integrity Constraints and Transaction Boundary.

3.9.6 View Updating

Any view that can be defined using combination of base tables, and theoretically updatable, must also be capable of being updated by the RDBMS.

3.9.7 High-Level Update, Insert and Delete

An RDBMS must do more than just be able to retrieve relational data sets. It must also be possible to insert, update and delete data items from the relational set.

3.9.8 Physical Data Independence

Changes made to physical storage representation or access methods do not require changes to be made to the application programs used to manipulate data in tables.

3.9.9 Logical Data Independence

Application programs should not be affected by the changes made to the base tables. Changes made to tables should not require changes to be made to application programs, operating on the table.

3.9.10 The Distribution Rule

An RDBMS package must have distribution-independence. Thus, RDBMS package must make it possible for the database to be distributed across multiple computers even though they are having heterogeneous platforms both for hardware and operating system. This is one of the most attractive aspects of the RDBMS. Database systems built on the relational framework are also well-suited for today's Client/Server database design.

3.9.11 Non-Subversion

If the RDBMS supports facilities allowing application programs to operate on table a row at a time, then an application program using this type of database access is prevented from bypassing entity-integrity or referential-integrity constraints that may be defined for the database.

3.9.12 Integrity Rule

Integrity constraints specific to a particular relational database must be definable in SQL or some other data sub-language. These integrity constraints must be storable in the catalogue and not in the application programs.

☞ *An RDBMS package should satisfy at least six of the 12 rules to be accepted as an RDBMS software package. There is no RDBMS package commercially available that satisfies all of the 12 rules, given as CODD's rules.*

REVIEW QUESTIONS WITH ANSWERS

1. Multiple Choice Questions

1. A collection of data items organized and manageable is:
   a. Attribute
   b. Database
   c. Tuples
   d. None of the above
2. The set of all possible values of a data items is called:
   a. Domain
   b. Attribute
   c. Tuples
   d. None of the above
3. A field in a column of a table is called:
   a. Database
   b. Tuple
   c. Attribute
   d. Data
4. A field used to access a specific record is called:
   a. Key b. Attribute
   c. Domain d. None of the above
5. A super key is a set of one or more attributes that taken collectively, allow us:
   a. To identify uniquely an entity in the entity set
   b. To make the key most powerful for faster retrieval
   c. To increase effectiveness of database access
   d. None of the above
6. The union of primary keys of the related entity sets becomes a ___________ of the relation.
   a. Super key b. Candidate key
   c. Foreign key d. Primary key
7. File is the collection of all related:
   a. Database b. Fields
   c. Records d. File
8. The following entities/attributes in a relational database should not have null values:
   a. keys b. Relations
   c. Variables d. All of these
9. In a relational database a referential integrity constraint can be specified with the help of:
   a. Primary Key b. Foreign key
   c. Secondary Key d. None of the above
10. Which one is correct statement?
    a. Attribute corresponds to a column and entity corresponds to a row in a relational table
    b. Attribute corresponds to a column and entity corresponds to relational table
    c. Attribute correspond to a row and entity corresponds to a column in a relational table
    d. Attribute corresponds to a column and an occurrence of an entity corresponds to a row in a relational table
11. Data integrity means:
    a. Providing fast access to stored data
    b. Ensuring correctness and consistency of data
    c. Providing data sharing
    d. None of the above
12. Which key provide the basic tuple-level address in mechanism in a relational system?
    a. Candidate keys b. Alternative keys
    c. Primary keys d. None of these

2. State True or False for the following:

1. In a table each column is assigned a distinct headings.
2. All data and relationship are represented in a two dimensional table called a relation.
3. All possible values of data items is called tuples.
4. Data are raw facts which can be manipulated.
5. Raw facts or figures are known as information.
6. The number of rows associated with the relations are called as the degree.
7. RDBMS supports the concepts of Null values.
8. A key is a property of the entity set, rather than of the individual entities.
9. Foreign key values can be left blank.

10. A base table is a table, which is derived from other table.
11. In a table duplicate rows are not allowed.
12. A database constructed using relations is referred to as a relational database.
13. Key attribute values can be used to identify each entity uniquely.
14. A relationship is an association among several entities.
15. A relationship can also have attributes.
16. Referential integrity states that if table A contains a foreign key that matches the primary key in table B. Then values of their foreign key either match the value of the primary key for some in table B and must not be null.

3. Match the following:

1. Two dimensional table	a. Cardinality
2. Permitted value for the attribute	b. 12 rules
3. Derived relations	c. Emp_code
4. The number of rows in the table	d. Domain
5. Base relation	e. Created prior to use
6. Entity	f. Relation
7. Entity set	g. Views
8. E.F. Codd	h. Entities of same type
9. Row of a relation	i. Object that exists
10. Key-attribute	j. Capturing of data
11. Referential constraints	k. Degree
	l. Tuple of relation
	m. Foreign key

4. Fill in the blanks:

1. The smallest piece of meaningful information in a file is called a __________.
2. The collection of related fields are called__________.
3. __________ is a collection of related files.
4. The __________ in a record is a unique data item.
5. __________ is the manipulation of data.
6. A group of similar information or data, which is inherent to an organization is called an __________.
7. The __________ relations are those relations which are derived from a base relation.
8. Rows of the relation are referred to as __________ of the relation.
9. The number of columns associated with the table or relations is called as the __________.
10. __________ attribute is a key of the employee entity in an organization.
11. An entity set that has a primary key is termed as __________.
12. The degree of a relation is ________ of its relation schema.
13. A _______ value is used when an entity does not have a value for an attribute.
14. An entity is an object that is distinguishable from other objects by a specific set of __________.

Answers

1.

1. b	2. a	3. c	4. a	5. a	6. a
7. c	8. a	9. b	10. a	11. b	12. a

2.

1. T	2. T	3. F	4. T	5. F	6. F
7. T	8. T	9. T	10. F	11. T	12 T
13. T	14. T	15. T	16. T		

3.

1. f	2. d	3. g	4. a	5. e	6. i
7. h	8. b	9. l	10. c	11. m	

4.

1. Data item	2. Records
3. Database	4. Keyfield
5. Information	6. Entity
7. Derived	8. Tuples
9. Degree	10. Emp_code
11. Strong entity set	12. Number of attributes
13. Null	14. Attributes

Short Answers Questions

1. What is relation in RDBMS?

Ans All data items and relationships among them are represented in a two dimensional table called a *relation*. A database constructed using relations is referred to as a *relational database*. Relational database is constructed from flat arrangement of data items.

2. Define relation. Explain different types of relations.

Ans All data and relationships are represented in a two dimensional table called a *relation*.

There are two types of relations. These are:

(a) Base Relation
(b) Derived Relation

Base Relation

The *base relations* are those relations that are created prior to their use. They are also called as '*tables*' and they exist as physical file.

Derived Relation

The *derived relations* are those relations which are derived from a base relation. They do not exist as physical files. The derived relations are also called as *views*.

3. Explain Entities and Entity sets giving example.

Ans An *entity* is an object that exists and is distinguishable from any other object. An *entity set* is represented by a set of attributes. For example, Employee entity has three attributes Name, Address, and Age.

4. Define attributes.

Ans Each entity has particular properties called attributes that describe it. For example, an *Employee* entity may be described by employee's Name, Address and Age.

5. What is Degree and Cardinality?

Ans The number of columns associated with a table or relation among them is called the *Degree*.
The number of rows in a table is called as *Cardinality*.

6. What do you mean by Domain?

Ans A domain is a collection of all possible values from which the values for a given column or attribute is drawn. There are domains defined for every attribute in each table.

7. Write few properties of Relational Database Management System (RDBMS).

Ans A Relational Database Management System (RDBMS) has the following properties:

(a) Stores data in the form of tables.
(b) Does not require the user to understand its physical implementation.
(c) Provides information about its content and structure in the system table.
(d) Supports the concepts of NULL values.

8. What do you mean by Candidate Key and Alternate keys?

Ans A *Candidate Key* is an attribute or set of attributes that uniquely identifies a record. These attributes or combinations of attributes are called candidate keys. In such a case, one of the candidate key is chosen to be a primary key. The remaining candidate keys are called *Alternate keys*.

9. Can we have more than one primary keys in a table?

Ans No, there is only one primary key in a table. But there can be multiple candidate keys.

10. What do you mean by integrity and Referential Integrity? Explain with example.

Ans ***Entity Integrity:*** If an attribute of a table is prime attribute (unique identifier), it can not accept null values, i.e., no component of a primary key values may be null.
Referential Integrity: To ensure that a value which appears in one relation for a given set of attributes will also appear for certain set of attributes in another relation. This condition is called as referential integrity.

11. What is an Entity type?

Ans It is a collection (set) of entities that have same attributes.

12. What is an Entity set?

Ans It is a collection of all entities of particular entity type in the database.

13. What is degree of a Relation?

Ans It is the number of attribute of its relation schema.

14. What is Relationship?

Ans It is an association among two or more entities.

15. Explain the relationship between entity, entity class, and entity instance.

Ans An entity is something that can be identified in the users' work environment, something that the users want to track.
Entities of a given type are grouped into entity classes. An entity instance is the representation of a particular entity.

16. Explain the terms primary key, candidate key and foreign key. Give an example for each.

Ans Primary Key: Primary key is one of the candidate keys that uniquely identifies each row in the relation.
Candidate Key: A candidate key of an entity set is a minimal superkey, that uniquely identifies each row in the relation.
Foreign Key: Let there are two relations (tables) R and S. Any candidate key of the relation R which is referred in the relation S is called the foreign key in the relation S and referenced key in the relation R. The relation R is also called as parent table and relation S is also called as child table.

17. Explain entity, attribute and relationship with an example.

Ans Entity is a real-world thing. Attribute is characteristics or properties of an entity. Relationship is dependency or association between two entities.
For example:
Customer and Product are two entities. Customer number and Name are attributes of the Customer entity and Product name and Price are attributes of product entity.
Sale is the relationship between the Customer and Product

18. Write short note on Foreign key.

Ans In a relation, the column whose data values correspond to the values of a key column in another relation is called a Foreign Key.

EXERCISE

1. Write short note on the following:
   (a) Secondary Key
   (b) Foreign Key
   (c) Super Key
   (d) Domain
   (e) Base relation
2. State any five rules formulated by E.F. Codd for RDBMS.
3. Write short notes on entity integrity.
4. What is referential integrity?
5. Define Relation and Domain as applicable to RDBMS.
6. What is Composite Key?
7. Explain Primary key with example.
8. What do you mean by Attributes and Tuples?
9. Explain the distinction among the term Primary key, Candidate key and Super key?
10. Compare and Contrast Primary key and foreign key.
11. What are keys? How many type of keys used in Database? Explain each.
12. What are Tuples and Domain in relational model?
13. List some of the properties of a relation.

CHAPTER 4

Database Design

4.1 NORMALIZATION

Normalization is the name given to the process of simplifying the relationship among data elements in a record. Normalization replaces a collection of data in a record structure by another record design which is simpler, more predictable and therefore more manageable.

The goal of a relational database design is to generate a set of relation schemes that allow us to store information without any redundant (repeated) data. It also allow us to retrieve information easily and more efficiently.

The first step towards Normalization is to convert E-R model into *Tables* or *Relations*. The next step is to examine the tables for redundancy and if necessary, change them to non-redundant forms. This non-redundant model is then converted to a database definition, which achieves the objective of the database *Design Phase*.

4.1.1 Need for Normalization

Normalization reduces redundancy. Redundancy is the unnecessary *repetition* of a field. It can cause problems with storage, retrieval and updation of data. Redundancy can lead to:

(a) Inconsistencies—errors are more likely to occur when facts are repeated.

(b) Update anomalies—inserting, modifying and deleting data may cause inconsistencies. Inconsistency occurs when we perform updation or deletion of data in one relation, while forgetting to make corresponding changes in other relations.

☞ *During the process of normalization, we can identify dependencies, which do cause problems when deleting or updating. Normalization helps in simplify the structure of the tables.*

A fully normalized record consists of:

(a) A primary key that identifies that entity.

(b) A set of attributes that describe that entity.

Salesperson				Sales		
Employee number	Employee name	Store branch	Department	Item number	Item description	Sale price(Rs.)
21130680	Anand K	Downtown	Hardware	TR10	Router	35.00
				SA 1	Saw	19.00
				PT 6	Drill	21.00
				AB16	Lawnmover	245.00
30142101	Zadoo S	Dadeland	Home appliances	TT 1	Humidfier	114.00
				DS10	Dishwasher	262.00
41984620	Balwant	Cutter point	Auto parts	MC16	Snow tire	85.00
				AC146	Alternator	65.00
				BB100	Battery	49.50
61204721	Bhagwan	Fashion spot	Men's clothing	HS10	Suit	215.00

Figure 4.1 Unnormalized file for sales

In the process of normalization, data are grouped in the simplest possible way so that changes can be made later with minimum impact on the data structure. Various steps in normalization process are described later in this chapter.

4.2 FIRST NORMAL FORM (1NF)

A table is in the *First Normal Form* when it contains no repeating groups. The repeating columns or fields present in an unnormalized table are removed from the table and put into separate table or tables. These tables are dependent on the parent table from which it is derived. The key to these tables must also be a part of the parent table, so that the parent table and the derived tables can be related to each other.

Isolate repeating groups from an entity because they are easier to process separately, from rest of the entity. Figure 4.1 shows an unnormalized table structure.

☞ *When a table has no repeating groups, it is said to be in first normal form (1 NF). That is, for each cell in a table (one row and one column), there can be only one value. This value should be atomic in the sense that it cannot be decomposed into smaller pieces.*

As seen in Figure 4.1, the first four attributes (Employee number, Employee name, Store branch and Department) are virtually constant. The remaining three attributes (Item number, Item description, and Sale price) contain data that change and are repeated with different sales persons. Therefore, the repeating group should be separated from the entity "salesperson."

The normalized file is shown in Figure 4.2. It consists of two files:

* = Key

* Employee number	Employee name	Store branch	Department
21130680	Anand K	Downtown	Hardware
30142101	Zadoo S	Dadeland	Home appliances
41984620	Balwant	Cutter point	Auto parts
61204721	Bhagwan	Fashion spot	Men's clothing

Salesperson Data File

* Employee number	* Item number	Item description	Sale price(Rs.)
21130680	TR10	Router	35.00
21130680	SA 1	Saw	19.00
21130680	PT 6	Drill	21.00
21130680	AB16	Lawnmover	245.00
30142101	TT 1	Humidfier	114.00
30142101	DS10	Dishwasher	262.00
41984620	MC16	Snow tire	85.00
41984620	AC146	Alternator	65.00
41984620	BB100	Battery	49.50
61204721	HS10	Suit	215.00

Salesperson Item File

Figure 4.2 First normalized file for sales

(a) The *salesperson data* file with employee number as the primary key.

(b) The *salesperson item* file with employee number and item number as new attributes. These two attributes are added to relate the records in this file to the salesperson data file. The two attributes are used together for accessing data. Therefore, two keys are used together and such a key is called a *concatenated* key.

4.3 FUNCTIONAL DEPENDENCIES

Functional dependencies play an important role in differentiating good database design from not so good database design. Functional dependencies are the consequence of the interrelationships among attributes of an entity represented by a relation. Alternatively, it may be due to the relationship between entities that are also represented by a relation. Given a relation R, attribute Y of R is functionally dependent on attribute X of R *if and only if* each X-value in R is associated with it precisely one Y-value in R.

☞ *A functional dependency is denoted by X → Y, between two sets of attributes X and Y.*

To understand functional dependencies in a better way, let us see the database containing information concerning suppliers (S) and parts (P). The suppliers and parts are uniquely identified by Supplier numbers (SNo) and Part no (PNo).

	SNo	Name	Status	City
S ⇒	S1	Shyam	20	Mumbai
	S2	Ram	10	Kolkata
	S3	Amit	30	Kolkata
	S4	Chirag	20	Delhi
	S5	Raj	30	Kolkata

	PNo	Name	Colour	Weight	City
P ⇒	P1	Nut	Red	12	Mumbai
	P2	Bolt	Green	17	Kolkata
	P3	Screw	Blue	17	Goa
	P4	Screw	Red	14	Mumbai
	P5	Handle	Blue	12	Mumbai
	P6	Wire	Red	19	Delhi

In the Supplier and parts databases, attributes Name, Status and City of relation S are each functionally dependent on attribute SNo, because given a particular value for SNo, there exists precisely one corresponding value for each of Name, Status and City. Symbolically we can write:

S.SNo →S.Name
S.SNo →S.Status
S.SNo →S.City

The statement "S.SNo → S.City" is read as "attribute S.City is functionally dependent on attribute S.SNo".

The statement "S.SNo → S. (Name, Status, City)" can be similarly interpreted if we consider the combination (Name, Status, City) as composite key of relations. Functional dependency can be shown diagrammatically as in Figure 4.3.

☞ *Note that in relation S, we have both S.SNo → Name and Name → S.SNo because Name is an alternate key for relation S.*

Similarly, in the Student (Name, Address, Subject, Grade) relation, following functional dependencies should hold.

Name → Address
Name Subject → Grade

The underlying semantics of these two functional dependencies are that the address of a Student is unique and in each subject a student gets a unique grade.

Consider an Employee database as Employee (Emp_Code; Emp_Name, Dept, Grade, Salary, Age, Address) relation.

The following functional dependencies hold:

f1: Emp_Code → Emp_Name;

(each employee has a unique Emp_Code)

f2: Emp_Code → Dept;

(an employee can work in one department only)

f3: Emp_Code Grade Age → Salary;

(employee's salary depends on his age and grade)

f4: Emp_Code → Age;

(each employee has a unique age)

f5: Emp_Code → Address;

(each employee has unique address)

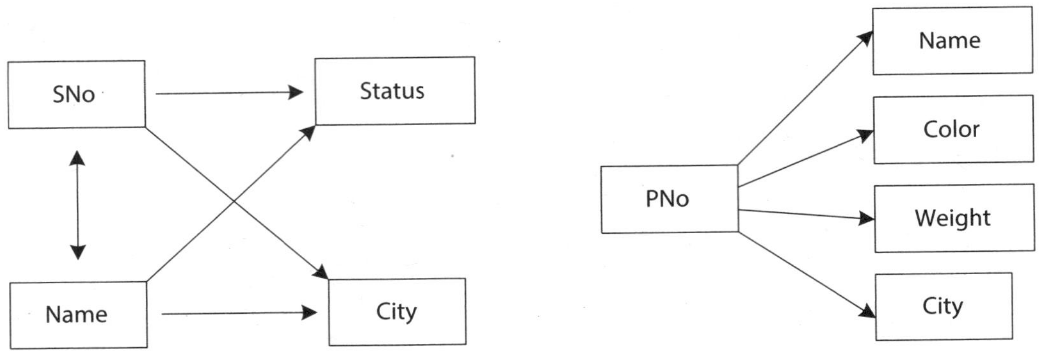

Figure 4.3 Functional dependencies in relation S and P

In this relation Emp_Code is not functionally dependent on Salary or Age, because more than one employee can have the same salary and can be of the same age.

4.3.1 Full Functional Dependency

X → Y is a full functional dependency, because removal of any attribute A from X would result into the cancellation of dependency. In other words, for any attribute A ∈ X, it does not functionally determine Y. For example, in the relation S, the attribute CITY is functionally dependent on the composite attribute (SNo, Status). However CITY is not *fully* functionally dependent on this composite attribute because it is also functionally dependent on SNo. (If Y is functionally dependent on X but not fully so, then X must be composite).

☞ *When all non-key attributes are dependent on the key attribute, it is called full functional dependency (See Figure (4.4)*

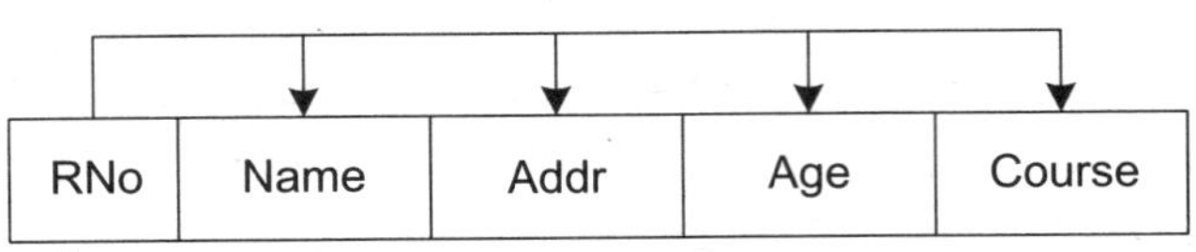

Figure 4.4 Concept of full functional dependency

In the above example non key attributes (Name, Addr, Age and Course) are dependent on key attribute RNo. Here RNo stands for Roll Number.

4.3.2 Partial Dependency

A functional dependency X → Y is a partial dependency if some attributes A ∈ X can be removed from X and the dependency still holds. Partial dependency in a record type occurs when some non-key attribute depends on the *key* attribute, and the remaining non-key attributes depend on key attribute and on one or more non-key attributes. In other words, all the non-key attributes are not dependent on the key attribute. There is a partial dependency of non-key attributes either on the key attribute or on the non-key attribute. (See Figure 4.5)

In Figure 4.5, non-key attributes *Name, Addr* and *Age* are dependent on RNo, and *Date of Comp* (Date of Completion) i.e. non-key attribute depends on *RNo* (key attribute) as well as on *Course* (non-key attribute).

4.3.3 Transitive Dependency

A functional dependency X → Y in a relation scheme R, is a transitive dependency if there is a set of attributes Z that is neither a candidate key nor a subset key of R and both X → Z and Z → Y hold.

A general case of transitive dependencies is as follows:

A, B, C are three columns in a table
If C is related to B
If B is related to A
Then C is indirectly related to A.

This is the case when transitive dependency in a table exists. We can remove transitive dependency by splitting each relation into two separate tables, which are to be linked using a foreign key.

When one non-key attribute depends on other non-key attribute, it is called a transitive dependency (See Figure 4.6(a) and Figure 4.6(b)).

To calculate *Distance* in Figure 4.6(a), which is a non-key attribute, we must know *origin* and *Destination* which are also non-key attributes, i.e., one non-key attribute is dependent on one or more than one non-key attributes. Here, distance has the transitive dependency.

As seen in Figure 4.6(b), transitive dependency occurs because one non-key attribute is dependent on other non-key attribute i.e. if student is in I^{st} year then he has been assigned Hostel *Gandhi*, if he is in IInd year, Hostel assigned is *Jawahar*; IIIrd year the hostel assigned is *Indra*. Thus, Hostel assigned to a student is dependent on the year of study in the college.

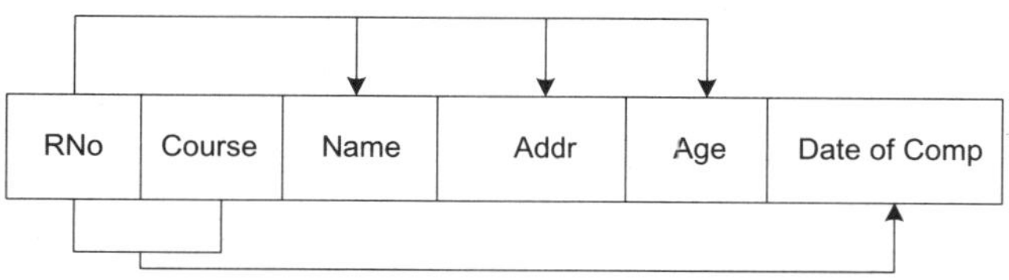

Figure 4.5 Concept of partial dependency

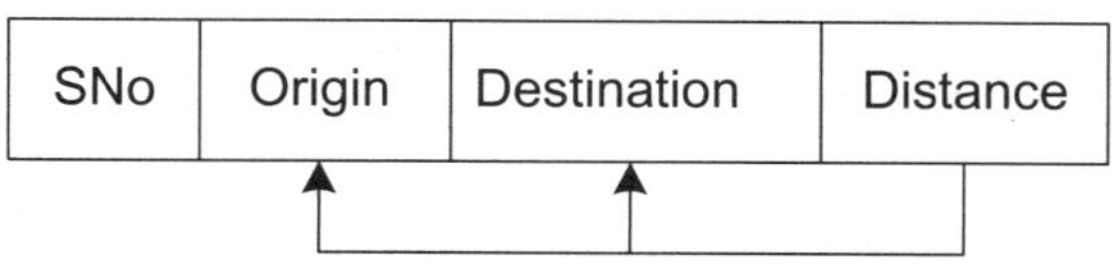

Figure 4.6(a) Concept of transitive dependency

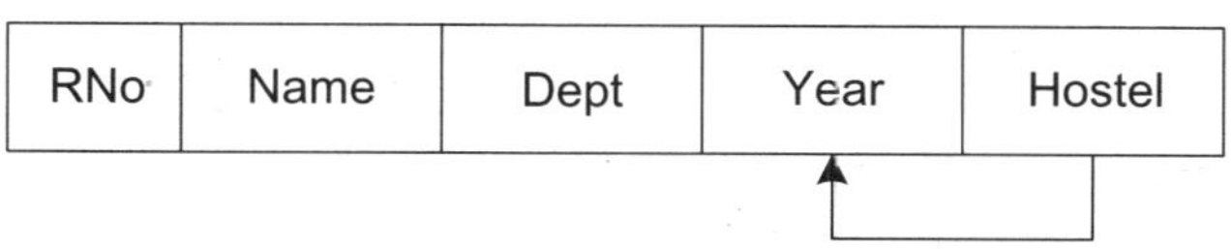

Figure 4.6(b) Concept of transitive dependency

4.3.4 Multivalued Dependency

Functional dependencies rule out certain tuples from being in a relation. If $A \rightarrow B$, then we cannot have two tuples with the same A value but different B values. *Multivalued* dependencies, on the other hand, do not rule out the existence of certain tuples, which have multiple dependencies. Instead, they require that other tuples of a certain form be present in the relation.

Multivalued dependencies are a consequence of first normal form. First normal form does not allow an attribute in a tuple to have more than one value. If we have two or more multivalued independent attributes in the same relation schema, then we would get into a problem of having to repeat every value of one of the attributes with every value of the other attribute to keep the relation instances consistent. This constraint is specified by a *multivalued dependency*.

☞ *Functional dependencies are also referred to as* ***equality generating dependencies****, and multivalued dependencies are also referred to as* ***tuple generating dependencies****.*

For example, consider the following relation EMP:

ENAME	PNAME	DNAME
Rajan	X	Ganesh
Ramesh	Y	Dinesh
Ram	X	Babu
Arjun	Y	Baskar

A tuple in this EMP relation represents the fact that an employer whose name is ENAME works on the project whose name is PNAME and has a dependent whose name is DNAME. An employee may work on several projects and may have several dependents. Also note that the employee, projects and dependents are not directly related to one another.

To keep the tuples in the relation consistent, we must keep a tuple to represent every combination of an employee's dependent and an employee's project. This constraint is specified as a multivalued dependency on the EMP relation. Informally, whenever two independent 1:N relationships A:B and A:C are mixed in the same relation, then multivalued dependencies may arise.

Consider the Course (Course#, Teacher, Student, Time, Room) relation as given in Figure 4.7. Consider an instance of multivalued dependencies

m1 : Course# $\rightarrow\rightarrow$ Time, Room

m2 : Course# $\rightarrow\rightarrow$ Student

Course#	Teacher	Student	Time	Room
BS03	Jain, S	Beena	M3	3
BS03	Jain, S	Aman	M3	3
PC02	Singh, S.	Bipin	M5	2
PC02	Singh, S.	Aman	M5	2
PC02	Singh, S.	Kamal	M5	2
BS03	Bose, V.	Vivek	Th7	1
BS03	Bose, V.	Beena	Th7	1
BS03	Bose, V.	Kamal	Th7	1
PC02	Arora, K.	Bipin	F7	1
PC02	Arora, K.	Aman	F7	1
PC02	Arora, K	Kamal	F7	1

Figure 4.7 An instance of the multivalued dependencies in relation Course (Course#, Teacher, Student, Time, Room)

The meaning of these two multivalued dependencies are that the same teacher is teaching a particular course irrespective of time or room in which the course is held. Moreover, students registered for a course are not determined by the time or room where the course is held.

4.3.5 Join Dependency

Join dependency is a constraint, similar to a Functional Dependency or a Multivalued Dependency. It is satisfied if and only if the relation concerned is the join of certain number of projections. And therefore, such a constraint is called a *join dependency*.

We now consider a special class of join dependencies which help to capture data dependencies present in a hierarchical data structure. For example, in the NURS_HOME database shown in Figure 4.8, data has an inherent hierarchical organization. It implies that information regarding wards and patients currently admitted to a ward depend only on the Nurs_home but not the facilities present in that hospital (and vice-versa). Since a Nurs_home can have multiple wards, functional dependencies are not adequate to describe the data dependency among NURS_HOME and WARDS or FACILITIES. In this case, Multivalued dependencies, NURS_HOME $\rightarrow\rightarrow$ WARD or NURS_HOME $\rightarrow\rightarrow$ FACILITIES hold.

Using, First Order Hierarchical Decomposition (FOHD) would enable us to represent data dependencies present in a hierarchical data structure in a more natural way.

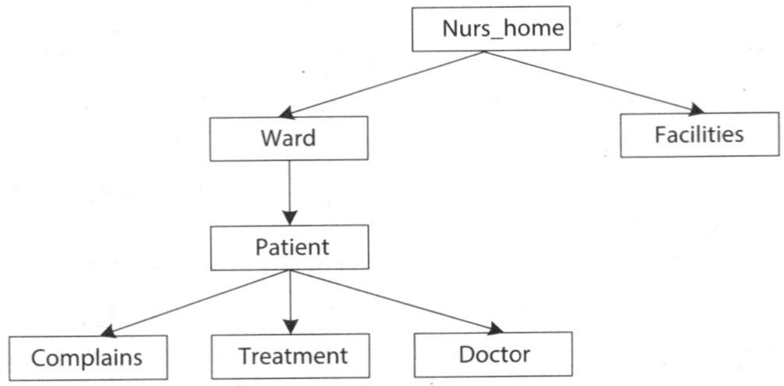

Figure 4.8 Hierarchical representation of a NURS_HOME database

The NURS_HOME database shown in Figure 4.8 when decomposed, has the following representations:

fh_1: NURS_HOME : WARD | FACILITIES
fh_2: NURS_HOME, WARD : PATIENT
fh_3: NURS_HOME, WARD, PATIENT : COMPLAINTS | TREATMENT | DOCTOR

Thus we can store NURS_HOME database as the lossless join of
NURS_FACILITY (NURS_HOME, FACILITY)
NURS_WARD (NURS_HOME, WARD, PATIENT, COMPLAINTS, TREATMENT, DOCTOR)
relations. We can use fh_2 and fh_3 to further decompose NURS_WARD relation.

4.4 SECOND NORMAL FORM (2NF)

A table is in the *Second Normal Form* if all its non-key fields are fully dependent on the whole key. This means that each field in a table, must depend upon the entire key. Those that do not depend upon the combination key, are moved to another table on whose key they depend on. Structures which do not contain combination keys are automatically in the second normal form.

The second normalization makes sure that each non-key attribute depends on a key attribute or on a composite key. Non-key attributes that do not meet this condition are split into simpler entities. In Figure 4.9, each attribute in the salesperson data file depends on the primary key "Employee#." In the salesperson item file, the attribute "Sales price" depends on a composite key ("Employee#" and "Item#"). Note that the sales price is firmly related to the salesperson number and the item number of the sale. Also, the attribute "Item description" tags to "Item#," which is part of the composite key. "Item#" is not related in any way to the "Employee#" field. This causes several concerns. An employee transfer would make it difficult to maintain records because the sales information would be dropped when the salesperson leaves the department. This is because sales information (Item#, Sale price) is linked with "Employee#" in the salesperson item file.

To solve such a problem, we create new independent tables for "Item description" and "Sales price". In one file, we create the item description attribute with item number keys from the Salesperson Item file. The remaining attributes (Employee number, Item number, and Sales price) become the second table or file. (See Figure 4.9).

☞ *A table is in Second normal form (2NF) if every non-key column depends on the entire key (not just part of it). This issue arises only for composite keys (with multiple columns).*

The creation of the second table offers several benefits. These are:

(a) Sales items can be added without being tagged to a specific salesperson.

(b) If the item changes we need to change only the item file.

(c) If a salesperson leaves the department, it would have no direct effect on the status of the items sold.

4.5 THIRD NORMAL FORM (3NF)

A table is said to be in the *Third Normal Form*, if all the non-key fields of the table are independent of all other non-key fields of the table.

In Figure 4.9 we can observe that there is further room for improvement. In the salesperson data file, the attribute "Store branch" is tagged to the primary key "Employee#" while the attribute "Department" which is a non-key attribute is related to "Store branch," which is another non_key attribute. Making "Store branch" a key attribute requires isolating "Department" along with "Store branch" and placing them in a new table as shown in Figure 4.10.

* Employee #	Employee name	Store branch	Department
21130680	Anand K	Downtown	Hardware
30142101	Zadoo S	Dadeland	Home appliances
41984620	Balwant	Cutter point	Auto parts
61204721	Bhagwan	Fashion spot	Men's clothing

Salesperson Data File

1

2

* Employee #	* Item #	Sale price (Rs.)
21130680	TR10	35.00
21130680	SA 1	19.00
21130680	PT 6	21.00
21130680	AB16	245.00
30142101	TT 1	114.00
30142101	DS10	262.00
41984620	MC16	85.00
41984620	AC146	65.00
41984620	BB100	49.50
61204721	HS10	215.00

Salesperson Item File

* Item #	Item description
TR10	Router
SA 1	Saw
PT 6	Drill
AB16	Lawnmover
TT 1	Humidfier
DS10	Dishwasher
MC16	Snow tire
AC146	Alternator
BB100	Battery
HS10	Suit

Item File

Figure 4.9 Second normalization

Employee #	Employee name	Store branch
21130680	Anand K	Downtown
30142101	Zadoo S	Dadeland
41984620	Balwant	Cutter point
61204721	Bhagwan	Fashion spot

Salesperson Data File

Store branch	Department
Downtown	Hardware
Dadeland	Home appliances
Cutter point	Auto parts
Fashion spot	Men's clothing

Store Branch File

Employee #	Item #	Sale price (Rs.)
21130680	TR10	35.00
21130680	SA 1	19.00
21130680	PT 6	21.00
21130680	AB16	245.00
30142101	TT 1	114.00
30142101	DS10	262.00
41984620	MC16	85.00
41984620	AC146	65.00
41984620	BB100	49.50
61204721	HS10	215.00

Salesperson Item File

Item #	Item description
TR10	Router
SA 1	Saw
PT 6	Drill
AB16	Lawnmover
TT 1	Humidfier
DS10	Dishwasher
MC16	Snow tire
AC146	Alternator
BB100	Battery
HS10	Suit

Item File

Figure 4.10 Third normalization

Note that, after completing the third normalization, we can store branch information independent of the salespersons in the branch. We can also make changes in the "Department" without having to update the record of the employee in it. In this respect, normalization simplifies relationships and provides logical links between files without losing information.

One inherent problem with normalization is data redundancy. For store branch, the system goes through three steps:

(a) Computes total sales for each salesperson from the salesperson item file.

(b) Goes to the employee data file to look up the store branch to which the sales person is assigned.

(c) Accumulates each salesperson's sales in a specified field in the store branch file.

This procedure is repeated for each salesperson in the file. Figure 4.11 illustrates the processing cycle for salesperson 21130680.

☞ *A relation is in the third normal form if it is in second normal form and no non-prime attribute is functionally dependent on other non-prime attributes.*

4.6 BCNF (BOYCE-CODD NORMAL FORM)

Boyce-Codd Normal Form (BCNF) was proposed as a simpler form of Third Normal Form (3NF), but it is much more strict than 3NF, meaning that every relation in BCNF is also in 3NF. However, a relation in 3NF is not necessarily be in BCNF.

Consider a relation scheme in third normal form that has a number of overlapping composite candidate keys. In particular consider the relation GRADE (Name, Student#, Course, Grade) of Table 4.1. Here the functional dependencies are {Name Course $\rightarrow$ Grade, Student# Course $\rightarrow$ Grade, Name $\rightarrow$ Student#, Student# $\rightarrow$ Name}. Thus, each student has a unique name and a unique student number. The relation has two candidate keys, (Name, Course) and (Student#, Course). Each of these keys is a composite key and contains a common attribute Course. The relation scheme satisfies the criterion of the third normal form relation, i.e., for all functional dependencies X → A in GRADE.

The problem in the relation GRADE is that it had two overlapping candidate keys. In the Boyce Codd normal form (BCNF), which is stronger than the third normal form, the intention is to avoid the above anomalies. This is done by ensuring that for all non-trivial functional dependencies implied by the relation, determine the functional dependencies that involve a candidate keys.

The relation GRADE of Table 4.1 is not in BCNF because the dependencies Student# → Name and Name → Student# are non-trivial and their determinants are not superkeys of GRADE.

4.7 FOURTH NORMAL FORM (4NF)

In order to avoid undesirable updating problem in presence of multi-valued dependencies, Fourth Normal Form was introduced as an extension of Boyce Codd normal form.

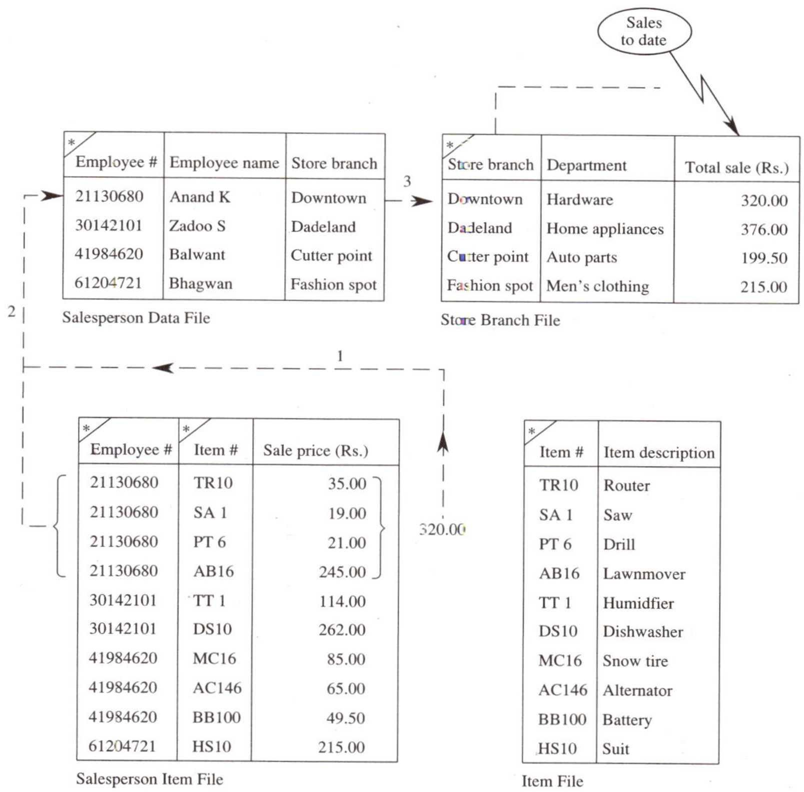

*Employee #	Employee name	Store branch
21130680	Anand K	Downtown
30142101	Zadoo S	Dadeland
41984620	Balwant	Cutter point
61204721	Bhagwan	Fashion spot

*Store branch	Department	Total sale (Rs.)
Downtown	Hardware	320.00
Dadeland	Home appliances	376.00
Cutter point	Auto parts	199.50
Fashion spot	Men's clothing	215.00

*Employee #	*Item #	Sale price (Rs.)
21130680	TR10	35.00
21130680	SA 1	19.00
21130680	PT 6	21.00
21130680	AB16	245.00
30142101	TT 1	114.00
30142101	DS10	262.00
41984620	MC16	85.00
41984620	AC146	65.00
41984620	BB100	49.50
61204721	HS10	215.00

*Item #	Item description
TR10	Router
SA 1	Saw
PT 6	Drill
AB16	Lawnmover
TT 1	Humidfier
DS10	Dishwasher
MC16	Snow tire
AC146	Alternator
BB100	Battery
HS10	Suit

Figure 4.11 Processing cycle

Table 4.1 The GRADE relation

Name	Student#	Course	Grade
James	23714539	353	A
Neelam	42717390	329	A
James	23714539	328	in prog
Mohan	38815183	456	C
Dilip	37116259	293	B
Deepak	82317293	491	C
Deepak	82317293	353	in prog
James	23714539	491	C
Raj	11011978	353	A+
Vikas	83910827	379	in prog

Fourth Normal Form eliminates cases in which the composite key of a record type contains two or more data items that are independent, multivalued facts of an entity.

The fields are independent if there are no combinations that are logically related.

In the example given in Figure 4.12, skill and languages are multivalued (many different skills and many different languages), but there is no logical dependency between a language and a skill.

To put it in Fourth Normal Form, the data must be separated by creating two separate tables.

☞ *A generalization of the Boyce Codd normal form to a relation which includes the multivalued dependencies is called Fourth Normal Form.*

4.8 FIFTH NORMAL FORM (5NF)

The Fourth Normal Form is by no means the "ultimate" normal form. As we saw earlier, multivalued dependencies help us understand and tackle some forms of repetition of information that cannot be understood in terms of functional dependencies. There are types of constraints called *join dependencies* that generalize multivalued dependencies, and lead to another normal form called *project-join normal form (PJNF)*. The PJNF is called *Fifth Normal Form*. There is a class of even more general constraints, which leads to a normal form called *domain-key normal form*.

A practical problem with the use of these generalized constraints is that they are not only hard to reason with, but there is also no set of sound and complete inference rules for reasoning about the constraints. Hence, PJNF and domain key normal form are used very rarely.

Employee	Skill	Language

must be separated as

Employee	Skill

and

Employee	Language

Figure 4.12 Fourth Normal Form

☞ *The concept of Project-join-Normal form (PJNF) is an extension of the Fourth Normal form definition when join dependencies are also considered.*

4.9 DOMAIN-KEY NORMAL FORM

The process of normalization and the process of discovering undesirable dependencies was carried through Fifth Normal Form (5NF) as a meaningful design activity. However, it has been possible to define stricter normal forms that take into account additional types of dependencies and constraints. The idea behind domain-key Normal Form (DKNF) is to specify the ultimate normal form that takes into account all possible types of dependencies and constraints.

The domain key normal form (DKNF) does not exhibit insertion and deletion anomalies. However, unlike the other normal forms, DKNF is not defined in terms of functional dependency, multivalued dependency, or join dependency. The central requirements in DKNF are the basic concepts of domains, keys and general constraints. A *domain constraint* is a statement that the values of a certain attribute lie within some prescribed set of values. *Key constraints* is a statement that a certain attribute or attribute combination is a candidate key. A *general* constraint is expressed as a simple statement or predicate and specifies some special requirement. Each tuple of a relation must specify this predicate i.e. general constraint for it to be a valid tuple.

☞ *A relation scheme is in DKNF, if every general constraint can be inferred from the knowledge of the attributes involved in the scheme, their underlying domains, and the sets of attributes that form the keys.*

An insertion anomaly in the case of DKNF occurs when a tuple is inserted in a relation and the resulting relation violates one or more general constraints. Similarly, a deletion anomaly occurs when a tuple from a relation is deleted and the remaining relation violates one or more general constraints. We show these dependencies and general constraints in the following example.

Example 1

Consider the relation scheme TRANSCRIPT (*SNo, Course, Grade). Suppose the* attributes *SNo* and *Course* are numeric, 8 and 3 digits long, respectively. The attribute *Grade* is a letter grade and could be A, B, C, D, P, F. The general constraint is that for *Courses* 000 through 900, the *Grade* can only be A, B, C, D, F. The domain constraints for this relation are the following:

SNo is required to be 8 digits long, *Course* is 3 digit long, and *Grade* has to be from the set {A,B,C,D,P,F}.

The key constraint for the relation is that no two tuples can exist with the same values for the key attributes, which are *SNo* and *Course*. Obviously,

SNo Course → Grade.

Finally, the general constraint can be expressed by the following:

if Grade > 900 then Grade ∈ {P, F}
else Grade ∈ {A, B, C, D, F}

☞ *The DKNF is considered to be the highest form of normalization, since all insertion and deletion anomalies are eliminated and all general constraints can be verified by using only the domain constraints and key constraints.*

The problem with this relation is that a tuple such as (12345678, 991, A), which satisfies all the domain constraints and key constraints, can be inserted in the relation TRANSCRIPT of Table 4.2. However, since the tuple does not satisfy the general constraint, the relation TRANSCRIPT becomes illegal after the insertion.

Table 4.2 The TRANSCRIPT relation

SNo	Cours e	Grade
23714539	353	A
42717390	329	A
23714539	928	P
38815183	456	F
37116259	293	B
82317293	491	C
82317293	953	F
23714539	491	C
11011978	353	A
83910827	379	P

Example 2

The TRANSCRIPT relation discussed above can be decomposed into the following relations:

TRANSCRIPT_REGULAR (*SNo, Course, Grade*) with the domain constraints (*SNo* being 8 digit, *Course* being 3 digit in the range 000 through 900, and Grade in the set {A, B, C, D, F}). The key as before is *SNo Course.*

TRANSCRIPT_SPECIAL (*SNo, Course, Grade*) with the domain constraints (*SNo* being 8 digit, *Course* being 3 digit in the range 000 through 999, and Grade in the set {P, F}). The key as before is *SNo Course.*

4.10 DENORMALIZATION

In some exceptional cases, database designers use the redundancy to improve performance for specific applications. They select such a *schema* that has redundant information that means it is not normalized.

For example, suppose that the name of an account holder has to be displayed along with the account number and cash balance, every time the account is accessed. In our normalized schema, this requires a join of *account* with *depositor*. One alternative is to create a relation containing all the attributes of *account* and *depositor*. This makes displaying the account information faster. However, the balance information for an account is repeated for every person who owns the account, and all copies must be updated by the application, whenever the account balance is updated. This process of taking a normalized schema and making it non-normalized is called *denormalization*. Designers of database use it to tune performance of systems that require time-critical operations.

A better alternative is to use views. A materialized view is a view whose result is stored in the database, and reflected in the data when the relations used in the view are updated. Like denormalization, using materialized view does have space and time overheads, but it has the advantage that keeping the view up-to-date is the job of database system, not the application programmer.

4.11 CASE STUDY 1

Normalize the following data of CUSTOMER table to 2NF using appropriate relation. Give brief explanation for each level.

XYZ LTD.

Cust_no : 001
Cust_name : Dev and Co. LTD.
Addr : DWARKA Sec. 7, Pl. no. 2
Order_no : 2240
Order_date : 5/11/19
Deli_date : 15/11/19

Item_no	Desc	Rate	Qty
001	Pendrive	170	5
024	Printer (Inkjet)	5500	2
035	CD	450	5
039	Keyboard	1000	3

Solution

Step 1

Firstly, we have to write down the data in the unnormalized form. Without normalization, the data appears as follows:

Unnormalized Data:

Cust_no
Cust_name
Addr
Order_no
Order_date
Deli_date
Item_no
Desc
Rate
Qty

Step 2

The First Normal Form (1NF) is any data structure without repeating groups. So to achieve First Normal Form, remove all repeating groups. In this example, *Item_no, Desc, Rate, Qty* etc. repeats with each customer.

The primary key from the original structure is to be brought into repeating group structure. Also the key field from the new structure (repeating group) is to be found out. The new structure is named with appropriate name.

1
*Cust_no *Item_no Desc Rate Qty

1
*Cust_no Cust_name Addr Order_no Order_date Deli_date

☞ *Note that * denotes key field for an entity.*

In the first file structure *Cust_no* is the main key or the primary key and *Item_no* is the partial or secondary key.

Step 3

The Second Normal Form (2NF) is a data structure in which all non-key data elements are fully functionally dependent on the primary key. If a relation is 1NF then we can go for its 2NF. In the 2NF we look for Functional Dependence. For example, *Desc* of item is dependent on *Item_no*, *Rate* is dependent on *Item_no.*

Similarly, *Cust_name* is dependent on *Cust_no*, customer *Addr* is dependent on *Cust_name* and so on. We group such functionally dependent attributes and achieve 2NF.

In the 2NF the element depending upon the whole key and partial key are separated and formed into new data structure.

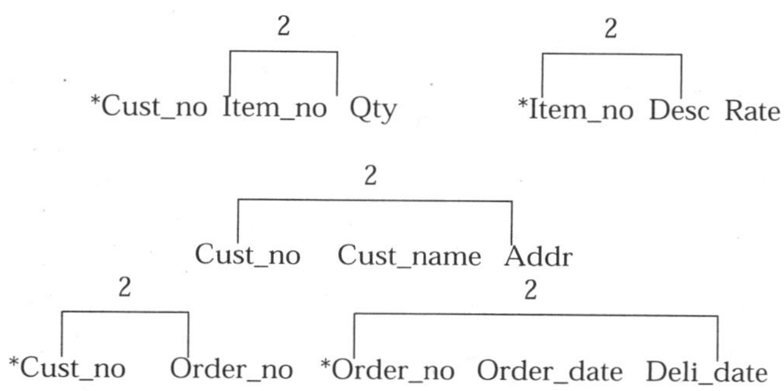

4.12 CASE STUDY 2

Normalize the following data of personal employees table to 3NF using appropriate relations. Note that key fields are denoted by *.

Unnormalized Data

Personal Employee Table

* Emp_code	Employee code
Dept_code	Department code
Mgr_code	Manager code
Course_code	Course code
Course_title	Course title

Solution

Step 1

The first stage of normalization is to remove all repeating groups. So there are two tables; employee table and training table, with the key field Emp_code appearing in each.

First Normal Form (1NF)

Employee table	Training table
* Emp_code	*Emp_code
Dept_code	*Course_code
Mgr_code	Course_title

Step 2

In Second Normal Form (2NF) we have to remove partial key dependencies. This is done by examining those records possessing a compound key (i.e. a key comprising more than one item) and checking to see whether each data field in the record relates to the whole key. If the field relates to only part of the key, it is removed with its key to form another table. In the above example Course_title relates only to Course_code, so it is removed with its key to form another table as Course table.

Second Normal form (2NF)

Employee table	Training table	Course table
*Emp_code	*Emp_code	*Course_code
Dept_code	*Course_code	Course_title
Mgr_code		

Step 3

In Third Normal Form (3NF) involves examining each record to see whether any items are mutually dependent. In this example, Dept_code and Mgr _code are mutually dependent because the manager of each department will always be the same. Thus new table department is being created for departments, the key being Dept_code. Now data is completely normalized.

Third Normal Form (3NF)

Employee table	Training table
*Emp_code	*Emp_code
Dept_code	*Course_code

Department table	Course table
*Dept_code	*Course_code
Mgr_code	Course_title

4.13 E-R MODEL

In a database management system (DBMS), a group of similar information or data, which is of interest to an organization, is called an *Entity*. A model that represents system data by entity and relationship sets is called E-R (Entity-Relationship) model. E-R modeling is a conceptual level model.

☞ *Entities are real-world objects about which we collect data.*

The entity-relationship (E-R) data model is based on a perception of a real world which consists of a set of basic objects. The E-R model was introduced by *P.P. Chen.* He introduced not only E-R model but also corresponding diagramming techniques.

☞ *The overall logical structure of a database can be expressed graphically by an E-R diagram.*

4.14 COMPONENTS OF E-R MODEL

The E-R Model consist of the following major components:
(a) Entity
(b) Attributes
(c) Relationships
(d) Key attributes

4.14.1 Entity

An *entity* is a class of persons, places, objects, events or concepts about which we need to collect and store data.

Each entity is distinguishable from the other entities. Categories of different entities include:

- Persons
- Places
- Objects
- Events
- Concepts

Persons : Employee, customer, students, supplier etc.
Places : Branch Office, Building, Room etc.
Objects : Book, Machine, Vehicle etc.
Events : Sale, Reservation, Registration, Order etc.
Concepts : Qualification, Account, Course, Stocks etc.

The instance of an *entity* is a single occurrence of that entity. For example, the entity EMPLOYEE may have multiple instances or occurrences such as Raj, Mohan, Ravi, Shiva, etc. In data modeling, we do not concern overselves with individual instances because we recognize that each instance is described by similar data items.

Entity Set

An *entity set* is the collection of entities of the same type i.e. the entities which share common properties or attributes. For example, the set of all employees of an organization can be called as the entity set *Employee*. Similarly, the set of all persons who are customers at a given bank, can be called as the entity set *Customer*.

☞ *An entity set is a collection of similar types of entities.*

Entity type

It is a collection (set) of entities that have same attributes.

4.14.2 Attributes

Each entity can have a number of characteristics. The characteristics of an entity are called *Attributes*. For example, an entity, say client, can have characteristics like name, address, phone number, balance due etc. If an entity is something about which we want to store data, then we need to identify what specific pieces of data we want to store about each instance of a given entity. We call these pieces as data attributes.
Attributes have a domain. There exists a domain or range of values that can be assigned to attributes. For example, a student's name cannot be a numeric value. It has to be alphabetic. A student's age cannot be negative. The domain for a company's date of hire attribute consists of all dates that fit in a range (company startup date to current date) etc.

☞ *An attribute is a descriptive property or characteristic of an entity.*

Some attributes can be logically grouped into super attributes called compound attribute. For example, an Employee's name is a compound attribute consisting of first_name, middle_name and last_name.

☞ *A compound attribute is the one that actually consist of all other attributes.*

4.14.3 Types of Attributes

In E-R diagram, attributes associated with an entity set may be of the following types:

Simple attributes

Simple attributes are those attributes which can not be divided further. For example, a student's phone number is an atomic value of 10 digits.

Composite attributes

Composite attributes are those attributes which are composed of many other simple attributes. For example, a student's complete name may have first_name and last_name.

Single valued attributes

Single valued attributes are those attributes which can take only one value for a given entity from an entity set. For example Adhar_Number.

Multivalued attribute

Multivalued attribute may have more than one value for an entity. For example, a person can have more than one phone number, email_address, etc. In E-R diagram, multivalued attribute is represented by double oval.

Derived and Stored Attribute

Derived attributes are those attributes which can be derived from other attribute(s). An attribute that cannot be derived from another attribute is known as stored attribute. In some cases, two or more attribute values are related, for example, Age and BirthDate attributes of a person. For particular person entity, the value of Age can be determined from the current date and the value of that person's BirthDate. Hence, the attribute Age is called as derived attribute and the attribute BirthDate is called as stored attribute. In E-R diagram, derived attribute is represented by dashed oval.

Null valued attribute

An attribute, which has no value for an entity is known as null valued attribute. For example, assume Student is an entity and its attributes are Name, Age, Address and Phone_no. There may be chance when a student has no phone_no. In that case, phone_no is called null valued attribute.

Key attributes

Key attributes are those attributes which can identify an entity uniquely in an entity set. For example, the attribute "Roll_no" is a key attribute as it can identify any student uniquely. In ER diagram, key attribute is represented by an oval with underlying lines.

Identifiers

The E-R model uses identifiers, that is, one or more attributes that uniquely identify each entity instance. In the relational model, such identifiers are mapped to primary keys in tables. Identifiers are underlined in the E-R diagram.

☞ *Identifiers are attributes that name, or identify, entity instances..*

4.14.4 Relationships

The association among entities is called a relationship. For example, an employee works_at a department, a student enrolls in a course. Here, Works_at and Enrolls are called relationships.

To understand what we mean by relationships among data items, we need some familiarity with data model terminologies. An entity is a thing which can be easily identified. It may be an object, place, person, concept or activity for which data need to be recorded. In diagramming technique, entities are named and represented inside a box as shown in Figure 4.13. In this Figure, *Instructor* and *Student* are the entities:

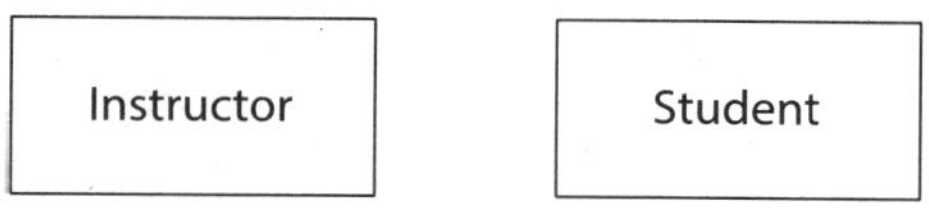

Figure 4.13 Entities Instructor and Student

An association among entities leads to *relationships*. For example, there is some relationship between *Instructor* and *Student* as seen in Figure 4.14.

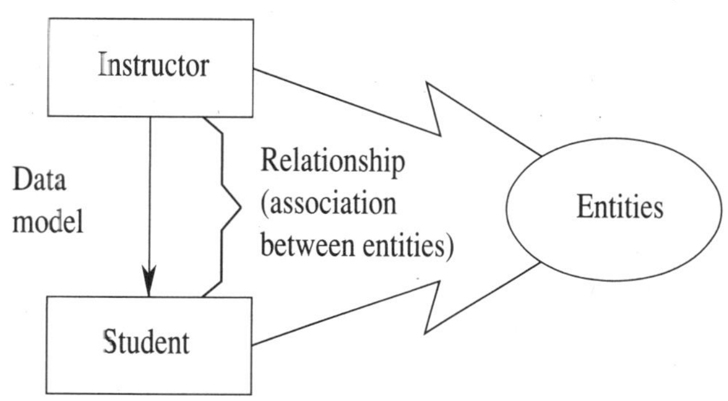

Figure 4.14 Entities and Relationships

This relationship represents the fact that an instructor teaches several students and a student is taught by several instructors.

4.14.5 Relationship Set

A set of relationships of similar type is called a relationship set. Like entities, a relationship too can have attributes. These attributes are called descriptive attributes.

4.14.6 Degree of Relationship

The number of participating entities in a relationship defines the degree of the relationship. When there is only ONE entity set participating in a relation, the relationship is called as unary relationship. For example, one person is married to only one person. When there are TWO entities set participating in a relation, the relationship is called as binary relationship. For example, Student is enrolled in Course. When there are n entities set participating in a relation, the relationship is called as n-ary relationship.

4.14.7 Mapping Cardinalities

Cardinality defines the number of entities in one entity set, which can be associated with the number of entities of other set via relationship set. The cardinality ratios for a relationship type specifies the maximum number of relationship instances that an entity can participate in. The possible cardinality ratios for relationship types are one-to-one (1:1), one-to-many or many-to-one (1:M or M:1), and many-to-many (M:M).

4.14.8 Participation Constraints

The participation constraint specifies whether the existence of an entity depends on its being related to another entity via the relationship type. This constraint specifies the minimum number of relationship instances that each entity can participate in. It is sometimes called the minimum cardinality constraint. There are two types of participation constraints:

Total Participation

Each entity in the entity set must participate in the relationship. If each student must enroll in a course, the participation of student will be total.

Partial Participation

The entity in the entity set may or may NOT participate in the relationship. If some courses are not enrolled by any of the student, the participation of course will be partial.

4.14.9 Types of Relationships

Three types of relationships exist among entities. These are:

(a) One-to-one
(b) One-to-many or Many-to-one
(c) Many-to-many

One-to-One Relationship (1:1)

A *one-to-one* (1:1) relationship is an association only between two entities. For example, in a university each department has only one head of the department. Moreover, one faculty member cannot head more than one department. This shows one-to-one relationship between department and the person as head.

Another example of such a relationship is between Automobile and Engine. If we assume that a car does not have two engines and that a car must be fitted with one engine to be considered a car. (See Figure 4.15).

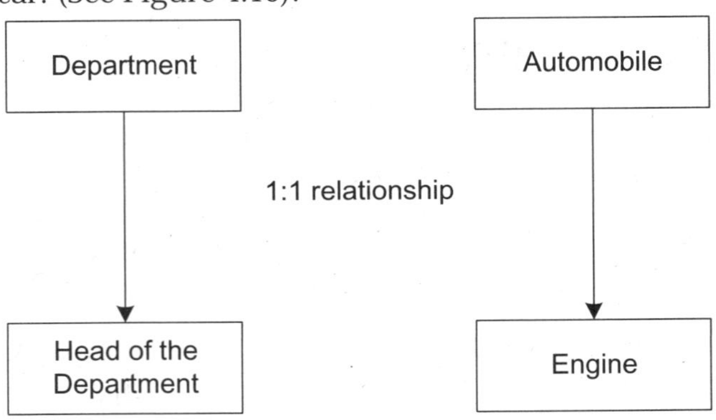

Figure 4.15 1:1 Relationships examples

One-to-Many Relationship (1:M)

One-to-many (1:M) relationship exists when one entity is related to more than one entity. For example a father may have many children but a child has one father.

Another example, two entity sets namely courses and Teacher. If we assume that more than one subject or course is taught by one teacher, then the relationship is one-to-many between Teacher and Courses (See Figure 4.16).

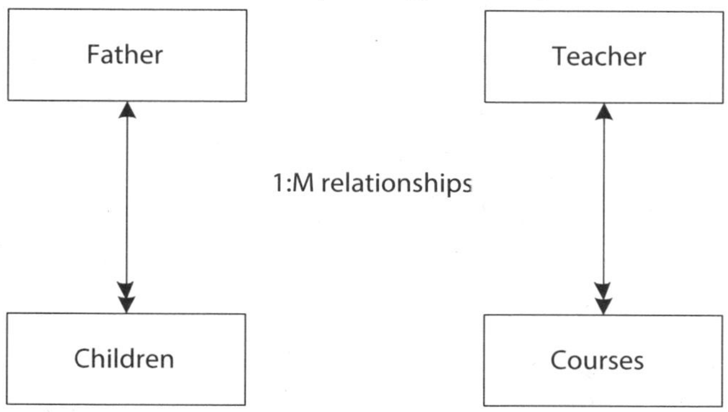

Figure 4.16 1:M Relationships examples

Many-to-One Relationship (M:1)

When entities in one entity set can take part only once in the relationship set and entities in other entity set can take part more than once in the relationship set, cardinality is many to one. For example, many employees are associated with one project.

Many-to-Many Relationship (M:M)

A *many-to-many* (M:M) relationship describes entities that may have many relationships among each other. For example, one customer may buy many items and one item may be bought by many customers.

Another example is that a student can take many courses in a university, and many students can register for a given course. Many-to-many relationships are depicted in Figure 4.17.

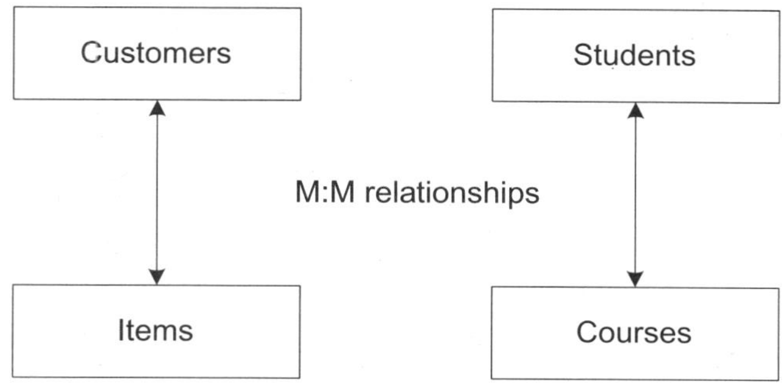

Figure 4.17 Many to Many Relationship examples

4.14.10 Key Attribute

The key attribute is an attribute that uniquely identifies an entity in the entity set. For example, *Employee_code* can be the key attribute for the entity set *Employee* because it uniquely identifies each Employee entity.

4.15 SYMBOLS OF E-R MODEL

E-R modelling uses the following symbols:

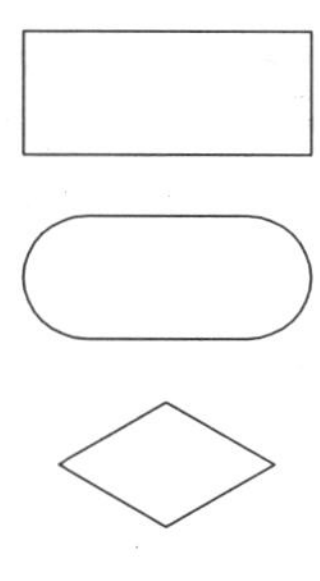

Name	Symbol	Meaning
Rectangle		Representing entity sets
Oval		Representing attributes
Diamond		Represents relationships among entity sets
Line		Links attributes to entity sets and entity sets to relationships

☞ *An association of several entities in an Entity-Relation model is called* ***relationship****. When the relationships such as, married to, parent of, child of, member of, and works for are added, then we know that we are talking about a group of related people, a family, or a corporation.*

Example

Consider the entity relationship diagram shown in Figure 4.18.

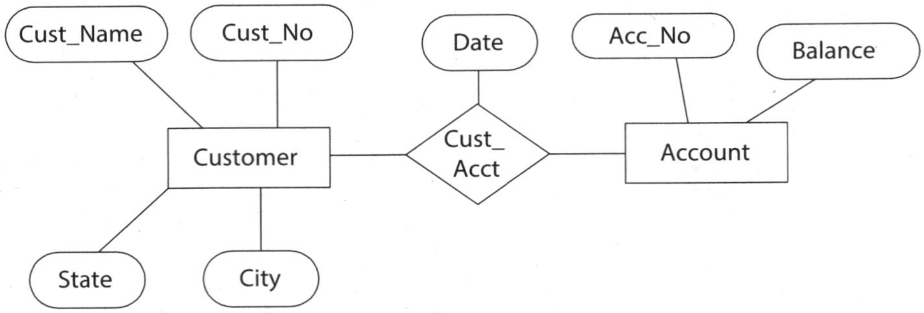

Figure 4.18 Entity-Relationship diagram for customer account

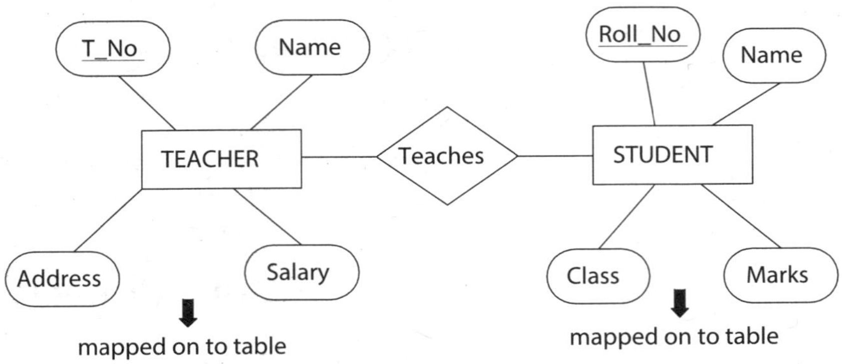

Teacher.dbf

T_No	Name	Address	Salary

Student.dbf

Roll_No	Name	Class	Marks

Figure 4.19 Mapping entities and attributes on a table

The diagram as seen in Figure 4.18 consists of two entity sets. *Customer* and *Account* and relates through a binary relationship set Cust_Acct. The attributes associated with Customer are Cust_Name, Cust_No, State and City. The attributes associated with Account are Acc_No and Balance.

4.15.1 E-R Diagram to Design Database Tables

A database which conforms to an E-R diagram can be represented by a set of tables. For each entity set and for each relationship set in the database, there is a unique table which is assigned the name of corresponding entity set or relationship set. Each table has a number of columns which are given unique names. For example, in Figure 4.19, the entities TEACHER and STUDENT are mapped on two separate tables say Teacher and Student. The attributes of entities TEACHER and STUDENT will map onto fields in the relevant tables. The key attributes become the key fields when mapped in the form of a table.

☞ *Note that T_No and Roll_No attributes are underlined because they are the key attributes. Key attribute has unique value for each student. (See Figure 4.18).*

4.15.2 Strong and Weak Entities

There are two types of entities namely, dependent entities (also called weak entities) and independent entities (also called regular or strong entities).

The *dependent entity* is the one whose existence depends on another entity. An entity set is called a weak entity set if its existence depends on the existence of another weak entity or any other strong entity. A weak entity set does not have sufficient attributes to form a primary key.

☞ *A weak entity set is represented by a double outlined rectangle in the E-R diagram.*

Consider an entity type *marks* which represents the marks obtained by a student. Now the existence of *marks* depends upon the existence of entity type *student* (See Figure 4.20).

☞ *Every weak entity set can be converted to a strong entity set by adding appropriate attributes.*

Let us take a real life situation to understand types of entity. Suppose, a student say "Swati" can have many instances of marks say Eng_marks, Sci_marks, SST_marks etc. related to it. If the instance "Swati" is deleted, then all the entity *marks* dependent upon *Swati* will also be removed.

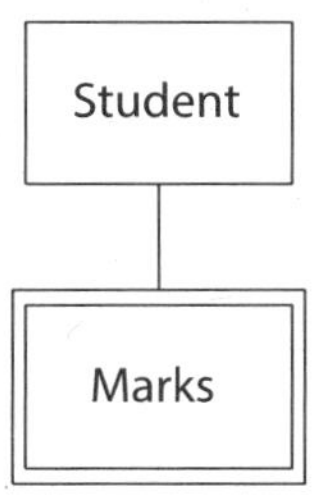

Figure 4.20 Marks is dependent (weak) entity that is dependent on entity Student

☞ *An entity set which has a primary key is termed as a strong entity set.*

For example in Figure 4.21, the entities Employee and Student are strong entities, because they have the primary keys Emp_No and Adm_No.

☞ *Note that Emp_No and Adm_No are the primary keys in Figure 4.21 (a) and (b).*

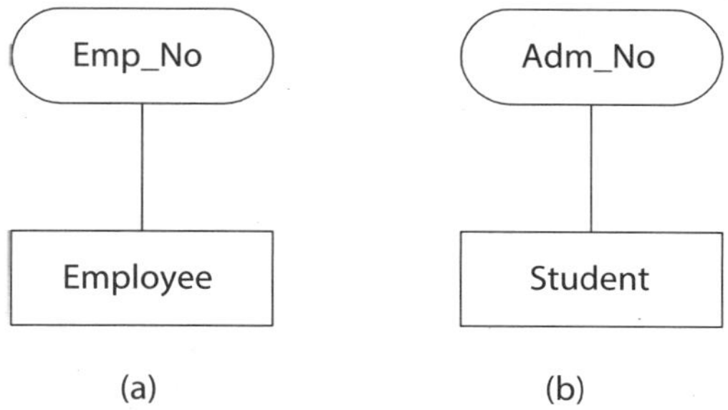

Figure 4.21 Examples of strong entities

4.15.3 How to Draw E-R Diagram?

While designing database using E-R diagrams, you should use the following guidelines:

(a) Do not introduce unwanted attributes.
(b) Merge the entities with common attributes or purposes.
(c) Decompose complex entities to simplify them. Do it by decomposing complex attributes into sub-attributes. (See Figure 4.22).

4.16 SUPERCLASS AND SUBCLASS TYPES

4.16.1 What is a Class?

The concept of class is best understood with an analogy. Out of the several objects in a room, let us talk about the picture on the wall. There is a class, which we can call the class of "Pictures" of which the picture on the wall is an *instance* (meaning an occurrence or example). The picture in the room belongs to the class of pictures, which consists of all pictures in the world.

☞ *A set of objects that share a common structure and a common behaviour is called* ***class***.

4.16.2 What is an object?

Putting it in the layman language, an object is something that has a fixed shape or well defined boundary. If you look at your computer desk, you would notice several objects of varying descriptions. They may be connected to or related to adjacent objects. For example, a keyboard may be attached to a PC, and it is also easy to see that different parts of PC are distinct objects.

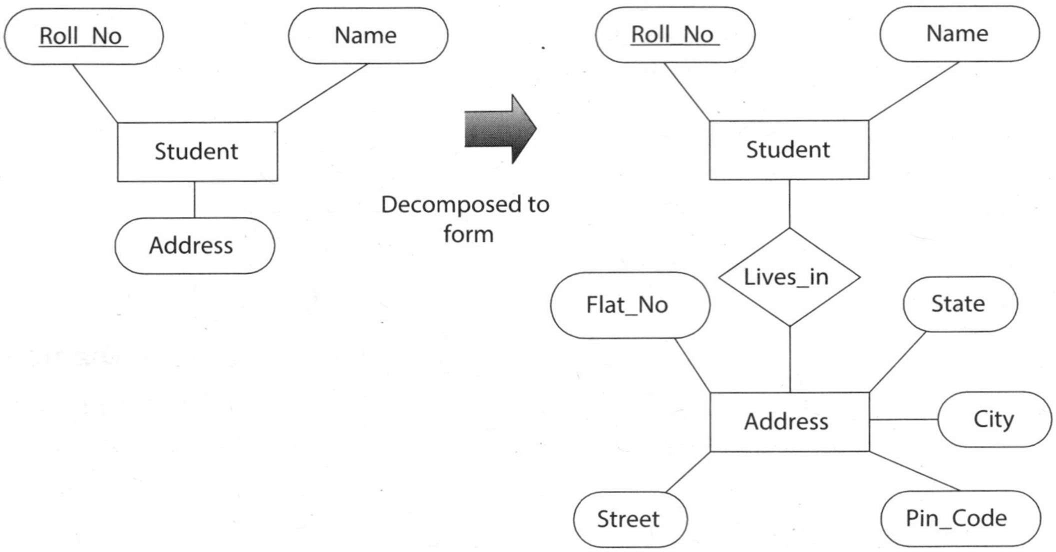

Figure 4.22 Decomposing of complex attribute Address to simpler attributes like Flat_No, Street, City, State and Pin_Code

☞ *In the ordinary sense, an **Object** is something which is capable of being seen, touched or sensed.*

4.16.3 Inheritance

Inheritance means the methods and/or attributes defined in an object class which can be inherited or reused by another object class.

A class ***supertype*** is an object whose instances store attributes that are common to one or more class subtypes of the object.

A class ***subtype*** is an object class whose instances inherit some common attributes from a class supertype and then add other attributes that are unique to an instance of the subtype.

☞ *Inheritance means that the behaviour and data associated with child classes are always an extension of the properties associated with parent classes. A subclass must have all the properties of the parent class, and other properties as well.*

Inheritance is always transitive i.e. can be transferred. A class can inherit features from superclasses many *levels* away. For example, if cat is a subclass of class Mammal, and class Mammal is in turn a subclass of class Animal, then cat will inherit attributes both from Mammal and from Animal. (See Figure 4.23).

The class whose objects store attributes which are common to its subclasses, is known as the *supertype* class. For example, a class *shopkeeper* is a supertype. Its objects store such attributes which are common to all shopkeepers like bakers, grocers, stationers, toy store owners, etc. These shopkeepers belong to the supertype class, *shopkeeper*. Thus, we can expect a florist to accept money for the sale of flowers because *florist* object is a subclass of *shopkeeper* class. Such an activity is not unique to florists, but is common to all shopkeepers.

The class *subtype* is the class which inherits qualities from a supertype class and also adds on its own qualities. For example, the florist inherits all the qualities that a shopkeeper should have. In addition he also has its own qualities like he sells flowers, etc.

Similarly, in terms of the hierarchy shown in Figure 4.23, we only need to define the distinguishing features of the cat family, provided the superclass of mammal is well defined. Thus, we only need to define that members of cat family have claws, eat meat and so on. Characteristics of mammals and animals are automatically included.

The concept of Inheritance is also known as *Generalization/specialization.* Supertype class is known as the *Generalization* class and the subtype class is known as the *Specialization* class. For example, furniture is referred to as a generalization class whereas chair, table and cupboards are specialization classes.

Generalization/specialization is a technique wherein the attributes and behaviours that are common to several types of object classes are grouped into their own class, called a super type. The attributes and methods of the supertype object class are then inherited by those object classes.

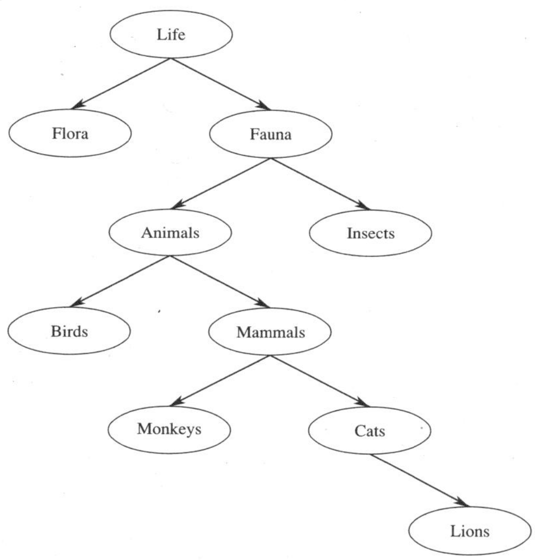

Figure 4.23 Hierarchy of life forms

4.17 ATTRIBUTE INHERITANCE

Attribute inheritance is the property of the higher and lower-level entities created by specialization and generalization. The attributes of the higher-level entity sets are inherited by the lower-level entity sets. For example, *customer* and *employee* inherit the attributes of person. So the, customer is described by his or her name, locality, city and customer_id attributes. In the same way employee is described by his or her name, locality, city and additional emp_code and salary attributes.

A lower-level entity set (or subclass) also inherits its participation in the relationship sets in which its higher-level entity (or superclass) participates. The officer and secretary entity sets can participate in the works_for relationship set, since the superclass employee participates in the works_for relationship. The above entity sets can participate in any relationships in which the person entity set participates.

4.18 GENERALIZATION

Generalization is used to emphasize the similarities among lower-level entity sets and to hide the differences. It also permits an economy of representation so that shared attributes are not repeated. In terms of an E-R diagram, generalization is depicted through a triangle component labeled "IS A", as seen in Figure 4.24.

There are similarities between *Saving account* entity set and *Current account* entity set in a bank account. These similarities are in the sense that they have several attributes in common. This commonalty can be expressed by generalization, which is a containment relationship that exists between a higher and lower-level entity set.

☞ ***Generalization** is the result of taking the union of several lower level entity sets to produce higher-level entity set.*

In Figure 4.24, *Account* is the higher-level entity set and *Saving account* and *Current account* are lower-level entity sets. Higher and lower-level entity sets may also be designated by the term superclass and subclass respectively. The *Account* entity set is the superclass of *Saving account* and *Current account* subclasses.

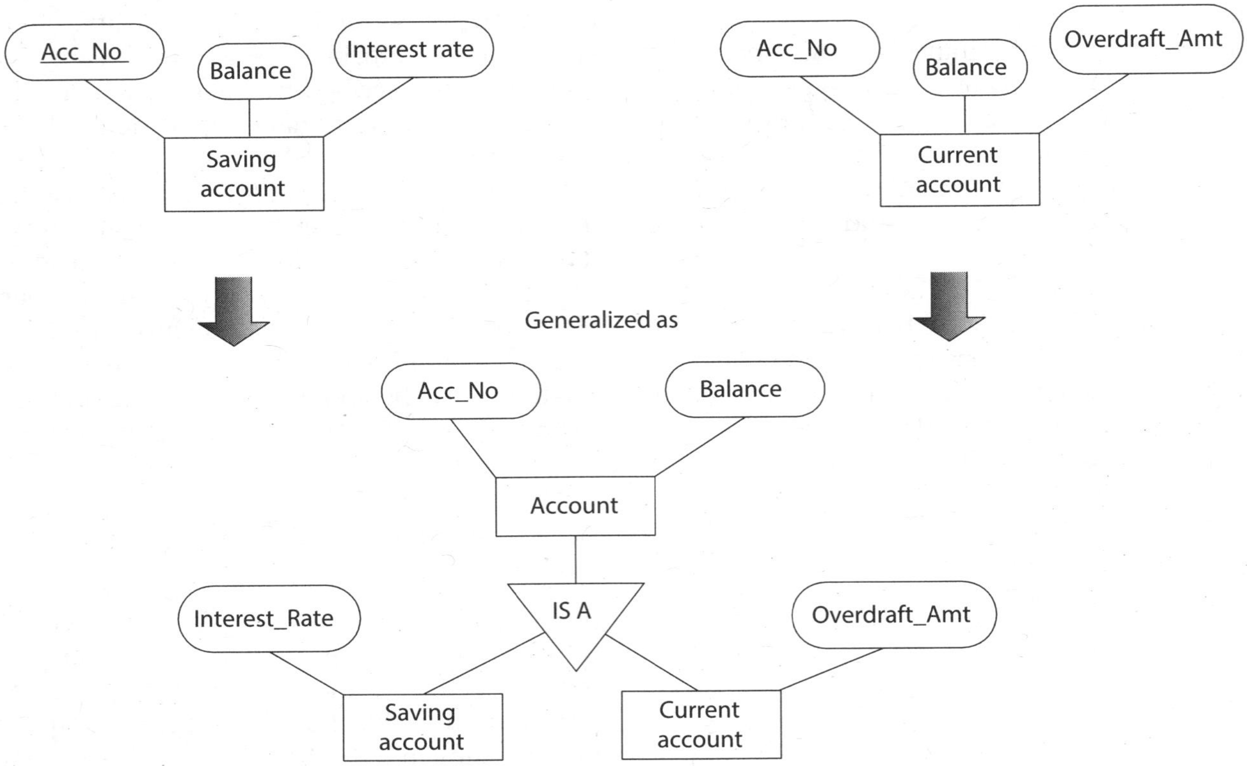

Figure 4.24 Generalization where saving account and current account are put together to generalize the banking account

4.19 SPECIALIZATION

Specialization is the process of defining a set of subclasses of an entity type. This entity type is called the *superclass* of the specialization.

☞ *The set of subclasses that form a specialization is defined on the basis of some distinguishing characteristic of the entities in the superclass.*

For example, Specialization of the *Employee* entity type may yield the set of subclasses namely, *Salaried_Employee* and *Hourly_Employee.* Note that this specialization differentiates among employees based on the method of payment. Figure 4.25 shows another example clarifying this concept.

☞ ***Specialization** is the result of taking subsets of a higher level entity set to form lower level entity sets.*

Note that *Pressure* applies only to *Steam* based Power House. *Radiation* applies only to *Nuclear* based Power House and *Flow* applies only to *Hydro* based Power House.

4.19.1 Difference between Generalization and Specialization

Generalization proceeds from the recognition that a number of entity sets share some common features which are described by the same attributes and participate in the same relationship sets. On the basis of their commonalties, generalization synthesizes these entity sets into a single, higher level entity set.

Specialization stems from a single entity set. Specialization emphasizes differences among entities within the set by creating *distinct* lower-level entity sets. These lower-level entity sets may have attributes, or may participate in relationships, that do not apply to all entities in the higher-level entity set.

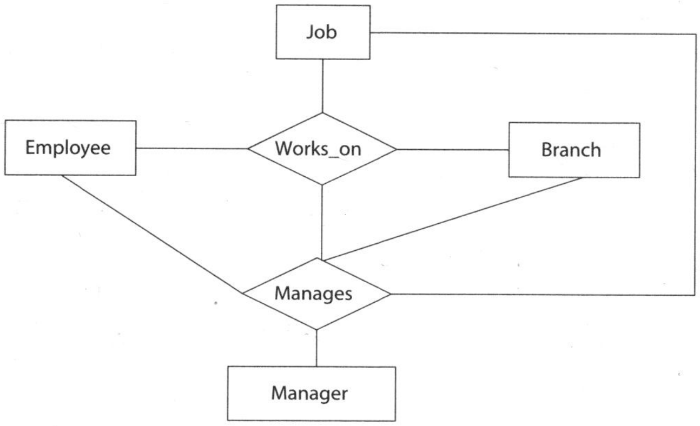

Figure 4.25 Concept of Specialization where three different types of Power Houses are based on the use of Steam, Nuclear and Hydro energy

4.20 AGGREGATION

Aggregation is the process of compiling information on an object, thereby abstracting a higher level object. One limitation of the E-R model is that it cannot express relationships within relationships. To illustrate the need for such a construct, consider the ternary relationship *works_on*, between an employee, branch and job as shown in Figure 4.26.

The best way to model a situation shown in Figure 4.26 is by the use of *aggregation*. Thus, the relationship set *Works_on* relating the entity sets *Employee*, *Branch* and *Job* is a higher level entity set. Such an entity set is treated in the same manner as in any other entity set. We can then create a binary relationship *Manages* between *Works_on* and *Manager* to represent who manages what tasks. Figure 4.27 shows a notation for such an aggregation.

4.21 CATEGORIZATION

In object-oriented system development, objects are categorized according to classes and subclasses. Identifying classes realizes numerous benefits. For example, consider the fact that a new attribute of interest, called *gender*, needs to be added to teacher and student objects. Because the attribute is common to both, the attribute could be added once, with the class person implying both objects within its class share that attribute.

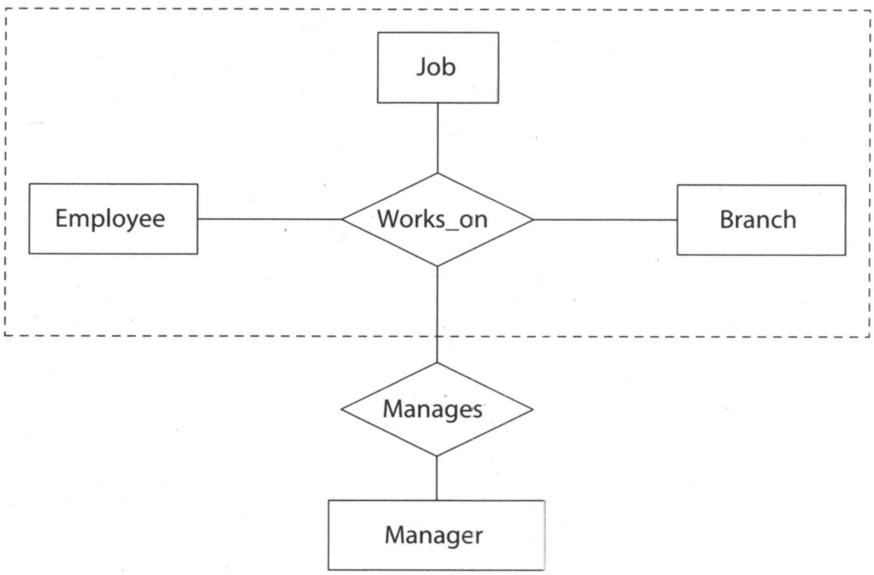

Figure 4.26 E-R diagram with redundant relationships

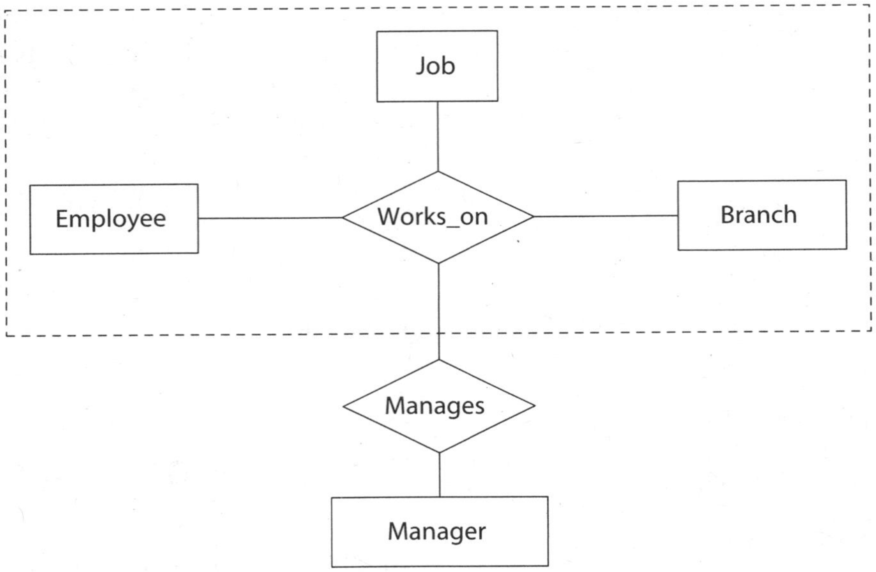

Figure 4.27 E-R diagram with aggregation

REVIEW QUESTIONS WITH ANSWERS

1. Multiple Choice Questions

1. Advantage(s) of normalizing database are:
   a. No duplicate entries
   b. Saves storage space
   c. Boasts the query performances
   d. All of the above
2. An association of several entities in an Entity-Relation model is called:
   a. Tuple b. Record
   c. Relationship d. Field
3. The overall logical structure of a database can be expressed graphically by
   a. Data flow chart b. Flow chart
   c. Directed graph d. Entity-relationship diagram
4. Course(course_id,sec_id,semester)
   Here the course_id, sec_id and semester are __________ and course is a _________
   a. Relations, Attribute
   b. Attributes, Relation
   c. Tuple, Relation
   d. Tuple, Attributes
5. The number of entities to which another entity can be associated via a relationship set is expressed as
   a. Entity b. Cardinality
   c. Scheme d. Attributes
6. One limitation of the entity-relation model is that it cannot
   a. Use generalization
   b. Express relationship among relationships
   c. Use single primary key
   d. None of the above
7. Every weak entity set can be converted to a strong entity set by
   a. Simply adding appropriate attribute
   b. Using generalization
   c. Using aggregation
   d. Repeating the entity set several times
8. Every Boyce-Codd normal form (BCNF) is in
   a. 1 NF b. 2 NF
   c. 3 NF d. None of the above
9. Which normal form is most desirable?
   a. Domain key normal form (DKNF)
   b. Boyce-Codd normal form (BCNF)
   c. Third normal form (3 NF)
   d. Fourth normal form (4 NF)
10. Complex entities can be constructed using the following operation:
    a. SUM b. Union
    c. Aggregation d. Collection
11. A relation in third normal form is:
    a. In first normal form also
    b. Second normal form also

c. From transitive dependencies
d. All of the above

12. Which one is not true?
    a. A relation is in BCNF if it is in 4NF
    b. BCNF is stricter than 3NF
    c. A relation is in BCNF if ever determinant of the relation is a candidate key.
    d. All are true

13. If every non-key attribute is functionally dependent on the primary key, then the relation will be in
    a. 1NF   b. 2NF
    c. 3NF   d. 4NF

14. A table is in 2NF if it is in 1NF and if
    a. No column that is not a part of the primary key is dependent on only a portion of the alternate key
    b. No column that is not a part of the primary key is dependent on only a portion of the primary key
    c. No column that is not a part of the primary key is dependent on only a portion of the foreign key
    d. None of the above

15. A ________ in a table represents a relationship among a set of values.
    a. Column   b. Key
    c. Row   d. None of the above

16. A domain is atomic if elements of the domain are considered to be ____________ units.
    a. Different   b. Indivisible
    c. Constant   d. Divisible

17. Which one of the following cannot be taken as a primary key?
    a. Id   b. Register number
    c. Dept_id   d. Street

18. Most of the time, modification anomalies are serious enough that tables should be normalized into:
    a. 1NF   b. 2NF
    c. 3NF   d. BCNF

19. When assessing the table structure of an acquired set of tables with data, determining functional dependencies is (part of) the:
    a. First step   b. Second step
    c. Third step   d. Fourth step

20. Normalization ________ data duplication.
    a. Eliminates   b. Reduces
    c. Increases   d. Maximizes

21. In a 1:N relationship, the foreign key is placed in:
    a. Either table without specifying parent and child tables
    b. The parent table
    c. The child table
    d. Either the parent table or the child table

22. In a 1:1 relationship, the foreign key is placed in:
    a. Either table without specifying parent and child tables
    b. The parent table
    c. The child table
    d. Either the parent table or the child table

23. E-R model uses this symbol to represent weak entity set.
    a. Dotted rectangle
    b. Diamond
    c. Doubly outlined rectangle
    d. None of these

24. An entity in A is associated with any number of entities in B, however an entity in B is associated with almost one entity in A.
    a. One to one
    b. Many to many
    c. Many to one
    d. One to many

2. State True or False for the following:

1. A weak entity set has a primary key.
2. Every weak entity set can be converted into a strong entity set by adding appropriate attributes.
3. A candidate key can be a subset of a super key.
4. Many-to-many relationship between two entities can be represented by two DBTG sets.
5. In a relational database, the foreign key of a relation would be the primary key of an another relation.
6. Boyce-Codd Normal Form is also in Third normal form.

7. The subschema must contain all the description of certain data that are in the scheme.
8. Codd gave 12 rules for any RDBMS to be accepted as a full fledged RDBMS.
9. Aggregation operation is used to construct complex entities.
10. An E-R model uses doubly outlined rectangle to represent weak entity set.
11. In an E-R diagram attributes are represented by ellipse. Rectangles or squares represent the entity sets and triangles represent the generalization and specialization.
12. Keys are the constraints in a relation.
13. Attribute is a specific domain in the relation which has entries of all tuples.
14. In a one-to-many relationship, the entity that is on the one side of the relationship is called a parent entity.
15. One-to-Many Relationship is a single-entity instance of one type related to many entity instances of another type.
16. An attribute that names or identifies entity instances is identifier.
17. Properties that describe the characteristics of entities are called attributes.
18. Generalization is the result of taking the union of several lower level entity sets to produce higher-level entity set.
19. Admission_No. is an example of weak entity type in student database.
20. Specialization is the process of defining a set of subclasses of an entity type.
21. Rectangle symbol represents the relationships among entity sets.
22. An association of several entities in a E-R model is called a relationship.

3. Match the following:

1. Specialization	a. Functional dependency
2. Relationship	b. Multivalued dependency
3. Entity integrity	c. Doubly outlined box
4. Virtual tables	d. Primary key values
5. Weak entity set	e. User views
6. Fourth normal form	f. Inheritance
7. Attribute that are not divisible	g. Atomic attributes
8. Update anomaly	h. Diamond
9. Union rule	i. Aggregation
10. Complex entities	j. First normal form
11. Doubly outlined rectangle	k. Weak entity
12. Each entity is represented as	l. Table

4. Fill in the blanks:

1. A view of the database that appears to an application program is known as _________.
2. If relation is in __________, it is in 3 NF also.
3. _________ represents relationship between the tables.
4. ____________ is the name given to the process of simplifying the relationship among data elements in a record.
5. Complex entities can be constructed using the __________ operation.
6. In a relational data model the columns of a table are called _________.
7. In a hierarchical database, modeling of many-to-many relations is achieved by _________.
8. In a hierarchical database, a hashing function is used to locate ___________.
9. E-R model is used to describe ___________ model.
10. ___________ contains the structure of the database.
11. When a table has no repeating groups, it is said to be in _________.
12. The relation is said to be in _________ when every non-key attribute is fully functionally dependent on the primary key.

13. Every relation in BCNF is also in ________.
14. A functional dependency is denoted by ________, between two sets of attributes x and y.
15. When one non-key attribute depends on other non-key attribute, it is called a ________ dependency.
16. In an E-R diagram an entity set is represent by a _______.
17. A ________ is always established between two entities.
18. The identifier of an entity will become the ________ of the new table.

Answers

1.	1. d	2. c	3. d	4. b	5. b	6. b
	7. a	8. c	9. a	10. c	11. d	12. d
	13. b	14. b	15. c	16. b	17. d	18. d
	19. b	20. a	21 c	22. a	23. c	24. d
2.	1. F	2. T	3. T	4. T	5. T	6. T
	7. F	8. T	9. T	10. T	11. T	12. T
	13. T	14. T	15. T	16. T	17. T	18. T
	19. F	20. T	21. F	22. T		
3.	1. f	2. h	3. d	4. e	5. c	6. b
	7. g	8. j	9. a	10. i	11. k	12. l

4.	1. Subschema	2. BCNF
	3. Foreign key	4. Normalization
	5. Aggregation	6. Attributes
	7. Record replication	8. Root
	9. Relational	10. Data dictionary
	11. 1NF	12. 2NF
	13. 3NF	14. x→y
	15. Transitive	16. Rectangle
	17. Relationship	18. Primary key

Short Answers Questions

1. Define normalization. Why normalization is carried out?

Ans Normalization is a process of simplifying the relationships between data elements in a record.

Normalization is carried out for the following four reasons:

(a) To structure the data between tables so that data maintenance is simplified.

(b) To permit simple retrieval of data in response query and report requests.

(c) To simplify the maintenance of data through updates, insertion and deletions.

(d) To reduce the need to restructure or reorganize data when new application requirements arise.

2. What is Entity and Attribute?

Ans An Entity is an object whose information is stored in the database. For example, in student database the entity is student.

An attribute is a characteristic of interest about an entity. For example, in case of student database Roll No, Name, Class, Address etc. are attributes of entity student.

3. What is weak entity set?

Ans An entity set that does not have sufficient attributes to form a primary key is a weak entity set.

4. Define attributes. Explain different types of attributes with example of each.

Ans The various kinds of data that describe an entity are known as its *attributes*.

Types of attributes are:

(a) Composite attributes

(b) Single valued attributes

(c) Multi-valued attributes

(d) Derived and stored attributes

Composite attributes can be divided into smaller sub parts, which represent more basic attribute with independent meaning of their own. For example, the address attribute of an employee entity can be subdivided into locality, city, and pin_code etc.

Single valued attributes have a single value for a particular entity. For example *Age* is a single valued attribute of an employee entity.

Multivalued attributes may have upper and lower limits on the number of values for an individual entity. For example, the colour attribute of a car may have between one to seven values, if we assume that car can have at most seven colours.

Derived and stored attribute: Some times two or more attribute values are related with one another. For example, the age and date_of_birth attributes of an *employee* entity are related to each other, because to calculate the age of an employee, we have to determine the current_date and the birth_date. Hence the *age* attribute is called *derived attribute* and birth date is called *stored attribute.*

5. What do you mean by the terms specialization and generalization?

Ans Specialization is the process of defining a set of subclasses of an entity type. This entity type is called the superclass of the specialization.
Generalization is the result of taking the union of several lower level entity sets to produce higher-level entity set.

6. Write short note on attribute inheritance.

Ans Attribute inheritance is the property of the higher and lower-level entities created by specialization and generalization. The attributes of the higher-level entity sets are inherited by the lower-level entity sets. For example, *customer* and *employee* inherit the attributes of person. So the, customer is described by his or her name, locality, city and customer_id attributes. In the same way employee is described by his or her name, locality, city and additional emp_code and salary attributes.

7. Explain class and object with an example of each.

Ans A set of objects that share a common structure and a common behaviour is called class. In the ordinary sense, an Object is something which is capable of being seen, touched or sensed.

8. What is Join dependency?

Ans Join dependency is a constraint, similar to a Functional Dependency or a Multivalued Dependency. It is satisfied if and only if the relation concerned is the join of certain number of projections. And therefore, such a constraint is called a *join dependency.*

9. What is null valued attribute? Explain with an example.

Ans An attribute, which has no value for an entity is known as null valued attribute. For example, assume Student is an entity and its attributes are Name, Age, Address and Phone_no. There may be chance when a student has no phone_no. In that case, phone_no is called null valued attribute.

10. Explain one-to-one (1:1) relationship.

Ans A one-to-one (1:1) relationship is an association only between two entities. For example, in a university each department has only one head of the department.

11. What is Key Attribute?

Ans The key attribute is an attribute that uniquely identifies an entity in the entity set. For example, *Employee_code* can be the key attribute for the entity set *Employee* because it uniquely identifies each Employee entity.

12. What is Many-to-Many (M:M) relationship?

Ans A *Many-to-Many* (M:M) relationship describes entities that may have many relationships among each other. For example, one customer may buy many items and one item may be bought by many customers.

EXERCISE

1. Write short note on the following:
   (a) Denormalization
   (b) Fourth Normal Form
   (c) Transitive Dependency
   (d) Multivalued Dependencies
   (e) One-to-Many Relationship
2. Define Normalization and why is it done?
3. Explain Third Normal Form (3NF) with an example.
4. With the help of an example, what do you understand by Boyce Codd Normal Form. How does it differ from Third Normal Form.

5. Explain Partial Dependency with an example.
6. What is join dependencies? Explain with an example.
7. What are the various symbols used to draw an E-R diagram?
8. Design an E-R diagram for airline reservation system consisting of flights, aircrafts, airports, fares, reservations, tickets, pilot, crew and passengers. Clearly highlight the entities, the relationships, the primary keys and the mapping constraints.
9. What is attribute inheritance? How does it help in developing a system?
10. What do you mean by specialization? Explain giving examples.
11. Explain super class and sub class with an example.
12. Give an example of each of the following relationships:
    a. One to one
    b. One to many
    c. Many to many
13. Explain E-R Modelling Symbol.
14. Define Normalization also differentiate between 3NF and BCNF.
15. Describe the purpose of normalizing data. How is the concept of functional dependency associated with the process of normalization?
16. Consider a relation:
    R(A,B,C,D,E,F,G,H,I,J)
    Given Functional Dependency:
    F={AB->C,A->DE,B->F,F->GH,D->IJ}
    Identify the keys
    Decompose the relation into 2NF and 3NF.

CHAPTER 5

MariaDB

5.1 INTRODUCTION TO MariaDB

MariaDB came out first in the market in 2009, introduced from the same MySQL founder Michael Widenius. It can be said as an advanced version of MySQL, as it carries various optimized features of existing SQL. It includes support for JSON APIs, replication of parallel data, various storage engines like Aria, ColumnStore, InnoDB, Cassandra, and others. It is owned by MariaDB Corporation, which provides training, migration services, remote database management and various other specialized features to its subscribers. The initiatives of the MariaDB Foundation are to support the continuity of the MariaDB and serve as a global contact point for open collaboration.

The RDBMS offers data processing capabilities for both small and enterprise tasks. This DBMS is an improved version of MySQL. It comes with numerous in-built powerful features and many usabilities, security and performance improvements that you cannot find in MySQL.

5.1.1 Features of MariaDB

- It is an Open-source Software and is based on the MySQL Community Version.
- It operates under GPL, BSD, or LGPL licenses.
- MariaDB supports a popular and standard querying language.
- It offers the advance Galera cluster technology.
- MariaDB supports PHP, a popular language for web development.
- Offers Backward Compatibility.

5.1.2 Limitations of MariaDB

- The engine is still pretty new, so there's no guarantee further updates and versions will be oncoming.
- As with many other free database engines, you have to pay for support.

5.2 WHAT IS MySQL?

MySQL is an open source Relational Database Management System (RDBMS) that uses Structured Query Language (SQL), the most popular language for adding, accessing and processing data in a database. MySQL runs as a server providing multi-user access to a number of databases. It is also used in many high-profile, large-scale World Wide Web products, including Wikipedia, Google and Facebook.

MySQL is a relational database (RDBMS) created by Michael Monty Widenius and David Axmark in year 1995. In 2008, MySQL was first acquired by Sun Microsystems-renowned tech brand. In 2010, Oracle took over Sun Microsystems and its subfields including MySQL. The most significant aspect about MySQL is that it comes up with a GNU General Public License (GPL), which effectively makes its usage applicable for the entire community. It is supported by major operating systems including Linux, UNIX, MacOS, Windows and others.

MySQL is an RDBMS that helps you to keep the data that exists in a database organized. It is used with the combination of PHP and Apache Web Server, on top of a Linux distribution. MySQL uses the SQL language to query the database.

5.2.1 Features of MySQL

- MySQL is an open-source software.
- MySQL runs with very fast speed. It is easy to use and is reliable.

- MySQL is a platform independent application which works on many operating systems like Windows, UNIX, LINUX etc., and has compatibility with many languages including JAVA, C++, PHP, PERL, etc.
- MySQL is an easy to install RDBMS and is capable of handling large databases.
- It is fully multi-threaded using kernel threads.
- MySQL database server is very fast, reliable and easy to use. The server can provide error messages to the clients in many languages.
- MySQL provides many data types to support different types of data.

5.2.2 Limitations of MySQL

- It is hard to scale.
- Oracle owns it, so it has lots of restrictions.
- It is Invisible from client applications.
- Triggers can impose a high load on the database server.

5.2.3 Difference between MariaDB and MySQL

- MariaDB has 12 new storage engines such as (PBXT, XtraDB, Maria, FederatedX etc.). Storage engines handle data at the physical level. Storage engines are designed to efficiently manage data files, the data, and the index caches. MySQL has fewer options for storage compared to MariaDB.
- MariaDB shows an improved speed when compared to MySQL.
- With the Memory storage engine of MariaDB, an INSERT statement can be completed 24% faster than in the standard MySQL.
- MariaDB comes with an advanced thread pool capable of running faster and supporting up to 200,000+ connections.
- MariaDB, replication can be done safer and faster. Updates can also be done 2x faster compared to the traditional MySQL.
- MariaDB comes with new features and extensions including the JSON, WITH and KILL statements. The new MariaDB features are not provided in MySQL.

5.3 DOWNLOAD AND INSTALL MariaDB

Step 1. Start installation

To download MariaDB, you go to URL https://downloads.mariadb.org/ and select the latest version to download. However we are downloading MariaDB 10.4.12 Stable 2020-01-28. (See Figure 5.1). It displays screen similar to Figure 5.2 check Windows and MSI Package and double-click the installer to start the installation process. It displays MriaDB Foundation screen and after sometime it displays MariaDB Server 10.4.12 screen followed by MariaDB 10.4(x64) Setup Wizard as shown in Figure 5.3.

Step 2. Accept the end-user license agreement

Read the end-user license agreement and accept the license agreement by activating the checkbox then click the Next button.

Step 3. Select features

Choose the features that are to be installed i.e., choose the directory that stores the MariaDB files and click the Next button. The default location on Windows is C:\Program Files\MariaDB 10.4\.

Step 4. Set root's password

In the next window, that appears, change the password for the root user by entering the password and confirm it by retyping the same password. The root user is the default user of the MariaDB, which has all privileges.

If you want to permit access from remote machines, activate the necessary checkbox. If you don't want the root user to login from a remote machine, you need to uncheck the Enable access from remote machines for 'root' user checkbox. The Use UTF8 as the default server's character set option allows you to use the UTF8 as the default character set when you create new databases and tables. Once you complete selecting all options, click the Next button to go to the next step.

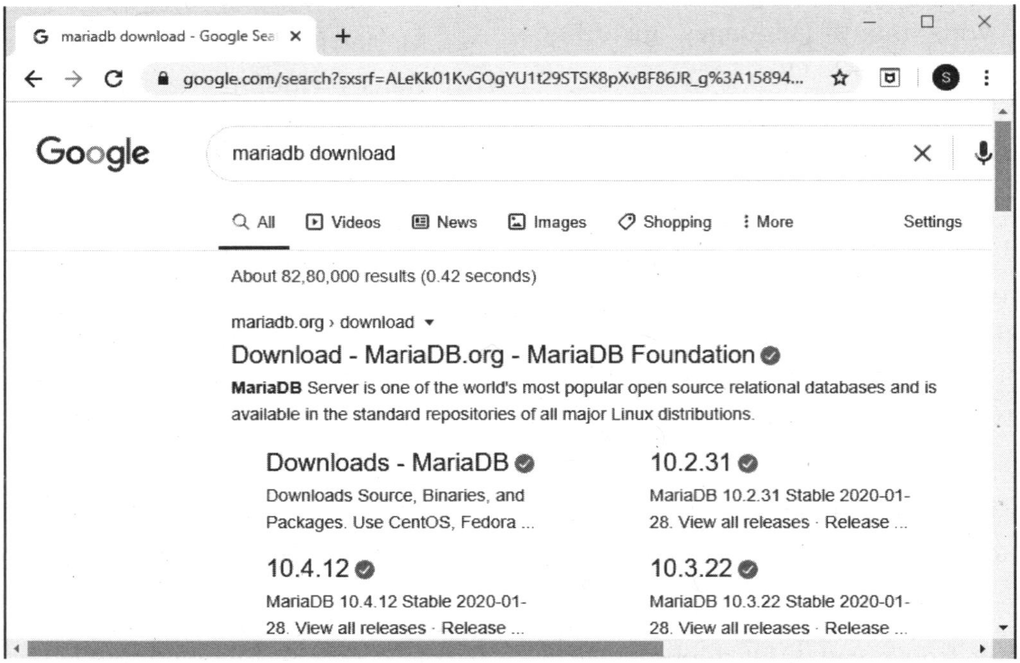

Figure 5.1 MariaDB download screen

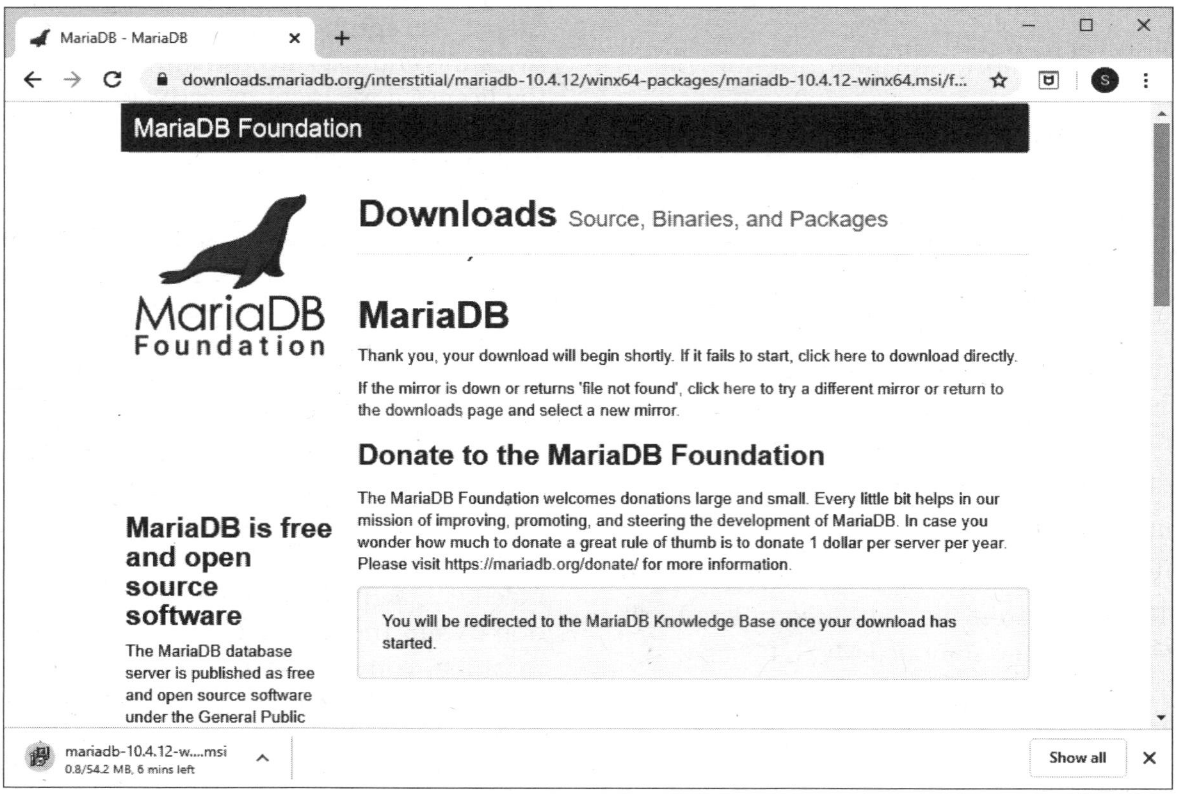

Figure 5.2 MariaDB Foundation screen

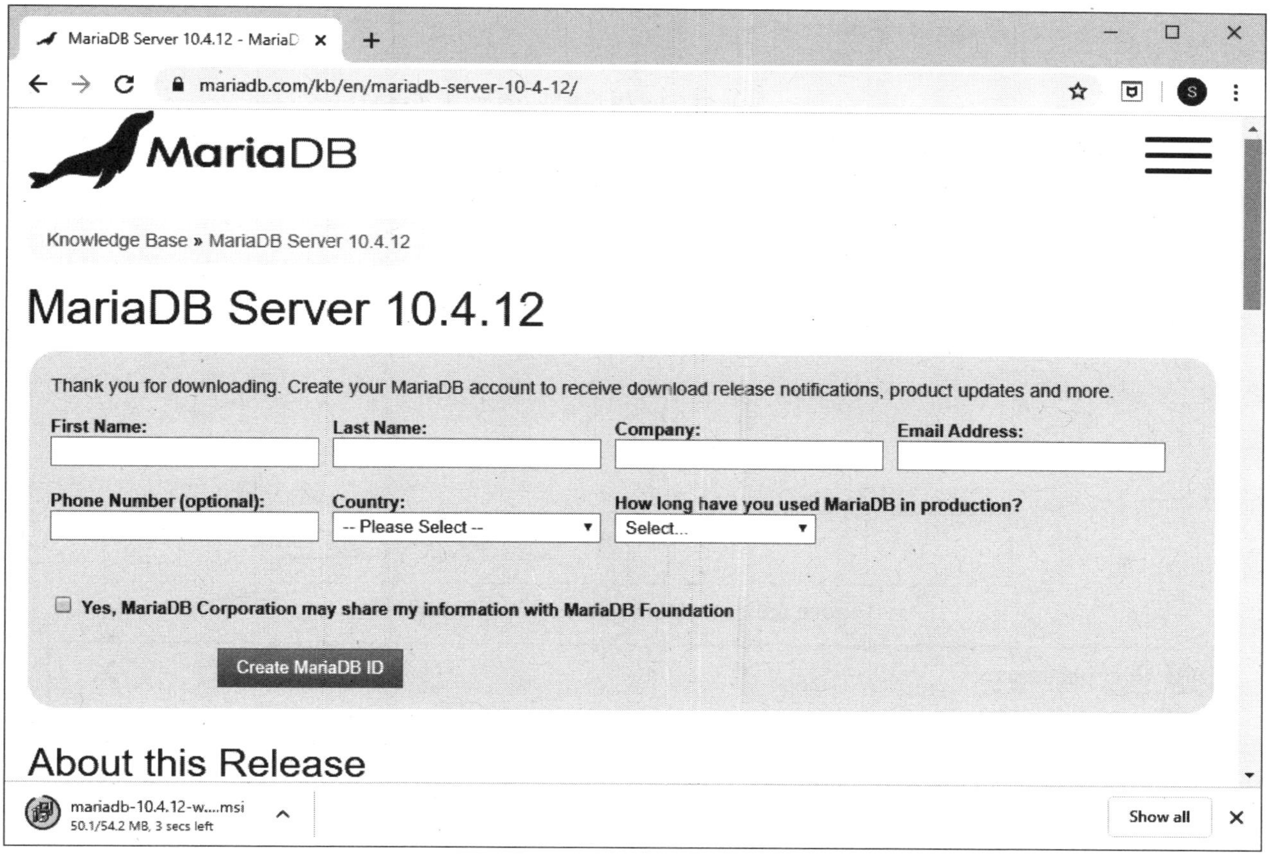

Figure 5.3 MariaDB welcome Setup wizard screen

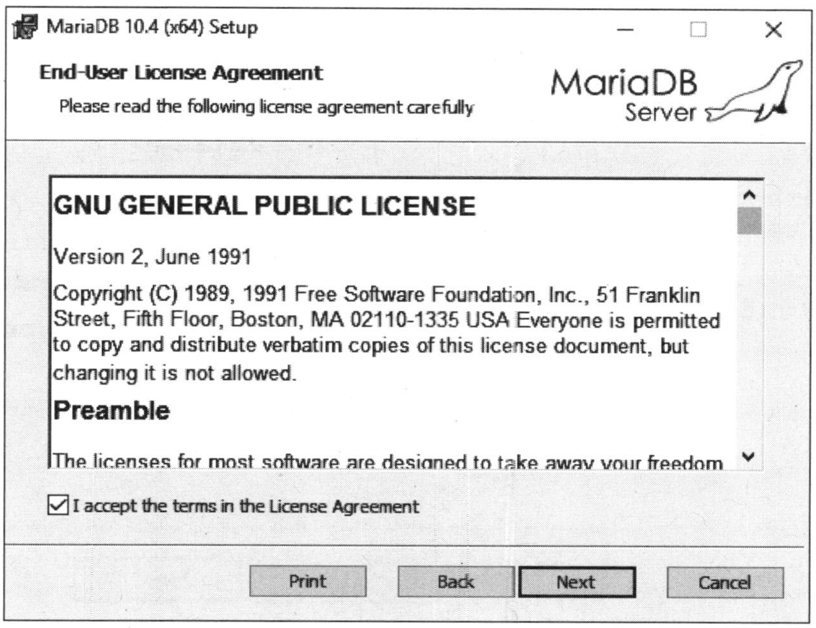

Figure 5.4 MariaDB end-user license agreement screen

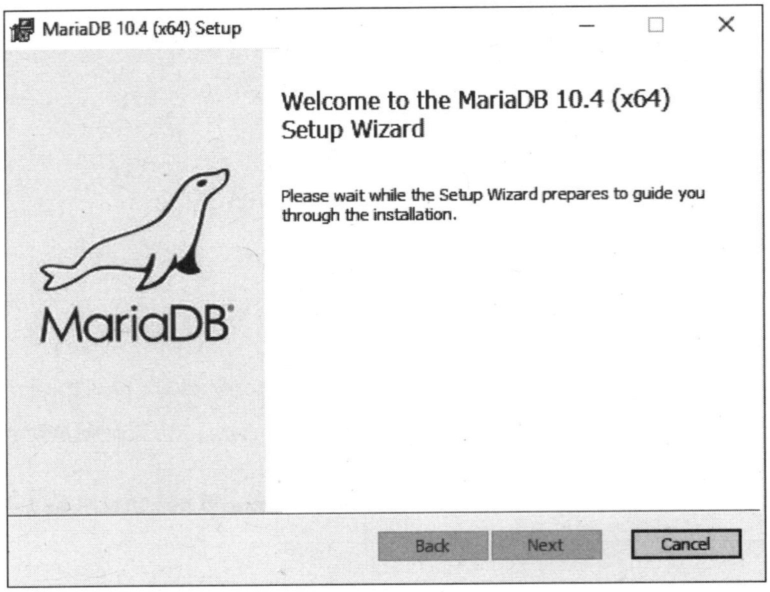

Figure 5.5 MariaDB custom setup screen

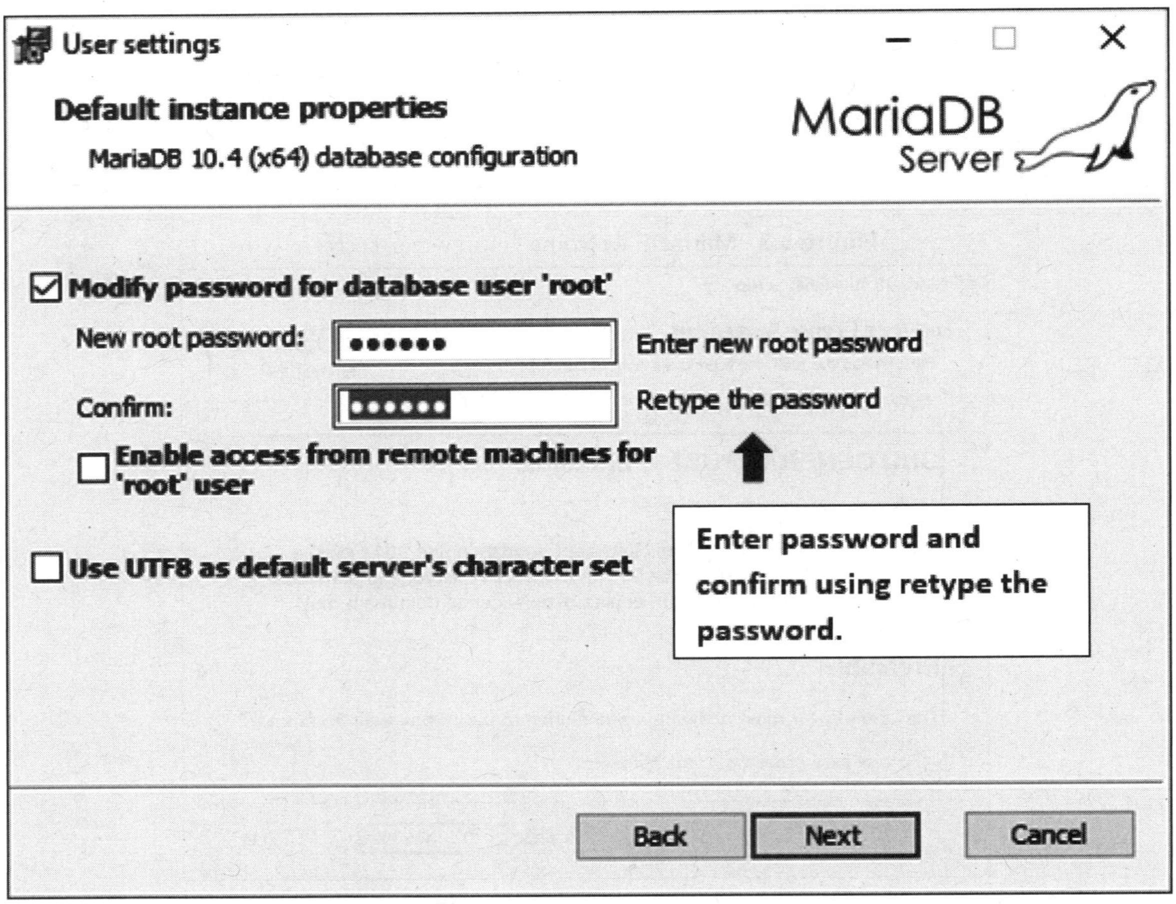

Figure 5.6 MariaDB user settings dialog box screen

Step 5. Configure Database

In the next window, type a name for the instance, choose the port number, and set the necessary size. Installing MariaDB as a service by selecting the Install as service option allows you to rename the service name. Configure the port for the MariaDB. By default, MariaDB uses 3306 port. However, you can change it to your port if you want. And finally, specify the parameters for the Innodb engine settings including buffer pool size and page size. 16KB page size is suitable for most databases. Now, click the Next button.

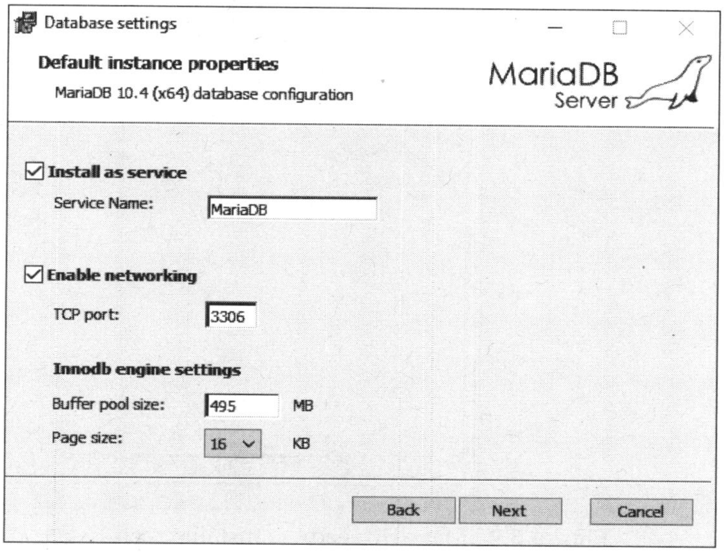

Figure 5.7 MariaDB database configure screen

Step 6. Submit usage information

If you want to submit anonymous usage information so that MariaDB developers can improve the system, check the checkbox and click the Next button.

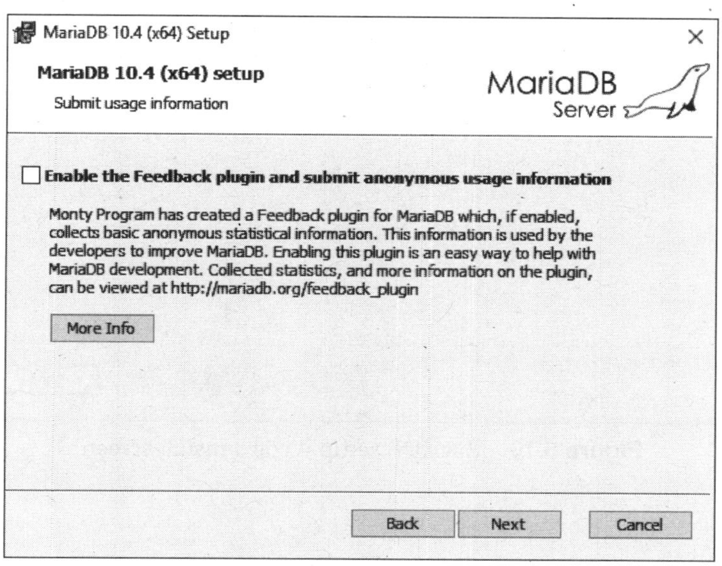

Figure 5.8 MariaDB usage information screen

Step 7. Ready to install MariaDB

In Ready to install MariaDB box click the Install button. A progress bar showing the progress of the installation will be shown. It will take a few minutes depending on the system and displays screen as show in Figures 5.9 to 5.14.

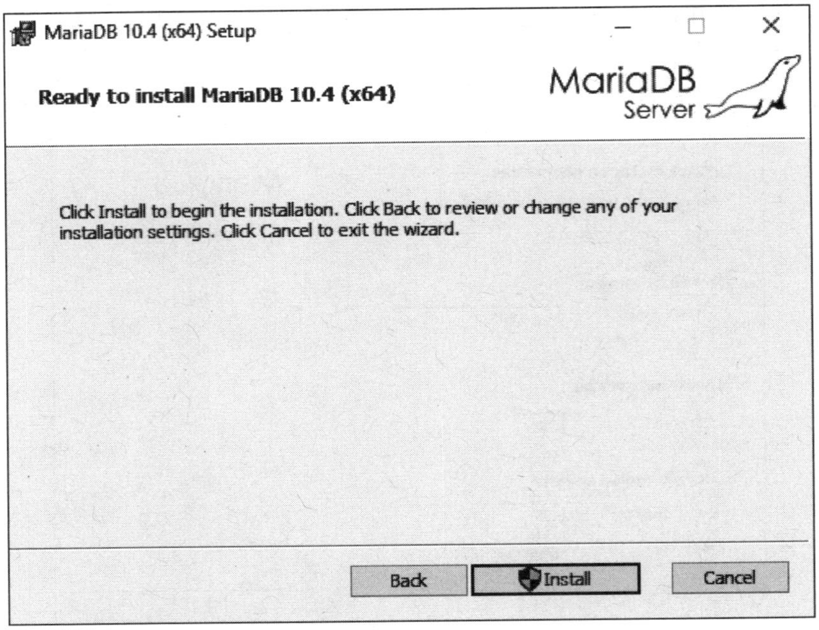

Figure 5.9 MariaDB ready to install screen

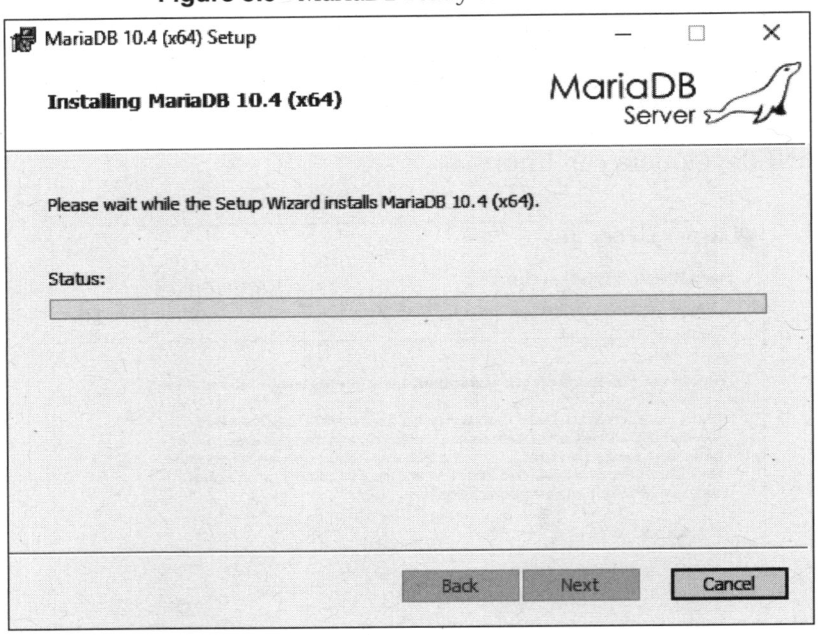

Figure 5.10 MariaDB setup wizard install screen

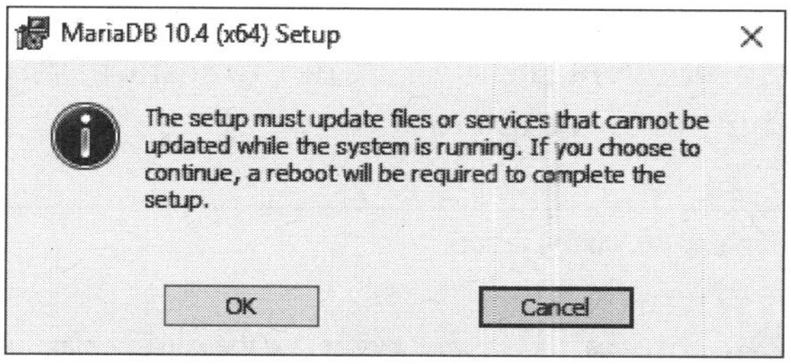

Figure 5.11 MariaDB setup dialog box

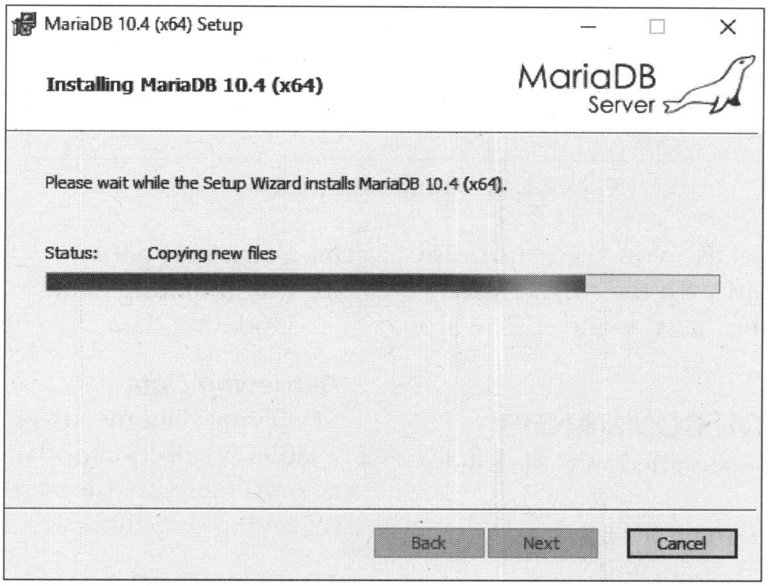

Figure 5.12 MariaDB setup with status copying new files

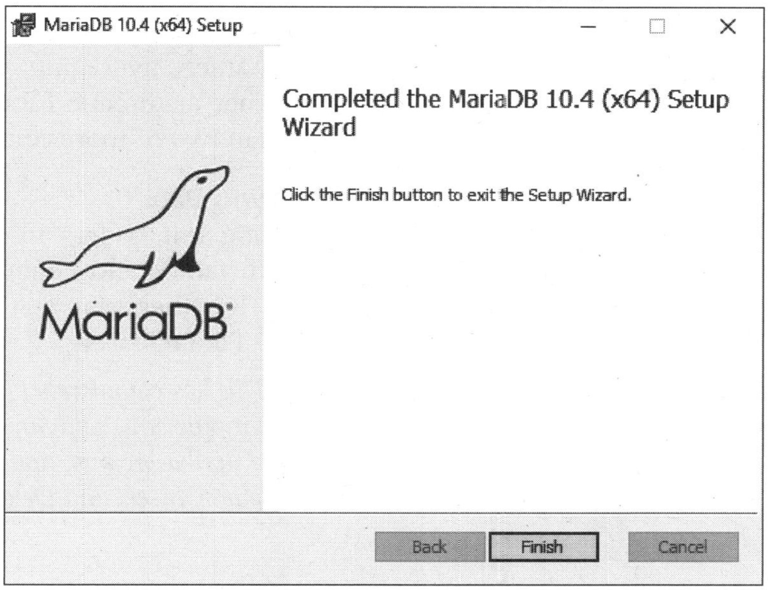

Figure 5.13 Complete MariaDB setup box

Step 8. Complete the MariaDB setup

Once the installation is complete, you will see the Finish button. Click the Finish button to complete MariaDB setup. Then it displays MariaDB dialog box to restart system. Click Yes.

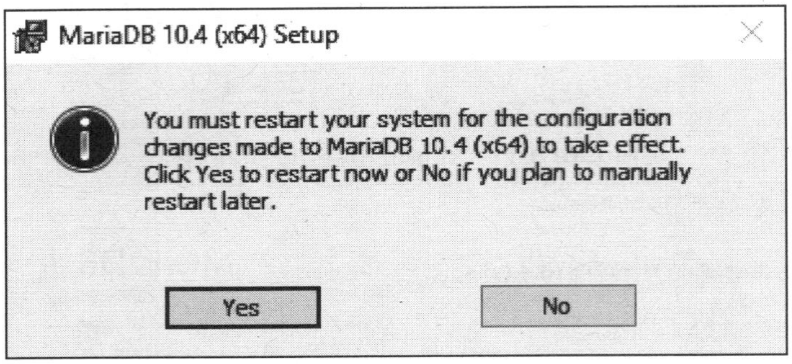

Figure 5.14 Complete MariaDB setup box

To connect to MariaDB, you can use any MariaDB client program with the correct parameters such as hostname, user name, password, and database name.

5.4 TYPES OF SQL COMMANDS

SQL commands can be classified into the following types:

(a) Data Definition Language(DDL)
(b) Data Manipulation Language(DML)
(c) Data Control Language(DML)
(d) Transaction Control Language(TCL)

5.4.1 Data Definition Language

Data Definition Language (or DDL) is a part of SQL which consists of those commands that create the objects (tables, indexes, views, etc.) in the database. *Create, Drop* and *Alter* are a few commands of DDL language.

5.4.2 Data Manipulation Language

Data Manipulation Language (DML) is that part of SQL which consists of a set of commands that determine which values are present in the tables at any given time. Data Manipulation Language is divided into three categories:

(a) Retrieving data
(b) Manipulating data
(c) Updating data

Retrieving Data

Retrieving data means getting information out of a table. A selection of data items stored in a table is presented on the screen. The command for retrieving data items is *SELECT*.

Manipulating Data

Manipulating data refers to the DML features that allow us to perform statistical functions on data, namely averaging and summing columns and other arithmetic functions like multiplying values in two or more columns of a table.

Updating Data

Updating data refers to inserting and deleting rows in tables and changing values in the columns. In other words it performs the maintenance of a database.

☞ *DML has commands for dealing with retrieving, manipulating and updating a database. For manipulation and updation, the commands are Update, Insert and Delete.*

5.4.3 Data Control Language

Data Control Language (DCL) is another portion of SQL which allows definition of a security mechanism or scheme for protecting data from unauthorized access. DCL consists of features that determine whether a user is permitted to perform a particular action. It contains commands like *Grant, Revoke* etc.

5.4.4 Transaction Control Language

Transaction means a sequence of information exchange and related work for the purposes of satisfying a request and for ensuring database integrity. Transactions are supported by SQL. A transaction is completed successfully, if and only if all the constituent steps are successfully carried out. When a transaction is completed successfully, it is said to be *committed* and when a transaction does not complete, it said to be *rolled back*. Transaction Control Language contains commands like *Commit, Rollback* etc.

5.5 STARTING MariaDB

Now, MariaDB is already installed on your computer, it is time for you to launch it and begin to use it. Follow the steps given below:

- Click Start-> choose All Programs then click MariaDB as shown in Figure 5.15.
- Choose a MariaDB Command Prompt and login as the root user by typing the following command:

`MySQL -u root -p`

Here -u specifies the username and -p specifies the password of the username.

☞ *To connect to MariaDB on a specific host, you use the -h option:*
-u [username] -p[password] -h [hostname]
To connect to a specific database, you need to specify the database name after all the options:
-u [username] -p[password] -h [hostname] database_name

It will prompt for a password by displaying "Enter password:" type the root password and press Enter key.

After entering password you will see a welcome screen (See Figure 5.16) with the following command-line:

`MariaDB [none]>`

In the prompt, [none] means that no default database is selected. This means that, every time a table is named in a statement, the name of the database where it is located must be specifically specified. The USE statement selects a default database, whose name will appear in the prompt.

☞ *The MariaDB client has a prompt that normally appears at the beginning of a new line.*

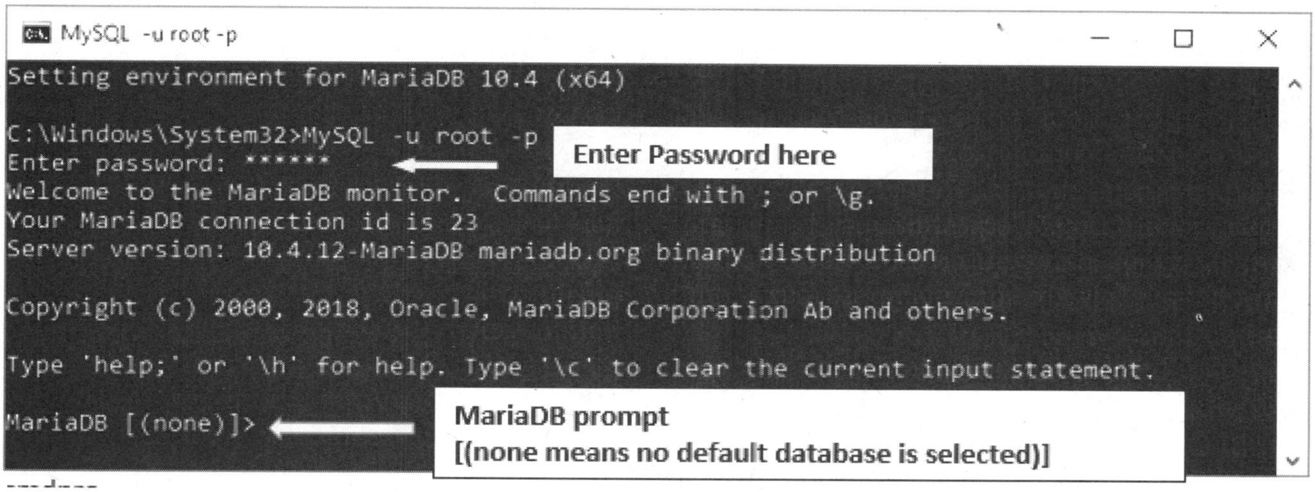

Figure 5.15 Starting MariaDB

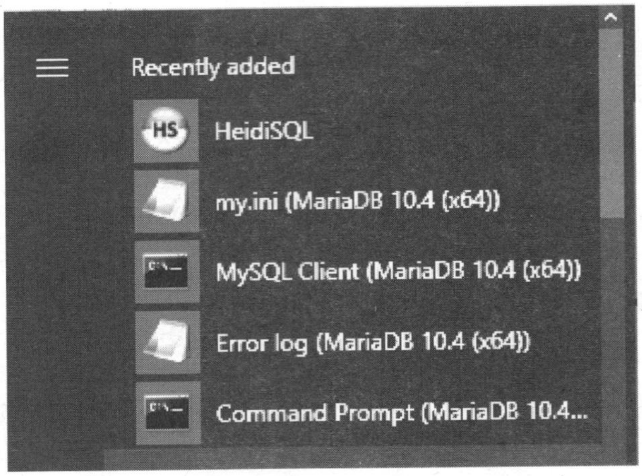

Figure 5.16 MariaDB Client prompt

☞ *You can also log in by selecting* ***MYSQL client(MariaDB 10.4(x64))****. It will ask for the password and MariaDB client has a prompt* ***MariaDB [none]****> will be displayed.*

5.6 SHOW DATABASES

SHOW statement in MariaDB is used to find out what databases currently exist on the server.

To show databases, open MariaDB Command Prompt window. Type the following SQL statement, after the **MariaDB [none]**> prompt window (See Figure 5.17).

```
SHOW DATABASES;
```

This will display the database list exist on the server (See Figure 5.17). The list of databases displayed by the above statement may vary from machine to machine. This statement does not show databases that you have no privileges.

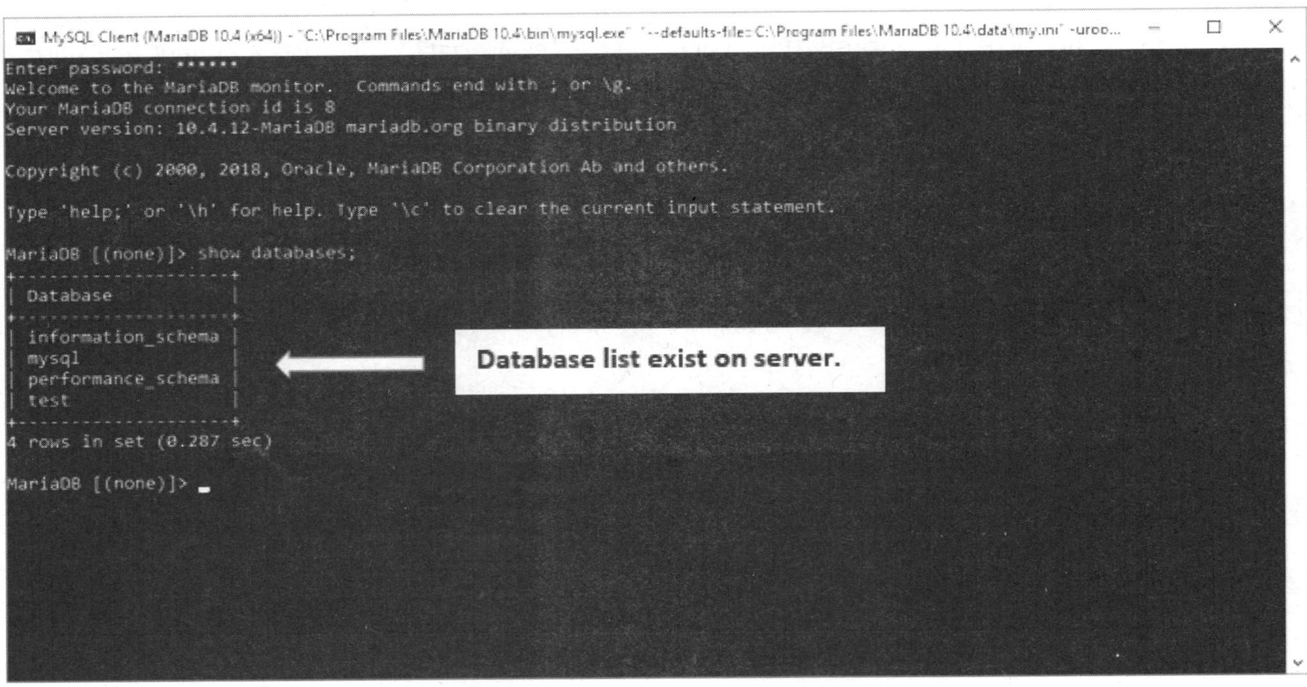

Figure 5.17 Showing Databases

☞ *MariaDB for windows is not case-sensitive, so you can write SQL statement in any case i.e., upper-case or lower-case.*

5.7 HeidiSQL

HeidiSQL is free software, and has the aim to be easy to learn. Invented in 2002 by Ansgar, HeidiSQL belongs to the most popular tools for MariaDB and MySQL worldwide. HeidiSQL is a Windows client for MariaDB and MySQL.

HeidiSQL is a so called client application, only usable when you have some server available. So, make sure you have some MariaDB, MySQL, MS SQL, PostgreSQL server or SQLite database file to connect to.

A simple setup is to have a MariaDB server installed on localhost (equivalent to the special IP address 127.0.0.1). In HeidiSQL's session manager, you click on the "New" button to create a new connection, and most default settings are already set for you, except from the password, which is mostly not an empty one on a newly installed MariaDB server. (See Figure 5.18).

You can organize your stored sessions in folders. To create a folder, click the dropdown arrow on the "New" button, then click "Folder in root folder" or "Folder in selected folder". Once you have a folder, you can create connections in it, or drag existing connections into that folder.

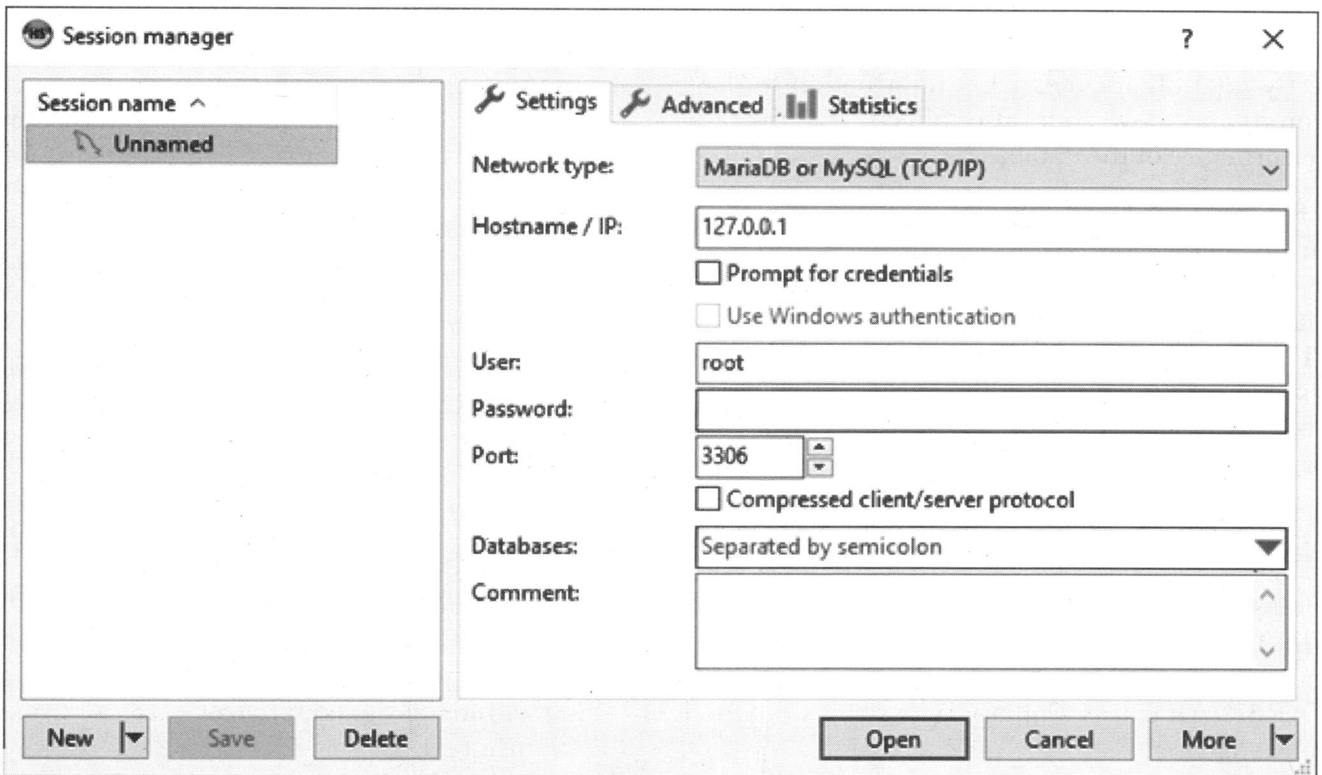

Figure 5.18 Heidi Session manager

5.8 MariaDB DATA TYPES

Every field or column in a table is given a data type when a table is defined. These data types describe the kind of information which can be stored in a column. Each data type has the following properties:

- The value that it can present.
- Its storage size

- The values can be indexed or not.
- How values can be compared.

Since relational-database systems are based on the relationships between pieces of information, various types of data must be clearly distinguished from one another, so that the appropriate processes and comparisons can be applied. In MariaDB, this is done by assigning each field a data type that indicates the kind of values the field will contain. There are three standard ANSI SQL data types which is true for almost every database software:

(a) String
(b) Numbers
(c) Date and Time

Within each of these, there are a number of variants–some of which are MariaDB specific–you can use. Choosing your column types correctly not only dictates what information can be stored and how, but also affects the overall performance of the database.

5.8.1 String Data Types

String literals are character sequences enclosed by quotes. The string type values supported by MariaDB are as follows:

CHAR: A fixed-length field from 0 to 255 characters long right-padded with spaces to the specified length when stored. Values must be enclosed in single quotes or double quotes. Its default value is 1.

VARCHAR: A variable-length field from 0 to 65535 characters long. Values must be enclosed in single quotes or double quotes.

BINARY: It is a binary byte strings, with maximum size of 255 characters.

VARBINARY: It is a binary byte strings of variable length.

TINYBLOB: It is a blob column with a maximum length of 255 bytes. In storage, each uses a one-byte length prefix indicating the byte quantity in the value.

BLOB: It is a blob column with a maximum length of 65,535 bytes. In storage, each uses a two-byte length prefix indicating the byte quantity in the value.

MEDIUMBLOB: It is a blob column with a maximum length of 16,777,215 bytes. In storage, each uses a three-byte length prefix indicating the byte quantity in the value.

LONGBLOB: It is a blob column with a maximum length of 4,294,967,295 bytes. In storage, each uses a four-byte length prefix indicating the byte quantity in the value.

TINYTEXT: A text column with a maximum length of 255 characters. In storage, each uses a one-byte length prefix indicating the byte quantity in the value.

TEXT: A text column with a maximum length of 65,535 characters. In storage, each uses a two-byte length prefix indicating the byte quantity in the value.

MEDIUMTEXT: It is a text column with a maximum length of 16,777,215 characters. In storage, each uses a three-byte length prefix indicating the byte quantity in the value.

LONGTEXT: It is a text column with a maximum length of 4,294,967,295 or 4GB characters. In storage, each uses a four-byte length prefix indicating the byte quantity in the value.

ENUM: Short for enumeration, which means that each column can have one of several possible values.

SET: Like ENUM except that each column can have more than one of several possible values. SET values present internally as integer values.

5.8.2 Numeric Data Types

The numeric data types supported by MariaDB are as follows:

TINYINT: It explains about the small integers falling within the signed range of –128 to 127 or 0 to 255 unsigned.

BOOLEAN: This data type associates a value 0 with 'false', and a value 1 with 'true'.

SMALLINT: This data type represents integers within range of –32,768 to 32,767 or 0 to 65535 unsigned.

MEDIUMINT: This data type represents integers in the signed range of –8,388,608 to 8,388,607 or 0 to 16,777,215 unsigned.

INT(also INTEGER): It explains about an integer of normal size in the range of –2,147,483,648 to 2,147,483,647 or 0 to 4,294,967,295 unsigned.

BIGINT: This data type represents integers within the range of –9,223,372,036,854,775,808 to 9,223,372,036,854,775,807 or 0 to 18,446,744,073,709,551,615 unsigned.

DECIMAL(also called DEC, NUMERIC, FIXED): This data type represents precise fixed-point numbers. Decimals are stored using a binary format, with the integer and the fraction stored separately.

FLOAT: This data type represents a small number with a floating decimal point.

DOUBLE (also called REAL and DOUBLE PRECISION): This data type represents a large number with a floating decimal point.

BIT: A bit is Boolean data type. Very small integer value that is equivalent to TINYINT(1).

5.8.3 Date and Time Data Types

The date and time data types supported by MariaDB are as follows:

DATE: It explains about a date range in the format of YYYY-MM-DD.

TIME: It explains about a time range in the format of HH:MM:SS.

DATETIME: This data type represents in the format of YYYY-MM-DD HH:MM:SS.

TIMESTAMP: It explains about a timestamp in the format of YYYYMMDDHHMMSS.

YEAR: It explains about a year in 2 or 4-digit format. The default is 4-digit format. The four-digit format allows values in the range of 1901 to 2155, and 0000.

5.8.4 How to Choose the right Data Type in MariaDB?

MariaDB Relational Database Management System (RDBMS) supports a wide range of data types. The data type that we choose for our table is important because it determines how MariaDB will store our data. It is possible that any one of multiple data types could be used to store a piece of data, but which one is the best or optimal data type to use?

For example, if an integer column is used for values in the range from 1 to 99999, **MEDIUMINT UNSIGNED** is the best type.

Because MariaDB supports various data types in several categories: numeric types, date and time types, and string (character) types, therefore, while creating tables it is best practice to understand which type of data each column will be storing and choose the appropriate data type.

5.8.5 Example of Incorrect Data Type Usage

The **TEXT** and **VARCHAR** data type are designed to store string types and has a maximum length of 65,535 bytes. Therefore it is intended for storing relatively large strings. The storage required for **TEXT** columns is the length of the data plus 2 bytes, whereas the **VARCHAR** columns require the length of the data plus one byte.

To store numbers, we could use **TEXT** or **VARCHAR** data types. However, it is much better to store the number in one of MariaDB's numeric data types.

☞ *Storing a number using the optimal data type means that it uses less storage space and our table can be searched faster.*

5.8.6 Examples and Best Practices

Numbers

Numbers should usually be stored using one of MariaDB's numeric data types such as **TINYINT**, **SMALLINT**, **MEDIUMINT**, **INT**, and **DECIMAL**. The first four numeric data types are used to store integers including negative numbers with varying minimum and maximum values. For example, **TINYINT** columns can store integers ranging from -128 to 127 and **INT** can store integers ranging from -2147483648 to 2147483647. The storage requirement for **TINYINT** columns is 1 byte and for **INT** columns it is 4 bytes. Therefore, if we know that a column will hold integers ranging from 1 to 99, we should use the **TINYINT** data type because it requires less storage.

We can also extend the numeric range of these numeric data types by giving them the *UNSIGNED* attribute. This means that negative values are not permitted and allows **TINYINT** columns to store integers ranging from 0 to 255 and **INT** columns to store integers ranging from 0 to 4294967295. This means that we can use a data type with a smaller storage requirement for a larger number of negative values are not needed.

If we want to store monetary values, we could store these values as strings i.e., **VARCHAR**, but the optimal data type is **DECIMAL**. This numeric data type is used to store exact numeric data values with a decimal point. When declaring a **DECIMAL** column, the precision and scale are specified. For example,

DECIMAL(5,2)

where **5** is the precision (the number of significant digits that are stored for values) and **2** is the scale (the number of digits that can be stored following the decimal point).

☞ *Decimals are stored using a binary format, with the integer and the fraction stored separately.*

Strings

Strings can also be stored using a number of different data types. The main types that we will come across are **CHAR**, **VARCHAR** and **TEXT**. **TEXT** and **VARCHAR** data types are used to store large strings (65,535 bytes) so we would usually use this to store larger amounts of text. **CHAR** data type is used to store short strings and can hold between 0 and 255 bytes.

(a) **CHAR**: The length of a **CHAR** column is fixed to the length that we declare while creating the table. So, if we define a column as **CHAR(255)** even if we only insert a few characters, the storage requirement will be 255 bytes. Because **CHAR** columns are fixed-length, MariaDB can search **CHAR** columns faster than variable-length columns.

(b) **VARCHAR**: **VARCHAR** column values are variable-length strings. **VARCHAR** values are stored as a one-byte length prefix plus data. For example, if we define a column as **VARCHAR(255)** and insert only 5 characters the storage requirement will only be 6 bytes. Therefore if the strings will be of variable length, the VARCHAR data type will require less storage.

☞ *If table will contain only **fixed-length** columns then use **CHAR** to take advantage of MariaDB's faster searching. But, if any columns will be **variable length** then use **VARCHAR** for its smaller storage requirement.*

ENUM

ENUM columns provide an efficient way to define columns that can contain only a given set of values. For example, if a column will contain 'var 1', 'var 2' or 'var 3', we should use the **ENUM** data type.

Another example of using **ENUM** data type is, suppose if we want to set a switch to specify whether a user account is active or disabled. Instead of storing 'active' or 'disabled' as **VARCHAR** values, we can use **ENUM** data type.

Date

We could store a date as a text string, but MariaDB has more optimal ways of storing dates. **DATETIME** data type is used to store dates in MariaDB. This is designed specifically to store both the date and time as 2019-10-11 15:00:00.

Dates stored using **DATETIME** data type are human-readable straight out of the database and MariaDB has a whole host of built-in functions to work with **DATETIME** formats. We can add and subtract dates, calculate the difference between dates, output the date in preferred format and much more using MariaDB alone.

You can also use **DATE** data type represents a date in YYYY-MM-DD date format or **YEAR** data type represents a year in 2 or 4-digit format.

☞ *MariaDB can also store the year alone, the date alone and a number of related types.*

In MariaDB, although data can often be stored in various data type columns, there is usually one data type that is optimal for our data. Using that optimal data type will bring benefits in terms of storage and possibly speed.

5.9 CREATING DATABASE

Creating database is easy; just type the name of database in a **CREATE DATABASE** statement. The syntax for creating a new database is given below:

```
CREATE DATABASE databasename;
```

☞ *CREATE command is also used for creating tables.*

Let us create database named **COLLEGE**. Type the following SQL statement, after the **MariaDB [none]**> prompt, as shown in Figure 5.19).

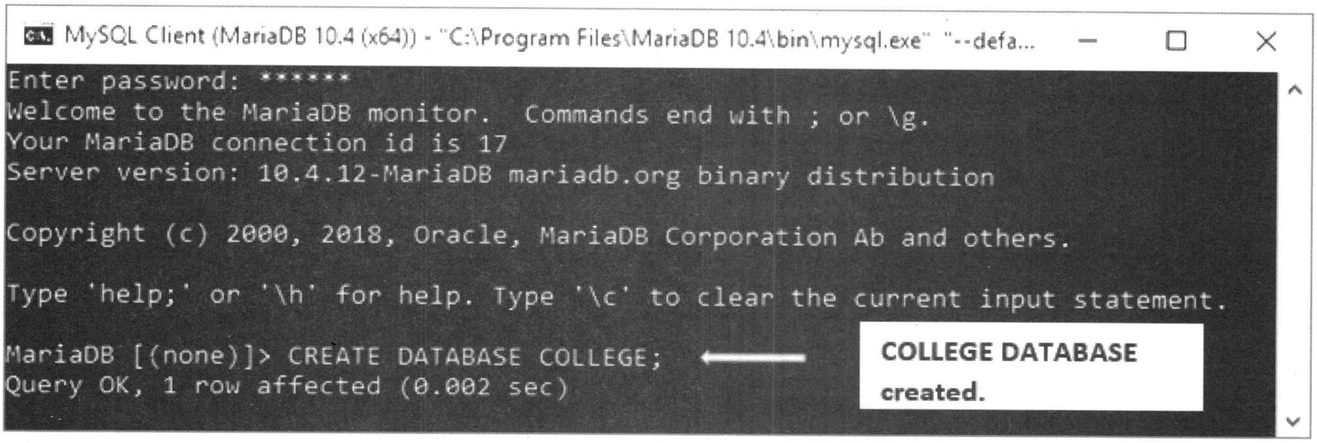

Figure 5.19 College database created

This will create an empty database means it would not contain any tables. To see whether the database is created or not, you can use the **SHOW** command at **MariaDB** prompt.

5.10 ACCESSING OR SELECTING DATABASE

Creating a database does not select it for use. Therefore, before start working with tables (i.e., creating or making queries) open the database for use. For example, to make **COLLEGE** the current database, type the following command:

```
USE COLLEGE;
```

Your database needs to be created only once, but you must select it for use each time you begin a MariaDB session. You can do this by issuing a **USE** statement as shown in Figure 5.19.

☞ *You can see at any time which database is currently selected using **SELECT DATABASE()**.*

5.11 CREATING TABLES

In order to learn MariaDB commands, we will create two tables, STUDENT and SUBJECT in database COLLEGE with structures as given in Table 5.1 and 5.2, respectively.

Table 5.1 The STUDENT table structure

Column Name	Type	Description
STU_ID	INT	Unique code assigned to each student [NOT NULL and PRIMARY KEY]
NAME	VARCHAR(30)	Name of the student with maximum size of 30 characters [NOT NULL]
SUB_CODE	VARCHAR(4)	Code of the subject i.e., course opted by the student [NOT NULL]

FEE	FLOAT	Fee charged for the course
GENDER	CHAR	Gender of the student
DOA	DATE	Date of admission

Table 5.2 The SUBJECT table structure

Column Name	Type	Description
SUB_CODE	INT(2)	Unique code assigned to each department
DEPT_NAME	VARCHAR(4)	Code of the subject i.e., course opted by the student [NOT NULL]
COURSE	VARCHAR(10)	Course taken by the student

To create tables in 5.2 and 5.3, type the following SQL statement, after the MariaDB [COLLEGE]> prompt, in the MariaDB window.

```
MariaDB [COLLEGE]> CREATE TABLE STUDENT
     -> (STU_ID INT NOT NULL,
     -> NAME VARCHAR(30) NOT NULL,
     -> SUB_CODE VARCHAR(4) NOT NULL,
     -> FEE FLOAT,
     -> GENDER CHAR,
     -> DOA DATE,
     -> PRIMARY KEY(STU_ID));
```

This will create STUDENT table as shown in Figure 5.20.

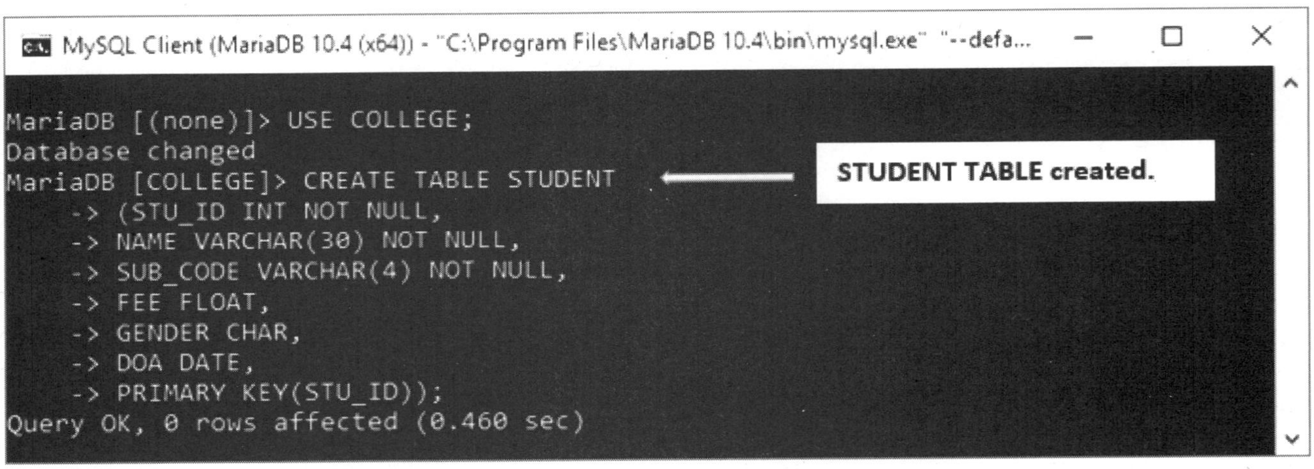

Figure 5.20 Creating table STUDENT

☞ *If table STUDENT already exists in database COLLEGE, then the error message "Table STUDENT already exists" is displayed.*

Similarly, create the SUBJECT table using the following SQL statements (See Figure 5.21).

```
MariaDB [COLLEGE]> CREATE TABLE SUBJECT
     -> (SUB_CODE VARCHAR(4) NOT NULL,
     -> COURSE VARCHAR(10));
```

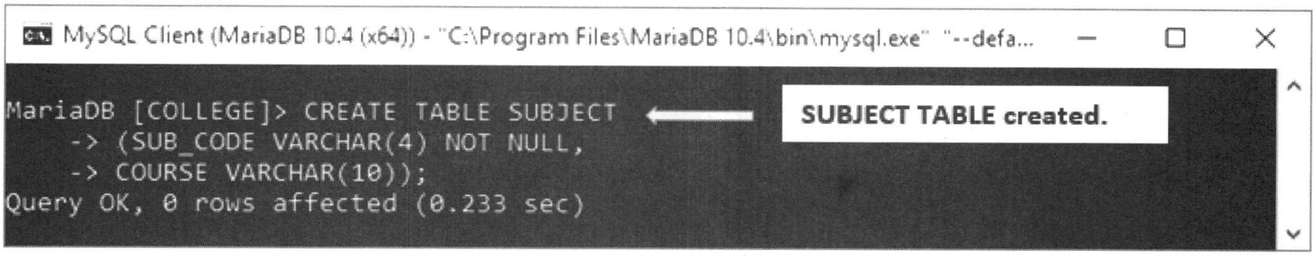

Figure 5.21 Creating table SUBJECT

The NULL is a special value in MariaDB. The NULL indicates that a value is missing or not applicable. NOT NULL constraint prevents a column from accepting null value. If you try to insert a null value in such a column, it will be rejected.

A primary key is a column or group of columns whose values uniquely identify every row in the table. The primary key constraint allows you to define the primary key for a table during table creation.

5.11.1 Describe Table Structure

The **DESCRIBE** statement can be used to see the structure of a table as indicated in the **CREATE** Statement. It displays the Column names, their data types, whether Column contain data, whether the Column is a Primary key etc. Syntax for describing table structure is given as under:

`DESCRIBE <table name>;`

OR

`DESC <table name>;`

For example to see structure of STUDENT and SUBJECT table type the following commands:

`MariaDB [COLLEGE]> DESCRIBE STUDENT;`

`MariaDB [COLLEGE]> DESCRIBE SUBJECT;`

Output is displayed in Figure 5.22 and 5.23 respectively.

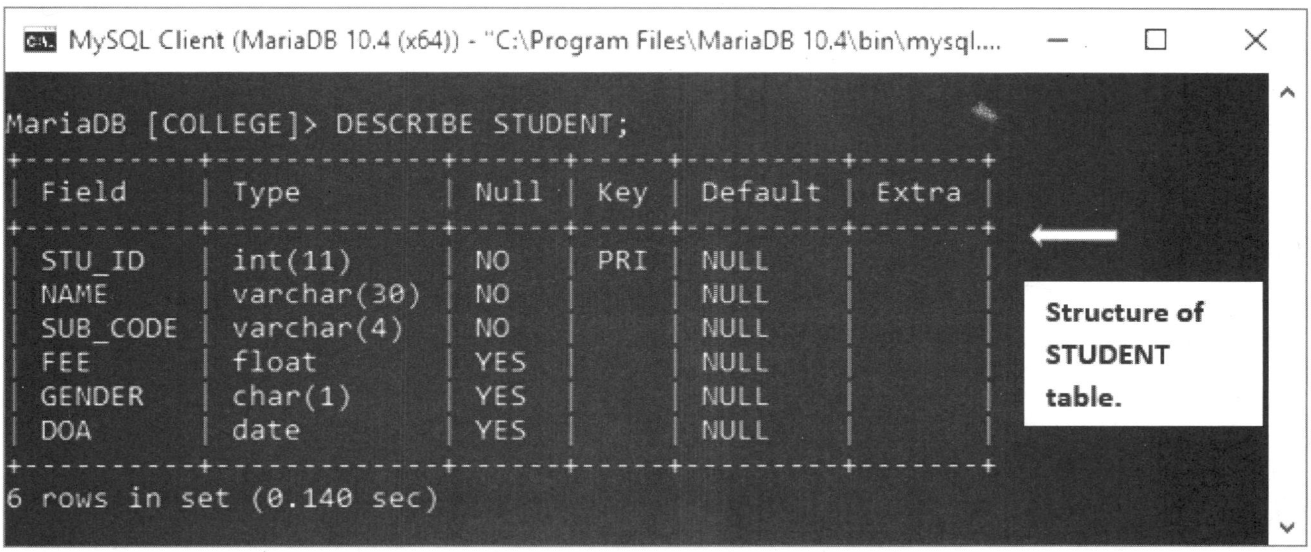

Figure 5.22 Structure of STUDENT table

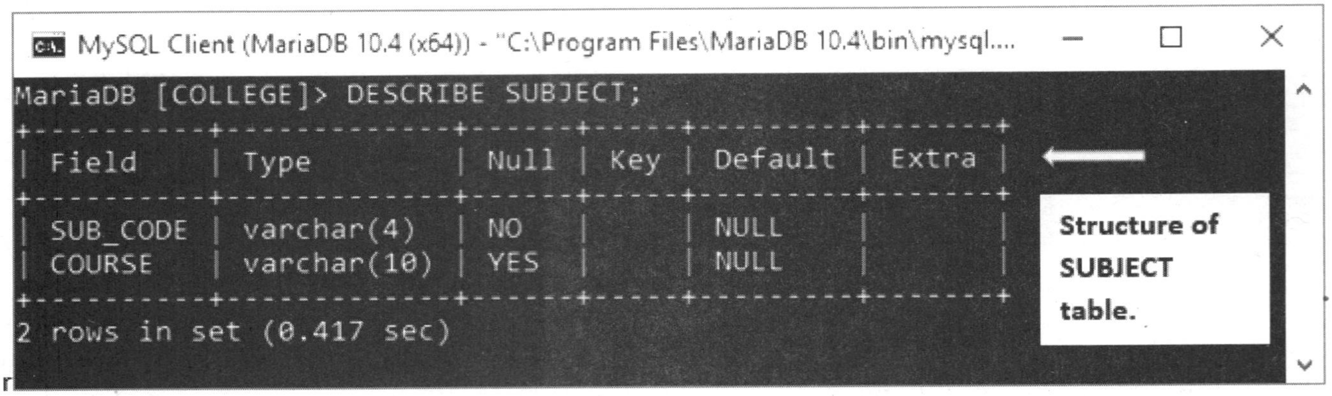

Figure 5.23 Structure of SUBJECT table

5.12 INSERT OPERATION

After creating the tables, namely STUDENT and SUBJECT, we shall insert data into the fields in these tables, using the SQL command *INSERT INTO*.

The inserted values into the tables STUDENT and SUBJECT are shown in Figure 5.24 and 5.25 respectively.

☞ *MariaDB insert statement is used to insert a row into a table.*

```
MariaDB [COLLEGE]> INSERT INTO STUDENT VALUES
    -> (1,'Meena','E1',15000,'F','2017-07-02'),
    -> (2,'Teena','E2',10000,'F','2017-07-01'),
    -> (3,'Reena','E1',15000,'F','2017-07-02'),
    -> (4,'Pankaj','E3',12000,'M','2017-07-07'),
    -> (5,'Tanya','E2',10000,'F','2017-07-01'),
    -> (6,'James','E1',15000,'M','2017-07-08'),
    -> (7,'Jaspreet','E2',10000,'F','2017-07-01');
MariaDB [COLLEGE]> INSERT INTO SUBJECT VALUES
    -> ('E1','B.TECH'),
    -> ('E2','BCA'),
    -> ('E3','B.SC');
```

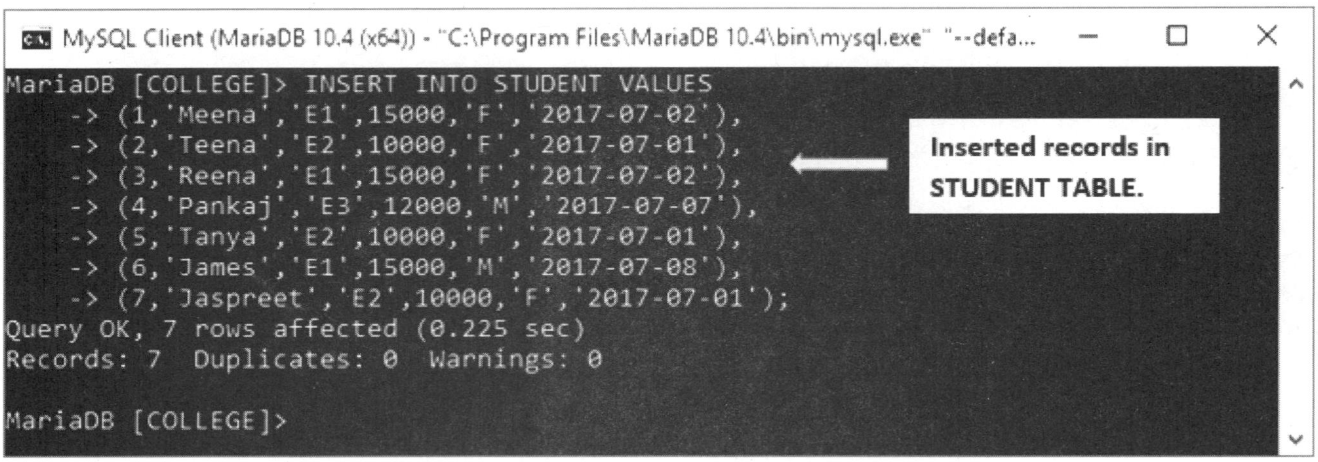

Figure 5.24 Inserting values into the STUDENT table

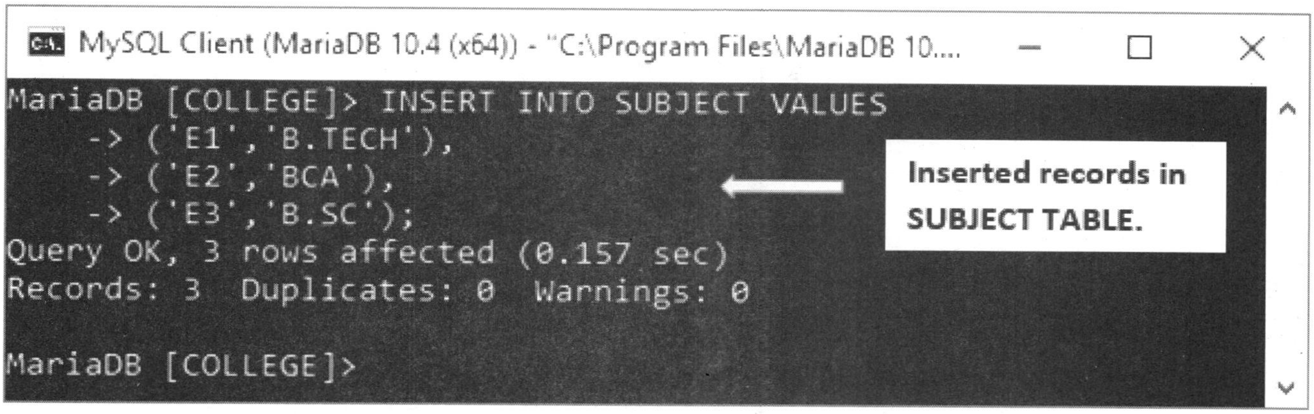

Figure 5.25 Inserting values into the SUBJECT table

5.13 SQL SELECT STATEMENT

The MariaDB SELECT statement retrieves data from one or more tables. The command also enables you to query a data item. This means that by executing SELECT statement, information currently available in table will be shown on the screen.

The syntax for *SELECT* command is:

`SELECT <columnname(s)> FROM <tablename>;`

The **`Select`** clause is followed by the column list. The **`From`** clause specifies the table from which such columns are to be extracted.

☞ *In MariaDB, the FROM clause is optional. It is convenient if you want to call a function or evaluate an expression.*

5.13.1 Selecting All the Columns

To select all the columns in a table, an asterisk (*) is used in place of the column list. For example, suppose you want to retrieve all the data stored in STUDENT table, then type the following statement, after MariaDB prompt:

`MariaDB [COLLEGE]> SELECT * FROM STUDENT;`

Similarly, to see all columns of SUBJECT table type the following statement after MariaDB prompt:

`MariaDB [COLLEGE]> SELECT * FROM SUBJECT;`

☞ *The asterisk (*) means "All". SELECT * means display all columns.*

On execution of above commands, you will see the details of all students available in the STUDENT table and SUBJECT table. In our case, the result will be as shown in Figure 5.26.

☞ *SELECT is the single most powerful query command in SQL. Many queries can be performed on tables using SELECT command.*

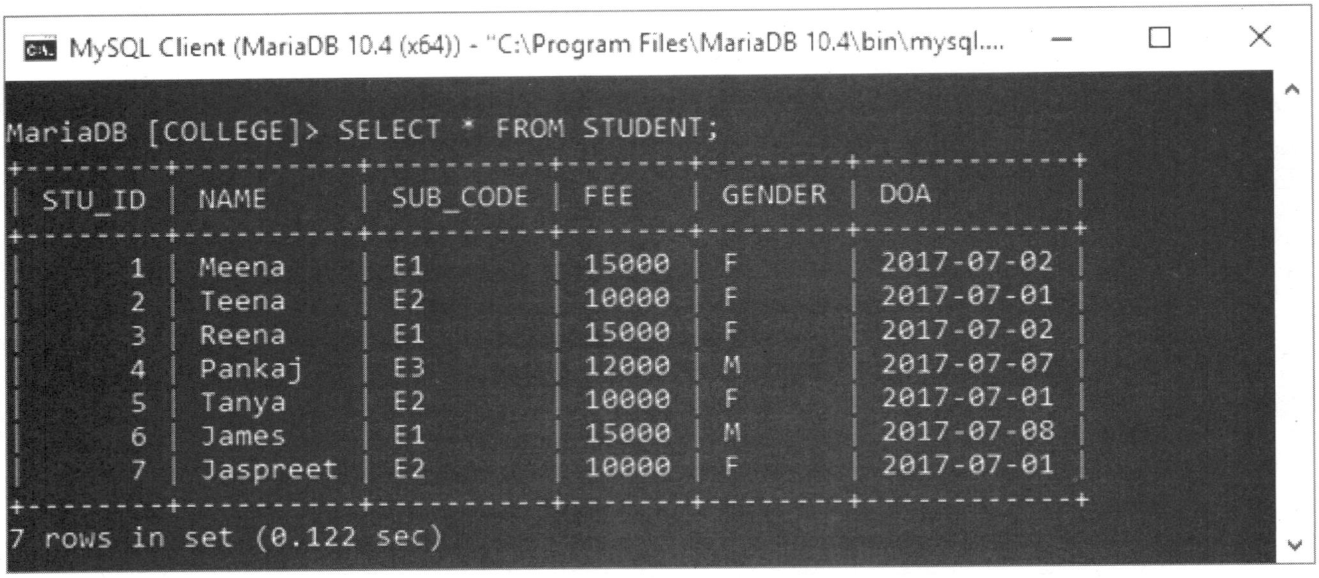

```
MySQL Client (MariaDB 10.4 (x64)) - "C:\Program Files\MariaDB 10.4\bin\mysql....

MariaDB [COLLEGE]> SELECT * FROM STUDENT;
+--------+----------+----------+-------+--------+------------+
| STU_ID | NAME     | SUB_CODE | FEE   | GENDER | DOA        |
+--------+----------+----------+-------+--------+------------+
|      1 | Meena    | E1       | 15000 | F      | 2017-07-02 |
|      2 | Teena    | E2       | 10000 | F      | 2017-07-01 |
|      3 | Reena    | E1       | 15000 | F      | 2017-07-02 |
|      4 | Pankaj   | E3       | 12000 | M      | 2017-07-07 |
|      5 | Tanya    | E2       | 10000 | F      | 2017-07-01 |
|      6 | James    | E1       | 15000 | M      | 2017-07-08 |
|      7 | Jaspreet | E2       | 10000 | F      | 2017-07-01 |
+--------+----------+----------+-------+--------+------------+
7 rows in set (0.122 sec)
```

Figure 5.26 Selecting all the data in all the columns from STUDENT table

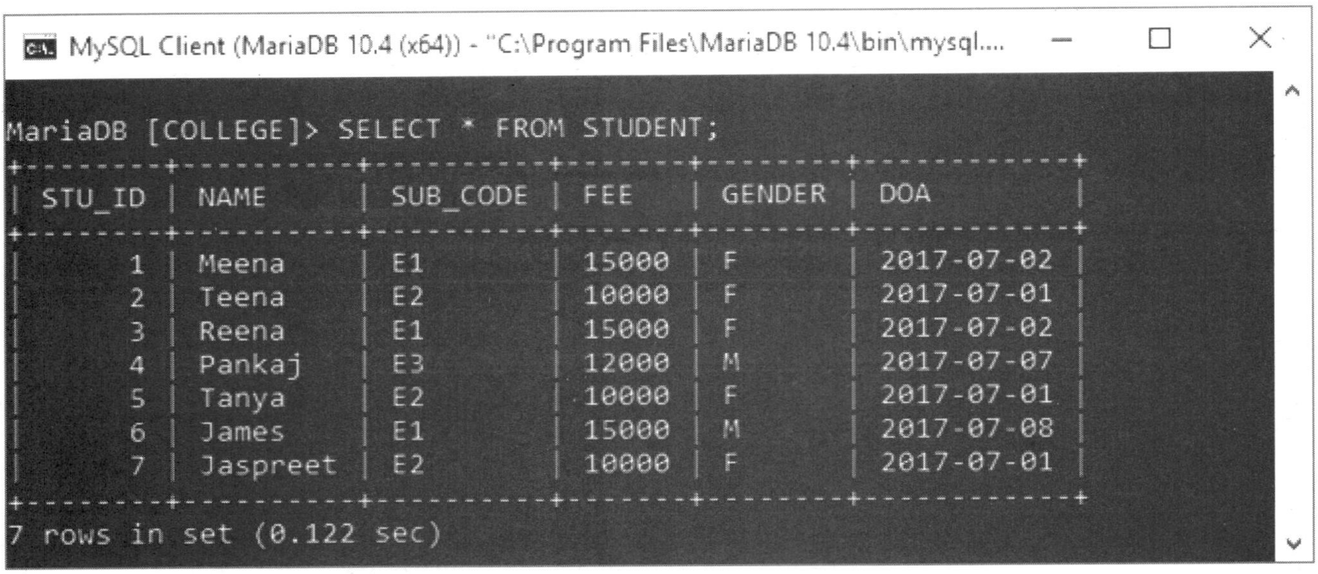

```
MySQL Client (MariaDB 10.4 (x64)) - "C:\Program Files\MariaDB 10.4\bin\mysql....

MariaDB [COLLEGE]> SELECT * FROM STUDENT;
+--------+----------+----------+-------+--------+------------+
| STU_ID | NAME     | SUB_CODE | FEE   | GENDER | DOA        |
+--------+----------+----------+-------+--------+------------+
|      1 | Meena    | E1       | 15000 | F      | 2017-07-02 |
|      2 | Teena    | E2       | 10000 | F      | 2017-07-01 |
|      3 | Reena    | E1       | 15000 | F      | 2017-07-02 |
|      4 | Pankaj   | E3       | 12000 | M      | 2017-07-07 |
|      5 | Tanya    | E2       | 10000 | F      | 2017-07-01 |
|      6 | James    | E1       | 15000 | M      | 2017-07-08 |
|      7 | Jaspreet | E2       | 10000 | F      | 2017-07-01 |
+--------+----------+----------+-------+--------+------------+
7 rows in set (0.122 sec)
```

Figure 5.27 Selecting all the data in all the columns from SUBJECT table

5.13.2 Selecting Specific Columns

Suppose you want to display STU_ID, NAME, and DOA of all students from the STUDENT table. Then, type the following statement:

```
MariaDB [COLLEGE]> SELECT STU_ID, NAME, DOA FROM STUDENT;
```

The records displayed on the monitor are shown in Figure 5.28.

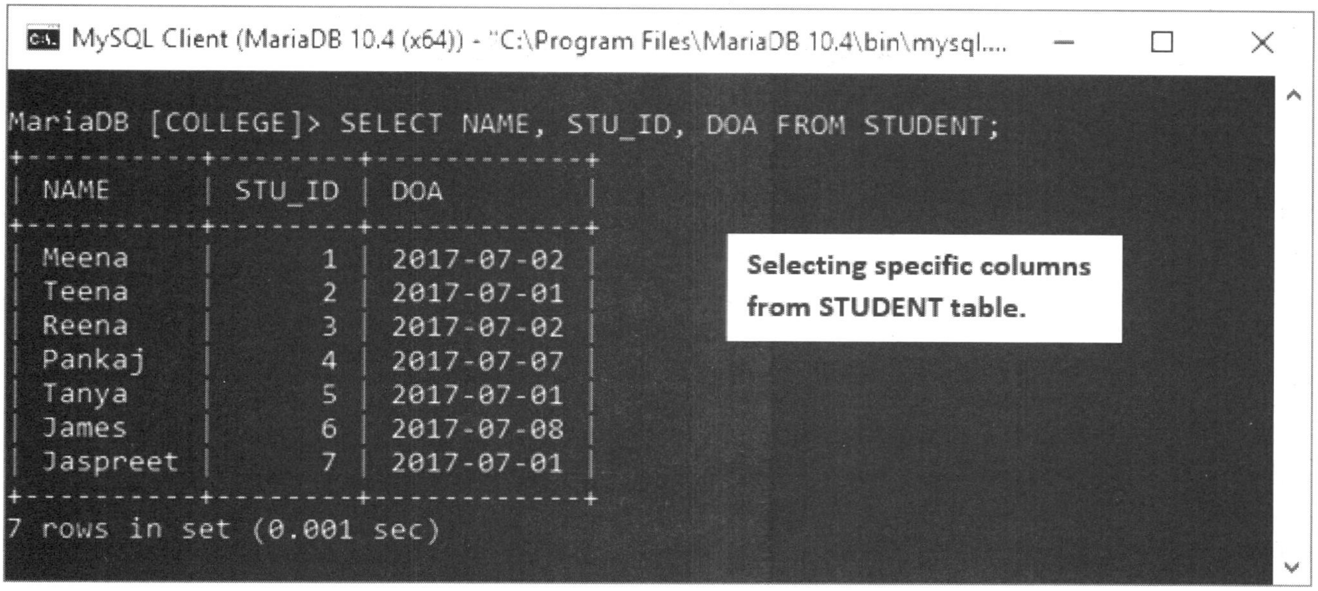

Figure 5.28 Selecting specific column

5.13.3 Changing the Order or Display of Columns

We can display columns in any order by specifying the columns in that order in **SELECT** statement. The following statement displays student names first and then student IDs from the STUDENT table.

```
MariaDB [COLLEGE]> SELECT NAME, STU_ID, DOA FROM STUDENT;
```

In the Figure 5.29, notice that the first column displaying student names and the second column displaying student IDs.

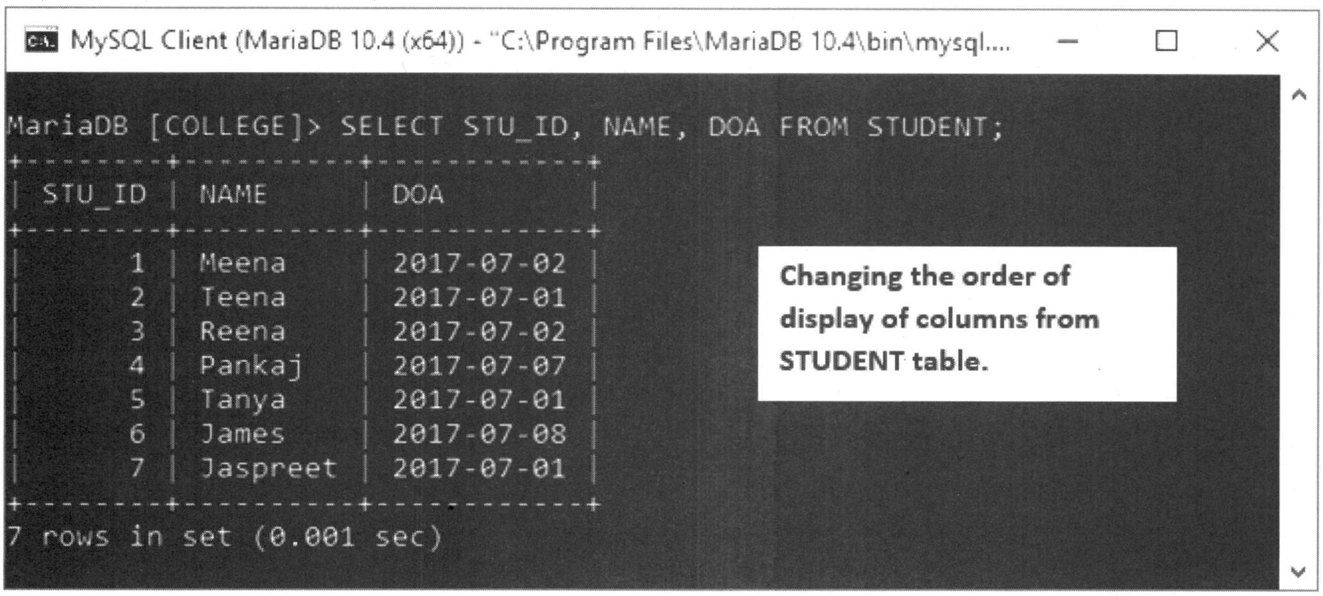

Figure 5.29 Changing order of display columns

5.14 ALTER TABLE COMMAND

We can change the definition of a table even after creating it. For this, ALTER TABLE command is used. This command can be used to add columns to the table, change their sizes, change their data-types or add or delete constraints. The syntax for ALTER TABLE command is as mentioned below:

```
ALTER TABLE <table name> [Options];
```

5.14.1 ADD Option

ADD keyword is used to add columns or constraints to the table. For example, the following statement will add a new column ADDRESS to the STUDENT table. The ADDRESS column will store the addresses of the students. (See Figure 5.30)

```
MariaDB [COLLEGE]> ALTER TABLE STUDENT
ADD ADDRESS VARCHAR(40);
MariaDB [COLLEGE]> DESCRIBE STUDENT;
```

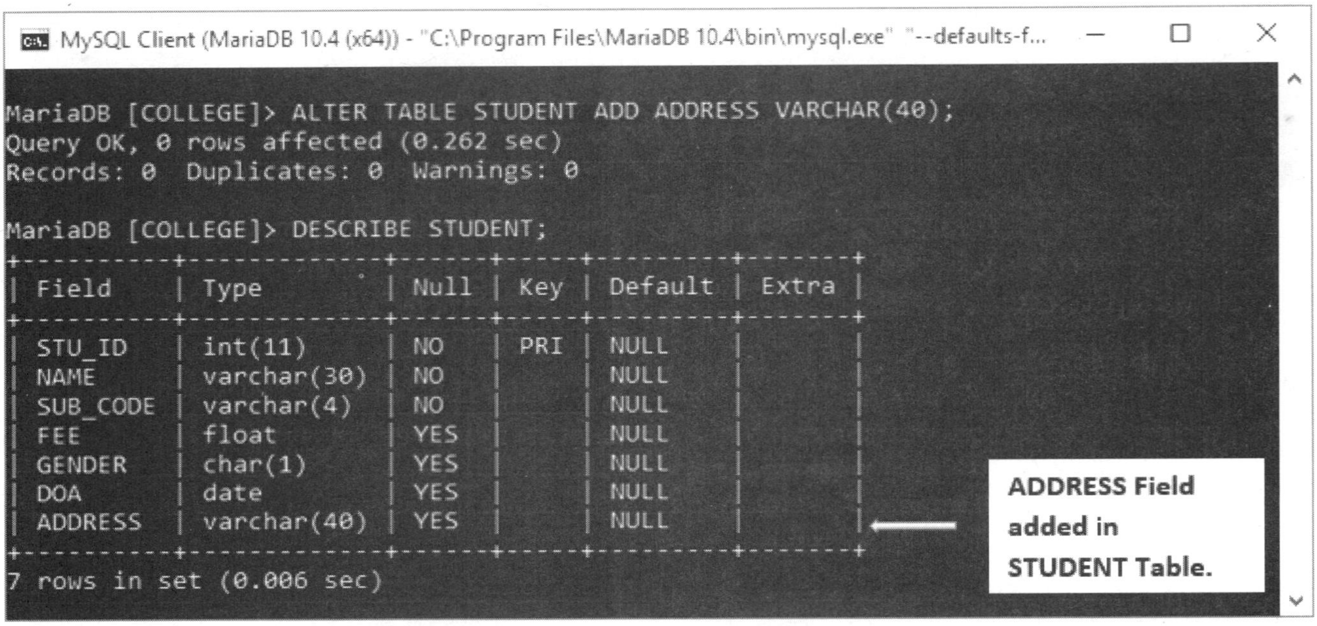

Figure 5.30 Alter table to add address column

The following statement will add CHECK constraint for FEE of STUDENT table (condition will be FEE should be greater than equal to 10000). (See Figure 5.31).

```
MariaDB [COLLEGE]> ALTER TABLE STUDENT
    -> ADD CONSTRAINT CHK_FEE CHECK
    -> (FEE>=10000);
```

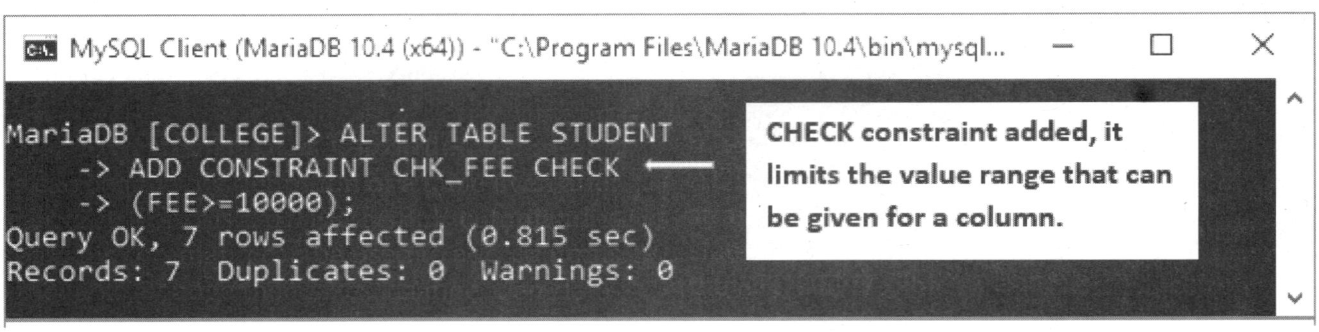

Figure 5.31 Alter table to add CHECK constraint for FEE column

5.14.2 MODIFY Option

Modify option can change the data type, column width and constraints of an existing column. For example to change the column width of NAME of STUDENT table, we can use the following statement. (See Figure 5.32).

```
MariaDB [COLLEGE]> ALTER TABLE STUDENT
    -> MODIFY NAME VARCHAR(40);
MariaDB [COLLEGE]> DESCRIBE STUDENT;
```

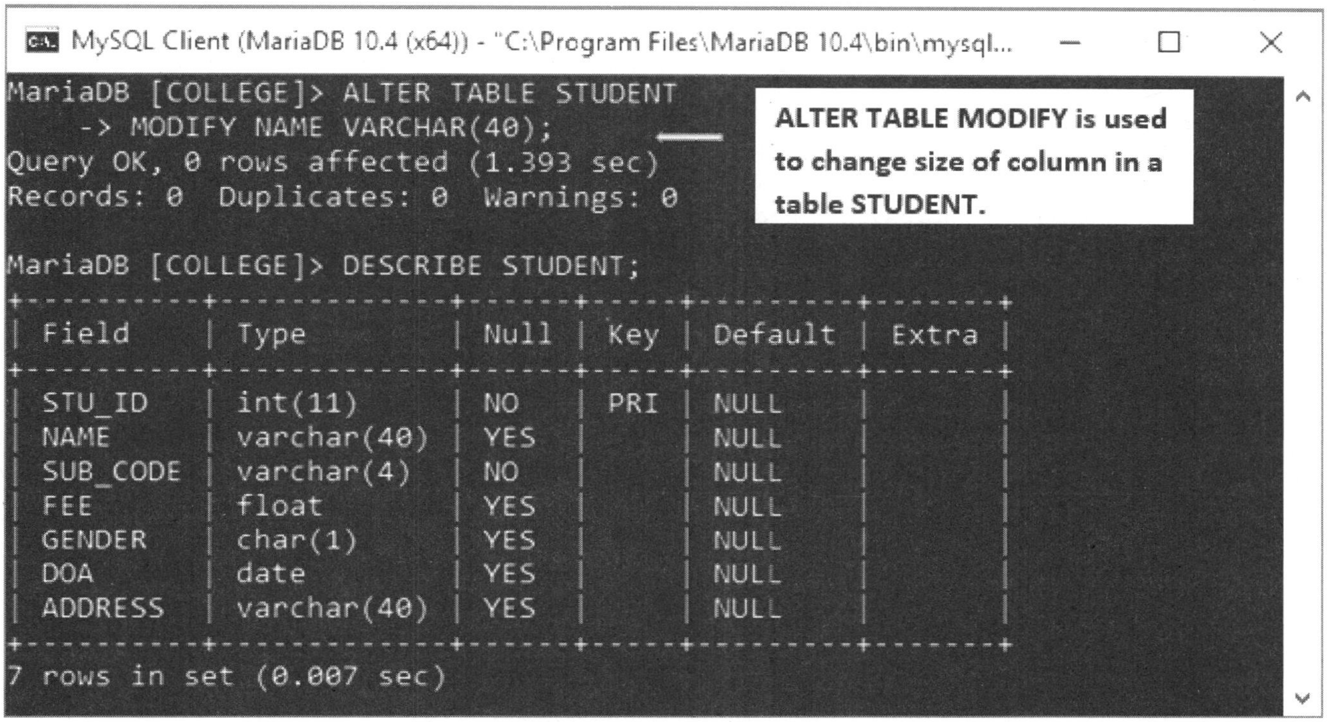

Figure 5.32 Alter table Modify option to change column width of NAME column

5.14.3 Drop Option

To remove the constraints imposed on the table, drop option can be used. For example, the following statement will remove the constraint CHK_FEE. (See Figure 5.33.

```
MariaDB [COLLEGE]> ALTER TABLE STUDENT
    -> DROP CONSTRAINT CHK_FEE;
MariaDB [COLLEGE]> ALTER TABLE STUDENT
    -> DROP ADDRESS;
MariaDB [COLLEGE]> DESCRIBE STUDENT;
```

5.15 UPDATE

UPDATE is the command that changes or modifies data values in a table.

The syntax for this is:

```
UPDATE <tablename>
SET <column name = new value>
[WHERE <condition>];
```

For example, suppose college has raised a fee of Rupees 200 for all students with SUB_CODE 'E2' i.e., course 'BCA', then this command will be as follows:

```
MariaDB [COLLEGE]> UPDATE STUDENT
    -> SET FEE = FEE + 200
    -> WHERE SUB_CODE = 'E2';
```

Now using SELECT statement, we can check whether the table STUDENT is changed or not.

```
MariaDB [COLLEGE]> SELECT * FROM STUDENT
WHERE SUB_CODE ='E1';
```

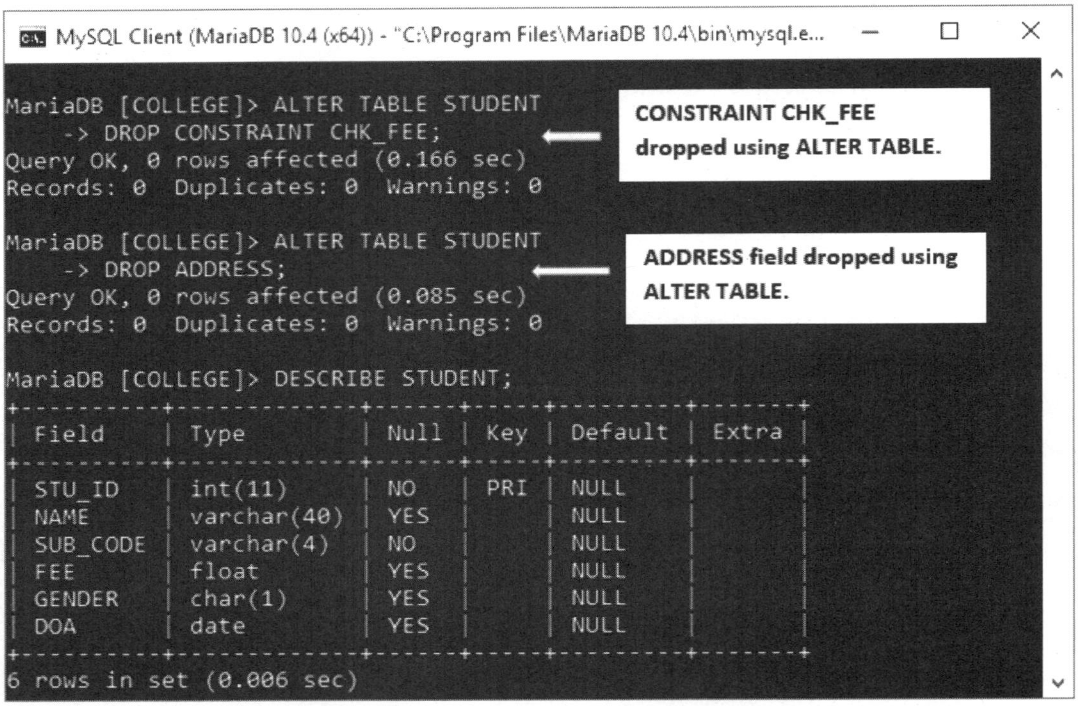


```
MariaDB [COLLEGE]> ALTER TABLE STUDENT
    -> DROP CONSTRAINT CHK_FEE;
Query OK, 0 rows affected (0.166 sec)
Records: 0  Duplicates: 0  Warnings: 0

MariaDB [COLLEGE]> ALTER TABLE STUDENT
    -> DROP ADDRESS;
Query OK, 0 rows affected (0.085 sec)
Records: 0  Duplicates: 0  Warnings: 0

MariaDB [COLLEGE]> DESCRIBE STUDENT;
+----------+-------------+------+-----+---------+-------+
| Field    | Type        | Null | Key | Default | Extra |
+----------+-------------+------+-----+---------+-------+
| STU_ID   | int(11)     | NO   | PRI | NULL    |       |
| NAME     | varchar(40) | YES  |     | NULL    |       |
| SUB_CODE | varchar(4)  | NO   |     | NULL    |       |
| FEE      | float       | YES  |     | NULL    |       |
| GENDER   | char(1)     | YES  |     | NULL    |       |
| DOA      | date        | YES  |     | NULL    |       |
+----------+-------------+------+-----+---------+-------+
6 rows in set (0.006 sec)
```

Figure 5.33 Alter table to drop CHECK constraint and column ADDRESS

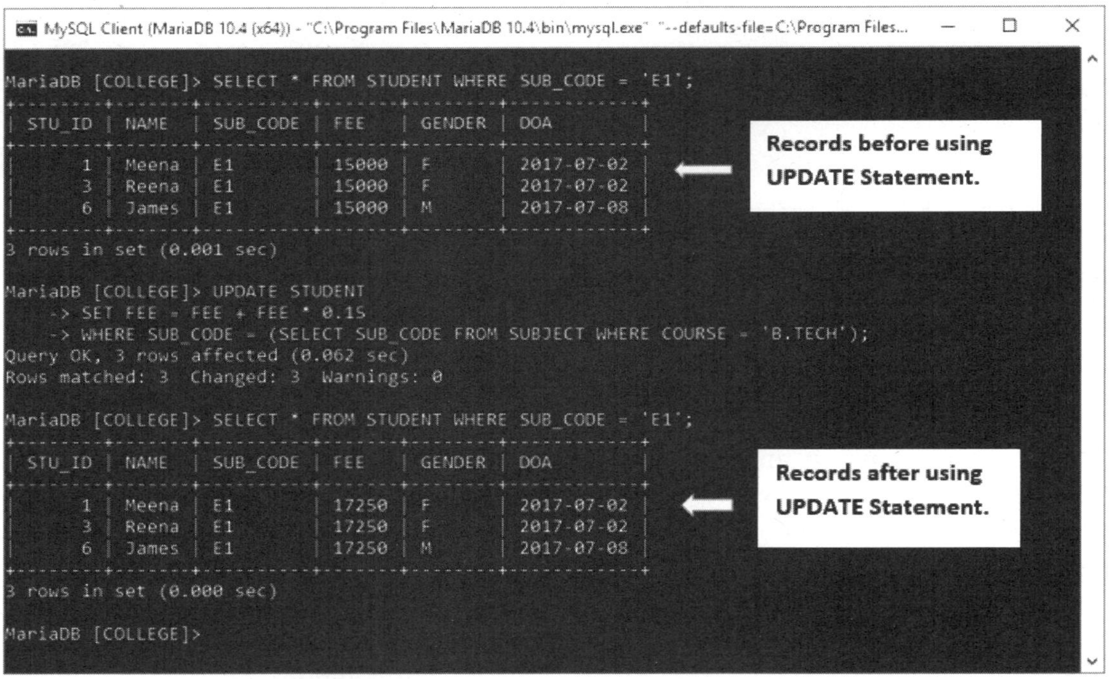


```
MariaDB [COLLEGE]> SELECT * FROM STUDENT WHERE SUB_CODE = 'E1';
+--------+-------+----------+-------+--------+------------+
| STU_ID | NAME  | SUB_CODE | FEE   | GENDER | DOA        |
+--------+-------+----------+-------+--------+------------+
|      1 | Meena | E1       | 15000 | F      | 2017-07-02 |
|      3 | Reena | E1       | 15000 | F      | 2017-07-02 |
|      6 | James | E1       | 15000 | M      | 2017-07-08 |
+--------+-------+----------+-------+--------+------------+
3 rows in set (0.001 sec)

MariaDB [COLLEGE]> UPDATE STUDENT
    -> SET FEE = FEE + FEE * 0.15
    -> WHERE SUB_CODE = (SELECT SUB_CODE FROM SUBJECT WHERE COURSE = 'B.TECH');
Query OK, 3 rows affected (0.062 sec)
Rows matched: 3  Changed: 3  Warnings: 0

MariaDB [COLLEGE]> SELECT * FROM STUDENT WHERE SUB_CODE = 'E1';
+--------+-------+----------+-------+--------+------------+
| STU_ID | NAME  | SUB_CODE | FEE   | GENDER | DOA        |
+--------+-------+----------+-------+--------+------------+
|      1 | Meena | E1       | 17250 | F      | 2017-07-02 |
|      3 | Reena | E1       | 17250 | F      | 2017-07-02 |
|      6 | James | E1       | 17250 | M      | 2017-07-08 |
+--------+-------+----------+-------+--------+------------+
3 rows in set (0.000 sec)

MariaDB [COLLEGE]>
```

Figure 5.34 Use of UPDATE statement to change existing data

5.15.1 Updating Rows based on Another Table

You can also update values in a table, based on the result of a subquery run on another table. For example, suppose you want to raise a fee in STUDENT table of all those students by 15%, who are persuing course in *B.TECH* in SUBJECT table. (See Figure 5.35). This can be done using the following UPDATE command:

```
MariaDB [COLLEGE]> UPDATE STUDENT
    -> SET FEE = FEE + FEE * 0.15
    -> WHERE SUB_CODE = (SELECT SUB_CODE
FROM SUBJECT WHERE COURSE = 'B.TECH');
MariaDB [COLLEGE]> SELECT * FROM STUDENT
WHERE SUB_CODE = 'E1';
```

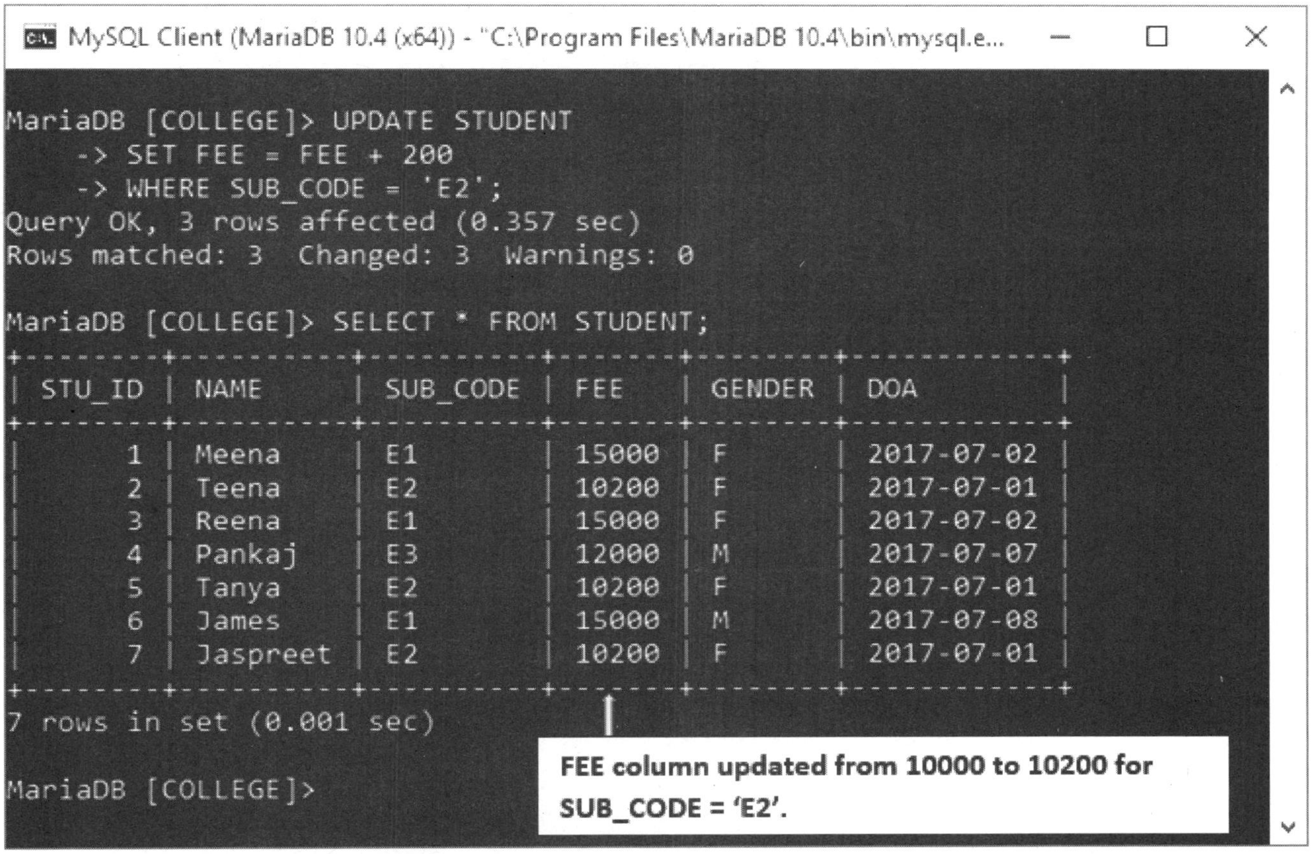

```
MySQL Client (MariaDB 10.4 (x64)) - "C:\Program Files\MariaDB 10.4\bin\mysql.e...

MariaDB [COLLEGE]> UPDATE STUDENT
    -> SET FEE = FEE + 200
    -> WHERE SUB_CODE = 'E2';
Query OK, 3 rows affected (0.357 sec)
Rows matched: 3  Changed: 3  Warnings: 0

MariaDB [COLLEGE]> SELECT * FROM STUDENT;
+--------+----------+----------+-------+--------+------------+
| STU_ID | NAME     | SUB_CODE | FEE   | GENDER | DOA        |
+--------+----------+----------+-------+--------+------------+
|      1 | Meena    | E1       | 15000 | F      | 2017-07-02 |
|      2 | Teena    | E2       | 10200 | F      | 2017-07-01 |
|      3 | Reena    | E1       | 15000 | F      | 2017-07-02 |
|      4 | Pankaj   | E3       | 12000 | M      | 2017-07-07 |
|      5 | Tanya    | E2       | 10200 | F      | 2017-07-01 |
|      6 | James    | E1       | 15000 | M      | 2017-07-08 |
|      7 | Jaspreet | E2       | 10200 | F      | 2017-07-01 |
+--------+----------+----------+-------+--------+------------+
7 rows in set (0.001 sec)

MariaDB [COLLEGE]>
```


Figure 5.35 Use of UPDATE statement to update rows based on another table

5.16 DELETE STATEMENT

We can remove rows from a table with the command DELETE. This command removes specific rows meeting the condition but not the individual field values. If no WHERE condition is specified, all rows will be removed from the table leaving the table structure intact.

```
DELETE FROM <tablename> WHERE <condition>;
```

For example, if Tanya (with STU_ID 5) has left the college, then there is no need to keep her record in this table.

The MariaDB statement to delete the record of Tanya will be as follows (See Figure 5.36):

```
MariaDB [COLLEGE]> DELETE FROM STUDENT
WHERE STU_ID = 5;
MariaDB [COLLEGE]> SELECT * FROM STUDENT;
```

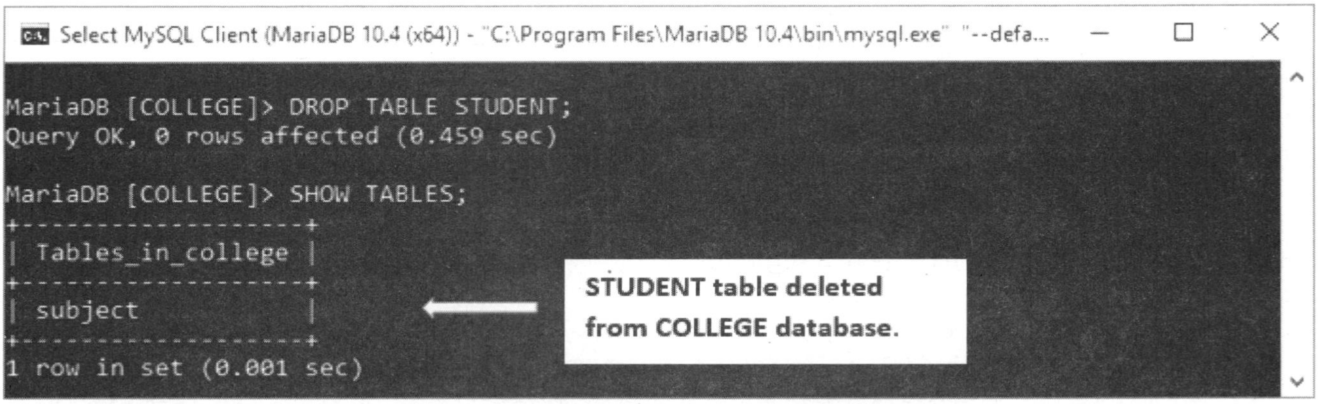

Figure 5.36 Use of DELETE statement to delete the record of Tanya

5.16.1 Deleting Rows based on condition from another Table

We can also use subqueries in the WHERE clause of a DELETE command. This will allow us to specify some sophisticated criteria for determining whether a row is to be deleted or not. For example, suppose the college has closed the *B.TECH* course, then we can use the following query to delete the records of all those students who are persuing B.TECH course (See Figure 5.37):

```
MariaDB [COLLEGE]> DELETE FROM STUDENT
    -> WHERE SUB_CODE = (SELECT SUB_CODE
FROM SUBJECT
    -> WHERE COURSE = 'B.TECH');
MariaDB [COLLEGE]> SELECT * FROM STU-
DENT;
```

☞ *To remove all the contents of a table, we would enter the following statement:*
`DELETE FROM <tablename>;`
The table would now be empty. Be very sure about your actions while using the DELETE command.

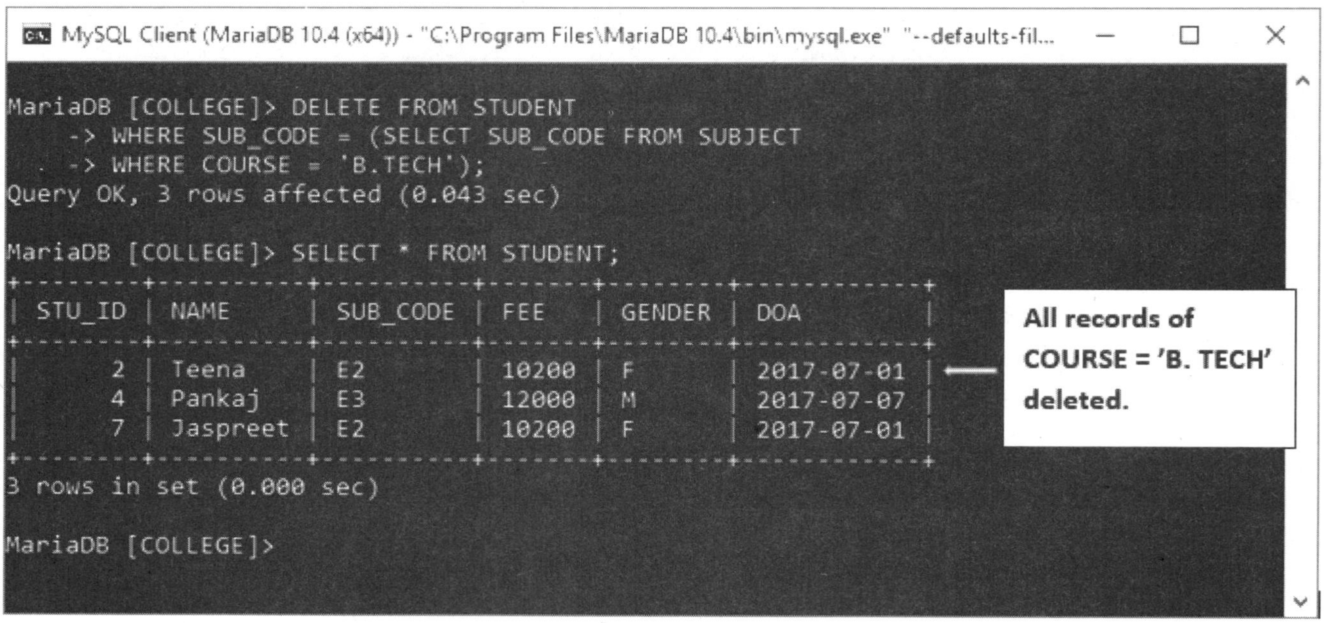

Figure 5.37 Use of DELETE statement to delete rows based on another table

5.17 DROPPING OR DELETING DATABASE

You can delete or drop database any time if you do not want. To delete an entire database, including every table therein and all its data, use the following command at MariaDB prompt:

```
DROP DATABASE databasename;
```

This query will permanently delete the database.

```
MariaDB [COLLEGE]> DROP TABLE STUDENT;
MariaDB [COLLEGE]> SHOW TABLES;
```

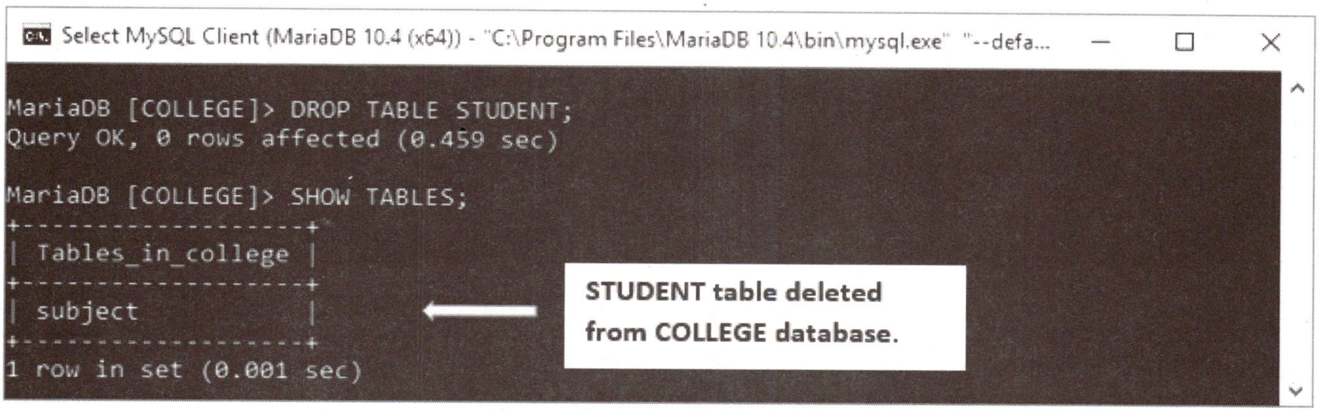

Figure 5.38 Dropping or deleting database

☞ *DROP DATABASE deletes all the tables in the database. So, be very careful before deleting a database.*

5.18 TRUNCATE TABLE STATEMENT

In MariaDB database, TRUNCATE TABLE statement is used to delete all records from a table. It is same as DELETE statement without a WHERE clause.

The syntax of the truncate table statement:

```
TRUNCATE [TABLE] [database_name.]table_name;
MariaDB [COLLEGE]> TRUNCATE TABLE COLLEGE.SUBJECT;
MariaDB [COLLEGE]> SHOW TABLES;
MariaDB [COLLEGE]> SELECT * FROM SUBJECT;
```

☞ *If you use the TRUNCATE table statement, the table will be deleted permanently and cannot be rolled back.*

Now drop the COLLEGE database (See Figure 5.40).

```
MariaDB [COLLEGE]> DROP DATABASE COLLEGE;
MariaDB [(none)]> SHOW DATABASES;
```

5.19 INDEXING

An index is a performance-tuning method of allowing faster retrieval of records. An index creates an entry for each value that appears in the indexed columns. There are two ways to create an index. You can either create an index when you first create a table using the CREATE TABLE statement or you can use the CREATE INDEX statement after the table has been created.

You can drop an index in MariaDB using the DROP INDEX statement.

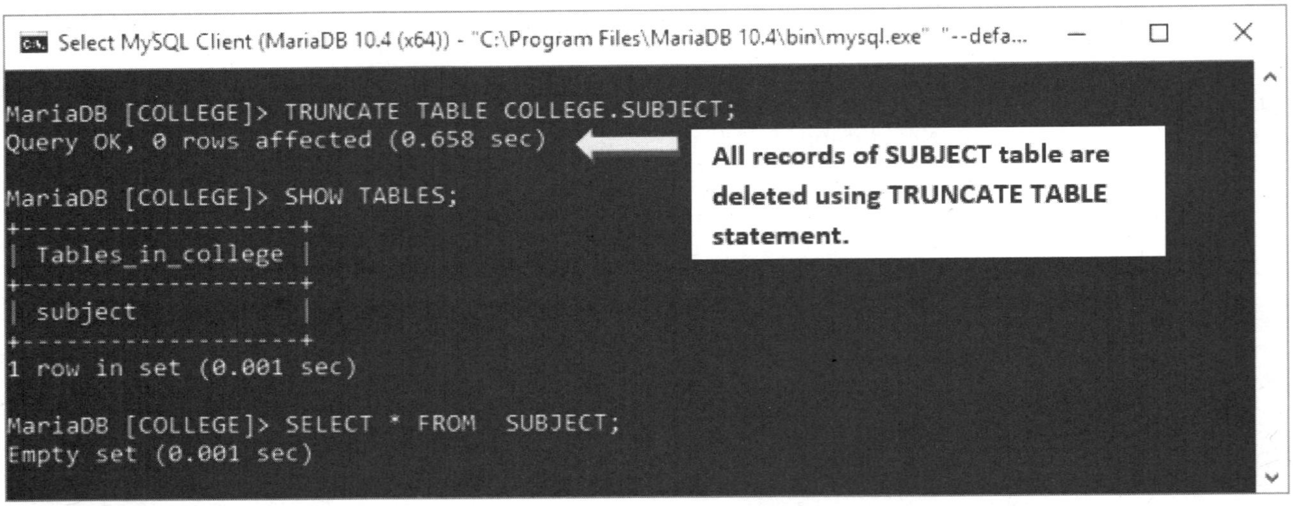

Figure 5.39 Truncating database

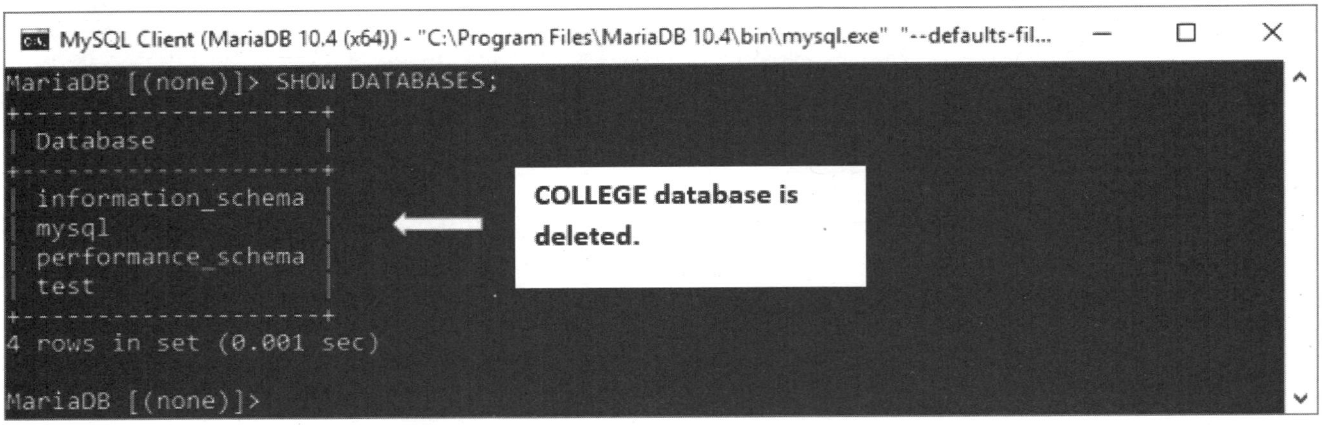

Figure 5.40 Truncating database

5.20 KEY

UNIQUE constraint ensures that values entered into a column will be different, i.e., unique. A column with this constraint will not accept any duplicate values. UNIQUE KEY constraint can be defined at the column level as well as the table level.

5.21 PRIMARY KEY

The primary key uniquely identifies each record in a table and must never be the same for two records. For example, emp_code can be primary key for the entity set Employees, Stu_Id can be primary key for entity set Student.

The primary key should be chosen such that its attributes are never or very rarely changed. For instance, the address field of a person should not be part of the primary key, since it is likely to change. Emp_code or Stu_Id, on the other hand, is not changed.

☞ *The primary key uniquely identifies each record in a table.*

5.22 FOREIGN KEY

In a relation, the column whose data values correspond to the values of a key column in another relation is called a *Foreign Key*. The supp_code key is a Foreign Key as seen in Figure 5.41.

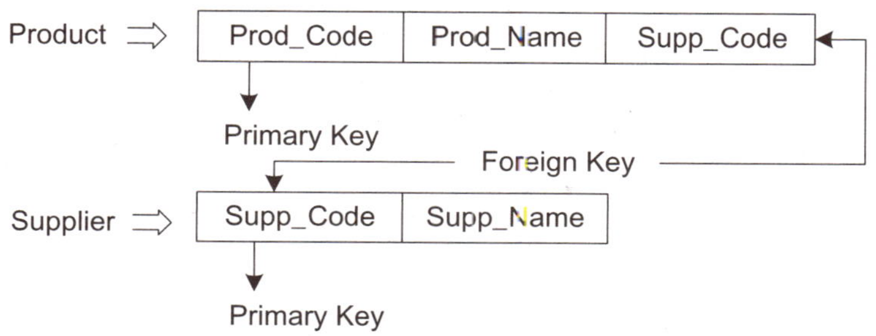

Figure 5.41 Concepts of foreign key

> ☞ *In a relational database, the foreign key of a relation may be the primary key of another relation.*

5.23 CONSTRAINTS

Constraints are created in the database to enforce a business rule or conditions in the database so as to ensure validity of data. This also specifies relationships among different tables.

> ☞ *A column can use more than one constraint each separated by space. Constraints are rules for restricting the values that can be placed in a table column.*

5.23.1 Integrity Constraints

While creating a table, you can place certain limitations on the values stored in the table. *Integrity constraints* would prevent bad data from being entered into a table. Different constraints as applicable to MariaDB are:

(a) NOT NULL
(b) UNIQUE KEY
(c) PRIMARY KEY
(d) CHECK
(e) DEFAULT

NOT NULL

NOT NULL constraint prevents a column from accepting null value. If you try to insert a null value in such a column, it will be rejected. Each column should be defined as NULL or NOT NULL. If this parameter is omitted, the database assumes NULL as the default.

> ☞ *NULL value does not mean a zero value. It just means absence of any data, in that column.*

A NOT NULL constraint is defined at the column level. It cannot be defined at the table level. For example:

```
EMP_ID VARCHAR(20) NOT NULL
```

Here, **EMP_ID** has a column constraint **NOT NULL**. It means the column **EMP_ID** cannot accept data with null value.

UNIQUE KEY

Sometimes, you may want to ensure values in a column or a set of columns are unique, for example, country codes of the countries, email addresses of customers, and so on. To enforce a column or a set of columns to store only distinct values, you use unique constraints. A UNIQUE constraint is a single field or combination of fields that uniquely defines a record. UNIQUE constraint ensures that values entered into a column will be different, i.e., unique. A column with this constraint will not accept any duplicate values. UNIQUE KEY constraint can be defined at the column level as well as the table level. For example:

```
EMP_ID VARCHAR(20) NOT NULL UNIQUE
```

Here, **EMP_ID** has the column constraint **NOT NULL** and **UNIQUE**. It means the column **EMP_ID** cannot accept data with null values and duplicate values.

> ☞ *A UNIQUE constraint specifies that two rows in a column cannot have the same value.*

PRIMARY KEY

A primary key is a column or group of columns whose values uniquely identify every row in the table. The primary key constraint allows you to define the primary key for a table. In order to declare a column as *primary key* of the table, use the PRIMARY KEY constraint. There can be only one *primary key* in a table. You can also use AUTO_INCREMENT (starting at 1, and incrementing by 1, unless otherwise specified.) constraint along with PRIMARY KEY constraint which tells MariaDB to go ahead and add the next available number to the ID field.

By default, primary key columns are implicitly imposed not null constraints, therefore, you don't need to explicitly specify the not null constraints for the primary key columns.

☞ *A PRIMARY KEY constraint defines a primary key on a table that uniquely identifies a row.*

CHECK

CHECK constraint is used to control the values entered into a field. A condition is specified along with the CHECK constraint which must be satisfied by all the values that are entered in the column. Otherwise the value will be rejected. For example,

```
CHECK (SALARY <= 100000)
```

If the value of salary entered is more than 100000, then it will be rejected. Here, `SALARY` is the column name.

☞ *A CHECK constraint restricts the data that users can enter into a particular column to specific value.*

If you create a check constraint without a name, MariaDB will automatically generate a name for it. However, you can explicitly specify a name for the check constraint by using the constraint clause.

DEFAULT

DEFAULT constraint is used to assign a default value to a column.

For example, SALARY DEFAULT 0 will assign the default value of the salary as 0.0. Even if the user does not enter any value into the SALARY column, the default value entered will be zero. Here, SALARY is the column name.

☞ *A DEFAULT constraint assigns a default value if no value is specified when a new record is inserted.*

5.24 REFERENCES

A *foreign key* has values which form the primary key in another table. A table that has the foreign key is called a child table while the table to which the foreign key references is known as a parent table. Typically, a foreign key column in a child table references to the primary key column of the parent table. The two tables thus get related by using the foreign key. Column(s) which are chosen as a foreign key should not have values other than that present in the primary key of a related table. MariaDB foreign key constraints enforce the referential integrity between tables. This referential integrity is implemented using the REFERENCES constraint.

☞ *REFERENCES constraint is followed by the name of the related table and its primary key.*

In a relational database, a table is associated with other tables via foreign key constraints. If you delete rows from the parent table, the corresponding rows from the child tables are automatically deleted if the foreign key constraints use on delete cascade action. For example, to relate a column DEPT_CODE with DEPT_NO column in another table called DEPARTMENT we will use the REFERENCES constraint as:

```
DEPT_CODE REFERENCES DEPARTMENT(DEPT_NO)
```

ON DELETE CASCADE OPTION

This option is used along with the REFERENCES constraint. If we use this option then whenever a parent row is deleted then all the corresponding child rows are also deleted from the related child table, because of this constraint.

5.24.1 Adding Constraints

We can add constraints in table in two ways:

(a) ***Column level:*** It is defined on a single column.

The syntax for the column level constraints is

```
<Column name> <Data type> <Constraint Type>
```

For example,

```
EMP_CODE INT(2) PRIMARY KEY
```

Here, **EMP_CODE** is column name, **INT(2)** is data type and **PRIMARY KEY** is the constraint type.

(b) ***Table level:*** This is applied on more than one column or may be whole table.

```
CONSTRAINT <constraint name> <constraint Type>
```

For example,

```
CREATE TABLE EMP(
SALARY DECIMAL(9,2),
BONUS DECIMAL(7,2),
CONSTRAINT CH_BONUS CHECK (BONUS >
0));
```

☞ *A name is provided for the constraints by specifying the keyword **CONSTRAINT** followed by the constraint name. If you do not provide a name for the constraint, Oracle assigns a system generated unique name that begins with SYS.*

For example, to create the DEPARTMENT table with the appropriate constraints defined, type the following statement:

```
CREATE TABLE DEPARTMENT
(
  DEPT_CODE INT(2) PRIMARY KEY,
  DEPT_NAME VARCHAR(10) NOT NULL
    UNIQUE CHECK (DEPT_NAME IN
    ('ACCOUNTS', 'RESEARCH',
       'SALES', 'OPERATIONS')),
  FLOOR SMALLINT(1) NOT NULL
);
```

Similarly, create the EMPLOYEE table using the following statement:

```
CREATE TABLE EMPLOYEE
(
  EMP_CODE INT(4) PRIMARY KEY,
  EMP_NAME VARCHAR(25) NOT NULL,
  DESIG CHAR(10) NOT NULL,
  HEAD INT(4),
  DOJ DATE NOT NULL,
  BASIC FLOAT DEFAULT 0,
  DEPT_CODE INT(2) REFERENCES
    DEPARTMENT(DEPT_CODE)
);
```

You can view the structure of the tables using the **DESCRIBE <table name>** statement.

Example

Create a table INV_PROD, used for managing inventory. Details of the columns for this table is given in Table 5.3.

Solution

```
CREATE TABLE INV_PROD
(
  ProductNo INT(4) Primary Key,
  Name Varchar(20) Not Null,
  QOH INT(5) Default 200,
  Class Char(1) check (Class
    in ('A', 'B', 'C')),
  UOM Char(4),
  ROL INT(5) Not Null
    Check (ROL > 0),
  ROQ INT(5) Not Null
    Check (ROQ > 0),
  Rate FLOAT(8, 2) Not Null,
  Check ((Class='A' AND
    Rate <= 2000) OR (Class='B' AND
    Rate<=6500 and Rate>2000) OR
    (Class='C' AND Rate>6500)),
  Unique (ProductNo, Name)
);
```

5.24.2 Dropping a Constraint

We can also remove the constraints imposed on a table, at a later time, using the ALTER TABLE command.

5.24.3 Disabling and Enabling Constraints

When we create a constraint, the constraint is automatically enabled. We can disable a constraint by using the DISABLE clause, in the ALTER TABLE command. When we disable UNIQUE OR PRIMARY KEY constraints, MariaDB drops the associated unique index.

Table 5.3 The INV_PROD table structure

Column Name	Type	Size	Description	Column Constraints
ProductNo	INT	4	Product Number	Primary Key
Name	VARCHAR	20	Product Name	Not Null
QOH	INT	5	Quantity on Hand	Default value 200
Class	CHAR	1	Category of the product	Class can be only 'A', 'B' or 'C'
UOM	CHAR	4	Unit of Measurement	
ROL	INT	5	Reorder Level	Not Null, Cannot be 0
ROQ	INT	5	Reorder Quantity	Not Null, Cannot be 0
Rate	FLOAT	8,2	Unit sale's price	Not Null

Table Constraints:
(a) Combination of columns ProductNo and Name should be Unique.
(b) Rate of any product under class 'A' should be less than or equal to 2000.00, rate of any product in class 'B' should be more than 2000.00 but less than or equal to 6500.00, and that of class 'C' should be more than 6500.00.

REVIEW QUESTIONS WITH ANSWERS

1. Multiple Choice Questions

1. Which of the following is correct?
   a. A SQL query automatically eliminate duplicates.
   b. SQL permits attribute names to be repeated in the same relation
   c. A SQL query will not work if there are no indexes on the relations
   d. None of the above
2. A set of definitions expressed by a special language is known as
   a. Data Manipulation Language
   b. Data Definition Language
   c. Data Declaration Language
   d. None of the above
3. The ________ command helps us to change or modify the records that have already been inserted into a table.
   a. UPDATE
   b. ALTER
   c. DROP
   d. None of the above
4. The ______ clause helps us to specify the exact location where we need to make a change.
   a. WHERE
   b. INSERT
   c. SELECT
   d. None of the above
5. Advantage(s) of MariaDB:
   a. It is fast and stable
   b. It has high availability and is very secure
   c. It provides different tools for disaster recovery
   d. All of the above
6. Which of the following commands is used to get all the columns in a table?
   a. # b. *
   c. % d. @
7. Which of the following is not as SQL command?
   a. Create b. Drop

c. Alter d. All are SQL Commands.

8. Create, Alter and Drop are example of:
   a. DML b. DQL
   c. DCL d. DDL
9. The keyword to eliminate duplicate rows from the query result in MariaDB is:
   a. DISTINCT b. NO DUPLICATE
   c. UNIQUE d. None of the above

2. State True or False for the following:

1. DROP VIEW command is used to dispose off a view not needed anymore.
2. Null value means string of characters.
3. Foreign key value should not be left blank.
4. Column constraints are specific to a column in a base table.
5. NULL value means absence of data.
6. Unique index can occur only one per table in database.
7. The DELETE statement is used to delete an existing column or columns from a table.
8. SQL is an abbreviation for simple query language.
9. Standard comparison operators cannot be used with NULL.
10. It is not possible for us to insert multiple records into a MariaDB table at a go.
11. In MariaDB database, TRUNCATE TABLE statement is used to delete all records from a table.
12. MariaDB comes with many storage engines, including the high-performance ones that can be integrated with other relational database management systems.
13. MariaDB is written in C, C++, Bash & Perl languages.
14. The primary key for a record must never be allowed to have a NULL value.
15. MariaDB is a community-development branch of the OpenSolaris database which uses the Maria engine by default.

3. Match the following:

1. View	a. Modify table's structure
2. DML	b. One record represents multiple records
3. Primary	c. Select a default database
4. USE!	d. They are tested easily whenever a new data item is entered into a database
5. DESCRIBE	e. One record represents all records
6. ALTER	f. Virtual table
7. DDL	g. Shows the structure of a table
8. Unique	h. This is used to specify the set of relations in a database
9. Domain constraint	i. Represents missing information
10. Null values	j. Query language

4. Fill in the blanks:

1. The CHECK clause in CREATE TABLE command can be used to enforce ___________.
2. When one column of a table refers to the values in another column of the same table, it introduces a ___________ integrity constraint.
3. _________ symbol in SQL indicates that all attributes of the relation are to be retrieved.
4. Range variables are defined using the ___________ statement.
5. The ___________ key can never allow null because it uniquely identifies a given row.
6. ________!is used to completely destroy an existing database.
7. MariaDB is an improved version of _________.

8. To see the structure of any particular table, you can use the DESCRIBE command, commonly abbreviated as ______.
9. The ________ statement helps us to view or see the contents of a database table.
10. MariaDB _________ Clause is used to remove duplicates from the result when it is used with SELECT statement.

Answers

1. 1. c 2. b 3. a 4. a 5. d 6. b
   7. d 8. d 9. a
2. 1. T 2. F 3. T 4. T 5. T 6. T
   7. F 8. F 9. T 10. F 11 T 12 T
   13. T 14. T 15. T
3. 1. f 2. j 3. e 4. c 5. g 6. a
   7. h 8. b 9. d 10. i
4. 1. Domain dependency 2. Self referential
   3. * 4. From
   5. Primary 6. DROP DATABASE
   7. MySQL 8. DESC
   9. SELECT 10. DISTINCT

Short Answers Questions

1. What is MariaDB?

Ans It is an Open-source software and is based on the MySQL Community Version. MariaDB supports a popular and standard querying language. MariaDB runs on a number of operating systems and supports a wide variety of programming languages.

2. Write Pros and Cons of MariaDB.

Ans Pros of MariaDB are:

(a) It has high scalability with easier integration.
(b) It provides real-time access to data.

Cons of MariaDB are:

(a) Password complexity plugin is missing.
(b) It has no optimiser trace.

3. What is MARIA Database?

Ans MariaDB is one of the MySQL database servers. It is a relational database management system developed by the original developers of MySQL.

4. What is a query?

Ans A query with respect to DBMS relates to user commands that are used to interact with a data base.

5. Define SQL.

Ans SQL is a nonprocedural language that is designed specifically for data access operations on normalized relational database structures.

6. Write short note on MySQL.

Ans MySQL is classified as a Relational Database Management System (RDBMS). It works with all the conventional properties of a relational database, i.e. building tables, constraints, views, etc. It uses core database processes to perform various functional operations, such as stored procedures, triggers, roles, and others.

7. Write features of MySQL.

Ans Features of MySQL Are:

(a) Scalability and Flexibility
(b) High Performance and Availability
(c) Robust Transactional Support
(d) Web and Data Warehouse Strengths

8. Write cons of using MySQL.

Ans Cons of using MySQL are:

(a) It is hard to scale.
(b) Oracle owns it, so it has lots of restrictions.

9. How MariaDB is different from MySQL?

Ans MariaDB vs MySQL

(a) Comparatively MariaDB is faster than MySQL
(b) MariaDB is Open Source whereas MySQL uses some proprietary code in its Enterprise Edition.
(c) In many scenarios, MariaDB offers improved performance.
(d) MariaDB is fully GPL licensed while MySQL takes a dual-license approach.

(e) MariaDB supports a lot of different storage engines whereas MySQL has lesser storage engines.

10. Write a command to create database in MariaDB.

Ans `CREATE DATABASE databasename;`

11. What is the use of Foreign key?

Ans A Foreign key serves as a link between two tables.

12. What are features of primary key?

Ans Features of primary key are:

(a) This refers to a unique, identifying value.

(b) This value cannot appear twice within a table.

(c) There is only one row associated with it.

13. What is use of Update in MariaDB?

Ans Update command is used to modify the existing fields and change the values. To specify the new values assigned and modify the specified columns we can use the SET clause. WHERE clause is used to specify conditions for an update.

14. In MariaDB [none]> prompt what is significance of [none]?

Ans In the prompt, [none] means that no default database is selected. This means that, every time a table is named in a statement, the name of the database where it is located must be specifically specified.

15. What is the command to select default database in MariaDB?

Ans The USE statement selects a default database, whose name will appear in the prompt. For example, you need to use the Try database. You can select it by running the following command:
USE Try;

16. In the BOOK table shown below what is use of PRIMARY KEY and AUTO_INCREMENT?

```
CREATE TABLE BOOK(
id INT NOT NULL AUTO_INCREMENT,
name VARCHAR(50) NOT NULL,
PRIMARY KEY (id));
```

Ans The PRIMARY KEY constraint has been used to set the id column as the primary key for the table. The AUTO_INCREMENT property will increment the values of the id column by 1 automatically for each new record inserted into the table. All the columns will not allow null values.

17. What is the use of INSERT in MariaDB? Write its syntax.

Ans To insert data into a MariaDB table, we should use the INSERT INTO statement. This command takes the syntax given below:

```
INSERT INTO tableName
VALUES
(value1, value2, ... ),
(value1, value2, ... ),
...;
```

18. What is HeidiSQL?

Ans HeidiSQL is a so called client application, only usable when you have some server available.

19. How will you delete a database in MariaDB?

Ans DROP DATABASE command is used to delete a database in MariaDB.

20. What is the use of DELETE statement in MariaDB?

Ans The MariaDB DELETE statement is used to delete one or more records from the table in the database.

21. How can you retrieve limited number of records from a table?

Ans LIMIT clause is used with SELECT statement to select a limited number of records from a table.

22. What is the purpose of Modify option of Alter table?

Ans Modify option can change the data type, column width and constraints of an existing column.

23. Differentiate between DROP TABLE and DELETE.

Ans Difference between DROP TABLE and DELETE are:

DROP TABLE	DELETE
The statement is used to delete a table.	This statement is used to REMOVE the rows in a table.
It is a DDL command.	It is a DML command
It is non conditional command.	It is a conditional command.
It cannot be rolled back.	It can be rolled back.
The structure of the table is deleted hence no more rows can be added after Drop Table command.	New rows can be added after the execution of this command.

24. What is DML? Discuss different operations performed by it.

Ans DML stands for Data Manipulation Language. A DML is a language that enables a user to access or manipulate data as organized by the appropriate data model. DML is used for performing the following operations:

(a) Retrieving information stored in the database.

(b) Inserting information into the database.

(c) Deleting information from the database.

(d) Modifying information stored in the database.

25. Differentiate between ALTER TABLE and UPDATE.

Ans Difference between ALTER TABLE and UPDATE are:

ALTER TABLE	UPDATE
This command is used to change definition of an existing table . It can add , modify columns, delete columns or change their size.	This command is used to modify existing data in a table.
It is DDL command.	It is DML command.
Conditions cannot be given.	Condition can be given.
It cannot be rolled back.	It can be rolled back.

EXERCISE

1. Write short note on the following:
   (a) MariaDB Data Types
   (b) DDL
   (c) DML
   (d) DCL
   (e) Primary key
2. Write any two advantages of MariaDB.
3. Describe DML statement in MariaDB.
4. Explain different constraints in MariaDB.
5. What are the main features of MariaDB database?
6. Write the syntax for Delete and Truncate query and explain the difference between them.
7. Write the query to check if table is present within Database.
8. How to install MariaDB in a Linux or Unix environment?
9. Create a simple table using MariaDB named Weather, consisting three fields Month, Day and Temperature. Set it as the current default database.

Manipulating Data with MariaDB

6.1 INTRODUCTION

In order to learn MariaDB commands, we will create two tables, EMPLOYEE and DEPARTMENT in database OFFICE, with structures as given in Table 6.1 and 6.2, respectively.

```
MariaDB [(none)]> CREATE DATABASE OFFICE;
Query OK, 1 row affected (0.002 sec)
MariaDB [(none)]> USE OFFICE;
Database changed
```

Since DEPT_CODE field of EMPLOYEE table is dependent on DEPARTMENT table, we need to first create DEPARTMENT table.

Table 6.1 The EMPLOYEE table structure

Column Name	Type	Description
EMP_CODE	INT	Unique code assigned to each employee
EMP_NAME	VARCHAR(25)	Name of the employee with maximum size of 25 characters
DESIG	CHAR(20)	Designation of the employee
HEAD	INT	EMP_CODE of the Manager under whom the employee is working
DOJ	DATE	Date of joining of the employee
BASIC	FLOAT	Salary of the employee
DEPT_CODE	INT	Code of the department in which the employee is working

Table 6.2 The DEPARTMENT table structure

Column Name	Type	Description
DEPT_CODE	INT	Unique code assigned to each department
DEPT_NAME	VARCHAR(10)	Department name with maximum size of 10 characters
FLOOR	SMALLINT	Location of the department

To create tables 6.1 and 6.2, open MariaDB command prompt. Type the following SQL statement, after the *MariaDB* prompt as shown in Figure 6.1:

```
MariaDB [OFFICE]> CREATE TABLE DEPARTMENT(
    -> DEPT_CODE INT,
    -> DEPT_NAME VARCHAR(10),
    -> FLOOR SMALLINT);
Query OK, 0 rows affected (0.460 sec)
```

Figure 6.1 Creating table DEPARTMENT

This will create the DEPARTMENT table Similarly, create the EMPLOYEE table using the following SQL statements (See Figure 6.2).

```
MariaDB [OFFICE]> CREATE TABLE EMPLOYEE(
    -> EMP_CODE INT,
    -> EMP_NAME VARCHAR(25),
    -> DESIG CHAR(20),
    -> HEAD INT,
    -> DOJ DATE,
    -> BASIC FLOAT,
    -> DEPT_CODE INT,
    -> PRIMARY KEY(EMP_CODE));
Query OK, 0 rows affected (0.595 sec)
```

Figure 6.2 Creating table EMPLOYEE

The **DESCRIBE** statement can be used to see the structure of a table as indicated in the **CREATE** Statement. It displays the Column names, their data types, whether Column contain data, or the Column is a Primary key etc. To see structure of DEPARTMENT and EMPLOYEE table type the following statements as in Figure 6.3 and 6.4 respectively.

```
MariaDB [OFFICE]> DESCRIBE DEPARTMENT;
+-----------+-------------+------+-----+---------+-------+
| Field     | Type        | Null | Key | Default | Extra |
+-----------+-------------+------+-----+---------+-------+
| DEPT_CODE | int(11)     | YES  |     | NULL    |       |
| DEPT_NAME | varchar(10) | YES  |     | NULL    |       |
| FLOOR     | smallint(6) | YES  |     | NULL    |       |
+-----------+-------------+------+-----+---------+-------+
3 rows in set (0.269 sec)
```

Figure 6.3 Structure of a DEPARTMENT table

```
MariaDB [OFFICE]> DESCRIBE EMPLOYEE;
+-----------+-------------+------+-----+---------+-------+
| Field     | Type        | Null | Key | Default | Extra |
+-----------+-------------+------+-----+---------+-------+
| EMP_CODE  | int(11)     | NO   | PRI | NULL    |       |
| EMP_NAME  | varchar(25) | YES  |     | NULL    |       |
| DESIG     | char(20)    | YES  |     | NULL    |       |
| HEAD      | int(11)     | YES  |     | NULL    |       |
| DOJ       | date        | YES  |     | NULL    |       |
| BASIC     | float       | YES  |     | NULL    |       |
| DEPT_CODE | int(11)     | YES  |     | NULL    |       |
+-----------+-------------+------+-----+---------+-------+
7 rows in set (0.144 sec)
```

Figure 6.4 Structure of a EMPLOYEE table

6.2 INSERT OPERATION

After creating the tables, namely EMPLOYEE and DEPARTMENT, we shall insert data into the fields in these tables, using the SQL command *INSERT INTO.*

The values to be inserted into the tables DEPARTMENT and EMPLOYEE are given in Tables 6.3 and 6.4 respectively.

Table 6.3 The DEPARTMENT table

DEPT_CODE	DEPT_NAME	FLOOR
10	Accounts	1
20	Research	2
30	Sales	3
40	Operations	4

Table 6.4 The EMPLOYEE table

EMP_CODE	EMP_NAME	DESIG	HEAD	DOJ	BASIC	DEPT_CODE
101	Raju	Manager	-	2000-12-17	8000	20
102	Amar Roy	Salesman	105	2000-02-20	4000	30
103	Raj	Assistant	101	2003-02-22	4500	20
104	Rajiv Kumar	As. Engineer	107	2001-04-02	6200	10
105	Suraj Patel	Area Manager	-	2001-09-28	7500	30
106	Binay Kumar	Salesman	105	2001-05-01	4270	30
107	Ramaswamy	Engineer	-	2001-06-09	6500	10
108	Jog Iyer	Assistant	105	2002-12-09	4250	30
109	Imran Khan	Steno	105	2001-11-17	4500	30
110	Tinu Anand	As. Engineer	107	2003-01-12	6000	10

INSERT INTO command adds (appends) new rows (records) to a table. For example, to add rows (records) to the DEPARTMENT table type the following statement in the MariaDB window as shown in Figure 6.5.

To add a record into the EMPLOYEE table type the following SQL statements shown in Figure 6.6:

```
MariaDB [OFFICE]> INSERT INTO DEPARTMENT VALUES
    -> (10, 'ACCOUNTS', 1),
    -> (20, 'Research', 2),
    -> (30, 'Sales', 3),
    -> (40, 'Operations', 4);
Query OK, 4 rows affected (0.203 sec)
Records: 4  Duplicates: 0  Warnings: 0
```

Figure 6.5 Inserting values into the DEPARTMENT table

6.3 SQL STATEMENTS

A statement is a combination of two or more clauses.

Keyword: A keyword refers to a special word that has a special meaning to MariaDB. For example, SELECT and FROM are keywords.

Clause: A clause is a portion of a statement. Each clause is identified by a keyword. For example, consider the statement:

`SELECT DEPT_NAME FROM DEPARTMENT;`

Here SELECT DEPT_NAME is a clause. SELECT is a statement as well as a clause. SELECT clause is everything from keyword SELECT until key-

word FROM. SELECT statement is the entire command.
FROM DEPARTMENT is a FROM clause, which specifies the table from which data has to be selected.

```
MariaDB [OFFICE]> INSERT INTO EMPLOYEE VALUES
    -> (101,'Raju','Manager',Null,'2000-12-17',8000,20),
    -> (102,'Amar Roy','Salesman',105,'2000-02-20',4000,30),
    -> (103,'Raj','Assistant',101,'2003-02-22',4500,20),
    -> (104,'Rajiv Kumar','As. Engineer',107,'2001-04-02',6200,10),
    -> (105,'Suraj Patel','Area Manager',Null,'2001-09-28',7500,30),
    -> (106,'Binay Kumar','Salesman',105,'2001-05-01',4270,30),
    -> (107,'Ramaswamy','Engineer',Null,'2001-06-09',6500,10),
    -> (108,'Jog Iyer','Assistant',105,'2002-12-09',4250,30),
    -> (109,'Imran Khan','Steno',105,'2001-11-17',4500,30),
    -> (110,'Tinu Anand','As. Engineer',107,'2003-01-12',6000,10);
Query OK, 10 rows affected (0.175 sec)
Records: 10  Duplicates: 0  Warnings: 0
```

Figure 6.6 Inserting values into the EMPLOYEE table

6.4 SELECT STATEMENT

SELECT statement in SQL, retrieves data items from a table. SELECT is the single most powerful query command in MariaDB. Many queries can be performed on tables using SELECT command. The statement also enables you to query a data item. This means that by executing SELECT statement, information currently available in table will be shown on the screen.

The syntax for *SELECT* command is:

SELECT <column_name(s)> FROM <table-name>;

The **Select** clause is followed by the column list. The **From** clause specifies the table from which such columns are to be extracted.

To select all the columns in a table, an asterisk (*) is used in place of the column list. For example, suppose you want to retrieve all the data stored in DEPARTMENT table, then type the following statement, after *MariaDB* prompt:

SELECT * FROM DEPARTMENT;

On execution of this command, you will see the details of all departments available in the DEPARTMENT table. In our case, the result will be as shown in Figure 6.7.

Similarly, to select all the columns in EMPLOYEE table, type the following statement, after *MariaDB>* prompt:

SELECT * FROM EMPLOYEE;

On execution of this command, you will see the details of all employees available in the EMPLOYEE table as shown in Figure 6.8.

```
MariaDB [OFFICE]> SELECT * FROM DEPARTMENT;
+-----------+------------+-------+
| DEPT_CODE | DEPT_NAME  | FLOOR |
+-----------+------------+-------+
|        10 | ACCOUNTS   |     1 |
|        20 | Research   |     2 |
|        30 | Sales      |     3 |
|        40 | Operations |     4 |
+-----------+------------+-------+
```

Figure 6.7 Displaying all the data in all the columns from DEPARTMENT table

```
MariaDB [OFFICE]> SELECT * FROM EMPLOYEE;
+----------+------------+-------------+-----+-----------+------+----------+
| EMP_CODE | EMP_NAME   | DESIG       | HEAD| DOJ       | BASIC| DEPT_CODE|
+----------+------------+-------------+-----+-----------+------+----------+
|      101 | Raju       | Manager     | NULL| 2000-12-17| 8000 |       20 |
|      102 | Amar Roy   | Salesman    |  105| 2000-02-20| 4000 |       30 |
|      103 | Raj        | Assistant   |  101| 2003-02-22| 4500 |       20 |
|      104 | Rajiv Kumar| As. Engineer|  107| 2001-04-02| 6200 |       10 |
|      105 | Suraj Patel| Area Manager| NULL| 2001-09-28| 7500 |       30 |
|      106 | Binay Kumar| Salesman    |  105| 2001-05-01| 4270 |       30 |
|      107 | Ramaswamy  | Engineer    | NULL| 2001-06-09| 6500 |       10 |
|      108 | Jog Iyer   | Assistant   |  105| 2002-12-09| 4250 |       30 |
|      109 | Imran Khan | Steno       |  105| 2001-11-17| 4500 |       30 |
|      110 | Tinu Anand | As. Engineer|  107| 2003-01-12| 6000 |       10 |
+----------+------------+-------------+-----+-----------+------+----------+
10 rows in set (0.345 sec)
```

Figure 6.8 Displaying all the data in all the columns from EMPLOYEE table

6.5 MariaDB OPERATORS AND THEIR PRECEDENCES

We may need operators to do arithmetic operations on data items stored in a table. Such operations may be as addition, subtraction, etc. on column values. Similarly, we may need to perform comparison for which we need relational operators like greater than (>), less than (<), less than or equal to (<=), greater than or equal to (>=) etc.

MariaDB operators may be classified as:

- Arithmetic operators
- Comparison operators
- Logical operators

6.5.1 Arithmetic Operators

An arithmetic operator is represented as a symbol. It performs an arithmetic operation such as *addition, subtraction*, etc. The operators +, -, *, / and % can be used in SQL statements and they have their usual mathematical meanings, namely + for addition, - for subtraction, * for multiplication, / for division and % returns remainder or modules of a division.

We can perform simple arithmetic computations on data using **SELECT** statement. For example, what if all employees's Basic is increased by 1,000, then we have to enter the following statement to display Basic increased by 1000 at the MariaDB> command prompt:

```
SELECT BASIC+1000 FROM EMPLOYEE;
```

BASIC column is displayed increased by 1000 (See Figure 6.9). The actual values are not increased in the table.

In the above example, arithmetic calculations were based on EMPLOYEE table. Arithmetic calculations may not always be based on tables. Suppose, we want to compute 54*2+1 or 67%3, there is no table to be referenced as shown in Figure 6.10. In such queries no **FROM** clause is used:

```
SELECT 54*2+1;
SELECT 67%3;
```

```
MariaDB [OFFICE]> SELECT BASIC+1000 FROM EMPLOYEE;
+------------+
| BASIC+1000 |
+------------+
|       9000 |
|       5000 |
|       5500 |
|       7200 |
|       8500 |
|       5270 |
|       7500 |
|       5250 |
|       5500 |
|       7000 |
+------------+
10 rows in set (0.136 sec)
```

Figure 6.9 Arithmetic operation on Data using SELECT Statement

```
MariaDB [(none)]> SELECT 54*2+1;
+--------+
| 54*2+1 |
+--------+
|    109 |
+--------+
1 row in set (0.090 sec)

MariaDB [(none)]> SELECT 67%3;
+------+
| 67%3 |
+------+
|    1 |
+------+
1 row in set (0.000 sec)
```

Figure 6.10 Arithmetic calculations without using any table

6.5.2 Comparison Operators

Comparison operators such as greater than (>) or less than (<) are used to compare two values. It gives a boolean result on comparison, namely TRUE or FALSE.

☞ *Using operators on tables does not create new columns in the tables or change the actual data values. The results of the calculations appear only in the output.*

Table 6.5 Comparison Operators

Operator	Action
>	Greater than
>=	Greater than or equal to
<	Less than
<=	Less than or equal to
=	Equal to
!=	Not equal to

Comparison (Relational) operators are given in Table 6.5.

☞ *When we use relational operators with character data type, < means earlier in the alphabet and > means later in the alphabet. 'Amir' < 'Aryan' as 'm' comes before 'r' in alphabet.*

6.5.3 Logical Operators

Logical operators such as AND, OR, NOT are used to determine logical relationship among various values. We use the rules of Boolean Algebra, for this purpose. Logical expression connected by logical operators AND, OR, NOT will give TRUE or FALSE results. Here, FALSE is zero, while any nonzero number is TRUE.

AND: The AND operator evaluates TRUE if both the operands are TRUE else it returns FALSE. For example, if A is true and B is true, then A AND B is true, else, in all other cases, its value is false.

OR: The OR operator evaluates to TRUE if either operand is TRUE. But if both the operands are FALSE then it returns FALSE. For example, if A is true and B is false, then A OR B is true. But, if A as well as B is false, then A OR B is false.

NOT: The NOT operator is used to reverse the result. It returns TRUE if the operand is FALSE, and returns FALSE if the operand is TRUE. For example, if A is true then NOT A is false and vice-versa.

6.5.4 BETWEEN Operator

BETWEEN operator is used to test the range of values. For example **BETWEEN A AND B** evaluates to TRUE if the value being checked is greater than or equal to **A** and less than or equal to **B**.

6.5.5 IN and NOT IN Operator

IN operator is used to test whether the particular value is present in a list of data items or not. It returns TRUE if value is present in list otherwise returns FALSE.

NOT IN operator is just opposite to IN operator. It returns TRUE if value is not present in the list otherwise returns FALSE.

6.5.6 LIKE Operator

LIKE operator is used to match a character or a string of characters. Two characters _ and % are used for pattern matching. The _ is just like ? wild card in DOS and is used to match any single character. But, % (same as * wild card in DOS) is used to match multiple characters. For example, **LIKE sim%** will match all strings that start with *sim*. And, **LIKE sim_** will match all 4-letter strings that start with *sim*.

☞ *The keyword **NOT LIKE** is used to select the rows that do not match the specified pattern.*

☞ *MariaDB pattern matching allows you to use '_' to match any single character and '%' to match an arbitrary number of characters (including zero characters).*

6.5.7 IS NULL and IS NOT NULL Operator

IS NULL operator is used to find the NULL values. It returns TRUE if the value is NULL. But, IS NOT NULL returns TRUE when the value is not NULL.

All these operations will be used and further discussed in queries, in a later section.

Table 6.6 shows the precedence or the order of calculations of the various operators. Precedence determines which operation will be performed first in an expression comprising of multiple operators. You can always use parenthesis to change the order of execution of an operator. Parenthesis have the highest precedence.

Table 6.6 Precedence of Operators

Operator	Precedence
( )	Highest
!	↑
– (unary minus)	
^	
* /	
+ –, ||	
< <= > >=	
LIKE IN BETWEEN	
NOT	
AND OR	Lowest

6.6 SIGNIFICANCE OF NULL VALUES

NULL values signify the absence of data items, which means the missing information. They form another data type in MariaDB. NULLs are not same as zeros, low-values or spaces. Fields containing NULL values are not considered for processing. They are ignored. Keyword 'NULL' can be used to specify NULL values. For example, to list the names and departments of those employees whose head column is NUll, the query can be as follows:

SELECT EMP_CODE, EMP_NAME FROM EMPLOYEE WHERE HEAD IS NULL;

```
MariaDB [OFFICE]> SELECT EMP_CODE, EMP_NAME FROM EMPLOYEE
    -> WHERE HEAD IS NULL;
+----------+-------------+
| EMP_CODE | EMP_NAME    |
+----------+-------------+
|      101 | Raju        |
|      105 | Suraj Patel |
|      107 | Ramaswamy   |
+----------+-------------+
3 rows in set (0.101 sec)
```

Figure 6.11 Use of NULL

6.7 DEFINING AND USING COLUMN ALIAS

By default, the column headings in a query, shows that name which we gave at the time of table creation. We can also change this name or we can also give a different name i.e., an alias name of a column for an output. Suppose you want to change the DESIG to DESIGNATION for a different output, we can write the following command:

SELECT EMP_NAME, DESIG DESIGNATION FROM EMPLOYEE;

See the output as shown in Figure 6.12.

If a column alias consists of more than one word, then it should be enclosed in quotes as in "HIS DESIGNATION", otherwise error message is displayed.

Column Alias does not rename a column. It simply displays a different column name in the output. The **AS** keyword between the column name and alias is optional. We can also write:

```
SELECT EMP_NAME, DESIG "HIS DESIGNATION"
FROM EMPLOYEE;
```

(See Figure 6.13).

```
MariaDB [OFFICE]> SELECT EMP_NAME, DESIG DESIGNATION FROM EMPLOYEE;
+-------------+-------------+
| EMP_NAME    | DESIGNATION |
+-------------+-------------+
| Raju        | Manager     |
| Amar Roy    | Salesman    |
| Raj         | Assistant   |
| Rajiv Kumar | As. Engineer |
| Suraj Patel | Area Manager |
| Binay Kumar | Salesman    |
| Ramaswamy   | Engineer    |
| Jog Iyer    | Assistant   |
| Imran Khan  | Steno       |
| Tinu Anand  | As. Engineer |
+-------------+-------------+
10 rows in set (0.039 sec)
```

Figure 6.12 Alias name for Column heading

```
MariaDB [OFFICE]> SELECT EMP_NAME, DESIG "HIS DESIGNATION" FROM EMPLOYEE;
+-------------+-----------------+
| EMP_NAME    | HIS DESIGNATION |
+-------------+-----------------+
| Raju        | Manager         |
| Amar Roy    | Salesman        |
| Raj         | Assistant       |
| Rajiv Kumar | As. Engineer    |
| Suraj Patel | Area Manager    |
| Binay Kumar | Salesman        |
| Ramaswamy   | Engineer        |
| Jog Iyer    | Assistant       |
| Imran Khan  | Steno           |
| Tinu Anand  | As. Engineer    |
+-------------+-----------------+
10 rows in set (0.001 sec)
```

Figure 6.13 Alias name for Column heading

6.8 PUTTING TEXT IN QUERY OUTPUT

We can also make the query output more presentable by inserting items such as symbols or text in the query output. For example,

```
SELECT EMP_NAME, 'IS A', DESIG, 'AND
BASIC IS', BASIC FROM EMPLOYEE;
```

The text 'IS A' and 'AND BASIC IS' are displayed with every row of the table (See Figure 6.14).

```
MariaDB [OFFICE]> SELECT EMP_NAME, 'IS A', DESIG, 'AND BASIC IS', BASIC FROM
EMPLOYEE;
+-------------+------+--------------+--------------+-------+
| EMP_NAME    | IS A | DESIG        | AND BASIC IS | BASIC |
+-------------+------+--------------+--------------+-------+
| Raju        | IS A | Manager      | AND BASIC IS |  8000 |
| Amar Roy    | IS A | Salesman     | AND BASIC IS |  4000 |
| Raj         | IS A | Assistant    | AND BASIC IS |  4500 |
| Rajiv Kumar | IS A | As. Engineer | AND BASIC IS |  6200 |
| Suraj Patel | IS A | Area Manager | AND BASIC IS |  7500 |
| Binay Kumar | IS A | Salesman     | AND BASIC IS |  4270 |
| Ramaswamy   | IS A | Engineer     | AND BASIC IS |  6500 |
| Jog Iyer    | IS A | Assistant    | AND BASIC IS |  4250 |
| Imran Khan  | IS A | Steno        | AND BASIC IS |  4500 |
| Tinu Anand  | IS A | As. Engineer | AND BASIC IS |  6000 |
+-------------+------+--------------+--------------+-------+
10 rows in set (0.002 sec)
```

Figure 6.14 Text added in Query Output

6.9 DISTINCT KEYWORD

DISTINCT keyword eliminates rows containing duplicate records before giving output. This would ensure that the resulting rows are unique.

For example, to find the unique DESIGNATIONS from EMPLOYEE table, type the following query:

```
SELECT DISTINCT DESIG FROM EMPLOYEE;
```

```
MariaDB [OFFICE]> SELECT DISTINCT DESIG FROM EMPLOYEE;
+--------------+
| DESIG        |
+--------------+
| Manager      |
| Salesman     |
| Assistant    |
| As. Engineer |
| Area Manager |
| Engineer     |
| Steno        |
+--------------+
7 rows in set (0.330 sec)
```

Figure 6.15 Use of DISTINCT keyword

6.10 WHERE CLAUSE

We have so far selected all the rows of EMPLOYEE or DEPARTMENT table. But suppose we want to see only a certain number of rows that contain specific values. For this, we would need to place *WHERE* clause along with the *SELECT* statement. The syntax is:

```
SELECT <column_name(s)>
FROM <tablename>
WHERE [<column_name><operator><value>;
```

Suppose we want to see details of only those employees who are Salesmen. The command for such a query is:

```
SELECT EMP_CODE, EMP_NAME, DESIG, BASIC
    -> FROM EMPLOYEE
    -> WHERE DESIG = 'Salesman';
```

Here, the display of rows will be restricted to those where the condition (Desig = 'Salesman') is satisfied. Output of the above query is shown in Figure 6.16.

☞ *Note that strings are written inside single quotes.*

```
MariaDB [OFFICE]> SELECT EMP_CODE, EMP_NAME, DESIG, BASIC
    -> FROM EMPLOYEE
    -> WHERE DESIG = 'Salesman';
+----------+-------------+----------+-------+
| EMP_CODE | EMP_NAME    | DESIG    | BASIC |
+----------+-------------+----------+-------+
|      102 | Amar Roy    | Salesman |  4000 |
|      106 | Binay Kumar | Salesman |  4270 |
+----------+-------------+----------+-------+
2 rows in set (0.556 sec)
```

Figure 6.16 Extracting data of 'Salesman' from Employee table

All comparison operators, namely `>`, `<`, `=`, `>=`, `<=` and `<>` (not equals) are supported by MariaDB. Moreover, MariaDB also supports Boolean operators NOT, AND and OR. For example, type the following command to extract records (rows) of those Salesmen who are earning a basic salary less than or equal to (<=) 4000. The following statement will extract such records.

```
SELECT EMP_CODE, EMP_NAME, DESIG, BASIC
    -> FROM EMPLOYEE
    -> WHERE BASIC <= 4000 AND DESIG =
'Salesman';
```

Figure 6.17 shows one such record.

```
MariaDB [OFFICE]> SELECT EMP_CODE, EMP_NAME, DESIG, BASIC
    -> FROM EMPLOYEE
    -> WHERE BASIC <= 4000 AND DESIG = 'Salesman';
+----------+----------+----------+-------+
| EMP_CODE | EMP_NAME | DESIG    | BASIC |
+----------+----------+----------+-------+
|      102 | Amar Roy | Salesman |  4000 |
+----------+----------+----------+-------+
1 row in set (0.278 sec)
```

Figure 6.17 Extracting records of Salesmen drawing Basic $\leq$ 4000

Special operators available in SQL namely, IN, BETWEEN, LIKE and NOT BETWEEN can also be used while making a query. For example, to list the name of the employees whose employee codes are 103, 105, 106, 107 and 110, we can use the IN operator as follows:

```
SELECT EMP_NAME FROM EMPLOYEE
    -> WHERE EMP_CODE IN(103, 105, 106,
107, 110);
```

Output of this query is shown in Figure 6.18.

```
MariaDB [OFFICE]> SELECT EMP_NAME FROM EMPLOYEE
    -> WHERE EMP_CODE IN(103, 105, 106, 107, 110);
+-------------+
| EMP_NAME    |
+-------------+
| Raj         |
| Suraj Patel |
| Binay Kumar |
| Ramaswamy   |
| Tinu Anand  |
+-------------+
5 rows in set (0.856 sec)
```

Figure 6.18 Query using operators IN

Similarly, to list the name of the employees whose employee codes are **not** 103, 105, 106, 107 and 110, we can use the NOT IN operator as follows:

```
SELECT EMP_NAME FROM EMPLOYEE
    -> WHERE EMP_CODE NOT IN (103, 105,
106, 107, 110);
```

Output of the above query is shown in Figure 6.19.

```
MariaDB [OFFICE]> SELECT EMP_NAME FROM EMPLOYEE
    -> WHERE EMP_CODE NOT IN (103, 105, 106, 107, 110);
+-------------+
| EMP_NAME    |
+-------------+
| Raju        |
| Amar Roy    |
| Rajiv Kumar |
| Jog Iyer    |
| Imran Khan  |
+-------------+
5 rows in set (0.001 sec)
```

Figure 6.19 Query using operators NOT IN

The operator BETWEEN is used to specify a range of values. For example, to list the names of the employees who joint after 1st JANUARY 2000 and before 31st DECEMBER 2000, meaning who joint during the year 2000, we will use the following statement:

```
SELECT EMP_NAME, DOJ FROM EMPLOYEE
    -> WHERE DOJ BETWEEN '2000-01-01' AND
'2000-12-31';
```

Output of the above query is shown in Figure 6.20.

```
MariaDB [OFFICE]> SELECT EMP_NAME, DOJ FROM EMPLOYEE
    -> WHERE DOJ BETWEEN '2000-01-01' AND '2000-12-31';
+----------+------------+
| EMP_NAME | DOJ        |
+----------+------------+
| Raju     | 2000-12-17 |
| Amar Roy | 2000-02-20 |
+----------+------------+
2 rows in set (0.001 sec)
```

Figure 6.20 Query using BETWEEN operator

Suppose we want to see those employee names which begin with letter 'S'. We will use the following statement:

```
SELECT EMP_NAME FROM EMPLOYEE
    -> WHERE EMP_NAME LIKE 'S%';
```

☞ *Note that the patterns are case sensitive i.e., upper case letters do not match lower case letters.*

Output of the above query is shown in Figure 6.21.

```
MariaDB [OFFICE]> SELECT EMP_NAME FROM EMPLOYEE
    -> WHERE EMP_NAME LIKE 'S%';
+-------------+
| EMP_NAME    |
+-------------+
| Suraj Patel |
+-------------+
1 row in set (0.113 sec)
```

Figure 6.21 Query using LIKE operator

Example

To find names beginning with 'R'.

```
SELECT EMP_NAME FROM EMPLOYEE
    -> WHERE EMP_NAME LIKE 'R%';
```

Output of the above query is shown in Figure 6.22.

```
MariaDB [OFFICE]> SELECT EMP_NAME FROM EMPLOYEE
    -> WHERE EMP_NAME LIKE 'R%';
+-------------+
| EMP_NAME    |
+-------------+
| Raju        |
| Raj         |
| Rajiv Kumar |
| Ramaswamy   |
+-------------+
4 rows in set (0.001 sec)
```

Figure 6.22 Query using LIKE operator

Example

To find names ending with 'ar'.

```
SELECT EMP_NAME FROM EMPLOYEE
    -> WHERE EMP_NAME LIKE '%ar';
```

Output of the above query is shown in Figure 6.23.

```
MariaDB [OFFICE]> SELECT EMP_NAME FROM EMPLOYEE
    -> WHERE EMP_NAME LIKE '%ar';
+-------------+
| EMP_NAME    |
+-------------+
| Rajiv Kumar |
| Binay Kumar |
+-------------+
2 rows in set (0.000 sec)
```

Figure 6.23 Query using LIKE operator

Example

To find names containing a letter 't'.

```
SELECT EMP_NAME
    -> FROM EMPLOYEE
    -> WHERE EMP_NAME LIKE "%t%";
```

Output of the above query is shown in Figure 6.24.

```
MariaDB [OFFICE]> SELECT EMP_NAME
    -> FROM EMPLOYEE
    -> WHERE EMP_NAME LIKE "%t%";
+-------------+
| EMP_NAME    |
+-------------+
| Suraj Patel |
| Tinu Anand  |
+-------------+
2 rows in set (0.001 sec)
```

Figure 6.24 Query using LIKE operator

Example

To find names containing exactly eleven characters, use the '_' pattern character.

```
SELECT EMP_NAME
    -> FROM EMPLOYEE
    -> WHERE EMP_NAME LIKE "___________";
```

```
MariaDB [OFFICE]> SELECT EMP_NAME
    -> FROM EMPLOYEE
    -> WHERE EMP_NAME LIKE "___________";
+-------------+
| EMP_NAME    |
+-------------+
| Rajiv Kumar |
| Suraj Patel |
| Binay Kumar |
+-------------+
3 rows in set (0.001 sec)
```

Figure 6.25 Query using LIKE operator

Example

To find employee names whose second character is an alphabet 'a'.

```
SELECT EMP_NAME
    -> FROM EMPLOYEE
    -> WHERE EMP_NAME LIKE "_a%";
```

Output of the above query is shown in Figure 6.26.

```
MariaDB [OFFICE]> SELECT EMP_NAME
    -> FROM EMPLOYEE
    -> WHERE EMP_NAME LIKE "_a%";
+-------------+
| EMP_NAME    |
+-------------+
| Raju        |
| Raj         |
| Rajiv Kumar |
| Ramaswamy   |
+-------------+
4 rows in set (0.001 sec)
```

Figure 6.26 Query using LIKE operator

6.11 ORDER BY CLAUSE

In general, the rows displayed from a query do not have any specific order. But if you want them to be shown in ascending or descending order in a particular field, then you can control this order even for the selected rows. This is done by adding the clause **ORDER BY** to the *SELECT* command. The syntax is as follows:

```
SELECT <column_name(s)>
FROM <tablename>
WHERE <condition>
ORDER BY <column to be ordered>
[<ASC/DESC>];
```

The command, *Order by*, will sort the selected rows as specified. For example, the clause *ASC* sorts and displays in the ascending order, from lowest value to largest value. Even if you do not specify the ASC clause, still the sorting of the rows would be done in the ascending order by *default*.

☞ *MariaDB will automatically order the output rows from lowest to highest order, unless you specify the clause DESC.*

The order *DESC* sorts and displays rows in descending order, namely from highest value to lowest value for the specified attribute.

6.11.1 Sorting in Ascending /Descending Order

If you want the list of all employees name in ascending order then type the following MariaDB statement:

```
SELECT EMP_CODE, EMP_NAME, DESIG, BASIC
    -> FROM EMPLOYEE
    -> ORDER BY EMP_NAME;
```

The result will be displayed as shown in Figure 6.27.

If you want to show the employees BASIC salary in the descending order, then type the following:

```
SELECT EMP_CODE, EMP_NAME, DESIG, BASIC
    -> FROM EMPLOYEE
    -> ORDER BY BASIC DESC;
```

The result will be displayed as shown in Figure 6.28.

```
MariaDB [OFFICE]> SELECT EMP_CODE, EMP_NAME, DESIG, BASIC
    -> FROM EMPLOYEE
    -> ORDER BY EMP_NAME;
+----------+------------+--------------+-------+
| EMP_CODE | EMP_NAME   | DESIG        | BASIC |
+----------+------------+--------------+-------+
|      102 | Amar Roy   | Salesman     |  4000 |
|      106 | Binay Kumar| Salesman     |  4270 |
|      109 | Imran Khan | Steno        |  4500 |
|      108 | Jog Iyer   | Assistant    |  4250 |
|      103 | Raj        | Assistant    |  4500 |
|      104 | Rajiv Kumar| As. Engineer |  6200 |
|      101 | Raju       | Manager      |  8000 |
|      107 | Ramaswamy  | Engineer     |  6500 |
|      105 | Suraj Patel| Area Manager |  7500 |
|      110 | Tinu Anand | As. Engineer |  6000 |
+----------+------------+--------------+-------+
10 rows in set (0.002 sec)
```

Figure 6.27 Sorting in Ascending Order by EMP_NAME

```
MariaDB [OFFICE]> SELECT EMP_CODE, EMP_NAME, DESIG, BASIC
    -> FROM EMPLOYEE
    -> ORDER BY BASIC DESC;
+----------+------------+--------------+-------+
| EMP_CODE | EMP_NAME   | DESIG        | BASIC |
+----------+------------+--------------+-------+
|      101 | Raju       | Manager      |  8000 |
|      105 | Suraj Patel| Area Manager |  7500 |
|      107 | Ramaswamy  | Engineer     |  6500 |
|      104 | Rajiv Kumar| As. Engineer |  6200 |
|      110 | Tinu Anand | As. Engineer |  6000 |
|      103 | Raj        | Assistant    |  4500 |
|      109 | Imran Khan | Steno        |  4500 |
|      106 | Binay Kumar| Salesman     |  4270 |
|      108 | Jog Iyer   | Assistant    |  4250 |
|      102 | Amar Roy   | Salesman     |  4000 |
+----------+------------+--------------+-------+
10 rows in set (0.003 sec)
```

Figure 6.28 Sorting in Descending order by BASIC

6.11.2 Sorting on Multiple Columns

You can also specify more than one column in the ORDER BY clause. In such a case, the result will be set by the first column in the ORDER BY clause, then by the second column and so on. The following query shows how to sort on multiple columns:

```
SELECT DEPT_CODE, DOJ, EMP_NAME
    -> FROM EMPLOYEE
    -> ORDER BY DEPT_CODE, DOJ DESC;
```

The output of the above query is shown in Figure 6.29. Note that the records are first sorted on DEPT_CODE in ascending order. If more than one record appears with the same DEPT_CODE, then such records are further sorted on DOJ in descending order.

```
MariaDB [OFFICE]> SELECT DEPT_CODE, DOJ, EMP_NAME
    -> FROM EMPLOYEE
    -> ORDER BY DEPT_CODE, DOJ DESC;
+-----------+------------+-------------+
| DEPT_CODE | DOJ        | EMP_NAME    |
+-----------+------------+-------------+
|        10 | 2003-01-12 | Tinu Anand  |
|        10 | 2001-06-09 | Ramaswamy   |
|        10 | 2001-04-02 | Rajiv Kumar |
|        20 | 2003-02-22 | Raj         |
|        20 | 2000-12-17 | Raju        |
|        30 | 2002-12-09 | Jog Iyer    |
|        30 | 2001-11-17 | Imran Khan  |
|        30 | 2001-09-28 | Suraj Patel |
|        30 | 2001-05-01 | Binay Kumar |
|        30 | 2000-02-20 | Amar Roy    |
+-----------+------------+-------------+
10 rows in set (0.001 sec)
```

Figure 6.29 Sorting on multiple columns

6.12 MariaDB FUNCTIONS

Functions are a powerful feature of MariaDB. Using these functions, we can find sum of values stored in a column or convert all characters of a name to lowercase or round off salaries in a column to two decimal places and so on. MariaDB supports functions that can be used to manipulate data.

Such functions can be classified into the following two types:

(a) *Single-row functions:* They work with a single row at a time. A single row function returns a result for every row of the table, on which a query is made.

(b) *Multiple-row (Aggregate) functions:* They work with data of multiple rows at a time and return aggregated or total values. For example, SUM(), AVG() and COUNT() are some multiple-row functions.

6.13 SINGLE-ROW FUNCTIONS

The single-row functions can be further classified into the following three types:

(a) String (Character) Functions

(b) Numeric (mathematical) Functions

(c) Date and Time Functions

Let us begin with the String Functions. The examples in this chapter refers to the tables Employee and Department.

6.13.1 String Functions

String (Character) functions accept a character input and returns character and/or numeric values. String functions are used to extract, change, format or alter character strings. These are discussed in the following sub-sections.

CHAR()

The *CHAR()* function returns the character for each integer passed. Syntax for *CHAR()* function takes the following form:

CHAR(V1, V2, ...Vn)

CHAR() interprets each argument *V* as an integer and returns a string consisting of the characters given by the code values of those integers. NULL values are ignored. For example,

SELECT CHAR(77,79,66,73,76,69);

will give the output as seen in Figure 6.30.

```
MariaDB [OFFICE]> SELECT CHAR(77,79,66,73,76,69);
+------------------------+
| CHAR(77,79,66,73,76,69) |
+------------------------+
| MOBILE                 |
+------------------------+
1 row in set (0.000 sec)
```

Figure 6.30 Use of CHAR() function

```
MariaDB [OFFICE]> SELECT CHAR(65);
+----------+
| CHAR(65) |
+----------+
| A        |
+----------+
1 row in set (0.001 sec)
MariaDB [OFFICE]> SELECT CHAR('97');
+------------+
| CHAR('97') |
+------------+
| a          |
+------------+
1 row in set (0.002 sec)
```

Figure 6.31 Use of CHAR() function

CONCAT(string1, string2,....)

The *CONCAT(string1, string2,....)* returns the string that results from concatenating the arguments. It may have one or more arguments. For example the query :

SELECT CONCAT('MY', 'S', 'QL');

and the query:

SELECT CONCAT('CARE','LESS');

will give the following as shown in Figure 6.32.

```
MariaDB [OFFICE]> SELECT CONCAT('MY', 'S', 'QL');
+------------------------+
| CONCAT('MY', 'S', 'QL') |
+------------------------+
| MYSQL                  |
+------------------------+
1 row in set (0.119 sec)

MariaDB [OFFICE]> SELECT CONCAT('CARE','LESS');
+----------------------+
| CONCAT('CARE','LESS') |
+----------------------+
| CARELESS             |
+----------------------+
1 row in set (0.000 sec)
```

Figure 6.32 Use of CONCAT() functions

INSTR()

The INSTR() function is used to find out where the particular pattern of characters occur in the given string. It is of the following form:

INSTR(string1, string2[, m[, n]])

Its first argument is the target string. The second argument is the pattern to match. The optional third and fourth arguments are numbers representing where to start looking and which match to report. For example,

SELECT INSTR('FOOTBALL','BALL');

The above statement will give the following output as shown in Figure 6.33.

```
MariaDB [OFFICE]> SELECT INSTR('FOOTBALL','BALL');
+-------------------------+
| INSTR('FOOTBALL','BALL') |
+-------------------------+
|                       5 |
+-------------------------+
1 row in set (0.106 sec)
```

Figure 6.33 Use of string function INSTR()

Suppose we want to find out the first occurrence of the character *u*, then use the following command:

```
SELECT EMP_NAME, INSTR(EMP_NAME,'u')
    -> FROM EMPLOYEE;
```

The above statement will give the following output as shown in Figure 6.34.

```
MariaDB [OFFICE]> SELECT EMP_NAME, INSTR(EMP_NAME,'u')
    -> FROM EMPLOYEE;
+------------+--------------------+
| EMP_NAME   | INSTR(EMP_NAME,'u') |
+------------+--------------------+
| Raju       |                  4 |
| Amar Roy   |                  0 |
| Raj        |                  0 |
| Rajiv Kumar |                 8 |
| Suraj Patel |                 2 |
| Binay Kumar |                 8 |
| Ramaswamy  |                  0 |
| Jog Iyer   |                  0 |
| Imran Khan |                  0 |
| Tinu Anand |                  4 |
+------------+--------------------+
10 rows in set (0.002 sec)
```

Figure 6.34 Use of string function INSTR()

LOWER(string) or LCASE(string)

The *LOWER(string)* or *LCASE(string)* converts all the characters in the string to the lowercase letters. For example,

SELECT LCASE('BPB PUBLICATIONS');

```
MariaDB [OFFICE]> SELECT LCASE('BPB PUBLICATIONS');
+---------------------------+
| LCASE('BPB PUBLICATIONS') |
+---------------------------+
| bpb publications          |
+---------------------------+
1 row in set (0.104 sec)
```

Figure 6.35 Use of string functions LCASE()

UPPER(string) or UCASE(string)

UPPER (string) or *UCASE(string)* converts all the characters in the string to uppercase letters. For example, 'bpb publication' will be changed to 'BPB PUBLICATION', by this function. For example, the query:

SELECT UCASE('bpb publication');

will give the output as shown in Figure 6.36.

```
MariaDB [OFFICE]> SELECT UCASE('bpb publication');
+--------------------------+
| UCASE('bpb publication') |
+--------------------------+
| BPB PUBLICATION          |
+--------------------------+
1 row in set (0.050 sec)
```

Figure 6.36 Use of string function UCASE()

Now write following MariaDB command to display EMP_NAME in lower and upper case:

```
SELECT LOWER(EMP_NAME), UPPER(EMP_NAME)
    -> FROM EMPLOYEE;
```

```
MariaDB [OFFICE]> SELECT LOWER(EMP_NAME), UPPER(EMP_NAME)
    -> FROM EMPLOYEE;
+-----------------+-----------------+
| LOWER(EMP_NAME) | UPPER(EMP_NAME) |
+-----------------+-----------------+
| raju            | RAJU            |
| amar roy        | AMAR ROY        |
| raj             | RAJ             |
| rajiv kumar     | RAJIV KUMAR     |
| suraj patel     | SURAJ PATEL     |
| binay kumar     | BINAY KUMAR     |
| ramaswamy       | RAMASWAMY       |
| jog iyer        | JOG IYER        |
| imran khan      | IMRAN KHAN      |
| tinu anand      | TINU ANAND      |
+-----------------+-----------------+
10 rows in set (0.001 sec)
```

Figure 6.37 Use of string functions LCASE() and UCASE()

LEFT(string,n)

LEFT(string,n) returns the specified number of characters (*n*) from the left side of string or NULL if any argument is NULL. For example,

SELECT LEFT('FOOTBALL',5);

will give the output as shown in Figure 6.38.

```
MariaDB [OFFICE]> SELECT LEFT('FOOTBALL',5);
+--------------------+
| LEFT('FOOTBALL',5) |
+--------------------+
| FOOTB              |
+--------------------+
1 row in set (0.000 sec)
```

Figure 6.38 Use of string functions LEFT()

RIGHT(string,n)

RIGHT(string,n) returns the specified number of characters (*n*) from the right side of string or NULL if any argument is NULL. For example,

SELECT RIGHT('FOOTBALL',5);

will give the output as shown in Figure 6.39.

```
MariaDB [OFFICE]> SELECT RIGHT('FOOTBALL',5);
+---------------------+
| RIGHT('FOOTBALL',5) |
+---------------------+
| TBALL               |
+---------------------+
1 row in set (0.002 sec)
```

Figure 6.39 Use of string functions RIGHT()

Now let us use LEFT() and RIGHT() functions on DEPARTMENT table as shown in Figure 6.40.

```
MariaDB [OFFICE]> SELECT LEFT(DEPT_NAME,3),
    -> RIGHT(DEPT_NAME,3) FROM DEPARTMENT;
+-------------------+--------------------+
| LEFT(DEPT_NAME,3) | RIGHT(DEPT_NAME,3) |
+-------------------+--------------------+
| ACC               | NTS                |
| Res               | rch                |
| Sal               | les                |
| Ope               | ons                |
+-------------------+--------------------+
4 rows in set (0.002 sec)
```

Figure 6.40 Use LEFT() and RIGHT() functions on DEPARTMENT table

LENGTH(string)

LENGTH(string) returns the length of its character argument in bytes. For example, the statement:

```
SELECT EMP_NAME, LENGTH(EMP_NAME)
    -> FROM EMPLOYEE;
```

will give the output as shown in Figure 6.41.

```
MariaDB [OFFICE]> SELECT EMP_NAME, LENGTH(EMP_NAME)
    -> FROM EMPLOYEE;
+-------------+------------------+
| EMP_NAME    | LENGTH(EMP_NAME) |
+-------------+------------------+
| Raju        |                4 |
| Amar Roy    |                8 |
| Raj         |                3 |
| Rajiv Kumar |               11 |
| Suraj Patel |               11 |
| Binay Kumar |               11 |
| Ramaswamy   |                9 |
| Jog Iyer    |                8 |
| Imran Khan  |               10 |
| Tinu Anand  |               10 |
+-------------+------------------+
10 rows in set (0.008 sec)
```

Figure 6.41 Use of string function LENGTH()

LTRIM(string)

The *LTRIM(string)* function returns the string with leading space characters removed i.e., removes spaces from the left side of the string.

For example,

SELECT LTRIM('   BPB PUBLICATIONS');

will give the following output (See Figure 6.42):

```
MariaDB [(none)]> SELECT LTRIM('     BPB PUBLICATIONS');
+-------------------------------+
| LTRIM('     BPB PUBLICATIONS') |
+-------------------------------+
| BPB PUBLICATIONS              |
+-------------------------------+
1 row in set (0.001 sec)
```

Figure 6.42 Use of LTRIM() function

RTRIM(string)

The *RTRIM(string)* function returns the string with trailing space characters removed i.e., removes spaces from the right side of the string.

For example,

SELECT RTRIM('BPB PUBLICATIONS   ');

will give the following output (See Figure 6.43):

```
MariaDB [(none)]> SELECT RTRIM('BPB PUBLICATIONS      ');
+----------------------------------+
| RTRIM('BPB PUBLICATIONS      ') |
+----------------------------------+
| BPB PUBLICATIONS                 |
+----------------------------------+
1 row in set (0.098 sec)
```

Figure 6.43 Use of RTRIM() function

TRIM()

The *TRIM()* function removes both leading and trailing spaces from the string. Syntax of *TRIM()* function are given below:

TRIM([{BOTH | LEADING | TRAILING} [remstring] FROM] string)

TRIM([remstring FROM] string)

If none of the specifiers *BOTH, LEADING*, or *TRAILING* is given, *BOTH* is assumed. *remstring* is optional and, if not specified, spaces are removed. For example,

SELECT TRIM('   BPB PUBLICATIONS   ');

will give the following output (See Figure 6.44):

```
MariaDB [(none)]> SELECT TRIM('      BPB PUBLICATIONS      ');
+-------------------------------------+
| TRIM('      BPB PUBLICATIONS     ') |
+-------------------------------------+
| BPB PUBLICATIONS                    |
+-------------------------------------+
1 row in set (0.000 sec)
```

Figure 6.44 Use of TRIM() function

Suppose, we want to remove the 'R' from the left side of the Employee name in Employee Table, then we have to give the following command (See Figure 6.45 for the output):

SELECT EMP_NAME, TRIM(LEADING 'R' FROM EMP_NAME)
-> FROM EMPLOYEE;

```
MariaDB [OFFICE]> SELECT EMP_NAME, TRIM(LEADING 'R' FROM EMP_NAME)
    -> FROM EMPLOYEE;
+-------------+---------------------------------+
| EMP_NAME    | TRIM(LEADING 'R' FROM EMP_NAME) |
+-------------+---------------------------------+
| Raju        | aju                             |
| Amar Roy    | Amar Roy                        |
| Raj         | aj                              |
| Rajiv Kumar | ajiv Kumar                      |
| Suraj Patel | Suraj Patel                     |
| Binay Kumar | Binay Kumar                     |
| Ramaswamy   | amaswamy                        |
| Jog Iyer    | Jog Iyer                        |
| Imran Khan  | Imran Khan                      |
| Tinu Anand  | Tinu Anand                      |
+-------------+---------------------------------+
10 rows in set (0.002 sec)
```

Figure 6.45 Examples showing TRIM()function

Now suppose, we want to remove the 'r' from the right side of the Employee name from Employee Table, then we have to give the following command:

SELECT EMP_NAME, TRIM(TRAILING 'r' FROM EMP_NAME)
-> FROM EMPLOYEE;

will give the output as shown in Figure 6.46.

```
MariaDB [OFFICE]> SELECT EMP_NAME, TRIM(TRAILING 'r' FROM EMP_NAME)
    -> FROM EMPLOYEE;
+-------------+--------------------------------+
| EMP_NAME    | TRIM(TRAILING 'r' FROM EMP_NAME) |
+-------------+--------------------------------+
| Raju        | Raju                           |
| Amar Roy    | Amar Roy                       |
| Raj         | Raj                            |
| Rajiv Kumar | Rajiv Kuma                     |
| Suraj Patel | Suraj Patel                    |
| Binay Kumar | Binay Kuma                     |
| Ramaswamy   | Ramaswamy                      |
| Jog Iyer    | Jog Iye                        |
| Imran Khan  | Imran Khan                     |
| Tinu Anand  | Tinu Anand                     |
+-------------+--------------------------------+
10 rows in set (0.001 sec)
```

Figure 6.46 Examples showing TRIM()function

SUBSTR(string, M, N) or SUBSTRING(string, M, N) Or MID(string, M, N)

The *SUBSTR(string, M, N)* function returns a sub-string, *N* characters long, from the *string* (source string), starting from position *M*. If the number of characters, *N*, is not specified, the string is extracted from position M to end. Note that blank spaces are also counted. For example,

SELECT SUBSTR('I WILL KILL YOU', 8,4);

will give the output as shown in Figure 6.47. This is so because from 8th character position, the word 'K' starts and the 4 characters will give output 'KILL'.

It is also possible to use a negative value for the second argument. In such a case, the beginning of the substring is positioned from the end of the string (See Figure 6.47). For example,

SELECT SUBSTR('I WILL KILL YOU', -3);

SELECT SUBSTR('I WILL KILL YOU', -8,4);

```
MariaDB [(none)]> SELECT SUBSTR('I WILL KILL YOU', 8,4);
+--------------------------------+
| SUBSTR('I WILL KILL YOU', 8,4) |
+--------------------------------+
| KILL                           |
+--------------------------------+
1 row in set (0.000 sec)

MariaDB [(none)]> SELECT SUBSTR('I WILL KILL YOU', -3);
+-------------------------------+
| SUBSTR('I WILL KILL YOU', -3) |
+-------------------------------+
| YOU                           |
+-------------------------------+
1 row in set (0.105 sec)
```

(Conti...)

```
MariaDB [(none)]> SELECT SUBSTR('I WILL KILL YOU', -8,4);
+---------------------------------+
| SUBSTR('I WILL KILL YOU', -8,4) |
+---------------------------------+
| KILL                            |
+---------------------------------+
1 row in set (0.000 sec)
```

Figure 6.47 Examples of SUBSTR()

The following statement will return a substring from Employee Table (See Figure 6.48).

```
SELECT MID(EMP_NAME,3,2)
    -> FROM EMPLOYEE;
```

```
MariaDB [OFFICE]> SELECT MID(EMP_NAME,3,2)
    -> FROM EMPLOYEE;
+-------------------+
| MID(EMP_NAME,3,2) |
+-------------------+
| ju                |
| ar                |
| j                 |
| ji                |
| ra                |
| na                |
| ma                |
| g                 |
| ra                |
| nu                |
+-------------------+
10 rows in set (0.001 sec)
```

Figure 6.48 Example MID() function

ASCII(string)

ASCII(string) returns the ASCII value of the left-most character of the string. It returns 0 if string is an empty string and NULL if string is NULL. For example (See Figure 6.49):

```
MariaDB [(none)]> SELECT ASCII('dall');
+---------------+
| ASCII('dall') |
+---------------+
|           100 |
+---------------+
1 row in set (0.000 sec)
```

(Conti...)

```
MariaDB [(none)]> SELECT ASCII('');
+-----------+
| ASCII('') |
+-----------+
|         0 |
+-----------+
1 row in set (0.000 sec)
MariaDB [(none)]> SELECT ASCII(NULL);
+-------------+
| ASCII(NULL) |
+-------------+
|        NULL |
+-------------+
1 row in set (0.000 sec)
```

Figure 6.49 Examples showing the use of ASCII() function

6.13.2 Numeric or Mathematical Functions

The Numeric functions accept numeric values and after performing the required operation, return numeric values. Some numeric functions are discussed in the following sections.

POWER(M, N)

The *POWER(M, N)* returns M raised to the power N. Note that N must be an integer.

For example the query:

```
SELECT POWER(2,4);
```

will give output 16 as shown in Figure 6.50.

```
SELECT BASIC, POWER(BASIC,2)
    -> FROM EMPLOYEE;
```

will give the square of Basic salary as output as shown in Figure 6.50.

ROUND(m,n)

The *ROUND(m,n)* function returns a number rounded as required. It takes two integer arguments. The first argument (*m*) is the number to be rounded off and the second argument (*n*) specifies the number of places to which the number should be rounded off.

For example, the following statement will round 1543.286 to 1 place because if positive value is specified for precision, it counts off that value right from the decimal point.

```
SELECT ROUND(1543.286,1);
```

The output of the above statement is shown in Figure 6.51.

If number of decimal places is not specified or is zero, the number rounds to the nearest integer OR (0 decimal places).

```
SELECT ROUND(1543.286);
```

The output of the above statement is shown in Figure 6.51.

If negative value is specified for precision, it counts off that value left from the decimal point. For example (See Figure 6.51),

```
SELECT ROUND(1543.286,-1);
```

The output of the above statement is shown in Figure 6.51.

TRUNCATE(X,D)

The *TRUNCATE(X,D)* function returns a number (*X*) with specified number of digits (*D*) to be truncated. For example, the following function will truncate 1543.286 to 2 decimal places.

```
SELECT TRUNCATE(1543.286,2);
```

The output will be 1543.28 as shown in Figure 6.52.

Here, .286 is truncated after two decimal places. Hence, the result is .28.

If *D* is 0, the result has no decimal point or fractional part. For example,

```
SELECT TRUNCATE(1543.286,0);
```

The output of the above statement will be 1543.

If D is negative, it causes D digits left of the decimal point of the value X to become zero. For example,

```
SELECT TRUNCATE(1543.286,-2);
```

The output of the above statement will be 1500 as shown in Figure 6.52.

```
MariaDB [OFFICE]> SELECT POWER(2,4);
+------------+
| POWER(2,4) |
+------------+
|         16 |
+------------+
1 row in set (0.325 sec)
MariaDB [OFFICE]> SELECT BASIC, POWER(BASIC,2)
    -> FROM EMPLOYEE;
+-------+----------------+
| BASIC | POWER(BASIC,2) |
+-------+----------------+
|  8000 |       64000000 |
|  4000 |       16000000 |
|  4500 |       20250000 |
|  6200 |       38440000 |
|  7500 |       56250000 |
|  4270 |       18232900 |
|  6500 |       42250000 |
|  4250 |       18062500 |
|  4500 |       20250000 |
|  6000 |       36000000 |
+-------+----------------+
10 rows in set (0.001 sec)
```

Figure 6.50 Examples showing the use of POWER() function

```
MariaDB [OFFICE]> SELECT ROUND(1543.286,1);
+-------------------+
| ROUND(1543.286,1) |
+-------------------+
|            1543.3 |
+-------------------+
1 row in set (0.000 sec)
MariaDB [OFFICE]> SELECT ROUND(1543.286);
+-----------------+
| ROUND(1543.286) |
+-----------------+
|            1543 |
+-----------------+
1 row in set (0.000 sec)
MariaDB [OFFICE]> SELECT ROUND(1543.286,-1);
+--------------------+
| ROUND(1543.286,-1) |
+--------------------+
|               1540 |
+--------------------+
1 row in set (0.001 sec)
```

Figure 6.51 Examples showing the use of ROUND() function

```
MariaDB [OFFICE]> SELECT TRUNCATE(1543.286,2);
+----------------------+
| TRUNCATE(1543.286,2) |
+----------------------+
|              1543.28 |
+----------------------+
1 row in set (0.000 sec)

MariaDB [OFFICE]> SELECT TRUNCATE(1543.286,0);
+----------------------+
| TRUNCATE(1543.286,0) |
+----------------------+
|                 1543 |
+----------------------+
1 row in set (0.000 sec)

MariaDB [OFFICE]> SELECT TRUNCATE(1543.286,-2);
+-----------------------+
| TRUNCATE(1543.286,-2) |
+-----------------------+
|                  1500 |
+-----------------------+
1 row in set (0.000 sec)
```

Figure 6.52 Examples showing the use of TRUNCATE() function

TRUNCATE () does not round a number. It simply chops off digits from a number.

6.13.3 Date and Time Functions

Date and Time functions operate on data of the type Date. The default date format in MariaDB is YYYY-MM-DD. Some of these are discussed in following sections.

CURDATE() or CURRENT_DATE()

CURDATE() function returns the current date in YYYY-MM-DD format or YYYYMMDD format, depending on whether the function is used in a string or numeric context. For example,

```
SELECT CURDATE();
```

The output of the above statement is 2020-05-19 where 19th May, 2020 is the date on which the command was used and thus, the system's current date is shown (Figure 6.53).

DATE(expr)

DATE(expr) extracts the date part of a date or datetime expression. For example (See Figure 6.53),

```
SELECT DATE('2020-05-19 09:02:56');
```

MONTH(date)

MONTH(date) function returns the numeric month from the date passed, in the range 0 to 12. For example, the following statement will return 11 as a month (See Figure 6.53):

```
SELECT MONTH('2020-05-19');
```

Now take another example, suppose, we want to know the employee's name and the month at which they join the office, then we have to give the following statement (See Figure 6.54):

```
SELECT EMP_NAME,DOJ, MONTH(DOJ)
    -> FROM EMPLOYEE;
```

```
MariaDB [OFFICE]> SELECT CURDATE();
+------------+
| CURDATE()  |
+------------+
| 2020-05-19 |
+------------+
1 row in set (0.128 sec)
MariaDB [OFFICE]> SELECT DATE('2020-05-19 09:02:56');
+----------------------------+
| DATE('2020-05-19 09:02:56') |
+----------------------------+
| 2020-05-19                  |
+----------------------------+
1 row in set (0.000 sec)
MariaDB [OFFICE]> SELECT MONTH('2020-05-19');
+--------------------+
| MONTH('2020-05-19') |
+--------------------+
|                  5 |
+--------------------+
1 row in set (0.001 sec)
```

Figure 6.53 Examples of CURDATE() or CURRENT_DATE and DATE() functions

```
MariaDB [OFFICE]> SELECT EMP_NAME,DOJ, MONTH(DOJ)
    -> FROM EMPLOYEE;
+-------------+------------+------------+
| EMP_NAME    | DOJ        | MONTH(DOJ) |
+-------------+------------+------------+
| Raju        | 2000-12-17 |         12 |
| Amar Roy    | 2000-02-20 |          2 |
| Raj         | 2003-02-22 |          2 |
| Rajiv Kumar | 2001-04-02 |          4 |
| Suraj Patel | 2001-09-28 |          9 |
| Binay Kumar | 2001-05-01 |          5 |
| Ramaswamy   | 2001-06-09 |          6 |
| Jog Iyer    | 2002-12-09 |         12 |
| Imran Khan  | 2001-11-17 |         11 |
| Tinu Anand  | 2003-01-12 |          1 |
+-------------+------------+------------+
10 rows in set (0.001 sec)
```

Figure 6.54 Examples of MONTH() function

YEAR(date)

YEAR(date) returns the year for date passed in the range 0 to 9999. For example (See Figure 6.55),

`SELECT YEAR('2020-05-19');`

```
MariaDB [OFFICE]> SELECT YEAR('2020-05-19');
+--------------------+
| YEAR('2020-05-19') |
+--------------------+
|               2020 |
+--------------------+
1 row in set (0.000 sec)
```

Figure 6.55 Examples of YEAR() function

To know the employee's name and the year when they join the office, then we have to give the following statement (See Figure 6.56):

```
SELECT EMP_NAME, DOJ, YEAR(DOJ)
    -> FROM EMPLOYEE;
```

The above statement will display output as shown in Figure 6.56.

```
MariaDB [OFFICE]> SELECT EMP_NAME, DOJ, YEAR(DOJ)
    -> FROM EMPLOYEE;
+-------------+------------+-----------+
| EMP_NAME    | DOJ        | YEAR(DOJ) |
+-------------+------------+-----------+
| Raju        | 2000-12-17 |      2000 |
| Amar Roy    | 2000-02-20 |      2000 |
| Raj         | 2003-02-22 |      2003 |
| Rajiv Kumar | 2001-04-02 |      2001 |
| Suraj Patel | 2001-09-28 |      2001 |
| Binay Kumar | 2001-05-01 |      2001 |
| Ramaswamy   | 2001-06-09 |      2001 |
| Jog Iyer    | 2002-12-09 |      2002 |
| Imran Khan  | 2001-11-17 |      2001 |
| Tinu Anand  | 2003-01-12 |      2003 |
+-------------+------------+-----------+
10 rows in set (0.001 sec)
```

Figure 6.56 Examples of YEAR() function

DAYNAME(date)

DAYNAME(date) returns the name of the day for date passed. Suppose, you want to know which day you were born on. For this you can use *DAYNAME()* function. For example,

```
SELECT DAYNAME('2020-05-19');
```

The above statement will display output as shown in Figure 6.57.

DAYOFMONTH(date)

DAYOFMONTH(date) returns the day of the month in the range 0 to 31. For example,

```
SELECT DAYOFMONTH('2020-05-19');
```

The output of the above statement is shown in Figure 6.57.

DAYOFWEEK(date)

DAYOFWEEK(date) returns the day of week in number such as 1 for Sunday, 2 for Monday and so on. For example (See Figure 6.57),

```
SELECT DAYOFWEEK('2020-05-19');
```

DAYOFYEAR(date)

DAYOFYEAR(date) return the day of the year for the given date in numeric format in the range 1 to 366.

```
SELECT DAYOFYEAR('2020-05-19');
```

will give the output as shown in Figure 6.57.

```
MariaDB [OFFICE]> SELECT DAYNAME('2020-05-19');
+-----------------------+
| DAYNAME('2020-05-19') |
+-----------------------+
| Tuesday               |
+-----------------------+
1 row in set (0.092 sec)
MariaDB [OFFICE]> SELECT DAYOFMONTH('2020-05-19');
+--------------------------+
| DAYOFMONTH('2020-05-19') |
+--------------------------+
|                       19 |
+--------------------------+
1 row in set (0.002 sec)
MariaDB [OFFICE]> SELECT DAYOFWEEK('2020-05-19');
+-------------------------+
| DAYOFWEEK('2020-05-19') |
+-------------------------+
|                       3 |
+-------------------------+
1 row in set (0.000 sec)
MariaDB [OFFICE]> SELECT DAYOFYEAR('2020-05-19');
+-------------------------+
| DAYOFWEEK('2020-05-19') |
+-------------------------+
|                    2020 |
+-------------------------+
1 row in set (0.000 sec)
```

Figure 6.57 Examples of DAYNAME(), DAYOFMONTH(), DAYOFWEEK(), DAYOFYEAR() functions

The following command will return the day of the year of employee's date of joining in numeric format. (See Figure 6.58).

```
SELECT DOJ, DAYOFYEAR(DOJ)
    -> FROM EMPLOYEE;
```

```
MariaDB [OFFICE]> SELECT DOJ, DAYOFYEAR(DOJ)
    -> FROM EMPLOYEE;
+------------+----------------+
| DOJ        | DAYOFYEAR(DOJ) |
+------------+----------------+
| 2000-12-17 |            352 |
| 2000-02-20 |             51 |
| 2003-02-22 |             53 |
| 2001-04-02 |             92 |
| 2001-09-28 |            271 |
| 2001-05-01 |            121 |
| 2001-06-09 |            160 |
| 2002-12-09 |            343 |
| 2001-11-17 |            321 |
| 2003-01-12 |             12 |
+------------+----------------+
```

Figure 6.58 Example of DAYOFYEAR() function

NOW()

NOW() returns the current date and time in 'YYYY-MM-DD HH:MM:SS' or YYY-YMMDDHHMM format, depending on whether the function is used in a string or numeric context. For example (See Figure 6.59),

SELECT NOW();

SYSDATE()

SYSDATE() returns the current date and time in 'YYYY-MM-DD HH:MM:SS' or YYY-YMMDDHHMM format, depending on whether the function is used in a string or numeric context. For example (See Figure 6.59),

SELECT SYSDATE();

```
MariaDB [OFFICE]> SELECT NOW();
+---------------------+
| NOW()               |
+---------------------+
| 2020-05-19 12:29:12 |
+---------------------+
1 row in set (0.000 sec)
MariaDB [OFFICE]> SELECT SYSDATE();
+---------------------+
| SYSDATE()           |
+---------------------+
| 2020-05-19 12:30:35 |
+---------------------+
1 row in set (0.000 sec)
```

Figure 6.59 Execution of NOW() and SYSDATE() function in MariaDB window

☞ ***SYSDATE()*** *returns the time at which the function executes. But,* ***NOW()*** *returns a constant time that indicates the time at which the statement began to execute.*

Statements given below will illustrate the difference between *NOW()* and *SYSDATE()*:

SELECT NOW(), SLEEP(10), NOW();

```
MariaDB [OFFICE]> SELECT NOW(), SLEEP(10), NOW();
+---------------------+-----------+---------------------+
| NOW()               | SLEEP(10) | NOW()               |
+---------------------+-----------+---------------------+
| 2020-05-19 12:31:10 |         0 | 2020-05-19 12:31:10 |
+---------------------+-----------+---------------------+
1 row in set (10.001 sec)
```

Figure 6.60 Execution of NOW() function

When we execute the first statement, NOW() function will return the same result even if we use it multiple times in same statement, even after creating delay using SLEEP() function (See Figure 6.60). But, when we execute the second statement, SYSDATE() function returns the different results if we use it multiple times in the same statement:

SELECT SYSDATE(), SLEEP(10), SYSDATE();

☞ ***SLEEP(S)*** *pauses for the number of seconds given by the argument, where* ***S*** *is the number of second.*

6.14 GROUP FUNCTIONS

Group functions work upon groups of rows, rather than on a single row. MariaDB Aggregate functions such as SUM, AVG, MAX, MIN, COUNT etc. produce a single value for the entire group of table entries. Group functions are also called *Aggregate Function* or *Multiple row functions*. There are five common Aggregate functions as given below:

(a) SUM function

(b) AVG function

(c) MAX function

(d) MIN function

(e) COUNT function

SUM function returns the sum of values in given column or expression.

AVG function returns average of given data.

MAX function returns the maximum value from a given column or expression.

MIN function returns the minimum value from a given column or expression.

COUNT function counts the number of rows in a given column or expression.

In order to learn Aggregate functions we will use EMPLOYEE table under OFFICE database which we created earlier.

6.14.1 SUM()

SUM() function calculates the arithmetic SUM of all selected values in a particular column. For example, to find the SUM of BASIC salary from the EMPLOYEE table, we would enter the following command:

```
SELECT SUM(BASIC) FROM EMPLOYEE;
```

The output of the sum of the basic salary calculated by this command is shown in Figure 6.61.

```
MariaDB [OFFICE]> SELECT SUM(BASIC) FROM EMPLOYEE;
+------------+
| SUM(BASIC) |
+------------+
|      55720 |
+------------+
1 row in set (0.122 sec)
```

Figure 6.61 Application of SUM function

More examples of SUM function are given below:

(a) To find the total Basic salary for DEPT_CODE 30 (See Figure 6.62).

```
SELECT SUM(BASIC) FROM EMPLOYEE
  -> WHERE DEPT_CODE = '30';
```

```
MariaDB [OFFICE]> SELECT SUM(BASIC) FROM EMPLOYEE
    -> WHERE DEPT_CODE = '30';
+------------+
| SUM(BASIC) |
+------------+
|      24520 |
+------------+
1 row in set (0.025 sec)
```

Figure 6.62 The total Basic salary for DEPT_CODE 30

(b) To find the total Basic salary for employee whose desig is 'Salesman' (See Figure 6.63).

```
SELECT SUM(BASIC) FROM EMPLOYEE
-> WHERE DESIG = 'Salesman';
```

```
MariaDB [OFFICE]> SELECT SUM(BASIC) FROM EMPLOYEE
    -> WHERE DESIG = 'Salesman';
+------------+
| SUM(BASIC) |
+------------+
|       8270 |
+------------+
1 row in set (0.104 sec)
```

Figure 6.63 The total Basic salary for employee whose desig is 'Salesman'

6.14.2 AVG()

The function *AVG()* calculates the average (mean value) of all selected values of a given field.

For example, to find the average of Basic salary, (See Figure 6.64) enter the following command:

```
SELECT AVG(BASIC) FROM EMPLOYEE;
```

```
MariaDB [OFFICE]> SELECT AVG(BASIC) FROM EMPLOYEE;
+------------+
| AVG(BASIC) |
+------------+
|       5572 |
+------------+
1 row in set (0.001 sec)
```

Figure 6.64 Application of AVG function

More example of AVERAGE function are given below:

(a) To find the average Basic salary of employees whose DOJ is before '2003-02-22'

```
SELECT AVG(BASIC) FROM EMPLOYEE
 -> WHERE DOJ < '2003-02-22';
```

(See Figure 6.65).

```
MariaDB [OFFICE]> SELECT AVG(BASIC) FROM EMPLOYEE
    -> WHERE DOJ < '2003-02-22';
+-------------------+
| AVG(BASIC)        |
+-------------------+
| 5691.111111111111 |
+-------------------+
1 row in set (0.112 sec)
```

Figure 6.65 The average Basic salary of employees whose DOJ is before '2003-02-22'

(b) To find the average Basic salary for employees whose DEPT_CODE = '20'.

```
SELECT AVG(BASIC) FROM EMPLOYEE
 -> WHERE DEPT_CODE = 20;
```

(See Figure 6.66).

```
MariaDB [OFFICE]> SELECT AVG(BASIC) FROM EMPLOYEE
    -> WHERE DEPT_CODE = 20;
+------------+
| AVG(BASIC) |
+------------+
|       6250 |
+------------+
1 row in set (0.001 sec)
```

Figure 6.66 The average Basic salary for employees whose DEPT_CODE = '20'

6.14.3 MAX()

MAX() function calculates the largest of all selected values of a given column. For example, using the EMPLOYEE table, the following command displays the maximum salary value in the column Basic:

```
SELECT MAX(BASIC) FROM EMPLOYEE;
```

The result of the above query is shown in Figure 6.67.

```
MariaDB [OFFICE]> SELECT MAX(BASIC) FROM EMPLOYEE;
+------------+
| MAX(BASIC) |
+------------+
|       8000 |
+------------+
1 row in set (0.001 sec)
```

Figure 6.67 Application of MAX function

More example of MAX function are given below:

(a) To find the maximum Basic salary for a year.
```
SELECT MAX(BASIC*12) FROM EMPLOYEE;
```
(See Figure 6.68).

```
MariaDB [OFFICE]> SELECT MAX(BASIC*12) FROM EMPLOYEE;
+---------------+
| MAX(BASIC*12) |
+---------------+
|         96000 |
+---------------+
1 row in set (0.017 sec)
```

Figure 6.68 The maximum Basic salary for a year

(b) To find the maximum Basic salary for employees whose DEPT_CODE = '10'. (See Figure 6.69).

```
SELECT MAX(BASIC) FROM EMPLOYEE
  -> WHERE DEPT_CODE = '10';
```

```
MariaDB [OFFICE]> SELECT MAX(BASIC) FROM EMPLOYEE
    -> WHERE DEPT_CODE = '10';
+------------+
| MAX(BASIC) |
+------------+
|       6500 |
+------------+
1 row in set (0.000 sec)
```

Figure 6.69 The maximum Basic salary for employees whose DEPT_CODE = '10'

6.14.4 MIN()

MIN() function calculates the smallest of all selected values of a given column. For example, using the EMPLOYEE table, the following command displays the minimum salary value in the column Basic.

SELECT MIN(BASIC) FROM EMPLOYEE;

The result of the above query is shown in Figure 6.70.

```
MariaDB [OFFICE]> SELECT MIN(BASIC) FROM EMPLOYEE;
+------------+
| MAX(BASIC) |
+------------+
|       4000 |
+------------+
1 row in set (0.001 sec)
```

Figure 6.70 Application of MIN function

More examples of MIN function are given below:

(a) To display joining date of seniormost employee. (See Figure 6.71).
SELECT MIN(DOJ) FROM EMPLOYEE;

```
MariaDB [OFFICE]> SELECT MIN(DOJ) FROM EMPLOYEE;
+------------+
| MIN(DOJ)   |
+------------+
| 2000-02-20 |
+------------+
1 row in set (0.001 sec)
```

Figure 6.71 To display joining date of seniormost employee

(b) To find the minimum Basic salary for employees whose DEPT_CODE = '10'.
SELECT MIN(BASIC) FROM EMPLOYEE
-> WHERE DEPT_CODE = '10';
(See Figure 6.72).

```
MariaDB [OFFICE]> SELECT MIN(BASIC) FROM EMPLOYEE
    -> WHERE DEPT_CODE = '10';
+------------+
| MIN(BASIC) |
+------------+
|       6000 |
+------------+
1 row in set (0.001 sec)
```

Figure 6.72 To find the minimum Basic salary for employees whose DEPT_CODE = '10'

6.14.5 COUNT()

This function counts the number of rows in the output table. The function COUNT with the asterisk (*) counts the number of rows in the resulting table. Count(DISTINCT) eliminates rows containing duplicate field values before counting them in the output table. For example, to find how many employees are in the EMPLOYEE table, type the following query:

SELECT COUNT(*) FROM EMPLOYEE;

The result of the above query is shown in Figure 6.73.

```
MariaDB [OFFICE]> SELECT COUNT(*) FROM EMPLOYEE;
+----------+
| COUNT(*) |
+----------+
|       10 |
+----------+
1 row in set (0.001 sec)
```

Figure 6.73 Application of COUNT function

Let us now find out the number of departments in the EMPLOYEE table eliminating the duplicate ones. For getting this, enter the following statement:

SELECT COUNT(DISTINCT DEPT_CODE) FROM EMPLOYEE;

The result of the above query is shown in Figure 6.74.

```
MariaDB [OFFICE]> SELECT COUNT(DISTINCT DEPT_CODE) FROM EMPLOYEE;
+---------------------------+
| COUNT(DISTINCT DEPT_CODE) |
+---------------------------+
|                         3 |
+---------------------------+
1 row in set (0.392 sec)
```

Figure 6.74 Application of COUNT function with DISTINCT

☞ *COUNT (DISTINCT) eliminates duplicate fields values before calculating the COUNT. Similarly, SUM(DISTINCT) eliminates duplicate fields values before determining the SUM. Similarly, AVG(DISTINCT) eliminates duplicate fields values before determining the average.*

☞ *With Aggregate functions such as COUNT, MAX, and MIN, both numeric and character fields can be used, whereas only numeric fields can be used for SUM and AVG.*

More examples of COUNT function are given

below:

(a) To count different department codes (DEPT_CODE) of employees present in EMPLOYEE table. (See Figure 6.75).

```
SELECT COUNT(DEPT_CODE) FROM EMPLOYEE;
```

```
MariaDB [OFFICE]> SELECT COUNT(DEPT_CODE) FROM EMPLOYEE;
+------------------+
| COUNT(DEPT_CODE) |
+------------------+
|               10 |
+------------------+
1 row in set (0.001 sec)
```

Figure 6.75 To count different department codes (DEPT_CODE) of employees

(b) To find distinct department codes (DEPT_CODE) present in EMPLOYEE table. (See Figure 6.76).

```
SELECT COUNT(DISTINCT DEPT_CODE) FROM EMPLOYEE;
```

```
MariaDB [OFFICE]> SELECT COUNT(DISTINCT DEPT_CODE) FROM EMPLOYEE;
+---------------------------+
| COUNT(DISTINCT DEPT_CODE) |
+---------------------------+
|                         3 |
+---------------------------+
1 row in set (0.001 sec)
```

Figure 6.76 To find distinct department codes (DEPT_CODE)

(c) To count the records of employees whose BASIC salary is greater than 7000. (See Figure 6.77).

```
SELECT COUNT(BASIC)
    -> FROM EMPLOYEE
    -> WHERE BASIC > 7000;
```

```
MariaDB [OFFICE]> SELECT COUNT(BASIC)
    -> FROM EMPLOYEE
    -> WHERE BASIC > 7000;
+--------------+
| COUNT(BASIC) |
+--------------+
|            2 |
+--------------+
1 row in set (0.001 sec)
```

Figure 6.77 The records of employees whose BASIC salary is greater than 7000

6.15 GROUP BY

The GROUP BY clause combines all those records that have identical values in a particular field or a group of fields. Assume that you want to know the total salary offered to each Department (i.e., Accounts, Research, Sales and Operations) which are Groups in the EMPLOYEE table, then the clause GROUP BY can be used. The *GROUP BY* clause allows you to form groups based on the given conditions.

The MariaDB statement to query the total Basic salary offered in each department in the

EMPLOYEE table would be:

```
SELECT DEPT_CODE, SUM(BASIC)
  -> FROM EMPLOYEE
  -> GROUP BY DEPT_CODE;
```

The result of the query is shown in Figure 6.78.

```
MariaDB [OFFICE]> SELECT DEPT_CODE, SUM(BASIC)
    -> FROM EMPLOYEE
    -> GROUP BY DEPT_CODE;
+-----------+------------+
| DEPT_CODE | SUM(BASIC) |
+-----------+------------+
|        10 |      18700 |
|        20 |      12500 |
|        30 |      24520 |
+-----------+------------+
3 rows in set (0.338 sec)
```

Figure 6.78 Extracting information using GROUP BY

More examples of GROUP BY function are given below:

(a) To display the maximum BASIC salary for each department (DEPT_CODE) from EMPLOYEE table. (See Figure 6.79).

```
SELECT DEPT_CODE, MAX(BASIC)
  -> FROM EMPLOYEE
  -> GROUP BY DEPT_CODE;
```

```
MariaDB [OFFICE]> SELECT DEPT_CODE, MAX(BASIC)
    -> FROM EMPLOYEE
    -> GROUP BY DEPT_CODE;
+-----------+------------+
| DEPT_CODE | MAX(BASIC) |
+-----------+------------+
|        10 |       6500 |
|        20 |       8000 |
|        30 |       7500 |
+-----------+------------+
3 rows in set (0.001 sec)
```

Figure 6.79 The maximum BASIC salary for each department (DEPT_CODE)

(b) To display department wise total Basic salary with total number of departments. (See Figure 6.80).

```
SELECT DEPT_CODE, SUM(BASIC), COUNT(DEPT_CODE)
  -> FROM EMPLOYEE
  -> GROUP BY DEPT_CODE;
```

6.16 HAVING

Sometimes we do not want to see the whole output produced by a statement with GROUP BY clause. We want to see the output only for those groups which satisfy some condition. It means we want to put some condition on individual groups (and not on individual records). A condition on groups is applied by HAVING clause. Suppose you want to see the list of only those departments where the total salary is greater than 15000. In such a case, you cannot use the aggregate functions, namely SUM, etc. in the *WHERE* clause.

```
MariaDB [OFFICE]> SELECT DEPT_CODE, SUM(BASIC), COUNT(DEPT_CODE)
    -> FROM EMPLOYEE
    -> GROUP BY DEPT_CODE;
+-----------+------------+------------------+
| DEPT_CODE | SUM(BASIC) | COUNT(DEPT_CODE) |
+-----------+------------+------------------+
|        10 |      18700 |                3 |
|        20 |      12500 |                2 |
|        30 |      24520 |                5 |
+-----------+------------+------------------+
3 rows in set (0.001 sec)
```

Figure 6.80 Display department wise total Basic salary with total number of departments

☞ *The HAVING clause restricts grouped rows that appear in the result table.*

It means you could *not* do something like the following:

```
SELECT DEPT_CODE, SUM(BASIC)
  -> FROM EMPLOYEE
  -> WHERE SUM(BASIC) > 15000
  -> GROUP BY DEPT_CODE;
```

This command would be rejected. To see the total salary over 15000, you have to use the *HAVING* clause. The *HAVING* clause defines criteria used to eliminate certain *groups* from the output, just as the WHERE clause does for individual rows. The correct command would thus be:

```
SELECT DEPT_CODE, SUM(BASIC)
  -> FROM EMPLOYEE
  -> GROUP BY DEPT_CODE
  -> HAVING SUM(BASIC) > 15000;
```

The output for this query is shown in Figure 6.81.

```
MariaDB [OFFICE]> SELECT DEPT_CODE, SUM(BASIC)
    -> FROM EMPLOYEE
    -> GROUP BY DEPT_CODE
    -> HAVING SUM(BASIC) > 15000;
+-----------+------------+
| DEPT_CODE | SUM(BASIC) |
+-----------+------------+
|        10 |      18700 |
|        30 |      24520 |
+-----------+------------+
2 rows in set (0.334 sec)
```

Figure 6.81 Extracting information using the HAVING clause

☞ *HAVING and WHERE clauses work in a similar manner. The difference is that clause WHERE works on rows, while clause HAVING works on groups. Expressions in HAVING clause must be single_value per group.*

More examples of HAVING clause are discussed in the following paragraph.

(a) To display number of employees and basic salary whose BASIC salary is greater than 4400. (See Figure 6.82).

```
SELECT COUNT(*), BASIC
  -> FROM EMPLOYEE
  -> GROUP BY BASIC
  -> HAVING BASIC > 4400;
```

```
MariaDB [OFFICE]> SELECT COUNT(*), BASIC
    -> FROM EMPLOYEE
    -> GROUP BY BASIC
    -> HAVING BASIC > 4400;
+----------+-------+
| COUNT(*) | BASIC |
+----------+-------+
|        2 |  4500 |
|        1 |  6000 |
|        1 |  6200 |
|        1 |  6500 |
|        1 |  7500 |
|        1 |  8000 |
+----------+-------+
6 rows in set (0.001 sec)
```

Figure 6.82 Number of employees and basic salary whose BASIC salary is greater than 4400

(b) To display the maximum BASIC salary of each department that has a maximum salary more than 7000.(See Figure 6.83).

```
SELECT DEPT_CODE, MAX(BASIC)
  -> FROM EMPLOYEE
  -> GROUP BY DEPT_CODE
  -> HAVING MAX(BASIC) > 7000;
```

```
MariaDB [OFFICE]> SELECT DEPT_CODE, MAX(BASIC)
    -> FROM EMPLOYEE
    -> GROUP BY DEPT_CODE
    -> HAVING MAX(BASIC) > 7000;
+-----------+------------+
| DEPT_CODE | MAX(BASIC) |
+-----------+------------+
|        20 |       8000 |
|        30 |       7500 |
+-----------+------------+
2 rows in set (0.001 sec)
```

Figure 6.83 The maximum BASIC salary of each department that has a maximum salary more than 7000

6.17 GROUP FUNCTIONS AND NULL VALUES

The group functions such as SUM, AVG, COUNT etc. pay no attention to the NULL values. For example, the COUNT function will not count the column values that are NULL. They automatically disregard NULLs and does not raise a warning message for the same.

For example, the query:

```
SELECT COUNT(HEAD) FROM EMPLOYEE;
```

would give the result as 7, instead of 10. This is because the COUNT function has counted only NOT NULL values of the HEAD column. Had it counted NULL values also, it would have given the result as 10 since there are 10 rows in employee table. (See Figure 6.84).

```
MariaDB [OFFICE]> SELECT COUNT(HEAD) FROM EMPLOYEE;
+-------------+
| COUNT(HEAD) |
+-------------+
|           7 |
+-------------+
1 row in set (0.001 sec)
```

Figure 6.84 The COUNT function has counted only NOT NULL values of the HEAD column

6.18 NESTED GROUPING OF RECORDS

With GROUP BY clause, you can also create groups within groups. To create a group within a group, you need to specify multiple fields in the GROUP BY clause, separated by commas.

For example, to group records DEPT_CODE wise, within DESIG wise, the query is:

```
SELECT DEPT_CODE, DESIG, COUNT(EMP_CODE)
  -> FROM EMPLOYEE
  -> GROUP BY DEPT_CODE, DESIG;
```

The output of the query is shown in Figure 6.85:

```
MariaDB [OFFICE]> SELECT DEPT_CODE, DESIG, COUNT(EMP_CODE)
    -> FROM EMPLOYEE
    -> GROUP BY DEPT_CODE, DESIG;
+-----------+--------------+-----------------+
| DEPT_CODE | DESIG        | COUNT(EMP_CODE) |
+-----------+--------------+-----------------+
|        10 | As. Engineer |               2 |
|        10 | Engineer     |               1 |
|        20 | Assistant    |               1 |
|        20 | Manager      |               1 |
|        30 | Area Manager |               1 |
|        30 | Assistant    |               1 |
|        30 | Salesman     |               2 |
|        30 | Steno        |               1 |
+-----------+--------------+-----------------+
8 rows in set (0.001 sec)
```

Figure 6.85 Example of nested grouping

6.19 USING NULL WITH GROUP FUNCTIONS

If a query returns no rows (or there are no rows in a group), so that the group function has no data to be applied on, the group function returns NULL. However, the function COUNT returns a value 0. As an example, let us insert a record, (See Figure 6.86) into the EMPLOYEE table, of an employee who works for department 40 and gets NULL salary. The INSERT query for this will be as follows:

```
INSERT INTO EMPLOYEE
   -> (EMP_CODE, EMP_NAME, DESIG, DOJ,
DEPT_CODE)
          -> VALUES (111,'Sonia
Wallia','Clerk','2003-07-25',40);
```

Now to see added record type the following command:

```
SELECT * FROM EMPLOYEE;
```

The output of the query is shown in Figure 6.86:

```
MariaDB [OFFICE]> SELECT * FROM EMPLOYEE;
+----------+-------------+-------------+------+------------+-------+-----------
+
| EMP_CODE | EMP_NAME    | DESIG       | HEAD | DOJ        | BASIC | DEPT_CODE |
+----------+-------------+-------------+------+------------+-------+-----------
+
|      101 | Raju         | Manager      | NULL | 2000-12-17 |  8000 |        20 |
|      102 | Amar Roy     | Salesman     |  105 | 2000-02-20 |  4000 |        30 |
|      103 | Raj          | Assistant    |  101 | 2003-02-22 |  4500 |        20 |
|      104 | Rajiv Kumar  | As. Engineer |  107 | 2001-04-02 |  6200 |        10 |
|      105 | Suraj Patel  | Area Manager | NULL | 2001-09-28 |  7500 |        30 |
|      106 | Binay Kumar  | Salesman     |  105 | 2001-05-01 |  4270 |        30 |
|      107 | Ramaswamy    | Engineer     | NULL | 2001-06-09 |  6500 |        10 |
|      108 | Jog Iyer     | Assistant    |  105 | 2002-12-09 |  4250 |        30 |
|      109 | Imran Khan   | Steno        |  105   2001-11-17 |  4500 |        30 |
|      110 | Tinu Anand   | As. Engineer |  107   2003-01-12 |  6000 |        10 |
|      111 | Sonia Wallia | Clerk        | NULL   2003-07-25 |  NULL |        40 |
+----------+-------------+-------------+------+------------+-------+-----------
+
11 rows in set (0.111 sec)
```

Figure 6.86 Display of newly inserted record

Now type the following command:

SELECT DEPT_CODE, AVG(BASIC) FROM EMPLOYEE
-> GROUP BY DEPT_CODE;

The output of the query is shown in Figure 6.87:

```
MariaDB [OFFICE]> SELECT DEPT_CODE, AVG(BASIC) FROM EMPLOYEE
    -> GROUP BY DEPT_CODE;
+-----------+-----------------+
| DEPT_CODE | AVG(BASIC)      |
+-----------+-----------------+
|        10 | 6233.333333333333 |
|        20 |            6250 |
|        30 |            4904 |
|        40 |            NULL |
+-----------+-----------------+
4 rows in set (0.050 sec)
```

Figure 6.87 The group function returns NULL

6.20 CORELATED AND NESTED QUERIES

You can nest the MariaDB queries, i.e. include one query within another. Nested query or subquery is an MariaDB SELECT statement inside another SELECT or action statement. MariaDB first evaluates the inner-most query. Further, the result of the inner query is returned to the outer query.

☞ *A subquery is a query made within another statement to produce a set of values that are used by the rest of the outer statement.*

For example, suppose we want to see the names of those employees who are working in the department in which the employee Mr. Amar Roy is working. For this purpose, we will use the following query:

```
SELECT EMP_NAME FROM EMPLOYEE
  -> WHERE DEPT_CODE = (SELECT DEPT_CODE
FROM EMPLOYEE
  -> WHERE EMP_NAME = 'Amar Roy');
```

In the above statement, the inner query will return the DEPT_CODE where *Amar Roy* is working. This DEPT_CODE is then used as data for the outer query which returns the names of employees working in department where *Amar Roy* is working. The output of the query is shown in Figure 6.88.

```
MariaDB [OFFICE]> SELECT EMP_NAME FROM EMPLOYEE
    -> WHERE DEPT_CODE = (SELECT DEPT_CODE FROM EMPLOYEE
    -> WHERE EMP_NAME = 'Amar Roy');
+-------------+
| EMP_NAME    |
+-------------+
| Amar Roy    |
| Suraj Patel |
| Binay Kumar |
| Jog Iyer    |
| Imran Khan  |
+-------------+
5 rows in set (0.631 sec)
```

Figure 6.88 List of employees who work in same department as Amar Roy

6.21 TABLE ALIASES

Instead of typing in table names repeatedly, in case of joins, one can assign aliases (temporary labels) to the tables. For example, in the following query we have assigned the alias E to the EMPLOYEE table and alias D to DEPARTMENT table:

```
SELECT E.EMP_CODE, E.EMP_NAME,
E.DEPT_CODE, D.DEPT_NAME
  -> FROM EMPLOYEE E, DEPARTMENT D
  -> WHERE E.DEPT_CODE = D.DEPT_CODE;
```

Note, in the above query, that we have specified the aliases in the FROM clause and used it in the SELECT and WHERE clause.

```
MariaDB [OFFICE]> SELECT E.EMP_CODE, E.EMP_NAME, E.DEPT_CODE, D.DEPT_NAME
    -> FROM EMPLOYEE E, DEPARTMENT D
    -> WHERE E.DEPT_CODE = D.DEPT_CODE;
+----------+--------------+-----------+------------+
| EMP_CODE | EMP_NAME     | DEPT_CODE | DEPT_NAME  |
+----------+--------------+-----------+------------+
|      101 | Raju         |        20 | Research   |
|      102 | Amar Roy     |        30 | Sales      |
|      103 | Raj          |        20 | Research   |
|      104 | Rajiv Kumar  |        10 | ACCOUNTS   |
|      105 | Suraj Patel  |        30 | Sales      |
|      106 | Binay Kumar  |        30 | Sales      |
|      107 | Ramaswamy    |        10 | ACCOUNTS   |
|      108 | Jog Iyer     |        30 | Sales      |
|      109 | Imran Khan   |        30 | Sales      |
|      110 | Tinu Anand   |        10 | ACCOUNTS   |
|      111 | Sonia Wallia |        40 | Operations |
+----------+--------------+-----------+------------+
```

Figure 6.89 Table Aliases

6.22 JOIN

Using the SELECT command, you can retrieve data from several related tables also. But this is possible only if the tables are related with one other. Join operation is used to combine columns from multiple tables. In a join, the tables to be included in the query are specified in the FROM clause, separated by commas. The condition required for specifying the relationship between the tables is given in the WHERE clause.

The syntax for SELECT statement where we *join* two tables is given below:

```
SELECT <column_name(s)>
FROM <table1>, <table2>, .., <tableN>
WHERE <table1.col1> = <table2.col1>
  AND <table3.col2> = <table2.col4>
    AND  ...  AND  <table2.col3  =  tab-
leN.colN>;
```

A Join statement is used to combine data or rows from two or more tables based on a common field between them. Different types of Joins are:

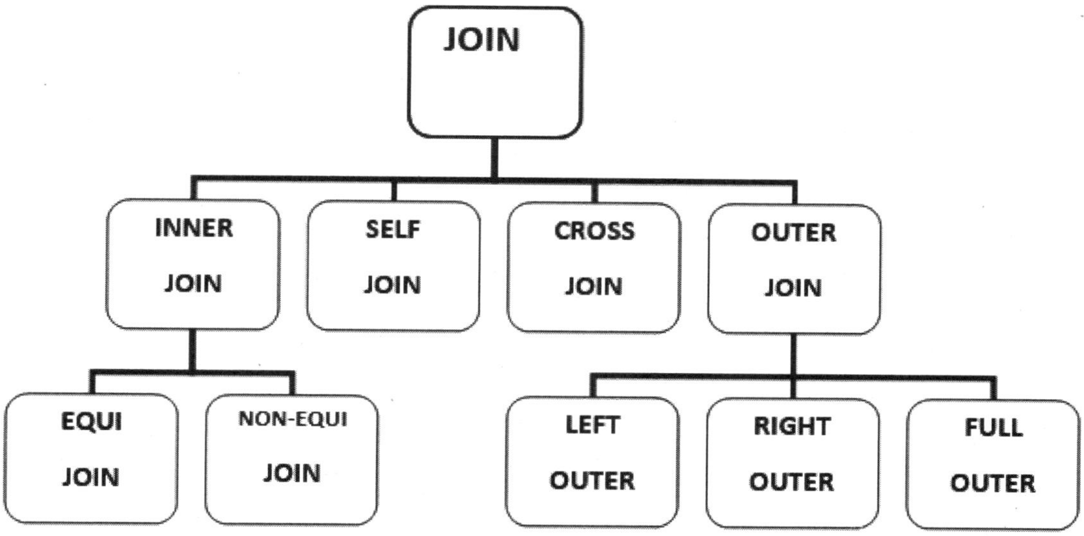

Figure 6.90 Different types of SQL join

Let's create database PUBLISHER and two tables BOOK and PRICE as shown in Figure 6.91.

```
MariaDB [(none)]> CREATE DATABASE PUBLISHER;
Query OK, 1 row affected (0.472 sec)

MariaDB [(none)]> USE PUBLISHER;
Database changed

MariaDB [PUBLISHER]> CREATE TABLE BOOK(
    -> ID CHAR(4),
    -> TITLE VARCHAR(25),
    -> PUBLISHER VARCHAR(10));
Query OK, 0 rows affected (0.892 sec)
```

(Conti...)

```
MariaDB [PUBLISHER]> CREATE TABLE PRICE(
    -> ID CHAR(4),
    -> PRICE FLOAT);
Query OK, 0 rows affected (0.316 sec)
```

Figure 6.91 Creation of Database and tables

Now insert values in BOOK and PRICE using INSERT INTO statement as shown below:

```
INSERT INTO BOOK
  -> VALUES ('A1','A-LEVEL MOD1', 'BPB'),
  -> ('A2','A-LEVEL MOD2', 'BPB'),
  -> ('A3','A-LEVEL MOD3', 'BPB'),
  -> ('A4','A-LEVEL MOD4', 'BPB'),
  -> ('A5','A-LEVEL MOD5', 'BPB');
```

```
INSERT INTO PRICE
  -> VALUES ('A1', 450),
  -> ('A2', 350),
  -> ('A3', 360),
  -> ('A4', 390);
```

Now type the following statements as shown in Figure 6.92 to see entered records.

```
MariaDB [PUBLISHER]> SELECT * FROM BOOK;
+------+--------------+-----------+
| ID   | TITLE        | PUBLISHER |
+------+--------------+-----------+
| A1   | A-LEVEL MOD1 | BPB       |
| A2   | A-LEVEL MOD2 | BPB       |
| A3   | A-LEVEL MOD3 | BPB       |
| A4   | A-LEVEL MOD4 | BPB       |
| A5   | A-LEVEL MOD5 | BPB       |
+------+--------------+-----------+
5 rows in set (0.032 sec)

MariaDB [PUBLISHER]> SELECT * FROM PRICE;
+------+-------+
| ID   | PRICE |
+------+-------+
| A1   |   450 |
| A2   |   350 |
| A3   |   360 |
| A4   |   390 |
+------+-------+
4 rows in set (0.000 sec)
```

Figure 6.92 Display of records of BOOK and PRICE tables

6.23 INNER JOIN

Returns records that have matching values in both tables i.e., value of the common field will be same.

```
MariaDB [PUBLISHER]> SELECT BOOK.TITLE, PRICE.PRICE
    -> FROM BOOK
    -> INNER JOIN PRICE
    -> ON BOOK.ID=PRICE.ID;
+---------------+-------+
| TITLE         | PRICE |
+---------------+-------+
| A-LEVEL MOD1  |   450 |
| A-LEVEL MOD2  |   350 |
| A-LEVEL MOD3  |   360 |
| A-LEVEL MOD4  |   390 |
+---------------+-------+
4 rows in set (0.145 sec)
```

Figure 6.93 INNER join

6.23.1 Equi Join

When two tables are joined together using equality of values in one or more columns, they would make an *Equi join*. This equality condition is put on the common column of the tables.

```
MariaDB [PUBLISHER]> SELECT * FROM BOOK, PRICE
    -> WHERE BOOK.ID = PRICE.ID;
+------+---------------+-----------+------+-------+
| ID   | TITLE         | PUBLISHER | ID   | PRICE |
+------+---------------+-----------+------+-------+
| A1   | A-LEVEL MOD1  | BPB       | A1   |   450 |
| A2   | A-LEVEL MOD2  | BPB       | A2   |   350 |
| A3   | A-LEVEL MOD3  | BPB       | A3   |   360 |
| A4   | A-LEVEL MOD4  | BPB       | A4   |   390 |
+------+---------------+-----------+------+-------+
4 rows in set (0.002 sec)
```

Figure 6.94 Equi Join

```
MariaDB [PUBLISHER]> SELECT TITLE, PUBLISHER, B.ID, PRICE
    -> FROM BOOK B, PRICE P
    -> WHERE B.ID=P.ID;
+---------------+-----------+------+-------+
| TITLE         | PUBLISHER | ID   | PRICE |
+---------------+-----------+------+-------+
| A-LEVEL MOD1  | BPB       | A1   |   450 |
| A-LEVEL MOD2  | BPB       | A2   |   350 |
| A-LEVEL MOD3  | BPB       | A3   |   360 |
| A-LEVEL MOD4  | BPB       | A4   |   390 |
+---------------+-----------+------+-------+
4 rows in set (0.002 sec)
```

Figure 6.95 Natural join

In the natural join also, the comparison operator is always the equality operator =, but only the equi join contains two identical columns from the relation being joined. It is possible to eliminate one of those two columns. An equi join with one of the two identical columns eliminated is called a *natural join*. Thus, natural join will also give a new table that does not have any duplicate columns.

Example

Consider following two relations R1 and R2:

R1: (A, B, C)

A	B	C
I	1	Y
J	3	Y
K	3	Z
L	2	Y
M	1	Z
N	7	Y

R2: (B, D, E)

B	D	E
1	p	S
2	q	T
5	p	U
7	q	T

Equi Join will produce the following result:

A	B	C	B	D	E
I	1	Y	1	p	S
L	2	Y	2	q	T
M	1	Z	1	p	S
N	7	Y	7	q	T

In above relation R1 and R2, Natural join will produce the following result:

A	B	C	D	E
I	1	Y	p	S
L	2	Y	q	T
M	1	Z	p	S
N	7	Y	q	T

☞ *Note that all the columns from joining table appears in the output even if they are identical.*

☞ *In equi join, the comparison operator = is only used. The result of an equi join will always have one or more pairs of columns that have identical values in every record. Equi Join is also called simple join.*

☞ *In natural join one of the two identical column is eliminated.*

6.23.2 Non Equi-Join (Theta join)

A *Non-equi-join* is a query that specifies some relationship between tables other than equality. In general, this Theta join is used to specify operators or conditions.

6.24 SELF JOIN

SELF JOIN is joining of a table to itself. In this, each row of the table is combined with itself and with every other row of the table. This can be viewed as a join of two copies of the same table. For distinguishing between the two copies, one can use table aliases.

It syntax is:

```
SELECT column_name(s)
FROM table1 T1, table1 T2
```

```
WHERE condition;
T1 and T2 are different table aliases for
the same table.
```

6.25 CROSS JOIN

A CROSS join returns all rows for all possible combinations of two tables. It generates all the rows from the left table, which is then combined with all the rows from the right table. This type of join is also known as a Cartesian product(A*B).

```
MariaDB [PUBLISHER]> SELECT * FROM BOOK CROSS JOIN PRICE;
+------+-------------+-----------+------+-------+
| ID   | TITLE       | PUBLISHER | ID   | PRICE |
+------+-------------+-----------+------+-------+
| A1   | A-LEVEL MOD1 | BPB      | A1   |   450 |
| A1   | A-LEVEL MOD1 | BPB      | A2   |   350 |
| A1   | A-LEVEL MOD1 | BPB      | A3   |   360 |
| A1   | A-LEVEL MOD1 | BPB      | A4   |   390 |
| A2   | A-LEVEL MOD2 | BPB      | A1   |   450 |
| A2   | A-LEVEL MOD2 | BPB      | A2   |   350 |
| A2   | A-LEVEL MOD2 | BPB      | A3   |   360 |
| A2   | A-LEVEL MOD2 | BPB      | A4   |   390 |
| A3   | A-LEVEL MOD3 | BPB      | A1   |   450 |
| A3   | A-LEVEL MOD3 | BPB      | A2   |   350 |
| A3   | A-LEVEL MOD3 | BPB      | A3   |   360 |
| A3   | A-LEVEL MOD3 | BPB      | A4   |   390 |
| A4   | A-LEVEL MOD4 | BPB      | A1   |   450 |
| A4   | A-LEVEL MOD4 | BPB      | A2   |   350 |
| A4   | A-LEVEL MOD4 | BPB      | A3   |   360 |
| A4   | A-LEVEL MOD4 | BPB      | A4   |   390 |
| A5   | A-LEVEL MOD5 | BPB      | A1   |   450 |
| A5   | A-LEVEL MOD5 | BPB      | A2   |   350 |
| A5   | A-LEVEL MOD5 | BPB      | A3   |   360 |
| A5   | A-LEVEL MOD5 | BPB      | A4   |   390 |
+------+-------------+-----------+------+-------+
20 rows in set (0.001 sec)
```

Figure 6.96 Cross Join

Example

In a database there are two tables X and Y shown as follows:

X:

Emp_No	Emp_name
101	Rita
103	Ritu
104	Setu
106	Leela
107	Neena

Y:

Project
AX10
AX11

There cartesian product will contains 10 (i.e 5X2) rows. The operation X × Y gives the resulting combinations as follows:

X × Y:

Emp_No	Emp_name	Project
101	Rita	AX10
101	Rita	AX11
103	Ritu	AX10
103	Ritu	AX11
104	Setu	AX10
104	Setu	AX11
106	Leela	AX10
106	Leela	AX11
107	Neena	AX10
107	Neena	AX11

Note that above commands will give all combinations of employees working on *project AX10* and also on project AX11.

☞ *A cartesian join is used when you join every row of one table to every row of another table.*

6.26 OUTER JOIN

In an EQUI JOIN, if there are any values in one table that do not have corresponding value(s) in the other table, that row will **not be** selected. On joining tables with a SQL inner join, the output returns only matching rows from both the tables. When using a SQL outer join, not only it will list the matching rows, it will also list the unmatched rows from the other tables.

6.26.1 Left Outer Join

Returns all records from the left table, and the matched records from the right table. The rows for which there is no matching row on right side, the result-set will contain null. LEFT OUTER JOIN is also known as LEFT JOIN as shown in Figure 6.97.

```
MariaDB [PUBLISHER]> SELECT BOOK.TITLE, PRICE.PRICE
    -> FROM BOOK
    -> LEFT JOIN PRICE
    -> ON BOOK.ID=PRICE.ID;
+---------------+-------+
| TITLE         | PRICE |
+---------------+-------+
| A-LEVEL MOD1  |   450 |
| A-LEVEL MOD2  |   350 |
| A-LEVEL MOD3  |   360 |
| A-LEVEL MOD4  |   390 |
| A-LEVEL MOD5  |  NULL |
+---------------+-------+
5 rows in set (0.001 sec)
```

Figure 6.97 Left Outer Join

6.26.2 Right Outer Join

Returns all records from the right table, and the matched records from the left table. The rows for which there is no matching row on left side, the result-set will contain null. RIGHT OUTER JOIN is also known as RIGHT JOIN as shown in Figure 6.98.

```
MariaDB [PUBLISHER]> SELECT BOOK.TITLE, PRICE.PRICE
    -> FROM BOOK
    -> RIGHT JOIN PRICE
    -> ON BOOK.ID=PRICE.ID;
+---------------+-------+
| TITLE         | PRICE |
+---------------+-------+
| A-LEVEL MOD1  |   450 |
| A-LEVEL MOD2  |   350 |
| A-LEVEL MOD3  |   360 |
| A-LEVEL MOD4  |   390 |
+---------------+-------+
4 rows in set (0.002 sec)
```

Figure 6.98 Right Outer Join

6.26.3 Full Outer Join

Returns all records when there is a match in either left or right table. The result-set will contain all the rows from both the tables. The rows for which there is no matching, the result-set will contain NULL values. Full outer join can potentially return very large result-sets.
Its syntax is:

```
SELECT column_name(s)
FROM table1
FULL OUTER JOIN table2
ON   table1.column_name   =   table2.co-
lumn_name
WHERE condition;
```

☞ *Full outer join is the union of left outer join and right outer join.*

6.27 UNION

The set operators UNION, INTERSECT and MINUS can be used to combine information from several tables.
The UNION operator *merges* outputs of two or more queries into a set of rows and columns. The rows and columns which are to be merged must be of the same data type. For example, the following query will display the names of employees working in department 10 and 20.

```
SELECT EMP_NAME FROM EMPLOYEE
  -> WHERE DEPT_CODE = 10
  -> UNION
  -> SELECT EMP_NAME FROM EMPLOYEE
  -> WHERE DEPT_CODE = 20;
```

The query will generate the output shown in Figure 6.99.

```
MariaDB [OFFICE]> SELECT EMP_NAME FROM EMPLOYEE
    -> WHERE DEPT_CODE = 10
    -> UNION
    -> SELECT EMP_NAME FROM EMPLOYEE
    -> WHERE DEPT_CODE = 20;
+-------------+
| EMP_NAME    |
+-------------+
| Rajiv Kumar |
| Ramaswamy   |
| Tinu Anand  |
| Raju        |
| Raj         |
+-------------+
5 rows in set (0.137 sec)
```

Figure 6.99 Use of UNION operator

Example

X and Y are two relations, with X holding the details of employees working on Project J1 and Y holding the details of those who are working on Project J2. The two tables are as under:

X:

Emp_No	Emp_name
101	Rita
103	Ritu
104	Setu
106	Leela
107	Neena

Y:

Emp_No	Emp_name
101	Rita
105	Isha
107	Neena
112	Seema

To select all those employees who are working on either in Project J1 or in J2 or in both projects J1 and J2, we write X ∪ Y. The result of union operation is given below:

X ∪ Y:

Emp_No	Emp_name
101	Rita
103	Ritu
104	Setu
105	Isha
106	Leela
107	Neena
112	Seema

6.28 TRANSACTION RECOVERY

A single DBMS operation such as updation, insertion, selection or deletion is not a single task but involves many tasks. For example, in the EMPLOYEE table, to update the designation of an employee from MANAGER to ANALYST, following operations need to be performed.

1. Locating the required record in the secondary storage medium (hard disk, etc.).
2. Copying the record to primary memory.
3. Performing the required updation.
4. If successful, perform *commit*[1] action. Else perform *rollback*[2] action.

Figure 6.100 shows the above tasks diagrammatically.

Thus, the updation, insertion or deletion operation requires a number of distinct tasks or steps to be performed by the DBMS. Such a collection of tasks or steps for execution of a single database operation (like insertion, updation, deletion, etc.) is called a *Transaction.*

A transaction is a unit of work that must be done in logical order and successful as a group or not done at all. Each transaction has a beginning and an end. If anything goes wrong in between the execution of transaction, the entire transaction will be cancelled. If it is successful, then the entire transaction should be saved to the database. In other words a transaction is a sequential group of database manipulation operations, which is performed as a single unit. A transaction will never be complete unless each individual operation within the group is successful. If any operation within the transaction fails, the entire transaction will fail.

☞ *A transaction is a program unit whose execution may or may not change the contents of a database. Transaction is executed as a single unit. If the database was in a consistent state before a transaction, then after execution of the transaction also, the database must be in a consistent state. Once committed, a database cannot be rolled back.*

Before and after execution of a transaction, the database must be in a consistent state. After the transaction execution, either the database has changed consistently or there has been no change at all. But in between the start of the execution of a transaction and its termination, database can be in an inconsistent state. Let us study the following transaction algorithm, that updates Employee table:

This algorithm would update the DEPT_CODE of OPERATIONS department from 40 to 50 in the DEPARTMENT table. The DEPT_CODE of employees working in OPERATIONS department (DEPT_CODE = 40) are also updated in the EMPLOYEE table. The algorithm is:

```
begin
    define action update DEPARTMENT as
    do until no more DEPT_CODE
       get next where DEPT_CODE = 40;
       DEPT_CODE = 50;
    end;
end;
begin
    define action update EMPLOYEE as
       do until no more EMP_CODE
       get next where DEPT_CODE = 40;
       DEPT_CODE = 50;
    end;
end;
if error then
    rollback update DEPARTMENT;
    rollback update EMPLOYEE;
else
    commit update DEPARTMENT;
    commit update EMPLOYEE;
```

Note that the above algorithm requires repeated access of database and also repeated changes to the database. The steps written in the algorithm can only occur at the rate of one at a time. Therefore, at any moment in between the start of execution of transaction and the termination of execution, the database would be in an inconsistent state.

For example, after the DEPARTMENT updation has taken place, i.e. DEPT_CODE of OPERATION department has been changed from 40 to 50, there will be no *referential integrity*. This is so because the employees working in OPERATION department will be shown as working in a department

---

1 The commit command is used to make changes to database permanent.

2 The Rollback command is used to undo part or all the work the user has done.

with DEPT_CODE 40 in the EMPLOYEE table. But there is no department in DEPARTMENT table with DEPT_CODE = 40.

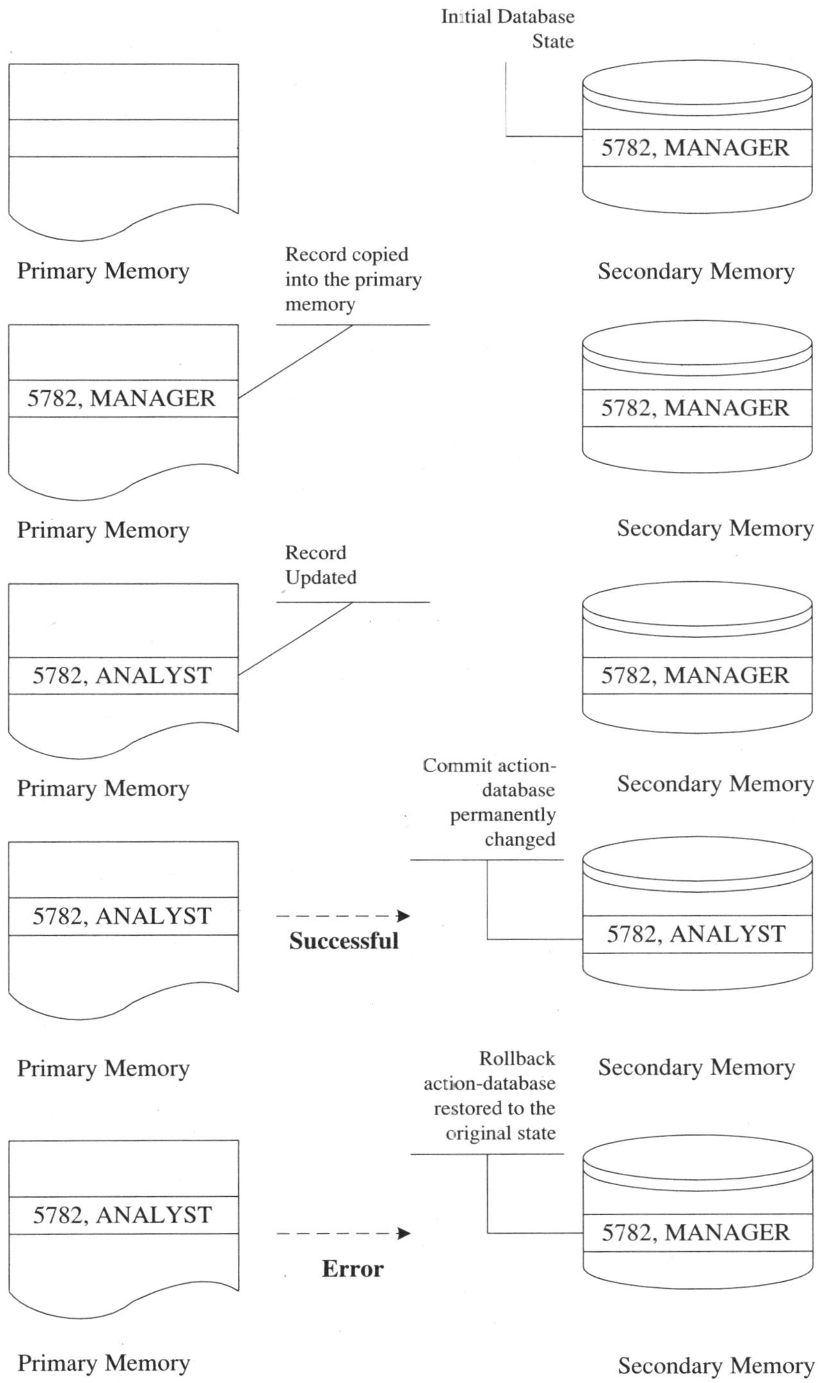

Figure 6.100 Tasks involved in an updation operation

Hence, though database will be in the consistent state after the complete execution of a transaction, there is no guarantee that the database will be in a consistent state *between transaction tasks*. The commit action is therefore performed at the end of execution of all transaction tasks. This ensures that either all the changes are made permanent in the database or the database remains unchanged. This method helps to view transaction as a single operation called *atomic operation*, which will be either completely successful or not.

A transaction can be terminated in three ways. These are:

1. **Suicidal Termination:** The Transaction detects an error while processing and decides to terminate itself by performing a rollback operation.
2. **Murderous Termination**: The Database Management Software or the operating system can force the Transaction to be terminated due to some specified reasons.
3. **Successful Termination:** The Transaction is terminated after executing it successfully.

6.29 TRANSACTION LOGS

The transaction log is stored on a storage media, so that it is not affected by any type of failure except for disk failure or any catastrophic failure. In addition, the log is periodically backed up (for example on a tape) to recover from such catastrophic failures.

Following is the list of entries (called *log records*) and the action each entry performs. These are written in the form of a log book on the hard disk:

(a) *[start_transaction, T]*:
Indicates that transaction with transaction-id *T* has started execution.

(b) *[write_item, T, A, old_value, new_value]*:
Indicates that transaction *T* has changed the value of data item *A* from *old_value* to *new_value*.

(c) *[read_item, T, A]*:
Indicates that the transaction *T* has read the value of data item *A*.

(d) *[commit, T]*:
Indicates that transaction *T* has been done successfully and that its effect can be recorded permanently on the database. After the commit point, the transaction is said to be committed and its effect is assumed to be permanently recorded in the database.

(e) *[abort, T]*:
Indicates that the transaction *T* has been aborted.

6.29.1 Write–Ahead Logging (WAL)

In Write–Ahead logging strategy, the updates are first written to the log before it is applied to the database. In this strategy, a transaction is not allowed to modify a database until the current value of the database (value before modification is applied) is written to a stable storage device. This ensures that database can be recovered to its previous consistent state if any failure occurs in the middle of the update transaction execution.

6.29.2 Checkpoints

A *checkpoint* is another type of entry in the log and is represented as *[checkpoint]*. The *[checkpoint]* record is written into the log when all the changes upto this point are reflected in the database. Consequently, all those transactions which have *[commit, T]* entry before *[checkpoint]* entry will not require their operations *undone* (if some failure occurs). This is because these operations have been reflected on the database.

Writing a checkpoint on the log consist of the following actions:

1. Suspend execution of transactions temporarily.
2. Write a *[checkpoint]* record to the log and make changes permanent to the database.
3. Resume execution of transactions.

6.30 TRANSACTION STATES

A transaction may go through multiple states during its lifetime. Figure 6.101 illustrates different paths a transaction process may take during its lifetime.

6.31 ACID PROPERTIES OF TRANSACTION

A transaction is expected to contain certain properties known as **ACID** test properties. These are:

(a) Atomicity
(b) Consistency
(c) Isolation
(d) Durability

6.31.1 Atomicity

The atomicity of a transaction implies that it will run to completion as an *individual unit* (*atomic unit*). At the end of a unit of transaction either there is no change to the database or the database has been changed in a consistent manner. No changes will be reflected in the database in the middle of execution of an atomic unit of transaction. Thus, only after a transaction unit has been executed completely that any updates made by it will be accessible to other transactions as well as the processes outside the transaction.

6.31.2 Consistency

Consistency property of a transaction implies that if a database was in the consistent state before the execution of the transaction, then after execution of the transaction also, the database will be in the consistent state.

6.31.3 Isolation

Isolation property of a transaction process implies that actions performed by a database will be isolated or hidden from other transactions or processes until it is either executed or terminated. This property gives transaction a measure of relative independence.

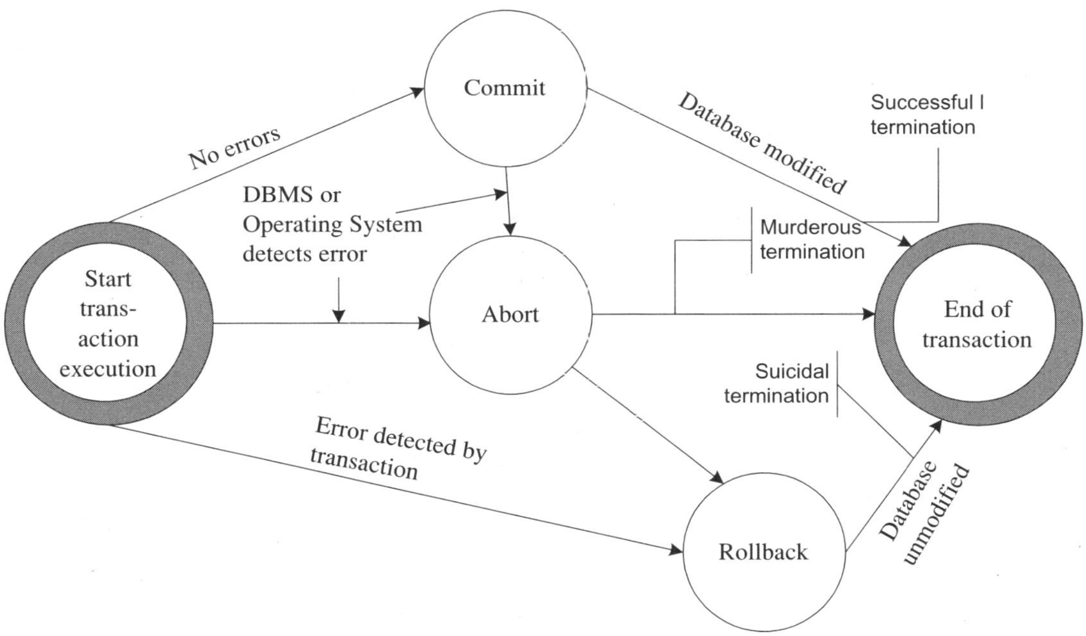

Figure 6.101 Various states of a Transaction process

6.31.4 Durability

Durability property of a database transaction implies that the updates made by a transaction will be reflected in the database on the termination of committed action. Therefore, any loss or failure after the committed action will not cause loss of updates made by the transaction. Once committed, rollback of the transaction cannot be performed, if the transaction has the property of durability.

6.32 CONCURRENCY CONTROL

In multiprogramming environment, programs are executed concurrently i.e. simultaneously or at the same time. The phrase 'same time' is not very appropriate to use in case of single processor computers, but in these computers multiprogramming is implemented in such a way that it appears that many programs are getting executed together.

In multiprogramming / multiuser computer systems, resources are shared among multiple users or programs. Database thus becomes a shared resource. Some DBMS packages allow many users and application programs to access data in a concurrent manner. An example is *airline reservation system*, where the database containing available seats may be accessed by many agents throughout the world.

The concurrent usage of a single database can lead to inconsistencies in a database. For example, suppose two transactions T1 and T2 are simultaneously accessing a data item in a database and are modifying its value. This would lead to false values for the data item created by first transaction and generate an inconsistent database.

This would be more clear by the example given in Table 6.7. In this example, both the transactions T1 and T2 are concurrently modifying data item A.

Table 6.7 Transaction Inconsistency

Transaction T1	Transaction T2	Permanent State of Database
		Initially, A = 200
Read (A)		
A = A -100		A is still 200. A's value in the database will be changed only after the write(A) command
	Read (A) (T2 will read the value of A as 200)	
	A = A * 10	
Write (A)		A = 100 (modification done by transaction T1)
	Write (A)	A = 2000 (as written by transaction T2)

You will observe in the example, that the results are unexpected. The updates made by transaction T1 is lost. This is known as *lost update problem* of concurrency. Had this problem be not there, the value of A should have been 1000 (T1 caused 100 to be subtracted from A and T2 caused the value of A to be multiplied with 10). But the result we got is 2000 due to the lost update problem.

Another problem that exists with concurrent database access is the *inconsistent read problem.* Suppose A and B represent two different accounts in a bank. Let us assume that transaction T1 transfers Rs 100 from A to B. That is T1 should reduce Rs 100 from A and add Rs 100 to B. But at the same time another transaction T2 is running. T2 has the job of calculating the total amount in A and B accounts. Let us see what happens after the execution of these two transactions, as shown in Table 6.8.

Table 6.8 Inconsistent read problem

Transaction T1	Transaction T2	Permanent State of Database
		Initially, A = 200, B = 500 and Sum = 0
Read (A)		
	Read (A)	
A = A - 100		
Write (A)		A = 100, B = 500, Sum = 0
	Sum = Sum + A (Sum = 200 now)	A = 100, B = 500, Sum = 0 (value of sum has not been saved in the database yet)
Read (B)		
B = B + 100		
Write (B)		A = 100, B = 600, Sum = 0
	Read (B)	
	Sum = Sum + B	
	Write (Sum)	A = 100, B = 600, Sum = 800

Sum = 800, but it actually should have been 700. This is because T2 read the value of A before it was changed by T1 and read the value of B after the change was made. This is called *inconsistent read problem.*

The problem would not have occurred if T2 was not using the data items A and B while they were being modified by the transaction T1. That is T2 was not allowed to use A and B.

6.32.1 Serializability

The transaction execution shown in Table 6.7 and Table 6.8 are not serial, because the operations of the transactions T1 and T2 are not executed consecutively. The execution would have been serial, if operations of each transaction are executed one after the other, without any interleaved operations from the other transactions. The serial execution is shown in Table 6.9.

Table 6.9 Serial execution of Transactions

Transaction T1	Transaction T2
Read (A)	
A = A - 100	
Write (A)	
Read (B)	
B = B + 100	
Write (B)	
	Read (A)
	Sum = Sum + A
	Read (B)
	Sum = Sum + B
	Write (Sum)

Note that in the serial transaction execution given above, all the problems associated with concurrent execution of transaction are eliminated. If every transaction executes serially, without interference from other transactions, the results are always correct. But this limits concurrency. The trick is to plan a schedule, which is equivalent to a serial schedule in giving correct results and at the same time also provides some degree of concurrency. Such a schedule is known as *serializable schedule*.

6.32.2 Recoverability

In some schedule, recovery from transaction failures is easy. Such schedules are called recoverable schedules. A schedule is recoverable, if no transaction T in a schedule commits, until all the transactions in the schedule that have written a data item which T reads, are committed.

For example, consider the schedule given in Table 6.10.

The above schedule is not recoverable, because T2 reads data item A from T1 and commits. But T1 aborts afterwards, thus invalidating the value of A read by T2. For the schedule to be recoverable, T2 should not commit until T1 commits. If T1 aborts, T2 should also abort.

Table 6.10 Non-recoverable Transaction Schedule

Transaction T1	Transaction T2
Read (A)	
A = A - 100	
Write (A)	
	Read (A)
	A = A + 200
Read (B)	
	Write (A)
	Commit
Abort	

The schedule given in Table 6.11 is recoverable.

Table 6.11 Recoverable Transaction Schedule

Transaction T1	Transaction T2
Read (A)	
A = A - 100	
Write (A)	
	Read (A)
	A = A + 200
Read (B)	
	Write (A)
Abort	
	Abort

6.32.3 Concurrency Control Schemes

Following are some of the techniques used for controlling concurrent execution of transactions.

Locking

A data item can be locked by a transaction in order to prevent this data item from being accessed and modified by any other transaction. The part of the database system which is responsible for locking or unlocking the data items is known as the *lock manager*.

Locks are of the following two types:

(a) Exclusive lock

(b) Shared lock

Exclusive Lock

This type of locking mechanism provides exclusive use of a data item to one transaction. Transactions which want to read as well as modify a data item must make exclusive lock on that data item. Hence it is also known as *update lock* or *write lock*. No other transaction can lock a data item when it is exclusively locked by another transaction.

☞ *A data item locked in the exclusive mode cannot be locked in the shared mode by any other transaction.*

If a Transaction T locks a data item A in an exclusive mode, no other transaction can access A, not even read A, until T releases its lock i.e. unlocks A.

Shared Lock

Transactions which want to read a data item only and do not modify it, can make shared lock on the data item. Hence, it is also known as *read* lock. Any number of transactions can make shared lock and read the data item. But they cannot modify the data item unless the shared lock is released by all the transactions that are holding locks on that data item.

☞ *A data item locked in shared lock cannot be locked in the exclusive mode by any other transaction but can still be locked as shared lock.*

We will assume that a data item *A* can be locked in the *shared* mode using the command *locks (A)*. Similarly, *A* can be locked in the *exclusive* mode using the command *lockx (A)*.

Suppose a transaction T1 wishes to do the following operations:

Transaction T1
Locks (A) Read (A) A = A - 100 Write (A) Unlock (A) Lockx (B) Read (B) B = B + 100 Write (B) Unlock (B)

Now suppose another transaction T2 is running concurrently with the following operations.

Transaction T2
Lockx (Sum) Sum = 0 Locks (A) Read (A)Sum = Sum + A Unlock (A) Locks (B) Read (B) Sum = Sum + B Write (Sum) Unlock (B) Unlock (Sum)

Due to the use of the lock – unlock commands in the two transactions, the schedule of execution of T1 and T2 would be as shown in Table 6.12.

Table 6.12 Schedule of Execution of T1 and T2

Transaction T1	Transaction T2
	Lockx (Sum) Sum = 0 Locks (A) Read (A) Sum = Sum + A Unlock (A)
Lockx (A) Read (A) A = A - 100 Write (A) Unlock (A) Lockx (B) Read (B) B = B + 100 Write (B) Unlock (B)	
	Locks (B) Read (B) Sum = Sum + B Write (Sum) Unlock (B) Unlock (Sum)

Note that in the above schedule there is *inconsistent read problem*. Transactions T1 and T2 are performing operations containing many steps. The database is in the inconsistent state after Transaction T1 has taken 100 units from A but not added to B. Allowing Transaction T2 to read the values of A and B before transaction T2 is complete leads to the inconsistent read problem.

A possible solution to the such a problem is to extend the time period of keeping the data items in locked state, even though the transaction no longer need these items. This principle is used in *Two Phase Locking.*

Concepts of Two Phase Locking

The concept of *two phase locking* emphasizes that all locks on required data items are first acquired before any of the locks are released. It has two phases namely a *growing phase* and a *contracting phase.* In the growing phase, the number of locks increase from zero to maximum for a transaction. In the contracting phase, the number of locks held decrease from maximum to zero. The transaction must first acquire locks on all the required data items. It cannot unlock a data item unless it has locked all the data items it needs for the execution of transaction. Once a transaction starts releasing locks, it is not allowed to request any further locks. For example, the Transactions T1 and T2 in two phase locking scheme will be working as shown in Table 6.13.

Table 6.13 Two phase locking of Transaction T1 and T2

Transaction T1	Transaction T2
Lockx(A)	
Read(A)	
A = A - 100	
Write (A)	
Lockx (B)	
Unlock (A)	
Read (B)	
B = B + 100	
Write (B)	
Unlock (B)	
	Lockx (Sum)
	Sum = 0
	Locks (A)
	Read (A)
	Sum = Sum + A
	Locks (B)
	Read (B)
	Sum = Sum + B
	Write (Sum)
	Unlock (A)
	Unlock (B)
	Unlock (Sum)

You will notice that the above method leads to lower degree of concurrency among Transactions.

Two-Phase Locking are of the following different types:

(a) Basic two-phase locking
(b) Conservative two-phase locking
(c) Strict two-phase locking
(d) Rigorous two-phase locking

Basic two-phase locking

The two phase locking technique just described is the basic two phase locking.

Conservative two-phase locking

In the conservative two-phase locking mechanism, a transaction locks all the required data items before a transaction is being executed. If any of the data item it needs cannot be locked, the transaction does not lock any item, instead it waits until all the items required are available for locking. This is a deadlock free mechanism. [*Deadlocks are explained in the following sections*]

Strict two-phase locking

In the Strict two-phase locking method, a transaction T does not release any of its exclusive (write) locks until it commits or aborts. No other transaction can read or write a data item until T commits or aborts.

☞ *Strict two-phase locking is not deadlock free but it makes recovery from failures easier.*

Rigorous two-phase locking

In rigorous two-phase locking method, a transaction does not release any of its locks (exclusive or shared) until it commits or aborts. Thus rigorous two-phase locking is rather more strict than strict two-phase locking.

Granularity

Granularity refers to the size of a data item. If the size or granularity of a data item is very large, for example an entire relation, then the overhead associated with the mechanism of locking it, is very low. Hence, the lock manager only has to manage a few data items. But this reduces the degree of concurrency because the transaction locked the entire relation and any other transaction cannot use tuples from this relation before the previous transaction releases its lock.

On the other hand, if the granularity or size of a data item is very small, the degree of concurrency will be very high. But overhead of managing these locks will also be high. This is because a transaction that needs many records and fields will have to request many locks, all of which have to be managed by the lock manager.

Hence, granularity chosen should be such that it neither reduces the concurrency nor increases the overhead of lock manager.

Deadlocks

Consider the situation–Transaction T1 has claimed data item A and is waiting for data item B. Data item B is claimed by transaction T2, which in turn is waiting for data item C. Data item C is locked by a transaction T3. T3 is waiting for data item A. But A will not be released by T1 unless T1 gets B and the *chain of waiting* continues. This condition is knows as *deadlock.* A deadlock would occur under the following four conditions.

1. A data item can be accessed by only one transaction at a time. Another transaction cannot use a data item unless it is released by the transaction which locked it.
2. The transaction which requires a data item continues to wait for its release by the other transaction which locked it.
3. There is no provision of pre-emption of data items. Pre-emption means that a high priority transaction is allowed to have data item if it is being locked by a lower priority transaction.
4. A circular wait condition as explained above.

☞ *A deadlock is said to occur when there is a circular chain of transactions, each waiting for the release of a data item held by the next transactions in the chain.*

Such a wait chain can be drawn as a *wait–for graph* (See Figure 6.102). The wait–for graph is a directed graph that contains *nodes* and directed *arcs.* The nodes of the graph represent various transactions. The directed arc is inserted between two nodes if the transaction at the tail of the arc requires a data item locked by the transaction located at the head of the arc.

In the wait–for graph of Figure 6.102 (a),

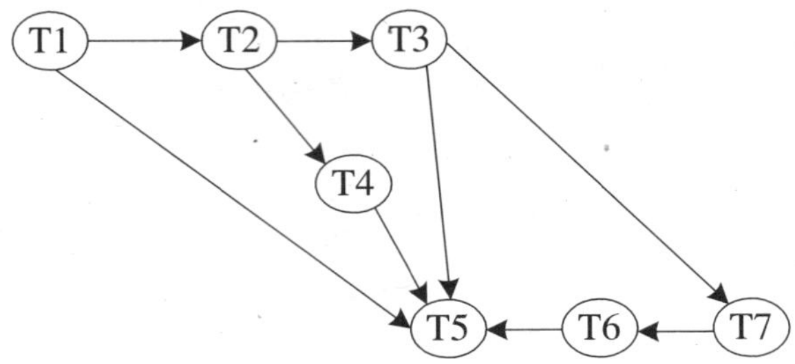

(a)

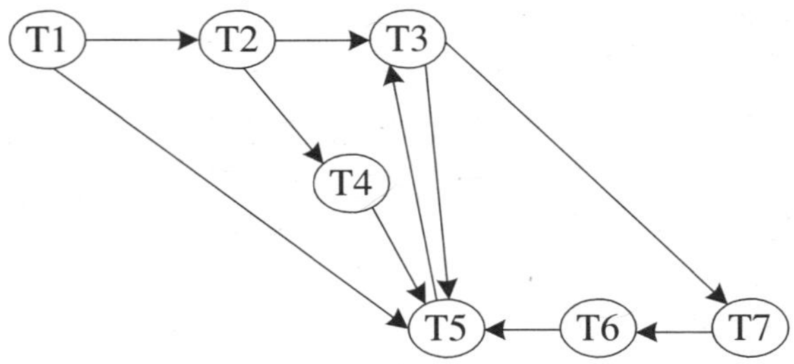

(b)

Figure 6.102 (a) Wait–for graph with no cycle and hence no deadlock
(b) Wait–for graph with cycle and hence a deadlock

Transaction T1 is waiting for data items locked by transaction T2 and T5.

T2 is waiting for data item locked by T3 and T4.

T3 is waiting for data item locked by T5 and T7

T4 is waiting for data item locked by T5
T6 is waiting for data item locked by T5
T7 is waiting for data item locked by T6

Since there is no cycle in the wait–for graph of Figure 6.102 (a), the problem of deadlock cannot occur. But in Figure 6.102 (b), the transaction T5 makes a request for a data item held by transaction T3. The addition of arc from T5 to T3 has resulted in a cycle in the wait–for graph. And hence a deadlock has occurred.

Deadlock Detection

The presence of a cycle in the wait–for graph is the reason for deadlock to occur. Therefore, a deadlock can be detected by examining the wait–for graph. If a cycle is detected in the graph, it is inferred that a deadlock has occurred.

Deadlock recovery

To recover from deadlock, the cycles in the wait–for graph must be broken. The cycles can be broken, by performing a *rollback* operation on one of the transactions forming the cycle.

Deadlock Avoidance

Deadlock can be avoided by using any one of the following methods:

(a) Lock all the required data items at the beginning of a transaction.

(b) Alternatively, all the data items are assigned an order. A transaction can only request locks in given order say ascending order. The data item may be assigned ranks as having rank 1, 2, 3, etc. A transaction T requiring data items A (having a rank j) and B (having a rank i) and if i < j, then T must first acquire a lock on B (having lowest rank) before it can lock A. All transaction must follow the same order, even if the data items are not required in that order by the transaction.

(c) Another method to avoid deadlock is to make run time decisions about what a transaction must do if it detects that it has to wait for a data item. For this, each transaction is assigned a unique time stamp. The system uses these time stamps to decide whether the transaction should wait for the data item, abort or rollback the transaction. There are two approaches for making such a decision namely,

   (i) wait–die
   (ii) wound–wait

Wait–Die

In the wait–die approach, if the requesting transaction is older than the transaction which is holding the lock on the required data item, the requesting transaction is allowed to wait. But if the requesting transaction is younger than the transaction that is holding the lock, then the requesting transaction is aborted and rolled back (die).

Wound–Wait

In the wound–wait approach, if the requesting transaction is older than the transaction which is holding the lock on the required data item, the younger transaction will be aborted and rolled back (the younger transaction is aborted by the older transaction and dies). But if the requesting transaction is younger than the transaction which is holding the required data item, then the requesting transaction is allowed to wait.

Concurrency control based on Timestamps

Another method of controlling access to shared resources, by multiple transactions, is *time-stamp ordering*. In this, each transaction, Ti, is associated with a unique timestamp TS(Ti). The timestamp is associated as soon as BEGIN_TRANSACTION is encountered. Timestamps are assigned in an increasing order. For example, if a transaction T1 is given TS(T1), then a new transaction T2 will have a timestamp
TS(T2) > TS(T1).

Also, with each data item A, two timestamp values are associated, namely *W-timestamp(A)* and *R-timestamp(A)*. W-timestamp(A) is equal to the largest timestamp of a transaction, that has executed the Write(A) operation successfully. That is, the timestamp value of the oldest transaction that has executed the Write(A) operation successfully. Similarly, R-timestamp(A) is equal to the largest timestamp of a transaction, that has executed the Read(A) operation successfully. That is, the timestamp value of the oldest transaction that has executed the Read(A) operation successfully.

The timestamp-ordering protocol or algorithm works as follows:

(a) If a transaction Ti tries to execute a read(A) command, then

   (i) If timestamp of Ti, TS(Ti) is less than W-timestamp(A), then read operation is rejected and Ti is rolled back. This is because another older transaction has overwritten A. If Ti is allowed to read A, it will read a wrong value.

(ii) If TS(Ti) ≥ W-timestamp(A), then read operation is executed and R-timestamp(A) is set to either TS(Ti) or R-timestamp(A), whichever is the largest.

(b) If a transaction Ti tries to execute a write(A) command, then

(i) If timestamp of Ti, TS(Ti) < R-timestamp(A), then write operation is rejected and Ti is rolled back. This is because another older transaction has read A and it has assumed that the A will not be changed.

(ii) If TS(Ti) < W-timestamp(A), write operation is rejected and Ti is rolled back. This is because, Ti is attempting to overwrite an already updated data item.

(iii) In all other cases, write operation is executed and W-timestamp(A) is set to TS(Ti).

Since, no transaction waits in this *timestamp-based concurrency control*, there is no possibility of deadlock. But, there are possibilities of starvation if a young transaction is rolled back again and again.

6.33 TRANSACTION CONTROL COMMANDS

MariaDB offers a set of commands for transaction control purpose. These subset of commands are known as TCL (Transaction Control Language) commands. The Transaction Control Language consist of following commands:

6.33.1 Start Transaction

Start Transaction command of MariaDB commits the current transaction and starts a new transaction. It tells MariaDB that the transaction is beginning and the statements that follow should be treated as a unit, until the transaction ends. We can use BEGIN or BEGIN WORK or START TRANSACTION command to mark the beginning of a transaction. Here WORK is a keyword and is optional.

6.33.2 Commit

The command **COMMIT;** is used to make changes to a database permanent. That is, if you want to permanently save the modifications you have made to the table(s), use **COMMIT;** command. COMMIT ends the current transaction.

6.33.3 Rollback

The **ROLLBACK;** command is however used to undo all the work the user has done. If you want to undo the changes and want to get the previous values of the table(s), use the **ROLLBACK;** command. The ROLLBACK command cancels the entire transaction i.e. It rolls the transaction to the beginning. It aborts any changes made during the transaction and the state of database is returned to what it was before the transaction began to execute and does not save any of the changes made to the database during the transaction.

6.33.4 Savepoint

The `SAVEPOINT` command is used for partially committing a transaction, while still being able to rollback the rest of the transaction. The `SAVEPOINT` command is followed by a name, that will be used as a reference in subsequent commit or rollback statements. For example,

```
SAVEPOINT emp_insert;
```

In the above statement a marker (savepoint) with the name emp_insert is defined. It becomes a bookmark in the transaction.

6.33.5 Autocommit

By default, Autocommit mode is on in MariaDB. If Autocommit is *on* then each SQL statement is considered a complete transaction, and is committed by default when it finishes. If it returns an error then either Rollback or Commit happens depending on the type of error.

The following statement sets the autocommit mode to ON. It also commits and terminates the current transaction.

```
SET AUTOCOMMIT=1;
```

If we do not want individual statements of SQL to be automatically committed, we should set the autocommit mode to off. When Autocommit is *off* then we have to issue COMMIT statement explicitly to save changes made to the database. The transactions that need to be manually configured by the users are known as *explicit transactions*.
The following statement sets the autocommit mode to off. It also starts a new transaction

```
SET AUTOCOMMIT=0;
```

Example

Let us create a BANK database and Account table (See Figure 6.103) to store customers information with the following fields:

Field Name	Type	Width	Description
ACC_NO	INT		Account Number(NOT NULL)
NAME	VARCHAR	20	Customer's Name
BALANCE	DOUBLE	10,2	Balance Amount

```
CREATE DATABASE BANK;
USE BANK;
CREATE TABLE ACCOUNT
  -> (ACC_NO INT NOT NULL,
  -> NAME VARCHAR(20),
  -> BALANCE DOUBLE(10,2));
```

```
MariaDB [(none)]> CREATE DATABASE BANK;
Query OK, 1 row affected (0.034 sec)

MariaDB [(none)]> USE BANK;
Database changed

MariaDB [BANK]> CREATE TABLE ACCOUNT
    -> (ACC_NO INT NOT NULL,
    -> NAME VARCHAR(20),
    -> BALANCE DOUBLE(10,2));
Query OK, 0 rows affected (0.518 sec)
```

Figure 6.103 Creating table ACCOUNT

After creating Account table we will insert data values using INSERT INTO command, which adds appends new rows(record) to a table. (See Figure 6.104).

```
INSERT INTO ACCOUNT
  -> VALUES
  -> (101, 'Abhishek', 5000.00),
  -> (103, 'Shiva', 8000.00);
```

```
MariaDB [BANK]> INSERT INTO ACCOUNT
    -> VALUES
    -> (101, 'Abhishek', 5000.00),
    -> (103, 'Shiva', 8000.00);
Query OK, 2 rows affected (0.161 sec)
Records: 2  Duplicates: 0  Warnings: 0
```

Figure 6.104 Inserting values in ACCOUNT table

Now type the following command to retrieve all the data stored in ACCOUNT table.

```
SELECT * FROM ACCOUNT;
```

On execution of this command, we will see the details of ACCOUNT table. The result is shown in Figure 6.105.

```
MariaDB [BANK]> SELECT * FROM ACCOUNT;
+--------+----------+---------+
| ACC_NO | NAME     | BALANCE |
+--------+----------+---------+
|    101 | Abhishek | 5000.00 |
|    103 | Shiva    | 8000.00 |
+--------+----------+---------+
2 rows in set (0.001 sec)
```

Figure 6.105 Displaying records from the ACCOUNT table

Now we will use START TRANSACTION command to mark the beginning of a transaction. A transaction is one logical unit of work consisting of one or more logically related statements.
UPDATE command is used to change some or all the values of existing row. The UPDATE command specifies the rows to be changed using the WHERE clause, and new data using SET keyword. The command **COMMIT;** is used to make changes to a database permanent. Type the following statements as shown in Figure 6.106. and Figure 6.107.

```
MariaDB [BANK]> START TRANSACTION;
Query OK, 0 rows affected (0.000 sec)

MariaDB [BANK]> UPDATE ACCOUNT
    -> SET BALANCE = BALANCE + 1000
    -> WHERE ACC_NO = 101;
Query OK, 1 row affected (0.001 sec)
Rows matched: 1  Changed: 1  Warnings: 0

MariaDB [BANK]> SELECT * FROM ACCOUNT;
+--------+----------+---------+
| ACC_NO | NAME     | BALANCE |
+--------+----------+---------+
|    101 | Abhishek | 6000.00 |
|    103 | Shiva    | 8000.00 |
+--------+----------+---------+
2 rows in set (0.000 sec)
```

Figure 6.106 Updated record for ACC_NO 101

```
MariaDB [BANK]> UPDATE ACCOUNT
    -> SET BALANCE = BALANCE - 4000
    -> WHERE ACC_NO = 103;
Query OK, 1 row affected (0.108 sec)
Rows matched: 1  Changed: 1  Warnings: 0

MariaDB [BANK]> COMMIT;
Query OK, 0 rows affected (0.051 sec)
```

(Conti...)

```
MariaDB [BANK]> SELECT * FROM ACCOUNT;
+--------+----------+---------+
| ACC_NO | NAME     | BALANCE |
+--------+----------+---------+
|    101 | Abhishek | 6000.00 |
|    103 | Shiva    | 4000.00 |
+--------+----------+---------+
2 rows in set (0.000 sec)
```

Figure 6.107 Updated record for ACC_NO 103

Note that START TRANSACTION command is used to start new transaction and we updated Abhishek's account balance (with account no. 101) from 5000 to 6000 and the balance in Shiva's account (with account no. 103) is decreased by 4000. COMMIT ends the transaction by saving database changes.

Example

Let us now understand the function of ROLLBACK command which is executed when we want to discard the changes made to the database and returning to what it was before the transaction began to execute. (See Figure 6.108).

```
MariaDB [BANK]> START TRANSACTION;
Query OK, 0 rows affected (0.000 sec)

MariaDB [BANK]> UPDATE ACCOUNT
    -> SET BALANCE = BALANCE + 1500
    -> WHERE ACC_NO = '101';
Query OK, 1 row affected (0.001 sec)
Rows matched: 1  Changed: 1  Warnings: 0

MariaDB [BANK]> SELECT * FROM ACCOUNT;
+--------+----------+---------+
| ACC_NO | NAME     | BALANCE |
+--------+----------+---------+
|    101 | Abhishek | 7500.00 |
|    103 | Shiva    | 4000.00 |
+--------+----------+---------+
2 rows in set (0.000 sec)

MariaDB [BANK]> ROLLBACK;
Query OK, 0 rows affected (0.361 sec)

MariaDB [BANK]> SELECT * FROM ACCOUNT;
+--------+----------+---------+
| ACC_NO | NAME     | BALANCE |
+--------+----------+---------+
|    101 | Abhishek | 6000.00 |
|    103 | Shiva    | 4000.00 |
+--------+----------+---------+
2 rows in set (0.001 sec)
```

Figure 6.108 Demo of ROLLBACK command

Note that due to ROLLBACK command Abhishek's account balance is not updated and it is displayed as it was before the transaction started.

Example

Let us consider ACCOUNT table once again and understand SAVEPOINT command. SAVEPOINT command is a point in a transaction uptil which all changes have been saved permanently. Here START TRANSACTION command starts the transaction and INSERT INTO command inserts one new record in ACCOUNT's table. SAVEPOINT marker TILLHERE is defined. UPDATE command is used to update amount of newly added record. Note that the ROLLBACK TO SAVE POINT TILLHERE command cancels the effect of UPDATE command. (See Figure 6.109).

```
MariaDB [BANK]> START TRANSACTION;
Query OK, 0 rows affected (0.000 sec)

MariaDB [BANK]> INSERT INTO ACCOUNT
    -> VALUES (105, 'Vivek', 3000.00);
Query OK, 1 row affected (0.001 sec)

MariaDB [BANK]> SAVEPOINT TILLHERE;
Query OK, 0 rows affected (0.000 sec)

MariaDB [BANK]> UPDATE ACCOUNT
    -> SET BALANCE = BALANCE + 500
    -> WHERE ACC_NO = '105';
Query OK, 1 row affected (0.001 sec)
Rows matched: 1  Changed: 1  Warnings: 0

MariaDB [BANK]> ROLLBACK TO SAVEPOINT TILLHERE;
Query OK, 0 rows affected (0.020 sec)

MariaDB [BANK]> COMMIT;
Query OK, 0 rows affected (0.175 sec)

MariaDB [BANK]> SELECT * FROM ACCOUNT;
+--------+----------+---------+
| ACC_NO | NAME     | BALANCE |
+--------+----------+---------+
|    101 | Abhishek | 6000.00 |
|    103 | Shiva    | 4000.00 |
|    105 | Vivek    | 3000.00 |
+--------+----------+---------+
3 rows in set (0.001 sec)
```

Figure 6.109 Demo of SAVEPOINT command

Example

When AUTOCOMMIT is set to 0, by giving SET AUTOCOMMIT = 0 command, the subsequent series of statements act like a transaction and no activities are committed until we give COMMIT command explicitly. (See Figure 6.110)

```
MariaDB [BANK]> SET AUTOCOMMIT = 0;
Query OK, 0 rows affected (0.157 sec)

MariaDB [BANK]> SELECT * FROM ACCOUNT;
+--------+----------+---------+
| ACC_NO | NAME     | BALANCE |
+--------+----------+---------+
|    101 | Abhishek | 6000.00 |
|    103 | Shiva    | 4000.00 |
|    105 | Vivek    | 3000.00 |
+--------+----------+---------+
3 rows in set (0.001 sec)

MariaDB [BANK]> INSERT INTO ACCOUNT
    -> VALUES (107, 'Raja', 9000.00);
Query OK, 1 row affected (0.001 sec)

MariaDB [BANK]> SELECT * FROM ACCOUNT;
+--------+----------+---------+
| ACC_NO | NAME     | BALANCE |
+--------+----------+---------+
|    101 | Abhishek | 6000.00 |
|    103 | Shiva    | 4000.00 |
|    105 | Vivek    | 3000.00 |
|    107 | Raja     | 9000.00 |
+--------+----------+---------+
4 rows in set (0.001 sec)

MariaDB [BANK]> ROLLBACK;
Query OK, 0 rows affected (0.114 sec)

MariaDB [BANK]> SELECT * FROM ACCOUNT;
+--------+----------+---------+
| ACC_NO | NAME     | BALANCE |
+--------+----------+---------+
|    101 | Abhishek | 6000.00 |
|    103 | Shiva    | 4000.00 |
|    105 | Vivek    | 3000.00 |
+--------+----------+---------+
3 rows in set (0.000 sec)
```

Figure 6.110 Demo of AUTOCOMMIT OFF command

Note that ROLLBACK command will explicitly ends the current transaction and changes to inset new record in ACCOUNT's table is rolled back.

Example

When AUTOCOMMIT is ON then every single SQL statement is a new transaction and all the changes will be committed at the end of the statement execution. (See Figure 6.111).

```
MariaDB [BANK]> SET AUTOCOMMIT = 1;
Query OK, 0 rows affected (0.000 sec)

MariaDB [BANK]> INSERT INTO ACCOUNT
    -> VALUES (107, 'Raja', 9000.00);
Query OK, 1 row affected (0.119 sec)

MariaDB [BANK]> SELECT * FROM ACCOUNT;
+--------+----------+---------+
| ACC_NO | NAME     | BALANCE |
+--------+----------+---------+
|    101 | Abhishek | 6000.00 |
|    103 | Shiva    | 4000.00 |
|    105 | Vivek    | 3000.00 |
|    107 | Raja     | 9000.00 |
+--------+----------+---------+
4 rows in set (0.000 sec)

MariaDB [BANK]> ROLLBACK;
Query OK, 0 rows affected (0.000 sec)

MariaDB [BANK]> SELECT * FROM ACCOUNT;
+--------+----------+---------+
| ACC_NO | NAME     | BALANCE |
+--------+----------+---------+
|    101 | Abhishek | 6000.00 |
|    103 | Shiva    | 4000.00 |
|    105 | Vivek    | 3000.00 |
|    107 | Raja     | 9000.00 |
+--------+----------+---------+
4 rows in set (0.001 sec)
```

Figure 6.111 Demo AUTOCOMMIT ON command

Note that when AUTOCOMMIT is enabled Raja's record is added in ACCOUNT's table and is committed. Even ROLLBACK command cannot undo the insertion operation.

☞ *By default AUTOCOMMIT mode is ON.*

6.34 GRANT AND REVOKE COMMANDS

To change the privileges in MariaDB, GRANT and REVOKE commands are used. The GRANT command is used to create users and give them privileges. The REVOKE command is used to take privileges away from a user. A privilege is the right to perform a particular action on a particular object, and is associated with a particular user. The concept is very similar to file permissions. When you create a user within MariaDB, you grant him/her a set of privileges to specify what he/she can and cannot do within the system.

The principle of least privilege can be used to improve the security of any computer system. A user (or process) should have the lowest level of privilege required in order to perform his assigned task.

6.35 DATABASE BACKUPS

Database Backup is the activity of copying database to a permanent storage (such as magnetic tape) so that they will be preserved in case of equipment failure or other disasters. Equipment failures include system crashes, disk damage etc.

Disasters include fire, flood or earthquakes. The backup copy can then be used to restore data. The backup must be kept synchronized with the primary copy of the database, regularly. That is, one should copy the primary database onto the backup everyday, every week or every month depending on the need. Generally, the backup copy of the database is kept separated from the primary copy. This is because a disaster at the primary location should not damage the backup site.

Keeping a backup increases the availability of data. That is, data is available to the user in spite of system failures or environmental disasters. Latest copy of the backup is loaded from the tape to the system and thus the normal operations are restarted.

6.35.1 Why to Plan Backups?

An important part of database planning is backup planning. Planning backup means to make sure that a current copy of the database is always available even in case of catastrophes. Any disaster, be it fire, flood, earthquake, terrorist or virus attacks, disk drive crash, power failure or accidental deletion may not block the normal functioning the system.

One major problem with backup activity is that while the database copy is being made, changes could still be made to the primary copy. For example, in Figure 6.112, backup copy contains only a snapshot of database at any point of time. New changes are made in the primary copy. That is, a backup copy just made can also become outdated. For all such cases, the Database Administrator has to determine how often to perform a partial backup. In a partial backup, recently made changes are stored in a log. The administrator also has to determine how often to perform a full database backup.

Emp_code	Emp_name	Basic
101	Raju	6120
102	Amar Roy	2000
103	Raj	2550
104	Rajiv Kumar	4284

Primary Copy

Emp_code	Emp_name	Basic
101	Raju	6120
102	Amar Roy	2000
103	Raj	2550

Backup

Figure 6.112 Backup of a changing Database, where data of Rajiv Kumar is not present in the backup copy

☞ *Partial backups are faster to create and requires less storage space but takes more time to restore, in case of disaster.*

Changes recorded in the log are reflected on to the backup copy, periodically as specified in the backup plan.

A schedule must be planned for backup activity and this schedule must be revised regularly. This is so because the log (partial backup area) may become full because of many changes at any time. In that case, backup has to be run earlier than scheduled. If such a situation occurs very often, the backup schedule must be modified.

☞ *The backup copy and backup logs must be kept away from the primary database site, so that disasters, such as theft or fire, do not destroy them also. The backup logs must be moved to a different place at least once in a day.*

6.35.2 Types of Backups

Backups are of two types:

(a) Immediate Backup

(b) Archival Backup

Immediate Backups are kept in a Hard disk, zip disk, or pen drives. These comes handy when a technical fault occurs in the primary database such as system failure, disk crashes, network failure or accidental erasure of data. Damage due to virus attacks are also repaired using the immediate backup.

Archival Backups are kept in mass storage devices such as external hard disk, CDs, DVDs, Internet Servers etc. They are useful for recovering data after a disaster such as fire, earthquake, flood, terrorist attack etc. Archival backups should be kept at a different site other than where the system is functioning. Archival backup at a separate place remains safe from thefts and intentional destruction by user staff.

6.36 DATABASE SYSTEM RECOVERY

All electronic devices are subject to failures in one form or another. A computer system is also an electronic device and hence is subject to failures of various forms. Since DBMS forms part of the computer system, it is also prone to failures and errors of various kinds.

☞ *Failures in DBMS can be due to transaction, system or media failures. Database Recovery deals with the techniques used for database recovery (restore) from failures.*

Following are likely reasons for a transaction to fail in the middle of execution.

(a) *System crash*: A hardware, software or network error can occur in the computer system during transaction execution. Hardware crash may also occur due to main memory failure.

(b) *Transaction error*: Some erroneous operation, such as integer overflow or division by zero, etc., in the transaction may cause a failure in between.

(c) Transaction might be terminated before completion due to the detection of a deadlock condition.

(d) *Disk failure*: Some disk blocks may lose their data because of a read or write malfunction or because of a disk read/write head error.

(e) *Natural catastrophes*: This refers to a number of problems including power failure, fire, theft, overwriting tapes or disks by mistake.

Failures due to reasons given in sub-para (a) to (c) are more common than failures given in sub para (d) and (e), above.

Database recovery means that the entire data items in the database are re-entered to the most recent consistent state of the database as it was, just before the time of failure.

☞ *Recovery means restoration of database to the most recent correct state, if a failure occurs.*

For this, the system keeps record of the changes by transactions in the database, in a *log*. An ideal strategy for recovery is the following:

(a) If there occurs a wide damage to the database, due to disk crash or fire, the recovery method restores a past copy of the database from the archive storage. All the committed transactions in the log file are then redone on this restored database.

(b) If the database is not physically damaged, but has become erratic due to some logical error or system crash, the recovery method would undo the operations that caused the error. In this case, data in archive storage is not needed, only the log file is required for undoing.

6.36.1 Data Storage

In order to understand database recovery procedures, we need to have some knowledge about storage media and their access methods. Storage media can be classified as volatile or non-volatile storage media.

Volatile Storage Media

Data stored in volatile storage media gets deleted when the power is switched off. Volatile storage media includes main memory and cache memory. These are made up of IC chips and hence data access is very fast. Data stored in volatile storage media cannot survive when system crashes. However, power failure is normally backed by uninterrupted power supply (UPS) facility.

Non-volatile Storage Media

Data stored in non-volatile storage media can survive system crashes. It includes hard disks and pendrives etc. Non-volatile storage devices are subject to failures when head crashes or power supply is fluctuating.

Stable Storage Device

Data stored in stable storage device is never lost. Such a storage media is impossible to obtain, but techniques can be used to implement such a system where data loss is practically nil. Replicating the needed information in several nonvolatile storage media, with independent failure mechanisms is one such technique. The information stored must be updated regularly to ensure that failure at one site does not affect the normal functioning of the system.

6.36.2 Recovery Facilities

Following are some DBMS recovery facilities:

(a) Checkpoint Facility (discussed previously) that enables *updates* to database be made permanent.

(b) Recovery manager module of the DBMS. It is the role of the Recovery Manager module, available in DBMS package, to guarantee durability and atomicity in case of unpredictable failures.

6.36.3 Recovery Techniques

The different recovery techniques used are discussed in the subsequent sections.

Recovery using Backups

Backups, as discused, are particularly useful if there has been extensive damage to database.

Mirroring

Two complete copies of the database are maintained on-line on different stable storage devices. This method is mostly used in environments that require non-stop, fault-tolerant operations.

Recovery using Transaction Logs

In case of recovery using transaction logs, the following steps are followed:

(a) The log is searched for all the transactions that have recorded a *[start transaction, ' ']* entry, but have not recorded a corresponding *[commit, ' ']* entry.

(b) These transactions are rolled back.

(c) Transactions which have recorded a *[commit, ' ']* entry in the log, must have recorded the changes, they did to the database, in the log. These changes are followed to undo their effects on the database.

Shadow Paging

In a single user environment, *Shadow Paging* System can be used for data recovery instead of using transaction logs.

In the Shadow Paging scheme, a database is divided into a number of fixed–sized disk pages, say *n*. Thereafter, a *current directory* is created that will be having *n* entries with each entry pointing to a disk page in the database. The current directory is transferred to the main memory.

When a transaction begins executing, the current directory is copied into a *shadow directory*.

The shadow directory is then saved on the disk. The transaction will be using the current directory. Hence during the transaction execution, all the modifications are made on the current directory and the shadow directory is never modified.

☞ *When a transaction performs the* ***write*** *operation, a new copy of the modified database page is created. This is done to ensure that the old copy of the database page is not overwritten until the transaction commits.*

The current directory is modified to point to the new database page while the shadow directory continues to point to the old database page.

Figure 6.113 illustrates the concept of shadow paging. To recover from a failure occurring during the transaction execution what we have to do is to just remove the new database pages as well as the current directory. The previous database version is safe in the old database pages pointed to by the entries in the shadow directory.

If the transaction executes successfully, the current directory is copied to a stable storage. The only thing we have to do is to change the pointer entries in the shadow directory which can be done by just overwriting the entries in shadow directory with the current directory.

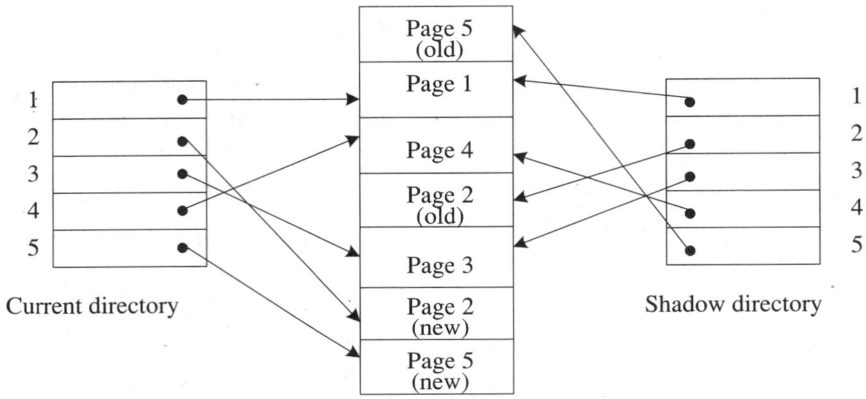

Figure 6.113 Shadow Paging scheme

☞ *Thus the shadow paging scheme reduces the need of transporting the updated database pages from the main memory to the disk storage.*

For example, in Figure 6.113, the current directory is pointing to the pages 1, 2 (new), 3, 4 and 5 (new). The new pages (2 and 5) are created as a result of changes made by the transaction. Note that the shadow directory points to the old pages (2 and 5) as well as the pages 1, 3 and 4 where there are no changes. Besides, the main memory contains both the old and the new pages. Hence, if there occurs any failure, the old pages remain intact, pointed to by the shadow directory. If the transaction commits successfully and the changes has to be written on to the stable storage, the contents of the shadow entry is overwritten by the contents of current directory. Also, the old pages (2 and 5) are removed from the memory and only the new modified pages are retained.

6.36.4 Recovery Procedures

Recovering from any type of system failure requires the following steps to be performed:

(a) Determining which data items are intact and which ones would need recovery.
(b) Follow the appropriate recovery methods (i.e. implement any of the methods discussed under recovery techniques).
(c) Restarting the database so that it can resume normal operations.
(d) Ensure that no data items are lost and no incorrect data items are entered in the database.

6.37 DETACHED TRANSACTION ACTIONS

A transaction is executed on occurrence of any of the following events:

(a) Some operation on the database is to be done such as insertion or deletion of a tuple, updation of an attribute etc.

(b) Another transaction raises an event in the middle of its execution such as abort or start of a transaction.

(c) An event raised by a clock at some particular point in time.

(d) An event raised because some error has occurred in the database.

If an event occurs within a centralized system, the transaction executed relative to the event can be:

(a) **Immediate:** in which case the transaction is executed as soon as the event occurs.

(b) **Deferred:** in which case the event is evaluated from within the same transaction that triggered the event.

(c) **Detached:** in which case the event is handled from within a different transaction other than the one in which the event took place.

☞ *Detached transaction is a transaction that is evaluated as a separate transaction and that retains any transactional locks acquired in a previous activity.*

There are two types of detached transaction actions:

(a) **Dependent Detached Transaction Action:** In which case the execution of the action is dependent upon committing of the transaction where the event took place.

(b) **Independent Detached Transaction Action:** in which case the execution of the action is independent of the committing of the transaction where the event took place.

Out of these, the dependent detached transaction is the preferred one. This is because if the transaction, where the event took place, aborts then the dependent *detached* transaction will not get executed. The dependent detached transaction will only commit if the transaction where the event took place got committed successfully. Whereas an independent detached transaction is an autonomous transaction and does not depend on any other transaction for its execution, therefore, may cause errors and hence not preferred.

In distributed database management systems, parts of the database resides at different sites that are connected by a communication network. Each site will be having its own recovery and transaction management techniques. Similarly, in systems that makes use of multiple database systems such as relational, object-oriented, hierarchical etc. each database system employs different recovery and transaction management techniques. In such situations, parts of transaction actions are executed at different sites or using different database systems. The transaction actions executing at a particular site use the resources of that site and are under the control of a local transaction coordinator. They have local recovery manager and local log tables. Such transaction actions are called detached transaction actions.

In addition, in distributed database management systems, there is a global recovery manager or coordinator that controls all these transaction actions as a whole and work towards maintaining the atomicity of the transaction. The protocol followed in such cases is known as the *two-phase commit protocol.* The two phases of the commit protocol are the following:

(a) **Phase I:** The participating sites or database systems signal the coordinator that the transaction actions at their end has concluded. The global coordinator will then send a "prepare to commit" signal to each site. The participating sites will then force-write all log records and send a "ready to commit" signal to the coordinator. If the participating sites cannot commit due to some reason or disk failure in between, they will send a "cannot commit" signal to the coordinator.

(b) **Phase II:** Upon receiving the "ready to commit signal" from all the participants, the coordinator will send a "commit" signal to all participating sites. The sites will then write a *[commit]* entry in the log. If any of the participating sites had sent a "cannot commit" signal, the global coordinator will send a "roll back" signal to all the sites. Each site will then *undo* their transaction actions, using the log.

☞ *The principal behind the two-phase commit protocol is that either all the participating database systems or sites commit successfully, or none of them commit at all.*

6.38 DATABASE SECURITY

Database security is process of protecting a database from unintended activity. Unintended activity can be categorized as authenticated misuse, malicious attacks or inadvertent mistakes made by authorized individuals or processes.

Database Security includes policies framed to protect data, falling in the hands of unauthorized users. Security also includes the techniques used to ensure that data elements are not changed or deleted by viruses or by unauthorized persons.

In short, data security addresses the following issues:

(a) Privacy of certain data elements.
(b) Preserving Policies of the Organization.
(c) System related security level.
(d) Maintaining integrity of database.

6.38.1 Privacy of certain Data Elements

Privacy relates to the legal and ethical rights regarding the access to certain personal data items. Some critical information may be regarded as private say for example the medical records of a person. Such records should not be accessed, read or modified by unauthorized persons.

6.38.2 Preserving Policies of the Organization

Some governmental, institutional or corporate level organizations have specific policies as to what kind of information should be made public. For example a person's credit rating and medical records should never be made public.

6.38.3 System related Security Level

The level of the system at which the security should be enforced. For example, whether a security should be enforced at the hardware level, operating system level or DBMS level.

6.38.4 Maintaining Integrity of Database

Data items stored in the database should be valid and consistent. Besides integrity constraints in the database management system, controlling access to the database can greatly help to preserve the database integrity.

6.39 DATA SECURITY RISKS

A database involves the following threats to its security:

(a) An unauthorized user can get access to a database and damage its files or alter it.
(b) The authorized users can accidently or deliberately give privileges to users, who have no time to access databases.
(c) Improper usage of concurrent transaction processing can cause variations in the data values read and written, by two users at the same time.
(d) An unauthorized person could get access to a database through a communication channel, via a terminal, and even insert virus and destroy data completely.
(e) A database user (such as an operator or programmer) can intentionally bypass the security mechanisms and make unauthorized copies of secret data, for malicious purposes.
(f) Authorized persons could transmit secret information under force or for personal gain (such as bribe or other favours).
(g) Failure of memory protection against virus attack may lead to errors in the DBMS package.
(h) Due to some system malfunctioning, a user may get access to the portion of a database, which he is not authorized under normal conditions.

6.40 DATABASE SECURITY REQUIREMENTS

Database security requires the following:

(a) Ethical and social culture of the employees of the organization should forbid an individual from obtaining something by unfair means and forcibly entering into an organizations computing facility. Legislation and security laws that make it illegal to obtain an unauthorized access to an organization's computer systems should be implemented.

(b) Computers and terminals should be kept locked and their access should be limited to authorized users. Physical storage devices (such as magnetic tapes, disk drives) should be secured both within the organization and while they are being sent from one location to another.

(c) Usernames and passwords should be kept confidential. The database administrator determines whether a user should be given the privilege or not and if yes, what privileges should be given.

(d) The operating system should have some built-in safety features such as identification and authentication of users, avoiding direct access to data in primary files, memory access as well as resource management including thread synchronization.

6.41 LEVELS OF SECURITY

Database management systems (DBMSs) provide different levels of security. These are the following:

(a) **Network Level Security:** Network Software Level security is required in case of distributed database systems. Network Software have built-in method for *login security controls*, permitting authorized users to log in and gain access to resources on the network. Another level of security provided by network software is the *rights security*. Rights security controls the files, sub directories and directories, a user or a group of users can access. Another level of security is *attribute security*. Attribute security determines if a particular file (or directory) can be viewed, shared, renamed, modified or deleted by a user or not. Therefore, even if a user or group of users have the privilege to delete a particular file, but they cannot do so, if the attribute of file does not allow.

(b) **Operating System (OS) Level Security:** Even if you have a strong DBMS software, a weak operating system may serve as a means of unauthorized deletion of database files. So, secure OS is important.

(c) **Database System Level Security:** Some database users may be allowed to access only a portion of the database and denied access to other portions. A user, Ram Lal, may be given permission to view information but not to modify data. That is, he can issue SELECT queries but not INSERT, UPDATE or DELETE queries.

(d) **Program Level Security:** It debars unauthorized users from using particular programs that may access the database. For example, a bank clerk may be allowed to use a program that retrieves details of a customer account, but not a program that modifies the balance amount.

(e) **Record Level Security:** It dabars unauthorized users from accessing or updating certain records, such as records of managers in the EMPLOYEE table.

(f) **Field Level Security:** It dabars unauthorized users from accessing or updating data in certain fields such as Salary field.

6.42 DATABASE SECURITY MEASURES

The data stored in a database is confidential and should not be accessible by unauthorized users or application programs (such as viruses). To prevent the database from being accessed by unauthorized users, different security measures need to be adopted. These are discussed in the following sections.

6.42.1 Controls

Identification and Authentication of a user can be done through any of the following methods:

(a) *What you know.* The simplest and the most common method is the usage of user's account number and password for authentication purpose. Instead of a simple password, the database system may also ask the user one or more questions. Only an authenticated user will have the right answers to such questions.

(b) *What you have.* In an another method, each user is given a badge, card or key to be used for identification purposes. A password or question-answer scheme as above can be used for authentication purpose.

(c) *What you are.* Special hardware or software can be used to identify a user, using some of his/her physical or physiological characteristics, such as thumb print.

6.42.2 Audit Trail

Database system keeps track of all the operations that a user performs during a *log-in session.* When a user logs in, the DBMS records the user's account number and then associates it with the terminal from which the user logged in. All operations done from that terminal are attributed to that user account number till the user logs-off.

If any tampering with the database is suspected, a *database audit* is performed. Database audit consists of reviewing the database accesses and operations done by a user account during a certain period of time. When an illegal or unauthorized operation is found, the DBA can determine the account number which performed such an operation.

☞ *A database log that is used mainly for security purposes is called an audit trail.*

6.42.3 Statistical Databases

Statistical Databases are such databases which store confidential information about users or organizations. Examples include database storing medical record, income of individuals, etc.

☞ *Statistical databases answers only statistical queries like computing total, average, etc.*

The goal of a statistical database is to maximize information-sharing and at the same time preserving the privacy of individuals. In order to maximize sharing, statistical database allows every user full access to the data in a database. In order to preserve privacy of individual information, only queries that involve large records are processed by statistical databases. For example, it is not possible to get a response from a database to a query that asks for the salary of an individual.

But if a malicious user has some knowledge about certain records in a database, he can still find out the salary of an individual. For example, suppose Mr. Ram Lal knows that there are only two people including him in the Accounts department. He knows his own salary. He can now find out the salary of Mr. Raju Chadha using the following query:

```
SELECT SUM(EMP.SALARY) FROM EMP
WHERE DEPT_CODE = 10
```

Suppose answer to the above query comes to be 50,000. Then, Mr. Ram Lal's salary being Rs. 20000, Raju Chadha's salary can be computed as Rs. 50000 - Rs. 20000 = Rs. 30000.

To prevent oversmart users from using such smart methods for accessing private information, one can use the following techniques:

(a) Rejection of those queries that involve only a small number of records in a database.

(b) Rejection of queries if the number of intersection records with previous queries made by the user is very large. This is to prevent such users as Mr. Ram Lal. For this, the system should maintain a history of records that were used in queries asked by a particular user.

(c) A third method is random falsification. In this approach, a small amount of data is randomly made wrong. The result of statistical computation of such data remains correct so that normal users do not suffer.

(d) A random sample of data representing the entire database is selected. Then this sample data is used to respond to any query. The normal user thus will not suffer and at the same time there will not be any danger to the database.

(e) There can also be an audit trail of activities on the database. This trail will record the identity of the users and their interactions with the database. The very fact that this can be done will discourage users with malicious intentions.

6.42.4 Data Encryption

Confidential data may be stored in an encrypted (coded) form in a database. This encrypted data cannot be read by anyone, unless he knows how to decipher (decrypt) it. The process requires an *encryption device* for converting the original message into a meaningless code, as well as a *decryption device* for translating the code back into the original text. In business data processing, this can be accomplished by using specialized computer software.

An algorithm known as encryption algorithm can be used for encrypting the data. A good encrypting algorithm has the following features:

(a) It should be very simple for authorized users to encrypt and decrypt data.

(b) It is very difficult to keep the algorithm secret. Hence, the security of data should not depend on the secrecy of the algorithm, but on a parameter of the algorithm. This parameter is known as *key*. The key should be known only to authorized users.

(c) The *key* used should be very difficult for an intruder to determine.

Public-key Encryption

Public-key encryption is one of the commonly used technique for data encryption. In this technique, two separate keys are used. It uses one key for encryption, say A and another related key for decryption, say B. The encryption key is placed in a public register and is known as the *public key*. The decryption key is kept secret and is known as *private key*.

Each user, U_i is given a public key, A_i and a private key, B_i. The public key is known to everyone. The private key is known only to the user to whom it belongs to. If a user U_1 wants to store encrypted data, he encrypts them using public key A_1. Decryption is done using the private key B_1, known only to U_1. But, if the user U_1 wants to share this data with user U_2, he encrypts it using A_2. U_2 can decrypt the data safely using his private key, B_2.

6.43 ROLE OF DBA

Restricting database access only to authorized users can be implemented by the access control mechanism. Access control is made available by creating user's accounts and passwords. The Database Administrator (DBA) has the responsibility of granting access permissions and user accounts to various users of a database.

DBA has the following responsibilities:

(a) *Account Creation*	Creating a new account and password for a user or a group of users.
(b) *Privilege Granting*	Allowing a user account to have access to certain parts of database.
(c) *Privilege Revocation*	Take away the privileges from a user account that were previously given to him.
(d) *Security Level Assignment*	Assigning user accounts to the appropriate security level.

Whenever a user or a group of users need to access a database, they must first apply for the user account. The DBA then may or may not grant a user account and password. If these are given, the user(s) will then log in to the DBMS by providing his user account and password. The DBMS will then check the validity of user account and password. If they are valid, user is permitted to access specified portion of the database.

☞ *Application programs are also considered as users by the DBMS and are required to supply user account and password.*

REVIEW QUESTIONS WITH ANSWERS

1. Multiple Choice Questions

1. What are the different types of clauses used in MariaDB?
   a. Where Clause
   b. Like Clause
   c. Both a and b
   d. None of the above
2. What are the types of JOIN in MariaDB?
   a. Inner Join
   b. Outer Join
   c. Left and Right Join
   d. All of the above
3. MariaDB is a community-developed branch of the ________ database, which uses the Maria engine by default.
   a. Solaris (operating system)
   b. OpenSolaris
   c. OpenOffice.org
   d. None of the above
4. Types of aggregate function:
   a. COUNT Function
   b. SUM Function
   c. MAX Function
   d. All of the above
5. If D1, D2,... Dn are domains in a relational model then the relation is a table which is a subset of
   a. {D1, D2,.....Dn}
   b. D1 × D2 × ... Dn
   c. D1 ∪ D2 ∪ Dn
   d. Maximum {D1, D2 ... Dn}
6. In order to undo the work of transaction after last commit which one should be used?
   a. View b. Commit
   c. Rollback d. Flashback
7. In order to maintain the consistency during transactions database provides:
   a. Commit b. Atomic
   c. Flashback d. Retain
8. The operation of a relation X, produces Y, such that Y contains only selected attributes of X. Such an operation is
   a. Projection b. Intersection
   c. Union d. Difference
9. The table generated on compilation of data stored in language (DDL) are stored in:
   a. Data abstraction b. Data Dictionary
   c. Data file d. Meta data
10. The following entities / attributes in a relational database should not have null values
    a. Keys b. Relations
    c. Variables d. All of these
11. This is an authorization command of SQL
    a. Access
    b. Grant
    c. Allow
    d. None of the above
12. Which one of the clause is useful in defining that notion of tuple variables?
    a. As b. By
    c. From d. None of these
13. Which one of the following is an aggregate function in SQL?
    a. AVG
    b. SELECT
    c. ORDER BY
    d. None of the above
14. Transactions are initiated by BEGIN TRANSACTION and terminated:
    a. By COMMIT TRANSACTION
    b. By ROLLBACK TRANSACTION
    c. Either by COMMIT TRANSACTION or by ROLLBACK TRANSACTION
    d. None of the above
15. Which of the following is an aggregate function?
    a. Union
    b. Like
    c. Group By
    d. Max
16. Which of the following is not a proper state of transaction?
    a. Partially aborted
    b. Partially committed
    c. Aborted
    d. Committed
17. Rollback of transaction is normally used to:
    a. Recover from transaction failure
    b. Update the transaction

c. retrieve old records
d. Repeat a transaction

18. GRANT is a command from:
a. DDL b. DML
c. DCL d. None of the above

19. Which of the following aggregate functions does not ignore nulls in its results?
a. Count b. Count(*)
c. Max d. Min

20. In order to recover from a failure, all the transaction that have not yet committed are:
a. undone b. redone
c. committed d. None of the above

21. In case of partial commit, recovery from failure is performed by __________ operations after the checkpoint.
a. Committing b. Undoing
c. Redoing d. None of the above

22. Rollback of transaction is normally used to
a. Recover from transaction failure
b. Update the transaction
c. Retrieve old records
d. Repeat a transaction

23. What is not true about two-phase locking?
a. All locks precede all unlocks
b. It ensures serialisability
c. Problem of deadlock does not arise with this scheme
d. None of these

24. Which one is true statement?
a. With fines degree of granularity of locking a high degree of concurrency is possible
b. Locking prevents non-serializable schedules
c. Locking cannot-take place at field level
d. An exclusive lock on data item x is granted even if a shared lock is already held

25. Media recovery refers to recovering database
a. After a system crash
b. After some individual transaction has failed
c. After database has been physically damaged
d. None of the above

26. Before a transaction is committed, the following is updated:
a. Log b. Query processor
c. Database d. Database manager

27. The two-phase commit protocol may introduce:
a. Deadlock b. Starving
c. Blocking d. None of the above

28. When the detection algorithm detects a deadlock, recovery is normally accomplished by
a. Rollback of transactions
b. Consistency checking
c. Locking of data
d. Calling back the same transaction

29. A directed graph which detects a deadlock is called
a. Cyclic graph b. Wait-for graph
c. Deadlock graph d. Deadlock detection graph

30. The user who controls the database structure and implements access control is
a. MD b. Chairman
c. DBA d. Database Operator

31. This is NOT one of the functions of a database administrator:
a. Granting of authorization for data access
b. Schema definition
c. Interaction with file manager
d. Storage structure and access method definition

32. What is used for database security?
a. Data encryption
b. A view
c. finger print
d. All of the above

33. The command used to allow access to specific parts of a database to a user is:
a. Access b. Grant
c. Allow d. None of these

34. If there exists a set of transactions such that every transaction the set is waiting for another transaction in the set, then the system is called:
a. Transaction failure
b. Transaction processing
c. Deadlock

d. Two-phase lock

2. State True or False for the following:

1. HAVING is used to eliminate groups in the same way as WHERE is used to eliminate rows.
2. Aggregate functions cannot appear with HAVING clause.
3. Equi-join is a natural join with duplicate columns eliminated.
4. Aggregate functions are also known as column functions.
5. The DISTINCT keyword is illegal for MAX and MIN.
6. When an INSERT statement using a query is executed, the query cannot contain an ORDER BY clause.
7. Transaction is a set of operation until commit.
8. The INTERSECT operator returns the rows that are common.
9. GROUP BY is not the same as ORDER BY.
10. COUNT (DISTINCT) eliminates duplicate field values before calculating the COUNT.
11. SQL aggregate functions produce a single value for the entire group of table entries.
12. Systems that permit transactions to interact with multiple resource managers must use a protocol called two – phase commit, if they are to maintain the transaction atomicity property.
13. All data values are not atomic (scalar).
14. A deadlock exists in the system if and only if the wait-for graph does not contain a cycle.
15. Every two-phase schedule can be produced by a time stamp ordered scheduler.
16. Order in which statements belonging to different transactions, is executed, is called a schedule.
17. If a write-lock is applied to a data item then any number of transactions can read it but no transaction can update it.
18. Deadlock can be described precisely in terms of a directed graph.
19. Schedules generated by a scheduler using two-phase locking protocol would be free of deadlock.
20. An ODBC transaction can span multiple databases.
21. Basic timestamp based scheduler may cause cascading abort of transactions.
22. In a lock-based schedule deadlocks cannot occur.
23. Isolation is a desired property of a transaction.
24. Read lock of data item by a transaction prevents other transactions to write that item.
25. In a timestamp based scheduler, if a transaction T attempts to modify a data item, say X, such that both write and read stamps of X are smaller than the timestamp of T then the write operation of T is accepted.
26. An audit trail is nothing but a log that is used for security purposes.
27. If the size of two databases are 10kb and 20kb respectively, the size of a database created using JOIN command will be less than or equal to 30kb.
28. The UNION operator *merges* outputs of two or more queries into a set of rows and columns.
29. The operator BETWEEN is used to specify a range of values.
30. The operator EXISTS is used for checking the existence of values.

3. Match the following:

1. Transaction	a. The operation automatically eliminates duplicates
2. Union	b. A unit of program execution that accesses and possibly updates various data items
3. Domain constraint	c. Shadow copy

4.	Null values	d.	They are tested easily whenever a new data item is entered into a database
5.	Database Recovery	e.	This restricts the number of possible schedules
6.	SQL keyword used to sort the result	f.	This is a situation where a particular transaction never completes its designated task
7.	LIKE operator	g.	This is used to produce the number of log records that must be scanned when the system recovers from crash
8.	Concurrency control	h.	Order by
9.	Starvation	i.	Match a character or a string of characters
10.	Deadlock detection	j.	Two-phase commit
11.	Deadlock free	k.	WFG
12.	Blocking problem	l.	Two-phase locking
13.	Check point	m	commit
14.	Transaction Successful	n.	Active
15.	Transaction State	p	Represents missing information

4. Fill in the blanks:

1. The list of tuples selected using the SQL SELECT FROM command may contain __________ entries.
2. Along with the GROUP BY clause, one can use the ________ clause to define a condition on the group of tuples associated with each value of the grouping attributes.
3. The CHECK clause in CREATE TABLE command can be used to enforce ___________.
4. A transaction completes its execution is said to be _________.
5. In database terms, a(n) ________ is any action that reads from and/or writes to a database.
6. A user with ______________ system privilege can modify a database by adding new files to it.
7. Data about data is normally termed as __________ .
8. The maximum number of rows returned by the following SQL query is __________.
   Select empno, empname from emp where salary = (select min (salary) from emp;
9. A(n) _________ is simple a SQL SELECT statement that returns a single row.
10. Transaction might be ________ before completion due to the detection of a deadlock condition.
11. __________ is a situation in which two or more transactions are in a simultaneous wait state.
12. A __________ is a unit of program execution that accesses and possibly updates various data items.
13. Deadlock may be detected using __________.
14. _________ refers to the database properties of a transaction.
15. The command ROLLBACK TO SAVEPOINT is used to ___________ rollback a transaction.
16. _________ of database system is concerned with maintaining of correctness and consistency of data.
17. The _________ is a situation where a transaction never completes its designated task.
18. In order to improve concurrency, Oracle supports __________ locking.
19. The primary key of a relation is minimal _________ key.
20. The CHECK clause in CREATE TABLE command can be used to enforce __________.
21. Data encrypted using public key can only be decrypted using __________ key.

22. Confidential data should be stored in _________ in database.
23. All the operations that a user performs on a database are recorded by a process known as ___________.
24. ___________ is SQL whose results are used in a search condition of another SQL query.
25. A lock placed automatically by the DBMS is called _________ lock.
26. MIN, MAX, AVG, SUM are all examples of _________ functions.

Answers

1.

1. c	2. d	3. c	4. d	5. b	6. c
7. b	8. a	9. b	10. a	11 b	12. d
13. a	14. c	15. d	16. b	17. a	18. c
19. a	20. a	21. b	22. a	23. c	24. b
25. c	26. a	27. c	28. a	29. b	30. c
31. c	32. d	33. b	34. c		

2.

1. T	2. T	3. T	4. T	5. F	6. F
7. T	8. T	9. T	10. T	11 T	12. T
13. T	14. F	15. F	16. T	17. F	18. T
19. T	20. F	21. T	22. F	23. T	24. F
25. T	26. T	27. F	28. T	29. T	30. T

3.

1. b	2. a	3. d	4. p	5. c	6. h
7. i	8. e	9. f	10. k	11. l	12. j
13. g	14. m	15. n			

4.

1. Duplicate	2. Having
3. Domain dependency	4. Committed
5. Transaction	6. Alter Database
7. Meta data	8. Unlimited
9. singleton SELECT	10. Terminated
11. Deadlock	12. Transaction
13. Wait-for-graph	14. ACID
15. Partially	16. Integrity
17. Starvation	18. Row-level
19. Super key	20. Domain dependency
21. private	22. encrypted
23. Database Audit	24. Sub query
25. Implicit	26. Aggregate

Short Answers Questions

1. What is a SQL view? Mention its two uses.

Ans A SQL view is a virtual table built from other tables or views. Views are used to:

(a) Hide columns or rows

(b) Show the results of computed columns

2. Write features of Where clause.

Ans Features of Where clause are:

(a) It is optional.

(b) It allows any condition to be specified.

(c) It allows for the specification of multiple conditions through using an AND or OR operator.

(d) Case sensitivity only applies to statements using LIKE comparisons.

3. What are the different types of Clause used in MariaDB?

Ans Different types of Clause used in MariaDB are Where, Order By, Like, Distinct etc.

4. What is use of Join?

Ans Join is used to retrieve data from multiple tables.

5. What is the use of ORDER BY clause in MariaDB?

Ans ORDER BY clause is used to sort the records in increasing or decreasing order.

6. What is function in MariaDB?

Ans MariaDB function is a stored program that is used to pass parameters into them and return a value.

7. Explain natural join with an example.

Ans Natural join is denoted as $R \bowtie S$. It is applicable only when there is at least one attribute common to R and S.

To compute $R \bowtie S$, do the following:

(a) Compute R × S
(b) Select those tuples from R × S whose components corresponding to the common attributes have the same values.
(c) Project out the columns corresponding to the attributes which have been considered once.

For example,

A	B	C
b	c	e
f	g	h
a	d	d
a	c	e

R

B	C	D
d	d	f
g	h	k
g	h	i
c	m	k

S

R ⋈ S

A	B	C	D
f	g	h	k
f	g	h	i
a	d	d	f

8. What do you understand by the term concurrency? How can we avoid deadlock?

Ans Most of today's DBMS allow multiple users to access a database at the same time. This is referred to as concurrency or concurrent access of database. The DBMS must include concurrency control software to ensure that several users trying to update the same data do so in a controlled manner so that the results of the updates are correct. For example, when several reservation clerks try to assign a seat on an airline flight, the DBMS should ensure that each seat can be accessed by only one clerk at a time for assignment to a passenger.

Deadlocks can be avoided by any of the following ways:

(a) Lock all the required data items at the beginning of a transaction.

(b) All data items are assigned an order. A transaction can only request locks in the given order say ascending order.

(c) Another method is to make run time decisions about what a transaction must do if it detects that it has to wait for a data item. For this, each transaction is assigned a unique timestamp. The system uses these timestamps to decide whether it should wait for the data item, abort or rollback the transaction.

9. Discuss the two-phase locking protocol. What benefits are provided by strict two-phase locking? What are its disadvantages?

Ans According to the two-phase locking protocol, locks on all the required data items must be acquired before the first unlock operation. Such a transaction can be divided into two phases, namely:

(a) *expanding* or growing phase during which the number of locks being acquired goes on increasing.

(b) *shrinking* or contracting phase, during which the existing locks can be released but no new locks can be acquired. That is during the shrinking phase, the number of locks acquired goes on decreasing.

Benefits of strict two phase locking scheme are:

(a) Strict two phase locking scheme follows a strict schedule. This leads to serializability in transaction execution.

(b) Recovery from system or disk failure is easier using this method since no other transaction can modify data items used by transaction T until T commits or aborts. Hence, during recovery only the changes made by T needs to be undone.

Disadvantages of strict two phase locking scheme are:

(a) It is not deadlock free.

(b) Degree of concurrency is greatly reduced.

(c) It can lead to starvation problem. This is because a lock is not released until the transaction commits or aborts. Some other transaction requiring a data item has to wait till the transaction having the lock is committed.

(d) Although it guarantees serializability, it does not permit all possible serializable schedules, i.e., some serializable schedules will be prohibited by this scheme.

10. What are the different states a of transaction?

Ans A transaction can be in one of the following states:

(a) **Active:** A transaction is in Active state, after it has started execution.

(b) **Partially committed:** A transaction is in Partially committed state, after the final statement has been executed.

(c) **Aborted:** A transaction is in Aborted state, after the transaction has been rollback.

(d) **Failed:** A transaction is in Failed state, after the discovery that normal execution of the transaction cannot be proceeded.

(e) **Committed:** A transaction is in Committed state, after it has been completed successfully.

11. What do you mean by a serial schedule and a serializable schedule?

Ans A schedule is said to be serial, if all the transactions involved in the schedule execute serially, that is one after the other. For example, a schedule involving two transactions, T1 and T2, will be a serial schedule if:

(a) all the operation of T1 are executed (in sequence) followed by the execution of all the operations of T2.

OR

(b) all the operation of T2 are executed (in sequence) followed by the execution of all the operations of T1.

A schedule is said to be a serializable schedule, if it is equivalent to some serial schedule of *n* number of transactions.

12. What do you understand by the term phantom deadlocks?

Ans Phantom deadlocks occur in case of distributed database systems. In distributed database systems, a site or node is chosen that creates a Global Wait For Graph (GWFG). If the GWFG is cyclic, it is assumed that a deadlock has occurred else not. This site or node then becomes the location for deadlock detection and selection of those transactions that have to be aborted in order to recover from deadlock. But suppose if the messages indicating which transactions are waiting for which resources and the release of resources by transactions are received out of order, then this site will falsely conclude that a deadlock has occurred. This falsely detected deadlock is called a *phantom deadlock.*

13. Define the violations caused by each of the following: dirty read, nonrepeatable read and phantoms.

Ans **Dirty read**: This condition occurs when a transaction T1 may read the update of a transaction T2, which has not yet committed. If T2 fails and is aborted then T1 would have a value that does not exist and is incorrect.

Nonrepeatable read: This condition occurs when a transaction T1 may read a given value from a table. If another transaction T2 later updates the value and T1 reads that value again, T1 will see a different value.

Phantoms: This condition occurs when a transaction T1 may retrieves a set of rows from a table, by giving a specific condition in the WHERE clause of the SQL statement. Now, suppose another transaction T2 inserts a new record into the table that meets the same condition used by T1. Then, if T1 is repeated, it will see a phantom, i.e. a row that was not previously existing.

14. Write short note on database security.

Ans Database security is process of protecting a database from unintended activity. Unintended activity can be categorized as authenticated misuse, malicious attacks or inadvertent mistakes made by authorized individuals or processes. Database Security includes policies framed to protect data, falling in the hands of unauthorized users. Security also includes the techniques used to ensure that data elements are not changed or deleted by viruses or by unauthorized persons.

15. Write short note on Data Encryption.

Ans Confidential data may be stored in an encrypted (coded) form in a database. This encrypted data cannot be read by anyone, unless he knows how to decipher (decrypt) it. The process requires an *encryption device* for converting the original message into a meaningless code, as well as a *decryption device* for translating the code back into the original text. In business data processing, this can be accomplished by using specialized computer software. An algorithm known as encryption algorithm can be used for encrypting the data.

16. What is Public-key Encryption?

Ans Public-key encryption is one of the commonly used technique for data encryption. In this technique, two separate keys are used. It uses one key for encryption, say A and another related key for decryption, say B. The encryption key is placed in a public register and is known as the *public key*. The decryption key is kept secret and is known as *private key*.

17. What is Audit Trail?

Ans Database system keeps track of all the operations that a user performs during a *log-in session*. When a user logs in, the DBMS records the user's account number and then associates it with the terminal from which the user logged in. All operations done from that terminal are attributed to that user account number till the user logs-off.

If any tampering with the database is suspected, a *database audit* is performed. Database audit consists of reviewing the database accesses and operations done by a user account during a certain period of time. When an illegal or unauthorized operation is found, the DBA can determine the account number which performed such an operation.

18. Create two relations, EMPS and DEPTS as follows:

```
EMPS (EMP_NO, NAME, SALARY, DEPT_NO)
DEPTS(DEPT_NO, DNAME, MANAGER)
```

Express the following integrity constraints:

(a) No employee earns more than Rs. 50000

(b) No employee in DEPT_NO 50 earns more than 5000.

Ans The two tables, EMPS and DEPTS, containing the required integrity constraints, are created as follows:

```
CREATE TABLE EMPS
(
EMP_NO NUMBER PRIMARY KEY,
NAME VARCHAR2(20),
SALARY NUMBER CHECK (SALARY <=
50000),
DEPT_NO NUMBER,
CHECK ((DEPT_NO <> 50) OR (SALARY <=
5000))
);

CREATE TABLE DEPTS
(
DEPT_NO NUMBER PRIMARY KEY,
DNAME VARCHAR(15),
MANAGER VARCHAR(25)
);
```

19. Given a relational database consisting of following relations:

```
EMP(E_NO, EMP_NAME, AGE, SALARY)
DEPT(DEPT_NAME, LOCATION, E_NO,
  MANAGER)
PROJECTS(P_NO, PROJ_DETAILS,
  START_DATE, E_NO, PERIOD)
```

Express the following query:

Get the name of employees who are working in the testing department on a project for more than fifteen days (i.e. PERIOD > 15) and list the P_NO of such projects.

Ans The query command to get the names of employees who are working in the Testing Department on a project for more than fifteen days (i.e. PERIOD > 15) and the list of P_NO of such projects, is given below:

```
SELECT EMP_NAME, P_NO
FROM EMP, DEPT, PROJECTS
WHERE PERIOD > 15 AND DEPT_NAME =
'TESTING'
AND EMP.E_NO = DEPT.E_NO
AND EMP.E_NO = PROJECTS.E_NO;
```

20. Consider the following relational database:

```
bank_emp(emp_name, street, city)
works(emp_name, company_name, sal-
ary)
Bank(bank_name, city)
manages(emp_name, manager_name)
```

(a) Give a DDL definition in SQL for the database. Identify referential integrity constraints that should hold, and include them in the DDL definition.

(b) Find the names of all employees who work for State Bank of India.

(c) Find all the employees in the database who live in the same city as the bank for which they work.

(d) Find the names, street and cities of residence of all employees who work for State Bank of India and earn more than Rs. 15,000.
Assume that all employees have distinct names.

Ans 20 a SQL DDL definition for the given database is as follows:

```
CREATE TABLE BANK_EMP
(
EMP_NAME VARCHAR2(20) PRIMARY KEY,
STREET VARCHAR2(15) NOT NULL,
CITY VARCHAR2(10)
);
CREATE TABLE BANK
(
BANK_NAME VARCHAR2(25),
CITY VARCHAR2(10)
);
CREATE TABLE WORKS
(
EMP_NAME VARCHAR2(20) REFERENCES
BANK_EMP(EMP_NAME),
COMPANY_NAME VARCHAR(25) REFERENCES
BANK(BANK_NAME),
SALARY NUMBER
);
CREATE TABLE MANAGES
(
EMP_NAME VARCHAR2(20) REFERENCES
BANK_EMP(EMP_NAME),
MANAGER_NAME VARCHAR2(20) REFERENCES
BANK_EMP(EMP_NAME)
);
```

20 b. The query to get the names of those employees who work for State Bank of India is:

```
SELECT EMP_NAME
FROM WORKS
WHERE COMPANY_NAME = 'State Bank of
India';
```

20 c. The query to find those employees in the database who live in the same city as the bank for which they work, is:

```
SELECT BANK_EMP.EMP_NAME
FROM BANK_EMP, BANK, WORKS
WHERE BANK_EMP.EMP_NAME =
WORKS.EMP_NAME
AND WORKS.COMPANY_NAME =
BANK.BANK_NAME
AND BANK_EMP.CITY = BANK.CITY;
```

20 d. The query to find the names, street and cities of all employees who work for State Bank of India and earn more than Rs. 15,000, is:

```
SELECT BANK_EMP.EMP_NAME, STREET,
CITY
FROM BANK_EMP, WORKS
WHERE BANK_EMP.EMP_NAME =
WORKS.EMP_NAME
```

```
AND COMPANY_NAME = 'State Bank of
India'
AND SALARY > 15000;
```

21. What are the criteria which determine whether base table updations are possible through views or not?

Ans Operations such as insertion, deletion, updation, etc. are not possible on views that are defined in any of the following ways:

(a) A column of the view is defined using aggregrate function.

For example, consider the following view definition:

```
CREATE OR REPLACE VIEW CLERK AS
SELECT DEP_CODE, COUNT(*)
FROM EMPLOYEE
GROUP BY DEPARTMENT;
```

The rows of above defined view, CLERK, cannot be updated, deleted or inserted because of the presence of an aggregate function COUNT.

(b) When the view definition contains DISTINCT, GROUP BY or HAVING clause.

(c) If the view definition contains nested queries.

(d) A column of the view is defined using some arithmetic expression.

(e) If the view has been created using two base tables, i.e a join operation has been performed in the view definition. (However, modern RDBMS packages such as Oracle 8.0 supports modifying such views subject to certain conditions).

22. Table DEP contains DEP_NO, DNAME. Table EMPY contains ENO, ENAME, DNO, SALARY.
Write a query to get total number of employees in each department having salary more than 20000 but only for departments where more than 5 employees work.

Ans The query to get total number of employees in each department having salary more than 20000 but only for departments where more than 5 people work is:

```
SELECT DNAME, COUNT(*)
FROM DEP, EMPY
WHERE DNO = DEP_NO
AND SALARY > 20000
GROUP BY DNAME
HAVING COUNT(*) > 5;
```

23. If X and Y are two relations as shown below:

a b c	b c a
d c a	c d f
b f e	b f e
X	Y

Find:

(a) $X \cup Y$ (c) $X \cap Y$
(b) $X - Y$ (d) $X \times Y$

Ans

(a) $X \cup Y$ =

a b c
d c a
b f e
b c a
c d f

(b) $X - Y$ =

a b c
d c a

(c) $X \cap Y$ =

b f e

(d)

$X \times Y$ =	a	b	c	b	c	a
	a	b	c	c	d	f
	a	b	c	b	f	e
	d	c	a	b	c	a
	d	c	a	c	d	f
	d	c	a	b	f	e
	b	f	e	b	c	a
	b	f	e	c	d	f
	b	f	e	b	f	e

EXERCISE

1. Write short note on the following:
   (a) Nested queries
   (b) Deadlock
   (c) Natural Join
   (d) Backup
   (e) Two-phase locking
2. Write main features of MariaDB database.
3. Explain the difference between Order by and Group by clause.
4. How left join is different from right join?
5. What is database security? Why is it important? Also discuss the various security issues.
6. Explain any three group functions.
7. What is the use of DISTINCT keyword?
8. Explain Union operator with example.
9. How count() is different from count(*)?
10. What is Single-row functions?
11. What are transactions? How do you define and control them in a database application?
12. Explain the concept of two phase locking and explain how it guarantees serialisability.
13. Explain how concurrency can lead to inconsistency. What is a deadlock? Can it occur in a serialisable schedule? If so, give an example? How can it be detected and resolved?
14. List the ACID properties. Explain the usefulness of each.
15. Consider the following Transactions:

Transaction T1
Read(A) Read(B) If A = 0 then B = B + 1 Write(B)

Transaction T2
Read(B) Read(A) If B = 0 then A = A + 1 Write(A)

Consistency requirement: $A = 0 \vee B = 0$
Initial values: $A = B = 0$

a. Show that the serial execution of these two transactions preserves the consistency of the database.
b. Show that concurrent execution of these two transactions produces a non-serializable schedule.
c. Is there a concurrent execution that produces a serializable schedule?

16. What are the different level of security that a DBMS provides?
17. Discuss the various measures that we can take to protect a database.
18. Write a note on data encryption techniques. List the possible threats or risks to a database.
19. Explain how audit trailing can help against malicious attacks to database.
20. Create two tables, EMPS and DEPTS as per the following structure:

```
EMP(EMP_CODE, EMP_NAME, BASIC, DEPT_CODE)
DEPT(DEPT_CODE, DEP_NAME, HEAD)
```

Express the following integrity constraints using SQL command

(a) No employee earns more than 1,00,0000

(b) No employee in DEPT_CODE 10 earns more than 50,000.

2. Create tables consisting of the following structures and enter some sample data:

```
EMP(E_NO, NAME, BASIC)
DEPT(DEPT_NAME, FLOOR, E_NO, HEAD)
PROJECTS(P_NO, PROJ_DETAILS, E_NO,
PERIOD)
```

Express the following query:

Get the names of employees who are working in the testing department and PERIOD > 15 and the list of P_NO of such projects.

3. Consider the following relational database:

```
bank_emp(emp_name, street, city)
works(emp_name, company_name, sal-
ary)
Bank(bank_name, city)
manages(emp_name, manager_name)
```

(a) Give a SQL DDL definition for the above database. Identify referential integrity constraints that should hold, and include them in the DDL definition.

(b) Find the names of all employees who work for State Bank of India.

(c) Find all the employees in the database who live in the same city as the bank for which they work.

(d) Find the names, street and cities of residence of all employees who work for State Bank of India and earn Basic more than 15,000 a month.

Assume that all employees have different names.

4. List the circumstances in which base table updations through views are not possible?

5. Table DEP contains DEP_NO, DEP_NAME. Table EMP contains E_NO, E_NAME, DEP_NO, SALARY. Write a query in SQL to get total number of employees in each department having salary more than 5000 but only for those departments where more than 3 persons work.

CHAPTER 7

NoSQL Database Technology–MongoDB

7.1 INTRODUCTION TO NoSQL DATABASES

NoSQL ('not only SQL') databases were developed in the late 2000s with a focus on scaling, fast queries, allowing for frequent application changes, and making programming simpler for developers. Relational databases accessed with SQL (Structured Query Language) were developed in the 1970s with a focus on reducing data duplication as storage was much more costly than developer time. SQL databases tend to have rigid, complex, tabular schemas and typically require expensive vertical scaling.

NoSQL databases offer many benefits over relational databases. NoSQL databases have flexible data models, scale horizontally, have remarkable fast queries, and are easy for developers to work with. NoSQL is not a relational database. It provides more flexibility since all records are not restricted by the same column names and types defined across the entire table.

Advantages of NoSQL Databases

- **Dynamic schemas**: NoSQL databases typically have very flexible schemas. A flexible schema allows you to easily make changes to your database as requirements change. You can iterate quickly and continuously integrate new application features to provide value to your users faster. NoSQL is used for Big data and real-time web apps like Twitter, Facebook, Google that collect terabytes of user data every single day. Thus, in real-time application changes can be made easily without the need to worry about service interruptions. This makes development faster, more reliable and less time consuming for the database administrator.
- **Horizontal scaling**: The system response time becomes slow when you use RDBMS for huge volumes of data. To resolve this problem, you could "scale up" our systems by upgrading your existing hardware. This process is expensive. Most SQL databases require you to scale-up vertically (switch to a larger, more expensive server) when you exceed the capacity requirements of your current server.
  The alternative for this issue is to distribute database load on multiple hosts whenever the load increases. This method is known as "scaling out". NoSQL databases allow you to scale-out horizontally, i.e., servers are added instead of increasing the capacity of a single server. It provide auto-sharding feature i.e., it automatically spread data across various numbers of servers. Also, a load of data and query are automatically balanced among the servers. If any server fails, then it is replaced quickly and transparently without disrupting the application. This type of scalabilty improves performance, allowing for continuous availability and very high read/write speeds.
- **Fast queries**: Queries in NoSQL databases can be faster than SQL databases. Data in SQL databases is typically normalized, so queries for a single object or entity require you to join data from multiple tables. As your tables grow in size, the joins can become expensive. However, data in NoSQL databases is typically stored in a way that is optimized for queries. Queries typically do not require joins, so the queries are very fast.

- **Easy for developers**: Some NoSQL databases like MongoDB map their data structures to those of popular programming languages. This mapping allows developers to store their data in the same way that they use it in their application code. This mapping can allow developers to write less code, leading to faster development time and fewer bugs.
- **Distributed**: NoSQL database is designed to distribute data at global scale, meaning it can use multiple locations involving multiple data centers and/or cloud regions for write and read operations. Also some sophisticated NoSQL databases provide automated recovery and are fully self-healing. Relational databases, in contrast, use a centralized application that is location-dependent (e.g. single location), especially for write operations.
- **Zero Downtime**: NoSQL database is zero downtime. This is made possible by a masterless architecture, which allows for multiple copies of data to be maintained across different nodes. If one node goes down, another node has a copy of the data for easy, fast access.

Drawbacks of NoSQL Databases

- No standardization rules. There are many types of NoSQL databases but there is almost no uniformity among them.
- Limited query capabilities. Also, no specific programming interface to the different databases. Each one varies in query language with another.
- Open source options which is not so popular for enterprises.
- RDBMS databases and tools are comparatively mature.
- NoSQL Databases do not support ACID (Atomicity, Consistency, Isolation, Durability) transactions across multiple documents. With appropriate schema design, single record atomicity is acceptable for lots of applications. However, there are still many applications that require ACID across multiple records.
- NoSQL stores the key name along with every document so when the volume of data increases it is difficult to maintain unique values as keys become difficult. Also, due to no functionality of joins, there is data redundancy. This results in increasing unnecessary usage of memory.
- Not all non-relational databases are good at automating the process of sharding, or spreading the database across multiple nodes.
- It does not offer any traditional database capabilities, like consistency when multiple transactions are performed simultaneously.

7.1.1 Difference between Relational and NoSQL Databases

The two main types of modern databases to choose from are relational (SQL) and non-relational (NoSQL) for query processing. Due to advanced technology and big data applications traditional SQL-based relational database was less equipped to handle rapidly expanding data volumes and the growing complexities of data structures. So, the non-relational, NoSQL databases became more popular for offering a more flexible, scalable, cost-efficient, alternative to the traditional SQL-based relational databases. Also unlike traditional, SQL based, relational databases, NoSQL databases can store and process data in real-time.

- SQL databases are known as relational databases, and have a table-based data structure, with a strict, pre-defined schema required. NoSQL databases, or non-relational databases, can be document based, graph databases, key-value pairs, or wide-column stores.
- In a relational database, you are required to define your schema before adding data to the system. Also all of your data must follow the same structure. Changing the schema structure in a relational database can be extremely expensive and time-consuming.

NoSQL databases don't require any pre-defined schema, i.e., NoSQL database has dynamic schema for unstructured data (such as texts, social media posts, photos, videos, email etc.) allowing you to work more freely with such data. Basically, this means you can build your application without having to first define the schema. No pre-defined schema makes NoSQL databases much easier to update as data and requirements change.

- Relational databases are vertically scalable i.e., you can increase the load on a single server, but usually more expensive. Since they require a single server to host the entire database, in order to scale, you need to buy a bigger, more expensive server. Whereas the horizontal scaling nature of NoSQL databases is more cost-efficient. This means that you handle more traffic by sharding, or adding more servers in your NoSQL database. Sharding means dividing a database into smaller chunks across multiple hardware servers instead of a single large server.
- Relational databases are table-based. NoSQL databases can be document based, graph databases, key-value pairs, or wide-column stores. While relational databases were built during a time that data was mostly structured and clearly defined by their relationships. We know that today data is much more complex. NoSQL databases are designed to handle such unstructured data. So, NoSQL databases can easily process structured, semi-structured, and unstructured data, while relational databases, are designed to handle primarily structured data.
- NoSQL databases are part of the open-source community. Relational databases are typically closed source with added licensing fees to use their software.
- Great support is available for all SQL database from their vendors. Also a lot of independent consultations are there who can help you with SQL database for a very large scale deployments but for some NoSQL database you still have to rely on community support and only limited outside experts are available for setting up and deploying your large scale NoSQL deployments.
- NoSQL database is designed to distribute data at global scale, meaning it can use multiple locations involving multiple data centers and/or cloud regions for write and read operations. Relational databases, in contrast, use a centralized application that is location-dependent (e.g. single location), especially for write operations.

Some examples of SQL databases include PostgreSQL, MySQL, Oracle and Microsoft SQL Server. NoSQL database examples include Redis, RavenDB Cassandra, MongoDB, BigTable, HBase, and CouchDB.

7.2 FEATURES OF NoSQL DATABASES

Features of NoSQL databases are discussed below:

- NoSQL databases never follow the relational model. Relations in a database establish connections between tables of data. For example, a list of transaction details can be connected to a separate list of delivery details. With a NoSQL database, this information is stored as an aggregate - a single record with everything about the transaction, including the delivery address.
- Never provide tables with flat fixed-column records.
- Doesn't require object-relational mapping and data normalization. In relational database theory, the goal is to normalize your data (that is, to organize the fields and tables to remove duplicate data). In NoSQL databases especially Document or Aggregate databases you often deliberately denormalize data, storing some data multiple times.
- A database schema is the description of all possible data and data structures in a relational database. NoSQL database offers a flexible schema design which can easily be altered without downtime or service disruption.

- No complex features like query languages, query planners, referential integrity joins, ACID etc.
- Offers heterogeneous structures of data in the same domain.
- Multiple NoSQL databases can be executed in a distributed fashion. The database allows automatic database replication. NoSQL databases don't need a dedicated high-performance server.
- It provides fast performance and horizontal scalability.
- NoSQL databases allow developers to store huge amounts of structured, semi-structured, and unstructured data with equal effect and giving them a lot of flexibility.
- NoSQL databases have integrated caching capability i.e., they keep frequently used data in system memory and remove the need for the separate caching layer.
- Distributed databases can store and process a set of information on more than one device. With a NoSQL database, a cluster of servers can be used to hold a single large database. For example, you need a distributed mechanism to effectively manage all data on Twitter and Facebook. Also, there is huge flexibility in the way the data is stored and this increases the performance in the NoSQL database.
- In relational databases, you join information and add constraints across tables at query time. This may require the database engine to evaluate many tables. The more query constraints you have across different tables, the more you reduce your query speed. In a NoSQL database, all the information you need to evaluate your query is in a single document. Therefore, you can quickly determine the list of matching documents.

7.3 TYPES OF NoSQL DATABASES

NoSQL databases are non-tabular, and store data differently than relational tables. NoSQL data models allow related data to be nested within a single data structure. They provide flexible schemas and scale easily with large amounts of data and high user loads.
NoSQL databases come in a variety of types based on their data model. There are mainly four categories of NoSQL databases. Each of these categories has its unique attributes and limitations. No specific database is better to solve all problems. You should select a database based on your product needs.

- Key-value Pair
- Column-oriented
- Graphs-based
- Document-oriented

7.3.1 Key-value Pair

These databases work on a simple data model that has a pair of unique keys and a value associated with it i.e., data is stored in key/value pairs (See Figure 7.1). Key-value pair storage databases store data as a hash table where each key is unique, and the value can be a JSON (JavaScript Object Notation), BLOB(Binary Large Objects), string, etc. It is designed in such a way to handle lots of data and heavy load.
It is one of the most basic types of NoSQL databases. This kind of NoSQL database is used as a collection, dictionaries, associative arrays, etc. Key value stores help the developer to store schema-less data. They work best for storing user profiles, blog comments, product recommendations, and session information. Redis and DynanoDB are popular key-value databases.

Figure 7.1 Key-value Pair Database

7.3.2 Column-oriented

Traditional relational databases are row-oriented, with each row having a row-id and each field within the row stored together in a table. Column-oriented Graph databases organize data in columns instead of rows. Every column is treated separately. Values of single column databases are stored contiguously. They can query large data sets faster than other conventional databases.

Column based NoSQL database deliver high performance on aggregation queries like SUM, COUNT, AVG, MIN etc., as the data is readily available in a column. Column-based NoSQL databases are widely used to manage data warehouses, business intelligence, Library card catalogs, fraud detection, and recommendation engines. It is also used for storing Internet of Things (IoT) data and user profile data. HBase, Cassandra, Hypertable are examples of some popular column based database. (See Figure 7.2).

7.3.3 Graphs-based

These databases organize data as nodes and edges that show connections between nodes. Nodes typically store information about people, places, and things while edges store information about the relationships between the nodes. Every node and edge has a unique identifier.

Compared to a relational database where tables are loosely connected, a Graph database is a multi-relational in nature. Traversing relationship is fast as they are already captured into the Database, and there is no need to calculate them. Graph databases are great for establishing data relationships especially when dealing with large data sets. Graph base database mostly used where you need to traverse relationships to look for patterns such as social networks, fraud detection, logistics, and recommendation engines. Neo4J, Infinite Graph, OrientDB, FlockDB are some popular graph-based databases. (See Figure 7.3).

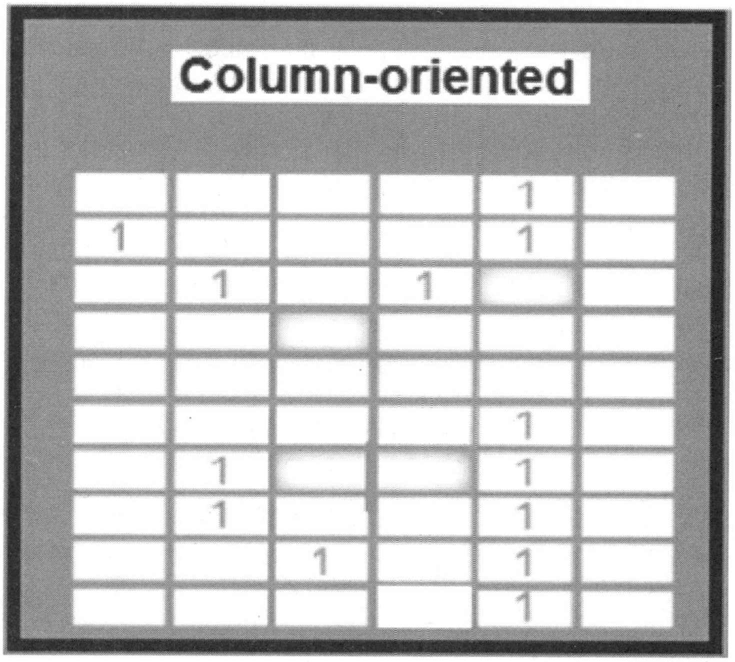

Figure 7.2 Column-oriented Database

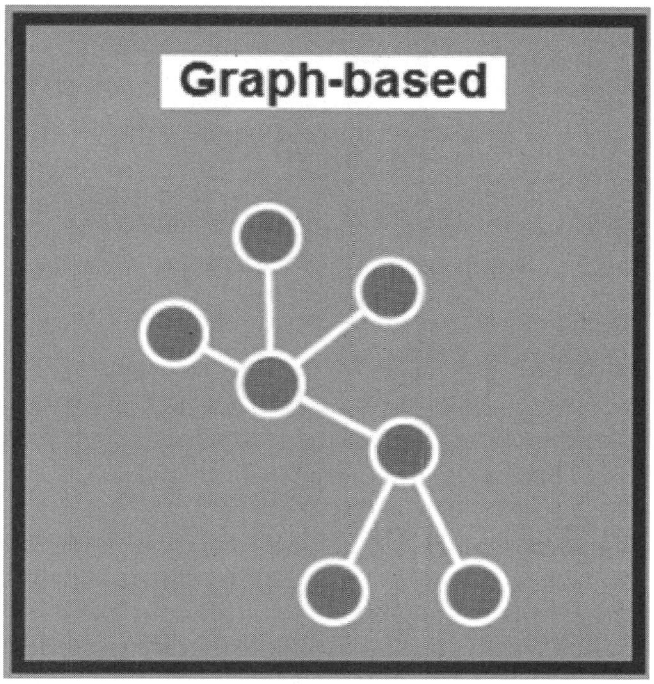

Figure 7.3 Graphs-based Database

7.3.4 Document-oriented

Document-oriented NoSQL Database stores store data in documents. Each document contains pair of fields and values. The values can typically be a variety of types including strings, numbers, booleans, arrays, or objects. They do not refer to master schema for creating and updating programs. The document is stored in JSON (JavaScript Object Notation) or XML (Extensible Markup Language) formats. Consider an order from an online retailer. The order could include product codes, quantities, item prices, and item descriptions, as well as information about the person ordering, such as delivery address and payment information. Rather than insert many rows in a variety of tables in a relational database, you can instead store a single structure for all of this order information in a JSON or XML document.

The document type is mostly used for CMS systems, blogging platforms, real-time analytics and E-commerce applications. It should not use for complex transactions which require multiple operations or queries against varying aggregate structures. Amazon SimpleDB, CouchDB, MongoDB, Riak, Lotus Notes, are Document originated DBMS systems. MongoDB is the most popular of these databases. (See Figure 7.4).

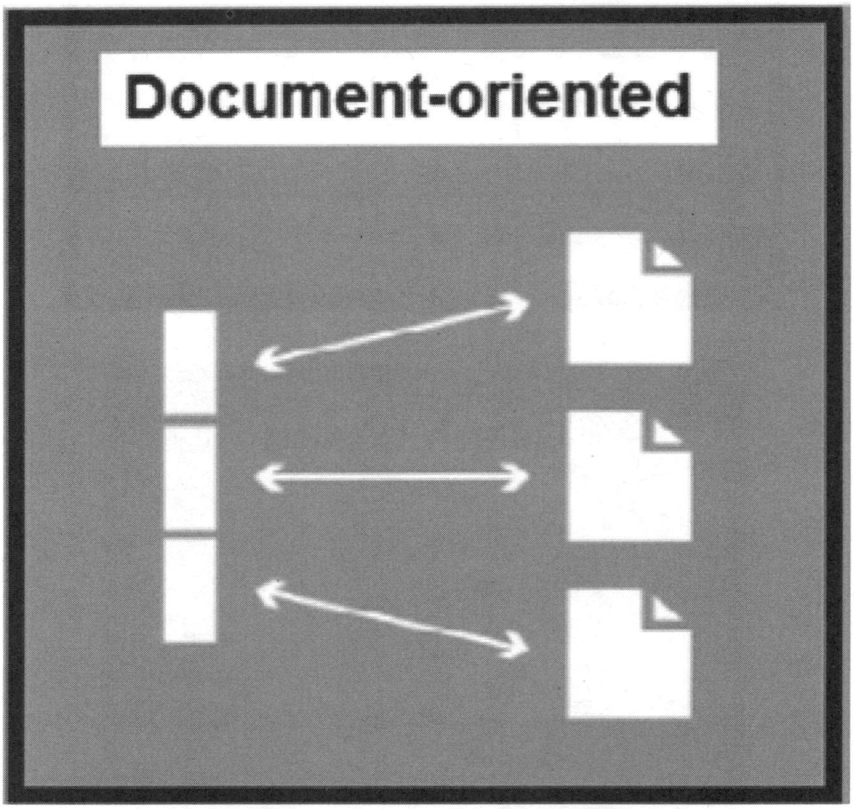

Figure 7.4 Document-oriented Database

7.4 INTRODUCTION TO MongoDB

MongoDB is an open-source document database, and leading NoSQL database. It is written in C++. The term NoSQL was coined in 2009 to unite together the many non-relational databases gaining in popularity at that time. One of their commonalties being that they use a query language other than SQL. NoSQL is not a relational database. It provides more flexibility since all records are not restricted by the same column names and types defined across the entire table.

MongoDB is a powerful, flexible, and scalable general-purpose database. It combines the ability to scale out with features such as secondary indexes, range queries, sorting, and aggregations. MongoDB is a cross-platform database that provides high performance, high availability, and easy scalability. It works on the concept of collection and document.

MongoDB is a document-oriented database, not a relational one. A document-oriented database replaces the concept of a "row" with a more flexible model, the "document". By allowing embedded documents and arrays, the document-oriented approach makes it possible to represent complex hierarchical relationships with a single record.

MongoDB document format is based on JSON (JavaScript Object Notation), a popular scheme for storing arbitrary data structures. JSON structures consist of keys and values and are analogous to the dictionaries in Python.

7.5 BASIC CONCEPTS OF MongoDB

Relational databases have tables, while MongoDB has collections. In other words, MySQL (a popular relational database) keeps its data in rows of tables, while MongoDB keeps its data in collections of documents, which you can think of as a group of documents. Mapping between RDBMS and MongoDB is given in Figure 7.5.

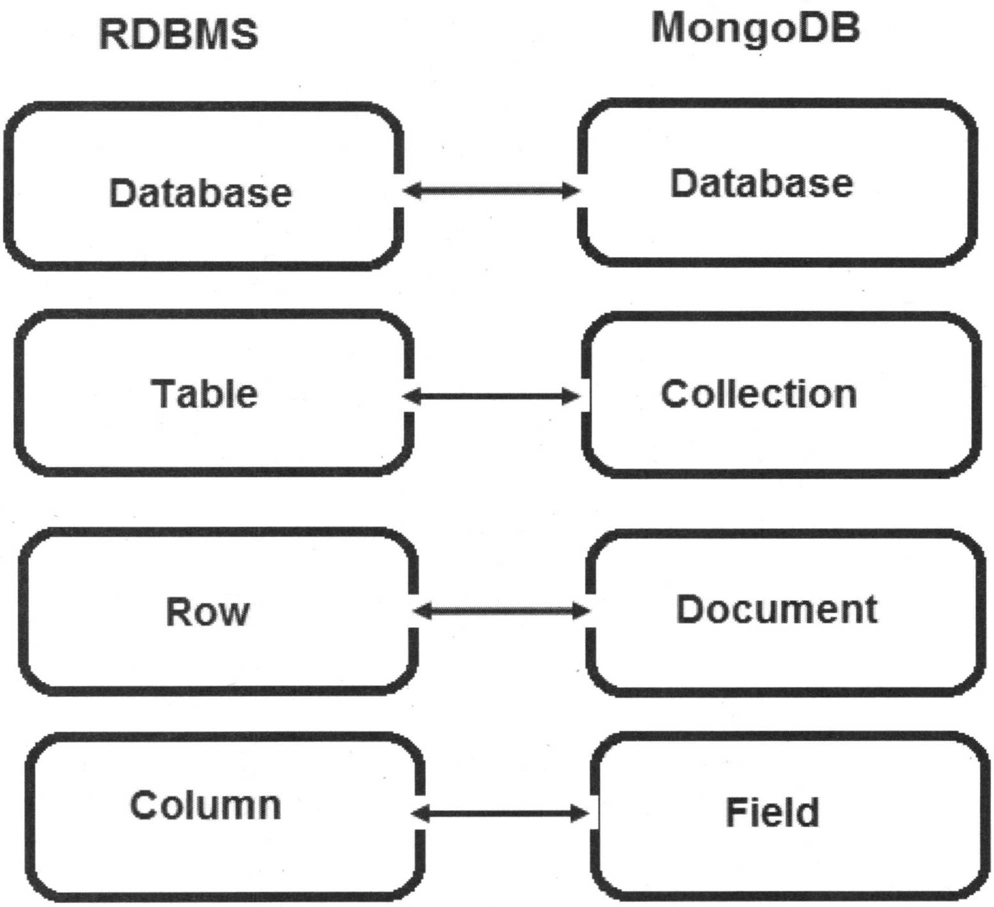

Figure 7.5 Mapping between RDBMS and MongoDB

7.5.1 Document

A *document* is the basic unit of data for MongoDB and is roughly equivalent to a *row* in a Relational Database Management System. MongoDB is the document i.e., an ordered set of keys with associated values. The keys in the document are strings. Key/value pairs in documents are ordered: {"x" : 1, "y" : 2}.

7.5.2 Collection

A *collection* is a group of documents. It is the equivalent of an RDBMS *table*. It exists within a single database. Documents within the collection can have different fields.

7.5.3 Field

A *field* is a name-value pair in the document. A

document has zero or more fields. Fields are analogous to columns in relational databases.

Every document has a special key, "_id", that is required in every MongoDB document. The _id field represents a unique value in the MongoDB document. The _id field is like the document primary key. Each document has a unique key id or object id which can both be user or system defined. If you create a new document without an _id field, MongoDB will automatically create the field.

☞ *MongoDB doesn't support primary key-foreign key relationship. MongoDB has _id key field for every document that uniquely identifies the particular document.*

7.5.4 Database

MongoDB group collections into *databases*. In simple words, it can be called as the physical container for data. Each of the databases has its own set of files on the file system with multiple databases existing on a single MongoDB server. A single instance of MongoDB can host several databases, each grouping together zero or more collections.

☞ *Cursor is a pointer to the result set of a query. Clients can iterate through a cursor to retrieve results.*

MongoDB comes with a simple but powerful JavaScript shell, which is useful for the administration of MongoDB instances and data manipulation. The mongo executable loads the shell and connects to a specified mongod process, or the one running locally by default.

☞ *MongoDB is type-sensitive and case-sensitive.*

7.6 ADVANTAGES OF MongoDB

Any relational database has a typical schema design that shows a number of tables and the relationship between these tables, while in MongoDB there is no concept of relationship.

MongoDB has a flexible schema. That means we can have any type of data in a separate document. Unlike in SQL databases, where you must have a table schema declared before inserting data, MongoDB collections do not enforce document structure. Without the fixed schema, adding or removing fields as needed becomes easier. Generally, this makes development faster as developers can quickly iterate.

MongoDB has deep query-ability. It supports dynamic queries on documents, using a document-based query language that's nearly as powerful as SQL.

MongoDB supports document-oriented storage. It is easy to access documents by indexing. Hence, it provides fast query response. The speed of MongoDB is much faster than the relational database. Since MongoDB is a NoSQL type database, instead of having data in a relational type format, it stores the data in documents. This makes MongoDB very flexible and adaptable to real business world situation and requirements. Data is stored in the form of JSON style documents. JSON is a simple representation of data. MongoDB queries are generally composed of JSON objects rather than text strings as in SQL. This makes them simpler to create and parse.

MongoDB supports searching by field, range queries, and regular expression searches. Queries can be made to return specific fields within documents. Moreover, Indexes can be created to improve the performance of searches within MongoDB.

We can store a large data by distributing it to several servers connected to the application. If a server cannot handle such a !big data then there will be no failure condition. This is called auto-sharding.

☞ *Auto-sharding process distributes data across multiple physical partitions called shards. Due to sharding, MongoDB has an automatic load balancing feature.*

A great advantage of MongoDB is that it is a horizontally scalable database. When you have to handle a large data, you can distribute it to several machines. MongoDB was designed to scale out. Its document-oriented data model makes it easier for it to split up data across multiple servers. It can run over multiple servers, balancing the load and/or duplicating data to keep the system up and running in case of hardware failure.

It supports MapReduce and flexible aggregation tools. MapReduce is a powerful and flexible tool for aggregating data. It can solve some problems that are too complex to express using the aggregation framework.

MongoDB supports GridFS feature. GridFS is the standard method for storing large files by dividing files into smaller parts and stores them as separate documents.

7.7 ARCHITECTURE OF MongoDB

MongoDB is a NoSQL database, which enables building and running applications using modern development techniques. Let us understand how MongoDB architecture works. (See Figure 7.6).

Being a NoSQL tool means that it does not use the usual rows and columns as the Relational Database Management. It is an architecture that is built on collections and documents. In simple words, database can be called the physical container for data. Each of the databases has its own set of files on the file system with multiple databases existing on a single MongoDB server. Each database contains collections which in turn contains documents. Each document can be different with a varying number of fields. The size and content of each document can be different from each other.

A database can have a mixture of sharded and unsharded collections. Sharded collections are partitioned and distributed across the shards in the cluster. Unsharded collections are stored on a primary shard. Each database has its own primary shard. A sharded cluster consists of the following components:

- **shard**: They contain the subset of sharded data. Each shard can be deployed as a replica set. MongoDB sharded collections are partitioned and distributed in clusters. A replica set is group of mongod processes that maintains same data set. It provides redundancy in order to provide high availability.
- **mongod**: It is the core database process. Arbiter is the mongod instance, it is a part of replica set but does not contain data.
- **mongos**: It is responsible for processing queries from the application layer. It also determines the location of this data in the sharded cluster to complete the task. You must connect to a mongos router to interact with any collection in the sharded cluster. This includes sharded and unsharded collections. Clients should never connect to a single shard in order to perform read or write operations.
- **mongo**: It is an interactive JavaScript shell interface to MongoDB, through which administrators and developers interact with MongoDB to test queries and run the operations.
- **config server**: They store metadata and configuration settings for the cluster. MongoDB automatically takes care of balancing data and load across a cluster, re-distributing documents automatically and routing user requests to the correct machines. This allows developers to focus on programming the application, not scaling it.

7.8 DYNAMIC SCHEMA

Schema design determines the way an application handles its data. With traditional relational databases, you must define your schema before you can add any data. MongoDB databases permit to insert the data without the pre-defined schema. Dynamic schema means that documents in the same collection do not need to have the same set of fields or structure, and common fields in a collection's documents may hold different types of data. With enhanced Dynamic schema you can improve your data without affecting the existing data. It provides excellent scalability and high performance.

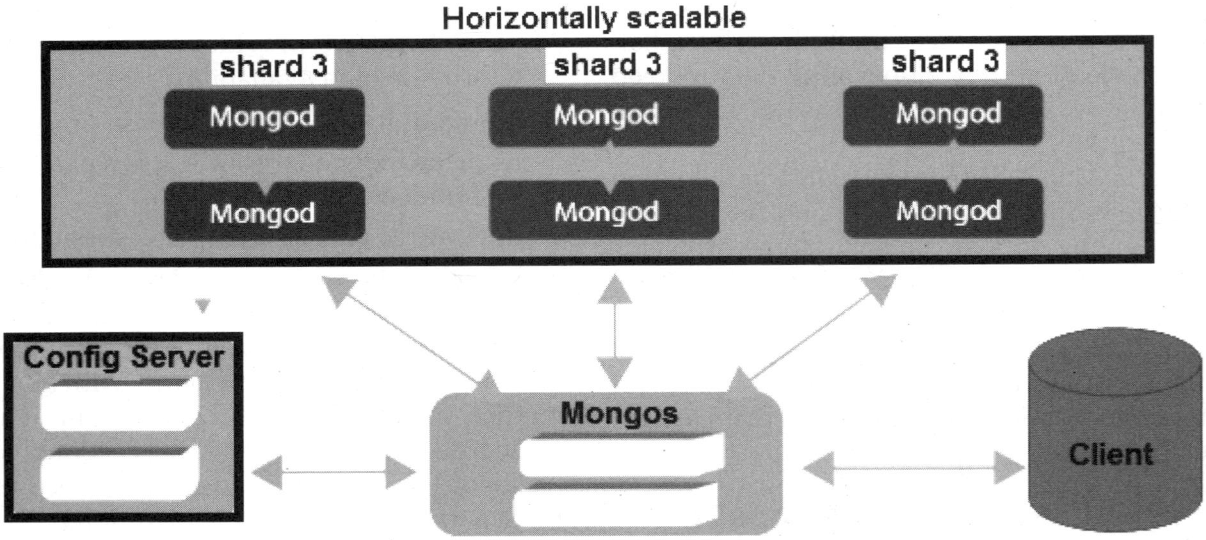

Figure 7.6 Architecture of MongoDB

7.9 MONGO SHELL

The mongo shell is an interactive JavaScript interface to MongoDB. You can use the mongo shell to query and update data as well as perform administrative operations. There are some global commands you can execute, like help or exit. Commands that you execute against the current database are executed against the db object, such as db.help() or db.status(). Commands that you execute against a specific collection, are executed against the db.COLLECTION_NAME object, such as db.student.help() or db.student.count(). The mongo shell is included as part of the MongoDB Server installation. MongoDB also provides the mongo shell as a standalone package.

☞ *To exit the shell, type quit() or use the* Ctrl+C *shortcut.*

7.10 MONGO SERVER AND CLIENT

NoSQL databases don't need a dedicated high-performance server. NoSQL databases, use multiple computers to store data for a single database, rather than have the whole database on a single server. Sharding distributes data across multiple physical partitions called shards. An advantage of distributing your database is that you can use cheaper servers, called commodity servers. Even for smaller datasets, it may be cheaper to buy three commodity servers instead of a single, higher powered server. Thus, it removes the dependency on a single server. The database never goes off-line. In other words, it provides 24/7 services.

Replication refers to having a single master MongoDB server, with one or more slave servers (replicas) associated with it. MongoDB can provide high availability with replica sets. A replica set consists of two or more MongoDB instances. Each replica set member may act in the role of the primary or secondary replica at any time. The primary replica is the master(main) server which interacts with the client and performs all the read/write operations. The secondary replicas maintain a copy of the data of the primary using built-in replication. When a primary replica fails, the replica set automatically switches over to the secondary and then it becomes the primary server.

MongoDB is a server-client database. Server usually runs with the binary file mongod and client runs with mongo. MongoDB supports Java-Script for server-side execution. MongoDB uses JSON format for data storage and retrieval at the client-side. In other words, it allows a developer to use a single programming language for both client-side and server-side code. MongoDB allows you to configure multiple clients. Using several clients works the same way as having a single client.

7.11 MongoDB DATA TYPES

MongoDB stores documents in BSON, which is the binary encoded format of JSON. Basically, the name BSON itself comes from Binary encoded JSON. The BSON data format provides various types, used when we store the JavaScript objects in the binary form. MongoDB supports many data types listed below:

String: The string is most commonly used data type to store the data.

Integer: This type is used to store an integer value. There are two forms available for this data type, 32 bits, and 64 bits depending upon your server.

Boolean: This type is used to store a boolean values i.e., true or false.

Double: The double data type is used to store floating point values.

Min/Max keys: This type is used to compare a value against the lowest and highest BSON elements. Min key compares the value of the lowest BSON element. Max key compares the value against the highest BSON element.

Arrays: This type is used to store arrays or list or multiple values into one key.

Timestamp: This can be handy for recording when a document has been modified or added.

Object: This data type is used to store embedded documents.

Null: This type is used to store a Null value.

Symbol: This data type is used identically to a string.

Date: This data type is used to store current date or time. There are various methods to return date. It can be either as a string or as a date object.

ObjectID: This data type is used to store the document's unique key Id. There is an _id field in MongoDB for each document. The data which is stored in _id is in hexadecimal format.

Binary data: This data type is used to store binary data.

Code: This data type is used to store javascript code into document.

Regular expression: This data type is used to store regular expression.

Undefined: This data type stores the undefined values.

7.12 MongoDB DOCUMENT STRUCTURE

There can be two ways to establish relationships between the data in MongoDB:

- Referenced Documents
- Embedded Documents

7.12.1 Referenced Documents

Reference is one of the tools that store the relationship between data by including links from one data to another. In such data, a reference to the data of one collection will be used to collect the data between the collections. Reference relationships should be used to establish one-to-many or many-to-many relationships between documents.

7.12.2 Embedded Documents

In RDBMS, data is sometimes spread across various tables and in order to show a complete view of all data, a join is sometimes formed across tables to get the data. In MongoDB, the data is normally stored in a single collection, but separated by using Embedded documents. So there is no concept of joins in MongoDB. Embedded documents create relationships between data by storing related data in a single document structure. These data models allow applications to retrieve and manipulate related data in a single database operation. Object data type is used for storing embedded documents. Embedded documents are particularly useful when a one-to-many relationship exists between documents.

☞ *If a document contains another document in the form of the key-value pair then such type of document is known as an embedded document.*

7.13 JSON FILE FORMAT

JSON! is known as JavaScript Object Notation. Douglas Crockford is the Creator or Father of JSON. This is a human-readable, plain text format for expressing structured data. JSON is currently supported in many programming languages such as MongoDB. MongoDB stores data in a binary JSON like format called BSON. MongoDB uses

BSON format to store the data into a document. BSON extends the JSON model to provide additional data types and to be efficient for the encoding and decoding within various languages.

Advantages of JSON

- Its lightweight text-based structure makes it easily readable. Also documents written in JSON format is easy to understand.
- We can generate embedded documents and arrays that reduce the need for Joins.
- MongoDB is a document-oriented database. These documents support embedded fields, so related data can be stored within them.
- It is widely used and recognized by almost all programming languages and JSON is language independent.
- Easier to read and best suited as files to non-programmers.
- JSON present a flexible and concise framework for specifying queries as well as storing records.
- JSON is commonly used to read data from a web server and display the data on a web page.

☞ *A JSON file has an extension of '.json'. Being in a text-based format, a JSON file can be viewed or edited using any text editor like notepad or notepad++.*

Disadvantages of JSON

JSON has several advantages over the other formats but at the same time, it also has some limitations. They are:

- JSON is not suitable for handling very complex large data.
- JSON doesn't have support for handling multimedia formats such as rich text or images.
- It doesn't support comments.

☞ *JSON is one of the simplest data interchange format, independent of programming language and platform.*

7.13.1 JSON objects

An object is defined as a set of key-value pairs. Data inside a JSON is arranged in key-value pair. The left side represents the key and the data on the right side represents value. A JSON starts with a left brace '{' and ends with another right brace '}'. Every key is followed by a colon ':' and the key-value pairs are separated from each other by using a comma ','. So, basically, the JSON object is a collection of keys along with their values arranged in a pre-specified JSON format.

For example,

```
{"name":"Vivek", "age":19,
 "class":"XII"}
```

Note that JSON objects are surrounded by curly braces {}. They are written in key or value pairs.

Arrays in JSON can be values of an object property. It is defined as:

```
{
"name":"Vivek",
"age":19,
"class": "XII"
"hobbies":[     "Singing",      "Reading",
"Painting" ]
}
```

7.13.2 Advantages of JSON over XML

XML, or eXtensible Markup Language, is a way to store accessible data that can be read by both humans and machines. The XML format is available for use across many programming languages. In many ways, XML is very similar to JSON, but it requires much more text so is longer in length and more time consuming to read and write. XML must be parsed with an XML parser, but JSON can be parsed with a standard function. Also unlike JSON, XML cannot use arrays.

- JSON is lighter and faster than the XML.
- JSON has object types but XML doesn't define objects as types. JSON has different object type for a different set of data such as string, integer, boolean, array, etc. All XML objects are categorized as just one data type, i.e., string.

- JSON data can be easily accessed as a JSON object using JavaScript. On the other hand, the XML data need to be parsed and allocated to the variables using APIs.
- The text-based lightweight nature makes JSON more accessible and useful than XML.
- JSON uses a map data structure whereas XML has a tree structure.

7.13.3 JSON Data Types

In JSON, values must be one of the following data types:

- **string**: Strings in JSON must be written in double quotes. For example:
  `{ "name":"Abhi" }`
- **number**: Numbers in JSON must be an integer or a floating point. For example:
  `{ "age":19 }`
- **object** : It is an unordered collection of key:value pairs. Objects as values in JSON must follow the same rules as JSON objects. Objects are enclosed in curly braces i.e., it starts with '{' and ends with '}'. Each name is followed by ':'(colon) and the key/value pairs are separated by , (comma). For example:
```
{
"student":{ "name":"Abhi", "age":19,
"city":"New Delhi" }
}
```
- **array**: It is an ordered sequence of values. These are enclosed in square brackets which means that array begins with '[' and ends with ']'. The values are separated by , (comma). For example:
```
{
"students":[ "Abhi", "Raj", "Shiva" ]
}
```
- **boolean**: The boolean data type represents either True or False values. For example:
  `{ "present":true }`
- **null**: The null value denotes that the associated variable doesn't have any value. For example:
  `{ "middlename":null }`

7.14 DOWNLOAD AND INSTALL MongoDB

To install the MongoDB on Windows, first download the latest release of MongoDB from http://www.mongodb.org/downloads. Make sure you get correct version of MongoDB depending upon your Windows version. To get your Windows version, open command prompt and execute the following command:

```
C:\>wmic os get osarchitecture
```

Your screen will display the message as shown in Figure 7.7.

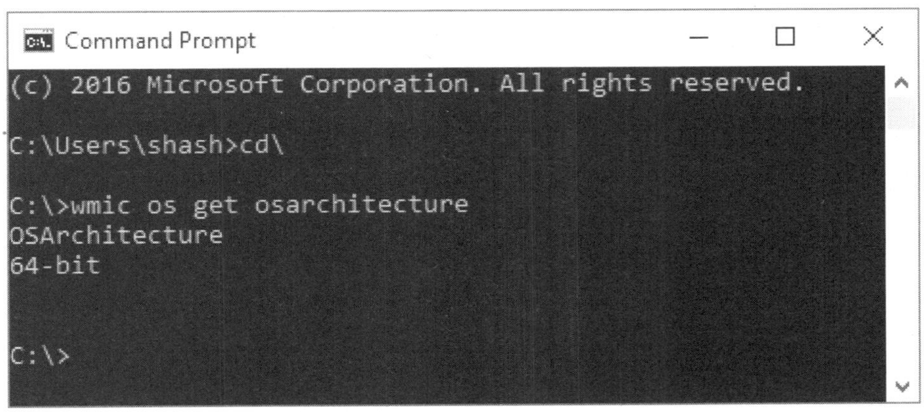

Figure 7.7 Getting your Windows Version

32-bit version of MongoDB only supports databases smaller than 2GB and suitable only for testing and evaluation purposes. Also, note that MongoDB does not support Windows XP, and in order to install it on Windows, you need to have Windows Server 2008 R2, Windows Vista, or latest versions.

Understand your requirements and download the suitable package from the following link - https://www.mongodb.com/download-center/community as shown in Figure 7.8.

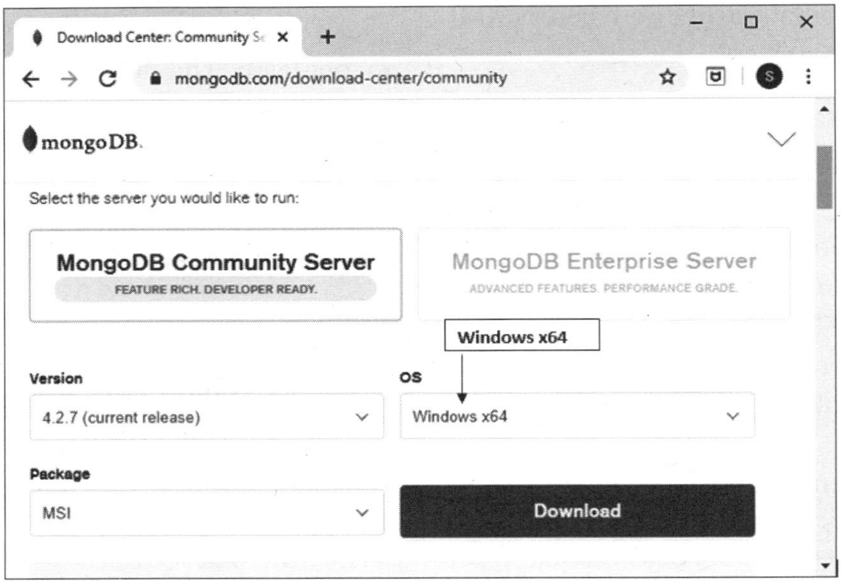

Figure 7.8 MongoDB Download centre screen

Select **Community Server**, then select the version, select OS as Windows x64 and click on **download**.

It will start downloading MongoDB msi file as shown in Figure 7.9.

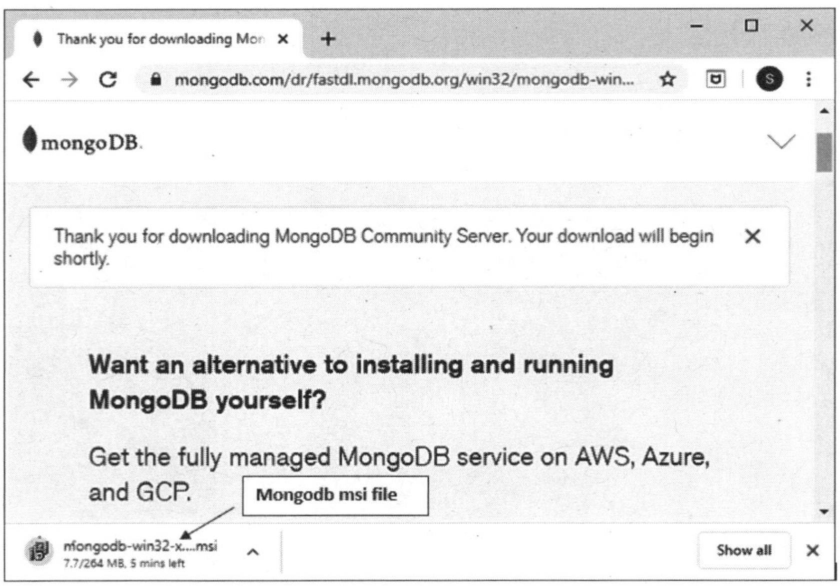

Figure 7.9 Thank you for downloading MongoDB Screen

Double click on the MongoDB.msi file which you downloaded from the site and follow through the instruction to successfully complete the installation. (Figure 7.10 to 7.16 demonstrate the installation process of MongoDB). In the Setup Wizard that opens, click Next. In next step, accept the agreement and click Next. You may read the Terms and Conditions, if desired so before clicking Next.

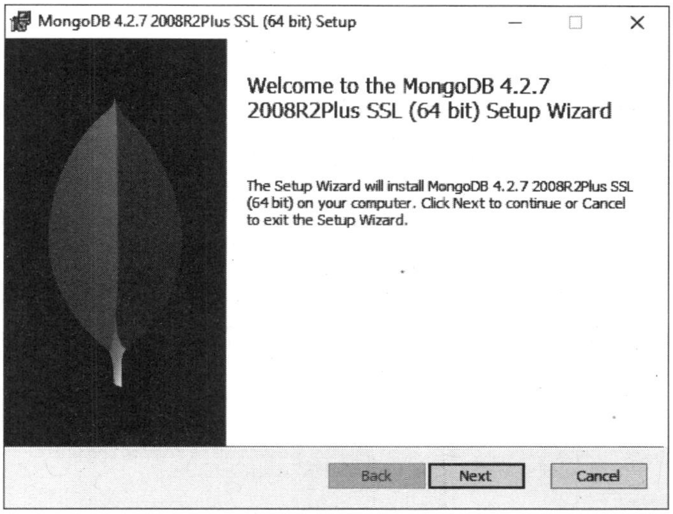

Figure 7.10 Click on the Next Button

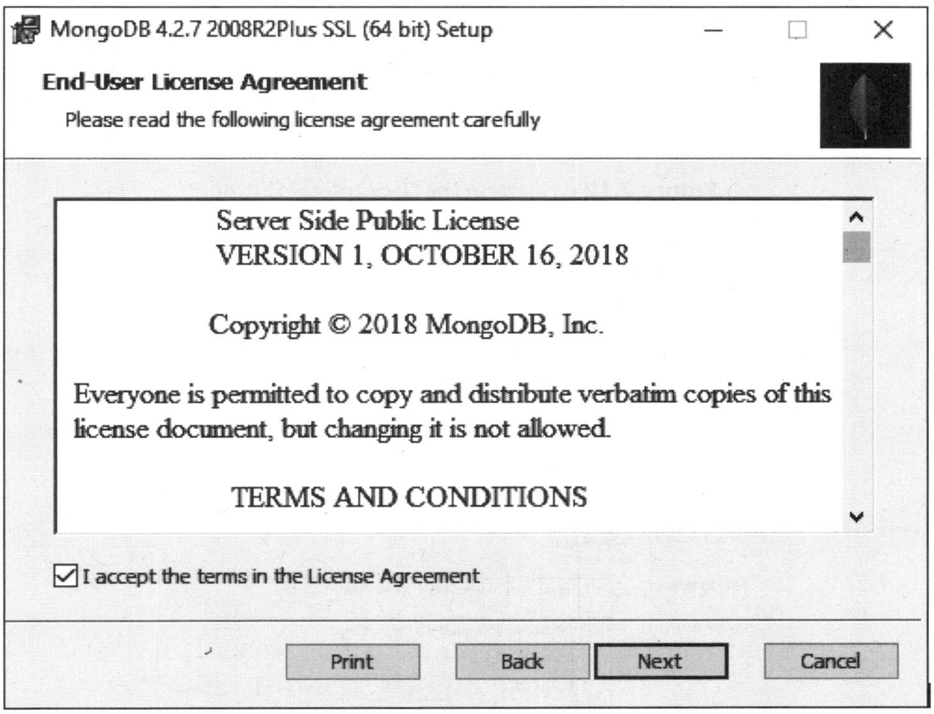

Figure 7.11 Click on the Next Button to Agree to the End User License Agreement

In next step, It will ask you to either choose from Complete or Custom Installation. Click on the "Complete" button to install all of the components. The Complete setup option installs MongoDB and the MongoDB tools to the default location. The "Custom" option can be used to install selective components or if you want to change the location of the installation. In service configration window click Next button. Now click Install button.

The installation will begin and it will take some time to install the MongoDB on your system. The progress bar will be displayed.

After some time, the MongoDB will be installed and completion dialog box will open. Click the Finish button.

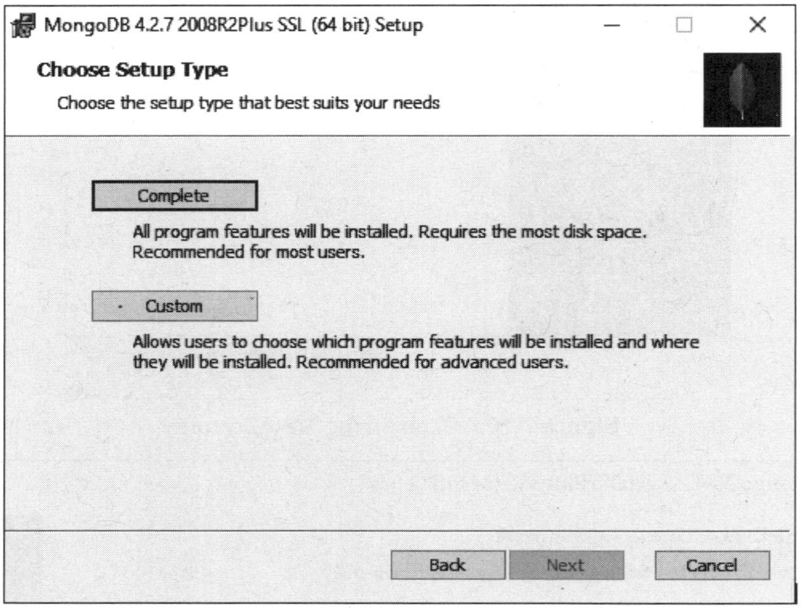

Figure 7.12 Click on the "Complete" Button

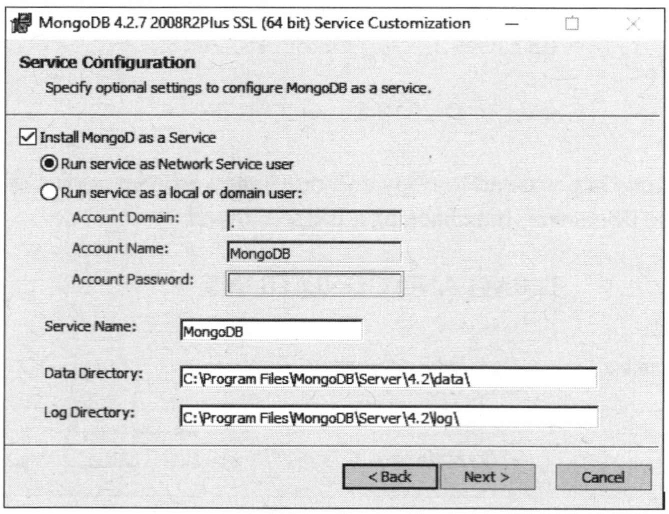

Figure 7.13 On MongoDB Service Configration Screen, Click on Next Button

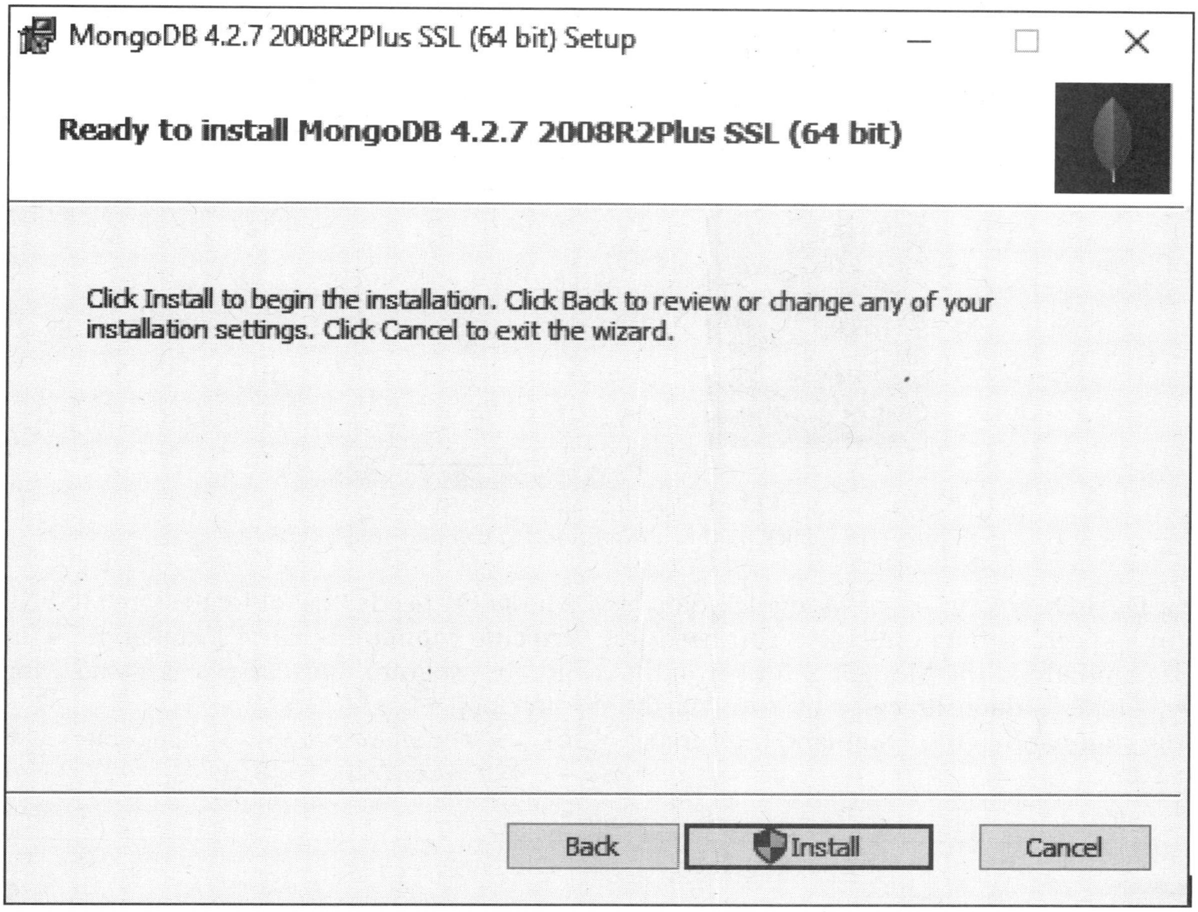

Figure 7.14 Click on the Install Button to start the Installation

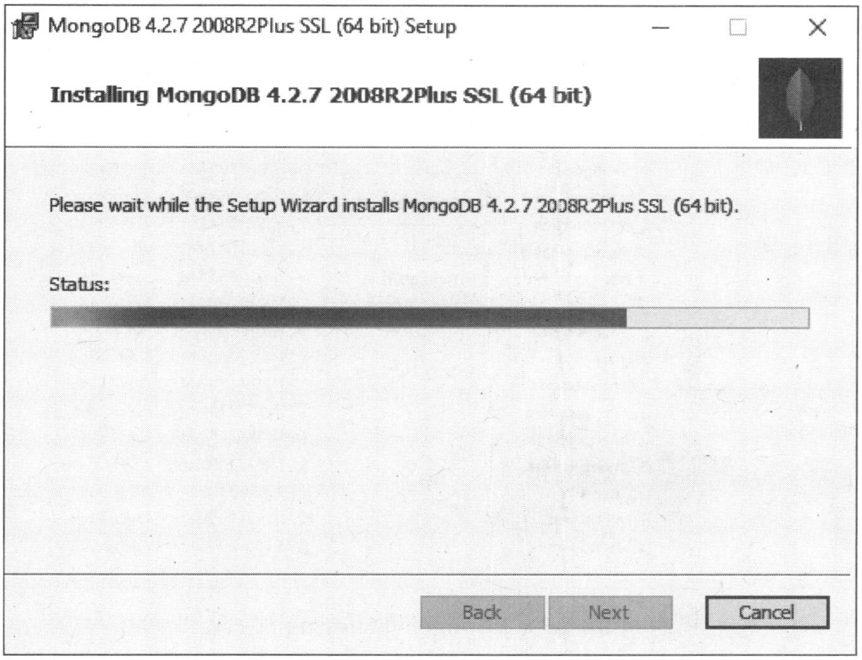

Figure 7.15 MongoDB Setup Wizard Installation Process

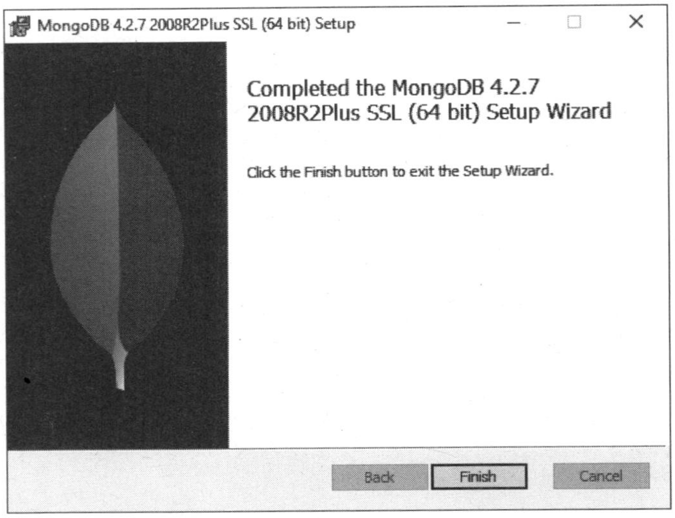

Figure 7.16 Click on the Finish Button to complete the installation

Create a Data Directory: All of MongoDB data is stored in a specified data directory. You need to create it manually in the MongoDB folder on the C drive. Create a data directory by running the following command in the Command Interpreter:

```
md\data\db
```

MongoDB needs this folder to store all the data.

Execute MongoDB: Once installation is finished, go to program files and select the MongoDB directory.

```
C: -> Program Files -> MongoDB -> Server
-> 4.2(version) -> bin
```

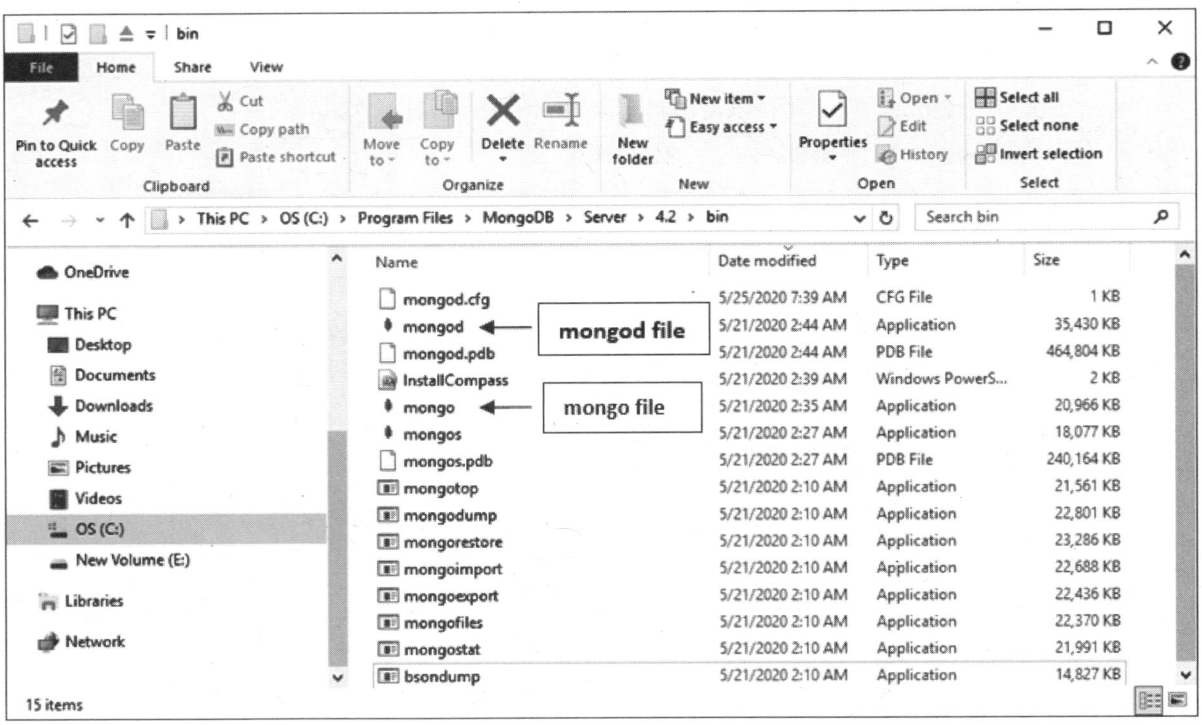

Figure 7.17 MongoDB Files are Stored

The bin directory contain several binary file along with mongod and mongo two executable files. mongod is a background process used by MongoDB. The main purpose of mongod is to manage all the MongoDB server tasks. For instance, accepting requests, responding to client, and memory management. mongo is a command line shell that can interact with the client (for example, system administrators and developers).

To start MongoDB you need to execute this command (See Figure 7.18). This will start the main MongoDB process.

Run MongoDB by executing *mongod.exe* on command prompt. For example,

```
"C:\Program Files\MongoDB\Server\4.2\bin
\mongod.exe"
```

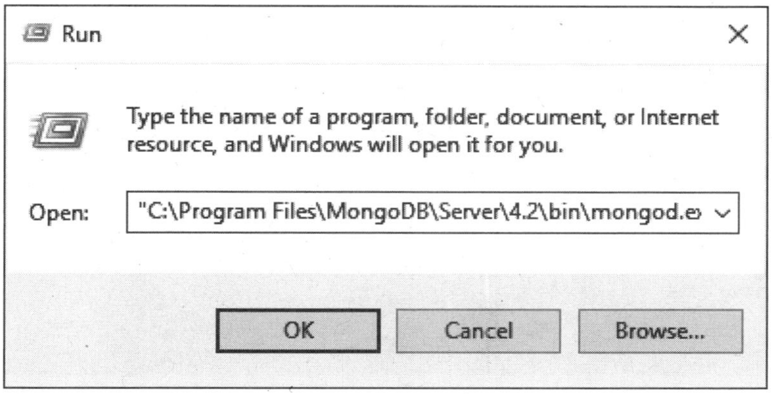

Figure 7.18 Running mongod.exe file

After executing the mongod.exe file, the process has begun. Now we need to connect it to the MongoDB server. We will connect it through mongo.exe shell by opening another command prompt (See Figure 7.19). Now you need to execute a command to connect with the shell. For example,

```
"C:\Program Files\MongoDB\Ser-
ver\4.2\bin\mongo.exe"
```

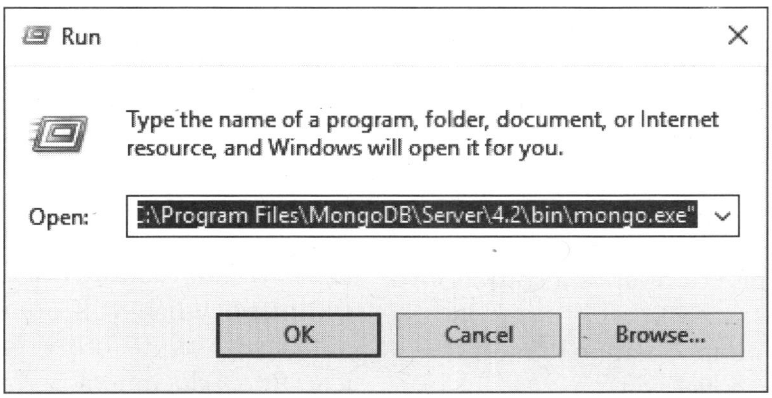

Figure 7.19 Running mongo.exe file

Now MongoDB is ready to use. It will show you the screen with the > prompt (See Figure 7.20). On the prompt, type db, and it will show test:

```
>db
test
```

By default it connects to the test database.

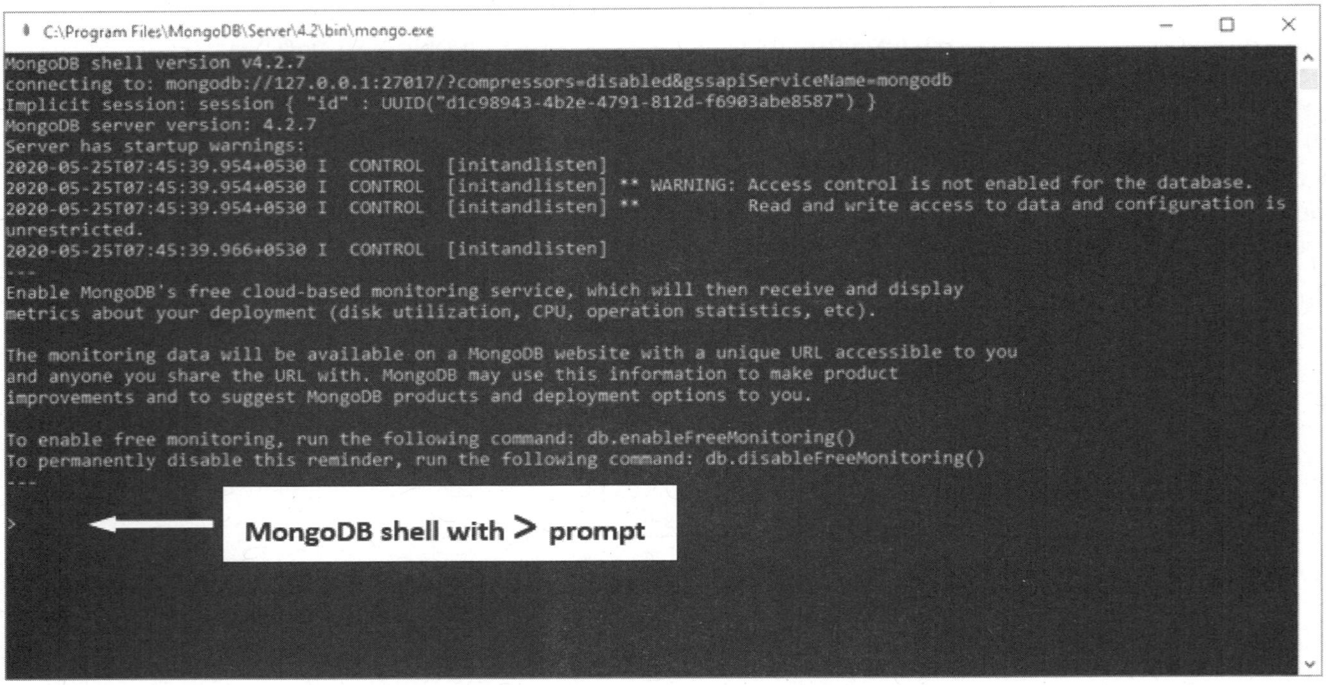

Figure 7.20 MongoDB command prompt

7.15 MongoDB CRUD OPERATION

CRUD operations refer to the basic Insert, Read, Update and Delete operations. These are the four basic database operations while building an application. For instance, any modern application will have the ability to create a new user, read the user data, update the user information and, if needed, delete the user account.

Create Operations: Create or insert operations add new documents to a collection. If the collection does not currently exist, insert operations will create the collection.

Read Operations: Read operations retrieves documents from a collection i.e., queries a collection for documents.

Update Operations: Update operations modifies existing documents in a collection.

Delete Operations: Delete operations remove documents from a collection.

7.16 CREATING DATABASE IN MongoDB

Once you are in the MongoDB shell, create the database in MongoDB by typing following command:

use database_name

For example, create a database "mydb". So, the command should be:

```
> use mydb
```

Note: If the database name you mentioned is already present, then this command will connect you to the database. However, if the database does not exist, then this will create the database with the given name and connect you to it.

Any time you can check the currently connected database by typing the command *db*. This command will show the database name to which you are currently connected. This is a very helpful command when you are working with several databases, as before creating a collection or inserting a document in database, you may want to ensure that you are in the right database.

```
> db
mydb
```

To list down all the databases, use the command *show dbs*. This command lists down all the databases and their size on the disk. (As shown in Figure 7.21).

Figure 7.21 Creating mydb database -> use mydb

We can see that the database "mydb" that we have created is not present in the list of all the databases. This is because a database is not created until you save a document in it. Now, create a collection *user* and insert a document in it by typing the following command in the MongoDB shell:

```
> db.user.insert({name: "Abhishek", age: 17})
> show dbs
```

You can now see that the database "mydb" is created. (See Figure 7.22).

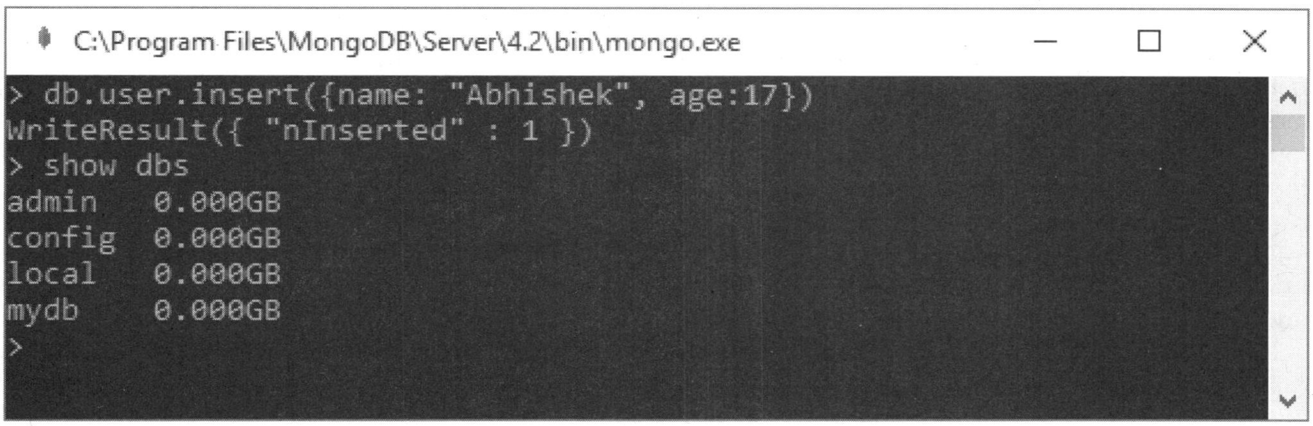

Figure 7.22 Creating a Collection user and Inserting a Document

7.17 DROP DATABASE IN MongoDB

Here, you will see how to drop a database in MongoDB. You can use db.dropDatabase() command to delete a database. You should be very careful while deleting the database, as this will remove all the data inside that database, including collections and documents stored in the database. The syntax to drop a database is as follows:

```
> db.dropDatabase()
```

You do not have to specify any database name in this command because this command deletes the currently selected database. Let's consider the steps to drop a database in MongoDB.

Switch to the database that needs to be dropped.

```
use database_name
```

For example, to delete the database "mydb", type:

```
> use mydb
switched to db mydb
```

Note that the currently selected database is mydb, so the command db.dropDatabase() would delete this database.

```
> db.dropDatabase()
{ "dropped" : "mydb", "ok" : 1 }
```

The command executed successfully, showing the operation "dropped" and status "ok" which means that the database is dropped.

To verify that the database is deleted successfully, type "show dbs" command. This will show the list of databases after deletion. Note that the database "mydb" is not present in the list; that means, it has been dropped successfully. (See Figure 7.23).

```
> show dbs
```

Figure 7.23 Dropping Database -> mydb

7.18 CREATING A COLLECTION IN MongoDB

Data in MongoDB is stored in the form of documents. These documents are stored in collection, and collection is stored in database. In MongoDB, you need not create collection before you insert document in it. With a single command, you can insert a document in the collection, and the MongoDB creates that collection. Its syntax is:

```
db.collection_name.insert({key:value,
key:value...})
```

Let us create a collection "details" in the database "studentsdb". This command will create the collection named "details" and insert a document in it with the specified key and value pairs. (See Figure 7.24).

```
> use studentsdb
switched to db studentsdb
> db.details.insert({
  name: "Abhishek",
  age: 17,
  Address: "C1, Vikaspuri"
})
```

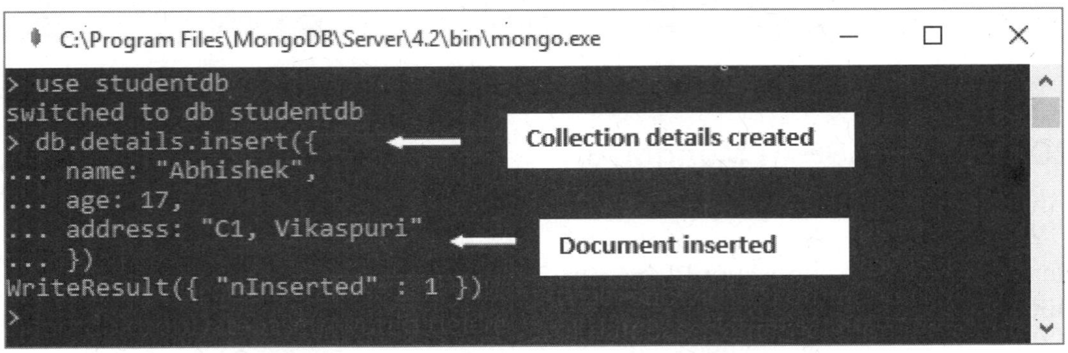

Figure 7.24 Creating the Collection Named "details" and Inserting a Document

To check whether the document is successfully inserted, apply the following syntax:

```
db.collection_name.find()
```

Now, type the following command:

```
db.details.find()
```

It shows all the documents in the given collection. (See Figure 7.25)

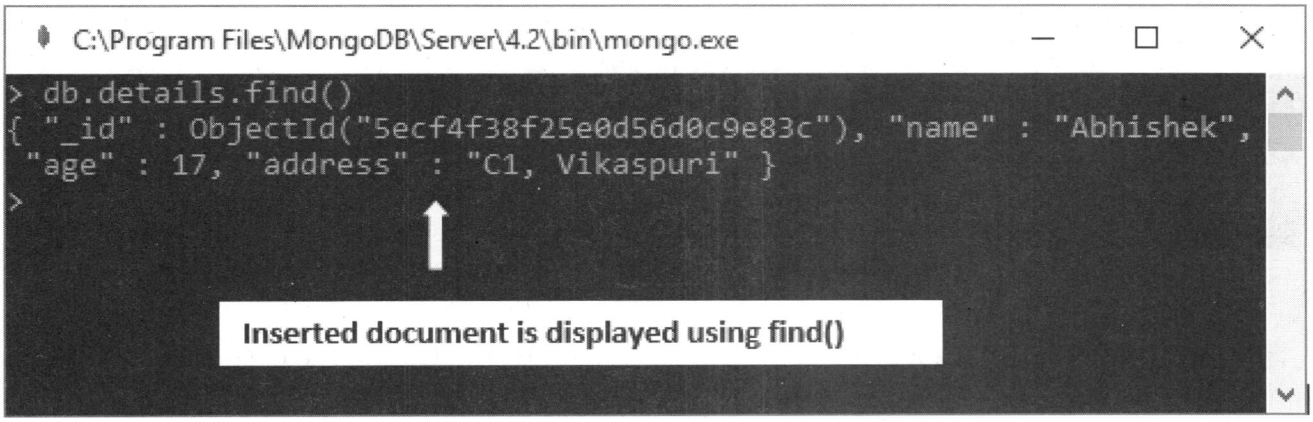

Figure 7.25 Applying find() method

To check whether the collection is created successfully, use the following command:

```
show collections
```

This command shows the list of all the collections in the currently selected database.

```
> show collections
details
```

You can also create collection before you actually insert data in it. This method provides you with the options that you can set while creating the collection. Its syntax is:

```
db.createCollection(name, options)
```

Here, *name* is the collection name, and *options* is an optional field that you can use to specify certain parameters, such as size and max number of documents, in the collection. First let's see how this command is used for creating collection without any parameters.

```
> db.createCollection("students")
{ "ok" : 1 }
```

Let's see the options that you can have while creating the collection:

capped: type: boolean. → This parameter takes only true and false. This specifies a cap on the max entries a collection can have. Once the collection reaches that limit, it starts overwriting old entries. The point to note here is that when you set the capped option to true, you also have to specify the size parameter.

size: type: number. → This specifies the max size of collection (capped collection) in bytes.

max: type: number. → This specifies the max number of documents a collection can hold.

autoIndexId: type: boolean → The default value of this parameter is *false*. If you set it true, then it automatically creates index field _id for each document.

Let's see an example of capped collection:

```
db.createCollection("staff", { capped : true, size : 9232768} )
{ "ok" : 1 }
```

This command will create a collection named "staff" with the max size of 9232768 bytes. Once this collection reaches that limit, it will start overwriting old entries.

When you type:

```
> show collections
```

It will display all the collection names:

```
details
staff
students
```

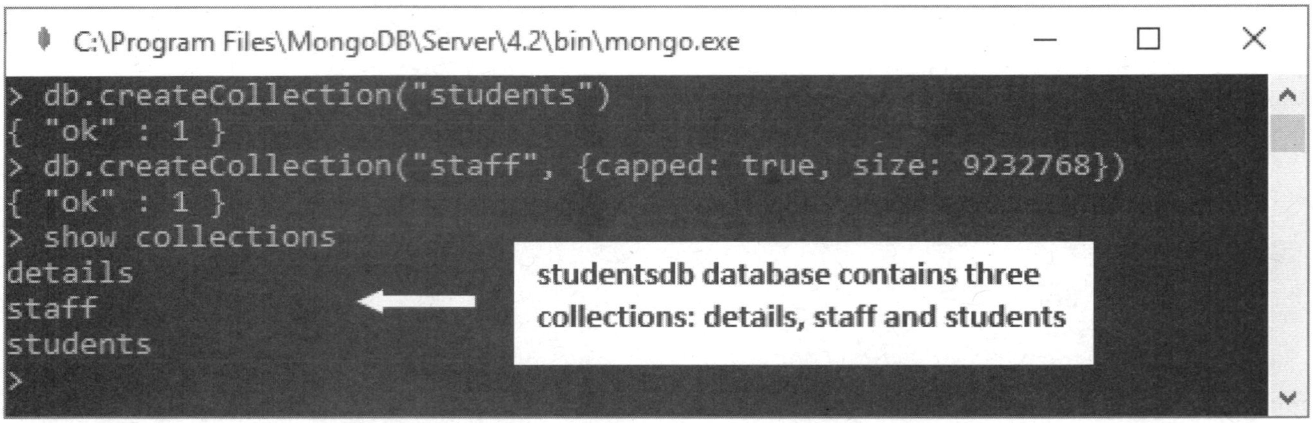

Figure 7.26 Creating collection students and staff

7.19 DROP COLLECTION IN MongoDB

MongoDB db.collection.drop() is used to drop a collection from the database. To drop the collection, first connect to the database in which you want to delete the collection, and then type the following command to delete the collection:

```
db.collection_name.drop()
```

Note: Once you drop the collection, all the documents and the indexes associated with it will also be dropped. To preserve the indexes, you can use remove() function that only removes the documents in the collection but does not remove the collection itself and the indexes created on it. For example, to delete the collection named "staff" in the database "studentsdb", write the following commands in the given sequence. (See Figure 7.27).

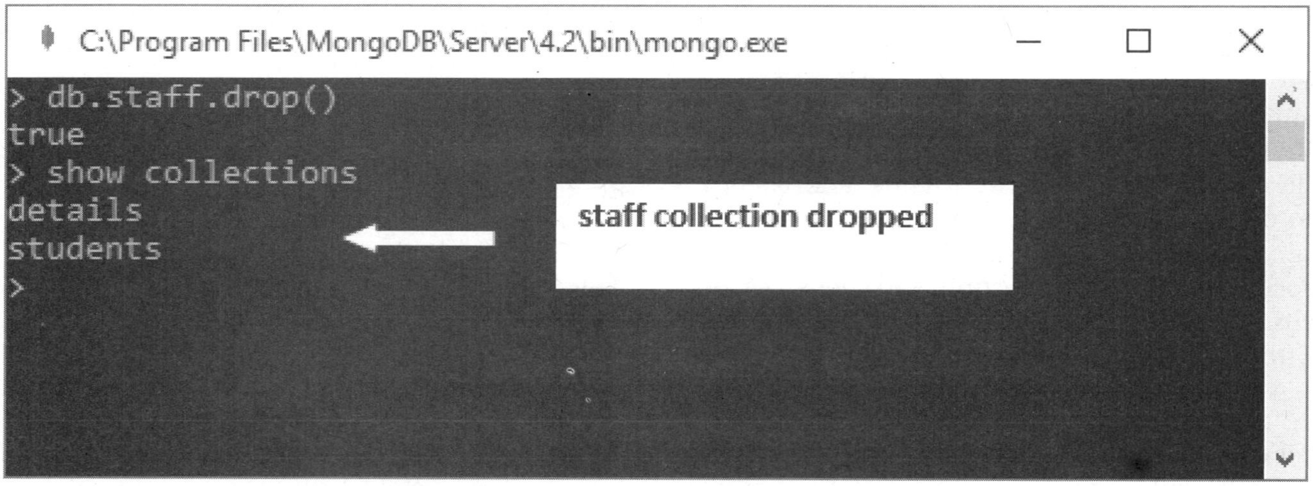

Figure 7.27 Deleting collection -> staff

```
> db.staff.drop()
true
> show collections
details
students
```

You can see that the command db.staff.drop() returned *true*, which means that the collection is deleted successfully. The same thing can be verified using the *show collections* command after deletion as shown in Figure 7.27.

☞ *drop() method will return true if the selected collection is dropped successfully; otherwise, it will return false.*

7.20 INSERTING DOCUMENT IN MongoDB

You will understand how to insert a document into the collection. With the help of the example. Syntax to insert the document into the collection is as follows:

db.collection_name.insert()

Here, you insert the document into the collection named "details". The field "course" in the example given below is an array that holds the several key-value pairs.

```
> db.details.insert(
... name: "Abhishek",
... age: 17,
... address: "C1, Vikaspuri",
... course: [{name: "MongoDB", duration: 10},
... {name: "IoT", duration: 20},
... {name: ""MariaDB", duration: 8}])
```

You will see a successful written message like this:

```
WriteResult({ "nInserted" : 1 })
```

The insert() method creates the collection if it does not exist, but if the collection is present then it inserts the document into it. (See Figure 7.28).

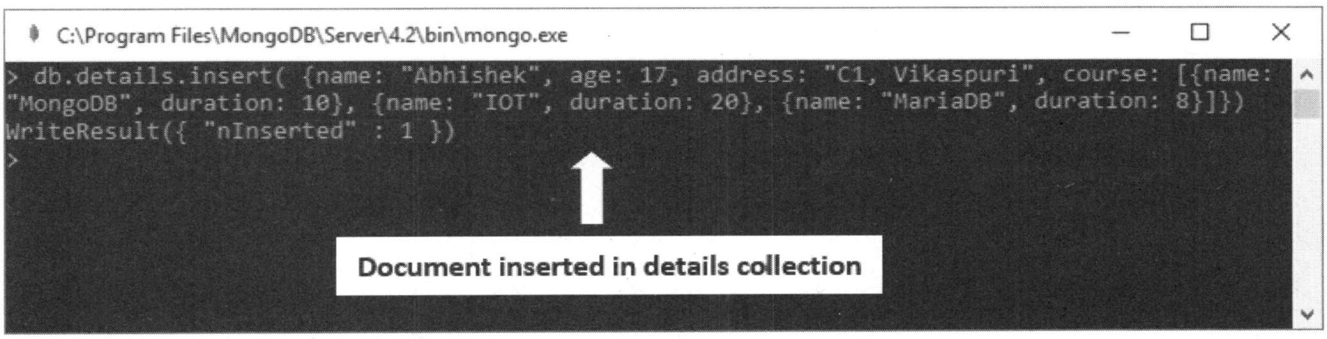

Figure 7.28 Inserting a Document into the Collection named "details"

You can also verify whether the document is successfully inserted by typing the following command:

db.collection_name.find()

In the above mentioned example, you inserted the document in the collection named "details", so the command should be:

```
> db.details.find()
{ "_id" : ObjectId("5ecf64a6ff06392910484d17"), "name" : "Abhishek", "age" : 17,
"address" : "C1, Vikaspuri", "course" : [ { "name" : "MongoDB", "duration" : 10 },
{ "name" : "IoT", "duration" : 20 }, { "name" : "MariaDB", "duration" : 8 } ] }
```

7.21 INSERTING MULTIPLE DOCUMENTS IN MongoDB

To insert multiple documents in collection, you can define an array of documents and later you can use the insertMany() method on the array variable as shown in the example given below (See Figure 7.29). Here, you insert the four documents in the collection named "students". The following command will insert the data in "students" collection; if the collection is not present, then it will create the collection and insert these documents. To insert data into MongoDB collection, you need to use MongoDB insert() or save() method. The basic syntax of insert() command is as follows:

db.COLLECTION_NAME.insertMany(document)

Now type, the following command:

```
> db.students.insertMany( [{
... ... "StudentId": 101,
... ... "Name": "Ravi Singh",
... ... "Age": 18,
... ... "Course": "MongoDB",
... ... "Fees": 4500
... ... },
... ... { "StudentId": 102,
... ... "Name": "Raman Sharma",
... ... "Age": 17,
... ... "Course": "MariaDB",
... ... "Fees": 4000
... ... },
... ... {"StudentId": 103,
... ... "Name": "Abhi Sharma",
... ... "Age": 17,
... ... "Course": "MongoDB",
... ... "Fees": 4500
... ... },
... ... {"StudentId": 104,
... ... "Name": "Swati Singh",
... ... "Age": 19,
... ... "Course": "IoT",
... ... "Fees": 5000
... ... },
... ... ])
```

After inserting data, your screen appears as shown in Figure 7.29.

You would see this output:

```
{
        "acknowledged" : true,
        "insertedIds" : [
                ObjectId("5ecf6cfcff06392910484d18"),
                ObjectId("5ecf6cfcff06392910484d19"),
                ObjectId("5ecf6cfcff06392910484d1a"),
                ObjectId("5ecf6cfcff06392910484d1b")
        ]
}
```

You can see that it shows four ObjectID created; this means that four documents have been inserted by this command. To verify that the documents are there in the collection, run the following command:

```
> db.students.find()
```

It will display four documents as shown in Figure 7.30.

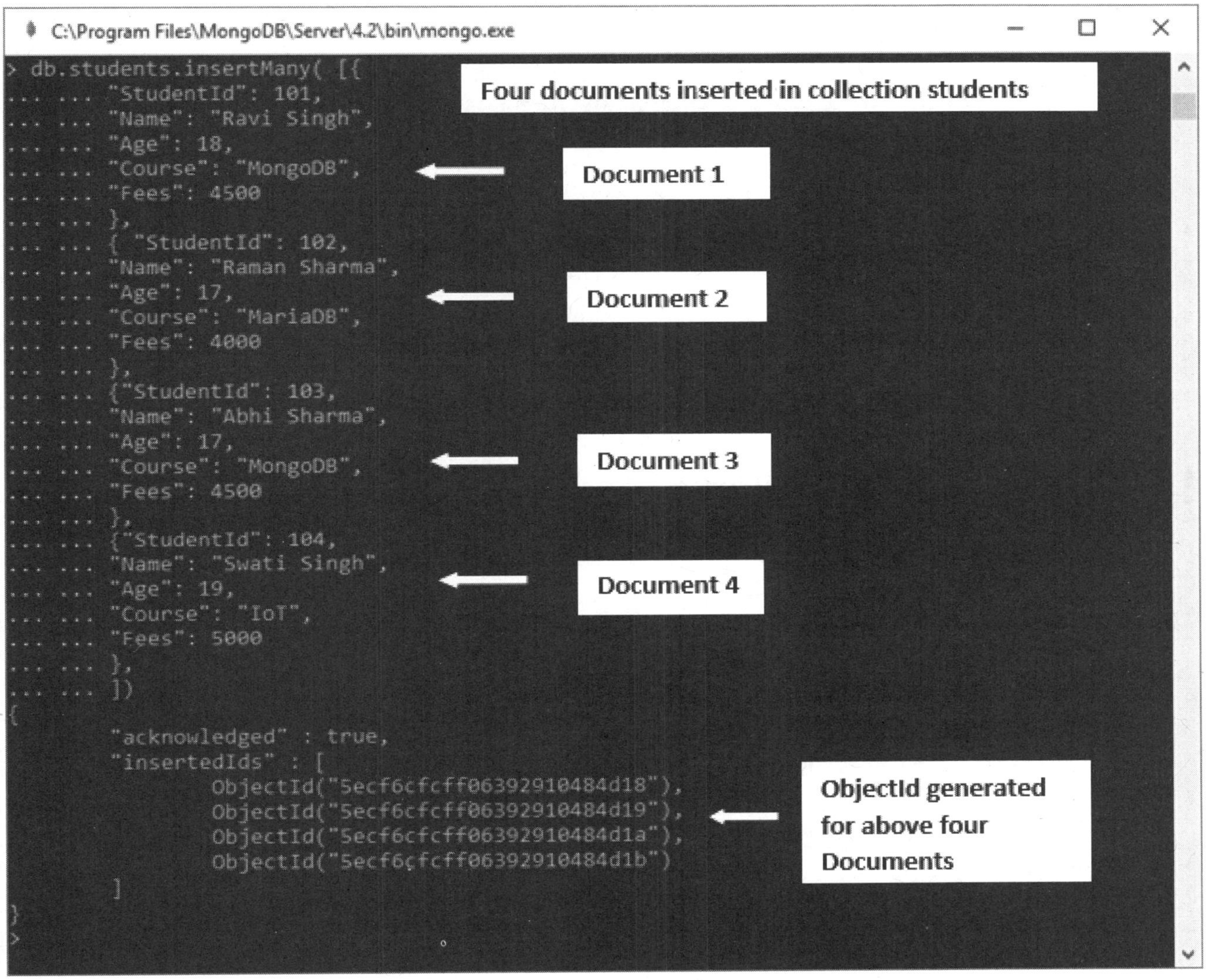

Figure 7.29 Four Documents inserted in the Collection 'students'

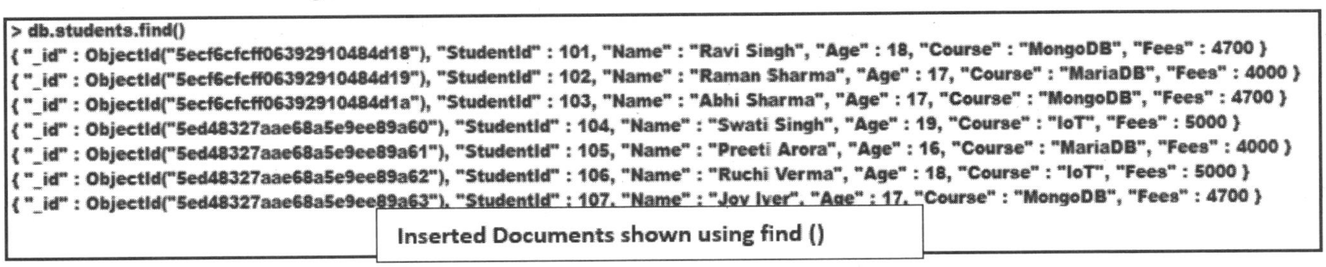

Figure 7.30 Documents displayed using db.students.find()

You can print the output data in a JSON format so that you can read it easily. In the Figures 7.30 and 7.31, you can see the difference. First, you have printed the documents using normal find() method, and then you printed the documents of same collection using JSON format. The documents in JSON format are neat and easy to read. (See Figure 7.31).

```
> db.students.find().pretty()
{
        "_id" : ObjectId("5ecf6cfcff06392910484d18"),
        "StudentId" : 101,
        "Name" : "Ravi Singh",
        "Age" : 18,
        "Course" : "MongoDB",
        "Fees" : 4500
}
{
        "_id" : ObjectId("5ecf6cfcff06392910484d19"),
        "StudentId" : 102,
        "Name" : "Raman Sharma",
        "Age" : 17,
        "Course" : "MariaDB",
        "Fees" : 4000
}
{
        "_id" : ObjectId("5ecf6cfcff06392910484d1a"),
        "StudentId" : 103,
        "Name" : "Abhi Sharma",
        "Age" : 17,
        "Course" : "MongoDB",
        "Fees" : 4500
}
{
        "_id" : ObjectId("5ecf6cfcff06392910484d1b"),
        "StudentId" : 104,
        "Name" : "Swati Singh",
        "Age" : 19,
        "Course" : "IoT",
        "Fees" : 5000
}
```

Documents displayed in JSON format

Figure 7.31 Documents displayed in JSON Format

```
> db.students.find().pretty()
```

In the inserted document, if you do not specify the _id parameter, then MongoDB assigns a unique ObjectId for this document. _Id is 12 bytes hexadecimal number, unique to every document in a collection. 12 bytes are divided as follows - _id: ObjectId(4 bytes timestamp, 3 bytes machine id, 2 bytes process id, 3 bytes incrementer)

☞ *To insert multiple documents in a single query, you can pass an array of documents in insert() command.*

7.22 QUERYING DOCUMENT USING find() METHOD

Earlier, you used the find() method to query all the documents from a collection. Now , you will understand the usage of find() method to query the documents from a collection based on the given criteria. Let's say you have a collection *students* in a database named *studentsdb*. To get all the documents, you can use this command:

```
> db.students.find()
```

☞ *Note that calling the find() method without any argument is equivalent to passing in an empty predicate; db.students.find() is the same as db.students.find({}).*

However, the output you get is not in any format and less-readable. To improve the readability, you can format the output in JSON format with this command:

```
> db.students.find().pretty()
```

It will show all the documents present in the collection in proper format.

7.23 QUERYING DOCUMENT BASED ON THE CRITERIA

Query criteria allow you to use one or more query selectors to specify the query results. Instead of fetching all the documents from collection, you can fetch selected documents based on the criteria. Query conditionals "$lt", "$lte", "$gt", and "$gte" are all comparison operators, corresponding to <, <=, >, and >=, respectively. They can be combined to look for a range of values.

Equality criterion: To fetch the data of "*Raman Sharma*" from *students* collection, type the following command :

```
> db.students.find({Name: "Raman Sharma"}).pretty()
```

This command returns the document matching the given criterion. (See Figure 7.32).

```
> db.students.find({Name: "Raman Sharma"}).pretty()
{
        "_id" : ObjectId("5ecf6cfcff06392910484d19"),
        "StudentId" : 102,
        "Name" : "Raman Sharma",
        "Age" : 17,
        "Course" : "MariaDB",
        "Fees" : 4000
}
```

Demo of equality operator

Figure 7.32 Equality criterion

Greater than criterion: Its syntax is:
`db.collection_name.find({"field_name":{$gt:criteria_value}}).pretty()`
To fetch the details of students having Age > 17, the query should be:
`>db.students.find({"Age":{$gt:17}}).pretty()`
The document matching the criterion is returned as shown in Figure 7.33.

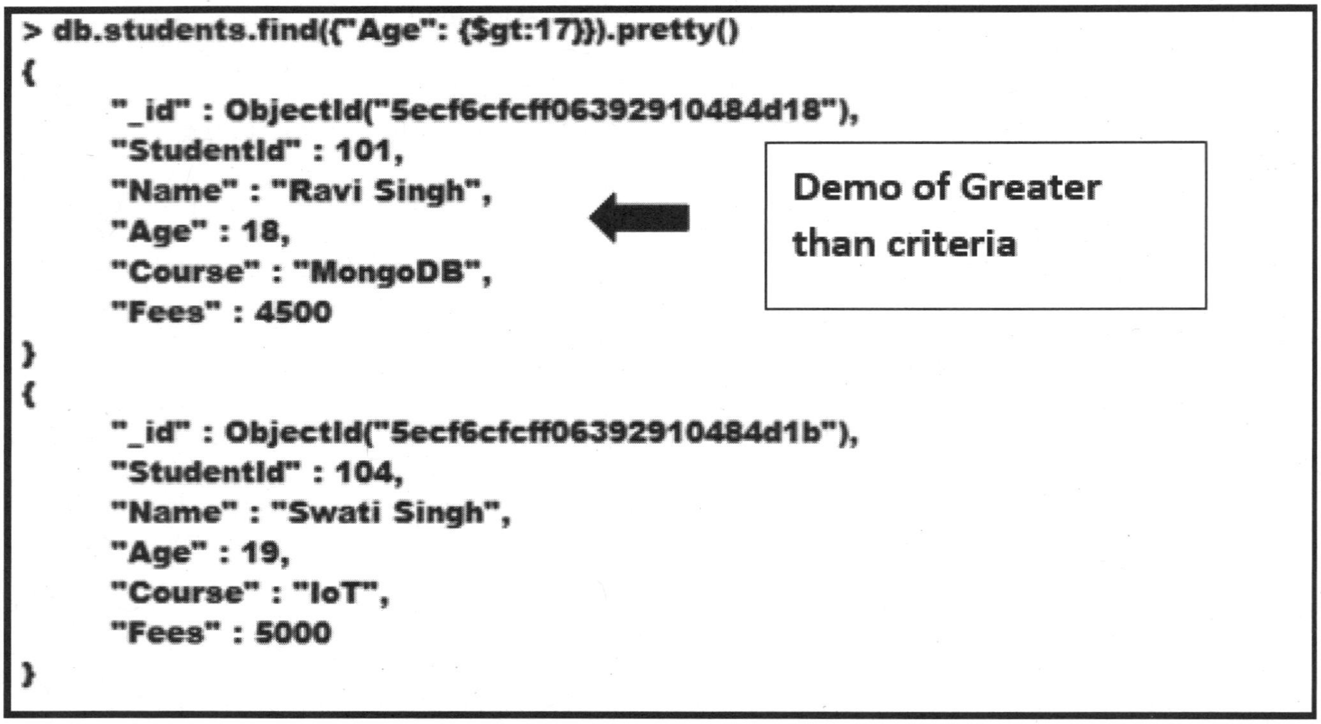

Figure 7.33 Greater Than Criterion

Less than criterion: Its syntax is:
`db.collection_name.find({"field_name":{$lt:criteria_value}}).pretty()`
To find all the students having Age less than 18, the command would be:
`>db.students.find({"Age":{$lt:18}}).pretty()`
Two documents matching the criterion are returned as shown in the Figure 7.34.

☞ *You can also issue range queries using the special $gt and $lt operators. They stand for greater than and less than, respectively.*

Not equals criterion: To query for documents where a key value is not equal to a certain value, you must use another conditional operator, "$ne", which stands for "not equal". Its syntax is:
`db.collection_name.find({"field_name":{$ne:criteria_value}}).pretty()`
To find all the students whose Age is not equal to 17, the command would be:
`>db.students.find({"Age": {$ne:17}}).pretty()` [See Figure 7.35].

Greater than equals criteria: Its syntax is:
`db.collection_name.find({"field_name":{$gte:criteria_value}}).pretty()`

Less than equals criteria: Its syntax is:
`db.collection_name.find({"field_name":{$lte:criteria_value}}).pretty()`

☞ *The pretty() method that we have added at the end of all the commands is not mandatory. It is just used for formatting purposes.*

```
> db.students.find({"Age": {$lt:18}}).pretty()
{
        "_id" : ObjectId("5ecf6cfcff06392910484d19"),
        "StudentId" : 102,
        "Name" : "Raman Sharma",
        "Age" : 17,
        "Course" : "MariaDB",
        "Fees" : 4000
}
{
        "_id" : ObjectId("5ecf6cfcff06392910484d1a"),
        "StudentId" : 103,
        "Name" : "Abhi Sharma",
        "Age" : 17,
        "Course" : "MongoDB",
        "Fees" : 4500
}
```

Demo of Less than criteria

Figure 7.34 Less than Criterion

```
> db.students.find({"Age": {$ne:17}}).pretty()
{
        "_id" : ObjectId("5ecf6cfcff06392910484d18"),
        "StudentId" : 101,
        "Name" : "Ravi Singh",
        "Age" : 18,
        "Course" : "MongoDB",
        "Fees" : 4500
}
{
        "_id" : ObjectId("5ecf6cfcff06392910484d1b"),
        "StudentId" : 104,
        "Name" : "Swati Singh",
        "Age" : 19,
        "Course" : "IoT",
        "Fees" : 5000
}
```

Demo of Not Equals criteria

Figure 7.35 Not Equals Criterion

Queries can go beyond the exact matching, they can match more complex criteria, such as AND-clause, OR-clause, and NOT-clause. You can also pass any number of key value pairs in find clause.

AND in MongDB

In the find() method, if you pass multiple keys by separating them by ',' then MongoDB treats it as AND condition. Basic syntax of AND is shown below:

```
db.mycol.find({key1:value1, key2:value2}).pretty()
```

For example, to look for students who are between the ages of 18 and 25, you can type this:

```
>db.students.find({"Age":  {"$gte":  18, "$lte" : 25}}).pretty()
```

This would find all documents where the "Age" field was greater than or equal to 18 AND less than or equal to 25. (See Figure 7.36).

```
> db.students.find({"Age": {"$gte": 18, "$lte" : 25}}).pretty()
{
        "_id" : ObjectId("5ecf6cfcff06392910484d18"),
        "StudentId" : 101,
        "Name" : "Ravi Singh",
        "Age" : 18,
        "Course" : "MongoDB",
        "Fees" : 4500
}
{
        "_id" : ObjectId("5ecf6cfcff06392910484d1b"),
        "StudentId" : 104,
        "Name" : "Swati Singh",
        "Age" : 19,
        "Course" : "IoT",
        "Fees" : 5000
}
```

Demo of and clause

Figure 7.36 AND Criterion

OR in MongoDB

OR is can be used to query for any of the given values across multiple keys.

To query documents based on the OR condition, you need to use $or keyword. Basic syntax of OR is shown below:

```
db.mycol.find(
{
$or: [
{key1: value1}, {key2:value2}
]
}
).pretty()
```

For example,

```
> db.students.find({ $or: [
... { "Course": "IoT"},
... { "Course": "MariaDB"}
... ]}).pretty()
```

The query returns both the Raman Sharma's and Swati Singh's documents. (See Figure 7.37).

$not(negation)

"$not" is a metaconditional. It can be applied on top of any other criteria. "$not" can be particularly useful in conjunction with regular expressions to find all documents that do not match the given criteria. (See Figure 7.38).

For example,

```
>db.students.find({ "Age": {$not: { $gt: 18} }}).pretty()
```

7.24 UPDATING DOCUMENT IN A COLLECTION IN MongoDB

MongoDB update() and save() methods are used to update document in a collection. The update() method is used when we need to update the values of an existing document, while the save() method is used to replace the existing document with the document that has been passed in it. To update a document in MongoDB, you can provide a criterion in command, and the document that matches that criterion is updated.

To updating document using update() method, use the following syntax:

```
db.collection_name.update(criteria,
update_data)
```

Now, suppose you want to update the "Fees" 4500 to "Fees" 4700 (See Figure 7.39). The command for this would be:

```
> db.students.update({"Fees": 4500},
{$set: {"Fees": 4700 }})
```

You can see that the document has been updated. By default, the update method updates a single document, i.e., it updates only the first document found that matches the criterion. If there are more matching documents, they will remain unchanged.

In the above mentioned example, there were two documents matching with the criterion, i.e., "Fees": 4500; however, only one document has been updated. To enable update() method to update multiple documents, you have to set "*multi*" parameter of this method to *true* as shown in Figure 7.40. To update multiple documents with the update() method, type:

```
> db.students.update({"Fees": 4500},
{$set: {"Fees": 4700 }}, {multi:true})
```

To update the document with save() method, use the following syntax:

```
db.collection_name.save( {_id:ObjectId(), new_document} )
```

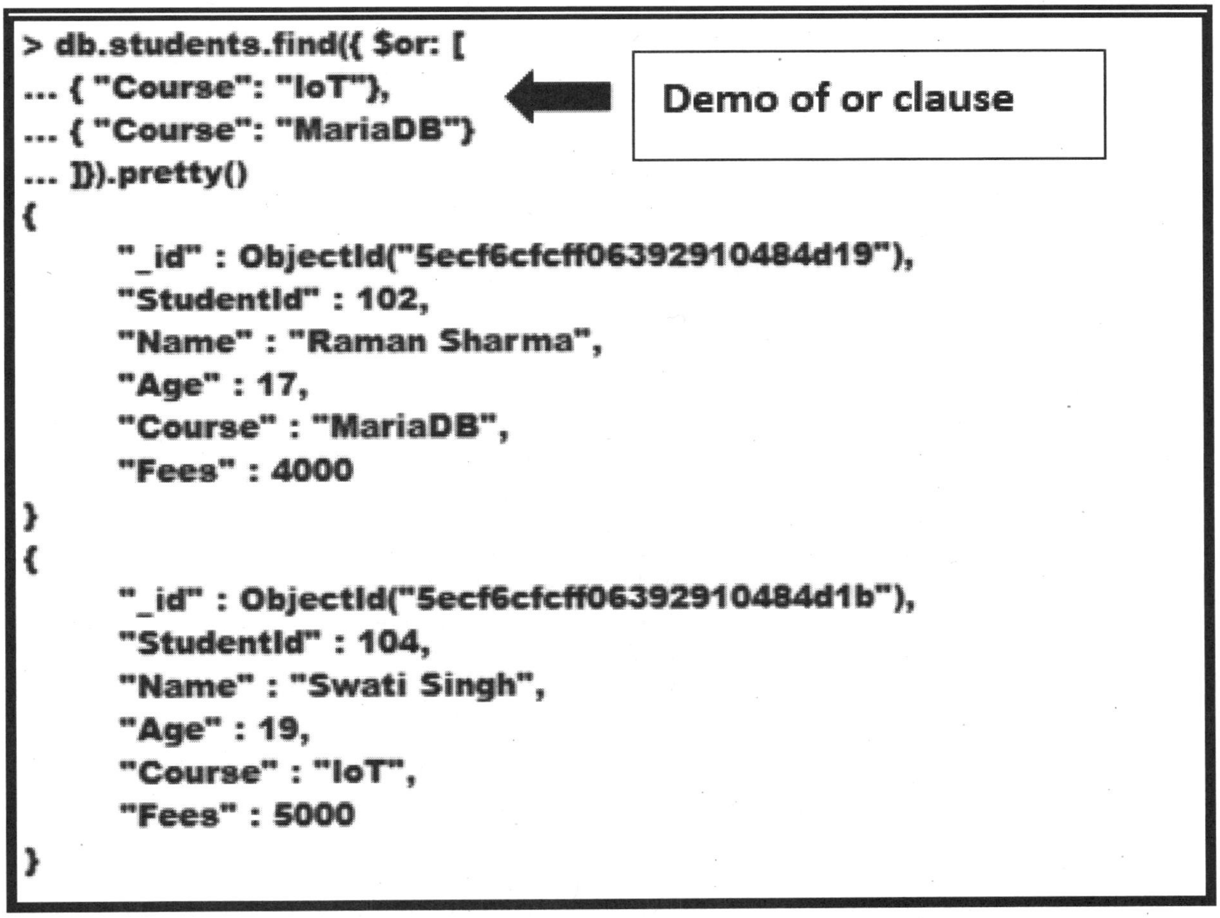

Figure 7.37 OR Criterion

```
> db.students.find({ "Age": {$not: { $gt: 18} }}).pretty()
{
        "_id" : ObjectId("5ecf6cfcff06392910484d18"),
        "StudentId" : 101,
        "Name" : "Ravi Singh",
        "Age" : 18,
        "Course" : "MongoDB",
        "Fees" : 4500
}
{
        "_id" : ObjectId("5ecf6cfcff06392910484d19"),
        "StudentId" : 102,
        "Name" : "Raman Sharma",
        "Age" : 17,
        "Course" : "MariaDB",
        "Fees" : 4000
}
{
        "_id" : ObjectId("5ecf6cfcff06392910484d1a"),
        "StudentId" : 103,
        "Name" : "Abhi Sharma",
        "Age" : 17,
        "Course" : "MongoDB",
        "Fees" : 4500
}
```

Demo of not clause

Figure 7.38 NOT Criterion

```
> db.students.update({"Fees": 4500}, {$set: {"Fees": 4700 }})
WriteResult({ "nMatched" : 1, "nUpserted" : 0, "nModified" : 1 })
```

Demo of updating single document

Figure 7.39 Updating single Document with update() Method

To work with save() method, you should know the unique _id field of that document. A very important point to note is that when you do not provide the _id field while using save() method, it calls insert() method, and the passed document is inserted into the collection as a new document. To get the _id of the document, you can type this command:

```
> db.students.find().pretty()
```

Here, you will get a collection name. This method

of finding unique _id is only useful when you have few documents; otherwise, scrolling and searching for that _id among huge number of documents are tedious. (See Figure 7.41).

```
> db.students.update({"Fees": 4500}, {$set: {"Fees": 4700 }}, {multi:true})
WriteResult({ "nMatched" : 1, "nUpserted" : 0, "nModified" : 1 })
```

Demo of updating multiple documents using multi parameter

Figure 7.40 Updating Multiple Documents with the update() Method

```
> db.students.find().pretty()
{
        "_id" : ObjectId("5ecf6cfcff06392910484d18"),
        "StudentId" : 101,
        "Name" : "Ravi Singh",
        "Age" : 18,
        "Course" : "MongoDB",
        "Fees" : 4700
}
{
        "_id" : ObjectId("5ecf6cfcff06392910484d19"),
        "StudentId" : 102,
        "Name" : "Raman Sharma",
        "Age" : 17,
        "Course" : "MariaDB",
        "Fees" : 4000
}
{
        "_id" : ObjectId("5ecf6cfcff06392910484d1a"),
        "StudentId" : 103,
        "Name" : "Abhi Sharma",
        "Age" : 17,
        "Course" : "MongoDB",
        "Fees" : 4700
}
{
        "_id" : ObjectId("5ecf6cfcff06392910484d1b"),
        "StudentId" : 104,
        "Name" : "Swati Singh",
        "Age" : 19,
        "Course" : "IoT",
        "Fees" : 5000
}
```

Updated document (annotation pointing to "Fees" : 4700 of StudentId 101)

Updated document (annotation pointing to "Fees" : 4700 of StudentId 103)

Figure 7.41 Getting the _id of a Document using find().pretty()

7.25 DELETING DOCUMENT IN A COLLECTION IN MongoDB

The remove() method is used for removing the documents from a collection in MongoDB. Syntax of remove() method is as follows:

```
db.collection_name.remove(delete_criteri
a)
```

To remove the student from this collection who has the "*StudentId*" equal to *104*, use remove() method.

Figure 7.42 Deleting Document using remove() Method

```
> db.students.remove({"StudentId": 104})
```

To verify whether the document is actually deleted, type the following command:

```
> db.students.find().pretty()
```

It will list all the documents of *students* collection.

☞ *The remove() operation does not actually delete the collection; it merely removes documents from the collection.*

When there are more than one document present in collection that match the criterion, then all those documents will be deleted if you run the remove command. However, there is a way to limit the deletion to only one document so that even if there are more documents matching the deletion criterion, only one document will be deleted. Its syntax is :

```
db.collection_name.remove(delete_criteri
a, justOne)
```

Here, remove() method accepts two parameters. One is *delete_criteria* and the other is *justOne* flag. According to deletion criteria, documents will be removed. It is optional.

Next, justOne is a Boolean parameter that takes only 1 or 0; if you give 1, then it will limit the document deletion to only 1 document. This is an optional parameter as you have seen above that the remove() method is used without this parameter.

☞ *If you do not specify deletion criteria, then MongoDB will delete all the documents from the collection.*

7.26 MongoDB PROJECTION

Projections are most commonly defined as a set of fields to return. They are used when you want to get the selected fields of the documents rather than all fields. For example, you have a collection where you have stored documents that have the fields such as name, _id, StudentId, and age, but you want to check only the StudentId of all the students. Then, in that case, you can use projection to get only the StudentId. Its syntax is:

```
db.collection_name.find({},{field_key:1
or 0})
```

You use the projection to limit the fields returned from the find() function. But if you specify any fields in the find projection, only those specified fields will be returned.

To get only the StudentId for all the documents, you will use the Projection like this:

```
> db.students.find({}, {"_id": 0, "Stu-
dentId": 1})
{ "StudentId" : 101 }
{ "StudentId" : 103 }
```

_id field, is a special case and is always included by default. However, can exclude the _id field by setting its value to 0 in the projection document as mentioned earlier.

☞ *An empty query document (i.e., {}) matches everything in the collection.*

Another way of doing the same thing is as follows:

```
> db.students.find({}, {"_id": 0,
"name": 0, "age": 0})
{ "StudentId" : 101 }
{ "StudentId" : 103 }
```

```
> db.students.find({}, {"_id": 0, "StudentId":1})
{ "StudentId" : 101 }
{ "StudentId" : 102 }
{ "StudentId" : 103 }
```

Projection to display only StudentId

Figure 7.43 Projection to display only StudentID

To get only the StudentId and name for all the documents, you can use the Projection as shown in Figure 7.44.

```
> db.students.find({}, {"_id": 0, "Stu-
dentId": 1, "Name":1})
```

Here, value 1 means show that field, and 0 means do not show that field. When you set a field to 1 in Projection, other fields are automatically set to 0 except _id. So, to avoid the _id you need to specifically set it to 0 in projection. The vice versa is also true, when you set few fields to 0, other fields are set to 1 automatically.

```
> db.students.find({}, {"_id": 0, "StudentId":1, "Name":1})
{ "StudentId" : 101, "Name" : "Ravi Singh" }
{ "StudentId" : 102, "Name" : "Raman Sharma" }
{ "StudentId" : 103, "Name" : "Abhi Sharma" }
```

Projection to display StudentId and Name

Figure 7.44 Projection to display StudentID and Name only

Some of you may get this error while using Projection in Query:

```
Error: error: {
  "ok" : 0,
  "errmsg" : "Projection cannot have a mix of inclusion and exclusion.",
  "code" : 2,
  "codeName" : "BadValue"
}
```

This happens when you set some fields to 0 and others to 1. In other words, you mix inclusion and exclusion; the only exception is the _id field. For example, the following query would produce this error:

```
> db.students.find({}, {"_id": 0, "Name": 0, "Age": 1})
```

This is because you have set Name to 0 and other field age to 1. You cannot mix these. You either set those fields that you do not want to display to 0 or set the fields to 1 that you want to display.

7.27 MongoDB limit() and skip() METHODS

The *limit()* method limits the number of documents returned in response to a particular query. Its syntax is :

```
db.collection_name.find().limit(number_of_documents)
```

For example,

```
> db.c.find().limit(3)
```

If there are fewer than three documents matching your query in the collection, only the number of matching documents will be returned; limit() sets only upper limit, not the lower limit.

The *skip()* method is used for skipping the given number of documents in the query result. Its syntax is :

```
db.collection_name.find().skip(number_of_documents)
```

For example,

```
> db.c.find().skip(3)
```

This will skip the first three matching documents and return the rest of the matches. If there are fewer than three documents in your collection, it will not return any documents.

7.28 MongoDB sort() METHOD

Using sort() method, you can arrange the documents in ascending or descending order, based on a particular field of document. This method accepts a document containing list of fields along with their sorting order. To specify sorting order, 1 and -1 are used. 1 is used for ascending order, while -1 is used for descending order. The default value is 1. Syntax of sort() method:

```
db.collection_name.find().sort({field_key:1 or -1})
```

Here, *field_key* are key names, and the values are the sort directions. Sort direction can be 1 (ascending) or -1 (descending).

```
> db.students.find({}, {"StudentId": 1, _id:0, "Name":1,}).sort({"Name": 1})
```

The default is ascending order, so if you do not provide any value in the sort() method, then it will sort the results in ascending order.

If multiple keys are given, the results will be sorted in that order. For instance, to sort the results by "username" in ascending order and "age" in descending order, you can do the following:

```
> db.c.find().sort({username : 1, age : -1})
```

7.29 INTRODUCTION TO INDEXING

Index is similar to a book index. Instead of looking through the whole book, the database takes a shortcut and just looks at an ordered list that points to the content, which allows it to do queries in large number efficiently.

Indexes plays a vital role in execution of queries in MongoDB. If no index is defined, MongoDB has to scan every document of the specified collection and if index is there, it has to scan less number of documents resulting in a faster result to select those documents that match the query criteria.

Indexes are special data structures that store a small portion of the data set in an easy-to-traverse form. They store the value of a specific field or set of fields, ordered by the value of the field as specified in index.

☞ *MongoDB indexing allows you to optimize your queries.*

MongoDB defines the indexes at the collection level and supports indexing on any fields in a MongoDB collection. MongoDB provides a method named createIndex() using this we can create the index, it has an alias method named ensureIndex().

By default, MongoDB creates a _id field if not specified in each collection and create a unique index on the _id field during the creation of a collection. The _id field acts like primary key and prevents users from inserting two documents with the same value for the _id field. The index on the _id field automatically created by MongoDB cannot be removed or dropped.

7.29.1 createIndex()

To create an index, you need to use createIndex() method of MongoDB.

Its syntax is:

```
db.collection_name.createIndex({field_name: 1 or -1})
```

Here, field_name is the name of field on which you want to create index. The value 1 is for ascending order, and -1 is for descending order.

7.29.2 ensureIndex()

To create an index you need to use ensureIndex() method.

Its syntax is:

```
>db.collection_name.ensureIndex({KEY:1})
```

Here key is the name of field on which you want to create index and 1 is for ascending order. To create index in descending order you need to use -1.

☞ *Default Index in MongoDB i.e., _id.*

Let us insert following documents into collection named students. (See Figure 7.45).

```
> db.students.insertMany( [
... {"StudentId" : 104, "Name" : "Swati Singh", "Age" : 19, "Course" : "IoT",
"Fees" : 5000 },
... {"StudentId" : 105, "Name" : "Preeti Arora", "Age" : 16, "Course" : "MariaDB",
"Fees" : 4000 },
... {"StudentId" : 106, "Name" : "Ruchi Verma", "Age" : 18, "Course" : "IoT",
"Fees" : 5000 },
... {"StudentId" : 107, "Name" : "Joy Iyer", "Age" : 17, "Course" : "MongoDB",
"Fees" : 4700 },
... ])
```

```
> db.students.insertMany( [
... {"StudentId" : 104, "Name" : "Swati Singh", "Age" : 19, "Course" : "IoT", "Fees" : 5000 },
... {"StudentId" : 105, "Name" : "Preeti Arora", "Age" : 16, "Course" : "MariaDB", "Fees" : 4000 },
... {"StudentId" : 106, "Name" : "Ruchi Verma", "Age" : 18, "Course" : "IoT", "Fees" : 5000 },
... {"StudentId" : 107, "Name" : "Joy Iyer", "Age" : 17, "Course" : "MongoDB", "Fees" : 4700 },
... ])
{
        "acknowledged" : true,
        "insertedIds" : [
                ObjectId("5ed48327aae68a5e9ee89a60"),
                ObjectId("5ed48327aae68a5e9ee89a61"),
                ObjectId("5ed48327aae68a5e9ee89a62"),
                ObjectId("5ed48327aae68a5e9ee89a63")
        ]
}
```

Inserted documents in students collection

Figure 7.45 Inserted documents in students collection

Now type following commands to display inserted documents (See Figure 7.46):

```
> db.students.find().pretty()
```

```
> db.students.find({}, {"_id":0})
{ "StudentId" : 101, "Name" : "Ravi Singh", "Age" : 18, "Course" : "MongoDB", "Fees" : 4700 }
{ "StudentId" : 102, "Name" : "Raman Sharma", "Age" : 17, "Course" : "MariaDB", "Fees" : 4000 }
{ "StudentId" : 103, "Name" : "Abhi Sharma", "Age" : 17, "Course" : "MongoDB", "Fees" : 4700 }
{ "StudentId" : 104, "Name" : "Swati Singh", "Age" : 19, "Course" : "IoT", "Fees" : 5000 }
{ "StudentId" : 105, "Name" : "Preeti Arora", "Age" : 16, "Course" : "MariaDB", "Fees" : 4000 }
{ "StudentId" : 106, "Name" : "Ruchi Verma", "Age" : 18, "Course" : "IoT", "Fees" : 5000 }
{ "StudentId" : 107, "Name" : "Joy Iyer", "Age" : 17, "Course" : "MongoDB", "Fees" : 4700 }
```

Display of all documents in students collection

Figure 7.46 Inserted documents displayed using find().pretty()

7.30 INTRODUCTION TO SINGLE INDEX

MongoDB supports user-defined indexes like single field index on any user defined key in the collection apart from the default _id index. A single field index is used to create an index on the single field of a document. This user created index can be ascending or descending indexes on a single field of a document as defined by the user.

Its syntax is:

```
db.collection.createIndex( { <field>: <Value>} )
```

where

Field : is the name of the key in the collection

Value : 1 for ascending , -1 for descending

For example, command to create a descending order index on field "Age":

```
> db.students.createIndex({"Age": -1})
{
        "createdCollectionAutomatically" : false,
        "numIndexesBefore" : 1,
        "numIndexesAfter" : 2,
        "ok" : 1
}
```

After executing the command, it displays:

"createdCollectionAutomatically": false → It is created by user

"numIndexesBefore": 1 → No. of indexes before the command (only _id)

"numIndexesAfter": 2 → No. of indexes after the command (_id and the other one)

"ok": 1 → It means an index has been created successfully

Here, an index has been created on "Age" which means when someone searches the document based on the "Age", the search will be faster because the created index will be used for the above search. (See Figure 7.47).

```
> db.students.createIndex({"Age": -1})
{
        "createdCollectionAutomatically" : false,
        "numIndexesBefore" : 1,
        "numIndexesAfter" : 2,
        "ok" : 1
}
            Demo of single index
```

Figure 7.47 Single Field Index

7.31 INTRODUCTION TO COMPOUND INDEXES

MongoDB supports a user-defined index on multiple fields as well. For this MongoDB has a compound index. A compound index is an index on two or more fields of a collection, and it can support queries based on those fields. In compound indexes, fields can be sorted inside other fields.

Its syntax is:

```
db.collection.createIndex( { <field1>: <value>, <field2>: <value>, ... } )
```

where

Field: is the name of the key in the collection

Value: 1 for ascending , -1 for descending

For example, let us create a compound index on two fields, i.e., Course (descending order) and Fees (ascending order), to do so, the command will be:

```
> db.students.createIndex({"Course": -1, "Fees": 1})
{
        "createdCollectionAutomatically" : false,
        "numIndexesBefore" : 2,
        "numIndexesAfter" : 3,
        "ok" : 1
}
```

```
> db.students.createIndex({"Course": -1, "Fees": 1})
{
        "createdCollectionAutomatically" : false,
        "numIndexesBefore" : 2,
        "numIndexesAfter" : 3,
        "ok" : 1
}
            Demo of compound index
```

Figure 7.48 Compound Index

After executing the command as shown in Figure 7.48, it displays:
"createdCollectionAutomatically": false → It is created by user
"numIndexesBefore": 2 → No. of indexes before the command (_id and "Age" created just before)
"numIndexesAfter": 3 → No. of indexes after the command (_id, "Age" and compound index of "Course and Fees")
"ok": 1 → It means an index has been created successfully
This compound index of "Course + Fees" sorts the collection first by "Course" and then, within each "Course" value, sort by "Fees".

7.31.1 Finding the indexes

The getIndexes() method in MongoDB is created on a collection and used to find all the indexes with details like version, name, unique or not etc. Whereas getIndexKeys() displays only index keys (field for which indexing done).
Its syntax is:
`db.collection_name.getIndexes()`
Example
To get all the indexes of students collection, the command will be:

```
> db.students.getIndexes()
[
        {
                "v" : 2,
                "key" : {
                        "_id" : 1
                },
                "name" : "_id_",
                "ns" : "studentsdb.students"
        },
        {
                "v" : 2,
                "key" : {
                        "Age" : -1
                },
                "name" : "Age_-1",
                "ns" : "studentsdb.students"
        },
        {
                "v" : 2,
                "key" : {
                        "Course" : -1,
                        "Fees" : 1
                },
                "name" : "Course_-1_Fees_1",
                "ns" : "studentsdb.students"
        }
]
```

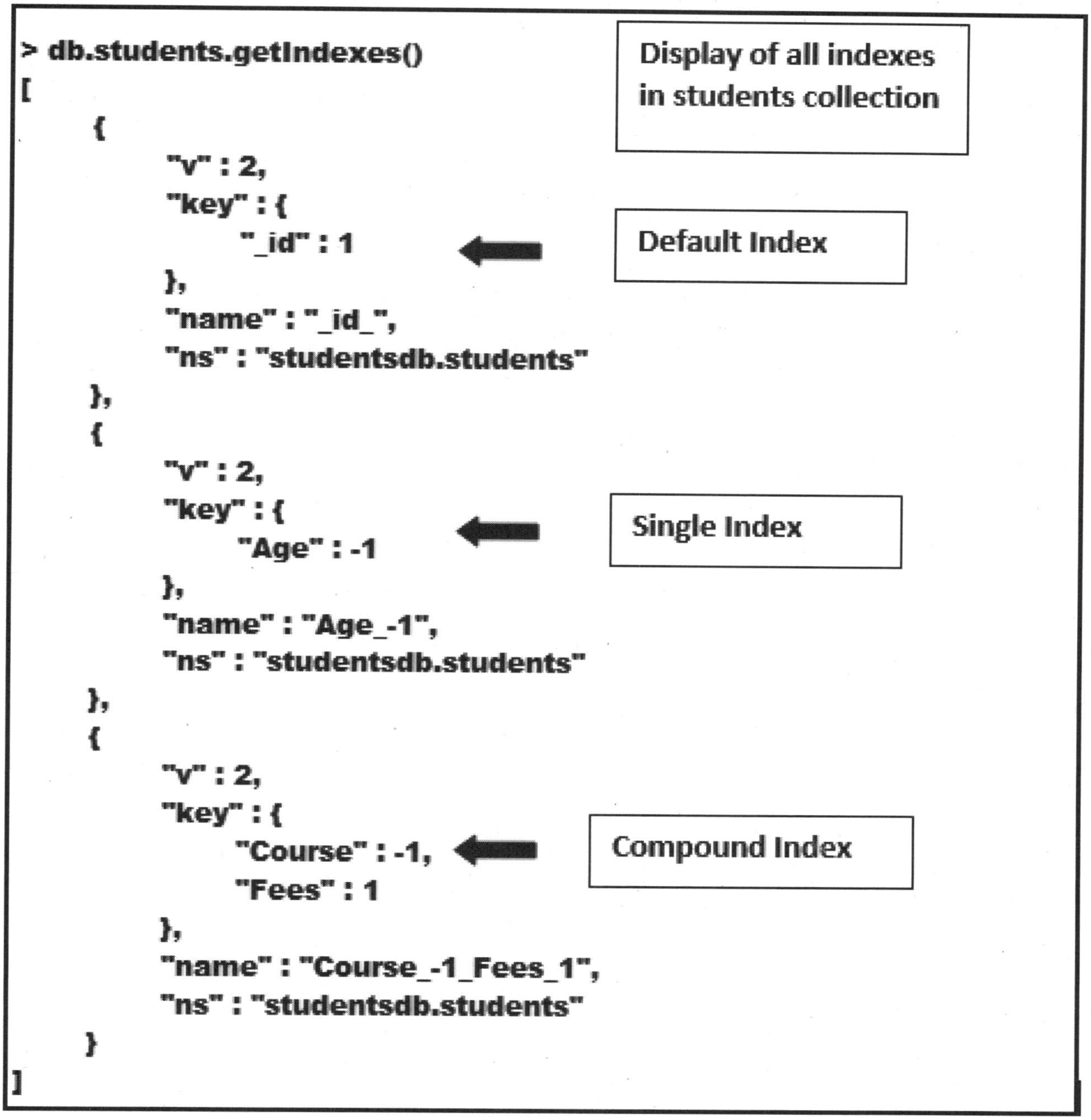

Figure 7.49 Finding the indexes in a collection using getIndexes()

The Figure 7.49 shows that three indexes are there in "students" collection. These are:

The default index created on _id with name "_id_",

The single index we have created on "Age" field with name "Age_-1",

The compound index we have created on "Course" and "Fees" with name "Course_-1_Fees_1".

7.31.2 Dropping index

We can use dropIndex(indexname) method to remove a specific index in a collection. You can specify the index either by the index name or by

the index specification document.
Its syntax is:

```
db.collection_name.dropIndex(index)
```

where index can be either "index_name" for example, "Age_-1" or "Course_-1_Fees_1", or "index specification document" for example, { "Age" : -1} or { "Course" : -1, "Fees" : 1}

Example

```
> db.students.dropIndex("Age_-1")
{ "nIndexesWas" : 3, "ok" : 1 }
```

will delete the index with index name "Age_-1".
nIndexesWas: 3 → shows how many indexes were there before this command got executed i.e., 3
ok: 1: → means the command is executed successfully.

7.31.3 Dropping compound index

The dropIndexes() method is are used to drop i.e. delete or remove, all the indexes on a collection except the index on the _id field.
Its syntax is:

```
db.collection_name.dropIndexes()
```

without any parameter it will delete all indexes except on _id field, if we specify the "index_name" or "index specification document", it will delete that particular index and act like db.collection_name.dropIndex() method.

```
> db.students.dropIndexes()
{
        "nIndexesWas" : 2,
        "msg" : "non-_id indexes dropped for collection",
        "ok" : 1
}
```

msg: "non-_id indexes dropped for collection" → means that the default index _id will still remain and cannot be dropped.
nIndexesWas: 2 → shows how many indexes were there before this command got executed i.e., 2
ok: 1: → It means the command is executed successfully.

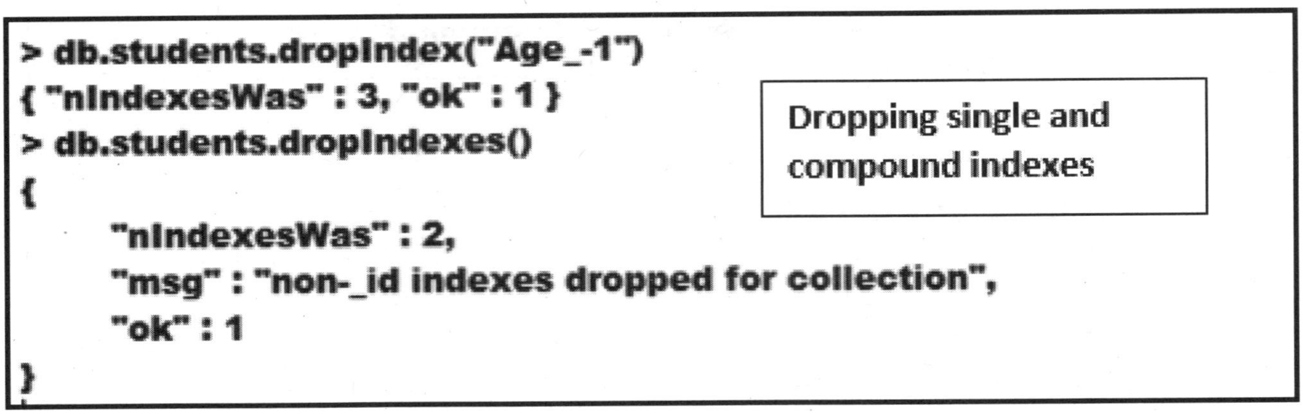

Figure 7.50 Dropping single and compound Index

7.32 INDEXING OBJECTS AND ARRAYS

Indexes are special data structures, that store a small portion of the data set in an easy to traverse form. The index stores the value of a specific field or set of fields, ordered by the value of the field as specified in index.
Arrays are values that can be interchangeably used for both ordered operations (as though they were lists, stacks, or queues) and unordered operations (as though they were sets).

In the following document, the key "things" has an array value:

```
{"things" : ["pie", 3.14]}
```

As we can see from the example, arrays can contain different data types as values (in this case, a string and a floating-point number). In fact, array values can be any of the supported values for normal key/value pairs, even nested arrays.

Now let us create marks collection and insert documents as shown in Figure 7.51.

```
> db.marks.insertMany([
... {"StudentId" : 101, "Name" : "Ravi Singh", "Course" : "MongoDB", "Marks": [55, 82, 72] },
... {"StudentId" : 102, "Name" : "Raman Sharma", "Course" : "MariaDB", "Marks": [65, 87, 55] },
... {"StudentId" : 103, "Name" : "Abhi Sharma", "Course" : "MongoDB", "Marks": [58, 77, 72] },
... {"StudentId" : 104, "Name" : "Swati Singh", "Course" : "IoT", "Marks": [85, 92, 82] },
... {"StudentId" : 105, "Name" : "Preeti Arora", "Course" : "MariaDB", "Marks" : [67, 43, 55]},
... {"StudentId" : 106, "Name" : "Ruchi Verma", "Course" : "IoT", "Marks" : [40, 45, 54] },
... {"StudentId" : 107, "Name" : "Joy Iyer", "Course" : "MongoDB", "Marks" : [93, 43, 67] },
... ])
{
        "acknowledged" : true,
        "insertedIds" : [
                ObjectId("5ed4a9fdaae68a5e9ee89a64"),
                ObjectId("5ed4a9fdaae68a5e9ee89a65"),
                ObjectId("5ed4a9fdaae68a5e9ee89a66"),
                ObjectId("5ed4a9fdaae68a5e9ee89a67"),
                ObjectId("5ed4a9fdaae68a5e9ee89a68"),
                ObjectId("5ed4a9fdaae68a5e9ee89a69"),
                ObjectId("5ed4a9fdaae68a5e9ee89a6a")
        ]
}
```

Creation of marks collection with array of Marks

Figure 7.51 Creation of marks collection

7.32.1 Multikey Index

MongoDB uses multikey indexes to index the content stored in arrays. To index a field that holds an array value, MongoDB creates an index key for each element in the array, i.e., creates separate index entries for every element of the array

These multikey indexes support efficient queries against array fields. Multikey indexes can be constructed over arrays that hold both scalar values (e.g. strings, numbers) and nested documents.

☞ *MongoDB uses multi key indexes basically to store the arrays. MongoDB creates a separate index for each element in an array.*

The multikey indexes, created by MongoDB, allow queries to select documents that contain arrays by matching on element or elements of the arrays.

Its syntax is:

```
db.collection_name.createIndex( { <field>: value } )
```

where

Field : is the name of the key in the collection

Value : 1 for ascending , -1 for descending

While creating an Index, it is not required to explicitly specify the multikey type, MongoDB automatically determines whether to create a multikey index, if the specified indexed field contains an array value.

Lets consider a collection marks. Now use following command to display all documents in marks collection as shown in Figure 7.52.

> **db.marks.find()**

```
> db.marks.find()
{ "_id" : ObjectId("5ed4a9fdaae68a5e9ee89a64"), "StudentId" : 101, "Name" : "Ravi Singh", "Course" : "MongoDB", "Marks" : [ 55, 82, 72 ] }
{ "_id" : ObjectId("5ed4a9fdaae68a5e9ee89a65"), "StudentId" : 102, "Name" : "Raman Sharma", "Course" : "MariaDB", "Marks" : [ 65, 87, 55 ] }
{ "_id" : ObjectId("5ed4a9fdaae68a5e9ee89a66"), "StudentId" : 103, "Name" : "Abhi Sharma", "Course" : "MongoDB", "Marks" : [ 58, 77, 72 ] }
{ "_id" : ObjectId("5ed4a9fdaae68a5e9ee89a67"), "StudentId" : 104, "Name" : "Swati Singh", "Course" : "IoT", "Marks" : [ 85, 92, 82 ] }
{ "_id" : ObjectId("5ed4a9fdaae68a5e9ee89a68"), "StudentId" : 105, "Name" : "Preeti Arora", "Course" : "MariaDB", "Marks" : [ 67, 43, 55 ] }
{ "_id" : ObjectId("5ed4a9fdaae68a5e9ee89a69"), "StudentId" : 106, "Name" : "Ruchi Verma", "Course" : "IoT", "Marks" : [ 40, 45, 54 ] }
{ "_id" : ObjectId("5ed4a9fdaae68a5e9ee89a6a"), "StudentId" : 107, "Name" : "Joy Iyer", "Course" : "MongoDB", "Marks" : [ 93, 43, 67 ] }
```

Display of marks document with default _id field

Figure 7.52 Display of documents of marks collection

Lets create an index on "Marks" key, which is an array on descending order:

```
> db.marks.createIndex({"Marks" : -1})
{
        "createdCollectionAutomatically" : false,
        "numIndexesBefore" : 1,
        "numIndexesAfter" : 2,
        "ok" : 1
}
```

And if we run the command getindexes(), it will display all the indexes in the collection result as shown in Figure 7.53.

```
> db.marks.getIndexes()
[
        {
                "v" : 2,
                "key" : {
                        "_id" : 1
                },
                "name" : "_id_",
                "ns" : "studentsdb.marks"
        },
        {
                "v" : 2,
                "key" : {
                        "Marks" : -1
                },
                "name" : "Marks_-1",
                "ns" : "studentsdb.marks"
        }
]
```

```
> db.marks.createIndex({"Marks" : -1})
{
        "createdCollectionAutomatically" : false,
        "numIndexesBefore" : 1,
        "numIndexesAfter" : 2,
        "ok" : 1
}
> db.marks.getIndexes()
[
        {
                "v" : 2,
                "key" : {
                        "_id" : 1
                },
                "name" : "_id_",
                "ns" : "studentsdb.marks"
        },
        {
                "v" : 2,
                "key" : {
                        "Marks" : -1
                },
                "name" : "Marks_-1",
                "ns" : "studentsdb.marks"
        }
]
```

Demo of multikey index

Figure 7.53 Multikey Index

It shows that an index on Marks key has been created with name "Marks_-1" and stored internally, but it will be a multikey index as it has been created on an array key.

7.32.2 Compound Multikey Index

Just like, creating a compound index, we may create a compound multikey index by specifying multiple keys in createIndex method.

Its syntax is:

```
db.collection.createIndex( { <field1>: <value>, <field2>: <value>, ... } )
```

where Field: is the name of the key in the collection

Value: 1 for ascending , -1 for descending

For example, let's create a compound multikey index on Course key in ascending order and Marks key in descending order.

```
> db.marks.createIndex({"Course":1, "Marks":-1})
{
        "createdCollectionAutomatically" : false,
        "numIndexesBefore" : 2,
        "numIndexesAfter" : 3,
        "ok" : 1
}
```

This will create a compound index combining both the specified key , Course key in ascending order and Marks key in descending order as we have specified the value as 1 in Course and -1 in Marks.

And if we display the created indexes on the marks collection, with getIndexes() method, it will display both the created indexes as follows:

```
> db.marks.getIndexes()
[
        {
                "v" : 2,
                "key" : {
                        "_id" : 1
                },
                "name" : "_id_",
                "ns" : "studentsdb.marks"
        },
        {
                "v" : 2,
                "key" : {
                        "Marks" : -1
                },
                "name" : "Marks_-1",
                "ns" : "studentsdb.marks"
        },
        {
                "v" : 2,
                "key" : {
                        "Course" : 1,
                        "Marks" : -1
                },
                "name" : "Course_1_Marks_-1",
                "ns" : "studentsdb.marks"
        }
]
```

```
> db.marks.createIndex({"Course":1, "Marks":-1})
{
	"createdCollectionAutomatically" : false,
	"numIndexesBefore" : 2,
	"numIndexesAfter" : 3,
	"ok" : 1
}
> db.marks.getIndexes()
[
	{
		"v" : 2,
		"key" : {
			"_id" : 1
		},
		"name" : "_id_",
		"ns" : "studentsdb.marks"
	},
	{
		"v" : 2,
		"key" : {
			"Marks" : -1
		},
		"name" : "Marks_-1",
		"ns" : "studentsdb.marks"
	},
	{
		"v" : 2,
		"key" : {
			"Course" : 1,
			"Marks" : -1
		},
		"name" : "Course_1_Marks_-1",
		"ns" : "studentsdb.marks"
	}
]
```

Demo of compound multikey index

Figure 7.54 Compound Multikey Index

7.32.3 Covered Query

In a covered query, all the fields used in the query have the index created. The results returned should also be part of the index. In other words, when all fields in the query are part of the index, MongoDB connects query conditions and returns the result by using the same index without looking inside the Document. Due to this, MongoDB fetches the results without actually looking inside documents, thus saving time and increasing efficiency.

7.33 AGGREGATION FRAMEWORK

The aggregation framework lets you transform and combine documents in a collection. Basically, you build a pipeline that processes a stream of documents through several building blocks such as filtering, projecting, grouping, sorting, limiting, and skipping. MongoDB also supports same concept in aggregation framework. There is a set of possible stages and each of those is taken as a set of documents as an input and produces a resulting set of documents (or the final resulting JSON document at the end of the pipeline). This can then in turn be used for the next stage and so on.

In aggregation operation, MongoDB processes the data records and returns a single computed result. It actually groups multiple documents and then performs aggregation operation on it and after that returns a single result to the end user. In simple words, Aggregation groups the data from multiple documents in a collection and operates in several ways on those grouped data in order to return one combined result i.e., total number(sum), average, minimum, maximum etc. out of the group selected.

☞ *In SQL count(*) and with "group by" is an equivalent of MongoDB aggregation. In MongoDB, aggregate() method is used for the aggregation.*

MongoDB provides three ways to perform aggregation. They are aggregation pipeline, the map-reduce function, and single purpose aggregation methods.

7.34 PIPELINE OPERATIONS

MongoDB supports an aggregation pipeline that allows you to build complex aggregations from simple pieces and allow the database to optimize it. Each operator receives a stream of documents, does some type of transformation on these documents, and then passes on the results of the transformation. If it is the last pipeline operator, these results are returned to the client. Otherwise, the results are streamed to the next operator as input. Operators can be combined in any order and repeated as many times as necessary. For example, you could "$match", "$group", and then "$match" again with different criteria.

The MongoDB aggregation pipeline consists various stages. Each stage transforms the documents passes through the pipeline. In this stage it is not needed to produce one output document for every input document. The pipeline stages can appear multiple times in the pipeline.

Its syntax is:

```
db.COLLECTION_NAME.aggregate(pipeline,
options))
```

Where, pipeline is a sequence of data aggregation operations or stages. The method can still accept the pipeline stages as separate arguments instead of as elements in an array; however, if you do not specify the pipeline as an array, you cannot specify the options parameter.

These are different stages of aggregation of Pipeline in MongoDB:

7.34.1 $match

The $match operator filters the documents matching the query, to the next stage of the pipeline. $match uses standard MongoDB queries. For each input document, outputs either one document (a match) or zero documents (no match). We can also apply additional constraints such as comparisons, where document values must be greater than, less than, or equal to some other value. Generally, good practice is to put "$match" expressions as early as possible in the pipeline so that it allows you to filter out unneeded documents quickly.

Its syntax is:

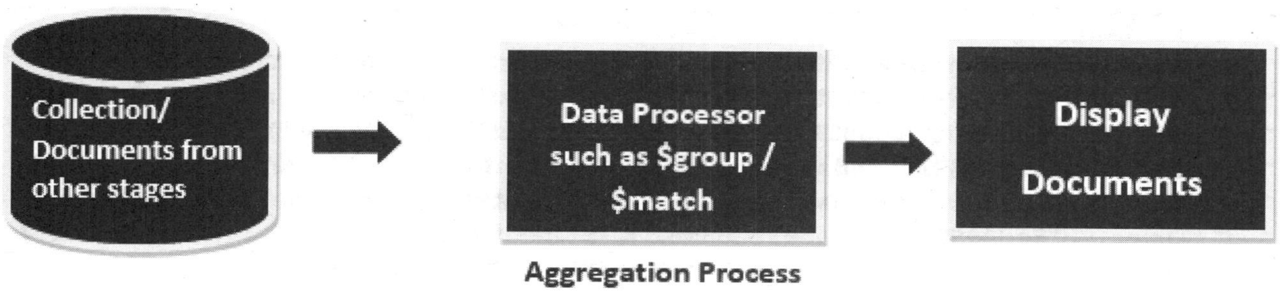

Figure 7.55 Aggregation process

```
{ $match: { <query> } }
```

☞ *$match can reduce the amount of documents that are given as input to the next stage.*

7.34.2 $project

The simplest operation "$project" can perform is simply selecting fields from your incoming documents. The $project function in MongoDB passes along the documents with only the specified fields to the next stage in the pipeline, i.e., it reshapes each document in the stream, such as by adding new fields or removing existing fields where the field may be the existing fields from the input documents or newly computed fields. By default, "_id" is always returned if it exists in the incoming document.

Its syntax is:

```
{ $project: { <specifications> } }
```

Where, the specification contain the inclusion of fields, the suppression of the _id field, the addition of new fields, and the resetting the values of existing fields.

Let's have a students collection as follows:

```
> db.students.aggregate( [ { $project : { StudentId: 1 , Name: 1 } } ] )
{ "_id" : ObjectId("5ecf6cfcff06392910484d18"), "StudentId" : 101, "Name" : "Ravi
Singh" }
{ "_id" : ObjectId("5ecf6cfcff06392910484d19"), "StudentId" : 102, "Name" : "Raman
Sharma" }
{ "_id" : ObjectId("5ecf6cfcff06392910484d1a"), "StudentId" : 103, "Name" : "Abhi
Sharma" }
{ "_id" : ObjectId("5ed48327aae68a5e9ee89a60"), "StudentId" : 104, "Name" : "Swati
Singh" }
{ "_id" : ObjectId("5ed48327aae68a5e9ee89a61"), "StudentId" : 105, "Name" : "Pre-
eti Arora" }
{ "_id" : ObjectId("5ed48327aae68a5e9ee89a62"), "StudentId" : 106, "Name" : "Ruchi
Verma" }
{ "_id" : ObjectId("5ed48327aae68a5e9ee89a63"), "StudentId" : 107, "Name" : "Joy
Iyer" }
```

```
> db.students.aggregate( [ { $project : { StudentId: 1 , Name: 1 } } ] )
{ "_id" : ObjectId("5ecf6cfcff06392910484d18"), "StudentId" : 101, "Name" : "Ravi Singh" }
{ "_id" : ObjectId("5ecf6cfcff06392910484d19"), "StudentId" : 102, "Name" : "Raman Sharma" }
{ "_id" : ObjectId("5ecf6cfcff06392910484d1a"), "StudentId" : 103, "Name" : "Abhi Sharma" }
{ "_id" : ObjectId("5ed48327aae68a5e9ee89a60"), "StudentId" : 104, "Name" : "Swati Singh" }
{ "_id" : ObjectId("5ed48327aae68a5e9ee89a61"), "StudentId" : 105, "Name" : "Preeti Arora" }
{ "_id" : ObjectId("5ed48327aae68a5e9ee89a62"), "StudentId" : 106, "Name" : "Ruchi Verma" }
{ "_id" : ObjectId("5ed48327aae68a5e9ee89a63"), "StudentId" : 107, "Name" : "Joy Iyer" }
```

Demo of $project to display selected fields but _id field is displayed by default

Figure 7.56 Demo of $project to display StudentId and Name

The command includes only the _id, std_id, and stu_name fields in its output documents as shown above. _Id field is included by default.

Let's take another example to suppress _id field in the output Documents.

```
> db.students.aggregate( [ { $project : { _id: 0, StudentId: 1 , Name: 1 } } ] )
{ "StudentId" : 101, "Name" : "Ravi Singh" }
{ "StudentId" : 102, "Name" : "Raman Sharma" }
{ "StudentId" : 103, "Name" : "Abhi Sharma" }
{ "StudentId" : 104, "Name" : "Swati Singh" }
{ "StudentId" : 105, "Name" : "Preeti Arora" }
{ "StudentId" : 106, "Name" : "Ruchi Verma" }
{ "StudentId" : 107, "Name" : "Joy Iyer" }
```

The above command suppresses i.e., excludes the _id field but includes the std_id, and stu_name fields in its output documents as we have given value as 0 for _id field.

```
> db.students.aggregate( [ { $project : { _id: 0, StudentId: 1 , Name: 1 } } ] )
{ "StudentId" : 101, "Name" : "Ravi Singh" }
{ "StudentId" : 102, "Name" : "Raman Sharma" }
{ "StudentId" : 103, "Name" : "Abhi Sharma" }
{ "StudentId" : 104, "Name" : "Swati Singh" }
{ "StudentId" : 105, "Name" : "Preeti Arora" }
{ "StudentId" : 106, "Name" : "Ruchi Verma" }
{ "StudentId" : 107, "Name" : "Joy Iyer" }
```

Demo of $project suppress _id field.

Figure 7.57 Demo of $project to suppress _id field

☞ *$project is used to select some specific fields from a collection.*

7.34.3 $group

Grouping allows you to group documents based on certain fields and combine their values. In MongoDB, the $group operator groups the input documents by the specified expression and groups the document for each distinct grouping. For every distinct group that is formed, it is passed to the next stage as a document with a unique _id field.

7.34.4 $sort

$sort will operate in the same way as sort() but this operator can be applied with aggregate() whereas sort() will works only with cursor (return result of find() methods). $sort is used to reorders the document stream by a specified sort key. It only changes the order not the documents. The $sort pipeline stage passes all documents to the next stage, sorted by the specified sort criteria.

Its syntax is:

```
{ $sort: { <field1>: <sort order>, <field2>: <sort order> ... } }
```

$sort takes a document that specifies the field(s) to sort by and the respective sort order. <sort order> can have one of the following values:

1 Sort ascending.

-1 Sort descending.

Let us sort name field of collection students in ascending order:

```
> db.students.aggregate( [ { $sort : {Name: 1 } } ] )
{ "_id" : ObjectId("5ecf6cfcff06392910484d1a"), "StudentId" : 103, "Name" : "Abhi Sharma", "Age" : 17, "Course" : "MongoDB", "Fees" : 4700 }
{ "_id" : ObjectId("5ed48327aae68a5e9ee89a63"), "StudentId" : 107, "Name" : "Joy Iyer", "Age" : 17, "Course" : "MongoDB", "Fees" : 4700 }
{ "_id" : ObjectId("5ed48327aae68a5e9ee89a61"), "StudentId" : 105, "Name" : "Preeti Arora", "Age" : 16, "Course" : "MariaDB", "Fees" : 4000 }
{ "_id" : ObjectId("5ecf6cfcff06392910484d19"), "StudentId" : 102, "Name" : "Raman Sharma", "Age" : 17, "Course" : "MariaDB", "Fees" : 4000 }
{ "_id" : ObjectId("5ecf6cfcff06392910484d18"), "StudentId" : 101, "Name" : "Ravi Singh", "Age" : 18, "Course" : "MongoDB", "Fees" : 4700 }
{ "_id" : ObjectId("5ed48327aae68a5e9ee89a62"), "StudentId" : 106, "Name" : "Ruchi Verma", "Age" : 18, "Course" : "IoT", "Fees" : 5000 }
{ "_id" : ObjectId("5ed48327aae68a5e9ee89a60"), "StudentId" : 104, "Name" : "Swati Singh", "Age" : 19, "Course" : "IoT", "Fees" : 5000 }
```

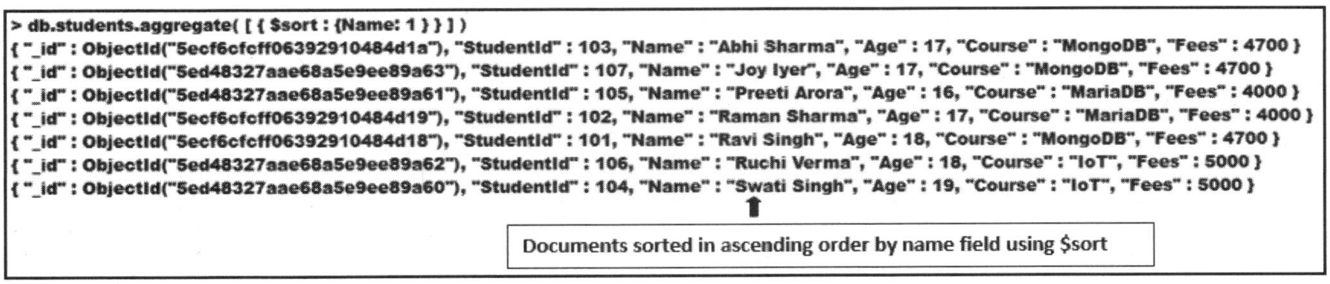

Figure 7.58 Demo of $sort to sort name field in ascending order

Now let us take another example to sort the documents in the students collection, in descending order by the Course field and then in ascending order according to the value in the Name field.

```
> db.students.aggregate( [ { $sort : {Course:-1, Name: 1 } } ] )
{ "_id" : ObjectId("5ecf6cfcff06392910484d1a"), "StudentId" : 103, "Name" : "Abhi Sharma", "Age" : 17, "Course" : "MongoDB", "Fees" : 4700 }
{ "_id" : ObjectId("5ed48327aae68a5e9ee89a63"), "StudentId" : 107, "Name" : "Joy Iyer", "Age" : 17, "Course" : "MongoDB", "Fees" : 4700 }
{ "_id" : ObjectId("5ecf6cfcff06392910484d18"), "StudentId" : 101, "Name" : "Ravi Singh", "Age" : 18, "Course" : "MongoDB", "Fees" : 4700 }
{ "_id" : ObjectId("5ed48327aae68a5e9ee89a61"), "StudentId" : 105, "Name" : "Preeti Arora", "Age" : 16, "Course" : "MariaDB", "Fees" : 4000 }
{ "_id" : ObjectId("5ecf6cfcff06392910484d19"), "StudentId" : 102, "Name" : "Raman Sharma", "Age" : 17, "Course" : "MariaDB", "Fees" : 4000 }
{ "_id" : ObjectId("5ed48327aae68a5e9ee89a62"), "StudentId" : 106, "Name" : "Ruchi Verma", "Age" : 18, "Course" : "IoT", "Fees" : 5000 }
{ "_id" : ObjectId("5ed48327aae68a5e9ee89a60"), "StudentId" : 104, "Name" : "Swati Singh", "Age" : 19, "Course" : "IoT", "Fees" : 5000 }
```

```
> db.students.aggregate( [ { $sort : {Course:-1, Name: 1 } } ] )
{ "_id" : ObjectId("5ecf6cfcff06392910484d1a"), "StudentId" : 103, "Name" : "Abhi Sharma", "Age" : 17, "Course" : "MongoDB", "Fees" : 4700 }
{ "_id" : ObjectId("5ed48327aae68a5e9ee89a63"), "StudentId" : 107, "Name" : "Joy Iyer", "Age" : 17, "Course" : "MongoDB", "Fees" : 4700 }
{ "_id" : ObjectId("5ecf6cfcff06392910484d18"), "StudentId" : 101, "Name" : "Ravi Singh", "Age" : 18, "Course" : "MongoDB", "Fees" : 4700 }
{ "_id" : ObjectId("5ed48327aae68a5e9ee89a61"), "StudentId" : 105, "Name" : "Preeti Arora", "Age" : 16, "Course" : "MariaDB", "Fees" : 4000 }
{ "_id" : ObjectId("5ecf6cfcff06392910484d19"), "StudentId" : 102, "Name" : "Raman Sharma", "Age" : 17, "Course" : "MariaDB", "Fees" : 4000 }
{ "_id" : ObjectId("5ed48327aae68a5e9ee89a62"), "StudentId" : 106, "Name" : "Ruchi Verma", "Age" : 18, "Course": "IoT", "Fees" : 5000 }
{ "_id" : ObjectId("5ed48327aae68a5e9ee89a60"), "StudentId" : 104, "Name" : "Swati Singh", "Age" : 19, "Course" : "IoT", "Fees" : 5000 }
```

Documents are sorted by Course in descending order and by Name in ascending order

Figure 7.59 Demo of $sort to sort two fields

☞ *$sort is used to sort all the documents.*

7.34.5 $skip

With $skip, it is possible to skip forward in the list of documents for a given amount of documents i.e., it skips the first n documents where n is the specified skip number and passes the remaining documents unmodified to the pipeline.

Its syntax is:

{ $skip: <positive integer> }

$skip takes a positive integer that specifies the maximum number of documents to skip.

Consider the following example:

```
> db.students.aggregate( [ { $skip : 3 } ] )
{ "_id" : ObjectId("5ed48327aae68a5e9ee89a60"), "StudentId" : 104, "Name" : "Swati Singh", "Age" : 19, "Course" : "IoT", "Fees" : 5000 }
{ "_id" : ObjectId("5ed48327aae68a5e9ee89a61"), "StudentId" : 105, "Name" : "Preeti Arora", "Age" : 16, "Course" : "MariaDB", "Fees" : 4000 }
{ "_id" : ObjectId("5ed48327aae68a5e9ee89a62"), "StudentId" : 106, "Name" : "Ruchi Verma", "Age" : 18, "Course" : "IoT", "Fees" : 5000 }
{ "_id" : ObjectId("5ed48327aae68a5e9ee89a63"), "StudentId" : 107, "Name" : "Joy Iyer", "Age" : 17, "Course" : "MongoDB", "Fees" : 4700 }
```

Demo of $skip to skip first three documents

Figure 7.60 Demo of $skip

```
> db.students.aggregate( [ { $skip : 3 } ] )
{ "_id" : ObjectId("5ed48327aae68a5e9ee89a60"), "StudentId" : 104, "Name" : "Swati Singh", "Age" : 19, "Course" : "IoT", "Fees" : 5000 }
{ "_id" : ObjectId("5ed48327aae68a5e9ee89a61"), "StudentId" : 105, "Name" : "Pre-eti Arora", "Age" : 16, "Course" : "MariaDB", "Fees" : 4000 }
{ "_id" : ObjectId("5ed48327aae68a5e9ee89a62"), "StudentId" : 106, "Name" : "Ruchi Verma", "Age" : 18, "Course" : "IoT", "Fees" : 5000 }
{ "_id" : ObjectId("5ed48327aae68a5e9ee89a63"), "StudentId" : 107, "Name" : "Joy Iyer", "Age" : 17, "Course" : "MongoDB", "Fees" : 4700 }
```

This operation skips the first 3 documents.

7.34.6 $limit

This limits the amount of documents to look at by the given number starting from the current position. i.e., $limit operator passes the first n documents to the pipeline where n is the specified limit.

Its syntax is:

{ $limit: <positive integer> }

$limit takes a positive integer that specifies the maximum number of documents to pass along.

Consider the following example:

```
> db.students.aggregate( [ { $limit : 5 } ] )
{ "_id" : ObjectId("5ecf6cfcff06392910484d18"), "StudentId" : 101, "Name" : "Ravi Singh", "Age" : 18, "Course" : "MongoDB", "Fees" : 4700 }
{ "_id" : ObjectId("5ecf6cfcff06392910484d19"), "StudentId" : 102, "Name" : "Raman Sharma", "Age" : 17, "Course" : "MariaDB", "Fees" : 4000 }
{ "_id" : ObjectId("5ecf6cfcff06392910484d1a"), "StudentId" : 103, "Name" : "Abhi Sharma", "Age" : 17, "Course" : "MongoDB", "Fees" : 4700 }
{ "_id" : ObjectId("5ed48327aae68a5e9ee89a60"), "StudentId" : 104, "Name" : "Swati Singh", "Age" : 19, "Course" : "IoT", "Fees" : 5000 }
{ "_id" : ObjectId("5ed48327aae68a5e9ee89a61"), "StudentId" : 105, "Name" : "Pre-eti Arora", "Age" : 16, "Course" : "MariaDB", "Fees" : 4000 }
```

This operation returns only the first 5 document.

☞ *The $limit stage limits the number of documents passed to the next stage.*

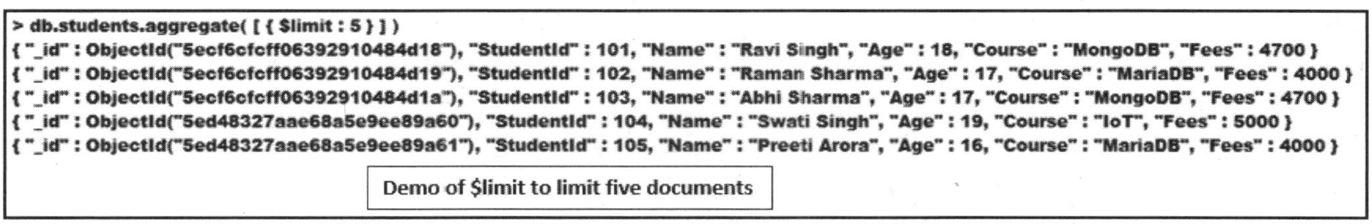
```
> db.students.aggregate( [ { $limit : 5 } ] )
{ "_id" : ObjectId("5ecf6cfcff06392910484d18"), "StudentId" : 101, "Name" : "Ravi Singh", "Age" : 18, "Course" : "MongoDB", "Fees" : 4700 }
{ "_id" : ObjectId("5ecf6cfcff06392910484d19"), "StudentId" : 102, "Name" : "Raman Sharma", "Age" : 17, "Course" : "MariaDB", "Fees" : 4000 }
{ "_id" : ObjectId("5ecf6cfcff06392910484d1a"), "StudentId" : 103, "Name" : "Abhi Sharma", "Age" : 17, "Course" : "MongoDB", "Fees" : 4700 }
{ "_id" : ObjectId("5ed48327aae68a5e9ee89a60"), "StudentId" : 104, "Name" : "Swati Singh", "Age" : 19, "Course" : "IoT", "Fees" : 5000 }
{ "_id" : ObjectId("5ed48327aae68a5e9ee89a61"), "StudentId" : 105, "Name" : "Preeti Arora", "Age" : 16, "Course" : "MariaDB", "Fees" : 4000 }
```
Demo of $limit to limit five documents

Figure 7.61 Demo of $limit

7.34.7 $unwind

Unwinding turns each field of an array into a separate document. The $unwind operator is used to deconstructing an array field from the input documents to output a document for each element. Each output document replaces the array with an element value i.e., every output document is the input document with the value of the array field replaced by the element.

Its syntax is:

```
{ $unwind: <field path> }
```

When you specify the field path, prefix the field name with a dollar sign $ and enclose in quotes. For example,

```
> db.stock.insert(
... { "_id":1,
... "Tshirt":"Half Sleeve",
... "Size" : ["Medium", "XL", "XXL"]
... },
... {"_id":2,
... "Tshirt":"Full Sleeve",
... "Size":[]})
WriteResult({ "nInserted" : 1 })

> db.stock.aggregate( [ { $unwind : "$Size" } ] );
{ "_id" : 1, "Tshirt" : "Half Sleeve", "Size" : "Medium" }
{ "_id" : 1, "Tshirt" : "Half Sleeve", "Size" : "XL" }
{ "_id" : 1, "Tshirt" : "Half Sleeve", "Size" : "XXL" }
```

Here from the result it shows that, each document is identical to the input document except for the value of the size field that contain the value from the original sizes array.

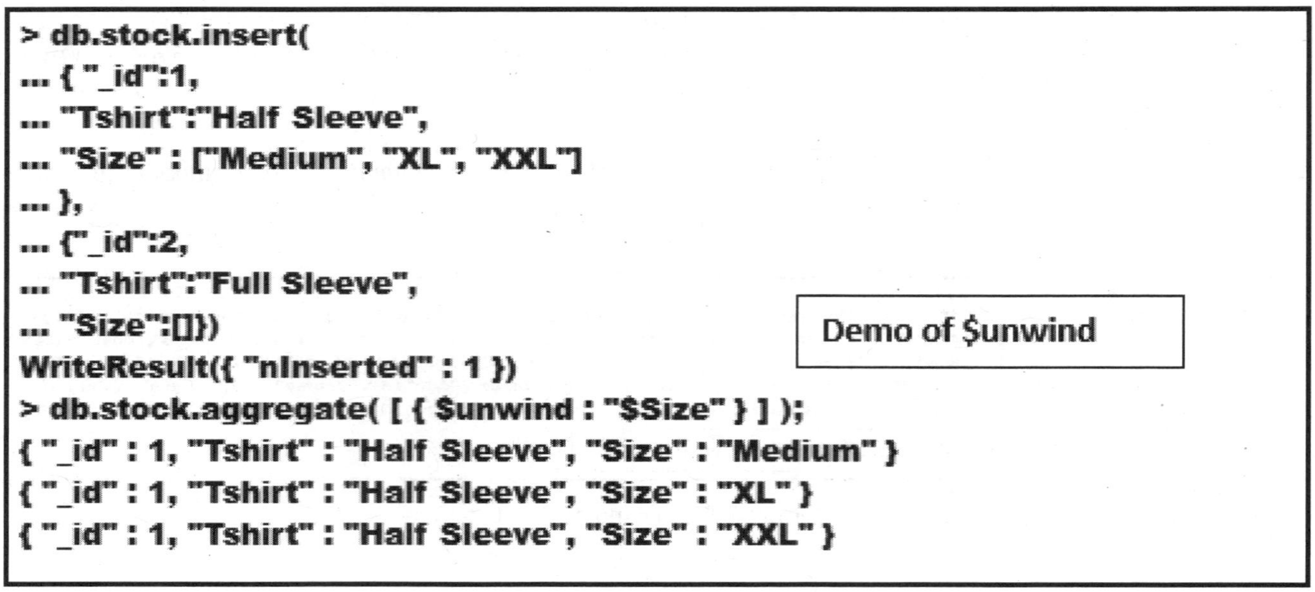

```
> db.stock.insert(
... { "_id":1,
... "Tshirt":"Half Sleeve",
... "Size" : ["Medium", "XL", "XXL"]
... },
... {"_id":2,
... "Tshirt":"Full Sleeve",
... "Size":[]})
WriteResult({ "nInserted" : 1 })
> db.stock.aggregate( [ { $unwind : "$Size" } ] );
{ "_id" : 1, "Tshirt" : "Half Sleeve", "Size" : "Medium" }
{ "_id" : 1, "Tshirt" : "Half Sleeve", "Size" : "XL" }
{ "_id" : 1, "Tshirt" : "Half Sleeve", "Size" : "XXL" }
```


Figure 7.62 Demo of $unwind

7.34.8 $set

$set, adds new fields to documents. Similar to $operator, $set reshapes each document in the stream; specifically, by adding new fields to output documents that contain both the existing fields from the input documents and the newly added fields.

7.34.9 $unset

Removes/excludes fields from documents.

7.35 AGGREGATION COMMANDS

The aggregate command does the aggregation operation using the aggregation pipeline. The aggregation pipeline allows the user to perform data processing from a record or other source using a stage-based application sequence. To understand the MongoDB group by multiple fields first, let's have a look at a list of all operators that can be used in $group:

7.35.1 $sum

Returns the sum of all numeric fields from all the documents in a collection.

7.35.2 $avg

Calculates the average values from all the documents in a collection.

7.35.3 $max

Return the maximum of all values of documents in a collection.

7.35.4 $min

Return the minimum of all values of documents in a collection.

7.35.5 $addToSet

Inserts values to an array but no duplicates in the resulting document

7.35.6 $push

Inserts values to an array in the resulting document.

7.35.7 $first

Gets only the first document from the grouped ones, usually for sorting.

7.35.8 $last

Returns the last document.

7.36 AGGREGATION PIPELINE

The aggregation pipeline is a framework for data aggregation modeled on the concept of data processing pipelines. Documents enter a multi-stage pipeline that transforms the documents into aggregated results.

The MongoDB aggregation pipeline consists of stages (aggregation states). Each stage transforms the documents as they pass through the pipeline. Pipeline stages do not need to produce one output document for every input document; for example, some stages may generate new documents or filter out documents based on the various operators and functions etc.

The most basic pipeline stages provide filters that operate like queries and document transformations that modify the form of the output document. Other pipeline operations provide tools for grouping and sorting documents by specific field or fields as well as tools for aggregating the contents of arrays, including arrays of documents. In addition, pipeline stages can use operators for tasks such as calculating the Average, Sum, Min, Max or concatenating a string also.

Lets take a collection result, having marks of various subjects for each students in various course given as under:

```
> db.result.insertMany( [
... {"Name" : "Raj", "Course" : "O Level", "Sub" : "Mod1", "Marks": 58 },
... {"Name" : "Raj", "Course" : "O Level", "Sub" : "Mod2", "Marks": 48 },
... {"Name" : "Raj", "Course" : "O Level", "Sub" : "Mod3", "Marks": 59 },
... {"Name" : "Raj", "Course" : "O Level", "Sub" : "Mod4", "Marks": 56 },
... {"Name" : "Imran", "Course" : "O Level", "Sub" : "Mod1", "Marks": 66 },
... {"Name" : "Imran", "Course" : "O Level", "Sub" : "Mod2", "Marks": 86 },
... {"Name" : "Imran", "Course" : "O Level", "Sub" : "Mod3", "Marks": 84 },
... {"Name" : "Imran", "Course" : "O Level", "Sub" : "Mod4", "Marks": 76 },
... {"Name" : "Gauri", "Course" : "O Level", "Sub" : "Mod1", "Marks": 96 },
... {"Name" : "Gauri", "Course" : "O Level", "Sub" : "Mod2", "Marks": 72 },
... {"Name" : "Gauri", "Course" : "O Level", "Sub" : "Mod3", "Marks": 64 },
... {"Name" : "Gauri", "Course" : "O Level", "Sub" : "Mod4", "Marks": 55 },
... ])
```

Use following command to see all the documents present in collection result:

```
> db.result.find({}, {"_id":0})
{ "Name" : "Raj", "Course" : "O Level", "Sub" : "Mod1", "Marks" : 58 }
{ "Name" : "Raj", "Course" : "O Level", "Sub" : "Mod2", "Marks" : 48 }
{ "Name" : "Raj", "Course" : "O Level", "Sub" : "Mod3", "Marks" : 59 }
{ "Name" : "Raj", "Course" : "O Level", "Sub" : "Mod4", "Marks" : 56 }
{ "Name" : "Imran", "Course" : "O Level", "Sub" : "Mod1", "Marks" : 66 }
{ "Name" : "Imran", "Course" : "O Level", "Sub" : "Mod2", "Marks" : 86 }
{ "Name" : "Imran", "Course" : "O Level", "Sub" : "Mod3", "Marks" : 84 }
{ "Name" : "Imran", "Course" : "O Level", "Sub" : "Mod4", "Marks" : 76 }
{ "Name" : "Gauri", "Course" : "O Level", "Sub" : "Mod1", "Marks" : 96 }
{ "Name" : "Gauri", "Course" : "O Level", "Sub" : "Mod2", "Marks" : 72 }
{ "Name" : "Gauri", "Course" : "O Level", "Sub" : "Mod3", "Marks" : 64 }
{ "Name" : "Gauri", "Course" : "O Level", "Sub" : "Mod4", "Marks" : 55 }
```

Now, lets execute the following aggregate command:

```
> db.result.aggregate([{$match:{"Course":"O Level"}},
... {$group:{_id:"$Name","Total_Marks":{$sum: "$Marks"}}}])
```

This command executed in two states, in first stage, $match stage filters the documents by the status field and passes to the next stage those documents that have Course equal to "O Level". In second stage, the $group stage groups the documents by the sub field to calculate the sum of marks.

```
> db.result.insertMany( [
... {"Name" : "Raj", "Course" : "O Level", "Sub" : "Mod1", "Marks": 58 },
... {"Name" : "Raj", "Course" : "O Level", "Sub" : "Mod2", "Marks": 48 },
... {"Name" : "Raj", "Course" : "O Level", "Sub" : "Mod3", "Marks": 59 },
... {"Name" : "Raj", "Course" : "O Level", "Sub" : "Mod4", "Marks": 56 },
... {"Name" : "Imran", "Course" : "O Level", "Sub" : "Mod1", "Marks": 66 },
... {"Name" : "Imran", "Course" : "O Level", "Sub" : "Mod2", "Marks": 86 },
... {"Name" : "Imran", "Course" : "O Level", "Sub" : "Mod3", "Marks": 84 },
... {"Name" : "Imran", "Course" : "O Level", "Sub" : "Mod4", "Marks": 76 },
... {"Name" : "Gauri", "Course" : "O Level", "Sub" : "Mod1", "Marks": 96 },
... {"Name" : "Gauri", "Course" : "O Level", "Sub" : "Mod2", "Marks": 72 },
... {"Name" : "Gauri", "Course" : "O Level", "Sub" : "Mod3", "Marks": 64 },
... {"Name" : "Gauri", "Course" : "O Level", "Sub" : "Mod4", "Marks": 55 },
... ])
{
        "acknowledged" : true,
        "insertedIds" : [
                ObjectId("5ed4ba9caae68a5e9ee89a6b"),
                ObjectId("5ed4ba9caae68a5e9ee89a6c"),
                ObjectId("5ed4ba9caae68a5e9ee89a6d"),
                ObjectId("5ed4ba9caae68a5e9ee89a6e"),
                ObjectId("5ed4ba9caae68a5e9ee89a6f"),
                ObjectId("5ed4ba9caae68a5e9ee89a70"),
                ObjectId("5ed4ba9caae68a5e9ee89a71"),
                ObjectId("5ed4ba9caae68a5e9ee89a72"),
                ObjectId("5ed4ba9caae68a5e9ee89a73"),
                ObjectId("5ed4ba9caae68a5e9ee89a74"),
                ObjectId("5ed4ba9caae68a5e9ee89a75"),
                ObjectId("5ed4ba9caae68a5e9ee89a76")
        ]
}
```

result collection with Marks in various subjects

Figure 7.63 The result collection with documents

This resulted into:

```
{ "_id" : "Gauri", "Total_Marks" : 287 }
{ "_id" : "Raj", "Total_Marks" : 221 }
{ "_id" : "Imran", "Total_Marks" : 312 }
```

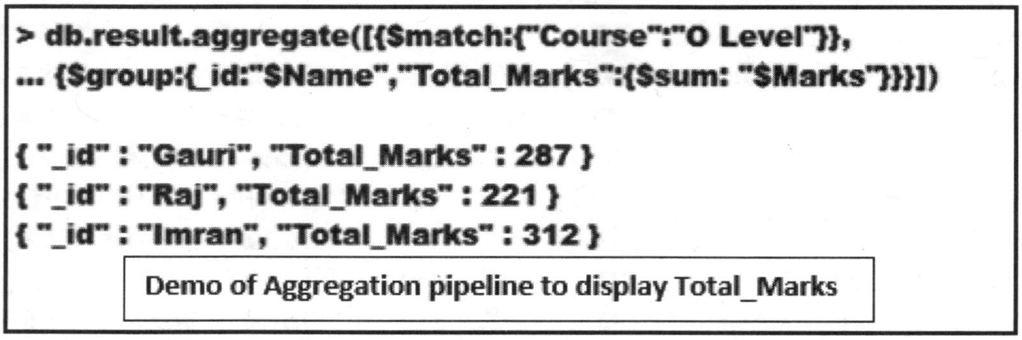

Figure 7.64 Demo of Aggregation pipeline to display Total_marks

Now run following aggregate command and see the output:

```
> db.result.aggregate([{$match:{"Course":"O Level"}},
... {$group:{_id:"$Sub",Max_marks:{$max:"$Marks"}}}])
```

This resulted into:

```
{ "_id" : "Mod1", "Max_marks" : 96 }
{ "_id" : "Mod3", "Max_marks" : 84 }
{ "_id" : "Mod2", "Max_marks" : 86 }
{ "_id" : "Mod4", "Max_marks" : 76 }
```

Here, in stage 1, students of Course "O Level" are filtered out and then Maximum marks of each module has been computed.

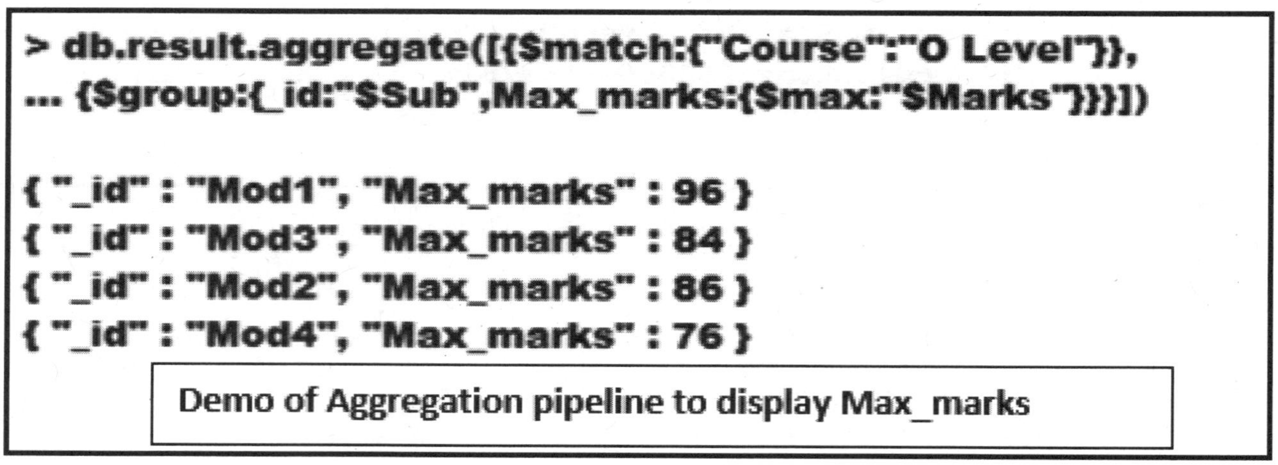

Figure 7.65 Demo of Aggregation pipeline to display Max_marks

Same way you can find Minimum by executing following command:

```
> db.result.aggregate([{$match:{"Course":"O Level"}},
...{$group:{_id:"$Sub",Min_marks:{$min:"$Marks"}}}])
```

This resulted into:

```
{ "_id" : "Mod2", "Min_marks" : 48 }
{ "_id" : "Mod3", "Min_marks" : 59 }
{ "_id" : "Mod1", "Min_marks" : 58 }
{ "_id" : "Mod4", "Min_marks" : 55 }
```

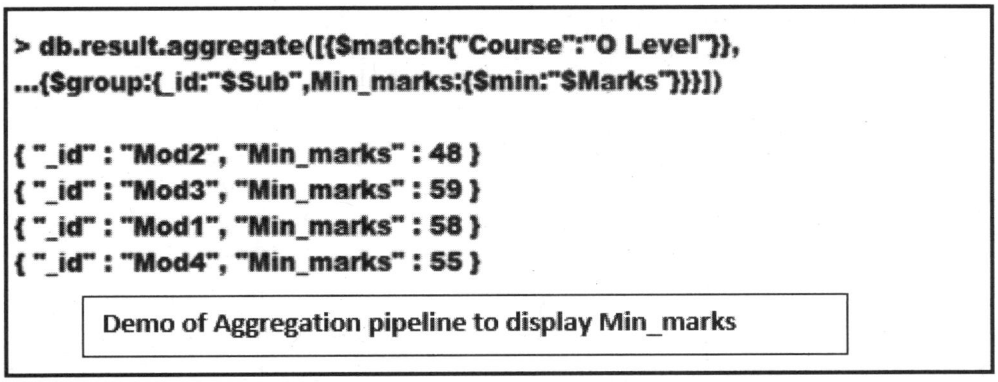

Figure 7.66 Demo of Aggregation pipeline to display Min_marks

Same way you can find average by executing following command:

```
> db.result.aggregate([{$match:{"Course":"O Level"}},
... {$group:{_id:"$Sub",Average_marks:{$avg:"$Marks"}}}])
```

This resulted into:

```
{ "_id" : "Mod4", "Average_marks" : 62.333333333333336 }
{ "_id" : "Mod1", "Average_marks" : 73.33333333333333 }
{ "_id" : "Mod3", "Average_marks" : 69 }
{ "_id" : "Mod2", "Average_marks" : 68.66666666666667 }
```

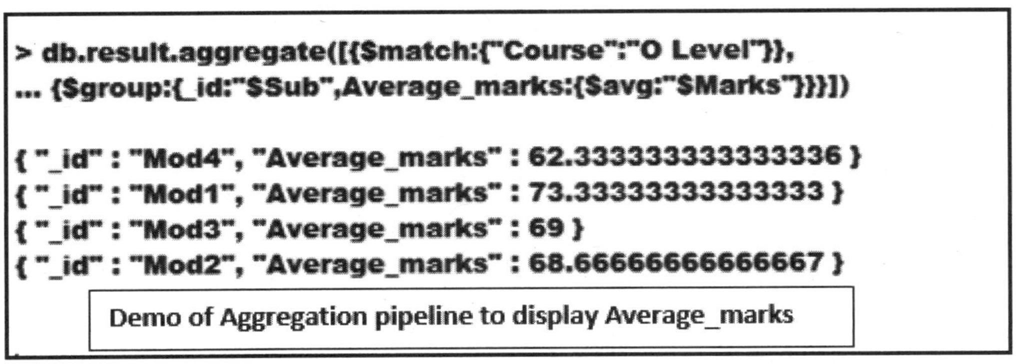

Figure 7.67 Demo of Aggregation pipeline to display Average_marks

7.37 MongoDB AND MapReduce

MapReduce is a powerful and flexible tool that condenses large volumes of data into aggregated results. It can solve some problems that are too complex to express using the aggregation framework. MapReduce can be easily parallelized across multiple servers. It splits up a problem, sends chunks of it to different machines, and lets each machine solve its part of the problem. When all the machines are finished, they merge all the pieces of the solution back into a full solution.

MapReduce tends to be fairly slow and should not be used for real-time data analysis. MapReduce can be used for batch processing of data and also for aggregation operations. MapReduce is nothing but a process, in which large datasets will process and generate results with the help of parallel and distributed algorithms on clusters. It consists of two sets of operations in itself, they are Map() and Reduce(). MapReduce is used for processing large data sets. Map() performs operations like filtering the data and then performing sorting on that dataset. Reduce() performs the operation of summarizing all the data after the map() operation.

The two phases of Map/Reduce is:

- map phase: filter / transform / convert data
- reduce phase: perform aggregations over the data

Map is a JavaScript function, which is used to generate key-value pairs. Reduce is a JavaScript function used for grouping all the documents which have the same key. The mapReduce function first queries the collection, then maps the result documents to emit key-value pairs, which is then reduced based on the keys that have multiple values.

Lets have the result collection having the student name, marks, course and subject marks in each document. Now, we will use a mapReduce function on result collection to select all sum of marks of all the students in course "O Level". The candidates of the course will be grouped based on the name and then the count the marks of each student. The output of the operation will be saved as a new collection "result_OLevel" and the documents in the newly created collection may be seen using find() command:

```
> db.result.mapReduce( function() { emit(this.Name,this.Marks); },
... function(key, values) {return Array.sum(values)}, {query:{Course:"O Level"},
...  out:"result_OLevel"})
{
        "result" : "result_OLevel",
        "timeMillis" : 1487,
        "counts" : {
                "input" : 12,
                "emit" : 12,
                "reduce" : 3,
                "output" : 3
        },
        "ok" : 1
}
```

```
> db.result_OLevel.find()
{ "_id" : "Gauri", "value" : 287 }
{ "_id" : "Imran", "value" : 312 }
{ "_id" : "Raj", "value" : 221 }
```

```
> db.result.mapReduce( function() { emit(this.Name,this.Marks); },
... function(key, values) {return Array.sum(values)}, {query:{Course:"O Level"},
... out:"result_OLevel"})
{
        "result" : "result_OLevel",
        "timeMillis" : 1487,
        "counts" : {
                "input" : 12,
                "emit" : 12,
                "reduce" : 3,
                "output" : 3
        },
        "ok" : 1
}
> db.result_OLevel.find()
{ "_id" : "Gauri", "value" : 287 }
{ "_id" : "Imran", "value" : 312 }
{ "_id" : "Raj", "value" : 221 }
```

Demo of mapReduce function on result collection to select sum of marks of all the students in Course "O Level"

Figure 7.68 Demo of MapReduce

7.38 SINGLE-PURPOSE AGGREGATE COMMANDS

Single-purpose aggregate commands are used for specific aggregation operations on sets of data. Single-purpose aggregate commands and methods are less complex but with limited scope compared to Pipeline and MapReduce operations. Single-purpose aggregate commands provide direct semantics for common data processing options.

7.38.1 count()

The count operation returns the number of documents in the collection. It takes a number of documents and depending on the match query returns the count of the documents. It is different from find() as find() returns the documents while it returns the number of documents matching the query. Counting the total number of documents in a collection is fast regardless of collection size. To find documents where the marks is greater than 70. The command will be:

```
> db.result.count({"Marks":{$gt:70}})
5
```

To find documents where the marks is less than 70. The command will be:

```
> db.result.count({"Marks":{$lt:70}})
7
```

7.38.2 estimatedDocumentCount()

The estimatedDocumentCount() method returns the count of all documents in a collection or view. The command to count all document in result collection command is:

```
> db.result.estimatedDocumentCount()
12
```

7.38.3 distinct()

The distinct() command finds the distinct values for a specified field across a single collection or view and returns the results in an array. It takes a document and depending on the match query returns the unique values for a field.

For example to find the distinct marks among the various documents from the collection, the command is:

```
> db.result.distinct("Marks")
[ 48, 55, 56, 58, 59, 64, 66, 72, 76,
84, 86, 96 ]
```

```
> db.result.count({"Marks":{$gt:70}})
5

> db.result.count({"Marks":{$lt:70}})
7

> db.result.estimatedDocumentCount()
12

> db.result.distinct("Marks")
[ 48, 55, 56, 58, 59, 64, 66, 72, 76, 84, 86, 96 ]
```

Figure 7.69 Demo of single-purpose aggregate commands

7.39 INTRODUCTION TO REPLICATION

Replication is a way of keeping identical copies of your data on multiple servers. For performing this task, MongoDB always maintains a log of operations or oplog which contains every writes information into the primary server.

Replication provides redundancy and increases data availability with multiple copies of data on different database servers, replication protects a database from the loss of a single server. Replication keeps your application running and your data safe, even if something happens to one or more of your servers. Replication also allows you to recover from hardware failure and service interruptions. The way MongoDB accomplishes this is by keeping a log of operations, or oplog, containing every write that a primary performs. This is a capped collection that exist in the local database on the primary. The secondaries query this collection for operations to replicate.

Each secondary maintains its own oplog, recording each operation it replicates from the primary. Oplog keep an ordered list of write operations that have occurred. Each member has its own copy of the oplog, which should be identical to the primary. This allows any member to be used as a sync source for any other member. The secondary server always first fetch the information related to the pending operations from the primary members, then apply that operation to their own data set and then writes down the logs about that operation into the oplog. If applying an operation fails (which should only happen if the underlying data has been corrupted or in some way differs from the primary), the secondary will exit.

If a secondary goes down for any reason when it restarts, it will start syncing from the last operation done by itself according to its oplog file. As operations are applied to data and then written to the oplog, the secondary may replay operations that it has already applied to its data.

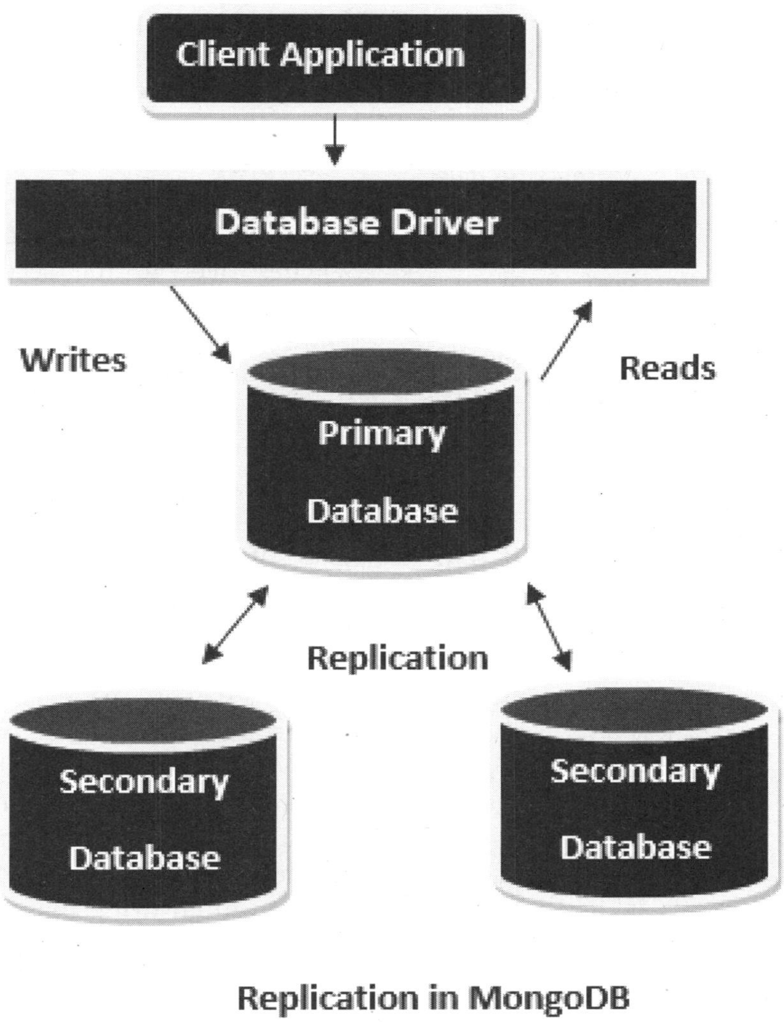

Figure 7.70 Replication in MongoDB

If you create a collection without an "_id" index, you will never be able replicate the mongod it lives on. Replication requires the "_id" index on every collection. It is important that replication can uniquely identify each document in a collection.

7.39.1 Benefits of Replication

- Replication helps you in recovering data in case a disaster takes place. You will have a backup of your data from which you can recover your lost files quickly.
- Your data remains available all the time. This means replication ensures you have 24X7 accessibility.
- The downtime of server maintenance reduces if you perform replication regularly.
- Replication enhances your reading scalability. Having multiple copies helps in scaling the reading of data.

Apart from the benefits replication has a drawback too. As you will store copies of your data, you will need to have more storage space. Although this is not a significant issue, it's worth noting. You might need to increase your server's storage capability.!

☞ *Replication is the process of synchronizing data across multiple servers.*

Difference between replication and sharding

Remember that replication creates an exact copy of your data on multiple servers, so every server is a mirror-image of every other server. Conversely, every shard contains a different subset of data.

7.39.2 How replication works?

MongoDB achieves replication by the use of replica set. A replica set is a group of mongod instances that host the same data set. In a replica, one node is primary node that receives all write operations. All other instances, secondaries, apply operations from the primary so that they have the same data set. Replica set can have only one primary node.

- Replica set is a group of two or more nodes (generally minimum 3 nodes are recommended).
- In a replica set one node is primary node and remaining nodes are secondary.
- In a replica set, all data replicates from primary to secondary node.
- At the time of automatic failover (or during maintenance), an election takes place for determining the primary and a new primary node is elected.
- After the recovery of failed node, it again join the replica set and works as a secondary node.

7.39.3 Configuring a Replica Set

The replica set is a group of mongod instances that maintain the same data set. Replication in MongoDB provides high availability with replica sets. A replica set consists of two or more MongoDB instances. Each replica set member may act in the role of the primary or secondary replica at any time. The primary replica is the main server which interacts with the client and performs all the read/write operations. The secondary replicas maintain a copy of the data of the primary using built-in replication. When the primary replica fails, the replica set automatically switches over to the secondary, and then it becomes the primary server.

Before we start creating the Replica Set in MongoDB, it is desired to create separate configuration file for each replica set i.e., for each new port. These replicas will be treated as separate instance of MongoDB Server. Suppose you have three servers, Server X, Server Y, and Server Z. Out of these three, Server X is the primary one, and Server Y and Z are the secondaries.

You already know that replication takes place from the primary server to the secondary ones. First, you have to make sure that all of the mongod instances are installed on various servers.

Connect a mongo shell to the mongod instance. Use rs.initiate() to initiate the new replica set. The replica set is now operational. To view the replica set configuration, use rs.conf(). This step will help you in ensuring that your replica is set up optimally and without any issues. To check the status of the replica set, use rs.status().

The basic procedure is to start the mongod instances that will become members of the replica set, configure the replica set itself, and then add the mongod instances to it.

You may create as many number of instances as required and feasible. To start replication, open mongo shell and run the following command:

```
> rs.initiate()
```

rs.initiate() will initiate replication (initiate system considered as primary).

Verify the initial replica set configuration by issuing following command:

```
> rs.conf()
```

Once the primary server is added, it is easy to add the other secondary nodes. Add the remaining members to the replica set by issuing following command:

```
> rs.add()
```

You may also check the status using following command:

```
> rs.status()
```

☞ *Host and Port options of mongo command can be used to connect to mongod instance running on different node connected to the network.*

7.39.4 Member Configration Options

After defining a replica set, we can change the replica set at any time. We can add new members, removing any existing members. To add members to this replica set, use the rs.add() method. This command adds members to the replica set. You can add mongod instance to replica set only if they are connected to primary node. db.isMaster() command is to check whether you are connected to primary or not. In our example, we had Server X, Server Y, and Server Z. Out of those three servers, Server X was the primary one in the replica set. We need to add the remaining servers as secondaries by using following command:

```
> rs.add()
```

Apart from establishing and adding servers, You might need to remove a server from the configuration group as well. For that purpose, you have to use the following command:

```
> rs.remove()
```

The rs.status command gives you the status of your replica set. The members of a replica set send some messages to one another. We call these messages "heartbeat". We call them heartbeat because these messages show that the member is working (i.e., alive).

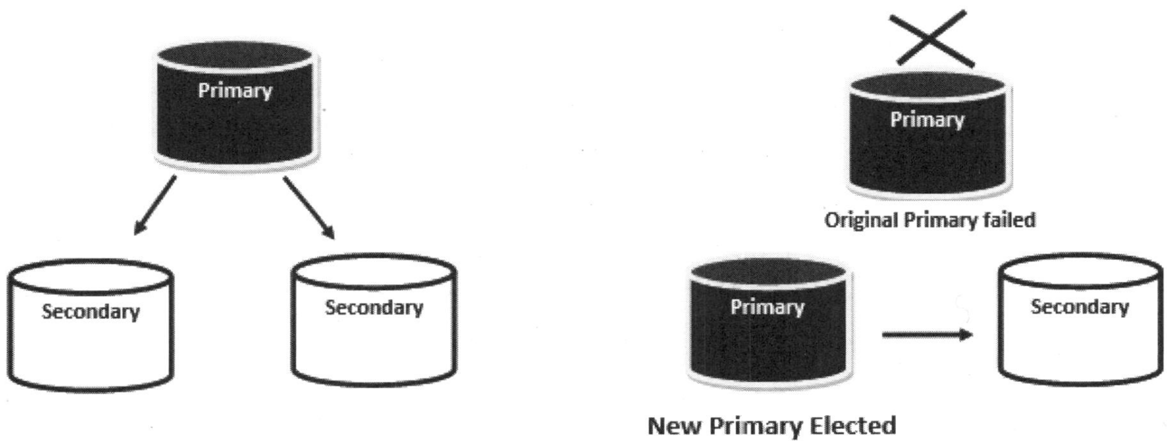

Figure 7.71 Working of Replica set

7.39.5 How Elections Work?

When a secondary cannot reach a primary, it will contact all the other members of the replica set and request that it be elected primary. If a member seeking election receives from a majority of the set, it becomes primary. If even one server vetoes the election, the election is cancelled. A member vetoes an election when it knows any reason that the member seeking election should not become primary. If it did not receive the majority of votes then it will remain as secondary and maybe try to become a primary node in the future.

If the network condition is healthy and most of the servers are up, then the entire elections process should be very fast. In this scenario, it will take two seconds to notify all the members that primary has gone down (since heartbeat response was not received yet) and the election process starts immediately.

7.39.6 Heartbeat

In replication, heartbeat is the process to identify the current status of the node servers within the replica set. In other words a heartbeat request is basically a short message that checks everyone's current state. MongoDB determines who to sync to based on ping time. When one member heartbeats (pings) another, it times how long that request took. MongoDB keeps a running average of these times. When it has to choose a member to sync from, it looks for the member that is closest to it and ahead of it in replication.

7.39.7 Calculating Lag

Lag is when the secondaries cannot keep up with the primary. One of the most important metrics to track for replication is how well the secondaries are keeping up with the primary. Lag is how far behind a secondary is, which means the difference in timestamp between the last operation the primary has performed and the timestamp of the last operation the secondary has applied.

REVIEW QUESTIONS WITH ANSWERS

1. Multiple Choice Questions

1. Which of the following statements is (are) true in MongoDB:
   a. A database holds a set of collections
   b. A collection holds a set of documents
   c. A document is a set of fields
   d. All of the above
2. Benefit(s) of JSON:
   a. The speed of processing
   b. The easiness of use
   c. It is recognized natively by JavaScript.
   d. All of the above
3. Which of the following line skips the first 5 documents in the fee collection and returns all remaining documents?
   a. db.fee.find().limit(5)
   b. db.fee.find().skip(1)
   c. db.fee.find().skip(5)
   d. None of the above
4. MongoDB provides high __________ with replica sets.
   a. Performance
   b. Availability
   c. Scalability
   d. None of the above
5. Documents enter a multi-stage __________ that transforms the documents into an aggregated result.
   a. pipeline
   b. pipelineView
   c. pipelineUser
   d. None of the above
6. Identify NoSQL Database(s) other than MongoDB:
   a. Cassandra b. HBASE
   c. CouchDB d. All of the above
7. MongoDB can handle:
   a. Structured data b. Semi structured data
   c. Unstructured data d. All of the above
8. Without a primary, a replica set cannot accept ________ operations.
   a. read b. write
   c. read-write d. All of the above
9. __________ is a part of the standard MongoDB distribution and provides a full JavaScript environment.
   a. mongod b. mongodb
   c. mongo d. None of these
10. Which of the following format is supported by MongoDB?
    a. SQL b. XML
    c. BSON d. All of the above
11. Initial release of MongoDB was in the year?
    a. 2000 b. 2005
    c. 2009 d. 2011
12. __________ command display the list of databases.
    a. show db b. show dbs
    c. show data d. display dbs
13. Which of the following method is used to query documents in collections?
    a. find b. move

c. shell d. replace

14. After starting the mongo shell, your session will use the ________ database by default.
    a. mongo b. master
    c. test d. primary
15. Which of the following method corresponds to Order by clause in SQL?
    a. sort() b. order()
    c. orderby() d. All of the above
16. The __________ method limits the number of documents in the result set.
    a. limit() b. limitOf()
    c. limitBy() d. None of these
17. MongoDB scales horizontally using _________ for load balancing purpose.
    a. Replication b. Partitioning
    c. Sharding d. None of the above
18. MongoDB supports fixed-size collections called ____________ collections.
    a. Primary b. Secondary
    c. capped d. All of the above
19. ____________ are operations that process data records and return computed results.
    a. Replication b. Partitioning
    c. Aggregations d. None of these
20. ________ passes the first n documents unmodified to the pipeline where n is the specified limit.
    a. $skip
    b. $limit
    c. $match
    d. None of the above
21. MongoDB also supports user-defined indexes on multiple fields called _________.
    a. compound
    b. composite
    c. candidate
    d. None of the above
22. The browsers that support JSON format?
    a. Internet Explorer
    b. Chrome
    c. Mozilla Firefox
    d. All of the above
23. Which of the following is a NoSQL Database Type?
    a. SQL
    b. Document databases
    c. JSON
    d. All of the above
24. Which of the following are the simplest NoSQL databases?
    a. Key-value
    b. Wide-column
    c. Document
    d. All of the mentioned

2. State True or False for the following:

1. An index is created with multiple keys then it is termed as multikey or Compound Index.
2. The drop() method will return true if the collection is dropped successfully, else it will return false.
3. MongoDB is schema-less, which means there is no need of defining a structure for the data before insertion.
4. All data replicates from primary to secondary nodes.
5. One of the most important activities of heartbeats is to check that the primary server is available to reach for all secondary servers.
6. MongoDB then uses this Oplog to replicate the writes to the other members in the replica set.
7. MongoDB is a popular NoSQL database management system that stores data as BSON (binary JSON) documents.
8. MongoDB is fault tolerant.
9. MongoDB can not be used for real time analytics.
10. Is it possible to run multiple Mongo Instances on the same computer.
11. By default, Mongo Daemon starts on the port 12707.
12. The use <database_name> command in mongo shell can be used to connect to a specific MongoDB Database.
13. Documents support nesting.
14. JSON files are used as a data interchange format.
15. JSON is short for JavaScript Object Notation.

16. Arbiters do not keep a copy of the data.
17. JSON is "self-describing" and easy to understand.
18. MongoDB has official drivers for a variety of popular programming languages and development environments.

3. Match the following:

1. MongoDB is	a. Schema free data structure
2. An index with the one key is termed as	b. Horizontally scalable.
3. JSON	c. Deletes collection
4. Example of structured data	d. Simple Index.
5. Example of unstructured data	e. Filtering operation to reduce the amount of documents to the next stages
6. show dbs	f. A spread-sheet or table
7. drop()	g. Sorts the documents
8. $project	h. Multimedia content
9. $match	i. To get the list of databases
10. $sort	j. Select some specific fields from a collection

4. Fill in the blanks:

1. MongoDB provides a method named createIndex() with an alias method named ________.
2. ________ method will sorts all input documents and returns them to the pipeline in sorted order.
3. In a replica set, one node is primary node and remaining nodes are ________.
4. ________ is the process to identify the current status of the node servers within the replica set.
5. ________ means that all clients see the same data at the same time, no matter which node they connect to.
6. ________ means that any client making a request for data gets a response, even if one or more nodes are down.
7. ________ means that the cluster must continue to work despite any number of communication breakdowns between nodes in the system.
8. ________ is a group of MongoDB Collections.
9. ________ is a data processing technique that condenses large volumes of data into aggregated results.
10. MongoDB's ________ method is used to remove document from the collection.
11. ________ groups all documents based on some keys.
12. ________ is used to sort all the documents.
13. JSON arrays are written inside ________ brackets.
14. Some of the columns of a relation are at different sites is ________.
15. MongoDB Queries can return specific fields of documents which also include user-defined ________ functions.
16. ________ is an unordered collection of key:value pairs.

Answers

1.	1. d	2. d	3. c	4. b	5. a	6. d
	7. d	8. b	9. c	10. c	11. c	12. b
	13. a	14. c	15. a	16 a	17. c	18. c
	19. c	20. b	21 a	22 d	23. b	24. A
2.	1. T	2. T	3. T	4. T	5. T	6. T
	7. T	8. T	9. F	10. T	11. T	12. T
	13. T	14. T	15. T	16. T	17. T	18. T
3.	1. b	2. d	3. a	4. f	5. h	6. i
	7. c	8. j	9. e	10. g		

4.	1. ensureIndex()	2. sort()
	3. Secondary	4. Heartbeat
	5. Consistency	6. Availability
	7. Partition tolerance	8. Database

9. Map Reduce
10. remove()
11. $group
12. $sort
13. Square
14. Vertical Partitioning
15. Javascript
16. Object

Short Answers Questions

1. What is MongoDB?

Ans MongoDB is a document database. Each database contains collections, which in turn contain documents. Each document can be different with varying number of fields. The size and content of each document can also be different from each other.

2. What is NoSQL?

Ans NoSQL is not a relational database. It provides more flexibility since all records are not restricted by the same column names and types defined across the entire table.

3. What is collection in MongoDB?

Ans Collection is a grouping of MongoDB documents. It is the equivalent of a table which is created in any other RDBMS, such as Oracle or SQL. It exists within a single database. It does not enforce any sort of structure.

4. What do you mean by Database and Document in MongoDB?

Ans Database - This is a container for collections like in RDBMS wherein it is a container for tables. Each database gets its own set of files on the file system. A MongoDB server can store multiple databases.

Document - A record in a MongoDB collection is basically called a document. The document in turn consists of field names and values.

5. What is the difference between MongoDB and RDBMS?

Ans The differences between MongoDB and RDBMS are as follows:

- In RDBMS, the table contains the columns and rows which are used to store the data whereas in MongoDB, this same structure is known as a collection. The collection contains documents, which in turn contain fields, which in turn are key-value pairs.
- In RDBMS, the row represents a single, implicitly structured data item in a table, whereas in MongoDB, the data is stored in documents.
- In RDBMS, the column denotes a set of data values whereas these, in MongoDB, are denoted by fields.
- In RDBMS, data is sometimes spread across various tables and in order to show a complete view of all data, a join is sometimes formed across tables to get the data. In MongoDB, the data is normally stored in a single collection, but separated by using Embedded documents. So there is no concept of joins in MongoDB.

6. How is MongoDB better than MySQL?

Ans

Criteria	MongoDB	MySQL
Data Models	Many alternatives	Relational Database Management System
Architecture	Without Schema	With Schema
Query Language	JSON Query	SQL
Scalability	Highly scalable	Not Scalable
Speed	Faster	Slower

7. Write any five features of MongoDB.

Ans Features of MongoDB are:

(a) Queries: It supports ad-hoc queries and document-based queries.

(b) Index Support: Any field in the document can be indexed.

(c) Replication: It supports Master/Slave replication. MongoDB uses native application to maintain multiple copies of data. Preventing database downtime is one of the replica sets features as it has self-healing shard.

(d) Auto-sharding: This process distributes data across multiple physical partitions called shards. Due to sharding, MongoDB has an automatic load balancing feature.

(e) Document-oriented Storage: It uses BSON format which is a JSON-like format.

8. What is JSON? Explain.

Ans JSON is the abbreviation of JavaScript Object Notation. It is one of the simplest data interchange format, independent of programming language and platform. Its lightweight text-based structure makes it easily readable. It is derived from JavaScript for presenting simple data in the form of key-value pairs.

9. Who is known as the father of JSON?

Ans Douglas Crockford is known as the father of JSON.

10. MongoDB is a schemaless database. Comment.

Ans MongoDB is a schemaless database. This means that we don't have to define a fixed schema for a collection. We just need to insert a JSON document into a collection. Documents in the same collection can have a completely different set of fields, and even the same fields can have different types on different documents. The same object can be a string in some documents and can be a number in other documents.

11. Write short note on Collection.

Ans Collection is a group of MongoDB documents. It is the equivalent of an RDBMS table. A collection exists within a single database. Collections do not enforce a schema. Documents within a collection can have different fields. Typically, all documents in a collection are of similar or related purpose.

12. Write short note on Document.

Ans A document is a set of key-value pairs. Documents have dynamic schema. Dynamic schema means that documents in the same collection do not need to have the same set of fields or structure, and common fields in a collection's documents may hold different types of data.

13. Explain two components of Graph database.

Ans Node: The entities themselves. In a social network this could be people.
Edge: The relationship between two entities. This relationship is represented by a line and has its own properties. An edge can have a direction.

14. Explain Insert() command.

Ans Insert() command is used to insert document in form of name/value combination to the specified collection. If collection is not already created, it will create the specified collection.

15. What are the equivalents of Tables and Rows in SQL to that of MongoDB?

Ans MongoDB Collections is equivalent to Tables and MongoDB Documents is equivalent to Rows of SQL.

16. What is a Document in MongoDB ? Explain with example.

Ans Document is an entity in which zero or more ordered field-value pairs are stored.
For example,

```
{
  name: "Vivek",
  class: "XII"
  hobbies: ["Singing", "Reading"]
}
```

17. Mention some names of NoSQL Databases.

Ans Some NoSQL Databases are MongoDB, Cassandra, HBASE, CouchDB, IBM Informix, Azure DocumentDB, ToroDB etc.

18. What is MongoDB Projection?

Ans In MongoDB projection means selecting only necessary data rather than selecting whole of the data of a document. If a document has 5 fields and you need to show only 3, then select only 3 fields from them.

19. Is primary key supported by MongoDB?

Ans There is no concept of primary key in MongoDB. But there is a key:value pair with key as _id that is used to store a unique value for each Document that is inserted to Collection. By default _id is provided by MongoDB. But _id:value could be provided by user also, but user must provide unique value for _id.

20. What are the similarities between JSON and XML?

Ans There are several similarities that can be found between JSON and XML. These are:

(a) Both JSON and XML are used to transfer data between different systems.

(b) Both JSON and XML have a simple structure and are readable by the human.

(c) Both are independent of programming language.

(d) Both of these can be parsed easily through several programming.

21. How will you create a MongoDB Collection?

Ans To create MongoDB Collection first select a database using use <database_name> command, to create a collection use db.<collection_name> to reference a collection. If the collection is not present, a new Collection is created.

22. What is MapReduce in MongoDB?

Ans MapReduce is an algorithm used for gathering some useful information and trends from the available data. It is generally used in data analytics associated with Big Data.

23. Explain following Logical Query operators.

(a) $and

(b) $not

(c) $or

Ans Logical Query operators:

(a) $and: Joins query clauses with a logical AND returns all documents that match the conditions of both clauses.

(b) $not: Inverts the effect of a query expression and returns documents that do not match the query expression.

(c) $or: Joins query clauses with a logical OR returns all documents that match the conditions of either clause.

24. Write short note on $unwind.

Ans The MongoDB $unwind stages operator is used to deconstructs an array field from the input documents to output a document for each element. Every output document is the input document with the value of the array field replaced by the element.
Syntax:
{ $unwind: <field path> }

25. Differentiate between $project and $match.

Ans The $project function in MongoDB passes along the documents with only the specified fields to the next stage in the pipeline. This may be the existing fields from the input documents or newly computed fields.
The MongoDB $match operator filters the documents to pass only those documents that match the specified condition(s) to the next pipeline stage.

26. What is Replication in MongoDB?

Ans Replication is the process of making copies of data (documents) across multiple MongoDB instances. This helps in failover, when a node goes down, the data is still present on the other nodes and application can continue to function.

27. Why replication is needed?

Ans The replication is needed:

(a) To keep your data safe.

(b) High (24*7) availability of data.

(c) Disaster Recovery.

(d) No downtime for maintenance (like backups, index rebuilds, compaction).

(e) Replica set is transparent to the application.

28. What are the advantages of Replication?

Ans The advantages of replication are:

(a) Increased reliability and availability.

(b) Queries requesting replicated copies of data are always faster.

(c) Less Communication Overhead.

(d) Helps in disaster recovery and backup of data.

(e) Load Balancing.

(f) No downtime for maintenance (like backups, index rebuilds, compaction).

29. What are the disadvantages of Replication?

Ans The disadvantages of replication are:

(a) Redundant data is stored, so more storage space and server processing is needed.

(b) Write operations are costly.

(c) Difficult to main data integrity.

(d) High Cost for Hardware and other infrastructure.

(e) Need connectivity with all the replicated servers.

30. What is replica set?

Ans Replica set is a group of two or more nodes. It is a group of Mongod instances that host the same data set. In a replica, one node is primary node that receives all write operations and all other instances called secondary instances, apply operations from the primary so that they have the same data set. Replica set can have only one primary node and rest all are the secondary nodes.

31. Explain working of replica set.

Ans Replica set works as follows:

(a) MongoDB is a single leader based system that can have multiple replicas. These replicas update themselves asynchronously from Primary/Leader's OpLog.

(b) Each node maintains the heartbeat of every other node to keep track if other replicas or leader is alive or dead.

(c) If the leader/primary node goes down, replicas can identify and elect a new leader based on priority, if they can form the majority.

32. Differentiate between $skip and $limit.

Ans $skip is used to skip forward in the list of documents for a given amount of documents.
$limit is used to limit the amount of documents to look at by the given number starting from the current position.

33. Explain JSON syntax rules.

Ans There are several rules that describe the structure of the JSON. These are:

(a) Data inside a JSON is arranged in key-value pair.

(b) The left side represents the key and the data on the right side represents value.

(c) Both key and value are separated by a colon ':'.

(d) Each set of key-value pair is separated from the other pair by using a comma ','.

(e) Curly braces define the JSON objects. Left curly brace '{' represents the start of the object and right curly brace '}' represents the end of an object.

(f) Arrays are defined inside a JSON object by using square brackets '[ ]'.

34. What is ObjectId?

Ans This data type in MongoDB stores the unique key Id of documents stored. There is an _id field in MongoDB for each document. The data which is stored in Id is in hexadecimal format. The size of ObjectId is 12 bytes which are divided into four parts.

35. What is Default Index?

Ans In MongoDB indexing, all the collections have a default index on the _id field. If we don't specify any value for the _id the MongoDB will create _id field with an object value. This index prevents clients from creating two documents with the same value _id field.

36. Differentiate between Single Field Index and Compound Index in MongoDB

Ans Single Field Index: MongoDB supports user-defined indexes like single field index. A single field index is used to create an index on the single field of a document. With single field index, MongoDB can traverse in ascending and descending order.
Compound Index: MongoDB supports a user-defined index on multiple fields as well. For this MongoDB has a compound index.

37. Write short note on BSON.

Ans BSON is designed to be efficient in space, but in some cases is not much more efficient than JSON. In some cases BSON uses even more space than JSON. The reason for this is that BSON adds some "extra" information to documents, like length of strings and subobjects. This makes traversal faster.
BSON is also designed to be fast to encode and decode. For example, integers are stored as 32 (or 64) bit integers, so they don't need to be parsed to and from text. This uses more space than JSON for small integers, but is much faster to parse.

In addition to compactness, BSON adds additional data types unavailable in JSON, notably the BinData and Date data types.

EXERCISE

1. Write short note on the following:
   (a) JSON
   (b) Replication
   (c) Embedded Documents
   (d) Indexing
   (e) Replica Set
   (f) Dynamic schemas
2. What do you mean by NoSQL?
3. Explain the difference: RDBMS vs. NoSQL.
4. What are the features of NoSQL?
5. What are the similarities between JSON and XML?
6. What are the different types of NoSQL databases?
7. How to create database in MogoDB?
8. How to insert documents in MongoDB?
9. What is the use of MongoDB _id key field?
10. Define Covered Query in MongoDB.
11. What is the difference between Save and Insert?
12. How to define database schema in MongoDB? Does MongoDB support foreign key elements?
13. Explain the reasons why JSON is useful over other notation types?
14. Name the data types supported by JSON object. Also write syntax to build JSON object.
15. State the difference between SQL and NoSQL.
16. What is MapReduce?
17. Explain different aggregation commands used in MongoDB.
18. Explain in detail about the advantages and features of JSON.
19. What is MongoDB Projection? Explain.
20. What is the difference between Drop database and Drop collection?
21. What are the advantages of MongoDB over SQL?
22. Explain following terms in MongoDB:
    Field, Document, Collection and Database.
23. What is JSON format?
24. What is the difference between Sorting and Indexing?
25. Create a new Database named *newdb*. Now create a collection 'student' and insert following data in it:
    "name": "Yug", "marks": 67
    "name": "Mona", "marks": 77
    "name": "Raj", "marks": 44
    "name": "Uma", "marks": 43
    "name": "Vivek", "marks": 97

(a) Write a query to list documents in a collection.
(b) Write a query to retrieve all students name where marks is less than 50.
(c) Write a query to find document of student with name "Vivek".
(d) Write a query to remove all documents where marks is less than 50.
(e) Write a query to set marks of Yug as 70.

CHAPTER 8

Selecting the Right Database

8.1 INTRODUCTION

The *database* is an organized or structured collection of data which make easy access, manage, retrieve and update of stored data. The *DBMS* manages the interaction between your applications and the underlying database. It assures that the correct data is available for the requested user group when needed.

The major characteristics of the database as follows:

- It uses a digital place on a server to manage and store data.
- It can store all kinds of real-time data.
- It provides data security, a clear and logical view of the process that manipulates data.
- It contains automatic and recovery procedures.
- It helps to reduce the complex relationships between data.
- It helps specified users to view data according to their viewpoints and supports the manipulation and processing of data.

Today in the market various type of database options are available like RDBMS, NoSQL, Big Data, Database Appliance, etc., developers can get very confused with all the choice. They do not understand why they should consider a newer, alternative database when RDBMSs have been around for past 40 years.

Historically, they have worked well, for the times when data structures were much more simple and static. However, as technology and big data applications advanced, the traditional SQL-based relational database was less equipped to handle rapidly expanding data volumes and the growing complexities of data structures. With the rise in data all around the world, businesses and organizations are seeking new methods to manage the flood of data and are drawn toward the alternate database management tools and systems that are different from the traditional relational database systems. In the last decade, the non-relational, NoSQL databases became more popular for offering a more flexible, scalable, cost-efficient, alternative to the traditional SQL-based relational databases.

The popularity of NoSQL databases over the last decade or so has been driven by an explosion of data. Before what's commonly described as 'the big data revolution', relational databases were the norm - these are databases that contain structured data. Structured data can only be structured if it is based on an existing schema that defines the relationships (hence relational) between the data inside the database. However, with the vast quantities of data that are now available to just about every business with an Internet connection, relational databases simply are not equipped to handle the complexity and scale of large datasets. NoSQL databases are designed to work with large distributed data sets. NoSQL databases are highly and flexible, they allow us to store and process unstructured as well as semi-structured data which cannot be easily handled by making use of a relational database system (RDBMS). These databases are basically used for processing big data in real-time web applications.

Cloud computing also rose in popularity, and developers began using public clouds to host their applications and data. They wanted the ability to distribute data across multiple servers and regions to make their applications flexible. Some NoSQL databases like MongoDB provided these capabilities.

MongoDB is a very useful NoSQL database that is being used by some of the biggest corporations in the world. Due to some of the most powerful features of MongoDB, it offers a never before seen set of features to enterprises in order to parse all their unstructured data. Due to its versatile and scalable nature, MongoDB can be used for datasets like social media, videos, and so on. MongoDB clients and users won't feel a need for any other kind of databases.

☞ *Many big enterprises are already using alternative databases and are saving money, innovating more quickly, and completing projects.*

8.2 NEED OF DATABASE

Any organization, be it a Bank, Manufacturing Company, Hospital, University, Trust or a Government Department, large datasets such as weblogs, shopping transactions, email services, manufacturing data from assembly line devices, scientific data collections, etc., requires huge amount of data in some form or the other. All such organizations need to collect data, manipulate them and store them for future use. It will be very difficult for any application to store numerous data for lakhs of its users without a database. Apart from storing data, a database makes it quite easy to modify or update any piece of data with fresh data or delete any existing unnecessary data. A database helps us to easily identify any duplicate set of data or incomplete set of data in database.

A DBMS is a software program that is used to store, handle and manage data values. It uses commands and syntax to load, retrieve or modify existing data from the system.

8.3 TYPES OF DATABASE

Different types of databases available in the market for different purpose depending upon the usage requirements. These are discussed below:

8.3.1 Personal Database

Collecting and storing data on the user's system defines a Personal Database. These databases are small and easily manageable. This database is basically designed for a single user.

8.3.2 End User Database

The end user is usually not concerned about the transaction or operations done at various levels and is only aware of the product which may be a software or an application. Each node acts like a small database in itself, which includes data in presentations, spreadsheets, Word files, downloaded files and Notepad files. All such small databases form a different type of database called the end-user database.

8.3.3 Commercial Database

These are the paid versions of the huge databases designed uniquely for the users who want to access the information for help. These databases are subject specific. Access to such databases is provided through commercial links.

8.3.4 Centralized Database

The information (data) is stored at a centralized location and the users can access this data from different locations. This type of database contains application procedures that help the users to access the data even from a remote location. Various kinds of authentication procedures are applied for the verification and validation of end users, to let users access data securely. Data consistency is maintained in Centralized database as it manages data in a central repository. The size of the centralized database is large, which increases the response time for fetching the data and if any failure occurs, entire data will be lost, which could be a huge loss.

8.3.5 Distributed databases

A distributed database is a single logical database that is spread physically across computers in multiple locations that are connected by a data communications network. In distributed database system, the data is not at one place and is distributed at various sites of an organization.

These sites are connected to each other through communication links which helps them to access the distributed data easily.

8.3.6 Relational Database

Relational Database are table-based. Each table (or relation) consists of rows (records) and columns (fields or attributes), with a unique identifier (key) per row. This makes the user easy to access particular values inside the table structured database. Relational databases a better option for applications that require multi-row transactions such as an accounting system or for legacy systems that were built for a relational structure. The RDBMS databases follow ACID properties (Atomicity, Consistency, Isolation and Durability). Examples of Relational databases are MySQL, Sybase, Microsoft SQL Server, Oracle, etc.

8.3.7 Operational databases

An operational databases creates and updates the database in real-time. Information related to operations of an enterprise is stored inside this database. It is basically designed for executing and handling the daily data operations in several businesses. For example, an organization uses operational databases for managing per day transactions.

8.3.8 Enterprise Databases

Very large organizations and enterprises use this database for managing a huge amount of data. It helps organizations to increase and improve their efficiency. Such a database allows simultaneous access to users. Multi processes are supportable over the Enterprise database. It also allows executing parallel queries on the system.

8.3.9 Data warehouses

It is required by many organizations and government bodies to store all relevant data for several years. These stored data be used for analyzing and retrieving various information and comparing the present year data with past year to determine key trends. All such data, collected over years, is stored in a large data warehouse. It is presumed that these stored data has gone through different kinds of editing, screening and integration, it may not require any more editing or modification.

8.3.10 Cloud Databases

Cloud Databases are the databases which are stored over clouds (also known as virtual environment). Cloud databases can be stored on either in a hybrid cloud, public or private cloud. Cloud-based storage is an excellent cost-saving solution, but requires data to be easily spread across multiple servers to scale up. Some cloud platforms available are Amazon Web Services(AWS), Google Cloud, Microsoft Azure etc.

8.3.11 Object-oriented Databases

The Object Oriented database uses the object-based data model approach for storing data in the database system. The data is represented and stored as objects which are similar to the objects used in the object-oriented programming language. There are various items which are created using object-oriented programming languages like C++, Java etc.

8.3.12 NoSQL Database

No-SQL(Not Only SQL) is a type of database presently used for storing a wide range of data sets mainly of distributed data. A NoSQL database has dynamic schema for unstructured data. Data is stored in many ways which means it can be document-oriented, column-oriented, graph-based or organized as a key-value store. This flexibility means that documents can be created without having defined structure first. Also each document can have its own unique structure. Users can quickly access data from the database through key-value. The NoSQL database follows the Brewers CAP theorem (Consistency, Availability and Partition tolerance). NoSQL database examples include Redis, RavenDB Cassandra, MongoDB, BigTable, HBase, Neo4j and CouchDB.

8.3.13 Graph Databases

A graph database is a database that uses graph structures with nodes, edges, and properties to represent and store data. It is a type of NoSQL database that uses graph theory to store, map and query relationships. Graph databases are mainly used for analyzing interconnections. For example, companies might use a graph database to mine data about customers from social media.

8.4 SELECTION OF RIGHT DATABASE

The two main types of modern databases to choose from are relational and non-relational, also known as SQL or NoSQL (for their query languages). Given the choice of a Relational Database (RDBMS) vs a NoSQL database, it has become more important to select the right type of database for storing data. RDBMS and NoSQL both databases are great in data management and both are used to keep data storage and retrieval optimized and smooth. It's hard to say which technology is better, not all the requirements fit in a NoSQL database or an RDBMS. So developer take decision according requirement and situations. There are a few main differences to be familiar with when deciding which database works best for your needs.

SQL is a common query language used when dealing with an RDBMS. RDBMSs are mainly related to managing, storing, and manipulating structured data where the data format, columns, data type, attributes, and schema are fixed, and the relationship between entities needs to be consistently maintained. Using an RDBMS is a choice for storing transactional data or records where the ACID (Atomicity, Consistency, Isolation, Durability) proprieties of transactions must be provided by an underlying database. An RDBMS is also a choice where the security, integrity and accessibility of data are of utmost importance like for defense, financial applications, and private health information. Typical use cases are financial records, financial transactions, OLTP, ERP, CRM systems, E-commerce applications, etc.

NoSQL (sometimes referred to as Not only SQL, non-SQL or non-relational) is a database that is suitable for managing data that is non-relational, i.e., not structured in tabular format or have fixed data type formats and variables that do not possess tabular relationships. There are various types of NoSQL databases that exist, like key-value, document-based, column-based, and graph-based. When it comes to scalability and performance of unstructured data, NoSQL is the obvious choice. Typical uses cases of NoSQL include data that is largely unstructured and needs flexibility in data models like content management, personalization, web search engines, storing large users profiles from heterogeneous sources, data streams, documents, digital communication such as storing messages and chats, big data, analytics, machine learning, and storing IoT data.

SQL databases are known as relational databases, and have a table-based data structure, with a strict, pre-defined schema required. They depend on defined relations between tables, use indexes to speed up selected queries, and use joins to query multiple tables at once. NoSQL databases, or non-relational databases, can be document-based, graph-databases, key-value pairs, or wide-column stores. NoSQL databases don't require any pre-defined schema, allowing you to work more freely with unstructured data. Relational databases are vertically scalable, but usually more expensive, whereas the horizontal scaling nature of NoSQL databases is more cost-efficient.

If your database schemas are unlikely to change significantly over time, and you want most fields to have consistent types from record to record, then SQL databases would be a good choice for you. Otherwise, NoSQL databases, might be better for your application. NoSQL is a non-relational DBMS, that does not require a fixed schema, avoids joins, and is easy to scale. NoSQL is used for Big data and real-time web apps where they have terabytes of data stored in big data centers. For example, companies like Twitter, Facebook, Google, Amazon collect terabytes of user data every single day. NoSQL is a type of database that can handle and sort all type of unstructured, messy and complicated data.

The concept of NoSQL databases became popular with Google, Facebook, Amazon, etc., who deal with huge volumes of data. The system response time becomes slow when you use RDBMS for such huge volumes of data. To resolve this problem, we could "scale up" our systems by upgrading our existing hardware. This process is expensive. The alternative for this issue is to distribute database load on multiple hosts whenever the load increases. This method is known as "scaling out. "NoSQL database is non-relational, so it scales out better than relational databases as they are designed with web applications in mind.

Relational databases require data to be put into tables and columns to be accessed and analyzed, the various data model capabilities of NoSQL databases make them extremely flexible when it comes to handling data. They can deal with structured, semi-structured, and unstructured data with equal ease, whereas relational databases are extremely rigid, handling primarily structured data. Different data models handle specific application requirements. Developers and architects choose a NoSQL database to more easily handle different lively application development requirements. Popular data models include graph, document, wide-column, and key-value. The idea is to support multiple data models, which allows you to use the same data in different data model types without having to manage a completely different database.

Cost is a consideration with relational databases. They tend to be more expensive to set up and grow. Horizontal scaling, or scaling by adding more servers, is usually both faster and more economical than vertical scaling, which involves adding more resources to a server. However, the structure of relational databases complicates the process. Sharding (where data is horizontally partitioned and distributed across a collection of machines) is necessary to scale out a relational database. Sharding relational databases while maintaining ACID compliance can be a challenge.

There are various factors to be considered while choosing the right database for your application. Your decision will depend on your budget, size of your organization, and what the database will be used for. Some of these factors are discussed here:

8.4.1 Performance

Truly, the speed and performance of your database systems incorporate a wide range of parameters and decisions that are made well before implementation. All database services and capabilities must be assessed and evaluated against requirements to determine the right mix of fault-tolerance, usability and performance for your application or business.

8.4.2 Speed and scalability

Speed addresses the time taken to service all incoming reads and writes to our application. When we consider different databases, some databases are faster at writes and some faster at reads and queries. The number of expected reads and writes from the application is a factor to consider while selecting the correct database.

8.4.3 Structure of data

The structure of the data is very important as it decides how it is stored and retrieved. The way your enterprise requires storage and retrieval of data depends on the structure of the data. The application in enterprise handles data existing in variety of formats. Therefore, choosing the appropriate database must incorporate going for the correct data structures for the purpose of storage and retrieval of data. Incorrect database selection with respect to the our data, our application will take more time to retrieve data from the database, and will also require more development efforts to work around any data issues. SQL databases are perfectly suited for storing and processing structured data, while NoSQL databases are the best solution for working with unstructured or semi-structured data.

8.4.4 Infrastructure and Cost

Following the consideration for present and future data volume requirements, the cost of implementation is also a critical consideration relative to organizational capacity and strategic goal. When comparing databases, it is important to remember that in addition to purchase price, there is a very real cost to any break-down your business suffers because of some defect of the database. Compatibility with existing technology infrastructure needs to be reviewed and aligned prior to software purchase. In the age of cloud infrastructure and software as a service (SaaS), it's critical to decide whether a database software is desktop-based, server-based, or cloud-based. All of these options have pros and cons over each other.

8.4.5 Size of data to be stored

To determine the size of the database, you must estimate how much data you will store. This factor takes care of the quantity of data an enterprise will require for the storage and retrieval purpose. For any enterprise, the amount of data it can store and retrieve might differ based on the combination of the data structure chosen, the capability of the database to distinguish data over various servers and file systems, and vendor-specific optimizations. So we need to choose our database keeping in mind the overall volume of data generated by the application at any specific time and also the size of data to be retrieved from the database. Hence, it's important for organizations to consider not only the present requirements for the volume of data but also the prospect and rate of data increase over the short-term and long-term.

8.4.6 Accessibility of data

The number of people or users simultaneously accessing the database and the level of computation involved in accessing any specific data are also important factors to consider while choosing the right database. Multi-threading is important feature to look for when assessing database performance and scalability. Multi-threading enables a database server to perform multiple operations at exactly the same time and is essential for most applications with multiple users or any application expected to grow to support a multiple users over time. Not only this the level of computation involved in accessing any specific data are also important factors to consider while choosing the right database. If the database chosen is not good enough to handle large loads it may adversely affect the processing speed of the application.

8.4.7 Frequency of accessing data

Business productivity is largely dependent on the user-friendliness of a software. It's important to understand the mode of accessing a database. This is why, while selecting a database software, there is a need to evaluate the mode, speed, and frequency of accessing the database with respect to business needs and requirements that are relative to the capacity of the software. It's important to pay attention to how the software is used with respect to user concurrency, which is a factor that represents the number of users that can connect to the database software at the same time. The ability of the users to learn the application part of database software may also be considered, especially for organizations with low training costs.

8.4.8 Safety and security of data

As database stores all user data, a database should be well-protected. That is why attention needs to be taken to ensure that security features are available in the software that guarantees user access control, data integrity, as well as backup and recovery functionalities as applicable to business goals and requirements. In addition to the above aspects, it is also necessary that your enterprise check for the level of security provided to the data stored into it by a particular database. In case where the data to be stored is highly confidential, we need to have a highly secured database. The safety measures implemented by the database in case of any system crash or failure is quite a significant factor to keep in mind while choosing a database.

Relational databases are capable to handle highly structured data. Moreover, it also offers a great support for ACID (Atomicity, Consistency, Isolation, and Durability) based transactions. ACID-compliant relational databases are more secure than non-relational databases. These kinds of databases are proficient at handling structured data but they found some difficulty with unstructured data. So you need to take additional steps to secure your NoSQL database.

The complex systems of today require multiple database engines to provide efficient solutions that a single engine of yesterday cannot. The major database vendors are adding cross-functionality support (relational and non-relational features) to their products in response to the needs of their customers.

8.5. TYPES OF NoSQL DATABASES

NoSQL Database is a database implementation method used for stacking, managing and fetching the data from the relational databases that are structured in any model, but not in the typical tabular formatted relationship model. These types of databases are also known as 'Not only SQL', 'non-SQL' or 'non-relational' databases, as it also allows and supports SQL programming languages. The NoSQL databases are progressively applied to big data applications, as well as many other web-based applications.

There are mainly four categories of NoSQL databases. Each of these categories has its unique attributes and limitations. No specific database is better to solve all problems. You should select a database based on your product needs.

- Key-value Pair Based
- Column-oriented Graph
- Graphs based
- Document-oriented

8.5.1 Key-value Pair Based

Data is stored in key/value pairs. It is designed in such a way to handle lots of data and heavy load. This kind of NoSQL database is used as a collection, dictionaries, associative arrays, etc. Key value stores help the developer to store schema-less data. These databases perform efficiently and show high scalability for caching in web applications and session management. They work best for shopping cart contents.

8.5.2 Column-oriented Graph

Column-oriented databases work on columns instead of rows. Every column is treated separately. Values of single column databases are stored contiguously. They can query large data sets faster than other conventional databases. They deliver high performance on aggregation queries like SUM, COUNT, AVG, MIN etc., as the data is readily available in a column. Column-based NoSQL databases are widely used to manage data warehouses, business intelligence, CRM (Customer Relationship Management), Library card catalogs, fraud detection, and recommendation engines.

8.5.3 Graphs based

A graph type database stores entities as well as the relations amongst those entities. Graph based database mostly used for social networks, logistics, spatial data, customer relationship or reservation systems management.

8.5.4 Document-oriented

These databases store semi-structured data and their descriptions in document format. They do not refer to master schema for creating and updating programs. Their usage has increased with the use of JavaScript and JSON (JavaScript Object Notation). These are used for mobile application data handling and content management.

Why should we use NoSQL Database?

- **Analytics**: NoSQL database is suitable for doing analytical queries. Querying language used for atomic queries can also be used for analytical queries.

- **Dynamic Schemas**: In NoSQL schema definition is not required, this solves the problem to modify the schema where a table is already present with huge datasets and new columns need to be added to the same table. RDBMS is not able to handle unstructured data.
- **Sharding**: Sharding means partitioning data into smaller databases to have faster access to data. This feature is present in NoSQL databases which allow us to fetch data from a server very quickly.
- **Scaling**: NoSQL databases scale out horizontally, when they grow. Data is divided and balanced among multiple nodes in a cluster and by default, aggregate queries are divided. Thus, they are cheaper to manage. RDBMS systems are not optimized for horizontal scaling out.
- **Redundancy**: The database is designed while keeping redundancy in concern. The database is designed to handle hardware failure instead of treating them. The problem of hardware failure is handled during the time of development.
- **Flexibility**: NoSQL offers flexibility to store structured, semi-structured or unstructured data, unlike a relational database which allows only structured data. Due to this huge flexibility in storing the data in NoSQL increases the performance in the NoSQL database.
- **Rapid Development**: NoSQL database can be customized by the user as per the need. The database provides an easy way to change the way data is stored or change the queries that are running.
- **Data storing**: A NoSQL database makes the most of cloud computing and storage. Cloud-based storage is an excellent cost-saving solution. It requires data to be easily spread across multiple servers to scale up.

8.6 SQL vs. NoSQL

Relational databases are efficient systems, which makes them a common choice for storing financial records, logistical information, personnel data, and other information in new databases. Because they are easier to understand and use than NoSQL databases, relational databases also frequently replace legacy hierarchical databases and network databases. Relational databases have the following properties:

- Values are atomic.
- All of the values in a column have the same data type.
- Each row is unique.
- Each column has a unique name.
- Integrity constraints maintain data consistency across multiple tables.
- Transactions with ACID properties - Atomicity, Consistency, Isolation & Durability.
- Adherence to Strong Schema of data being written/read.
- Execution of complex queries involving join and group by clauses.

NoSQL is a schema-less alternative to SQL and RDBMSs designed to store, process, and analyze extremely large amounts of unstructured data. In NoSQL databases, the principles of ACID (atomicity, consistency, isolation, and durability) are reduced. In addition, the process of normalization is not mandatory in NoSQL. Due to the size and speed of modern data, it is preferable for NoSQL databases to be de-normalized. NoSQL databases have the following properties:

- They have higher scalability i.e., it provides fast performance and horizontal scalability.
- NoSQL databases don't need a dedicated high-performance server. They use distributed computing.
- They are cost effective.

- They support flexible schema which can easily be altered without downtime or service disruption.
- They are able to process structured, semi-structured, and unstructured data with equal effect.
- No single point of failure.
- Never provide tables with flat fixed-column records. Also, There are no complex relationships such as the ones between tables in an RDBMS.
- It can serve as the primary data source for online applications.
- Handles big data which manages data velocity, variety, volume, and complexity.
- The operations of NoSQL are faster than relational databases due to the use of different data structures.
- In-memory caching option is available to increase the performance of queries.

Choosing between a NoSQL and a Relational database is depends on company's particular needs. And there may be situations for which you might want to use both types, as they can often complement each other. Most importantly, we need to select the database that supports the right structure, size, and speed to meet the needs of our application. If you deal with a lot of data types, and you need to build powerful web and cloud applications for a distributed and quickly growing user base, then you will need your database to be multi-model, flexible, easily scalable, distributed, and always on, which means you will use NoSQL.

SQL is one of the most versatile and widely-used options available which makes it a safe choice especially for great complex queries. But from other side it can be restrictive. SQL requires you to use pre-defined schemas to determine the structure of your data before you work with it. Also all of your data must follow the same structure.

Relational database engines do ACID (Atomicity, Consistency, Isolation, and Durability) very well. ACID compliance reduces anomalies and protects the integrity of your database by prescribing exactly how transactions interact with the database. Generally, NoSQL databases sacrifice ACID compliance for flexibility and processing speed, but for many e-commerce and financial applications, an ACID-compliant database remains the preferred option. NoSQL engines use BASE (Basic Availability, Soft-state, and Eventual consistency) to achieve the performance offered through horizontal scaling, high availability, and fault tolerance.

Let's compare the two types of databases on the following set of parameters.

(a) Scaling

RDBMSs scale vertically.

- Architecture design runs well on a single machine.
- To handle larger volumes of operations, it is better to upgrade the machine with a faster processor or more memory.
- There is a limitation to the level of scaling.

NoSQL databases scale horizontally

- NoSQL databases are intended to run on clusters of comparatively low-specification servers.
- To handle more data, more servers need to be added to the cluster.
- These databases are calibrated to operate with full throttle even with low cost hardware.
- It's a relatively cheaper approach to handle increased number of operations and can handle high volumes of data.

(b) Maintenance

RDBMSs are high maintenance databases.

- Maintaining high-end RDBMS systems is expensive and requires a trained workforce for database management.

NoSQL databases are low maintenance databases.

- These databases require minimal management and they offer many features.
- These include automatic repair, easier data distribution and simpler data models.

(c) Data model

RDBMSs have a rigid data model.

- RDBMSs require data in a structured format as per a defined data model.

NoSQL databases are based on a no schema data model.

- A NoSQL database is schemaless; so data can be inserted into it with ease, even without any pre-defined schema.
- The format or data model can be changed anytime, without application disruption.

8.7 ACID vs BASE

Before any database selection the first stage is to determine if you really need a NoSQL Database or a RDBMS already being used in your organization will fulfill. Understanding ACID vs BASE properties shall help you in this decision.

A *transaction* describes a sequence of operations performed by a transaction-processing system (e.g., database) as a single logical unit of work.

ACID is an acronym to describe database transaction properties, and includes Atomicity, Consistency, Isolation, and Durability. RDBMS are generally very focused on providing strong consistency and ACID transactions, tremendous functionality, stability, and strong reliability and robustness guarantees. They are also very well-suiting for complex querying and non-real time analytics applications. RDBMS is characterized by ACID properties which are as follows:

- **Atomicity**: It means each task in a transaction succeeds or the entire transaction is rolled back. Atomicity indicates that a transaction is all or nothing, which means that any failure in a transaction causes the entire transaction to fail and therefore leaves the database unchanged.
- **Consistency**: It means a transaction maintains a valid state for the database before and after its completion and cannot leave the database in an inconsistent state. Consistency ensures that all transactions result in a valid state of the database, and that all validation rules and constraints are met, and required actions are carried out.
- **Isolation**: It means a transaction not yet committed must not interfere with another transaction and must remain isolated. Isolation means that the database is able to perform concurrent transactions that result in the same database state as if the transactions had occurred one after the other.
- **Durability**: It means committed transactions persist in the database and can be recovered in case of database failure. Durability ensures that a committed transaction persists, or is permanently stored under any and all conditions.

BASE is an acronym used to describe eventually consistent services, and stands for Basically Available, Soft state, Eventual consistency. The alternative to ACID is BASE which is what NoSQL databases follow. The BASE systems allow horizontal scaling, fault tolerance and high availability at the cost of consistency. So, if your application requires high availability and scalability, a NoSQL Database built on BASE properties might be suitable. The NoSQL is characterized by BASE properties which are as follows:

- **Basically Available**: It means the system is guaranteed to be available in event of failure i.e., any data request should receive a response, but that response may indicate a failure or changing state as opposed to the requested data.
- **Soft State**: It means the state of the data could change without application interactions due to eventual consistency i.e., given eventual consistency, the system may be in a changing state until consistency is reached.

- **Eventual Consistency**: It means system will be eventually consistent after the application input. The data will be replicated to different nodes and will eventually reach a consistent state. But the consistency is not guaranteed at a transaction level i.e., the system will continue to serve requests without checking the consistency of previous transactions.

8.8 CAP Theorem

SQL databases follow ACID properties (Atomicity, Consistency, Isolation and Durability) whereas the NoSQL database follows the Brewers CAP theorem (Consistency, Availability and Partition tolerance). CAP theorem is also called brewer's theorem.

- **Consistency**: Consistency means, if you write data to the distributed system, you should be able to read the same data at any point in time from any nodes of the system. It means all replicas contain the same version of data. Client always has the same view of the data no matter what node it is. For example, after updating the order status, all the clients should be able to see the same data.
- **Availability**: Availability means the system should always perform reads/writes on any non-failing node of the cluster successfully without any error. The database should always be available (System remains operational) and responsive (All clients can always read and write). It should not have any downtime.
- **Partition Tolerance**: Partition Tolerance means that the system should continue to function even if the communication among the servers is not stable i.e., if part of the system fails, it is possible for the system as a whole to continue functioning.

REVIEW QUESTIONS WITH ANSWERS

1. Multiple Choice Questions

1. NoSQL is designed to support:
   a. High performance
   b. Big table
   c. Graph databases
   d. All of the above
2. Feature(s) of NoSQL:
   a. Using NoSQL, we can store the large amount of structured, semi-structured, and unstructured data.
   b. It has a scale-out architecture.
   c. It can be easily accessed.
   d. All of the above
3. MongoDB is known as best NoSQL database:
   a. Document Oriented
   b. High Performance
   c. Easily Scalable
   d. All of the above
4. Which of the following statement(s) is true about Centralized Database:
   a. The size of the centralized database is large, which increases the response time for fetching the data.
   b. It is not easy to update such an extensive database system.
   c. If any server failure occurs, entire data will be lost, which could be a huge loss.
   d. All of the above
5. Data is not lost even at the time of server failure:
   a. Atomicity
   b. Consistency
   c. Isolation
   d. Durability
6. Which of the following are the simplest NoSQL databases?
   a. Key-value b. Wide-column
   c. Document d. All of the above
7. Example(s) of NoSQL databases:
   a. Neo4j b. Cassandra
   c. Redis d. All of the above
8. ________ stores are used to store information about networks, such as social connections.
   a. Key-value b. Wide-column

c. Document d. Graph

9. Example(s) of Relational database:
   a. MySQL b. PostgreSQL
   c. SQL Server d. All of the above
10. NoSQL databases is used mainly for handling large volumes of ________ data.
   a. Unstructured b. Structured
   c. Semi-structured d. All of the above
11. The BASE systems allow:
   a. Horizontal scaling
   b. Fault tolerance
   c. High availability
   d. All of the above

2. State True or False for the following:

1. RDBMS uses various tables for storing data and relationships.
2. Replication takes the same data and copies it over multiple nodes.
3. Sharding puts different data on different nodes.
4. NoSQL provides an alternative to ACID called BASE.
5. BASE means Basic Availability Soft state Eventual consistency.
6. Non Relational databases require that schemas be defined before you can add data.
7. MongoDB is an a typical choice for unstructured data storage.
8. NoSQL stands for "Not Only SQL".
9. Relational databases use Structured Query Language (SQL) - a standard user application that provides an easy programming interface for database interaction.
10. In Distributed Database one server failure will not affect the entire data set.
11. Modular development is possible in a distributed database, i.e., the system can be expanded by including new computers and connecting them to the distributed system.
12. The vast majority of NoSQL technologies are ACID compliant.
13. CAP stands for Consistency, Availability and Partition Tolerance.
14. Partition Tolerance means that the system should continue to function even if the communication among the servers is not stable.

3. Match the following:

1. CAP theorem	a. BASE
2. NoSQL	b. ACID
3. RDBMS	c. Eric Brewer
4. Relational database	d. A stand-alone JavaScript Object
5. JSON	e. Library in a college
6. Centralized database	f. Oracle Database
7. Throughput	g. Single user
8. Consistency	h. Overall capability to process data
9. Atomicity	i. Same data at the same time
10. Personal Database	j. Ensures all-or-none rule

4. Fill in the blanks:

1. NoSQL databases are built to allow the insertion of data without a pre-defined ________.
2. MongoDB is a _______ database.
3. MongoDB database are _______ than SQL databases.
4. _______ is a highly scalable, flexible, and distributed NoSQL database.
5. A _________ system is a network that stores data on more than one node (physical or virtual machines) at the same time.
6. _________ databases are capable to handle highly structured data.
7. ________ stands for Basically Available Soft state Eventual consistency.
8. The properties of a transaction are termed ________ properties.
9. _________ gives us a guarantee that there will be a response for every request made to the system about whether it was successful or not.

10. ________ is the quality of NoSQL database management system which states that the system will work even if a part of the system has failed or is not working.

Answers

1. 1. d 2. d 3. d 4. d 5. d 6. a 7. d 8. d 9. d 10. a 11. d
2. 1. T 2. T 3. T 4. T 5. T 6. F 7. T 8. T 9. T 10. T 11. T 12. F 13. T 14. T
3. 1. c 2. a 3. b 4. f 5. d 6. e 7. h 8. i 9. j 10. g
4. 1. Schema 2. NoSQL 3. Faster 4. MongoDB 5. Distributed 6. Relational 7. BASE 8. ACID 9. Availability 10. Partition tolerance

Short Answers Questions

1. Write short note on Relational Database.

Ans Relational Database are table-based. Each table (or relation) consists of rows (records) and columns (fields or attributes), with a unique identifier (key) per row. This makes the user easy to access particular values inside the table structured database. Relational databases a better option for applications that require multi-row transactions such as an accounting system or for legacy systems that were built for a relational structure. The RDBMS databases follow ACID properties (Atomicity, Consistency, Isolation and Durability). Examples of Relational databases are MySQL, Sybase, Microsoft SQL Server, Oracle, etc.

2. What is the structure of the data?

Ans The data structure will dictate how it is stored and retrieved. As most apps deal with data in a variety of formats, the process of selecting the database should include the appropriate data structures for storing and retrieving the data.

3. What is a distributed database?

Ans A distributed database is a collection of multiple interconnected databases that are spread physically across various locations.

4. What is a database partitioning? What is its need?

Ans Database partitioning is a process where a logical database is divided into distinct independent parts. Partitioning is a powerful functionality that increases performance with decreased cost. It enhances the manageability and improves the availability of data.

5. Explain why volume of data is important for selecting right database?

Ans To determine the size of the database, you must estimate how much data you will store. The quantity of data need to store and retrieve as critical application data is very important factor while choose the right database. Different database management systems contain a different volume of records that can be stored and processed. Hence, it's important for organizations to consider not only the present requirements for the volume of data but also the prospect and rate of data increase over the short-term and long-term.

6. Define ACID Properties of database.

Ans ACID Properties of database are:

(a) Atomicity: It ensures all-or-none rule for database modifications.

(b) Consistency: Data values are consistent across the database.

(c) Isolation: Two transactions are said to be independent of one another.

(d) Durability: Data is not lost even at the time of server failure.

7. What do you mean by the term "Eventual consistency" in BASE?

Ans The term "Eventual consistency" in BASE means to have copies of data on multiple machines to get high availability and scalability.

8. Explain difference between scaling horizontally and vertically for databases.

Ans Horizontal scaling means that you scale by adding more machines into your pool of resources whereas Vertical scaling means that you scale by adding more power (CPU, RAM) to an existing machine. Examples of horizontal scaling are Cassandra, MongoDB, Google Cloud Spanner and a example of vertical scaling is MySQL - Amazon RDS (cloud version of MySQL).

9. Write one advantage and one disadvantage of Centralized Database.

Ans Advantage of Centralized Database

Data consistency is maintained as it manages data in a central repository.

Disadvantage of Centralized Database

If any server failure occurs, entire data will be lost, which could be a huge loss.

10. How Distributed database is different from Centralized database?

Ans Centralized Database stores data at a centralized database system and users to access the stored data from different locations through several applications. Unlike a centralized database system, in distributed systems, data is distributed among different database systems of an organization and users access the data via communication links.

11. What is the need of Data warehouses?

Ans Data warehouses enable organizations to collect, store, and analyze the data in large data warehouses over a number of years. Data analysis is performed on the data to make strategic business decisions for organizations.

12. What is the need of End-user databases?

Ans End-user databases is used for businesses with workstations that act like a small database in itself.

13. Write short note on No-SQL.

Ans No-SQL(Not Only SQL) is a type of database presently used for storing a wide range of data sets mainly of distributed data. A NoSQL database has dynamic schema for unstructured data. Data is stored in many ways which means it can be document-oriented, column-oriented, graph-based or organized as a key-value store. This flexibility means that documents can be created without having defined structure first. Also each document can have its own unique structure. Users can quickly access data from the database through key-value. The NoSQL database follows the Brewers CAP theorem (Consistency, Availability and Partition tolerance). NoSQL database examples include Redis, RavenDB Cassandra, MongoDB, BigTable, HBase, Neo4j and CouchDB.

14. Define BASE properties of Database.

Ans BASE properties of Database are:

(a) Basically Available: It means the system is guaranteed to be available in event of failure.

(b) Soft State: It means the state of the data could change without application interactions due to eventual consistency.

(c) Eventual Consistency: It means system will be eventually consistent after the application input. The data will be replicated to different nodes and will eventually reach a consistent state. But the consistency is not guaranteed at a transaction level.

15. What do you mean by Isolation?

Ans Isolation means that unfinished transactions remain isolated. It ensures that all transactions are processed securely and independently.

16. What do you mean by Durability?

Ans Durability means that the data is saved by the system even if the transaction fails.

17. Explain the term Consistency.

Ans Consistency means that only valid data that follows all rules can be written in the database. If input data is invalid the database returns to its state before the transaction. This ensures that illegal transactions can not corrupt the database.

18. Write short note on MySQL.

Ans MySQL is one of the most popular relational database management system created in 1995 and now managed by Oracle. This open-source database system has a huge user base and great support, and it works well with most libraries and frameworks.

19. Explain CAP Theorem.

Ans CAP stands for Consistency, Availability and Partition Tolerance. *Consistency* means, if you write data to the distributed system, you should be able to read the same data at any point in time from any nodes of the system or simply return an error if data is in an inconsistent state. Never return inconsistent data.

Availability means the system should always perform reads/writes on any non-failing node of the cluster successfully without any error.

Partition Tolerance means, if there is a partition between nodes or the parts of the cluster in a distributed system are not able to talk to each other, the system should still be functioning.

20. What is SQL?

Ans SQL (Structured Query Language) is a programming language used to communicate with data stored in databases. SQL language is relatively easy to write, read, and interpret.

21. Write drawback of Relational databases.

Ans Drawback of Relational databases are:

(a) It is expensive to set up and maintain.

(b) It require data in a structured format as per a defined data model.

22. Write drawback of non-relational databases.

Ans Drawback of non-relational databases are:

(a) ACID transactions are not supported by non-relational databases.

(b) Not all non-relational databases are good at automating the process of sharding, or spreading the database across multiple nodes.

EXERCISE

1. Write short note on the following:
   (a) ACID
   (b) BASE
   (c) Key-value stores
   (d) Operational database
   (e) Data warehouses
   (f) End user databases
2. What is NoSQL?
3. What do you understand by NoSQL in databases?
4. What is CAP theorem? How is it applicable to NoSQL systems?
5. Write down the differences between NoSQL and RDBMS.
6. Differentiate between ACID and BASE w.r.t. SQL and NoSQL databases.
7. Why volume of data to be stored is an important factor in selecting database?
8. Enlist differences between SQL and NoSQL databases.
9. Explain how the number of simultaneous users affects the database selection.
10. What are key considerations while choosing a database?
11. How database security is an important while choosing database?
12. Write any two drawbacks of relational databases.
13. What do you mean by document-oriented database?
14. What are various factors to consider while selecting the correct database?
15. What do you mean by DBMS?
16. What is a transaction? What are ACID properties?
17. How Relational is different from Non Relation Databases?
18. What are various types of Non-Relational databases? Explain.
19. Why database is needed?
20. What are advantages of NoSQL databases?

APPENDIX

System Design

A.1 DESIGN ELEMENTS

A system designer must consider the following factors while designing a system.

(a) **Data Flow:** The movement of data into, around and out of the system.

(b) **Data Stores:** Temporary or permanent collections of data.

(c) **Process:** Activities to accept, manipulate and deliver data and information which may be manual or computer-based.

(d) **Procedures:** Methods and routines for using the designed system is to achieve the intended results.

(e) **Controls:** Standards and guidelines for determining whether activities are occurring in the anticipated or accepted manner, that is "under control." Also they specify actions to take when problems or unexpected circumstances are detected. It may include the reporting of exceptions or procedures for correcting errors.

A.2 FILES

Computer programs are stored in computer files. Computer program files include:

(a) Source-language programs that are stored in the original programming language.

(b) Object programs that have been translated into machine language.

A.2.1 Specialized files

A commercial computer centre maintains a number of specialized files. Some of them are as under:

(a) Index files that help a computer system find information in other files.

(b) Data dictionaries store information that would be found in other documents.

(c) History files that consolidate transaction files into month-to-date and year-to-date files.

(d) Log files that maintain information about the jobs run at the computer centre.

A.2.2 File Processing

File Processing involves the following:

(a) **Updation of file:** Updation is the process of modifying a master file with current information according to a specified procedure.

(b) **Searching a file:** Searching is a function or mode that enables the user to locate a record in a sequential file. In this type of file, the search is made sequentially i.e. one after the other to locate a particular record. For example, a program might be asked to search for the record No. 15 containing the information about an employee.

(c) **Insertion in the file:** Insertion is the process of adding data or text or record in a file at the indicated location. A record is inserted in a sequential file at the end of the file. The file is then sorted or rearranged in a particular order, either ascending or descending. Inserting record in a sequential file is quite a cumbersome process.

A.2.3 Design of Files

The design of files includes decisions about the nature and contents of the file itself such as whether it is to be used for storing transaction details, historical data, or reference information. Among the decisions made during file design are the following:

(a) Which data items to include in a record format within the file?
(b) Length of each record, based on the characteristics of the data items on which it is based.
(c) The sequencing or arrangement of records within the file namely storage structure such as sequential, indexed or direct access files.

In some cases, master file may already exist because it is used in other existing applications. A new application may need to reference only the existing master file. In such cases, the details of the file are included in the application design specifications but the file itself may not be designed.

A.3 FORM DESIGN

Online systems include a dialogue or conversation between the user and the system. Users request system services through the dialogue and tell the system when to perform a certain function. The nature of online conversations often make the difference between a successful and unacceptable design.

The arrangement of messages and comments in online conversations, as well as the placement of data, headings and titles on display screens or source documents, is also part of input design. Sketches of each are generally prepared to communicate the arrangement to users for their review and other members of the system design team.

A form must be justified by assessing the following means:

(a) to obtain information most efficiently,
(b) to disseminate information efficiently, and
(c) to store information.

A.3.1 Design Stages

The stages for forms design are summarized as follows:

(a) Define objective of the form.
(b) Specify its data contents.
(c) Decide upon quantity required and likely methods of production.
(d) Using a guide sheet, enter title, enter form reference number, indicate position of any specially located material.
(f) Review with the user; revise using new guide sheet, if necessary.
(g) Produce fair specimen.
(h) Consider limited production run and field test.
(i) Revise as necessary.

A.3.2 Contents and Layout

Simple appearances of forms are important. Forms which look complicated and time-consuming to complete, or are unattractive to the eyes, are not likely to do the job they are intended to do. Words and phrases which may be familiar to the designer may be misunderstood by the user—so explanatory notes may be necessary.

☞ *Avoid using officious sounding words. A little politeness does get the response better. For example, use the words 'Please complete part B'... instead of, 'You must complete part B......'.*

A form produced by a computer line-printer has to be designed not only to convey information in a clear and unambiguous way to the recipient but also to facilitate its production on the line printer and other ancillary equipment. Increasingly, the user's interest is being regarded as paramount. Because, it is useless to process incorrect input data efficiently or producing confusing output information. The entries on a form should provide a logical sequence—bringing together related material. The flow should be left to right and from top to bottom. Grouping of information by the use of panels or blocks is helpful.

Stripping or shading is effective for highlighting parts of a form—but it may add to the cost of printing.

The form title should be as simple as possible—and the word 'form' should be avoided if possible. Instead use note, report, list, analysis, application, or some such meaningful word.

Care has to be taken over the allocation of space to headings describing data or information entries. A balance has to be struck between space needed by a heading and that needed for the actual entry; the amount of space should be determined by the entry requirements, not by the heading. (See Figure A.1)

Name	
Address	
Occupation	

(a) Too much space allowed for heading

Name
Address
Occupation

(b) Preferable alternative

Figure A.1 Space adjustment for column headings

A.3.3 Selecting a Choice

There are a number of ways in which selection or marking of choice can be dealt with. A few examples are shown in Figure A.1 and A.2.

It is preferable to stick to one method of indicating choice, otherwise the form appears confusing like the form given in Figure A.3.

The constraints of the output device will obviously limit the size of the form. Although line-printers are the most common type of output device employed, there are, in fact numerous alternatives. The choice between them depends on the following factors:

(a) The response time demanded by the system.
(b) What quality of output is required?
(c) What peripherals exist or can be obtained?
(d) Whether a hard copy record is desirable.
(e) Whether the system is integrated or not.
(f) The effective cost.

The analyst must give some thought to the presentation of information on the format and to the editing facilities needed in the programs.

A.4 DATA VALIDATION

A system designer should presume that mistakes will be made in entering data or in requesting the performance of certain functions. Some mistakes are very minor and not of great consequence. But others can be so serious that they could result in erasure of data or improper use of the system. Even if there is only a slight chance that a serious error will occur, a good information system design will offer the means for detecting and handling the error. The input controls provide ways for the following eventualities.

(a) To ensure that only authorized users access the system.
(b) To guarantee that transactions are acceptable.
(c) To validate the data for accuracy.
(d) To determine whether any necessary data have been omitted.

Data checking is an operation used to verify data quality or data integrity. There are the following three types of checks that can be preformed on the input data. These are:

(a) Validation checks
(b) Checks for the accuracy of data
(c) Confirming the relevance of data

A.4.1 Validation Checks

The term validation here means whether the input data is within the range of its value. For example, if an examiner awards marks out of a maximum of 100, then the marks awarded by him can not exceed 100. So if the marks input for that particular examiner is more than 100, they are invalid. Therefore, validation of data is important and it is the main function of the data management system to confirm that the entered data are within the valid limits. Following are some of the checks that may be carried out for validating data.

Colour preference (ring the one you like most)				
Black	Blue	red	Green	Brown

Colour preference (insert × in the appropriate box)

Black	Blue	red	Green	Brown
			×	

Figure A.2 Colour preference choice

Insert a cross if you are seeking special discount
We do/do not* purchase widgets from another supplier
* Delete as necessary
What is the name of your agent?
Circle the number of retail outlets you have

1 2 3 4 5

Figure A.3 Form for making a choice

Presence Check

The validation program checks that all mandatory items of data are present. For example, the customer account number could not be omitted on a sales order.

Character Count

Some items such as a customer code or product code are of fixed length, say 8 characters. The input is checked for the exact number of characters.

Picture Check

This check ensures that certain fields are in the correct format, for example 4 characters followed by 5 digits.

Range Check

This checks that a field lies within a particular range—for example week number must be between 1 and 53.

Check Digit Checks

Code numbers such as customer number, employee number or product number are often lengthy and prone to errors when being keyed in. One way of preventing these errors is to add an extra digit to the end of a code number, which has been calculated from the digits of the code number. In this way the code number with its extra check digit is self-checking. One of the methods of calculating check digits is the modulus-11 method. This method is able to detect 99% of the errors. The calculation of the check digit is done using the following steps:

(a) Each digit of the code number is assigned a weight. The right hand (least significant) digit is given a weight of 2. The next digit is given a weight 3 and so on.

(b) Each digit is multiplied by its weight and the products added together.

(c) The sum of the products is divided by 11 and the remainder obtained.

(d) The remainder is subtracted from 11 to give the check digit. If the remainder is 0 then the check digit is 0.

For example, to calculate the check digit for the number 1578, we do the calculations for the check digit as follows:

Original code ***1 5 7 8***

Weight for each position of the digit	5	4	3	2	
Multiply each digit by its weight	1×5 = 5	5×4 = 20	7×3 = 21	8×2 = 16	
Add products together	5 +	20 +	21 +	16	= 62

Divide the total 62 by 11 giving the remainder as 7.

Subtract the remainder 7 from 11 that is 11 – 7 = 4

Hence the check digit = 4. Therefore the complete code number including the check digit is 15784

A.4.2 Accuracy of Data

The entered data needs to be within the prescribed limit of accuracy. For example, if the entry of the number of persons appeared in an examination is say 20.5. Then such data are not accurate because the number of persons appearing in an examination can not be in the fractions. Similarly, if you are measuring the total price of gold sold to an accuracy of say rupee, then it may be important to measure the quantity of gold to an accuracy of third decimal place. It means, you have to measure the weight of gold as 3.145 kilograms and not as 3.1 kilograms.

A.4.3 Relevance of Data

The data entered in the information systems should be relevant to the output desired. The term GIGO (Garbage In Garbage Out) often used in information system emphasize the fact that if you input wrong data, the results will also be wrong.

A.5 OUTPUT DESIGN

While designing the output one should try to accomplish the following:

(a) Determine what information to present?

(b) Decide whether to display or print the information and accordingly select the output medium.

(c) Arrange the presentation of information in an acceptable format.

(d) Decide how to distribute the output to intended recipients.

The arrangement of information on a monitor screen or printed on a printer is termed as *layout*. Accomplishing the general activities listed above will require specific decisions, such as whether to use preprinted forms when preparing reports and documents, how many lines to be printed on a page, or whether to use graphics. The output design is specified on layout forms, sheets that describe the location characteristics (such as length and type) and format of the column headings and pagination.

Outputs can be categorize as follows:

(a) **External outputs:** These go outside the organization (e.g. invoices, orders, tax returns) and therefore call for special attention as they may directly affect the organization's business relations with its customers.

(b) **Internal outputs:** These remain within the organization but still require careful consideration because they may affect the operational efficiency of the total system.

(c) **Computer operations output:** These are required within the computer services department (e.g. usage statistics, control reports, etc.)

The output of a computer system is the primary contact between the system and most users. The quality of this output and its usefulness determines whether the system will be used, so it is essential to have the best possible output.

A.6 REPORT GENERATION

Files that are maintained by computer must be printed or displayed in order to be accessed by users. *Output* that is displayed on a screen is used for answering inquiries about the status of the file. *Printed reports*, on the other hand, are formal documents that provide users with the information they need to perform their jobs effectively. Because computer produces displays and prints reports that are to be read by people, therefore, they must be clear, neat and easy to understand. Where quickness and efficiency are the overriding considerations for designing disk and tape files, but clarity is the primary concern when designing displayed output and printed reports.

Several features must be considered while designing and preparing reports. These are described in the following sections.

A.6.1 Titles

Title, which supplies the report name, date, page number and field designations is essential for a clear and meaningful presentation of printed information.

Different types of Report Titles

Printed reports fall into three major categories.

(a) Transaction Reports

(b) Exception Reports

(c) Summary Reports

Transaction Reports These are the reports that include, specific output for each input record read. Customer bills generated from a master accounts receivable file would be an example of a detail report. Each input record results in one or more lines of output. Similarly, payroll cheques generated from a master payroll file would be a detail report. Finally, a listing of each part number stocked by a company would be a detail report. Detail output is produced when individualized output such as bills or cheques are needed.

Exception Reports Sometimes users ask for detail reports when in fact other types of output would be more appropriate. Suppose an insurance agent has requested a listing of all clients and their last payment date. When asked by a systems analyst why the detail report is necessary, he or she responds that he or she wants to contact all clients who have not made a payment within the last 90 days. An experienced computer professional would suggest an alternative type of output, one that lists only those clients who meet the criterion the insurance agent has set. This means, the listing of only those clients who have not made a payment within 90 days would save the time and effort necessary to print out all clients, but more importantly it would make the insurance agent's job easier. Rather than having to shift through numerous pages of a listing, the agent would have a list of only those people to be contacted. This type of output is called an *exception* report, which is a listing of individual records that meet (or fail to meet) certain criteria. Other examples of exception reports are a list of employees who are 65 or over and a list of part numbers in stock with a quantity on hand below some minimum value.

Summary Reports A summary report summarizes rather than itemizes. If summaries or totals should be generated rather than detail reports if they can serve the user's purpose.

Detail reports take a long time to generate. They tend to be voluminous and they often require some summarizing anyway before they are meaningful to users or managers. Illustration shown in Figure A.4 gives the summary of Payroll report department wise for different employees.

A.6.2 Subtitles

The reports may contain subtitles dealing with each aspect of the information in a clear manner. Figure A.5 shows the user training list containing several subheadings. For example, Notification, Functions, Forms, Equipment etc. are the subheadings to make the report more clear.

A.6.3 Date

Figure A.5 indicates the date of the generation of the report. The date clarifies as to the origination period for more clarification to the user of the reports.

☞ *Exception reports are produced by testing input records to see if they meet specified conditions. Some summary reports are produced by adding input data to total fields and simply printing those totals.*

A.6.4 Page Number

For the completeness of a report, it should be numbered on every page so that the recipient can come to know that all the information contained in the report is received by him. Page number also helps the user to quickly refer to any paragraph in the report for clarification.

A.6.5 Summary

A report containing a summary will be easily understood by the managers and other users who do not need the details of the contents. The summary could also be so made that the data is shown in graphical form such as bar chart etc.

ABC CO. LTD.
Payroll Report

Page: 1 Date: 01/7/19

EMP_NAME	DEPARTMENT	BASIC SALARY
Payroll for -- Production		
Manager	Employee Total:	8200.00
Assistant	Employee Total:	7150.00
Steno	Employee Total:	4700.00
	Subtotal:	20050.00
Payroll for -- Sales		
Area Manager	Employee Total:	7500.00
Salesman	Employee Total:	6270.00
	Subtotal:	13770.00
Payroll for -- Servicing		
Engineer	Employee Total:	11500.00
Asstt. Engineer	Employee Total:	6000.00
	Subtotal:	31000.00
	Grand Total:	64820.00

Figure A.4 Summary Report for ABC & Co.

A.7 FAULTS AND WEAKNESSES IN REPORT DESIGN

The reports generated using computerized systems may fall short of the expectation of the user or the management. The weakness in the report may be one or more of the followings:

(a) Completeness
(b) Appropriateness
(c) Method of Presentation
(d) Timing and Frequency

A.7.1 Completeness

A report should be so designed that it is complete as far as the user is concerned. If user needs any information immediately, then it must be present. Information should be complete so that a manager can take decisions confidently. Information received in bits and pieces may have to be connected together to make out the meaning. This may cause loss of time and relevance of information.

Company ____________________ Analyst ____________________
Project Name ____________________ Date ____________________

Activity	Start Date	Completion Date	Staff in Charge	Department in Charge	Comments
1. Notification					
Announcement to officers	10/06	10/20	P. Solen	Personnel Mgr.	
Announcement to employees	10/06	10/20	J. Hill	Auditing	
Coordinated customer activities	10/06	10/29	D. Stang	Cashier	
Coordinate computer service	10/06	10/29	C. Sibley	Sr. Vice Pres.	
2. Procedures					
Interdepartmental	10/14	11/01	A. Blake	Systems	
Interdepartmental	10/14	11/01	J. Hill	Auditing	
3. Forms					
Design	11/01	11/14	A. Blake	Systems	
Printing	11/01	11/20	A. Blake	Systems	
4. Equipment					
Terminals	11/01	12/15			
5. Training and orientation					
Manuals	12/01	21/16	A. Blake	Systems	
Training aids	12/01	12/16	A. Blake	Systems	
Special workshops	12/10	12/14	A. Blake	Systems	
6. Lobby layout	12/10	12/30	D. Stang	President	
7. Supplies	12/10	12/15	M. Steed	Perchasing Agent	
8. Personnel					
Transfers	12/10	12/12	P. Solen	Personnel Mgr.	
New hires	12/15	12/30	P. Solen	Personnel Mgr.	

Approved by: ____________________ ____________________
(Project leader) (Systems Department)

Figure A.5 User Training report containing different headings

A.7.2 Appropriateness

The report contents should contain data or information relevance with the expected output. If data is not correct or relevant, then the report will not have credence. In such a case, the user will not have confidence in the computer system. For example, the report is to give the total of two data items but the result in the report shows the difference of the two data items, in that case the user will not like to have the report because he can not have the correct result as desired.

☞ *Information is of value to a receiver only when he can make use of it. It will be useful only when it pertains to the field in which the user operates. For example, the variation in the price of bullion is relevant to a bullion merchant but may not be relevant to a grain merchant.*

A.7.3 Method of Presentation

The report should be so designed that it is direct and to the point. In addition, the presentation should be in simple form and give the figures in the form of graphs and pictures.

A.7.4 Timing and Frequency

The report is supposed to provide the information that it is fresh and the data which is shown is current. But more the number of times reports are generated, the more the expenses you need to bear. The information received late will be of little help to the managers because he may not need it for taking action. How often does he need the information is also important. In the case of regular reports, an immediate response time following each report would involve large volume of paper consumption and therefore the cost may be high. Thus, a compromise is often made.

☞ *The response time of a report should be short enough that the information does not lose its freshness and value, but it should be long enough to reduce cost of preparation.*

A.7.5 Frequency of Presentation of Reports

If the report is not current then the information is of no use. But more often the report is presented, more the cost to be borne. Therefore, the report frequency is to be optimized so that it is neither too frequent nor too late.

A.8 DOCUMENTATION

Documentation is the narrative and graphical description of a system. Good documentation should be so written, that any part of the document can be retrieved with out much effort. Moreover, the document should be updated regularly to serve the purpose. During the normal course of an analyst's work, charting techniques of one kind or another are found most useful for recording organizational structures, activities, functions and flows of data. Further, standard forms are found most useful for recording information about data—their content, organization, relationships and volumes, etc. The quantity and quality of programming documentation is difficult to determine for non-technical people. It depends on the programming language used as well as the conventions established in the programming department.

Documentation for an information system includes:

(a) System documentation
(b) Technical documentation
(c) User Manual

A.8.1 System Documentation

System documentation contains Data Dictionary— a description of the files and databases. It contains system flow chart i.e. description of the data as it flows from source document to report. It also contains application program documentation i.e. description of the inputs, processing and outputs for each data entry, query, update and report program in the system.

A.8.2 Technical Documentation

This document contains file structures and access methods, program flow charts, program source code, listing and machine functions.

A.8.3 User Manual

This includes the following:

(a) Instructions for turning the system on and getting the programs initiated (loaded).
(b) The instructions for obtaining source documents for data entry.
(c) Instructions for entering data at the terminal, which includes a picture of each screen layout the user will encounter.

It also includes a description of error messages that can occur and the alternative methods for handling them. Also a description of error messages that can occur and the alternative methods of handling them. A description of the defaults taken in the programs and the instructions for changing them and the instructions for distributing the computer's output which includes sample pages for each type of report.

A.9 TOOLS FOR DOCUMENTING SOLUTIONS

A.9.1 Decision Trees

A decision tree is a diagram that presents conditions and actions sequentially and thus shows which conditions to consider first, which second, and so on. It is also a method of showing the relationship of each condition and its permissible actions. The diagram resembles branches on a tree, hence is the name. The roots of the tree, on the left of the diagram, is the starting point of the decision sequence. The particular branch to be followed depends on the conditions that exist and the decision to be made. Moving from left to right along a particular branch is the result of making a series of decisions. Following each decision point is the next set of decisions to be considered. The right side of the tree lists the actions to be taken depending on the sequence of conditions that is followed.

Example 1

Draw a decision tree for the policy followed by a company in giving discount to its customers.

(a) If the transaction is on credit, and the customers credit record is good, then only accept his order but do not give any discount on credit. If the customers credit record is not good, then do not accept the order.
(b) If the transaction is on cash, and the sale amount is more than Rs. 100, then give a discount of 20%.
(c) If the transaction is on cash, and the sale amount is more than Rs. 50 but less than 100, then give a discount of 10%.
(d) No discount is to be given if the transaction is cash and it is less than Rs. 50. But accept the order.

Solution

The decision tree for this example is shown in Figure A.6. The decision tree is divided into two parts. First column shows the conditions and the second column gives the outcome of the condition or the actions.

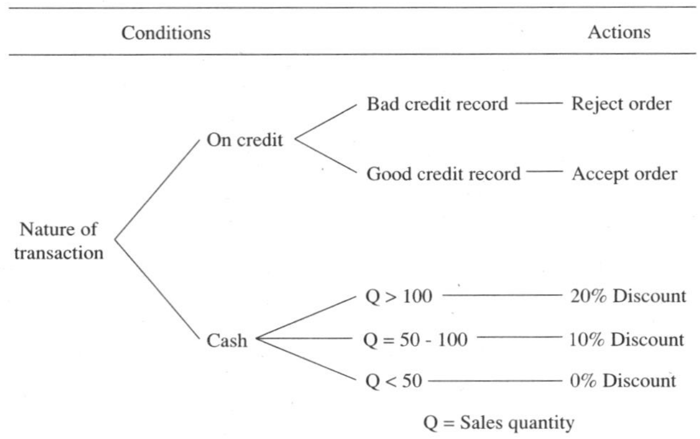

Figure A.6 Decision tree for example 1

Advantages of Decision Trees

(a) A decision tree describes conditions and actions and this forces a system analyst to identify the actual decisions that must be made.
(b) Decision tree forces analyst to consider the sequence of decision.

Disadvantages of Decision Trees

(a) A decision tree for a complex system with many sequences of steps and combinations of conditions will be unmanageable. A large number of branches with many paths through them will cloud rather than help in analysis. The analyst may not be able to determine which business policies or practices guide the formulation of specific decisions.
(b) Another major drawback of a decision tree is the lack of information in its format to tell us what other combinations of conditions to test. Whenever such problems arise, another analyst tool called Decision Tables should be considered.

A.9.2 Decision Tables

Decision Tables are used to define clearly and concisely the word statement of a problem in a *tabular* form. They can prove to be a powerful tool for defining complex program logic. As the name implies, decision tables reveal what decisions or actions the computer is to take as a result of the input data. When the computer has to make a large number of decisions or if there are a large number of different branches within a program, decision tables are particularly useful.

Steps in Writing Decision Tables

The steps to be followed for constructing a decision table are given below:

(a) Define the problem accurately that has to be solved by a computer.

(b) List out all the conditions to be tested in the problem.

(c) List out the corresponding actions that should be taken with each combination of conditions.

(d) Form a decision table using the two lists.

Most decision tables have six parts. The basic format of a decision table is shown in Figure A.7. The first part is the table heading that contains the name and/or number of the table. The second part of the table, known as condition stub, describes the conditions that could exist in the program logic.

Action stub, the third part of the decision table contains the action statements. These statements correspond to the statements located in non-decision symbols of a flowchart. While the condition statements reveal the possible states of the input data, the action statements describe the possible actions of the computer system. The right hand side of the decision table contains the decision rules (part 4), the condition entries (part 5), and the action entries taken by the computer (part 6). The condition entries correspond to the paths leading out from decision symbols in a flowchart. In order to understand a decision table, let us study the following three examples.

TABLE HEADING	DECISION RULES
CONDITION STUB	CONDITION ENTRIES
ACTION STUB	ACTION ENTRIES

Figure A.7 Format of a decision table

Example 2

The procedure to pick the largest of the three numbers is as follows: Read the three numbers, say, A, B, and C. A is compared with B. If A is larger, then it is compared with C. If A turns out to be the larger number again, then it is declared the largest number; else C is declared the largest number. If in the first step A is found less than or equal to B, then B is compared with C. If B is larger, it is the largest number; else C is the largest number. We are required to show this procedure in the form of a decision table.

		Rules						
		1	2	3	4	5	6	7
Conditions	A > B	Y	-	Y	Y	N	N	N
	B > C	Y	Y	-	N	Y	N	N
	C > A	-	Y	Y	N	N	Y	N
Actions	OUTPUT	A	B	C	A	B	C	Any
	STOP	X	X	X	X	X	X	X

Figure A.8 Decision table for Example 2

Solution

In this problem the conditions to be tested are:

(a) Is B

(b) Is C

(c) Is A

In the above figure, Y stands for Yes, N stands for No. In the decision table shown in Figure A.8, there are 7 rules. These rules are given below:

(a) Rule 1 states that if A > B and B > C, then the output is A. The dash against C > A in rule 1 means that this condition is irrelevant in arriving at the action. In fact if A > B, and B > C then C has to be less than A. C being greater than A is logically impossible.

(b) The second rule states that if B > C and C > A, then B is the largest number.

(c) The next rule states that if A > B, and C > A, then C is the largest number.

(d) Rule 4 states that if A > B, B < C and C < A, then A is the largest number.

(e) Rules 5 and 6 similarly determine that B and C are respectively the largest numbers under the conditions listed.

(f) Rule 7 considers the cases B < C, C < B, A < C. Under this combination of conditions A = B = C. Thus any one of the three numbers may be given as output.

Note the following points:

(a) The condition stub lists the conditions to be tested and the action stub lists the actions to be performed. The condition entries in this example list, for each rule, whether the condition is true or false or irrelevant (also known as *don't* care). The action entry tells us what action is to be carried out.

(b) All the conditions to be tested are listed and the order in which the testing is to be done is irrelevant. There are 3 conditions and thus 2^3 or 8 possible rules. Out of the 8 rules, one rule corresponding to the condition entries [Y Y Y] is logically impossible. The other seven rules take care of all the possibilities. A don't care entry corresponds to both true and false condition. For example, a rule [Y Y -] will split up into two rules [Y Y N] and [Y Y Y].

(c) The actions should be carried out in the order in which they are listed. For example in Rule 1, A is to be given as the output and then the STOP command is to be executed. A cross against the STOP in the action entry means the action is to be executed. A dash, on the other hand, will signify that the particular action is to be ignored.

(d) The condition entries in this example are binary, that is, the testing of the condition will lead to a Yes or No answer. Such decision tables are also called *limited entry decision tables.* When the condition entries are not binary, then the table is called an *extended decision table.*

Example 3

It is required to determine the procedure to pick the largest of 100 numbers. The method is to start with the first number A(1) in the list and call it X. Compare the current value of X with A(2). The larger of the two is then called X. Next X is compared with A(3) and the procedure is repeated. Thus X will contain the current largest number. After going through the 100 numbers, X will contain the largest number in the list.

Solution

A decision table corresponding to this example is shown in Figure A.9.

Table 1

X > A(J+1)	Y	N	N	Y
J = 99	N	N	Y	Y
X = A(J+1)		X	X	
J = J+1	X	X		
GO TO Table 1	X	X		
OUTPUT X			X	X
STOP			X	X

Figure A.9 Decision table for Example 3

A.10 DOCUMENTATION OF PROGRAM

Documentation of a software system involves collecting, organizing, storing and maintaining a complete historical record of programs and other documents used or prepared during different phases of the system development.

The documentation of a program is a continuous process. The program specifications, the algorithmic representation and the program itself can all be considered part of the documentation of a program. However, after successfully completing the program, we must ensure that our documentation is compete and it is in a finished, usable form. This includes both *technical documentation* for the programmers who may be working with and modifying the completed program and *user-level documentation* for the users of the program.

One of the mistaken ideas held by too many programmers is that the documentation for a program should be written only after the program is "finished". This is a very dangerous point of view! It will certainly lead to inadequate documentation and might result in an incomplete or incorrect program. Documentation is a continuous process. It starts when we first begin to formulate a clear problem statement and continues as we devise a solution, express the solution algorithmically, and code the algorithm as a computer program. The proper point of view is that documentation is an inherent part of a program. It is therefore meaningless to assert that documentation should be written after the program is finished.

Most programs that are written by professional programmers are used in a production environment. This means that once a program is deemed operational it is used on a regular basis, usually by people other than the author(s). For example, programs to process payrolls, maintain inventories, or handle hotel or airline reservations are invariably used by people who did not write them. Moreover, these people are usually not even programmers.

In this sort of environment, we can appreciate the need for the following two different kinds of documentation.

(a) User documentation
(b) Technical documentation

A.10.1 User Documentation

It provides the information that one needs in order to use a program. This information includes a number of different items. These items are:

(a) A description of the application area of the program or what will this program do?
(b) A description of the input data that the program requires.
(c) A description of the output produced by the program.
(d) A description of the commands needed to start the program.
(e) A description of the kinds of interactions that are possible with the program.
(f) An explanation of all the messages that the program can produce.
(g) A discussion (in nontechnical terms) of the performance capabilities and limitations of the program.

A.10.2 Technical Documentation

This kind of documentation is addressed to programmers who might be faced with the task of modifying the program at some time. Perhaps a mistake will become apparent after the program has been placed into use, or a decision may be made to enhance the program by adding a new feature. In either case, good technical documentation is a necessity.

A.10.3 Uses of Documentation

The uses of documentation are as follows:

(a) They facilitate communication about an application between the technical development personnel and the non-technical users.
(b) Documents are very helpful in initiating and training not just new employees, but old employees changing jobs or learning to use a computerized version of an old job. Good documentation will provide a self-instructional approach that will allow employees to advance at their own pace.

(c) The documents are essential during abnormal maintenance when a new programmer must maintain a system after the original programmer or analyst has left. This is a very common and serious problem. There are numerous cases where an application was left undocumented and could not be maintained. When this occurs, the application must be developed all over again.
(d) Documents are essential even among technical personnel not only during developing of a system but also during operations and normal maintenance.
(e) They provides a package that will contain the information needed to change the system should the environment or management's needs alter.
(f) Documentation prevents system dislocation and cost that might otherwise occur if knowledge of the system were centered in a few individuals who resigned, relocated or were subsequently reassigned other duties.

A.10.4 Limitations of Documentation

Documentation has the limitations inherent in human communication. The differences in the backgrounds of the user and the documenter, and the nature of the high technology that is being documented. This makes the test of a sound documentation more difficult.

Every thing can not be conveyed through documentation only. It may be difficult for an analyst to convey one's assumptions and one's view of how the system could and should be improved given changed circumstances (of technology or user), interaction which would be invaluable to maintenance and redevelopment.

A.11 TROUBLE SHOOTING

The process of *trouble shooting* involves discovering, locating, and correcting all errors that cause a program to produce either incorrect results or no results at all. Program debugging is the single most time-consuming phase in the overall program development process. Studies on the development of large programming systems indicate that it is not uncommon for 50 to 75% of the overall programming time to be spent on finding and correcting errors.

The ease of finding errors in a program is directly related to the clarity and lucidity of the structure of that program. Programs with complex, intricate, and "jumpy" logic are much more difficult to work with and to debug.

A.12 PROGRAM TESTING

It is the job of the programer to test, as far as possible, that all parts of the program work correctly. It should be realized that complete testing is not possible except in the case of the most trivial program; one can never be completely certain that all errors have been removed, but sufficient tests can be performed to give a reasonable measure of confidence in the program.

The situation is analogous to testing children on multiplication tables; once a child has answered a certain number of multiplication table tests correctly, at some point or other the teacher assumes that all other tests will be answered correctly and testing ceases.

A.12.1 Designing a Test Plan

Since we cannot test everything because there may be many number of if then else decision and all the test data may not be able to test all the loops. Each test must be carefully planned to provide more information about the program. A major benefit of preparing a comprehensive test plan with expected results is that it forces the programmer to think carefully about the program and often errors are spotted even before running the test.

Good testing requires the following:
(a) A thorough knowledge and understanding of what the program is supposed to do.
(b) Plan out in advance what ought to be tested.
(c) To work out expected results for each of the test cases.
(d) Writing out the test plan.

A.12.2 Methods of Testing

The objectives of testing can be stated in two basic questions:

(a) Does the logic work properly? This means, answering the following:
   (i) Does the program work as intended?
   (ii) Can it be made to crash?

(b) Is the necessary logic present? This means answering the following:
   (i) Are there any functions missing?
   (ii) Does the program or module do everything specified?

There are two different ways of testing. These are:

(a) Functional testing

(b) Logical or structural testing

Functional Testing

Functional testing is carried out independently of the code used in the program. It involves looking at the program specification and creating a set of test data that covers all types of inputs and getting outputs and program functions. This type of testing is also known as "*black box testing*". For example, to test the program that calculates check digits we could draw up the following test plan:

Table A.1 Test Plan for Check Digits

S. No.	Test for numerical data	Purpose	Expected result	Actual result
1	Enter 1234	Test validity of data	1234 Digits	3
2	Enter 8 digits	Test extreme case	are printed as it is	3
3	Enter 123W	Testing invalid data	Data not accepted	Error

From Table A.1 we will be able to make out whether the software is testing the data correctly or not. In Table A.1 we want to know if the input data is entered non numerical, then it should give an error. In row 3 column 2, we have entered data to contain numeral 123 and a character w and the result is error. Which indicates that the program is able to detect an entered data which is non numerical. If it had not pointed this error i.e. the program was not testing properly, then we may have to correct the program.

Logical (structural) Testing

Logical testing (*white box testing*) is dependent on the code logic, and derives from the program structure rather than its function. In other words, we study the program code and try to test each possible path in the program at least once. The problem with logical testing is that it will not detect the missing functions.

One method of devising a test plan is to start with a set of functional test cases, and then add additional tests to exercise each statement in the program at least once, making sure that each decision is tested for all outcomes.

A.13 DEBUGGING AIDS

Debugging aids refers to the software that help in finding the errors in the program logic. A debugger is a program that aids in debugging a program. It provides ways of stopping the program or capturing various system data at prescribed times. The debugger may be able to jump directly to the line in the source program that created the problem. Once the presence of logic errors has been detected with the help of test runs, there are various ways of finding where the error or errors lie. These include the following:

(a) A dry run through the program, building up a trace table while manually following the program steps.

(b) The inclusion of extra "write" statements to examine the contents of variables at various points in the program.

(c) An 'On line debugger' which allows a programmer to step through the program line by line and examine the values of variables at any point in the program.

A.14 TRACING ROUTINES

A trace routine allows the user to keep a track of the flow of the program while it is executed. He/she can request, for example, that the contents of certain registers or memory locations be printed every time a branch statement is executed or when the values of certain variables are changed. This allows the user to get a clear picture of what the program is doing and thus be able to correct any mistakes in the program.

Glossary

Abort

The abnormal end of a program because of the system fault error or operator intervention.

Abstraction

The act of representing the essential features of something without including much detail.

Account

A form of access to a computer or network for a specific user name and password usually with a home directory, an E-mail in box, and a set of access privileges.

ACID

ACID is an acronym to describe database transaction properties, and includes Atomicity, Consistency, Isolation, and Durability.

Aggregation framework

The aggregation framework lets you transform and combine documents in a collection. In aggregation operation, MongoDB processes the data records and returns a single computed result.

Aggregation pipeline

The aggregation pipeline is a framework for data aggregation modeled on the concept of data processing pipelines. The MongoDB aggregation pipeline consists of stages

Application Programming Interface (API)

A set of programmes that an application program uses to request and carry out lower-level services performed by a computer's operating system. On local area networks, an API such as IBM's NetBIOS, provides applications with a uniform means of requesting services from the lower levels of the network.

ASCII (American Standard Code for Information Interchange)

A standard coding system for computers. ASCII-7 is a 7-bit code and its extended version ASCII-8 is an 8-bit code.

ASCII File

It is a document file in the universally recognized text *format* called ASCII (American Standard Code for Information Interchange). An ASCII file contains characters, spaces, punctuation, carriage return, and sometimes tabs and an end-of-file marker, but it contains no formatting information.

Attribute

In relational database management, an attribute is a field within a record.

Audit trail

A feature of data processing systems that allows for the study of data as it is being processed step by step. In this, an auditor software can trace all transactions that affect an account.

Authentication

The process of determining the identity of a user that is attempting to access a system. Also the verification of the identity of a person or process.

Authentication Token

A portable device used for authenticating a user. Authentication tokens operate by challenge/response, time-based code sequences, or other techniques. This may include paper-based lists of one-time passwords.

Authorization

The process of determining what types of activities that are permitted. Usually, authorization is in the context of authentication: once you have authenticated a user, they may be authorized different types of access or activity on the PC system.

Automatic Teller Machine (ATM)

The ATM is a terminal of the bank's computer network and is operated by a customer himself through a VDU and a keyboard.

B-Tree

A method of TREE INDEXING that provides uniform performance regardless of how a file grows or shrinks.

Background processing

The automatic execution of lower-priority (background) computer programs when higher-priority (foreground) programs are not using the system resources.

Backup

Alternate facilities of programs, data files, hardware equipments, etc., that are used in case the original one is destroyed, lost, or fails to operate.

Backup files

These are the files which are generated automatically in MS-Word and other application programs when you save a document. These files help in protecting the document due to malfunctioning of the computer or power failure.

BASE

BASE is an acronym used to describe eventually consistent services, and stands for Basically Available, Soft state, Eventual consistency.

BLOB

It is a datatype. The full form is binary large object.

Bubble Memory

A compact data storage device made of thin wafers of garnet, a semiconductor material in a magnetic field. The data contained in them is not lost when the power is shut off.

Buffer

An area in memory used to hold input and output records.

Bug

An error in a computer program.

Checkpoint

A type of process that causes transactions to be either rolled back or committed to the underlying data; it creates a marker in the transaction log.

Client

Node or software program that requests services from a server.

Client/server

Distributed-computing network systems in which transaction responsibilities are divided into two parts: client and server. Clients rely on servers for services such as file storage, printing, and processing power.

Client/Server architecture

A configuration of computers on a network such that computing tasks are specialized—several computers (clients) interface to users while specialized operations are performed on another (typically smaller) group of one or more computers called servers. Structured Query Language (SQL) is typically used by clients to perform operations on data stored on servers.

Closed system

A system that is isolated from environmental influences.

Cloud Databases

Cloud Databases are the databases which are stored over clouds (also known as virtual environment).Some cloud platforms available are Amazon Web Services(AWS), Google Cloud, Microsoft Azure etc.

Clustered Index

An index that forces the rows in a table to be physically stored in sorted order, using one or more columns from the table.

Collection

A *collection* is a group of documents.

Column-oriented

Column-oriented Graph databases organize data in columns instead of rows.

Columns

The aspect of a table where field values are stored for each record or left null. The column contains data type information.

Constraints

Constraints are created in the database to enforce a business rule or conditions in the database so as to ensure validity of data. This also specifies relationships among different tables.

CRUD operations

CRUD operations refer to the basic Insert, Read, Update and Delete operations. These are the four basic database operations while building an application.

Data

A collection of facts in raw form that become information after proper organization or processing.

Data Control Language

Data Control Language (DCL) is another portion of SQL which allows definition of a security mechanism or scheme for protecting data from unauthorized access.

Data Control Statements

SQL Statements that are used to provide a way to protect a database from corruption.

Data Definition Language (DDL)

That portion of a data model which provides facilities for defining the structures in which data is to be stored.

Data Definition Statements

SQL Statements that are designed for defining a database, modifying its structure after it is created, and dropping it when you are done with it.

Data dictionary

It is a list of terms and their definitions for all data items and data stores of a system. The document that contains clear definitions of the data that will be used in setting up data base management systems.

Data element

A meaningful collection of related characters. Also called a field or data item.

Data entry

The process of writing new data into computer memory, typically from a keyboard.

Data file

A file consisting of data – text, numbers, or graphics as distinct from a program file of executable instructions.

Data Flow Chart

A flow chart showing the path of the data step by step in a problem solution or through a system.

Data Flow Diagram (DFD)

A diagram that depicts the flow of data through a system and the processes that manipulate data.

Data grouping

Categorizing data in groups in a report corresponding to a specified order. Headers and footers can be defined to print every time the value for a group changes.

Data hiding

A property whereby the internal data structure of an object is hidden from the rest of the program. The data can be accessed only by the functions declared within the class (of that object).

Data integrity

The extent to which the data used for processing are reliable, accurate, and free from errors.

Data Manipulation Language

Data Manipulation Language (DML) is that part of SQL which consists of a set of commands that determine which values are present in the tables at any given time.

Data Manipulation Statements

SQL Statements that are used for entering, changing and extracting data in a database.

Data Mart

A data storage facility or set of servers used to store departmental or divisional data.

Data Member

A variable that is declared in a class declaration.

Data model

A data model is a description of the organization of a database.

Data name

A data name is a name assigned to an item of data, such as a field or variable.

Data processing

A series of operations that convert raw facts (data) into useful information.

Data processing system

A system that accomplishes data manipulation or organization. It includes the necessary resources, which are people, materials, facilities, and equipments.

Data processor

A digital device that processes data.

Data store

An area in a network where application-layer data resides. A data store can be a server, a set of servers, a mainframe, a tape backup unit, a digital video library, or any device or component of an Internetwork where large quantities of data are stored. Sometimes called a *data sink*.

Data structure

A logically related set of data that can be decomposed into lower level data elements. It is a group of data elements handled as a unit.

Data type

The type of data that can be entered into a column.

Data warehouse

A storage system used to store virtually all the organization's data, which might be in various formats; it typically interacts with the client via the Online Application Processing server.

Database

A collection of data files integrated and organized into a single comprehensive file system, which is arranged to minimize duplication of data and to provide convenient access to information within that system to satisfy a wide variety of user needs.

Database administrator

The person responsible for defining, updating, and controlling access to a database in an organization.

Database Management System (DBMS)

A general-purpose software package such as Oracle, SQL Server etc. used as a tool for building individual database systems.

Database server

A system that receives requests from client applications over a network and responds by returning requested data (the answer set). Each database server is made up of a computer, an operating system, and database server software.

Database System

A combination of software and hardware for performing some task or group of tasks that involve handling large amount of data or information.

Deadlock

A situation in which two or more processes cannot proceed because each needs access to data that is being used by the other.

Debug

To identify program errors and their causes so that you can remove such errors.

Decision support system (DSS)

A "what if" approach that uses an information system to assist management in formulating policies and projecting the likely consequences of decisions.

Direct-access

Pertaining to storage devices where the access time is effectively independent of the location of data.

Documentation

Documentation of a software system involves collecting, organizing, storing and maintaining a complete historical record of programs and other documents used or prepared during the different phases of the system.

Dynamic schemas

NoSQL databases typically have very flexible schemas. A flexible schema allows you to easily make changes to your database as requirements change.

Embedded

Contained within. For example, the string "WEST COAST" is said to contain one embedded blank space.

Embedded object

Information (the object) inserted into a file (the destination file). Once embedded, the object becomes part of the destination file. When you double-click an embedded object, it opens in the program (source program) it was created in. Any changes, you make to the embedded object are also reflected in the destination file.

End user

Any individual who uses the information generated by a computer based system.

Field

In a record, it is a meaningful collection of one or more related characters treated as a unit.

File manager

A file manager is a data mangement software package that provides some of the features of a database management system, but works with only single files. Often erroneously called database managers, file managers provide the ability to create, enter, change, query and produce reports on only one file at a time. They have no relational capability and usually do not include a programming language for application development.

File volatility

It refers to the proportion of records changed during a time period.

Function

A preprogrammed calculation that can be carried out on request from any point in a DBMS program. Because a function takes in one or more arguments and returns a single value, it can be embedded in an expression.

Graphs-based

These databases organize data as nodes and edges that show connections between nodes. Nodes typically store information about people, places, and things while edges store information about the relationships between the nodes.

Hash function

A mathematical computation that results in a string of bits (digital code); the function is not reversible to produce the original input.

Hashing

A file-organization technique based on the idea of calculating rather than searching for the ADDRESS of RECORDS in a FILE.

Heartbeat

In replication, heartbeat is the process to identify the current status of the node servers within the replica set.

HeidiSQL

HeidiSQL is free software, and has the aim to be easy to learn. HeidiSQL belongs to the most popular tools for MariaDB and MySQL worldwide.

Hierarchical

A way of displaying text or graphics in a structure. In a hierarchical structure, items closer to the top of the structure are considered *parents* of the items connected to them, but which are lower down in the structure.

Index

A file containing a list or table of entries that identifies the sequence or record ordering of a database file, based on key fields.

Indexed file

A file that includes an index directory to facilitate random access.

Information

The result of data manipulation or processing which can be used to help people make decisions.

Information hiding

The principle which states that the implementation of an object or module should be private to that object or module and only accessible via its public interface. (same as encapsulation)

Input

The data entered into a data processing system.

Input device

A device used to enter information into a computer or other data processing devices; for example, the keyboard.

ISAM (Index Sequential Access Method)

Relating to a file design technique whereby records organized in a sequential order can be accessed directly through an index (directory) based on some key or characteristic. Permits both sequential and random access of records.

Item

A group of related characters treated as a unit. (A record is a group of related items, and a file is a group of related records).

Join Condition

A join condition specifies the relationship between two databases and is often a field common to both databases, such as a customer number or a transaction number.

JSON

This is known as JavaScript Object Notation. This is a human-readable, plain text format for expressing structured data. It is currently supported in many programming languages.

Key

An ATTRIBUTE or set of attributes for a RELATION whose values determine a unique TUPLE of that relation.

Key-value Pair

These databases work on a simple data model that has a pair of unique keys and a value associated with it i.e., data is stored in key/value pairs.

Key field

A unique field in a record used to distinguish one record from another.

Latency

1. Delay between the time a device requests access to a network and the time it is granted permission to transmit. 2. Delay between the time a device receives a frame and the time that frame is forwarded out the destination port.

Latency time

In case of disk storage, the time taken for the desired record to come under the read/write head positioned over that track. Maximum latency time equals the time taken by disk to rotate once.

limit()

The limit() method limits the number of documents returned in response to a particular query.

Log File

Every database has a log file, which is used to help recover a database, should it be damaged. A single database may have single log file or multiple log files if the original one runs out of room.

Log Processing

How audit logs are processed, searched for key events, or summarized.

Log Retention

How long audit logs are retained and maintained.

Logging

The process of storing information about events that occurred on the firewall or network.

Logical Database

A schema that describes the database as seen by one user. Different users or APPLICATIONS may have different views of the same database.

Logical drive

A drive that is not a physical drive, as in the floppy drive A or B. Instead, a logical drive is a drive created on a subpartition of an extended partition and given an arbitrary letter such as C, D or E.

Logical error

An error that occurs when the actual logic of a program is different from the desired logic.

Logical operator

An operator that produces logical result (true or false), sometimes called a Boolean operators.

Logical Records

The complete unit of information in a file is called a record. The records that a program reads or writes are called logical records. Logical records are placed in the storage medium's physical record — the pieces actually read or written to a diskette. A program sees logical records while the operating system performs translation between physical and logical records.

Mapping

Mapping is the transfer of a set of data or codes from one place to another. For example, program modules on disk are mapped into memory. A graphic image in memory is mapped onto the video screen. A logical database structure is mapped onto the physical database. Mapping is often used to refer to laying out anything.

MapReduce

MapReduce is a powerful and flexible tool that condenses large volumes of data into aggregated results.

MariaDB

It is an Open-source Software and is based on the MySQL Community Version. MariaDB supports a popular and standard querying language.

Mass storage

Storage systems that provide access to hundreds of billions of bytes of stored data. They are often referred to as archive storage because of the very large volumes of historical or backup data that they can store.

Master file

A file containing relatively permanent data. This file is often updated by records in a transaction file.

Memory

A device or medium that can accept data, hold them, and deliver them on demand at a later time.

Mongo shell

The mongo shell is an interactive JavaScript interface to MongoDB.

MongoDB

MongoDB is an open-source document database, and leading NoSQL database.

Non-clustered Index

A physical data structure, separate from the table, that points to the data in a table. The pointers themselves are sorted, making it easy to quickly locate data within a table. A table may include an index for every column in a table, although this would be uncommon. Generally, only columns that benefit from sorting have indexes.

Non-procedural

When a QUERY LANGUAGE requires the user to specify only what data is requested rather than how to retrieve the data, the language is said to be non-procedural. RELATIONAL CALCULUS is the most often cited example of a non-procedural query language.

Nonvolatile storage

A storage medium that retains its contents even in the absence of power.

Normalize

In programming, to adjust the exponent and fraction of a floating point quantity so that the fraction is within a prescribed range.

NoSQL Database

No-SQL(Not Only SQL) is a type of database presently used for storing a wide range of data sets mainly of distributed data. A NoSQL database has dynamic schema for unstructured data.

Object-oriented Programming

Implementation of programs using the objects in an object oriented language such as C++.

ObjectID

This data type is used to store the document's unique key Id in MongoDB.

Open Database Connectivity (ODBC)

component of the Windows Open Service Architecture (WOSA) that provides multi-database access by adding its own API (Application Programming Interface) layer on top of the native database layer, thus simplifying access. The developer needs to deal with only a single API to access numerous database servers, because ODBC can translate standard ODBC function calls into many different native database dialects.

Open system

A system that performs interactions across its boundary, receives inputs from and delivers outputs to the outside.

Output

The finished result of processing by a system.

Output unit

The unit of a computer system that supplies information and results of computation to the outside world.

Parent-child

In database management, a *parent* is a record or file that contains required data about a subject, such as employees and customers. The parent data must exist before it can have children; for example, the child of a customer file may be the order file. Parent-child relationships are used to express how data is related and accessed.

Password

A code by which a user gains access to a computer system. It is used for security purposes.

Path

In database management, a path is the route from one set of data to another, for example, from customers to orders.

Physical Database

The physical files that make up a database; composed of two or more physical operating–system files. At a minimum, one of these two files will contain the database information, and the other will contain the database's transaction log.

Projection

Projection is used when we want to get the selected fields of the documents rather than all fields.

Query

A statement that extracts information from the database, most often selecting the information based on a predicate.

Query Language

That portion of a data model which defines the permissible operations on data structures that are supported by the DDL.

Record

A collection of information, in one or more fields, about a specific item or person.

Record length

A measure of the size of a record, usually specified in units such as characters.

Record pointer

Shows which record number within a database that you are adding, editing, displaying, or deleting. Record numbers show the sequential position of a record within a database.

Relation

A rectangular array of data values. The relation forms the basic data-structure for the Relational Model.

Relational Data Base Management Package

Software that manages data in more than one file at a time, and these files are treated as tables with rows and columns rather than as lists of records. A database application back end that stores information in two-dimensional tables linked by common properties. SQL is used to create, manipulate, and extract data from relational databases.

Relational database

A type of database or database management system that stores information in tables (that is, rows and columns of data). A relational database uses matching values from two tables to relate information in one table to information in the other table. In a relational database, you typically store a specific type of information just once, which makes the database very efficient and reduces data entry errors.

Relationship

A connection between entities that has meaning for an application. A connection called *Owns* between Suresh and Bicycle can represent the fact that Suresh *owns* a bicycle.

Replica Set

The replica set is a group of mongod instances that maintain the same data set.

Replication

Replication is a way of keeping identical copies of your data on multiple servers.

Rollback

In recovery procedure, it is updating a prior valid copy of the database with the necessary changes to produce a current version.

Row

A row is a horizontal set of data or components that is also called the x-axis. Contrast with column, which is a vertical set of data or components.

RQBE

An acronym for Relational Query By Example.

Schema

A schema is the definition of an entire database. A subschema is the definition of a user's partial view of the database.

Script

A collection of one or more batches of SQL statements designed to perform some specific action.

Sequential File Organization

A file organization technique in which RECORDS are organized in order of the value of some FIELD.

Sequential processing

A technique in which a number of similar items or transactions to be processed are grouped together and processed in a designated sequence.

Serial Access

In serial access, the access is dependent on the position of the storage location and data must be processed serially.

skip()

The *skip()* method is used for skipping the given number of documents in the query result in MongoDB.

Software

The set of computer programs, procedures, and associated documentation related to the effective operation of a computer system.

Sort

A sort is the reordering of data into a new sequence. Sorting capabilities are provided within the operating system and many application programs, such as word processing and database management systems.

Spatial data management

Spatial data management is a technique for accessing both static data and animated video sequences by physically pointing or "steering" through the data, much like a player at an arcade game.

SQL

SQL is the abbreviated form of structured query language. A relational data-access language created by IBM. Most database server engines use SQL as a standard way of accessing data from client applications.

SQL Server

SQL Server is a database engine, or SQL engine. It runs on IBM compatible file servers and uses the SQL language as its primary interface.

Stored Procedure

Database objects that enable you to automate many tasks. They are made up of precompiled SQL statements that carry out a predetermined task or series of tasks.

Subschema

In database management, a subschema is an individual user's partial view of the database. The schema is the entire logical view of the database.

Transaction

A set of operations (SQL statements that change a database) that are to be completed at one time, as if they were a single operation.

Transaction log

Used to automatically record all changes made to a database before the changes are actually written to the database. This is a fault tolerant feature that prevents a database from getting corrupted.

Trigger

A special type of stored procedure that executes when specific events occur to a table. For example, when data in a table is inserted, updated or deleted, a trigger can be made to automatically fire, executing a series of SQL statements. SQL developers often use triggers to ensure data integrity and perform other tasks.

Tuple

In relational database management, a record or row is called a tuple. However, the term is not often used.

Updating

The process of keeping master files accurate and up-to-date by processing them with the latest transactions contained in the transaction file.

User

Any individual who supplies input data to, or uses information generated by, a computer based system.

Validation

The process of making sure that the forms and documents from a particular transaction are correct.

Variable

A value, usually the contents of a field within a database record or a memory variable. A variable may be a character string (made up of alphanumeric characters, spaces, and punctuation marks), a numeric value, a mathematical expression (equation), or a logical true or false, yes or no.

View

A virtual table created to provide alternative ways to view data stored in tables. Views can be created to display a subset of data from a table, or two or more tables can be linked and combined to create a view. Views themselves do not contain data; they only point to selected data and present it visually.

SOLVED SAMPLE PAPER – 1

Databases Technologies

Total Time : 3 Hours *Total Marks 100*

PART – ONE
(Answer all questions; each question carries one mark)

1. **Multiple Choice Questions**

1.1 One of the following is a valid record -based data models
   a. Object-oriented model
   b. Relational model
   c. Entity-relationship
   d. None of the above

1.2 A distributed database has Which of the following advantages over
   a. Software cost
   b. Software complexity
   c. Slow Response
   d. Modular growth

1.3 An abstraction concept for building composite objects from their component object is called
   a. Specialization
   b. Normalization
   c. Generalization
   d. Aggregation

1.4 What are the main features of MariaDB?
   a. MariaDB can run on different operating systems and support a wide variety of programming language
   b. MariaDB follows a standard and popular querying language
   c. MariaDB provides Galera cluster technology
   d. All of these

1.5 What are the different types of clauses used in MariaDB?
   a. MariaDB Where Clause
   b. MariaDB Like Clause
   c. Both a and b
   d. None

1.6 Duplicate data is referred to as
   a. Accurate data
   b. Redundant data
   c. Storage data
   d. Control data

1.7 Consider the relation scheme R (A,B,C,D,) where A is candidate key with no information about FDS involved, then R is in which normal form?
   a. First normal form
   b. Second normal form
   c. BCNF
   d. Third Normal form

1.8 In a relational database a referential integrity constraint is specified with the help of:
   a. Primary key
   b. Consistency key
   c. Foreign key
   d. None of the above

1.9 Which one is not an aggregate function in SQL?
   a. Count
   b. Min
   c. Max
   d. All are aggregate functions

1.10 4NF is designed to cope with:
   a. Transitive dependency
   b. Join dependency
   c. Multivalued dependency
   d. None of these

2. **State True or False for the following:**

2.1 Sharding solves the problem to modify the schema where a table is already present.

2.2 Cardinality of a relationship means the number of attributes in the relation.

2.3 MariaDB is a community-developed branch of the OpenSolaris database, which uses the Maria engine by default.

2.4 The DBA is the coordinator between the DBMS and application Programs.

2.5 DDBMS is designed for heterogeneous database platforms.

2.6 SELECT NULL is legal.

2.7 HAVING is used to eliminate groups in the same way as WHERE is used to eliminate rows.

2.8 The functional dependency X -> Y implies the multivalued dependency X -> -> Y.

2.9 NoSQL database are not ACID compliant.

2.10 The database schema is written in Data Definition Language.

3. Match the following:

	X		Y
3.1	E-R model	**A**	COMMIT
3.2	1NF	**B**	Elimination of repeating groups
3.3	SELECT operation	**C**	ROLLBACK
3.4	Join	**D**	Chen
3.5	DCL	**E**	Performs audits and analysis on operations within the database
3.6	DAS	**F**	Elimination of redundant data
3.7	DROP VIEW	**G**	Correctness and completeness of the data in a database
3.8	TCS	**H**	Codd
3.9	MINUS	**I**	Matches data from two or more tables
3.10	Data integrity	**J**	INSERT
		K	Acts as a filter
		L	Principal logical data definition statement.
		M	Controls the user access to the database objects
		N	UPDATE
		O	Set operation

4. Fill in the blanks:

A With	**B** BCNF	**C** Discriminator
D Recovery manager	**E** Static	**F** ACID
G Attributes	**H** Password	**I** Shadow
J Uncommitted	**K** Authorization	**L** Association
M Wait-for-graph	**N** Class	**O** Rollback
P Database manager	**Q** Committed	**R** Entity

4.1 An entity is an object that is distinguishable from other objects by a specific set of ________

4.2 The primary key of a week entity set is formed by the primary key of the identifying entity set, plus the weak entity set's ________.

4.3 ________ statement ends the current transaction and undoes any changes made during that transaction.

4.4 ________ is stricker than 3NF.

4.5 Deadlock may be detected using ________.

4.6 ________ refers to the database properties of a transaction.

4.7 In ______ paging, transaction logs are not required.

4.8 The ________, restores the database to a consistent state.

4.9 The undo logs rollback ________.

4.10 A(n) ________ granting of a privilege to a user.

Answers to Objective Type Questions

1.	1.1	b	1.2	d	1.3	a	1.4	d	1.5	c
	1.6	b	1.7	d	1.8	e	1.9	d	1.10	c
2.	2.1	F	2.2	F	2.3	T	2.4	F	2.5	T
	2.6	F	2.7	T	2.8	F	2.9	T	2.10	T
3.	3.1	D	3.2	B	3.3	K	3.4	I	3.5	M
	3.6	E	3.7	L	3.8	C	3.9	O	3.10	G
4.	4.1	G	4.2	C	4.3	O	4.4	B	4.5	M
	4.6	F	4.7	I	4.8	D	4.9	J	4.10	K

PART – TWO

(DESCRIPTIVE QUESTIONS to be answered in 2 Hours)

5. Explain the functions of Database Administrator
6. Construct an E-R diagram for a hospital with a set of patients and a set of a medical doctors. Associate with each patient a log of the various tests and examinations conducted.
7. (a) Explain in brief ACID properties of database transaction.
   (b) What is concurrency control? Explain with suitable example.
8. (a) Write short note on NoSQL - Document store Databases.
   (b) What are the main features of MariaDB?
9. (a) What do you understand by lock granularity ? Explain.
   (b) Write short note on No-SQL.
   (c) Explain difference between scaling horizontally and vertically for databases.

Answers to Descriptive Type Questions

Ans 5. The overall function of the database administrator include

i) **Schema definition:** The original database schema is created by writing a set of definitions which are translated by the DDL compiler to a set of tables that are permanently stored in the data dictionary.

ii) **Storage structure and access method definition:** appropriate storage structures and access methods are created by writing a set of definitions which are translated by the data storage and definition language compiler.

iii) **Schema and physical-organization modification:** The DBA carries out changes to the schema and physical organization to reflect the changing needs of the organization, or to alter the physical organization to improve performance.

iv) **Granting of authorization for data access:** DBA also maintains that the database is not accessible to unauthorized users. The DBA is responsible for granting permission to use the database and stores the profile of each user of a database. This profile describes the permissible activities of a user on that portion of the database which is authorized to him. The user profile can be used by the DBA to verify that a particular user is only allowed to perform a given operation on the database, within the limited time frame.

v) **Routine maintenance:** The DBA is responsible for defining procedures to recover data from failures due to human, natural or hardware malfunctioning with minimal loss. This recovery procedure would thus enable an organization to continue working with the available intact portion of the database.

He also ensures that enough free disk space is available for normal operations and upgrading disk space as required.

vi) **Maintaining integrity:** DBA ensures that appropriate measures are taken to maintain the integrity of a database. Integrity constraints are kept in a special system structure that is consulted by the database manager whenever an update takes place in the system.

Ans 6.

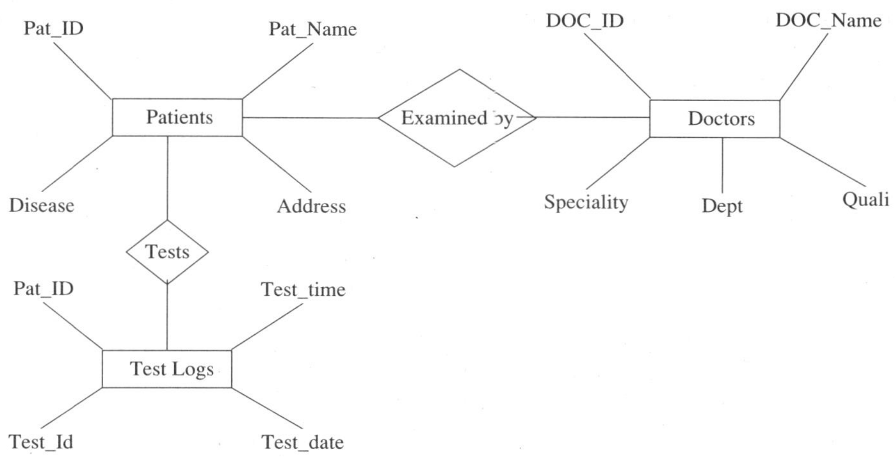

Figure 1 ER- diagram for a hospital

Ans 7a A transaction is expected to have certain properties called **ACID** test properties. These are:

a) Atomicity
b) Consistency
c) Isolation
d) Durability

Atomicity

The atomicity property of a transaction implies that it will run to completion as an *individual unit* (*atomic unit*). At the end of a unit of transaction either there is no change to the database or the database has been changed in a consistent manner. No changes will be reflected in the database in the middle of execution of an atomic unit of transaction. Thus, only after a transaction unit has been executed completely that any updates made by it will be accessible to other transactions and the processes outside the transaction.

Consistency

Consistency property of a transaction implies that if a database was in a consistent state before the execution of the transaction, then after execution of the transaction also, the database will be in a consistent state.

Isolation

Isolation property of transaction implies that actions performed by a database will be isolated or hidden from other transactions or processes until it is either executed or terminated. This property gives transaction a measure of relative independence.

Durability

Durability property of a database implies that the updates made by a transaction will be reflected in the database on the termination of committed action. Therefore, any loss or failure after the committed action will not cause loss of updates made by the transaction. It can also be inferred from this property of database that once committed, roll-back of the transaction cannot be performed.

Ans 7b In order to increase processor utilization and for better throughput, most operating system supports multiprogramming. In a multiprogramming environment, the execution of many programs are interleaved i.e. they execute concurrently. In a database environment such programs may try to access common data. The DBMS must include concurrency control software to ensure that several users trying to update the same data do so in a controlled manner so that the result of the updates is correct. For example, when several reservation clerks try to assign a seat on an airline flight, the DBMS should ensure that each seat can be accessed by only one clerk at a time for assignment to a passenger. Thus concurrency control is a method used to ensure that database transactions are executed safely without any data loss. The basic idea behind any concurrency control schema is to control concurrent data access such that database consistency is always preserved.

Ans 8.a Document-oriented databases, also known as document stores, are used to store and manage semi-structured or unstructured data. A document store is a nonrelational database that stores data in JSON, BSON, or XML documents. These databases supports a flexible schema. Due to the lack of a defined structure i.e., no schema of table is declared before inserting data, document stores don't enforce document structure. Documents can contain any data desired. Since the information of Document Stores cannot be arranged in tables, this data is not suitable for relational databases

Ans 8.b MariaDB can run on different operating systems and support a wide variety of programming language. It follows a standard and popular querying language. It also provides Galera cluster technology.

Ans 9.a Granularity refers to the size of data item. If the size or granularity of a data item is very large, for example an entire relation, then the overhead associated with the mechanism of locking it, is very low. Hence, the lock manager only has to manage a few data items. But this reduces the degree of concurrency because the transaction locked the entire relation and any other transaction cannot use tuples from this relation before the previous transaction release its lock.

On the other hand if the granularity or size of a data item is very small, the degree of concurrency will be very high. But overhead of managing these locks will also be high. This is because a transaction that needs may records and fields will have to request many locks, all of which have to be managed by the lock manger. Hence, granularity chosen should be such that it neither reduces the concurrency nor increases the overhead of lock manager.

Ans 9. b No-SQL(Not Only SQL) is a type of database presently used for storing a wide range of data sets mainly of distributed data. A NoSQL database has dynamic schema for unstructured data. Data is stored in many ways which means it can be document-oriented, column-oriented, graph-based or organized as a key-value store. This flexibility means that documents can be created without having defined structure first. Also each document can have its own unique structure. Users can quickly access data from the database through key-value. The NoSQL database follows the Brewers CAP theorem (Consistency, Availability and Partition tolerance). NoSQL database examples include Redis, RavenDB Cassandra, MongoDB, BigTable, HBase, Neo4j and CouchDB.

Ans 9. c Horizontal scaling means that you scale by adding more machines into your pool of resources whereas Vertical scaling means that you scale by adding more power (CPU, RAM) to an existing machine. Examples of horizontal scaling are Cassandra, MongoDB, Google Cloud Spanner and a example of vertical scaling is MySQL - Amazon RDS (cloud version of MySQL).

SOLVED SAMPLE PAPER – 2

Databases Technologies

Total Time : 3 Hours *Total Marks 100*

PART – ONE
(Answer all questions; each question carries one mark)

1. Multiple Choice Questions

1.1 Language used by programmes to communicate with database is:
a. DML c. QL
b. DDL d. None of these

1.2 The relational model is concerned with
a. Data structure and data integrity
b. Data manipulation
c. Both a and b
d. None of these

1.3 A top-to-bottom relationship among the items in a database is established by
a. Hierarchical schema c. Relational Schema
b. Network schema d. All of the above

1.4 Prevention of access to the database by unauthorized users is referred to as:
a. Integrity c. Security
b. Productivity d. Reliability

1.5 In an E-R, Y is the dominant entity and X is a subordinate entity, then which of the following is incorrect.
a. Operationally if Y is deleted, so is X
b. X existence is dependent on Y
c. Operationally, if X is deleted, so is Y
d. Operationally, if X is deleted, Y remains the same.

1.6 What are the types of JOIN in MariaDB?
a. Inner and Outer Join c. Both a and b
b. Left and Right Join d. None of the above

1.7 Object based data models are used in describing the abstraction of the following level(5).
a. Only physical c. Physical and conceptual
b. Conceptual and view d. None of the above

1.8 Type of constraints that specifies uniqueness of data stored in database are considered as
a. Semantics c. Controlled rules
b. Business rules d. Dtructural rules

1.9 Which of the following is a NoSQL Database Type?
a. SQL c. JSON
b. Document databases d. All of the mentioned

1.10 Most NoSQL databases support automatic __________, meaning that you get high availability and disaster recovery
a. Processing c. Replication
b. Scalability d. All of the mentioned

2. State True or False for the following:

2.1 LIMIT clause is used with SELECT statement to select a limited number of records from a table.

2.2 MariaDB provides different tools for disaster recovery.

2.3 If you want to see the list of all those employees whose name starts with **M**, then % operator is used.

2.4 While creating a table using CREATE TABLE statement atleast one column must be specified.

2.5 *NULL* values signify the absence of data, i.e., missing information in the column.

2.6 The database schema is written in Data Control Language.

2.7 NoSQL databases is used mainly for handling large volumes of semi-structured data.

2.8 MongoDB has official drivers for a variety of popular programming languages and development environments.

2.9 Locks that are placed expecting a conflict are termed pessimistic locks.

2.10 The vast majority of NoSQL technologies are ACID compliant.

3. **Match the following:**

	X		Y
3.1	Normalization	A	Douglas Crockford
3.2	The father of JSON	B	Table
3.3	Database Recovery	C	Primary Key
3.4	SQL keyword used to sort the result	D	Relationship
3.5	Two-Phase locking	E	Basically Available Soft state Eventual consistency
3.6	BASE	F	Functional dependency
3.7	Command is used to select and use a database in MariaDB	G	Order by
3.8	MongoDB is a __________ database that provides high performance, high availability, and easy scalability	H	Use database
3.9	Strong entity set	I	Document
3.10	Data dictionary	J	Growing and shrinking phase
		K	Shadow copy
		L	Foreign Key
		M	Meta data

4. **Fill in the blanks:**

A Aggregate B Javscript C Replication
D Partitioned E Implicit F admin.system.roles
G Union H Vertical Partitioning I Shared locks
J Deadlock K Schema L ACID
M Isolation

4.1 The __________ collection stores custom roles that administrators create and assign to users to provide access to specific resources.

4.2 In MariaDB, the SELECT statement can be used with__________ statement.

4.3 A lock placed automatically by the DBMS is called ________ lock.

4.4 The properties of a transaction are termed _______ properties.

4.5 Some of the columns of a relation are at different sites is ___________.

4.6 MongoDB Queries can return specific fields of documents which also include user-defined __________ functions.

4.7 The same storage capacity is a disadvantage of _____________.

4.8 MIN, MAX, AVG, SUM are all examples of ________ functions.

4.9 A distributed database________ into segments at different sites.

4.10 The characteristics of transactions ___________.

Answers to Objective Type Questions

1.	1.1	a	1.2	c	1.3	a	1.4	c	1.5	b
	1.6	c	1.7	b	1.8	a	1.9	b	1.10	c
2.	2.1	T	2.2	T	2.3	T	2.4	T	2.5	T
	2.6	F	2.7	F	2.8	T	2.9	T	2.10	F
3.	3.1	B	3.2	A	3.3	K	3.4	G	3.5	J
	3.6	E	3.7	H	3.8	I	3.9	C	3.10	M
4.	4.1	F	4.2	G	4.3	E	4.4	L	4.5	H
	4.6	B	4.7	C	4.8	A	4.9	D	4.10	M

PART – TWO

(DESCRIPTIVE QUESTIONS to be answered in 2 Hours)

5. (a) Explain the difference between two and three-tier architectures.

(b) Differentiate between Conceptual schema and Physical (internal) schema.

(c) How Logical Data Independence is different from Physical Data Independence?

6. (a) The LastName column of a table "Directory" is given below:

LastName
Batra
Sehgal
Bhatia
Sharma
Mehta

Based on this information, find the output of the following queries:

i. SELECT lastname FROM Directory WHERE lastname like"_a%";

ii. SELECT lastname FROM Directory WHERE lastname not like"%a";

7. (a) What do you mean by integrity and Referential Integrity? Explain with example.

(b) Explain one-to-one (1:1) relationship.

8. (a) In MariaDB [none]> prompt what is significance of [none]?

(b) What do you mean by Database and Document in MongoDB?

(c) What are Strengths and Weaknesses of Wide-column store.

(d) Write short note on Key-value store databases.

9. (a) What do you understand by the term concurrency? How can we avoid deadlock?

(b) Write short note on database security.

Answers to Descriptive Type Questions

Ans 5. (a) A three-tier architecture includes a client and two server layers. The application code is stored on the application server and the database is stored on the database server. A two-tier architecture includes a client and one server layer. The database is stored on the database server.

(b) The logical description of the entire database showing all the data elements and relationships among them is called the conceptual schema, whereas the specifications of how data from the conceptual schema are stored on physical media is termed the physical schema or internal schema.

(c) Logical data independence describes the degree up to which the logical or conceptual schema can be changed without modifying the external schema. The changes to data schema at the logical level are made either to enlarge or reduce the database by adding or deleting more entities, entity sets, or changing the constraints on data.

Physical data independence defines the extent up to which the data schema can be changed at the physical or internal level without modifying the data schema at logical and view level. The physical schema is changed if we add additional storage to the system or we reorganize some files to enhance the retrieval speed of the records.

Ans 6. The output of the queries are given below:

(a) i **LastName**
Batra

ii **LastName**
Sehgal

Ans 7. (a) ***Entity Integrity:*** If an attribute of a table is prime attribute (unique identifier), it can not accept null values, i.e., no component of a primary key values may be null.

Referential Integrity: To ensure that a value which appears in one relation for a given set of attributes will also appear for certain set of attributes in another relation. This condition is called as referential integrity.

(b) A one-to-one (1:1) relationship is an association only between two entities. For example, in a university each department has only one head of the department.

Ans 8. (a) In the prompt, [none] means that no default database is selected. This means that, every time a table is named in a statement, the name of the database where it is located must be specifically specified.

(b) Database - This is a container for collections like in RDBMS wherein it is a container for tables. Each database gets its own set of files on the file system. A MongoDB server can store multiple databases.

Document - A record in a MongoDB collection is basically called a document. The document in turn consists of field names and values.

(c) Wide-column stores are dynamic column-oriented nonrelational databases. Wide column stores are database management systems that organize related facts into columns. Some of the examples of wide-column store databases are Cassandra, HBase, Microsoft Azure Cosmos, Druid, Hypertable etc.

i Strengths: This type of database has some benefits of both relational and nonrelational databases. It deals better with both structured and semistructured data than other nonrelational databases, and it's easier to update. Columnar databases compress better than row-based systems. Also, large data sets are simple to explore. Columnar databases are highly scalable horizontally and faster at scale because they store data in columns rather than rows.

ii Weaknesses: Wide-column stores are slower than relational databases when handling transactions. Good for bulk write and updates but it's a costly affair in lower quantity like individual records.

(d) A key-value store database is a type of nonrelational database that uses a simple key-value method to store data. In key-value, each value is associated with a specific key. A key-value database stores data as a collection of key-value pairs where the key serves as a unique identifier. Both keys and values can be anything, ranging from simple objects to complex compound objects. It just has a one-way mapping from the key to the value to store data. A key-value store database are very flexible and able to handle a very wide array of data types easily. They can be moved from one system to another without rewriting code. i.e., easily Portable. It drawback is no query language to retrieve data. Only have some simple operations such as get, put and delete.

Ans 9. (a) Most of today's DBMS allow multiple users to access a database at the same time. This is referred to as concurrency or concurrent access of database. The DBMS must include concurrency control software to ensure that several users trying to update the same data do so in a controlled manner so that the results of the updates are correct. For example, when several reservation clerks try to assign a seat on an airline flight, the DBMS should ensure that each seat can be accessed by only one clerk at a time for assignment to a passenger.

Deadlocks can be avoided by any of the following ways:

i Lock all the required data items at the beginning of a transaction.

ii All data items are assigned an order. A transaction can only request locks in the given order say ascending order.

iii Another method is to make run time decisions about what a transaction must do if it detects that it has to wait for a data item. For this, each transaction is assigned a unique timestamp. The system uses these timestamps to decide whether it should wait for the data item, abort or rollback the transaction.

(b) Database security is process of protecting a database from unintended activity. Unintended activity can be categorized as authenticated misuse, malicious attacks or inadvertent mistakes made by authorized individuals or processes. Database Security includes policies framed to protect data, falling in the hands of unauthorized users. Security also includes the techniques used to ensure that data elements are not changed or deleted by viruses or by unauthorized persons.

UNSOLVED SAMPLE PAPER – 1

Databases Technologies

Total Time : 3 Hours *Total Marks 100*

PART – ONE
(Answer all questions; each question carries one mark)

1. Multiple Choice Questions

1.1 Which of the following are true about RDBMS:
- a. RDBMS store normalized data in form of data sets called relations.
- b. Data can be easily stored, modified and retrieved using SQL queries.
- c. RDBMS are expensive to set up and grow.
- d. All of the above are true

1.2 A distributed database has which of the following advantages over a centralized database?
- a. Software cost
- b. Software complexity
- c. Slow Response
- d. Modular growth

1.3 A relational database consists of a collection of:
- a. Tables
- b. Fields
- c. Records
- d. Keys

1.4 A ________ in a table represents a relationship among a set of values.
- a. Column
- b. Key
- c. Row
- d. Entry

1.5 The term _______ is used to refer to a row.
- a. Attribute
- b. Tuple
- c. Field
- d. Instance

1.6 Which one of the following attribute can be taken as a primary key?
- a. Name
- b. Id
- c. Address
- d. Department

1.7 The result which operation contains all pairs of tuples from the two relations, regardless of whether their attribute values match.
- a. Join
- b. Cartesian product
- c. Intersection
- d. Set difference

1.8 Normal forms are used to
- a. Reduce the size of tables so that less memory is required
- b. Make the query processing faster
- c. Avoid logical inconsistencies from operations which update tables
- d. None of these

1.9 Two phase commit
- a. Is used to avoid dead locks
- b. Is a form of transaction processing on multiple databases
- c. Locks tables in one phase and unlocks in the other
- d. None of these

1.10 Rollback of transaction is normally used to
- a. Recover from transaction failure
- b. Update the transaction
- c. Retrieve old records
- d. Repeat a transaction

2. State True or False for the following:

2.1 Some example of RDBMS are Oracle, MySQL, MS Server, Sybase, Informix, PostgreSQL.

2.2 RDBMS and typical SQL databases stores data in tables in form of rows and columns.

2.3 Even when transactions are allowed to write into the database only after they commit, undo operation would be required during recovery.

2.4 A key is a property of the entity set, rather than of the individual entities.

2.5 RDBMS engines implements ACID (Atomicity, Consistency, Isolation, and Durability) properties very efficiently and effectively while NoSQL database engines uses BASE (Basic Availability, Soft-state, and Eventual consistency).

2.6 If database takes too long to backup and restore, it may not be a suitable one.

2.7 Transaction files or tables contain records that describe business events. The data describing these events normally has a limited useful lifetime.

2.8 Database design should proceed only if the underlying logical data model is in at least 2NF.

2.9 Entity integrity dictates that every entity has exactly one primary key.

2.10 During the creation of database schemas, NULL means the field does not have to have a value; whereas, NOT NULL means the field must have a value.

3. Match the following:

	X		Y
3.1	Aggregation	A	Front end operation
3.2	Read lock	B	Shareable lock
3.3	Atomic entity	C	Entity which is not divisible
3.4	Select operation	D	Selects some of the columns
3.5	Back end	E	Information about structure of a database
3.6	Interface between database user and database	F	Building composite objects from components
3.7	Dictionary	G	Consistency
3.8	Mirroring	H	Guarantees serializability
3.9	Two phase locking	I	Selects some of the rows
3.10	Is a meaning of C in ACID properties of transactions	J	Database server
		K	This helps in case of disk failure
		L	Backup

4. Fill in the blanks:

A Distinct	B Read	C Member
D Allow	E Modify	F Undo
G DDL	H Duplicate	I SCHEMA
J Grant	K Attributes	L Combine
M No duplicate	N View	Having
P Records	Q Queries	R DML

4.1 A ____________ is a specification of the portion of the data which is oriented towards the needs of one or more application programs.

4.2 The primary key constraint does not allow ____________ data in the field.

4.3 Read lock of data item by a transaction prevents other transactions to ____________ that item.

4.4 To get rid of duplicate tuples selected by using SQL SELECT command ____________ option may be used.

4.5 ___________ is an SQL authorization command.

4.6 ___________ is used to specify database retrievals and updates.

4.7 ___________ is used along with GROUP BY clause to define a condition on the group.

4.8 Views combine the qualities of tables and ___________.

4.9 Recovery of data by first removing invalid changes and then reapplying valid ones is known as ___________.

4.10 A functional dependency is a relationship between ____________.

Module: A7–R5

PART – TWO
(DESCRIPTIVE QUESTIONS to be answered in 2 Hours)

5. (a) Discuss the main categories of data models.

(b) Describe the three-schema architecture. Justify the need for mappings between the schema levels with a suitable illustration.

(c) Discuss the integrity constraints supported in Relational database. Explain each constraint with suitable example.

(d) Why keys are important in relational model? Write about candidate keys, primary keys, alternate key and foreign key.

(e) What is database system? What are the benefits of database?

6. (a) Define Normalization also differentiates between 3NF and BCNF.

(b) Describe the purpose of normalizing data. How is the concept of functional dependency associated with the process of normalization?

(c) Consider a relation:

R(A,B,C,D,E,F,G,H,I,J)

Given Functional Dependency:

F={AB->C, A->DE, B->F, F->GH, D->IJ}

Identify the Keys.

Decompose the relation into 2NF and 3NF.

(d) Why keys are important in relational model? Write about candidate keys, primary keys, alternate key and foreign key.

(e) What is database system? What are the benefits of database?

7. (a) What are the main features of Maria database?

(b) Write the syntax for Delete and Truncate query and explain the difference between them.

(c) Write the query to check if table is present within Database.

(d) What is database security? Why is it important? Also discuss the various security issues.

8. (a) Define Transaction. Name the features available to maintain transaction.

(b) Discuss in brief about ACID Property.

(c) What is dead lock in database?

(d) How to set Schema privilages?

9. (a) Explain the reasons why JSON is useful over other notation types.

(b) Name the data types supported by JSON object. Syntax to build JSON Object.

(c) State the difference between SQL and NoSQL.

(d) How to define database schema in Mongo Db? Does MongoDB Support foreign key elements?

(e) Define Covered Query in MongoDB.

UNSOLVED SAMPLE PAPER – 2

Databases Technologies

Total Time : 3 Hours *Total Marks 100*

PART – ONE

(Answer all questions; each question carries one mark)

1. Multiple Choice Questions

1.1 Factors to be considered while choosing the right database:
a. Performance c. Volume of data to be stored
b. Structure of data d. All of the above

1.2 Storing a separate copy of the database at multiple locations is which of the following?
a. Data Replication
b. Horizontal Partitioning
c. Vertical Partitioning
d. Horizontal and Vertical Partitioning

1.3 Which of the following is a disadvantage of replication?
a. Reduced network traffic
b. If the database fails at one site, a copy can be located at another site
c. Each site must have the same storage capacity
d. Each transaction may proceed without coordination across the network

1.4 The _______ operator takes the results of two queries and returns only rows that appear in both result sets.
a. Union c. Difference
b. Intersect d. Projection

1.5 The _____________ is essentially used to search for patterns in target string.
a. Like c. In
b. Null d. Out

1.6 Which of the following is not a characteristic of a relational database model?
a. Table
b. Tree like structure
c. Complex logical relationship
d. Records

1.7 If there exists a set of transactions such that every transaction the set is waiting for another transaction in the set, then the system is called
a. Transaction failure c. Deadlock
b. Transaction processing d. Two-phase lock

1.8 5NF is designed to cope with
a. Transitive dependency
b. Multi valued dependency
c. Join dependency
d. None of these

1.9 A weak entity is an entity that
a. Has no key attributes
b. Has more than one candidate key
c. Cannot participate in any relationship
d. None of these

1.10 Which is not true in network model?
a. A member record may be stored without storing corresponding owner record
b. A set occurrence may contain only one owner type record and no member type records
c. Member and owner records may be of the same type
d. All are true

2. State True or False for the following:

2.1 All SQL databases have strong data consistency because all reads return the latest data.

2.2 MongoDB is a document-oriented NoSQL database used for high volume data storage.

2.3 MySQL, MariaDB, SQLite, Curbrid, PostgreSQL, FireBirdSQL, Drizzle, WebScaleSQL, Apache Derby etc., are some popular Relational DBMS.

2.4 MongoDB, Neo4j, OrientDB, CouchDB, Apache Cassandra, Redis, HBase, Titan etc., are examples of NoSQL DBMS.

2.5 A database schema and an instance of the database are the same thing.

2.6 When a computer program "reads" a record from a database, it actually retrieves a group or block (or page.) of records at a time. This approach minimizes the number of actual disk accesses.

2.7 If relation R satisfies the FD $A \rightarrow B$ and A is not a candidate key, then R will involve redundancy.

2.8 A foreign key is a field whose values identify one and only one record in the same file.

2.9 Foreign key refers to a column which belongs to a different table.

2.10 In relational database foreign key is used to specify a referential integrity constraints.

3. Match the following:

	X		Y
3.1	Union	A	This is the component of the database system which ensures that any schedule that gets executed will leave the database in the consistent state
3.2	Division	B	This restricts the number of possible schedules
3.3	Concurrency control	C	This operation is suited to queries that include the phrase "for all"
3.4	Locking protocol	D	They are tested easily whenever a new data item is entered into the database
3.5	Starvation	E	The operation automatically eliminates duplicates
3.6	Check point	F	This is the situation where a particular transaction never completes its designated task
3.7	Timestamp	G	This is used to produce the number of log records that must be scanned when the system recovers from crash
3.8	Domain constraint	H	This is used to specify the set of relations in a database
3.9	DDL	I	This is a function that takes a collection of values as input and return single value
3.10	max	J	A method to select an ordering among transaction in advance

4. Fill in the blanks:

A Domain	B Entity Set	C Null
D BCNF	E Attribute	F Join
G Alter	H Alternate Key	I Rectangle
J Row	K Primary Key	L Update
M Triangle		

4.1 An ________ is a set of entities of the same type that share the same properties, or attributes.

4.2 Minimum Super key is known as ________.

4.3 The descriptive property possessed by each entity set is ________.

4.4 The term tuple refers to a ________ of a table.

4.5 A set of possible data values is called ________.

4.6 ________ is stronger than 3NF.

4.7 Not applicable condition can be represented in relation entry as ________.

4.8 A data manipulation command that combines the records from one or more tables is called ________.

4.9 In E-R diagram generalization is represented by ________.

4.10 To delete a particular column in a relation the command used is ________.

PART – TWO

(DESCRIPTIVE QUESTIONS to be answered in 2 Hours)

5. (a) What is Database? Why it is needed?

(b) What are advantages of NoSQL databases?

(c) An university needs to maintain the information about its affiliated colleges as detail given below.

Student: Student's number, row, birth date, gender, age, address (consisting of street, area and city), hobbies phone numbers, courses taken.

College: College name, address (consisting of street, area and city)

Courses offered: course name, course credit

Draw E-R diagram for the above situation.

(d) Draw and explain the three level architecture of the database system.

6. (a) What is MongoDB? What are its features?

(b) What are Multikey Indexes? How it is different from Compound index.

(c) Why volume of data to be stored is an important factor? Explain.

(d) We can convert any weak entity set to a strong entity set by simply adding appropriate attributes. Why, then, do we have weak entity sets?

7. (a) Given a relation scheme R{A, B, C, D} with the functional dependencies

F{A -> B, B -> C, C -> D},

Can you determine its normal form? Justify your answer. Convert this relation into BCNF.

(b) Following is the description of a system and its information requirements. Identify the important entities and relations. Also draw E-R diagrams using standard methods.

A store has different counters managed by different employees. A counter has different items but no two counters have common items. Customers buy from different counters but bills are prepared at bill counter only. Once in a month performance of persons managing counters is evaluated in terms of sales. Items are also reviewed and slow moving items are identified.

(c) Consider the following tables in a relational database:

EMP (EMP_NO, E_NAME, DEPT, SALARY)

DEPARTMENT (EMP_NO, DEPENDENT_NAME, SEX, B_DATE, RELATION)

(Here EMP_NO is employee number of person related with dependent)

PROJECT (PROJ_NAME, PROJ_NO, LOCATION, CONT_DEP_NO)

(CONT-DEP_NO is project controlling department number)

WORKS_ON (P_NO, EMP_NO, HOURS_WORKED)

Write commands in any standard SQL to accomplish the following:

(i) Find the names of all employees who have a dependent with same name as employee.

(ii) Find employees with no dependent.

(iii) Find names of employees who work on all projects controlled by the department no. 5.

8. (a) Explain the following terms using suitable examples:

(i) Degree of a relation

(ii) Cardinality of a relation

(iii) Cartesian product

(iv) Binary relation

(v) Extension of a relation

(b) Explain the integrity constraints: Not Null, Unique, Primary Key with an example each.

(c) Describe the purpose of normalizing data. How is the concept of functional dependency associated with the process of normalization?

9. (a) Discuss the underlying objectives of database recovery procedures. Describe the basic techniques to implement database recovery in a centralized database.

(b) Explain the reasons why recovery of interactive transactions is more difficult to deal with than is recovery of batch transactions. Is there a simple way to deal with this difficulty?

(c) Explain checkpoints. How does it help in reducing the amount of time required during recovery?

(d) Explain how does encryption support in databases with an example.

Specimen Answersheet for Writing Answers to Objective Questions

PAPER CODE ____________ DATE ____________

1. Multiple Choice Questions

(shade the box corresponding to your answer)

	a	b	c	d
1.1.				
1.2.				
1.3.				
1.4.				
1.5.				
1.6.				
1.7.				
1.8.				
1.9.				
1.10.				

2. State True or False for the following:

(shade the box corresponding to your answer)

	True	False
2.1.		
2.2.		
2.3.		
2.4.		
2.5.		
2.6.		
2.7.		
2.8.		
2.9.		
2.10.		

3. Match the following:

(write the alphabet corresponding to your answer in the box)

3.1.	
3.2.	
3.3.	
3.4.	
3.5.	
3.6.	
3.7.	
3.8.	
3.9.	
3.10.	

4. Fill in the blanks:

(write the alphabet corresponding to your answer)

4.1.	
4.2.	
4.3.	
4.4.	
4.5.	
4.6.	
4.7.	
4.8.	
4.9.	
4.10.	

OTHER TITLES OF INTEREST

SQL, PL/SQL - The Programming Language of Oracle
ISBN: 9788176569644

Mastering **PL/SQL** Through **Illustrations**
ISBN: 9789389898484

SQL Interview Questions
ISBN: 9789389328462

PHP & MySQL in Easy Steps
ISBN: 9789386551405

Cracking **Kotlin Interview**
ISBN: 9789389845266

IT Interview Guide for **Freshers**
ISBN: 9789388511599

Writing Quality **Research** Papers
ISBN: 9789388176903

Fundamentals of
Soft Computing
ISBN: 9789386551566

Big Data Hadoop
Interview Guide
ISBN: 9789389898323

Big Data and Hadoop -
Learn by Example
ISBN: 9789386551993

Mastering **Sharepoint Framework**
ISBN: 9789389328875

SharePoint Online **Power User** Playbook
ISBN: 9789389845563

SharePoint Online **Modern Experience** Practical Guide
ISBN: 9789388511575

Getting Started with **Sharepoint Framework(SPFx)**
ISBN: 9788194334460

Theory of Computation and **Application**
ISBN: 9788183335287

Microprocessor
Data Handbook
ISBN: 9788176566124

Available on **www.bpbonline.com** and all leading book stores.

#1 PUBLISHER OF COMPUTER BOOKS

63 YEARS OF EXCELLENCE

90 MILLION BOOKS SOLD WORLDWIDE

bpb

OTHER TITLES OF INTEREST

100+ Solutions in **Java**
ISBN: 9789389845600

Advanced Analytics with
Excel 2019
ISBN: 9789389845808

Agile, **DevOps** and **Cloud Computing** with **Microsoft Azure**
ISBN: 9789388511902

Application Layering with
VMware App Volumes
ISBN: 9789389328769

Arduino Projects for **Engineers**
ISBN: 9788183335973

Artificial Intelligence and **Deep Learning** for Decision Makers
ISBN: 9789389328684

AutoCAD 2020 for **Engineers** and
Designers Basic and Intermediate
ISBN 9789389423099

Autodesk 3ds **Max 2021** for
3D Designers
ISBN: 9789389898897

Big Data and Hadoop -
Learn by Example
ISBN: 9789386551993

Bitcoin Blockchain
ISBN: 9789389898095

Biomedical Sensors Data Acquisition with **LabVIEW**
ISBN: 9789389845990

Blockchain for Business with
Hyperledger Fabric
ISBN: 9789388511650

Building Single Page App Using ASP .NET Core With Entity Framework Core and **Angular JS**
ISBN: 9788183335966

Computer Fundamentals –
8th Edition
ISBN: 9788176567527

Cookbook for **Mobile Robotic Platform** Control
ISBN: 9789388511674

Cracking
Microservices Interview
ISBN: 9788194334422

Available on **www.bpbonline.com** and all leading book stores.

#1 PUBLISHER OF COMPUTER BOOKS

63 YEARS OF EXCELLENCE

90 MILLION BOOKS SOLD WORLDWIDE

bpb